SPYING ON IRELAND

Spying on Ireland

British Intelligence and Irish Neutrality During the Second World War

EUNAN O'HALPIN

OXFORD
UNIVERSITY PRESS

OXFORD
UNIVERSITY PRESS

Great Clarendon Street, Oxford OX2 6DP

Oxford University Press is a department of the University of Oxford.
It furthers the University's objective of excellence in research, scholarship,
and education by publishing worldwide in

Oxford New York

Auckland Cape Town Dar es Salaam Hong Kong Karachi
Kuala Lumpur Madrid Melbourne Mexico City Nairobi
New Delhi Shanghai Taipei Toronto

With offices in

Argentina Austria Brazil Chile Czech Republic France Greece
Guatemala Hungary Italy Japan Poland Portugal Singapore
South Korea Switzerland Thailand Turkey Ukraine Vietnam

Oxford is a registered trade mark of Oxford University Press
in the UK and in certain other countries

Published in the United States
by Oxford University Press Inc., New York

British Library Cataloguing in Publication Data

Data available

Library of Congress Cataloging in Publication Data

O'Halpin, Eunan.
Spying on Ireland: British intelligence and Irish neutrality during
the Second World War / Eunan O'Halpin.
p. cm.
Includes bibliographical references and index.
ISBN 978–0–19–925329–6
1. World War, 1939–1945—Ireland. 2. World War, 1939–1945—Secret
service—Great Britain. 3. Espionage—Ireland—History—20th century.
4. Neutrality—Ireland. I. Title.
D754.I6O53 2008
940.54'8641—dc22   2007044982

Typeset by Laserwords Private Limited, Chennai, India
Printed in Great Britain
on acid-free paper by
Biddles Ltd, King's Lynn, Norfolk

ISBN 978–0–19–925329–6

1 3 5 7 9 10 8 6 4 2

For Conor Barrington

Preface

This book explores the activities of British intelligence organizations concerning Ireland during the second world war, and the relationship of those activities to British policy on independent Ireland. Many writers have discussed aspects of intelligence in relation to Ireland, especially German involvement. I and others have already touched on British activities, particularly regarding security operations and cooperation with the Irish authorities to thwart German espionage. This book attempts to go further in two respects. First, I place British dealings with Ireland in the wider context of the challenges facing British intelligence generally, just as did the intelligence officers who oversaw Irish affairs during the war years; secondly, I attempt what can be termed an 'all-agency' perspective.

I look at the various strands of intelligence activity of the various agencies and departments involved with Ireland in one way or another, and attempt to provide a coherent overview. This, of course, is not always easy where Ireland is concerned, any more than it is for any other state with which Britain had dealings during the war. Integration of activity and analysis remained a desideratum rather than an achievement in far more significant theatres of intelligence and security operations than the Irish one. There is a further point: historians writing from a broadly Irish perspective have generally viewed Anglo-Irish relations including questions of intelligence and security, in largely bilateral terms. Due to the release of so many British and American intelligence records in the last decade or so, it is now possible to look at Britain's Irish experience in the wider context of her intelligence dealings with other states and groups of states. Britain's perspective on issues such as the German legation's clandestine radio, for example, is far more understandable when discussed in terms of a generic problem, encountered with neutral states more or less within her sphere of influence—Iraq, Persia, and Afghanistan are instances—than as a uniquely Anglo-Irish question. We now know that in many neutral states the diplomatic missions of the belligerents housed clandestine radios. In Dublin two British sets operated with Irish blessing and, at least for a time, there were others undeclared; in London MI5 discovered that there were undeclared radios in the missions of two neutrals (Hungary and Sweden), and another in the Soviet embassy. The British hesitated to act for fear of reprisals against their own clandestine sets in neutral capitals. None of the intelligence people in London dealing with the issue of the German legation radio saw it as a unique problem: indeed, the final British push for its satisfactory resolution was delayed by a month because of possible reciprocity. British pressure on Ireland in relation to the Axis legations also invites comparison with the parallel case of Afghanistan, where London and Delhi concluded that on balance it was best to refrain from demanding the removal of the German legation's radio in Kabul because it allowed them to monitor and to thwart Axis efforts to manipulate the Indian independence movement, and very largely to take control of such activities through the use of double agents.

The 'American note' crisis of February 1944 should also be seen in the context of Allied action taken elsewhere against uncooperative neutrals. The dilatory manner in which the Persian government responded to Anglo-Soviet demands to expel Axis civilians in 1941 provided an excuse of sorts for joint occupation by British and Russian forces, while the British and Soviets made very forthright and threatening representations to Afghanistan about Axis activities against their interests. As in the Irish case, Churchill took a direct and forceful part in these matters, calling for action beyond what his policy advisers suggested and itching for a means of punishing neutrals, particularly those which had till recently been under British control, and which were unwilling or just slow to bend the knee to Allied demands.

The same considerations apply in respect of other intelligence questions. From July 1940 onwards Britain decoded a good deal of Irish diplomatic cable traffic. Almost all of this material can be found in the vast National Archives series HW12, where diplomatic decodes from across the globe are organized alphabetically and chronologically on a daily basis for every year from 1919 to 1945. It is clear that, with the exception of the latter half of 1941, Irish traffic was attacked not so much to gain an insight into Irish policy, as to secure miscellaneous intelligence from the dispatches of Irish diplomats in Europe. Churchill saw a surprising number of Irish cables from Rome in 1943 and from Berlin in 1944 and 1945 because they added some light and colour to other sources on the public mood in the beleagured Axis capitals. Britain also decoded a good deal of foreign diplomatic traffic to and from Dublin, and I deal with this at some length. In many instances, it is impossible to be certain that such decodes had any influence on policy, for the simple reason that all copies of and references to diplomatic decodes were normally weeded from the policy files of the various departments long before their release. Consequently, apart from the almost complete set of messages shown to Churchill as part of his daily selection of decodes from late September 1940, which are available in the National Archives series HW1, it is seldom possible to assess the impact of this kind of intelligence.[1] There is, however, one very important exception: some Dominions Office files dealing with Ireland were held back from release for many years—and by the time they finally reached the National Archives, sensitivity about diplomatic codebreaking had lessened, so that a lot of German and Italian decodes and British discussion of their significance can be seen. The decodes of foreign diplomatic traffic are also of use in themselves because they provide a partial insight into German, Italian, Vichy French, and even Japanese policy towards Ireland which could otherwise only be studied by consulting the records of their respective foreign ministries, a considerable research challenge which I have neither the time nor the language skills to undertake.

---

[1] Morton to C, 27 Sept. 1940, TNA, HW1/1, conveying the prime minister's instructions that he should see 'daily all the Enigma messages'. This proved impracticable, and he (or his deputy when he was not available) was instead sent a selection. See the interesting discussion of this class in respect of Turkish material in Denniston, *Churchill's Secret War*, 147–55.

In addition to the National Archives decodes series, the United States National Archives class RG457 contains 'Magic summaries', periodic digests of diplomatic decodes including European messages provided by the British codebreakers. These summaries sometimes contain extracts from German and other communications which cannot be found elsewhere.

Britain's twin-track policy of engaging with the Irish on a broad range of security and counter-espionage questions, and simultaneously mounting secret operations in Ireland, is neither surprising nor unique. All the documentary evidence, including not only MI5 records but documents from C (as the head of SIS is styled), show clearly that this approach was regarded as necessary although highly risky, because if the Irish got wind of clandestine activity they might withdraw cooperation. This was one of the reasons why SOE were hounded out when they attempted to get going in Ireland in 1941. This humiliation came not at the hands of the Irish but of SIS and MI5, the two agencies principally involved with Irish affairs. SIS argued that SOE's activities might jeopardize MI5's links with Irish military intelligence (G2), and might also lead to the uncovering of SIS's Irish operations. In fact the Irish had already penetrated the latter, but were content to observe them because in the main they were not directed against Irish interests. Much the same consideration applied in places such as Portugal, and for the same reasons: having penetrated British networks, it would have been counter-productive to roll them up because the British would most likely simply establish others, and would be far more careful in doing so, rendering them far harder to detect.

Another area where a comparative perspective is useful is cooperation on aspects of signals intelligence. Even in so secret a matter as codebreaking, Britain found herself constrained to sanction partial disclosure of important secrets in order to facilitate and elicit crucial contributions from the Irish, whose solitary code expert, Dr Richard Hayes, made two very important breakthroughs on Abwehr ciphers in 1943 and 1944 which—and the sources for this statement are MI5 documents—had considerable significance for British intelligence beyond the immediate sphere of German activities concerning Ireland. A key point about such cooperation—the existence of which is generally not even hinted at in the official history of British signals intelligence—is that it was an understandable and necessary part of wartime codebreaking across the globe. For one reason or another—for instance, the capacity to intercept radio traffic in areas of interest, local knowledge, access to complementary local sources through postal and telephone interception, long experience of a particular target (for example, the Finns on the Soviet Union)—small states were of necessity sometimes partners. However cautious and limited these exchanges, they unavoidably involved some disclosure of British capacity and interests.

It is important to note the striking continuity amongst the people in Whitehall and in Dublin who wrestled with Irish intelligence and security problems throughout the war. In MI5, Guy Liddell as deputy and then as head of B division watched Irish matters closely from first to last, as is reflected in the many references in his remarkable wartime diary which I draw on extensively, while his brother

Cecil established MI5's Irish section in 1939 and ran it throughout the war.[2] In SIS, the vice-chief Valentine Vivian, who controlled the counter-intelligence arm Section V, remained in place throughout the war, despite a breakdown in 1943. Within Section V Irish matters were handled from the end of 1940 until Ireland ceased to be a significant security concern after D-Day, by the brilliant Jane Archer in London and (from early 1941) by Captain V. B. Caroe in Northern Ireland, while Stewart Menzies, who became C in November 1939 on the death of Admiral 'Quex' Sinclair, remained head of SIS until 1952. In the armed services' intelligence directorates, there was also continuity: the able, though combative and overbearing, John Godfrey was director of naval intelligence (DNI) until removed at the behest of his joint intelligence committee (JIC) colleagues in September 1942, and F. N. Davidson was director of military intelligence (DMI) from the middle of 1940 until 1944. In the Dominions Office, similarly, the most senior officials dealing with Ireland, Ernest Machtig and John Stephenson, were in post throughout the war. Furthermore, the British Representative appointed to Ireland in September 1939, Sir John Maffey, remained in Dublin until 1949. In Belfast, the key RUC officers involved, the inspector-general Sir Charles Wickham, Captain Roger Moore who handled cross-border liaison, and Superintendent Moffat and Inspector Gilfillan of the Special Branch, were all involved more or less from start to finish.

The same general continuity of personnel can be seen on the Irish side: the high commissioner in London, John Dulanty, served from 1930 to 1950; the secretary and assistant secretary of External Affairs, Joseph Walshe and Fred Boland, were in those posts throughout the war; and while the director of G2 (Irish military intelligence), Liam Archer, left on promotion in June 1941, he was succeeded by his deputy Dan Bryan, who had spent almost all his revolutionary and military careers in intelligence. In the Garda (police), the key post of head of 3C (Security) was held throughout by Chief Superintendent Patrick Carroll.

Even at the political level the continuities are also substantially present. Crucially, as first lord of the Admiralty from September 1939 Winston Churchill was by far the most hawkish minister on the question of Irish neutrality, and continued in that vein as prime minister from May 1940 to July 1945. The nature of his prose is such that there is always a danger of overstating Churchill's particular interest in or passion about Ireland. While the records show that he did keep a constant and impatient watch on Ireland, we must remember that he was largely occupied with much greater questions. Churchill was incapable of writing an anodyne sentence, and in reading his fulminations about Ireland there is always a danger of ascribing too much significance to what were, by his literary standards, often mere throwaway lines. On the Irish side, the rather less prolix Eamon de Valera was minister for External Affairs as well as taoiseach throughout the war years, ensuring that security cooperation operated under his aegis.

This book touches on the approach and performance of the Irish police and military security agencies during the second world war. Here readers may suspect

---

[2] O'Halpin, 'The Liddell diaries'.

a tendency to overstate in particular the competence of the police in dealing with the IRA and its supporters, and the technical abilities and the perspicacity of Irish intelligence, and especially of Dan Bryan and the part-time codebreaker Richard Hayes. But, as I have said elsewhere, the most glowing estimates of their achievements come not from Irish but from secret British sources.

A final theme of the book is the question of the extent to which Ireland's status as a dominion and a former colony affected the conduct and extent of British intelligence activity relating to her. The fact that Ireland was a dominion was undoubtedly significant for other states in the empire. Australia, Canada, and South Africa themselves had sizeable anti-war minorities, largely defined by ethnicity and religion. Even when they deplored neutrality, they accepted the principle that Ireland had every right to choose whether or not to fight the Axis. They also had their own reasons to be sceptical about aspects of Britain's attitude towards her former colonies and their own vital national interests. Whether dominion opinion carried much weight remains a matter for debate: I argue that at crucial points both Canada and Australia did present arguments for a more considered attitude towards Ireland than that favoured by the British government, or more particularly its turbulent prime minister after May 1940, and that these had some impact on policy.

In researching this book I have consulted a wide range of sources, principally British. Of these, the most significant are the files of the Dominions Office, of MI5, of SOE, and of the codebreakers of GC&CS. Although these and other classes of records were subject to a certain amount of redaction within files, or withholding of records in their entirety, these series contain a wealth of material. We should, however, note that there are still significant gaps in the records available. I have found no material obtained through the clandestine opening of diplomatic bags passing through British control; again, with one exception, there is no trace of any product of telephone taps on the Irish high commission in London, or of penetration of that office by other means (suborning of servants, bugging, or whatever), techniques routinely deployed against other neutral diplomatic missions in London. Many MI5 records are still withheld, while others, such as that dealing with Frank Ryan, have been so heavily redacted as to make them very difficult to use. The reasons for most such redactions are, in the words of the official historian of SOE in France, M. R. D. Foot, 'inexplicable to the common man but supposedly defensible behind the scenes'. In most cases the intention is presumably to protect the identities of individuals, particularly if they worked for SIS, rather than to shield some terrible secret.[3] Historians must understand the restraints under which those authorizing the release or retention of material have to operate; we do not, however, have to applaud the underlying policies, which are generally inconsistent in principle and in application. The second world war ended over sixty years ago, a reality which those who determine the ground-rules for the release of historical materials appear not yet to have grasped fully.

---

[3] Foot, 'Foreword', in Mackenzie, *Secret History of SOE*, p. xiv.

NOTE ON CITATION AND TERMINOLOGY

The full titles of works cited in the footnotes are provided in the Bibliography.

For simplicity I have used the term 'decode' to describe all material, whether encoded or enciphered, which was read by codebreakers. I have also used the terms 'Persia' and 'Persian' throughout, save in direct quotations. Finally, I use 'Ireland' and 'Northern Ireland' for the two Irish jurisdictions.

Abbreviations are introduced on first usage, and a complete list is also provided.

Acknowledgements

I am grateful to the various archives and libraries which I have used during the research for this book. I particularly thank the staff of the National Archives, the National Archives of Ireland, the Military Archives of Ireland, UCD Archives, and Churchill College Cambridge Archives.

For guidance, recollections, advice, practical help, information, comments on the text, access to archives, hospitality, or general encouragement I must thank Richard Aldrich, Christopher Andrew, Liam Archer, Tom Bartlett, Gill Bennett, Sugata Bose, Pat Bourne, Pat Brady, Catriona Crowe, Colonel Ned Doyle, Ambassador Noel Fahey, Ronan Fanning, Geordie Fergusson, M. R. D. Foot, Sarah Frank, John and Amanda Gibbons, Mary Gibbons, Tom Hachey, Milan Hauner, Kieran Hefarty, Seamus Helferty, Michael Herman, Nicholas Hiley, Lisa Hyde, Peter Jackson, Keith Jeffery and Sally Visick, David Kahn, Patrick Kelly, Michael Kennedy, William Kingston, Commandant Victor Laing, Michael Lyons, Brigadier William and Mrs Maxine Magan, Bob Mahony, Barry McLoughlin, Deirdre McMahon, Alan Mac Simoin, Eve Morrison, Emmet O'Connor, Daithí Ó Corráin, Father Aodh O'Halpin, Ambassador Sean Ó hUiggín, Major-General the O'Morchoe, Kate O'Malley, Colonel Terry O'Neill, Alan Packwood, Amanda Piesse, Dorothy and Evelyn Podesta, Peter Rigney, Ambassador Sir Ivor Roberts, Jenny Scholtz, Mark Seaman, David Simms, Bradley Smith, David Spearman, David Stafford, Brian and Sally Stewart, Duncan Stuart, David Suckling, David Truesdale, Billy Vincent, Anne Walsh, Jill Walsh, Clair Wills, and Neville Wylie. I also owe much to people now departed, especially Colonel Tony Brooks, John Bruce Lockhart, Robin Cecil, Nigel Clive, Cleveland Cramm, Sir Harry Hinsley, Nicholas Mansergh, Sir Thomas Padmore, Sir Edward Playfair, Anthony Simkins, Sir John Stephenson, Harry Weber, Sir Dick White, Sir John Winnifrith, and Commandant Peter Young, and to the old G2 hands Douglas Gageby, Christopher Kelly, and, above all, Colonel Dan Bryan. Much of the research for the book was funded by grants from the Trinity College Dublin Arts and Social Sciences Benefactions Fund and the Institute for International Integration Studies. Finally, I must thank the anonymous Oxford reader, together with my successive patient editors Ruth Parr, Anne Gelling, and Rupert Cousens, copy-editors Jeff New and Kay Clement, and indexer Jackie Brind.

I thank the following institutions and holders of copyright for access to and permission to quote from collections of papers: the Bank of England (the Norman diaries and Bank records); the Bodleian Library (the Curtis and Sankey papers); the British Library (India Office records, and the Rich, Saklatvala, and Tegart MSS); the British Library of Political and Economic Science (the Dalton papers); the Controller of Her Majesty's Stationery Office; the Master, Fellows, and Scholars of Churchill College in the University of Cambridge (the Amery, Cadogan, Churchill, Drax, Gilchrist, Godfrey, Hankey, and Swinton papers); the Director of the National Archives of Ireland; the Dublin Diocesan Archives (the McQuaid papers); the Houghton Library, Harvard (the Moffat papers); the Keeper of the Public Records of Northern Ireland (the Savory papers); the Keeper of the Records of Scotland; the New York Public Library (the Joseph C. Walsh papers); the Podesta family (the Podesta papers); the Public Archives of Canada; the School of History and Archives, University College Dublin (the Bryan, de Valera, Fianna Fáil, Furlong, MacEntee, and Kathleen Barry Moloney papers); the Trustees of the Liddell Hart Centre for Military Archives (the Davidson papers); and the United States National Archives.

In the early stages of preparing this book I fell ill in 2002 with GIST, a rare cancer for which, luckily for me, an effective drug had just been developed. After surgery I experienced complications which left me with two curious craters in my skull and occasional bouts of fatigue. I owe a great deal to everyone who helped during that Gothic crisis and its aftermath, especially my former Dublin City University colleagues Pat Barker, John Horgan, John Hurley, Billy Kelly, Siobhain McGovern, Kathy Monks, and Gary Murphy, and my Trinity College colleagues Terry Barry, Ciaran Brady, Patricia Daly, David Dickson, Anne Dolan, Patrick Geoghegan, Louise Kidney, successive heads of department John Horne and Jane Ohlmeyer, Kevin O'Rourke and many students. I must also thank our tremendous neighbours, and friends from school, university, and civil service days, for their support. My greatest debt, however, is firstly to Rosemary, Patrick, Barry, Helen, and the Linders family; and secondly to my GP Dr Joseph Martin and to Professor Peter Daly and Ms Loreto Kissane of St James's Hospital, Dublin, for setting me on the road to recovery.

EOH

October 2007

Contents

List of Tables

Abbreviations and acronyms

AIDA	American Irish Defense Association
B1H	Designation for MIS's Irish section, hitherto B9
B1L	MI5's merchant-shipping security section
B9	Initial designation for MI5's Irish section in 1939
Barbarossa	German invasion of the Soviet Union on 22 June 1941
BJ	Diplomatic messages decoded by GC&CS
BL	British Library
BOAC	British Overseas Airways Corporation
BRO	British Representative's Office
BTNI	British Troops in Northern Ireland
BUF	British Union of Fascists
C	Head of SIS
CCCA	Churchill College Cambridge Archives
CID	Committee of Imperial Defence
CPGB	Communist Party of Great Britain
DMI	Director of Military Intelligence
DNI	Director of Naval Intelligence
Double Cross	The system developed by MI5 of running double agents in a coordinated manner so as to control enemy espionage and pass on deceptive information
FBI	Federal Bureau of Investigation
FIM	Federation of Irish Manufacturers
FOIS	Friends of India Society
G2	Irish military intelligence
GC&CS	Government Code and Cypher School
Garda	Garda Síochána (Irish police force)
GOC	General Officer Commanding
HMG	His Majesty's Government
INA	Indian National Army
IOR	India Office Records, British Library

IPI	Indian Political Intelligence
IRA	Irish Republican Army
ISC	Irish Situation Committee of the cabinet, 1932
ISIS	Irish Secret Intelligence Service (a G2 organisation in Cork and Kerry)
ISOS	Intelligence Service Oliver Strachey, a GC&CS acronym for decoded Abwehr traffic
ISSB	Inter Services Security Board
JIC	Joint Intelligence Committee
LOP	Look Out Post (Irish)
Magic	American summaries of decoded diplomatic traffic
MAI	Military Archives of Ireland
MI9	Escape and evasion organization
MI(R)	Military Intelligence (Research), 1939–40
MI5	Security Service
NAI	National Archives of Ireland
NARA	National Archives and Records Administration (United States)
NID	Naval Intelligence Department (Admiralty)
NSDAP	Nationalsozialische Deutsche Arbeiterpartei (Nazi Party)
NYPL	New York Public Library
OASA	Offences Against the State Act (Ireland)
O/C	Officer commanding
OSS	Office of Strategic Services (United States)
Overlord	Cover name for the invasion of France, 6 June 1944
PAC	Public Archives of Canada
Pandora	Decoded German diplomatic messages
PCO	Passport Control Officer
PWE	Political Warfare Executive
QRS	Acronym for periodic SIS political reports from Ireland from 1932 onward
RAF	Royal Air Force
RDF	radio direction finding
RNVR	Royal Naval Volunteer Reserve
RSS	Radio Security Service
RUC	Royal Ulster Constabulary

SIB	Manufactured rumour intended to confuse or deceive
Sigint	signals intelligence
SIS	Secret Intelligence Service (also known as MI6)
SOE	Special Operations Executive
TAR	T. A. Robertson, MI5 officer
TD	Member of Dáil Eireann, lower house of the Irish Parliament
TNA	The National Archives, London
Torch	Anglo-American invasion of French North Africa, November 1942
UCDA	University College Dublin Archives
UK	United Kingdom
W/T	wireless telegraphy

Biographical notes of key figures

Political figures are excluded on the basis that they are adequately identified in the text. Life dates are given where available.

Archer, Jane (née Sissmore). Married to Wing Commander Jo Archer of MI5. Joined MI5, 1923. Dismissed for insubordination in 1940, and joined SIS where she handled Irish affairs. Described by the Soviet agent Kim Philby as one of the two ablest officers he encountered in British intelligence (the other being Guy Liddell).

Archer, Colonel Liam (1892–1968). Participated in 1916 rising (wounded), but was reinstated in his Post Office position. Served in war of independence, 1919–21, and Irish army during the civil war. Director of intelligence, 1935–1941; assistant chief of staff, 1941–9; chief of staff, 1949–52.

Beppu, Fetsuya. Japanese consul (later consul-general) in Dublin, 1940–5.

Berardis, Count Vincenzo. Italian minister to Ireland, 1938–1944.

Boland, Frederick (1904–85). Assistant secretary, Irish Department of External Affairs, 1939–46.

Brennan, Robert (1881–1964). Under-secretary, Department of Foreign Affairs, 1921–2. Secretary, Irish Legation, Washington, DC, 1934. Minister to the United States, 1938–1947.

Bryan, Colonel Dan (1900–85). Medical student, University College Dublin, 1917. Served in IRA, 1919–21, and in Irish army during the civil war, mainly in intelligence. Acting director, G2, 1931; deputy director G2, 1935, and director, 1941–52. Commandant, Military College, 1952–5.

Collinson, Captain Charles Sydenham. SIS officer in Ireland, 1940–4. Retired from SIS, 1957.

Cremin, Cornelius 'Con' (1908–87). Irish chargé d'affaires in Berlin, 1943–5.

Denniston, Alastair (1881–1961) Director of GC&CS, 1919–42. Head of Diplomatic and Research section of GC&CS, 1942–5.

Dulanty, John (1883–1955). Irish high commissioner in London, 1930–49; ambassador, 1949–50. Previously honorary director of the United Irish League of Great Britain, where he supported Winston Churchill's campaign to win the North-West Manchester by-election. Joined Board of Education, 1913. Principal private secretary to Churchill at the Ministry of Munitions, 1917–18; assistant secretary, Treasury, 1920. Awarded CB and CBE. Resigned in protest at British policy towards Ireland, 1921. Chairman, Peter Jones Ltd., 1921–6. Irish trade commissioner in London, 1926–30.

Godfrey, Admiral John (1888–1971). Director of Naval Intelligence (DNI), Admiralty, 1939–42. Closely involved in Irish matters in 1939–40.

Hempel, Eduard (1887–1972). German minister in Dublin, 1937–45.

Kerney, Leopold (1881–1962). Irish minister to Spain, 1935–1946.

Liddell, Cecil (1890–1952). Captain, Kings Royal Rifle Corps, awarded MC, Order of the Crown of Belgium, 1918. Barrister and businessman. Established MI5's Irish section in 1939. Left MI5 in 1945.

Liddell, Guy (1892–1958), brother of Cecil. Captain, Royal Field Artillery, awarded MC, 1918. Joined MI5 1931. Deputy director and director, B Division (Counter-espionage), 1931–45. CBE, 1943. Deputy director general, MI5, 1945–52. CB, 1953. Described by the Soviet agent Kim Philby as one of the two ablest officers he encountered in British intelligence, the other being Jane Archer.

MacWhite, Michael (1882–1958). Irish minister to Italy, 1938–50. Awarded Croix de Guerre three times, and wounded at Gallipoli, during first world war service with French Foreign Legion.

Maffey, Sir John (1877–1969). Indian Civil Service, 1899–21; chief commissioner, North-West Frontier Province, 1921–4. KCVO, 1921, KCMG, 1931, KCB, 1934, and GCMG, 1935. Governor-general of Sudan, 1926–33. Permanent under-secretary, Colonial Office, 1933–7. British representative in Dublin, 1939–49. Created Lord Rugby, 1947.

Menzies, Sir Stewart (1890–1968). Major, Life Guards, awarded MC, 1915. Joined SIS in 1919, 'C' (director), 1939–52. CB, 1942, KCMG, 1943. Took a close interest in Irish matters, and controlled the flow of decoded enemy and neutral communications to the prime minister from September 1940.

Moore, J. Roger. Captain, RNVR. Joined RUC to deal with counter-espionage issues, 1940. Liaised closely with Garda headquarters until 1950.

Petrie, Sir David (1879–1961). Indian police, 1900–36. KBE, 1929. Director-general, MI5, 1941–6.

Pilger, Hans. German minister to Afghanistan, 1937–45.

Ryan, Frank (1902–1944). IRA man and volunteer in International Brigade in Spanish civil war. Captured and sentenced to death, 1938. Released with German assistance, July 1940. Embarked for Ireland on board U-boat, August 1940, but returned when his companion, IRA man Séan Russell, died on board. Occasionally employed by the Germans as an advisor on Irish matters. Died Dresden 1944.

Stephenson, Jo (John) (1910–97). Barrister. Joined MI5 Irish section, April 1940; Middle East, 1943–4; captain, 1943, major, 1944, lieutenand-colonel, 1946; headed MI5 traitor-catching unit in Northern Europe in 1944–5; high court judge, 1962–71; knighted, 1962; lord justice of appeal, 1971–85.

Vivian, Colonel Valentine (1886–1969). Joined Indian police, 1906. Joined SIS, 1923. Deputy head of SIS, 1939–51.

Walshe, Joseph (1886–1956). Secretary, Irish Department of External Affairs, 1927–46.

Warnock, William (1911–86). Irish chargé d'affaires in Berlin, 1939–43.

Wickham, Sir Charles (1879–1971). Served in Boer war, awarded DSO. Divisional commander, Royal Irish Constabulary, 1920–2; inspector-general, Royal Ulster Constabulary, 1922–45.

1

Britain's Irish security problem, 1922–1939

'WINSTON IS BACK'

On 3 September 1939 the Admiralty issued a general signal: 'Winston is back'. Churchill was restored to government as first lord of the Admiralty, the great office of state which he had occupied between August 1914 and July 1915. Prime minister Neville Chamberlain nominated Churchill just as war broke out because he could not possibly be excluded. Whatever his foibles and his failings, however irresponsible he might have been since 1929, he had vast experience of the higher conduct of war, as well as an unmatched fighting spirit.

Two days later, the new first lord called for

a special report . . . upon the questions arising from the so-called neutrality of the so-called Eire. Various considerations arise: (1) What does Intelligence say about possible succouring of U-Boats by Irish malcontents in west of Ireland inlets? If they throw bombs in London, why should they not supply petrol to U-Boats? Extreme vigilance should. be practiced, and the closest contact maintained between the DNI [director of naval intelligence] and 'C'.

Secondly, a study is required of the addition to the radius of our destroyers through not having the use of Berehaven or other south Irish anti-submarine bases: showing also the advantage to be gained by our having these facilities.

The Board [of Admiralty] must realise that we may not be able to obtain satisfaction, as the question of Eirish [*sic*] neutrality raises political issues which have not yet been faced, and which the 1st Lord is not certain he can solve. But the full case must be made for consideration.[1]

The next day he instructed the DNI to 'Ask "C" what is the position on the west coast of Ireland. Are there any signs of succouring U-boats in Irish creeks or inlets? It would seem that money should be spent to secure a trustworthy body of Irish agents to keep most vigilant watch. Has this been done? Please report'.[2] These instructions demonstrate two things: that from the moment he returned to the cabinet, Churchill saw the Irish ports as a crucial element in British maritime defence; and that he was still gripped by an *idée fixe* dating from the opening months of the first world war.

It is hardly surprising that Churchill should have recalled the Admiralty's fears in 1914 that U-boats were operating and receiving supplies along the west coast of Ireland. Such concerns had seen the dispatch of submarine-hunting patrols, and

---

[1] First lord to naval staff, 5 Sept. 1939, Churchill College Cambridge Archives (CCCA), Churchill papers, CHAR19/3.
[2] Ibid., 6 Sept. 1939.

the Naval Intelligence Department (NID) had also sent a large yacht, the *Sayonara*, crewed by ratings masquerading as Americans. This Gilbertian investigation merely added to the flood of scare stories which reached London of curious craft and suspicious characters turning up in small bays and inlets, asking veiled questions about submarines and separatists. Ireland was then part of the United Kingdom, and the Admiralty could rely on their own ships in Ireland, on the army, on the coastguard, harbourmasters, employees of the Post Office, the customs service, lighthouse-keepers, and above all on the loyal and efficient Royal Irish Constabulary (RIC) to keep their eyes open, and to report on mysterious goings on. Yet not one story of submarines sheltering or refuelling along the Irish coast turned out to be genuine. Submarines were twice used to infiltrate Irish rebels—Sir Roger Casement and a companion in 1916, and the hapless Corporal Joseph Dowling in 1918—but in each case the men disembarked at sea and made their way to shore in smaller craft. As post-war analysis of German navy records would have shown, there was no submarine-to-shore communication with Irish separatists, no docking of U-boats at remote piers, still less anything so technically complex as covert refuelling, during the first world war.[3] Yet no one in Whitehall seems to have drawn the obvious inference in 1939.

If the revival of the U-boat scare is puzzling, the re-emergence of the question of the ports is not. Throughout the first world war, Ireland was an integral part of the British Isles for naval purposes. In addition to operations based on Irish ports, the last two years of the war had also seen the development of naval aviation for anti-submarine operations.[4] Until the Anglo-Irish agreement of 1938, the Admiralty assumed that in a time of crisis, Irish ports and facilities such as airfields for coastal protection would again form part of their Atlantic defence network.

The curious intermingling in Churchill's directives of reheated old wives' tales about replenished U-boats, and actual strategic impairment due to the cession of the ports in 1938, begs the question of whether he deliberately sought to revive a powerful myth in order to prepare the way for action to remedy a real problem of naval defence. Is it possible that the U-boat scares were put into play precisely to legitimize a reoccupation of the ports? The answer is unequivocally no, if only because in the first months of the war the option was not open. Ireland, from being an integral part of the United Kingdom in 1914–18, had by 1939 become 'Hibernia incognita'. Even Churchill accepted that, before taking action to acquire the ports, information was needed on Irish affairs. The intelligence machinery to do this had to be built virtually from scratch. To understand how and why this was the case in respect of the only state with which the United Kingdom shared a land border, we must first look at British intelligence and Ireland between 1922 and 1939.

THE FAMILIAR UNKNOWN: IRELAND 1922–1932

The establishment of the Irish Free State in December 1922 saw the culmination of the withdrawal process from southern Ireland which Britain had begun in January

---

[3] These matters are more fully dealt with in O'Halpin, 'British Intelligence in Ireland', 54–77.
[4] Latham, *Naval Aviation in the first world war*, 31.

of that year. Almost all the residual civilian staff responsible for liaison with the new Irish regime since January 1922 quickly departed; the remaining military and naval personnel were withdrawn. The sole exception was the care-and-maintenance parties left in possession of the coastal defences and facilities of the treaty ports and installations. The British armed services continued to maintain bases in Northern Ireland, although after 1922 the internal security of the province became the exclusive preserve of the newly formed Royal Ulster Constabulary (RUC) including a part-time Special Constabulary.[5]

The ports aside, the departure from Ireland could scarcely have been more complete. Once the transfer of power and residual technicalities were dealt with, London left no one in Dublin either to speak to the new Irish authorities about matters affecting British defence or security interests, or to assess political and security developments. The Irish appointed a high commissioner to London, but Britain had no one in Dublin to do the equivalent job. During the civil war of 1922–3 the army and navy provided some logistical and intelligence support for Irish government forces, and there was some cooperation on action against republican activists in Britain. But these were ad hoc contacts which ceased almost immediately the civil war ended.[6] The office of governor-general might have provided a means for semi-official liaison, but the Irish ensured that this became simply a conduit for formal business between the new dominion and the Crown. In the other dominions governors-general were usually ex-military men or political grandees whose loyalties lay in London and whose approach was almost proconsular. They had considerable staffs, including some military officers, and they reported informally on affairs as well as relaying the wishes of the dominion governments. By contrast, the Irish governor-general had only a small retinue of secretaries without professional or informal links with Whitehall, and even these must have been hard pressed to find much to do beyond making social arrangements and maintaining the ceremonial decencies. The first governor-general was Timothy Healy, the fractious former MP and one-time scourge of Parnell. When not bickering with colleagues, Healy had spent his long career sniping at British rule in Ireland. London could expect no news or confidential guidance from him. Healy was succeeded in 1928 by the more emollient but no more biddable James McNeill. Although formerly a colonial official, his loyalties lay firmly with the new state.[7]

In Whitehall, the Home Office took on a liaison role with Northern Ireland. This amounted to little more than occasional correspondence on technicalities, because Belfast had its own government and legislature. Ireland became the responsibility first of the Colonial Office, and from 1925 of the newly established Dominions Office. Most Anglo-Irish matters were dealt with at departmental level: there was seldom need to bring issues to cabinet, and until de Valera's election in 1932 prompted the establishment of a dedicated committee there was no mechanism within the Cabinet

---

[5] Follis, *A State Under Siege*.

[6] A few officials remained in Dublin until as late as 1924 to help tie up administrative loose ends arising from the Government of Ireland Act 1920 and the Anglo-Irish treaty of 1921, but these had no diplomatic or intelligence role; O'Halpin, *Defending Ireland*, 21–3.

[7] On the governors general see particularly Sexton, *Ireland and the Crown*.

Office to bring together the views and knowledge of all departments interested in any aspects of Irish policy.

In matters of defence and security, the separation was even more marked. At the apex of defence policy was the Committee of Imperial Defence (CID), which had become a crucial instrument of strategic planning by the end of the first world war. In theory this provided a framework for inter-dominion dialogue on defence; in practice, because of her peculiar status and her lack of significant armed forces, Ireland took almost no part in the CID's work. There were no channels for regular liaison with the exiguous new Irish defence services on any aspect of military affairs. Once Lloyd George's coalition, at the price of some humiliation, narrowly avoided war with Turkey during the Chanak crisis in 1922, the CID concentrated on the possibilities of future conflict at sea with major powers which might pose a danger to the further reaches of empire, and on threats to the security of imperial communications. Any country with significant maritime capacity or ambitions—Japan, Italy, France, even the United States for a time—was regarded as a potential future enemy. The energies of defence planners were almost wholly engaged in anticipating such perils. There were also problems of imperial policing to consider: local disorder and insurgencies in various parts of the empire were a constant and enervating worry and a drain on military resources. Broadly speaking, for about a decade after Chanak the main strategic threats to empire which the CID anticipated were in far-flung corners of the globe or along Britain's lines of trade and communication. Consequently the security situation in Iraq often featured in the CID's deliberations; threats closer to home, such as possible Irish action against Northern Ireland, never did. Security was a jealously guarded responsibility of the Belfast government.[8]

The Anglo-Irish treaty provided for a defence conference after five years to discuss the transfer of responsibility for coastal defence from Britain to Ireland. Preliminary meetings eventually took place in 1926 on the margins of the Imperial Conference in London, but the definitive conference envisaged in the treaty never materialized. Among the small group of Irish officers involved in these inconsequential exchanges was Dan Bryan. He described the Irish assertion of readiness to assume responsibility for coastal defence as being dictated simply by considerations 'of general prestige': the new army was little more than a gendarmerie, and did not have the men, the equipment, or the ships to police the coastline and territorial waters and to defend the ports.[9] The Irish had no intention of building up their defence establishment—on the contrary, they were in the midst of reducing army numbers from a peak of over 50,000 in 1923 to about 7,000 by 1928, and they had already cancelled plans for a coastal patrol service.[10]

---

[8] Sir James Craig (prime minister of Northern Ireland) to Sir Henry Wilson, 28 Oct. 1921, made the case against raising 'a large Military Force in Ulster' and argued instead for the Special Constabulary under police control. Jeffery (ed.), *Wilson*, 303.

[9] 'Fundamental factors affecting Irish defence policy', marked 'G2/057, dated May 1936', with private secretary, minister for defence, to private secretary, minister for finance, 23 May 1936, UCDA (University College Dublin Archives), MacEntee papers, P67/91, 54. This document was very largely based on a paper prepared by Bryan while on a military college course in 1935. Dan Bryan interview, 1983.

[10] O'Halpin, *Defending Ireland*, 89.

The unreality of the Irish expression of willingness to take over coastal defence, and the emphasis which the Admiralty put on wartime coastal security, contributed significantly to Bryan's later analysis of Ireland's defence dilemma which was, uniquely, circulated to Irish ministers as 'Fundamental Factors affecting Irish Defence' in 1936. They also influenced his views while he was a highly effective deputy director (1935–41) and then director of intelligence (1941–52). Whitehall assumed that the external defence of the island of Ireland, its airspace, and surrounding seas, remained an exclusively British concern after 1922. There was no need to consult the Irish, and, as Paul Canning observes, despite generally good relations with the Cosgrave government, 'a lingering suspicion on both sides' about defence issues precluded serious discussions on such matters and the full involvement of Ireland in the CID's framework of dominions defence cooperation.[11] Threats to British Atlantic interests in any future war would be addressed, just as they had been between 1914 and 1918, by an appropriate naval and air presence in Ireland—commenting privately on the treaty in December 1921, one general observed that while 'the Naval Staff seem satisfied as regards the harbours, etc. . . . it seems obvious that only a loyal Ireland would ensure their protection in time of war'—but such reservations apparently did not register for long in the War Office.[12]

Of the three armed service intelligence organizations, NID had by far the most activist tradition. During the first world war they had secured control of both diplomatic and naval codebreaking, and under their charismatic director Reginald 'Blinker' Hall had played a crucial role in shaping—and on occasion distorting—British policy in key areas, including Ireland. NID ran their own agents in various countries, engaged on political as well as naval espionage, in places far outstripping SIS in the results obtained.[13] In the inter-war years NID concentrated on more technical subjects, but something of Hall's spirit remained. Much NID information came from naval attachés stationed abroad. The navy also intercepted signals traffic using its ships and radio stations across the world—direction finding and traffic analysis, as distinct from actual decoding, being crucial intelligence tools for naval operations. This traffic was analysed and, where possible, decoded locally, but some was forwarded to the Government Code and Cypher School (GC&CS), Britain's codebreaking organization. After 1922 NID had no reason to study Irish affairs except for security purposes: in 1926, following a warning that the IRA was planning to infiltrate the navy 'with motives of espionage, sabotage or propaganda', a system was devised of using retired officers living in Ireland to provide references for applicants. This procedure was to cost the elderly Vice-Admiral Boyle Somerville his life, as the IRA murdered him in 1936.[14]

[11] Canning, *British Policy Towards Ireland*, 182.

[12] Morland to Wilson, 9 Dec. 1921, in Jeffery, *Wilson*. 316. In 'naval' I include air units for shipping protection and anti-submarine operations, as anticipated in the treaty. The tangled story of British naval aviation between the wars is beyond the scope of this study. Sloan, *Geopolitics of Anglo-Irish Relations*, deals with the implications of the treaty for British strategy.

[13] Beesly, *Room 40*.

[14] Minute by 'head of naval branch' [signature illegible], 15 Apr. 1936, TNA, ADM178/144; O'Halpin, *Defending Ireland*, 125.

The army had been heavily engaged in combating insurgency in Ireland from 1919 until 1921 and, with the virtual collapse of police intelligence after 1919, an elaborate military intelligence machine was developed at command and unit levels.[15] But this was dismantled in 1922 when the army left. Thereafter the army's only direct interest lay in the small detachments assigned to guard the defence facilities retained under the treaty. Apart from one attack in Cork in 1924, which saw one soldier killed, the army's residual Irish experience was uneventful. Observation of the development of the Irish military presented no difficulties: many Irish personnel had served in the British army; Irish officers often took courses at British training establishments, and what little equipment the Irish possessed mainly came from Britain. No one in the War Office seriously considered Ireland as a future theatre of land operations, either offensive or defensive, and from the early 1920s the army vaguely hoped that the Irish would take over responsibility for coastal defence—'this awkward commitment', as it was termed in 1928.[16] The army continued to recruit men from Ireland, as did the Royal Air Force (RAF). The latter service had played only a minor part in operations in Ireland between 1919 and 1921, and had no reason to maintain any specialist intelligence interest after 1922. The codebreakers of GC&CS occasionally produced Irish-related material. GC&CS was an acknowledged department of government, but its main purpose—studying and decoding foreign cable and radio traffic—remained secret until the 1970s. GC&CS supplied decoded material to customers across Whitehall. MI5 and other agencies interested in the ramifications of international communism received decodes of Soviet diplomatic and clandestine radio and cable traffic having a bearing on Ireland, while the service departments saw anything of relevance to them. Thus the Admiralty were provided with American cables explaining the Irish delay in signing the Washington naval treaty in 1930; civilian departments such as the Board of Trade and the Dominions Office received copies of American and Belgian traffic concerning Irish trade policy.[17] Until 1932 such Irish-related decodes seem to have been acquired incidentally, and Irish government traffic was evidently not targeted.

Contiguity was one reason for a lack of unease about Ireland in Whitehall's secret world until 1932; another was probably sheer familiarity. Many soldiers and intelligence officers had served in Ireland at one time or another up to independence, and some were Irish themselves. An instructive example is provided by Indian Political Intelligence (IPI), a secret bureau established in London in 1910 to monitor the activities of Indian nationalists in Europe and America. During the first world war Germany had attempted to mobilize Indian nationalism for her own ends, building up links with Indians in Europe and with the émigré Ghadr party in the United States and encouraging rebellion in India.[18] The similarity with Ireland was clear.

[15] Towns-end, *The British Campaign in Ireland*; Hart (ed.), *British Intelligence in Ireland*.

[16] On this see Bond, *British Military Policy Between the Wars*, where Ireland is mentioned solely in respect of the war of independence. It was not until late May 1940 that the War Office began to plan for operations in both parts of Ireland to counter a German attack; Canning, *British Policy Towards Ireland*, 178–83.

[17] Such decodes are discussed in more detail in O'Halpin, ' "Weird Prophecies" ', 61–70.

[18] Jensen, *Passage from India*, 195.

After 1918, many Indian radicals were attracted towards communism because of its anti-imperialist doctrine. IPI studied the development of links, some of them Comintern-sponsored, between separatist movements throughout the empire, including Irish republicanism.[19] From 1924 IPI's small office was located in MI5 headquarters, greatly facilitating interchanges of information and ideas. When a new head of IPI was sought in 1925—'a good office man and as large part of work concerns Continent it is desirable he should have acquaintance with foreign languages, or at any rate French'—the first choice was Charles Tegart of the Calcutta police, a graduate of Trinity College Dublin, who had earlier worked on secondment to IPI.[20] In the event Tegart could not be spared. The job instead went to another Indian policeman and Trinity graduate with European experience and languages, Philip Vickery, who remained head of IPI until its incorporation into MI5 following Indian independence in 1947. His letter of acceptance was addressed from 'Carraig-na-Mara, Killiney', County Dublin.[21] The Irish backgrounds of such officials were thought an asset in understanding the interplay of nationalism and communism within the empire. So wrote David Petrie, a wartime head of MI5: 'Was Tegart ever an enemy of India's freedom? To those knowing his characteristically Irish make-up, the bare idea is ludicrous. He loved freedom for himself as he did for others, with all his ardent Irish nature . . . few were better constituted than he to understand what the mind of the bomb-and pistol-wallah was blindly groping after'.[22]

Ireland presented three main difficulties for British defence planners in the 1920s. Two of these—coastal security, and vulnerability to attack by a foreign power as part of a move against Great Britain—were centuries old. The third, the danger of military action by Ireland against Northern Ireland, was entirely new. In the early months of 1922 this seemed a possibility, as Dublin made plans for IRA operations along the border and inside Northern Ireland. This was potentially a means of papering over the treaty divide within the IRA, of exerting control over border units which might otherwise run amok, and of applying pressure on the new northern administration to protect the nationalist population from ethnic violence.[23] The possibility of concerted action quickly faded as civil war broke out. Britain provided weapons and other logistical support to the pro-treaty side, and there were some exchanges of information and concerted operations against republican support networks in Ireland and Britain. But the various British military and civilian intelligence, security, and police organizations involved in Ireland during the Anglo-Irish war all packed their bags in 1922. Ireland was no longer an intelligence and security problem. This attitude was reflected in the drastic 'Geddes Axe' cutbacks imposed in 1922, when the funding of the Secret Intelligence Service (SIS, also now known as MI6) was reduced from £200,000 to £180,000 because

---

[19] O'Malley, 'Indian Political Intelligence', 181–3.

[20] India Office to viceroy, 13 Mar. 1925, British Library, India Office records (IOR), L/PJ/12/39.

[21] Vickery to India Office, 1 Aug. 1926, BL, L/PJ/12/39. Vickery worked on secondment to IPI from 1915 to 1918 in Britain and the United States. BL, L/JP/12/9. So too did W. Somerset Maugham, whose *Ashenden* gives a fictionalized account of his activities in Switzerland against Indian émigrés.

[22] Tribute by Petrie, quoted in TS memoir of Tegart by K. F. Tegart, *c*.1948, BL, Tegart Mss. Eur C235.

[23] Hart, *Mick*, 380–4.

'secret operations in Ireland were surely unnecessary in view of the Anglo-Irish Treaty'.[24]

There was one obscure but important security matter where Anglo-Irish cooperation was essential. That was passport control, introduced during the first world war. The Passport Control Organization was established in 1919 as a subordinate office of SIS. It was, in the word's of Scotland Yard's Basil Thomson, 'a fine-meshed sieve through which the stream of alien visitors . . . is filtered', and 'provides an all important intelligence service on the movements of international revolutionaries'.[25] After the 1921 Anglo-Irish treaty, Britain continued to issue passports for citizens of the new state and visas for foreigners wishing to visit it, consulting Dublin about Irish applicants. Ireland's announcement of her intention to issue her own passports and visas as from April 1924 caused some alarm in Whitehall, because it threatened the integrity of the passport control system. A meeting involving SIS, MI5, Scotland Yard, the Home Office, the Foreign Office, the Colonial Office, and the India Office concluded that, because the British Isles formed a common travel area and the Irish border was unsealable, the Irish should be persuaded to operate the British passport watch lists, excluding only 'names which Scotland Yard and MI5 did not wish included' and 'all names of British Indians on [the] India Office Special List'.[26] Unless Irish cooperation were secured, undesirables could slip into the United Kingdom undetected simply by obtaining a visa to visit Ireland and either crossing the border or taking a ship across the Irish Sea. Anyone who sought a visa at an Irish mission abroad was first to be checked against the British watch list: anyone on it should also be denied an Irish visa or, depending on classification, their names should be notified to London. This arrangement worked satisfactorily enough, although in 1945 MI5's Irish section history observed that 'the Irish Immigration Service is not very efficient, and it seems certain that an alien wishing to enter . . . via Eire would have no difficulty in doing so, and [in] probably returning long before the notification of his landing in Eire reached the British Immigration authorities'.[27]

The operation of the common travel area and common external barrier around the British Isles made the control of movements between the United Kingdom and Ireland impossible. This had some bearing on wider economic and social policy, because it rendered impractical the imposition of restrictions on Irish immigration. In 1930 the cabinet considered Scottish demands, originating as much in prejudice against Roman Catholicism as in rational argument, to control Irish immigration in order to protect employment, discourage an influx of feckless indigents, and safeguard public morality. The prime minister Ramsay MacDonald, possessor of a stern Scottish nonconformist conscience despite his illegitimacy and his own

---

[24] O'Halpin, *Defending Ireland*, 15, 58–8, 69–70; Bennett, *Churchill's Man of Mystery*, 65. This work was published as one of the official histories of British intelligence, and the author had access to closed SIS and other records.

[25] Memorandum by Thomson, 29 Apr. 1921, in O'Halpin, 'Financing British Intelligence', 204.

[26] Note of a meeting, 11 Feb. 1924, National Archives (TNA), FO372/2091. Whitehall took considerable interest in Irish–Indian radical links. On these see particularly O'Malley, 'Ireland, India and Empire, 1919–1949'.

[27] O'Halpin, *MI5 and Ireland*, 35–6, cited hereafter as *Liddell History*.

marked taste for sexual adventure, believed 'we should refuse to be a dumping ground of Dominion refuse'. But the practical arguments against controls won the day. The problem was not to be addressed again until the second world war; even then, resentment of Irish neutrality and considerations of security had to be weighed against Britain's industrial and military need of Irish manpower.[28]

The question of which Whitehall secret agency, if any, should keep a discreet eye on Irish affairs was left open. Ireland was a loyal if somewhat assertive new member of the commonwealth. Ireland and the United Kingdom shared a common language, a common travel area, an open frontier, and effectively a common currency. Anyone wishing to take the temperature of affairs could simply take a boat across from Holyhead or Liverpool, or a train from Belfast, or just consult friends, relatives, or acquaintances who lived there.

So was there any need for intelligence on Ireland at all, apart from the particular problem of the republican movement in Britain, which was primarily a Special Branch task? Both SIS and the counter-espionage and security agency MI5 had been involved in monitoring aspects of separatist activities in and outside Ireland between 1914 and 1921. So too had Scotland Yard's Directorate of Intelligence, created in 1919 by the ambitious assistant commissioner Sir Basil Thomson, 'having in mind . . . the formation of a united military, naval, air and civil intelligence organization'.[29] He was forced out in November 1921, in part because of Irish controversies, and the directorate afterwards concentrated on the study of communism, drawing on the investigative work of the Metropolitan Police Special Branch.[30]

Under a rubric laid down in 1919, and reiterated in 1921, SIS were tasked to gather intelligence outside the empire. Answerable to the Foreign Office, SIS were chronically short of funds and of field staff. The main cover for intelligence gathering after 1919 was the system of passport control—most of its full-time representatives abroad operated under cover of the title passport control officer (PCO). This arrangement enabled the salaries of SIS officers abroad to be paid from Foreign Office funds, thereby reducing pressure on the small secret-service vote provided for unavowable expenditure; and it put them in a good position to study what was regarded as Britain's prime external target in the 1920s. That was not a country or an alliance of states but an ideology, communism. But PCOs had to run visa offices in addition to mounting covert intelligence operations. This was to prove a major difficulty in Europe in the 1930s, as thousands of refugees sought permission to travel to Britain or the empire. In addition, the PCO cover soon wore thin: in the mid-1930s the ambassador in Moscow flatly refused to allow such an

---

[28] Quoted in Canning, *British Policy Towards Ireland*, 117.

[29] Guy Liddell to Jock Curry, 24 May 1945, TNA, KV4/16.

[30] Sir Basil Thomson was assistant commissioner of the Metropolitan Police and in charge of the Special Branch from 1913 to 1921. A maverick who worked closely with the equally unconventional Blinker Hall on counter-espionage during the first world war, he made powerful enemies in Whitehall as he developed a wide-ranging security organization from 1919. He was eventually forced to resign after Sir Warren Fisher of the Treasury accused him of orchestrating a campaign of lies in 1919–20 against the inspector-general of the Royal Irish Constabulary, General Sir Joseph Byrne. Fisher sought to turn the tables completely by having Byrne replace Thomson, but the government instead chose a less controversial candidate. On this see O'Halpin, *Head of the Civil Service*, 91–5.

appointment because he believed it would damage relations with the Soviets.[31] He was probably right: in 1940 MI5's Jane Archer recorded how the Soviet intelligence defector Krivitsky 'incidentally asked me out of the blue—"I think your espionage abroad is carried out through your Passport Control Officers, in fact we were always certain of it"'. She demurred, but 'I am under the firm impression that he did not believe me'.[32]

Both because Ireland was a dominion, and because of the common travel area, the opportunity to station an SIS officer there under official cover did not arise until June 1940, when wartime movement controls were introduced. Significantly, these controls operated not only between the two Irish jurisdictions, but between the islands of Ireland and Great Britain, and they temporarily replaced the common travel area which had existed since 1922.

Imperial security, counter-espionage and counter-subversion were the business of MI5, an organization which, like SIS, did not exist officially. Most of its officers were ex-army men, contributing to confusion as to whether it was not simply a military security agency. MI5 spent most of the 1920s teetering on the brink of extinction. In 1919 it had a headquarters complement of over eighty officers and civilian officials, plus about 400 subordinate staff. By 1929 it had fewer than twenty officers and field-workers, plus a few clerical staff. As war loomed, a decade later, the officer strength had risen to just thirty, none of whom specialized in Irish affairs.[33]

Until the early 1930s MI5's main preoccupation was the ramifications of international communism within the United Kingdom and the empire. It was involved mainly in the collation and analysis of material supplied to it by other agencies, rather than in mounting independent investigations. No one minister oversaw its activities, but until 1931 it was nominally attached to the War Office; after a major reorganization that year, its closest links were with the Home Office. It also had some links with police forces throughout the United Kingdom through the Metropolitan Police Special Branch, an organization which was, it transpired, not free of the corruption which plagued Scotland Yard, since in 1929 it was discovered that two detectives had been selling information for years to the controller of a Soviet spy ring under MI5 investigation.[34] For a time after 1919 MI5 also had a handful of officers in dominions and colonies to liaise with local security and police authorities on counter-espionage and subversion. The exception was Ireland, with which it had no links at all.

This anomaly was not entirely the product of negligence. In February 1922 W. Phillips of MI5 set out the desirability of a structured security relationship with the new Dublin regime, analogous to those recently established with other dominions and colonies. His chief, Vernon Kell, a man whose long career at MI5 was marked by serial inability to avail of opportunities to develop his agency, sought

---

[31] Robert Cecil, 'Assessment and Acceptance of Intelligence', in Robertson, *British and American Perspectives*, 169.

[32] Note of Krivisky interview by Mrs K. M. Archer (neé Jane Sissmore), 8 Feb. 1940, TNA, KV2/804.

[33] *The Security Service 1908–1945: The Official History* (London, 1999), 99, 144, cited hereafter as *Curry History*.

[34] *Curry History*, 97; Guy Liddell to Curry, 24 May 1945, TNA, KV4/16.

a meeting with Winston Churchill, then the colonial secretary, but deferred the appointment due to the unsettled state of affairs in Dublin. The records do not show if the two did eventually meet to discuss Ireland. It is a fair question whether, given his love of secret intelligence, his appetite for political intrigue, his antagonism towards the Irish independence movement, and his disdain for local sentiment within the empire, Churchill would not have told Kell to make sure that, by hook or by crook, Britain retained the means of acquiring timely information on Irish affairs. As it was, 'in view of the present unsettled situation in Ireland (e.g. question of boundaries)', Kell was advised to 'work slowly on this question'.[35]

The onset of civil war prevented the establishment of a security link, although there was a good deal of ad hoc cooperation on republican activities in Britain. Chief constables throughout Britain were asked to keep an eye out for possible republican activity—in August 1922 the Northern Ireland education minister Lord Londonderry, a man almost crippled by pomposity, was outraged when police at Ardrossan insisted that standing orders required them to search his luggage on arrival from Belfast—but there was no significant spill-over from the new Irish conflict.[36] Phillips revisited the issue in December. He asked whether, 'in view of the complete withdrawal of British troops', it was not time to 'establish a liaison, either through the Colonial Office or direct with an official of the Free State'. The minute lay unanswered, although on 20 July 1923, by which time the civil war was over, Phillips added a note that matters affecting 'Southern Ireland' were dealt with by '(1) Scotland House (Colonel Carter)', which controlled the Special Branch; '(2) Colonial Office (Mr Lionel Curtis)'; and '(3) MO 3 (c) (Lieut [enant]. Col[onel]. Hill-Dillon)' of the War Office.[37] What these dispositions did not provide was a Dublin link dealing with security, espionage, and subversion.

Phillips returned to the charge after the Irish army mutiny of March 1924. He pointed to the revanchist sentiments on Ulster expressed by the leader of the mutineers, and argued that existing procedures for securing information on Ireland were cumbersome and incomplete. He identified three possible lines of action. The first was to establish an agreed link between MI5 and a designated Irish official. The second was to conduct enquiries from Northern Ireland. He knew 'unofficially' that Belfast ran agents across the border, but the 'Imperial Government' could not acknowledge such activities mounted against a dominion: 'if we used this service for our purposes, it might lead us into difficulties'. For the same reason he ruled out a third option, of stationing an undercover MI5 officer in Ireland.[38] Colleagues agreed, yet 'Southern Ireland is a far more likely potential enemy of ours during the next few years than many of the Foreign Powers whose activities we are now watching'. A temporary solution was to keep in touch with the 'Ulster Intelligence Service . . . our personal relations with certain of . . . the officers would probably enable us to ascertain what we want to know through them'.[39]

[35] Minutes by Phillips, 3 Feb. 1922, and by ?, same date, TNA, KV4/279.
[36] Scottish police report, 21 Aug. 1922, NAS, HH55/67.
[37] Minute by Phillips, 20 July 1923, ibid.
[38] Ibid., 12 June 1924, TNA, KV4/279.
[39] Minute by Ball, 18 June 1924, TNA, KV4/279.

This provincial 'secret service' had been created in 1922 as a military rather than a police or civilian agency. Responsibility for security generally was a contentious issue, and Belfast was determined to ensure the primacy of local civil forces in containing disorder.[40] Until the eventual abolition of the Irish boundary commission in December 1925, the Northern Ireland authorities and the army had strong reasons for studying the southern state in anticipation of any crisis arising from boundary commission findings, and also to thwart any efforts by the new Irish regime or its republican opponents to destabilize Northern Ireland. The War Office financed a small organization under Lieutenant R. A. Brown, who was attached to army headquarters in Northern Ireland. Its roles were to study Irish political and military developments, and to investigate possible Irish espionage.

These tasks made some sense, and were mirrored in arrangements in Dublin. Once the crises of the civil war and the army mutiny were successfully overcome, the Irish army's intelligence department put sustained efforts into the study of Northern Ireland. It was 'primarily interested in the activities of the Police Force, RUC, Specials etc. and collected data on their strength, organization, armament, location of units, etc. This was done largely through the use of agents'. Such material was included in a 'Topographical and Military Survey of Ulster', completed late in 1925. Army intelligence also had a counter-espionage role within Ireland, watching 'suspect agents of the Six Counties, and other elements likely to be in sympathy with the Northern Government'.[41]

For its part, Brown's agency garnered information of mixed quality on Irish political affairs and on the Irish police and army. One officer claimed to have uncovered eight Irish agents operating in Northern Ireland, reported accurately on the redesignation of Irish intelligence as the 'Second Bureau', and investigated the role of the German engineering firm Siemens in the vast Shannon hydroelectric scheme: 'the alien influx of late has been enormous and still continues . . . many of those with whom I have talked (as a perfectly *good Irishman*) evidently do *not* entertain the Locarno spirit towards Great Britain'. The writer was also involved in the case of a Belfast civil servant who imprudently used official notepaper in private correspondence with the 'Esoteric Club, Paris' — 'a *dirty affair* altogether . . . Fitzgerald Lombard came out *very badly* and had to go!!' He obligingly forwarded photographs to MI5 for their delectation, a gesture perhaps not unconnected with his hopes of employment by the agency, although MI5 had their eyes on Brown. He soon wrote again: 'I have heard nothing *official* regarding what is likely to be the ultimate disposal of self and my "travellers" though . . . when I visited the Ministry here to get the cheque to cover expenses etc a "hint" was given to me that "it was very unlikely that there would be many more such cheques to collect" — so that's that??'[42] Phillips incorporated much of this man's claims in a memorandum which argued that, since it was probably undesirable to start spying in Ireland, MI5 should appoint one of the Belfast specialists to maintain an eye on Irish

[40] Bew, Gibbon, and Patterson, *Northern Ireland 1921/2001*, 27–33; Follis, *State Under Siege*, 113; Donahue, 'The Special Powers Act', 1090–92.

[41] 'Review of North East Section 1926', in draft 'Annual Report of 2nd Bureau, General Staff Period 1st January '26 to 31st December, '26', Military Archives of Ireland (MAI).

[42] 'Fatty' to Phillips, 9 and 22 Feb. 1926, TNA, KV4/279.

matters. He stressed the point about alien penetration, and floated the possibility that the Irish might seek to spy in Britain. The director of military intelligence (DMI) was not persuaded: 'I am not unhappy about the Irish Free State, nor in the least frightened of it, and I don't believe it wants to, or is in a position to do us any harm'. As long as the Irish kept tabs on undesirable foreigners, he saw no need for an organization to collect intelligence in Ireland.[43] MI5 also had a spat with Scotland Yard about responsibility for thwarting Irish espionage in Britain, an activity which existed only in their imagination.[44]

The issue of Ireland did not arise again until 1931. Then, a major row with SIS about responsibility for studying communism in the United Kingdom prompted the incorporation into MI5 of Scotland Yard's Directorate of Intelligence, but Special Branch retained responsibility for 'Irish and anarchist' matters. SIS were debarred from running agents within the United Kingdom independently of MI5, forcing a degree of cooperation between the two feuding agencies. SIS established a counter-intelligence department, Section V, which was also to serve as the conduit for all its communications with other British security and police agencies.[45] These reforms provided more coherence to security work, and improved links between SIS, MI5, and Scotland Yard. MI5 took over responsibility for liaison with the RUC on 'revolutionary and seditious activities'. A year later, however, SIS established their own link with the RUC, through which 'they received information about events and suspect individuals in Northern and Southern Ireland'. This was a recipe for confusion, and it was eventually ended in 1938 when MI5 assumed responsibility for all security and intelligence exchanges (although the RUC continued to correspond separately with Scotland Yard on political crime).[46]

There were very occasional exchanges between Special Branch officers in towns and cities with significant Irish populations, and their counterparts in Dublin, mainly relating to the movements and activities of communists and suspect foreigners between Ireland and Britain. Traces of these exist in pre-war MI5 records.[47] So too do instances of occasional exchanges between Scotland Yard and the RUC about communists. So far as can be judged from the records, however, once the civil war was over there were no Anglo-Irish police exchanges on republican activities in the United Kingdom until 1939, and almost no north–south ones between the RUC and the Irish Garda (police).

There were also occasional exchanges with United States agencies. Irish radicals in America, and their international links with communist and anti-colonial movements, sometimes caught Uncle Sam's eye. Officials in the State Department, the Department of Justic, and the foreign service looked at such matters through the prism of anti-Bolshevism, a *lingua franca* which enabled American and British

[43] Director of military operations and intelligence to MI5, 14 Apr. 1926, TNA, KV4/279.

[44] Minute by 'B', 15 May 1926, TNA, KV4/279. Up to 1926 Irish army intelligence did run agents against the republican movement in Britain. O'Halpin, *Defending Ireland*, 57.

[45] *Curry History*, 101.

[46] Phillips to Gilfillan (RUC), 31 Oct. 1931, TNA, KV4/279; *Liddell History*, 24.

[47] Neligan (Garda) to Colonel Carter (Scotland Yard Special Branch), 12 Jan. 1932, and RUC to Major Phillips, MI5, 18 Dec. 1931, TNA, KV2/1180. For an earlier Carter–Neligan exchange see O'Halpin, *Defending Ireland*, 74.

officials to exchange material about the Comintern and all its works, as well as apparently related plagues such as Marcus Garvey's 'Back to Africa' movement and the Watch Tower movement (Jehovah's Witnesses). These perils were the stock in trade of Anglo-American security dialogue during the inter-war decades, and it was within that framework that occasional material concerning Ireland arose.

THE THREAT FROM IRISH REPUBLICAN LINKS WITH THE WIDER WORLD IN THE 1920S

The other side of the imperial defence coin was internal security. Here the challenges were clear enough: nationalism in various imperial territories, and Bolshevism. There was sporadic evidence of a link between the two impulses amongst the subject peoples of the empire, especially India. SIS collected both military and political intelligence in various corners of the globe, and in the territories of Britain's friends as well as in those of her likely enemies. SIS also collected strategic and military intelligence where they could, but it is important to stress how preoccupied they were with the Soviet threat until the mid-1930s. There ideology and geopolitics were intermixed because of Russia's historic ambitions, particularly in Asia and the Middle East: indeed, Britain and France had been rather let off the hook by the Bolshevik revolution, because had the Tsarist regime survived the war it would have been entitled to a share of the spoils of the former Ottoman empire.[48]

Ireland—or rather the defeated anti-treaty republican movement—sometimes featured in intelligence garnered by SIS and other agencies. There were sporadic indications that Irish republicans would continue to seek understandings with anyone who would help them in their struggle. The implications of this for British defence and security interests were, however, evidently not seen as terribly serious. Some outlandish material on links between Irish republicans and other anti-British movements turned up—in 1921 an Indian 'occasional correspondent', whom SIS regarded as 'usually well-informed', claimed that, 'in furtherance' of Tokyo's aim of ousting European influence from Asia, 'indirect Japanese influence is at work in Ireland'—but other reports were more credible.[49]

In the immediate aftermath of the civil war the republican movement, under the political direction of Eamon de Valera, sought to maintain the fiction that it was the legitimate Irish government, and pursued links with analogous movements elsewhere, both within the empire, particularly with Indian but also Egyptian separatists, and outside: in January 1925 de Valera was presented with a handsomely inscribed copy of *Montenegro: The Crime of the Peace Conference* by a visiting Montenegran separatist, and more significantly there was sporadic contact with the Soviet Union and with Soviet-sponsored international bodies.[50] A year later the Special Branch watched the London home of Shapurji Saklatvala, the Indian

[48] Busch, *Britain, India and the Arabs*, 35.
[49] SIS to Colonel Kaye (IPI), 29 Aug. 1921, BL, L/PJ/12/45.
[50] Warren, *Montenegro: The Crime of the Peace Conference*. The inscribed copy is in the Trinity College Dublin library; O'Halpin, 'Long Fellow, Long Story: MI5 and de Valera', 185–203.

radical and Britain's first communist MP, after an informant reported plans for a secret meeting involving de Valera and French and German extremists. Further, and probably more accurate, reports described de Valera's links with Indian separatists, including Jawaharal Nehru, and with the Comintern-sponsored League against Imperialism. As late as 1928, after he had qualified his personal theology of republicanism by accepting the legitimacy of the Irish state and taking his new party, Fianna Fáil, into the Dáil, de Valera reportedly visited the Berlin headquarters of the League, and various members of his party in its early years were also quite openly members of other radical international organizations 'affiliated to the Comintern'.[51]

Consequently it is no surprise that Irish-related material sometimes cropped up in SIS reports. The IRA occasionally sought to buy weapons in Germany, and Berlin was a hive of international radical political activity of both right and left: it housed the Comintern's western European headquarters, and was also the western European coordinating centre for Soviet espionage operations. In January 1923 SIS received a detailed report of an Asian freedom convention held in a villa in the Munich suburb of Schwabing. This brought together a kaleidoscope of European, Middle Eastern, and Asian delegates, mainly of the left but some from the opposite end of the political spectrum. Amongst them was an Irishman—'about forty, red hair, talkative'—who pledged 'every kind of moral and active support' for the oppressed nationalities of the British empire, and an Italian fascist who spoke in similar vein. Two representatives of Germany's new 'extremist Nationalist Party' offered their movement's sympathy; it was believed that one of the vehicles used to transport the delegates was normally used by their leader Herr Hitler, and that the villa might also be his.[52] This intelligence was not as incongruous as it might appear: Irish republicanism has always been characterized by extreme ideological flexibility, as its links both with the Soviet Union and with Nazi Germany were to show before and during the second world war.

Another SIS report in 1923 relayed a rumour that the German army had secured IRA agreement to gather military intelligence in Britain. At the time this was dismissed as incredible, because the source 'was an incorrigible liar'. In 1927, however, the matter was reconsidered by SIS because

reports concerning the German Band-Masters in Ireland; the visits of Republican Irishmen to Germany; the shipment of arms; and finally certain recent espionage cases in this country all point one way. Stripped of any detail, the present allegation arising out of all these facts is as follows:—

After the Irish treaty had become effective, the IRA organization in England tried for a while to continue creating trouble in Ireland. Finding no support, its leaders looked around for some method of employing the machine they had created, and incidentally of making money and doing harm to England. Already in touch with certain IIIrd International and German parties they . . . offered their services as an espionage organization, either to the International or the Germans or both. Having given proof that they possessed an organization

---

[51] Hanley, *The IRA*, 179; Childs (Special Branch) to MI5, 14 Dec. 1926, and MI5 to various departments, 22 Mar., enclosing text of intercepted letter from Bridgeman (a British communist) to Willi Muntzenberg (a Comintern agent in Berlin), 19 Mar. 1929, TNA, KV2/515. Saklatvala's papers throw little light on his Irish links. BL, MSS Eur D 1173/box 1.

[52] Hanley, *The IRA*, 33; SIS reports, 8 and 12 Jan. 1923, BL, L/PJ/12/102.

of couriers, collecting centres, fixed agents and so on, their services were accepted following a secret meeting in Glasgow as early as 1922, between representatives of the IRA and one or two delegates representing the German espionage service.

Whereas our Representatives aware of the above are on the lookout for information, it is clearly unlikely that we shall be the first to tumble on the full story, which is more likely to be found in England or Ireland.

For this reason C referred the memorandum to Scotland Yard, which raises the question of whether some form of enquiry was subsequently mounted in Ireland either with or without the knowledge of the Dublin authorities.[53]

Like so many reports, this was a melange of surmise, confusion, and inaccuracy. But it was not complete nonsense. The Irish had appointed a German, Fritz Brase, as head of the army school of music (providentially, this ardent Nazi dropped dead in 1940). Irish communists were few in number, but amongst them was James Larkin, the iconic labour agitator. The leader of the 1913 Dublin tramways strike, he had later moved to the United States, where for a time he was subsidized by the Germans to facilitate the sabotage of munitions ships sailing to Britain from east coast ports. Jailed for his labour activities in New York in 1919, upon his release and deportation in 1923 Larkin flung himself into communist affairs. He became a member of the executive committee of the Comintern, and set about building up a serious radical movement in Ireland. So far from being anyone's puppet, Larkin was the least manageable of men. He declined to take directions from anyone, whether in Ireland or in Moscow, and he generated as much friction within left-wing and labour organizations as he did conflict with employers. The Comintern despaired of him in 1925 and he went his own way.[54]

Other Irish communists were somewhat more disciplined. From the late 1920s a handful of promising young Irish people identified by the party were sent to the Comintern's Lenin School in Moscow.[55] This provided an ideological formation and practical training for activists; it was also a recruiting-ground for people regarded as suitable for clandestine work. Some of the Irish graduates of the Lenin School received secret training as couriers and radio operators. Brian Goold-Verschoyle played a significant role in London during 1935 in the Soviet spy ring handling material sold by the Foreign Office cipher clerk John Herbert King, before being sent to Spain during the civil war. His luck ran out in 1937, when he was decoyed onto a Soviet ship in Barcelona and arrested. He died in the Gulag in 1942. It is likely that some of the committed Irish volunteers who fought in the Spanish civil war were brought under Soviet control in the expectation of later use, both internationally and for the purpose of strengthening communist influence in the Irish labour and republican movements. British agencies picked up scraps of information about Soviet contacts with Irish socialists throughout the inter-war years, but such material was correctly viewed as further evidence of Comintern machinations rather than as representing a particularly Irish phenomenon.[56]

---

[53] SIS to MI5, 20 Apr. 1927, enclosing undated memorandum, TNA, KV3/11.

[54] O'Connor, *Reds and the Green*, 82–115.

[55] Decode of Comintern (Berlin) to Pollitt (CPGB), 14 Aug. 1931, re Irish students. TNA, HW17/70.

[56] McLoughlin, *Left to the Wolves*, 132–47 and 168–75.

In the 1920s and the 1930s the wider republican movement included many people of a left-wing persuasion, and as a whole it had no ideological aversion to cooperating with communists against a common enemy. During the Anglo-Irish war the underground Dáil government had attempted to establish links with the revolutionary regime in Moscow, and during the civil war de Valera sent an emissary to Geneva in a vain attempt to interest the Soviet foreign minister Chicherin in the Irish republican cause. Two years later three Irish republicans visited Moscow seeking weapons. This group reflected the heterogeneity of anti-treaty republicanism: Seán Russell was an apolitical physical force man, who was eventually to die en route to Ireland aboard a U-boat in 1940; Gerry Boland was soon to abandon the IRA and to become a key figure in de Valera's new Fianna Fáil party, and later as justice minister to be the scourge of republicanism during the second world war; and 'Pa' Murray was commander of the IRA in Britain. This troika found the Soviets still unwilling to provide direct help, although contact was established with a Soviet agent in Berlin, and an agreement reached under which for a time the IRA in Britain collected intelligence on military matters. The arrangement eventually became known in outline to both the British and Irish authorities.[57] In 1927 the IRA committed itself to siding with the Soviet Union in any future conflict with Britain, and in the following years the organization took a pronounced turn to the left. In 1929 a 'confidential and very delicate source' disclosed the views of an Irish employee of the Soviet trading company Arcos:

In the event of war with Russia, attacks . . . would be made in various directions by the IRA here . . . 'reliable' men had been selected to join the Army and Navy, in order to commit acts of sabotage. Both sections of the IRA . . . would be put under the charge of a 'new officer from Ireland', and would 'work independently of the Communist Party here'. Discussions had been held . . . on the whole matter. [J. R.] Campbell had pointed out that the position was dangerous . . . it would be more advantageous if the IRA acted on its own initiative, although it could keep in contact. M[ichael] Fitzpatrick, representing GHQ, IRA, said that that body would stand by the agreement which it signed some time ago, and would pull its 'full weight' with Russia, 'not only in Ireland and England, but America'.[58]

This report is credible in outline.

In an ironic replication of the edifice of imperialism which it sought to bring down, the Communist Party of Great Britain (CPGB) was assigned a directing role over all other national communist parties within the empire. This sometimes extended to subversive as well as to political matters, as was clear from clandestine Comintern radio traffic intercepted and decoded by GC&CS between 1931 and 1936. This included a good deal of Irish material, mainly concerned with the pitifully small subsidies which Harry Pollitt of the CPGB passed on to the Irish comrades, and calls for closer links between communists and the IRA.[59] Efforts were

[57] Undated report by McCartan [June 1920], in Fanning *et al.* (eds.), *Documents in Irish Foreign Policy* [*DIFP*], i. 148–54; O'Halpin, *Defending Ireland*, 24, 72–3.

[58] Special Branch to MI5, and enclosed report, 16 and 13 Aug. 1929, TNA, KV2/1180.

[59] O'Connor, *Reds and the Green*, 161–213. Decoded Comintern traffic concerning Ireland can be found in the TNA class HW17. HW17/80 contains an index of such decodes.

often made to maintain a distance between the CPGB and covert activities such as espionage, but while these may have convinced the naive, the party was clearly implicated: in 1943 the CPGB's Bob Stewart was recorded incautiously telling a comrade that Soviet agents 'over there [in Moscow], you see . . . they were always told as a last resort, you see, "Go to STEWART". . . .'.[60]

In September 1931 an SIS report 'obtained . . . from a Moscow source who is an official of the OGPU' (Soviet military intelligence) indicated that the head of the OGPU's 'Foreign Department', appropriately named Messing, had been purged, partly for 'bungling English and Irish affairs'.[61] The CPGB, under orders from Moscow to galvanize progressive forces in Ireland, dispatched Bob Stewart to Dublin. GC&CS decoded Comintern complaints about a lack of activity in Ireland and orders for a mass campaign to galvanise Irish workers and peasants against the Cosgrave regime and Ireland's residual links with Britain.[62] The intention was to harness the potential of the republican movement for wider revolutionary purposes in both parts of Ireland, as well as to extend communist influence in trade unions. Not all republicans were happy with what they regarded as an attempt to hijack the movement. Fissures developed, first with the formation of the radical Saor Éire in 1931 as a tolerated offshoot of the mainstream IRA, and secondly with the emergence of the openly communist Republican Congress in 1934 under the leadership of Peadar O'Donnell, a long-time IRA leftist who had been prominent in a number of Comintern-sponsored Irish and international bodies. This was in line with Comintern instructions to forge links with the IRA and to convert it to a genuinely revolutionary path.[63] Formation of the Congress led to a parting of the ways, with most of the IRA's socialists leaving the mainstream republican movement.[64] With them went most of the leftist impulses within the organization—as we shall see, within a year the IRA was making overtures to Nazi Germany, and there are also indications of contacts with Fascist Italy.

The episodic and contingent nature of Soviet interest in Ireland was reflected in the observations of the Soviet defector Krivitsky—'THOMAS'—who, when asked about one Comintern agent involved in Irish affairs, said that 'about 1926' three Irishmen 'asked for Soviet support':

THOMAS worked with them for a time and got quite useful information out of them, but he found he was dealing not with these men alone, but was getting involved in the affairs of the

[60] Extract of recorded conversation between Stewart and Jimmy Shields in CPGB headquarters, 22 June 1943, TNA, KV2/1180.

[61] Miller (MI5) to Robinson (MI5), 7 Oct. 1931, attaching SIS report of 24 Sept. 1931, TNA, KV3/13.

[62] Comintern (Berlin) to London, 20 Feb. and 20 June 1931, TNA, HW17/69 and 70; RUC to MI5, 18 Dec. 1931, re visit by Stewart to Belfast, and Neligan (Garda Special Branch) to Carter (Special Branch), re an unidentified Scotsman (Stewart) newly arrived in Dublin, 12 Jan. 1932; Special Branch report on Stewart, 10 Aug. 1932, TNA, KV2/1180. There is also a file on Stewart in the Public Record Office of Northern Ireland (PRONI), HA/5/2627.

[63] Comintern (Berlin) to London, 5 Apr. 1932, and Comintern (Stockholm) to London, 12 Apr. 1933, TNA, HW17/77 and 73. Those associated with the Republican Congress movement whom I met—Peadar O'Donnell, and our family friends Frank and Bobbie Edwards, and Charlie and Nora Harkin—always dismissed any suggestion of external control of the organization and resented any imputation that they were puppets of Moscow rather than free-thinking radicals.

[64] See English, *Radicals and the Republic*.

organization. Some time later about 1927 the Polit Bureau forbade any dealings with the Irish movement because they were trying to obtain Soviet credits here [in Britain].

Later THOMAS got in touch with these men again, but after a while these men suggested that THOMAS should give them assistance in a 'terrorist' plan. On this THOMAS thought these men might be agent provocateurs and . . . decided to drop them.

. . . THOMAS told me that if the OGPU . . . were finding it necessary to have an agent or contact in any particular place, their first recruiting ground was the Communist Party; if that failed they invariably tried to find out if there was any Irishman . . . who would make a good contact . . . purely on the basis that an Irishman was probably anti-British and would be more willing to work for them than an Englishman.[65]

Given the extent of the republican movement's links with Russia, it is perhaps surprising that Whitehall continued to regard the IRA simply as a residual irritant, not an organization capable of or even aspiring to threaten wider British interests. The explanation may lie partly in bureaucratic factors: MI5 was a tiny organization preoccupied with other matters. Scotland Yard's Special Branch, which held the watching brief for Irish affairs, was trained to investigate crime, rather than to accumulate information and to ruminate indefinitely about contingencies which might never materialize.

This was also the case with the RUC Special Branch, which naturally concentrated on the IRA but also kept an eye on communism in Northern Ireland. After 1931, although 'not well equipped to study foreign organizations and activities in Eire', it reported to SIS on 'events and suspect individuals in Northern and Southern Ireland'. These were mainly communists, feared not simply for ideological reasons but as possible saboteurs in the strategically significant aircraft- and shipbuilding industries, and occasional foreign visitors. From 1938 its London contacts on these matters were with MI5.[66] It was, however, only with the establishment of MI5's Irish section in 1939 that an officer was tasked with concentrating on all intelligence and security material relating to Ireland as a whole.

One other dimension of intelligence should be noted. Ireland retained sterling as its currency, and its banking and financial system was effectively a subset of Britain's. As a result, information on the Irish economy and public finances was readily to hand in London. The Treasury had acted as midwife and nanny to the Irish Department of Finance, and retained close contact with their protégés in Dublin. This remained so even at the height of the 'economic war' which began shortly after de Valera came to power, and these links played a significant part in the resolution of the trade and financial disputes underpinning the economic conflict, and of the 1938 agreement on the treaty ports.[67] The Bank of England also kept an eye on Irish financial and economic affairs, and the Irish remained in close and deferential touch: on the day that the 1938 Anglo-Irish agreement was signed, the secretary of the Irish Department of Finance called in to Threadneedle Street to mention that his government intended issuing a loan to cover the cost

---

[65] Krivitsky interview, 8 Feb. 1940, TNA, KV2/804. This plainly refers to the 1925 Moscow visit by Boland, Russell, and Murray already discussed.

[66] Liddell diary, 14 Nov. 1939, TNA, KV4/186.

[67] On these links see Fanning, *The Irish Department of Finance*, and Canning, *British Policy Towards Ireland*.

of the settlement, and 'asked—but did not expect a reply . . . whether the British government were likely to be launching a loan in the London market'. Just three days before Germany invaded Poland, the deputy governor of the Bank of Ireland met with the all-powerful governor of the Bank of England, Montagu Norman, to discuss technical problems which might arise once war broke out due to Irish reliance on the British financial system. The Bank of England routinely supplied economic and financial intelligence to SIS.[68] The position was broadly similar in relation to commodities such as coal and oil, where British companies were the main suppliers and carriers. All this meant that, when war broke out, reliable information on which to base decisions about trade and economic pressure on Ireland was to hand.

1932: IRELAND BECOMES AN INTELLIGENCE TARGET

For a decade after 1922, few in Whitehall seem to have worried much about intelligence on Ireland. She was now a dominion, albeit an assertive one, and that was that. The arrival in office in March 1932 of Eamon de Valera changed everything. For some months Ireland became a preoccupation. London had no diplomatic representative in Dublin to offer informed assessments of political developments, so the field of analysis and prediction was left entirely to outsiders and alarmists. The unsettling questions arose of what de Valera might attempt on partition, in Anglo-Irish relations, in wider dominions affairs, and at the League of Nations.[69] How influenced would he be by leftists—the outgoing Cosgrave government had portrayed him as a pawn of communism, and when the election outcome became known London was warned that he was at best a Kerensky, incapable of controlling the Moscow-inspired union of republicanism and socialism. The Tipperary man Sir Michael O'Dwyer, destined for assassination in the improbable setting of a lecture at Caxton Hall in 1940, warned that de Valera was a 'tool of Moscow'.[70] Within days of the change of government, MI5's Jasper Harker wrote of new dangers, not only for Northern Ireland but because independent Ireland could become a hotbed of revolutionary communism: 'we should ourselves run a small organization' to collect Irish intelligence, although the more modest innovation was adopted of making Ireland part of the brief of an MI5 officer.[71]

De Valera's accession to power came in the midst of a substantial scare about Soviet arms shipments. In May it appeared that a gun-running operation uncovered the previous winter was finally to begin. The navy was instructed to shadow the

---

[68] Report of meeting with McElligott, 25 Apr. 1938, and Montagu Norman diary, 20 and 24 May, and 29 Aug. 1939, Bank of England Archives, OB81/1.

[69] The intelligence response to de Valera's election is discussed in depth in O'Halpin, '"Weird prophecies"'.

[70] MI5 minute, 18 Apr. 1933, TNA, KV2/515, citing O'Dwyer; O'Dwyer, who was lieutenant-governor of the Punjab at the time of the Amritsar massacre in 1919, was shot in March 1940 by Udham Singh, an unbalanced Sikh who sometimes used the very Irish cover name 'Frank Brazil'. BL, L/PJ/12/500.

[71] Memorandum by Harker, 12 Mar. 1932, TNA, KV4/279.

suspect ships, and Dublin was informed: 'I feel it is my duty as one Dominion to another to inform you of the following facts'. Dublin refused permission for the navy to board and search the ships in Irish waters, and instead asked where the weapons were to be landed. It transpired that the ships were carrying legitimate cargoes. The crisis may have prompted allegations that Spanish boats were running guns to Ireland. MI5 found the claim baseless: some Welsh trawler-owners were angry because Spanish fishermen had moved into their traditional waters along the Irish coastline.[72] Yet the scares persisted. In December the dominions secretary J. H. Thomas, once a union leader of distinction, but in government an erratic buffoon, informed the Irish high commissioner John Dulanty that he had

demonstrable proof that both Russian arms and Russian money was being sent into Ireland, and . . . the Russians . . . would want their pound of flesh . . . It may have been that I looked incredulous because Mr Thomas said 'There is absolutely no doubt about this, and I can produce proof. I can give the date and particulars of the last cheque which was for £15,000. I can also give the date and particulars of a cheque . . . for another £15,000'. I pressed him for details . . . but he would say no more than that he knew as a fact . . . that Russian arms had been landed.[73]

What was most interesting about this scare is that London concluded they had no option but to consult de Valera on so delicate a matter as alleged IRA gun-smuggling. This was despite the fact that the cabinet's newly established Irish Situation Committee (ISC) was gravely concerned about his intentions. In April emissaries from Cosgrave had advised that Britain should make no concessions to de Valera and instead wait until his administration collapsed under the weight of its own ineptitude: even if his plans to amend the constitution won popular support, his determination to initiate a dispute over land annuities payable to Britain on foot of earlier land-purchase legislation would cause economic chaos and bring him down.[74] The inception of the land annuities dispute generated concerns in Britain, as 'it is possible that demonstrations or disturbances may arise amongst the Irish element of the population'. A Scottish chief constable reported that 'many of the Older School of Irishmen resident here are secretly, if not openly, hostile to Mr De Valera's Government', and in fact there was no trouble amongst the Irish diaspora during the years of the 'economic war'.[75]

The ISC continued to fret about Ireland—a further scare about arms shipments in August fanned fears that de Valera might be contemplating action against Northern Ireland—and it called for hard intelligence.[76] The chief of the imperial

---

[72] SIS report, 17 Nov., and Machtig to Walshe (Dublin), 19 Nov. 1931; undated draft communication [1932]; Kell (MI5) to Machtig, enclosing report, 19 June 1932, TNA, DO121/77.

[73] Dulanty to Walshe, 21 Dec. 1932, UCDA, de Valera papers, P150/2179. I am grateful to Michael Kennedy for drawing my attention to this document.

[74] McMahon, *Republicans and Imperialists*, 52–3; Canning, *British Policy Towards Ireland*, 128–52.

[75] Scottish Office circular to chief constables, 28 July, and reply from Coatbridge, 29 July 1932, National Archives of Scotland (NAS), HH55/700.

[76] Sankey diary, 24 Aug. 1932, Bodleian Library, Oxford, MS Eng. Hist. C 286. Sankey was lord chancellor and a member of the ISC.

general staff undertook to see if information 'both from the point of view of military intelligence and also of political intelligence' could be obtained.[77] MI5 were asked to gather intelligence in Ireland, just as Harker had advocated in March. 'After consideration', however, Kell declined this opportunity; instead SIS agreed to set up 'not an intelligence service, but a very restricted information service', which simply gave 'a limited cross section of private opinion on current events of public interest in Eire'. This, circulated to SIS's customers as 'QRS' reports, seems to have been little more than the table gossip of de Valera's critics, a kind of one-sided diplomatic reporting. SIS also liaised with the RUC about suspect foreigners in both parts of Ireland. It was probably around this time that SIS established the 'Irish section' to which Gill Bennett alludes.[78] There is no evidence that SIS solicited information or observations from inside de Valera's government or from the IRA, and they did not put any officers on the ground. But the fact that the task of watching Ireland was given to SIS reflected the prevailing confusion about how to treat Ireland under its new and determined leader, as well as to a lack of clear geographical delineation between SIS and MI5.

In July 1933 SIS produced further news of a supposed IRA–Comintern agreement, furnished by a White Russian émigré who lived by peddling such stories. The political element of this pact had supposedly been negotiated in New York, and the military section in Norway. The latter included a Soviet commitment to assist the IRA in purchasing arms in Germany. SIS tried to have it both ways with this report: 'Owing to the source we cannot . . . place any reliance upon it, but it strikes me as not by any means impossible, or even improbable, information'.[79] Such reports were significant not for their accuracy, but for the fact that the IRA were still cropping up from time to time in relation to other hostile movements and states. SIS also kept an eye on de Valera, reporting in December 1932 that he appeared among 'a long list of sympathisers' prepared by Breton nationalists recently seized by the French police. This might well have been the case during the 1920s, but in office de Valera steered well clear of such minority groups in countries with which Ireland had good relations. A Russian informant also claimed that de Valera, along with the oil magnate Calouste Gulbenkian, was interesting himself in the fate of ethnic Ukrainians in Poland while studiously ignoring Soviet treatment of their various minorities.[80]

Within a fortnight of de Valera's taking office, GC&CS began reading cable traffic between Dublin and Ireland's few missions abroad (GC&CS received copies of all encoded traffic on cables passing through British territory, as well as all encoded traffic on the direct Irish–North America cables). Not all codes were consistently easy to break, but in the early 1930s GC&CS were able to read some if not all Belgian, Italian, and American traffic to and from Dublin.[81] In such a backwater, most of this traffic dealt with routine political, economic, or consular matters. It

---

[77] Extract from ISC minutes, 5 Aug. 1932, TNA, ADM178/91.
[78] *Liddell History*, 20, 36; *Curry History*, 143–4; Bennett, *Churchill's Man of Mystery*, 354, n. 53.
[79] Undated memorandum, with SIS to MI5, 28 July 1933, TNA, KV2/819.
[80] SIS report, 9 Dec. 1932, TNA, KV2/515.
[81] Decodes of Sterling (US consul-general, Dublin) to Washington, and Dawes (US ambassador, London) to Washington, both 21 Oct. 1930; Sterling to Washington, 2 July, Mariani (Italian consul,

is a fair guess that some of the communications were so pedestrian that they were not even stored, let alone circulated to departments, and this makes it difficult to estimate the volume of GC&CS activity relating to Ireland. In any case, de Valera, who was minister for external affairs as well as president, was not a man to unburden himself unduly to foreign diplomats. Nor, as is clear from the Irish cables which the British did decode and preserve, did he have a great deal to say to his own diplomats abroad. Rather, their job was to report to him. Furthermore, Dulanty in London, much the most significant Irish diplomat so far as Britain was concerned, could easily and more safely communicate by courier or on visits home.

De Valera was aware of the vulnerability of codes, and within months of his coming to power Dublin told the Irish delegation at the Ottawa imperial trade conference that 'you understand codes are not secret'.[82] In MI5's view Irish decodes 'sometimes reflected . . . official opinion', though they were 'in no sense a source of counter-espionage information'.[83] The GC&CS records suggest that Irish traffic was initially targeted only for five months—from March to July 1932. The last Irish cables decoded were an exchange between Dublin and its representation at Geneva on 6 July.[84] The absence of Irish decodes over the succeeding years until July 1940 probably reflected British priorities—GC&CS were desperately short of staff—rather than any particular technical difficulties, or ethical concerns about reading the traffic of a dominion. Similarly pragmatic calculations presumably explain the fact that the Irish diplomatic bag seems to have remained inviolate in peacetime, a reflection of British priorities rather than of any ethical or technical obstacles. Once war came, such communications were considered fair game provided only that the fact of interception could be concealed. GC&CS did continue to decode some of the traffic of foreign missions in Dublin: thus in April 1939, when the American legation reported Irish complaints of Roosevelt's use of the phrase 'Great Britain and Ireland', the material was available in Whitehall almost as quickly as in Washington.[85]

The most significant inter-war decodes are of messages exchanged between Ireland and other dominions. The reading of such inter-dominion traffic was a clear breach of faith by London (which provided the codes for inter-dominion communications in the first place). The 1932 records contain two Irish cables to South Africa and Canada, and one from the Canadian government to Dublin, all relating to the forthcoming Ottawa conference (in 1942 the Canadian prime minister recalled how 'at Imperial Conferences . . . we had always counted on South Africa and Ireland').[86] This raises the question of whether GC&CS read similar bilateral inter-dominion traffic in the build-up to other imperial conferences (where Ireland, in concert with

Dublin) to Rome, and Goor (Belgian consul, Dublin) to Brussels, both 19 July 1932, TNA, HW12/136 and 157.

[82] Dublin to Walshe (Ottawa), 15 Aug. 1932, National Archives of Ireland (NAI), DFA Secretary's File S.1. I am grateful to Dr Michael Kennedy for drawing my attention to this document.
[83] *Liddell History*, 36.
[84] Lester, Geneva, to Dublin, and reply, 6 July, 1932, HW12/157.
[85] McVeagh (Dublin) to Washington, 19 Apr. 1939, HW12/238.
[86] Decodes of Dublin, Dublin, to Dublin, Pretoria, 30 May, Dublin, Dublin, to Prime Minister's Department, Canberra, 5 July, and Dublin, Ottawa, to Dublin, Dublin, 8 July 1932, TNA, HW12/156 and 157; Mackenzie King diary, 9 Apr. 1942.

other dominions, played a major role in redefining the nature of the commonwealth despite British objections).

The other question arising from London's alarm and incomprehension at de Valera's election is a straightforward one: is there any evidence that intelligence agencies sought to interfere in Irish politics, so as to bring down de Valera in favour of someone more amenable? On this the records are silent. In October 1932 there were extensive Anglo-Irish discussions. These contacts, while they provided little comfort and did not produce any compromise on the various constitutional and economic matters considered, at least familiarized Whitehall with de Valera. His plans might still appear outlandish and damaging, but so far from behaving like a capricious demagogue, he was clearly working systematically to a thought-out agenda.[87]

Once de Valera strengthened his position in a snap election in January 1933, London became more or less reconciled to having to deal with him. While there remained much regard in Whitehall for Cosgrave and his Cumann na nGaedheal party—their assertive attitude in dominions affairs was quite forgotten—there is nothing to suggest any active measures to help them. In 1934 a supporter sent a begging letter to Lionel Curtis, formerly the Colonial Office's great theoretician of empire and now a fellow of All Souls. This warned that the party was penniless, its coffers emptied by the demands of two general elections within a year, its best supporters drained and dispirited. Without financial assistance it would be impossible to rally it to mount a serious challenge. It seems unlikely, Whitehall's continuing affection for Cosgrave notwithstanding, that any British money reached Dublin (although it is conceivable that General Eoin O'Duffy's Blueshirt movement received financial support from Mussolini—Italy certainly gave money to Oswald Mosley's British Union of Fascists).[88]

Cumann na nGaedheal's vicissitudes resulted in a merging with O'Duffy's quasi-fascist organization, popularly known as the Blueshirts, to become Fine Gael, in September 1933. O'Duffy had been an outstandingly successful though partisan head of the Garda—he had attempted to organize a military coup should Fianna Fáil win the 1932 election—who was eventually dismissed from his position after refusing an alternative sinecure. He had then assumed the leadership of what had begun as an association of ex-soldiers.[89] He became president of Fine Gael. It was a brief and uncomfortable union. Cosgrave's followers were law-abiding men who had consolidated the new state between 1922 and 1932, and who had properly if fearfully relinquished power to de Valera. A few flirted with corporatist ideas, but by and large the party's cast of mind was democratic, and their natural milieu was the parliamentary chamber. By contrast, O'Duffy espoused the manly virtues of disciplined street-fighting, and spoke of the decay and obsolescence of democracy.[90] He was, unlike Cosgrave, bellicose about partition—as an IRA leader in Monaghan he had organized widespread sectarian reprisals along the new border in 1921—and

[87] Canning, *British Policy Towards Ireland*, 148–51.
[88] Senator Douglas to Curtis, and reply, 6 and 12 Apr. 1932, Bodleian Library, MS Curtis 90; Andrew, *Secret Service*, 474, 520–5.
[89] O'Halpin, *Defending Ireland*, 103–4.
[90] See Manning, *The Blueshirts*, and McGarry, *O'Duffy*, for contrasting assessments of the Blueshirts and their messianic leader.

he included England, along with de Valera and Bolshevism, in his catalogue of those responsible for Ireland's woes. He clearly aspired to be the Irish Duce, the strong man of action who would save Ireland from communism and bring her into alignment with the new ideological forces shaping Europe.[91]

Yet the emergence of O'Duffy's movement was initially greeted with relief in Whitehall. This was partly because it seemed the only way that Cosgrave could be saved, and partly because the charismatic O'Duffy appeared a genuine counterweight to de Valera. That the Blueshirts had most of the trappings of European fascism seems barely to have been noticed. The parliamentary wing eventually forced O'Duffy out of Fine Gael in September 1934. For a time he kept the Blueshirts alive, charging around the country making inflammatory speeches, but without a political arm the movement soon waned. In 1936 O'Duffy led some 700 committed supporters off to fight for Franco and Catholicism in the Spanish civil war, but their experience was ignominious. Their only casualties arose from friendly fire from Moorish soldiers, an ironic death for men involved in what O'Duffy termed a 'crusade in Spain'.[92] The Spanish fiasco finally did for the organization, but O'Duffy remained an awkward presence in the wings of Irish politics, surrounded by a small coterie of ideologues, thugs, and dodgy opportunists, and colloguing with the Italian and German legations, until his early death in 1944.

By 1935, when the first steps in Anglo-Irish rapprochement resulted in the 'coal–cattle pact', Whitehall had grown used to de Valera. Demands for Irish intelligence certainly diminished, if they did not cease. There was one exception: the fighting services continued to worry about IRA infiltration, but this was a minor concern addressed through routine enquiries.[93] At a meeting in London in 1937 held to encourage the dominions to establish wireless interception stations, Ireland was not even mentioned: it was assumed that the provisions of the 1921 treaty would apply, enabling Britain to use Irish facilities as needed (while most dominions expressed willingness, the South African representative said that for political reasons he could officially do nothing, although he would encourage sub rosa technical experiments. South Africa was to have its own difficulties in persuading its people to go to war in 1939).[94]

THE INTELLIGENCE AND SECURITY LESSONS OF THE ANGLO-IRISH CONFLICT, 1916–1921

It might be thought that the conflict in Ireland between 1916 and 1921 would have left its mark on military memory in terms of intelligence gathering, of counter-insurgency, and of irregular warfare. Surely there were lessons to be learnt from the IRA's campaign, not least in terms of their intelligence operations, and from

[91] McGarry, *O'Duffy*, 209.
[92] The best treatment of Irish involvement is McGarry, *Ireland and the Spanish Civil War*; see also O'Connor, *Reds and the Green*, 214–19. O'Duffy, *Crusade in Spain*.
[93] Minute by Troup (DNI), 30 Apr. 1936, TNA, ADM178/144.
[94] Note on meeting of 28 July 1937, with minutes of 'Y' committee, 31 Dec. 1939, TNA, HW42/5; Grundligh, 'The King's Afrikaners?', 353.

the army's response? Furthermore, was there not a danger that the IRA would be wooed by a willing partner for use against Britain, just as Germany had stoked the revolutionary fire in Ireland in 1916? In a future war might not Germany make an offer—whether to the IRA or even to the Irish government—to end partition in the event of victory (just as she had attempted in 1917 to tempt Mexico by promising to restore the vast territories she had lost to the United States)?[95] Yet evidence on the impact of the Irish experience on Britain's fighting and intelligence services is hard to find.

The fighting service with the greatest reason to reflect on its Irish experience during the first world war was the navy. The island's strategic significance for Britain's seaborne trade, and more particularly the harsh experience of submarine warfare in the Atlantic, naturally made a mark on the inter-war Admiralty's collective memory. Irish bases had played a major role in British and later American naval operations to protect Atlantic shipping. Experience had also shown that the scare-stories about U-boats along the Irish coast were just that.

The second area where lessons might have been learned was the management of decodes by the Admiralty—ironically, a matter frequently recalled as a series of brilliant coups by NID's Blinker Hall—which had resulted in the disastrous mishandling of excellent intelligence drawn from decodes of cables between the German embassy in Washington and Berlin. These disclosed the plans for the 1916 rising, yet Dublin Castle was left in the dark and was consequently caught by surprise when the rebellion broke out, having assumed that London had all the threads of the conspiracy in its hands. There were further occasions on which valid but problematic decodes were mishandled by NID.[96] On the conclusion of the Irish campaign in 1922, the army produced a number of studies as a 'Record of the Rebellion in Ireland', including one on intelligence. It is impossible to judge how much currency this volume had in inter-war Whitehall (though a copy in the Intelligence Corps Museum in Ashford was donated by an intelligence company operating in Londonderry in the early 1970s). Few British military thinkers sought to draw wider lessons from the Irish war of independence. A number of officers who were to make their name as intelligence or irregular warfare specialists, such as J. C. F. Holland of the War Office think-tank GS(R), which in 1939 developed into MI(R), Colin Gubbins of the Special Operations Executive (SOE), and Kenneth Strong, Eisenhower's chief of intelligence in 1944–5, had served in Ireland between 1919 and 1922 (Gubbins commanded the detachment which provided the field-gun with which Provisional Government troops shelled the Four Courts at the commencement of the civil war, and was also in charge of the handover of the gun-carriage lent to the Irish to bear the remains of Michael Collins).[97]

Undue emphasis has been placed on the importance for such officers of the experience of Irish rebellion and counter-insurgency. In 1969 M. R. D. Foot, the official historian of the Special Operations Executive (SOE) in France, presented a

[95] Beesly, *Room 40*, 204–24; TNA, ADM34/28.

[96] These matters are discussed in greater detail in O'Halpin, *Decline of the Union*, 113–15, 137–8, and 159–63, and in 'British Intelligence and Ireland, 1914–1921', 124–58; Hankey diary, 21 May 1918, CCCA, Hankey papers, 4/1.

[97] Wilkinson and Bright Astley, *Gubbins and SOE*, 27; Strong, *Intelligence at the Top*, 1.

celebrated lecture in Dublin on 'Michael Collins and Irregular Warfare'.[98] Amongst his audience was the British ambassador, Andrew Gilchrist, himself an old SOE hand, who thought the lecture brilliant. So too did Gilchrist's closest Irish friends, Colonel David Neligan and Major-General Sean Collins-Powell, respectively Collins's 'spy in the Castle' in 1920 and 1921, and Collins's nephew. Gilchrist bemoaned the absence of a single politician from the ruling Fianna Fáil party at the lecture.[99] But perhaps the Fianna Fáilers were right to doubt the weight of the speaker's argument, because a survey of inter-war British military thought and planning yields very few references to the intelligence, counter-insurgency, or irregular warfare lessons of the Irish campaign of 1919–21. Most inter-war British writers on counter insurgency operations, and those planning irregular warfare in the event of a further conflict with Germany, found plenty of examples in various far-flung parts of the empire, from Sudan to Iraq to India, and in conflicts such as the Russian civil war, the Sino-Japanese war, and the Spanish civil war, without reflecting on or even alluding to the Irish case.[100]

IRELAND AND THE GERMAN THREAT, 1935–1939

The republican movement's continued willingness to court England's enemies was clear from the IRA's intermittent dealings with Russia, fragmentary evidence of which had reached Whitehall. Such links were almost invariably regarded as evidence of Moscow's turpitude rather than of continuing republican potential to damage British interests. At the end of 1935 came an unexpected twist, in a decoded cable from the Italian consul-general in Dublin. He told Rome of discussions with IRA leaders. These, he believed, were willing to organize action 'in such a way as might be considered best in America' in support of Italian intervention in Abyssinia. Arrangements had been made for 'our agents' to contact a senior member of the IRA's American auxiliary Clan na Gael. A few months later he wrote that the IRA was the single most important political force in Ireland, the clear implication being that Italy should pursue an understanding with it.[101] These discussions probably came to nothing. The republican newspaper *An Phoblacht* opposed the invasion of Abyssinia, and the Italian's IRA contacts were unrepresentative: many, though by no means all, republicans were anti-Fascist, as the Spanish civil war was shortly to show. Yet the material might have served to remind Whitehall of enduring Irish republican willingness to do business with Britain's enemies irrespective of ideology.[102] The IRA also extended feelers to Germany, overtures which were to

[98] A later version was published as 'Michael Collins and the Origins of SOE', in Foot, *War and Society*, 57–69.

[99] Draft of Gilchrist to Foreign Office, 30 Jan. 1969, CCCA, Gilchrist papers, GILC 962/14A. Gilchrist served with SOE in the Far East in 1944–5, becoming a lieutenant-colonel.

[100] I have developed this argument in O'Halpin, 'The Irish Experience of Insurgency and Counterinsurgency'.

[101] Decodes of Lodi Fé to Rome, 9 Dec. 1935 and 1 July 1936, TNA, HW12/198 and 205. On Ryan see O'Halpin, *Defending Ireland*, 112–13.

[102] Hanley, *The IRA*, 174, discusses *An Phoblacht*'s line on the Spanish civil war.

mature as European war erupted. The reality was that no one in Whitehall in 1935–6 was studying Ireland and Irish republicanism in terms of threats to British strategic security, although the Special Branch in London and in Belfast continued to watch the IRA. MI5 were fully absorbed in studying the multiple perils of communism, Soviet espionage, British fascism, and to an increasing extent German espionage. This is probably why neither the Italian exchange nor the more enduring IRA–Soviet liaison receive even a passing mention in either the Curry or Liddell histories produced in the last year of the second world war.

Like many other states, during the inter-war years Ireland experienced a modest influx of Germans with technical, professional, and managerial skills. The great symbol of this was the Shannon hydroelectric scheme initiated in 1925, but Germans also played important roles in setting up new state industries such as the Electricity Supply Board and Bord na Móna (the turf board). As in other new states adjacent to British interests like Iraq, Turkey, Persia, and Afghanistan, this reflected a conscious desire to reduce dependence on Britain for necessary technical expertise and industrial goods; from the perspective of Germany, struggling to rebuild her industrial strength, such links provided opportunities to earn foreign currency, to secure employment abroad which could not be found at home, and to develop desperately needed new markets.[103] It was only after Hitler came to power that the Nazi regime began to impose political control on the German émigré community in Ireland as elsewhere, and to harness it for German foreign policy ends.

Discussion of intelligence on Ireland in the years leading up to the war must always be prefaced by the qualification that Ireland was very small beer in the wider scheme of challenges facing British defence and security officials. In 1934 a key committee concluded that Germany was the 'ultimate potential enemy' against which Britain should prepare her defences.[104] In 1935 a defence white paper made that conclusion public, in more diplomatic language, laying the ground for a massive rearmament campaign. The intelligence services played some part in that assessment, and took their lead from it. The threat from Soviet-inspired communism and espionage no longer preoccupied them. Germany was now the priority target both for offensive and for defensive intelligence operations. Their main concern about Ireland was still the machinations of a foreign power, but it was Hitler's hand rather than Stalin's that they feared.

In the autumn of 1936 MI5 and SIS exchanged views about possible German espionage in Ireland, noting that there were no Anglo-Irish channels for discussing matters such as the growing Irish activities of the NSDAP (the German Nazi Party).[105] Some months later the recently established joint intelligence committee (JIC) received copies of correspondence between Sir Robert Vansittart of the Foreign Office and Kell of MI5. This dealt with the possibility of Germany laying the foundations of a military alliance with de Valera. When the JIC finally considered the paper in September, as the final item on the agenda, they simply

---

[103] Nicosia, ' "Drang nach Osten" Continued?', 235–6; O'Driscoll, *Ireland, Germany and the Nazis*, 55–6, 58–63.

[104] Wark, *The Ultimate Enemy*, 17; O'Halpin, *Head of the Civil Service*, 228–31.

[105] Liddell to Vivian (SIS), 19 Dec. 1936, TNA, KV4/279.

noted its contents without comment. The committee never discussed Irish matters again up to the outbreak of war, despite some concerns about the gradual growth in the influence of the German community in Ireland, but MI5 grew increasingly concerned about the issue.[106]

At the culmination of intense Anglo-Irish negotiations to settle the 'economic war' and all other matters outstanding in relations between the two states in the spring of 1938, the cabinet decided that on balance Britain could afford to relinquish the defence rights enumerated in the 1921 treaty. De Valera had repeatedly stressed that he understood Britain's concerns about her Atlantic security, and that he would take all steps necessary to protect British interests. The chiefs of staff had reported, albeit after some prodding from on high and without particular conviction, that the port defences and facilities were in poor order and would require considerable investment. Furthermore, they could not be used in wartime without Irish cooperation unless very significant forces were deployed to protect them and their lines of supply against a presumably hostile local population.[107] The intelligence agencies were evidently not invited to provide assessments of the security implications of the cession of Britain's defence rights, of Irish political conditions, or of the likely Irish attitude in the event of a major war. This is not surprising: it was only after war broke out that Whitehall developed both an appetite for and the capacity for producing collective intelligence assessments through the JIC, and even then it was some time before that committee's conclusions carried much weight.[108]

While warmly welcoming the financial, trade, and defence settlements thus reached, de Valera stated unequivocally that attainment of sovereignty over the ports did not mean any departure from the policy of neutrality in any future war involving Britain, and expressed his regret that the negotiations had failed to address the one outstanding problem in Anglo-Irish relations, partition. He also publicly reiterated his long-held position that Ireland could not allow her territory to be used to harm British strategic interests.[109] This message was rather lost on Britain, although she might have learnt from developments elsewhere as small states reacted to the inability of the League of Nations to provide collective security. The Scandinavian countries had already adopted neutrality as a cornerstone of foreign policy, Denmark being particularly influenced by pacifist arguments despite, or perhaps because of, her undefended land border with Germany.[110] In October 1936 Belgium had abruptly repudiated her 1920 defence treaty with France (it included a secret agreement to violate the neutrality of Luxembourg if necessary). The Belgian action received widespread public backing—the Flemish population had always been suspicious of France, the treaty had complicated relations with the Dutch, and even the usually Francophile Walloons had been shocked by the Franco-Soviet rapprochement of 1935—and it was hailed internationally: 'the

---

[106] JIC 10th meeting, 28 Sept. 1936, TNA, CAB56/3; *Liddell History*, 37–8.
[107] Report of chiefs of staff subcommittee (COS 664), 12 Jan. 1938, TNA, CAB64/34. Fergusson, *War of the World*, 350, misinterprets the 1938 agreement as a formal recognition of Irish independence. So much for big history.
[108] Annan, *Changing Enemies*, 9.
[109] Extract from de Valera's speech to the Dáil, 27 Apr. 1938, NAI, DT, S. 10701A.
[110] Leistikow, 'Denmark's Precarious Neutrality', *Foreign Affairs*, 616.

action of the Belgian Government in emancipating itself from the post-war alliances by a bold announcement of its sovereign power was a masterstroke of diplomacy, one of rare courage and great statesmanship'.[111] Analysed in those terms, the Irish aspiration to stay neutral at all costs reflected a convergence with the small European democracies rather than an exercise in perverse particularism rooted solely in antagonism towards Britain. Britain's willingness to cede her Irish defence rights contrasts with the approach taken in the Middle East, where the treaties of 1930 and 1936 which recognized Iraqi and Egyptian independence respectively included provisions allowing Britain to maintain forces in these new states.

The period between the Anglo-Irish agreement and the outbreak of war in September 1939 saw very significant developments in security relations. These took place within the framework of continued Anglo-Irish dialogue on wider political questions. De Valera repeatedly indicated that if London could only take one further brave step to resolve the partition issue, the united island of Ireland would stand shoulder to shoulder with Britain to defend the British Isles (which was not the same as saying that a united Ireland would join Britain's wars). Although Neville Chamberlain had taken a particular interest in Ireland and had a high regard for de Valera, the succession of foreign policy crises which beset Britain rendered impossible any further push on the issue, even had the will been there. De Valera's continued promptings about partition, in the wake of the major concessions already agreed—the Irish took possession of the first of the Cork port defences on 11 July 1938 amidst a fanfare of self-congratulation—grated on London's nerves.[112] They might also have inspired some serious analysis of Ireland's likely position in a future war, had anyone in London had the time to reflect on such a question. Britain was confronted with further evidence of what must have appeared as Irish solipsism in April 1939, in the wake of her dramatic reversal of policy after the German occupation of Prague. The Chamberlain government guaranteed the borders of Poland and Romania, and so set Britain on a collision course with Germany. As part of this new policy, Chamberlain announced the introduction of conscription. In the midst of so many other woes, he then found himself under diplomatic barrage from Dublin. The Irish argued that conscription in Northern Ireland would be not merely an injustice to the nationalist minority—who would bear a disproportionate burden, since due to discrimination very few were employed in reserved occupations in industry and the public service—but would constitute an infringement of Irish sovereignty because these people were Irish citizens. There was also, as Joseph Walshe of External Affairs warned, 'real danger of bloodshed as people here and in Six Counties will resist to death imposition of conscription on Irish Nation by external power', and 'Britain has...no more right to conscript our people in the Six Counties than France or Germany'. Chamberlain was uncharacteristically terse in reply, although the Irish arguments eventually won the day despite the resentment of ministers at interference in Britain's internal affairs. The prime

---

[111] Lingelbach, 'Neutrality versus Alliances: Belgium and the Revolution in International Politics', 607–36; on the 1920 treaty see Helmreich, 'The Negotiation of the Franco-Belgian Military Accord of 1920', 363–73.
[112] Fisk, *In Time of War*, 9–11.

minister resignedly commented to Dulanty that de Valera 'had won his case but he felt sure that he would treat the decision with tact'.[113] The issue was to arise again in 1941.

By 1938 three strands of German clandestine interest in Ireland were already emerging, centred respectively on the German émigré community, on academic and cultural exchanges, and on German shipping using Irish ports. This clandestine activity was organized largely independently of the German legation, enthusiastic Nazis though most of its staff were. There were also indications of German interest in the IRA. Such developments were not particular to Ireland: much the same could be seen throughout the world wherever Germany had interests, for instance in Afghanistan, which shared an uncontrollable land border with British India as Ireland did with the United Kingdom.[114] In July 1937 Germany nominated new ministers to both Ireland and Afghanistan. The British ambassador reported that both men were middle-ranking officials. Edouard Hempel had served in the Far East and Norway, while Hans Pilger was a Near Eastern expert. Despite the promotion involved he viewed his translation to Kabul 'without enthusiasm'.[115] Pilger was prescient: his new posting nearly cost him his life. Neither Hempel nor Pilger were conspicuously enthusiastic Nazis, and neither had any background in intelligence, nor in the manipulation of religious, ethnic, or national minorities. Yet circumstances after 1939 were to see both men and their respective staffs involved in intelligence gathering and in political intrigues. In Pilger's case these were to become his *raison d'être* after 1940, as Germany used her Kabul mission for the organization of intelligence gathering, propaganda, sabotage, and subversion in India, Persia, Iraq, and the southern Soviet Union.[116]

Hempel's wartime experience was rather different: his primary task was the encouragement of Irish neutrality, and this has led some to argue that his legation played no significant intelligence role, a conclusion which also suited the Irish government. Yet as Mark Hull has conclusively shown, this was not the case. Hempel—and it is pointless to attempt to distinguish his approach and involvements from those of his subordinates—established good indirect links with the IRA even before war was declared, and in so doing provided the means for a range of clandestine activities. During the war, the legation's secret activities were circumscribed by the imperative of not provoking the Irish, and by Irish surveillance. Yet Hempel's communications with Berlin, once these became readable in 1943 as part of Pandora (the cover term for decoded German diplomatic material), showed that he had consistently passed on as much war information as could be obtained incidentally, had encouraged pro-Nazi fringe groups, had intrigued with a senior Irish army officer, had first denied possession of a secret transmitter and had then

---

[113] Walshe to de Valera, and to Brennan, 29 Apr., and Dulanty to Walshe, 27 Apr., 1 and 3 May 1939, in Crowe *et al.* (eds.), *DIFP* v. 447–8, 451–2, 455–6, and 459–60; Canning, *British Policy Towards Ireland*, 237–8.

[114] Much the best account of German intelligence interest in Ireland is Hull, *Irish Secrets*. The one exception is the case of Mrs Brandy, whose MI5 file was not open to research when Dr Hull was writing; Hauner, 'Afghanistan Between the Great Powers, 1938–1945', 482–3.

[115] British ambassador, Berlin, to London, 6 July 1937, BL, L/PS/12/1878.

[116] Hauner, 'Afghanistan Between the Great Powers', 490–2.

broken undertakings to the Irish not to operate it again, and had indirectly assisted German agents sent to Ireland.[117]

As elsewhere in Europe and the Americas, the NSDAP organized Germans in Ireland through its Auslandsampt organization. An Irish branch of the party was established in 1934, headed by the director of the National Museum, Dr Adolf Mahr. It did not engage in espionage as such before war broke out, apart from keeping tabs on the handful of German refugees and anti-Nazis who had managed to get into Ireland—this was formally the role of a sister organization, the Hafendienst, but the membership entirely overlapped—and possibly also accumulating topographical information. It was not simply an overt patriotic émigré organization but a potential support network for clandestine or military activities. There were two other German-sponsored organizations of some significance. One was the Irish branch of the news agency Deutsche Nachrichten Büro (DNB). Initially run by an Irish sympathizer, from December 1938 this was under the direction of Carl Petersen, who was appointed press attaché in the German legation shortly before war broke out. The other was the Deutscher Fichte Bund, a propaganda organization. The Red Bank restaurant in Dublin's D'Olier Street became the meeting-place for the Nazi groups, which worked closely with the German legation.[118] The Irish became very uneasy. In February 1939 Joseph Walshe spoke with the newly arrived German chargé d'affaires Henning Thomsen, who complained about a pastoral letter issued by the Catholic bishop of Galway which accused Germany of 'violence, lying, murder and the condemning of other races and peoples', and about press commentaries on the same lines. Walshe thought it best to 'let him run his full length before replying, as it seemed . . . important . . . to get to know the type we have to deal with'. Thomsen, Walshe records,

is insolent, bombastic, and apparently devoid of any sense of the real values of life. He is the first German I have met who seems to combine in himself all the worst ideas about the Nazi regime.

. . . I suggested to him, as I have frequently done to his Minister and his Minister's predecessor, that the . . . existence of a Nazi organization . . . and having as its chief member and organiser an employee of our state [Mahr], was not calculated to improve relations . . . He answered, not quite in so many words, that the Nazi organization in Dublin was really none of our business.

Walshe pointed out that 'we may expect an increase in anti-Nazi feeling and protests . . . No ordinary Civil Servant is allowed to be a member of a political organization, and it could not be regarded as an injustice' if Mahr 'were ordered to cease his membership of the Nazi Cell'.[119]

Opportunities for fostering links arose in disciplines such as linguistics and Celtic studies, where there was a strong tradition of German interest in Ireland (and, during the first world war, of related clandestine engagement). Two men sent by the

---

[117] Hull, *Irish Secrets*, 250–1. Hempel is more sympathetically portrayed in Fisk, *In Time of War*, and Duggan, *Herr Hempel at the German Legation*. These works were written without benefit of access to G2, MI5, and GC&CS records.

[118] *Liddell History*, 46; on Mahr see Mullins, *Dublin Nazi No. 1*.

[119] Walshe to de Valera, 22 Feb. 1939, in Crowe *et al.*, *DIFP* v. 411–12.

Deutsche Akademischer Austauschdienst (German Academic Exchange Bureau), Helmuth Clissmann and Jupp Hoven, used their time partly to build up contacts in republican circles. Hoven made visits to Northern Ireland in 1938 and 1939—he reportedly said he had come 'to see the beauties of the Glens of Antrim', but the RUC were not fooled—and Clissmann married into a prominent republican family.[120] Both men were to play significant parts in Irish-related German operations during the war as functionaries of the Abwehr (German military intelligence).

Ireland also attracted some Scottish, Welsh, Flemish, and Breton separatists, adding to this curious network of relationships. They shared broadly comparable narratives of linguistic, cultural, and political oppression, and provided potential cross-national networks for intelligence and related activities against Britain and France. One Breton who visited Ireland before the war and mixed in republican circles, Guy Vissault de Coetlogon, was executed in France in April 1945 for his collaborationist activities.[121] The use of cultural enthusiasts, academic specialists, and adventurers for covert political and intelligence work was neither particularly German nor a new clandestine technique: during and after the first world war the British and the French adopted much the same approach in East Asia and the Middle East, while the intellectual mainspring of German's subversive strategy in British Asia during the first world war, which hinged on manipulating Muslim opinion, was the orientalist Max von Oppenheim.[122]

By 1936 German naval intelligence had begun to collect information in Irish ports, both through crew members on German ships and through one or more Irish-based agents—after R. L. Brandy, a German who had 'submitted a number of reports' on naval matters, died in Dublin in 1937, his wife Gertrude carried on some covert work until detected.[123] It may be that this link was organized by Hoven: G2 wrote in 1942 that he had established an intelligence organization 'quite independent of the IRA and used to send . . . communications . . . through German boats calling at Cobh' (previously Queenstown), which went unnoticed by the Irish at the time. Hoven's undercover work was inspired by geography rather than by politics: Ireland was of interest to the German navy because of her Atlantic location and her shipping links with Britain. Clissmann, on the other hand, had a brief to develop relations with the republican movement in anticipation of a future war, although this was not clear at the time. G2 opened a file on German language classes in October 1938, and a few months later noted that 'Irish German Academic Bureau paid £10.9.0 in Clissman's Jan[uary] B[an]k A/[count]'.[124]

[120] *Liddell History*, 39–40; Gilfillan (RUC) to Vivian (SIS), 10 Oct. 1938, TNA, KV4/279, on Hoven. Clissmann appears in what seems to be the second file created in the G2 espionage series, dating from October 1938. MAI, G2/X/2.

[121] His MI5 file is TNA, KV2/303. While in Ireland he had some contact with another Breton separatist, Louis le Roux, author of *Patrick H. Pearse*, tr. Desmond Ryan (Dublin, n.d. [1932]), and with the naturalised Irishman Erwin Mill-Arden, later to be an important link between the IRA and the Abwehr.

[122] Hopkirk, *On Secret Service East of Constantinople*, 19 and 54. Von Oppenheim was scheduled for assassination, but this was not carried out. SOE war diaries, Feb. 1941, TNA, HS7/213.

[123] Climperman (US embassy, London) to Ms Paine (MI5), 21 May 1946, TNA, KV2/356.

[124] Note on 'German, IRA and related contacts' [undated], with Bryan to O'Donoghue, 14 Nov. 1942, MAI, G2/X/0093; undated MS note [Feb. 1939?], MAI, G2/X/2.

Assessment of German activity in Ireland was hampered by the fact that, as with communist material in the 1920s and early 1930s, the London agencies had no specialists on Irish affairs. Thus, 'information concerning Germans or Italians in Ireland was dealt with by the German or Italian section, just as information concerning the Nazi Party or the Fascio in Ireland was passed to the officers studying the Nazi Party and the Fascio generally'. The same was true of German espionage, a circumstance not addressed until Cecil Liddell joined MI5 in 1939 as the first officer in the new Irish Section B9, later redesignated B1H.[125]

Cecil Liddell's appointment provided rich grounds for confusion, since it meant that MI5's B Division now had two Captain Liddells, both holders of the Military Cross. His younger brother Guy, after service with the Royal Field Artillery, had become an intelligence officer, first in Scotland Yard and then, through amalgamation, in MI5. Cecil, an Etonian who also won a Belgian decoration while serving in the Kings Royal Rifle Corps, had made his post-war career in the City. The brothers were, by MI5 standards, unusually well got. Both their grandfather and their father, a younger son of the fourth Lord Ravensworth, had been attached to the royal household. Guy was married to Calypso Baring, a daughter of Lord Revelstoke, who owned Lambay Island off Dublin. The Liddell brothers also had family connections in County Down, they knew Ireland well, and they got on with Irish people. Even as Guy's wartime responsibilities mushroomed as deputy head and later head of B division, he remained very close to Irish issues. This is reflected in his remarkable diaries.[126]

Ireland had formed part of SIS's brief since 1932. Gill Bennett, writing with access to closed SIS records, states that from 1937 'the remit of SIS's Irish section increased considerably'. It is not possible to identify who in SIS handled this work, until the appointment of the feisty Jane Archer early in 1941 after she had been fired from MI5 for speaking her mind to her inept acting director-general, Jasper Harker.[127] Until the autumn of 1938, when what was termed 'the Dublin link' was established with Colonel Liam Archer of G2, there was no contact by either MI5 or SIS with the Irish authorities about German espionage.

The first substantial case of German activity in Ireland affecting British interests arose in 1937. A German visitor, Kurt Wheeler Hill, met a young Irishman through an advertisement for language classes. The Curry history identifies him as a bicycle salesman named Francis P. Campbell.[128] Campbell and his wife visited Hamburg in August 1937, and he agreed to collect intelligence for the Abwehr. He was to recruit Irishmen in the British forces as informants. Campbell returned home and did nothing, but in March 1938 returned to Germany and agreed to get started. Contact was maintained through an officer of the German ship *Finckenau,* which visited Dublin regularly. Campbell, evidently interested in extracting as much

---

[125] *Liddell History*, 18.

[126] O'Halpin, 'The Guy Liddell Diaries'; Carter, *Anthony Blunt*, 255–59.

[127] Philip Vickery to W. H. A. Rich, 19 Sept. 1977, BL, MSS Eur D1011; Liddell diary, 18 Nov. 1940, TNA, KV4/187. He wrote in response to Rich's request for information on Sir David Petrie for a *DNB* entry; Bennett, *Churchill's Man of Mystery*, 354, n. 53. This was researched and published as an official history.

[128] *Liddell History*, 45; *Curry History*, 135; private information.

money as possible before the Germans tired of him, subsequently reported that he had recruited two servicemen, both fictitious; he then approached the War Office and told them what he knew. At MI5's behest, he passed the Germans the name of a supposed right-wing journalist, in fact an MI5 officer. That man visited Dublin between 10 and 14 May and made contact through Campbell with the *Finckenau*. A few weeks later, Campbell received a reply from Hamburg. The MI5 man returned to Dublin, bringing with him some fairly harmless information on tanks. Campbell passed this on to his *Finckenau* contact, and brought the MI5 officer as his guest to a function at the Red Bank, where he was introduced to members of the German community, and heard Dr Mahr make a speech. Despite this promising start, nothing further materialized. Archer of G2 was informed of the case in September, and sent on a report on Kurt Wheeler Hill. But the suspect had left Ireland quite suddenly in May 1938, and the line went dead.[129]

From a British perspective, probably the most significant espionage cases which arose prior to September 1939 were those of the double agent *Snow* and of Mrs Gertrude Brandy. Curiously, neither of these feature in the Irish Section history, although Mrs Brandy is mentioned in passing elsewhere. *Snow*—his MI5 cover name—was Arthur Owens, a Welsh engineer recruited by the Germans in 1936. He collected some intelligence and passed it on while on visits to Europe, but also gathered scraps for SIS. In 1938 he disclosed his German contact to SIS. He was encouraged to keep up the link, and once war broke out MI5 were able to compel him to cooperate wholeheartedly under threat of prosecution for espionage. This was the genesis of what became the 'Double Cross' system, by which British intelligence first came to control all German espionage in the United Kingdom, and then gradually to use real and fictitious agents as instruments of strategic deception, an exercise which reached its apogee in the successful campaign to mislead the Germans about the intended location of the invasion of France in 1944.[130] *Snow*'s German controllers were interested in recruiting Welsh nationalists, and shortly after war was declared MI5 provided a retired police inspector to play the part of a Welsh saboteur. Before war broke out, the Germans also gave *Snow* a transmitter to deliver to Ireland. This he did in 1938, and neither the radio nor the person to whom he handed it over was ever traced (it seems unlikely that MI5 told G2 about it, as *Snow* remained a crucial part of the Double Cross system, an enterprise so secret that it was never disclosed to G2).[131]

The second big case was that of Mrs Brandy. In April 1938 SIS informed MI5 of arrests in Prague and New York which had uncovered a German espionage network using women as 'post boxes'—cover addresses—for correspondence from agents abroad. As the Curry history makes clear, this was a significant discovery in itself.[132]

---

[129] *Liddell History*, 44–7.
[130] Masterman, *Double-Cross System*; Hinsley and Simkins, *British Intelligence*.
[131] Hinsley and Simkins, *British Intelligence*, 41–4; Snow's MI5 records are in TNA, KV2/444–7. Dan Bryan told me that he was never told anything about Double Cross and would not have expected otherwise. He naturally assumed that some agents were being turned but he had no idea of the scale and sophistication of the British operation until the publication of Masterman's book. The British did, however, ask him to recruit and run a seaman double agent from Ireland. *Liddell History*, 67.
[132] *Curry History*, 126.

Amongst these was Gertrude Brandy in Dublin, who was receiving intelligence reports from France which she then passed on to Germany (most likely through the medium of German ships calling at Dublin). MI5 and SIS considered the possibility of an approach to the Irish about espionage problems—on 15 July the two agencies agreed that 'the most satisfactory thing' would be for MI5 'to establish relations in the first instance with Mr Walsh [*sic*], Minister of Foreign Affairs'.[133] British agencies soon learned the correct spelling of Walshe's name, but the crucial point that he was the secretary of External Affairs, and that the ministerial portfolio was held by de Valera, seldom registered in Whitehall's shadier precincts. This was an elementary and persistent error. While the Brandy case was under investigation, and MI5 and SIS were debating how best to broach the subject of counter-espionage liaison with the Irish, Dulanty, who as a former Treasury and Ministry of Munitions official had excellent Whitehall contacts, gave his government's first intimation of concern about possible German clandestine activity. MI5 believed that this approach had its origins in de Valera's appreciation for being taken into Britain's confidence about aspects of Atlantic defence immediately following the Anglo-Irish agreement. Guy Liddell met Dulanty and Walshe on 31 August 1938. This meeting marked the beginning of Anglo-Irish security cooperation. Walshe 'expressed . . . concern . . . about German activities' and expressed Irish 'desire to set up a Department similar to the Security Service. The Security Service representative expressed his readiness to assist them in every possible way and promised to supply a memorandum on the subject'.[134] Liddell explained that MI5 'had been built up over a period of years and was peculiarly English in character . . . it might be dangerous for anybody else, who had an opportunity of starting from scratch, to model themselves very closely on ourselves'. Nevertheless, key aspects were worth replicating: 'We . . . discussed the Ministry under which the counter-espionage organization . . . should function. We agreed that probably the Minister of Defence would be the best person to answer for it in the Dáil'. Walshe thought that, like MI5, the new agency 'should also be largely independent and self-contained'. He reiterated Irish anxiety about the NSDAP, which 'they did not like . . . as they felt its activities virtually infringed their sovereign rights'.[135]

This exchange was also significant for the simple reason of who Joseph Walshe was. The founding father of the Department of External Affairs in 1922, this fussy bachelor, a lawyer, former seminarian, and devout Catholic, was a curious mixture of ideologue and pragmatist. His career had been built firstly on the premise that Ireland should assert her independence constructively within the empire, a policy resolutely and successfully pursued by the Cosgrave government up to 1932; thereafter, he adroitly accommodated himself to the more confrontational Anglo-Irish diplomacy of de Valera's first years in office, which saw increased willingness to take unilateral action where London could not be persuaded to concede in the revision of the 1921 settlement. He had no experience of defence or security affairs, but he clearly believed that External Affairs should be centrally involved

---

[133] Harker's minute of talk with Vivian, 20 July 1938, TNA, KV4/279.
[134] *Liddell History*, 22.
[135] Note by Liddell of his talk with Walshe, sent to Vivian on 3 Sept. 1938, TNA, KV4/279.

in the management of Ireland's security relations with her nearest neighbour. Consequently External Affairs in 1938 acquired and retained control of policy in these matters. The functional departments—Justice and Defence—worked entirely under External Affairs's aegis.[136] As secretary of Extenal Affairs, Walshe worked directly to de Valera. From the start, therefore, security liaison operated under the taoiseach's personal control. This point is missed in the relevant volume of Sir Harry Hinsley's official history, where both the year of the meeting (Hinsley says August 1939) and Walshe's status (Hinsley describes him as the 'Minister for External Affairs') are mis-stated. The Curry history, by contrast, emphasized the origins of the Irish approach.[137] De Valera's approach to security cooperation contrasts with that of the Afghan prime minister when approached on much the same issues of potential Axis espionage and subversion in March 1939: while Delhi could 'rest assured that he was watching the activities of members of these states with care and that he would not hesitate to take any measures which might be necessary to restrain them in the event of war', he declined to sanction communication between the Delhi intelligence bureau and his own security organization. Although the British minister in Kabul was confident that, 'while preserving strict neutrality', the Afghans would 'co-operate wholeheartedly in . . . preventing subversive agents from penetrating the tribal areas or reaching India', the absence of a security link was to create severe difficulties during the war.[138]

MI5 provided Dulanty with a memorandum on the NSDAP, together with another outlining how a counter-espionage department might be organized. This 'contained suggestions based on our experience' trying to modernize a 'typically English organization' with powers and functions fragmented among a number of agencies. It also emphasized that

experience had shown that it was essential for such an organization to be adequately provided with measures for the control of—
(a) the entry and exit of aliens
(b) their supervision while in the country
(c) the interception of correspondence, telegraphic and telephonic communications.

The document suggested the employment of a retired police inspector to make enquiries, a recommendation which G2 quietly ignored for fear of damaging relations with the Garda.[139] A month afterwards, in discussing a forthcoming visit by Colonel Archer, Dulanty told MI5's Jasper Harker 'in strictest confidence' that the Irish minister for defence, Frank Aiken, was 'an extremist (left) and had done practically nothing since he took over' in 1932. Currently 'he was away sick and it was hoped that it would so remain for a long time!' This confidence found its way to the cabinet a month later, when ministers discussed a defence understanding with Ireland.[140] After war broke out, Aiken was consistently portrayed as virulently pro-German, a label which often annoyed the Irish. That Dulanty, presumably

[136] Kennedy, ' "A Voyage of Exploration" ', 8.
[137] Hinsley and Simkins, *British Intelligence*, 17; *Curry History*, 134.
[138] British minister, Kabul, to Delhi, 16 Apr. 1939, BL, L/PS/12/1758.
[139] Undated MI5 document with MS note dated 10 Sept. 1938, TNA, KV4/279.
[140] Note by Harker, 12 Oct., and extract from cabinet conclusions, 22 Nov. 1938, TNA, KV4/279.

acting under orders from Dublin, depicted Aiken as an anti-British bogeyman in 1938 may go some way to explain why the label stuck throughout the war (during which Aiken was elevated to the high-sounding role of minister for the coordination of defensive measures, a job which placed him at a remove from direct control over military affairs and contact with G2).

The Curry history observes that Archer's new service 'had to be built up from scratch under conditions of great secrecy without experience, personnel or funds; and subject to an internal political situation in which a factor was divergence of views . . . within the . . . Government itself'. This betrayed a certain naivety on MI5's part. What Archer established in 1938 was a defence security section under his deputy Dan Bryan. While chronically short of money and staff, G2 were not short of experience. Both Archer and Bryan had begun their intelligence careers in the IRA, and Bryan had continued in intelligence during and after the civil war. Archer had also been army director of signals, and consequently appreciated the more technical aspects of communications intelligence, matters which were to become crucial in Anglo-Irish security dialogue.[141] G2 were also able to avail themselves of good staff work done in the 1920s on problems of communications censorship in a war in which Ireland would wish to remain neutral, which drew extensively on British censorship memoranda outlining the experience between 1914 and 1918. This was dusted off in 1938 and became the basis of Irish censorship policy.[142]

During his October visit Archer was given a limited briefing on Mrs Brandy's activities. MI5's discovery that she had an anonymous correspondent 'created a tremendous impression' when SIS's Paris representative, 'Biffy' Dunderdale, informed the Deuxième Bureau, and led to the detention of a naval officer in Toulon, sous-lieutenant Marc Aubert. It transpired that he had been lured into espionage by his expensive mistress, who was also arrested and charged. SIS told Dunderdale that, 'for internal political reasons, it is very difficult to pursue enquiries [in Ireland] and the observance of the utmost secrecy is most urgently requested . . . The US authorities have given an assurance that they will do their best to exclude Mrs Brandy's name and address in the current proceedings . . .'[143] On his return to Dublin, Archer gathered some information about the Brandy family and forwarded it to MI5, who marked it 'LIAM REPORT'. Guy Liddell urged that the case be allowed to run on to see if Mrs Brandy had Irish contacts. G2 should be told 'quite frankly' that MI5 were intercepting her correspondence in transit through Britain, as otherwise the Irish 'may try to start opening' it, which 'in the existing arrangements over there, may well be disastrous'. On 5 November Archer again visited London. The deputy head of MI5

Spent most of the morning with Colonel Archer. Explained . . . the situation that had arisen in connection with Mrs BRANDY and discussed with him the possibilities. It is quite clear to me that . . . Archer (a) is certainly not prepared to act against Mrs BRANDY under the Official

---

[141] Despite taking part in the 1916 rising, in which he lost a toe, Archer had been reinstated in his Post Office job on the advice of a review committee which accepted his somewhat improbable account of events. Jeffery, *The GPO and the Easter Rising*, 201–4.

[142] O'Halpin, *Defending Ireland*, 57.

[143] The Deuxième Bureau was the French counter-espionage service. ? (SIS) to Hinchley Cooke, 19 Oct., copied to PCO Paris, 15 Oct. 1938, TNA, KV2/356. The New York proceedings involved the prosecution of a number of German spies using the same system of 'post boxes'. *Curry History*, 136.

Secrets Act; (b) is quite unable satisfactorily to intercept her correspondence and therefore quite rightly is not proposing to do so; (c) is very dubious as to how far he can safely employ the police in attempting to shadow . . . he is anxious to help . . . but I think we were right in getting him over as the information from Paris will undoubtedly strengthen his hand with the authorities . . . in order to get them to come round to his point of view as to what he requires in the way of personnel and powers.

I promised to let him know if and when we got any detailed information from Paris.[144]

G2 did arrange for Garda surveillance of Mrs Brandy, but she soon left Ireland. The MI5 records suggest that her departure may have been prompted by the *Daily Express* headline, 'Britain tracked down great naval plot'. Aubert lay 'manacled in cell' awaiting execution (which came the following month). Although the story had no Irish angle, MI5 thought this leak was 'a confounded nuisance from the Dublin end'.[145] On the other hand, Dan Bryan speculated decades later that Mrs Brandy's flight was attributable to overzealousness on the part of detectives involved in investigating her, though he thought the case valuable both in demonstrating that Germany was using Ireland for espionage, and in marking a constructive start to G2–Garda cooperation (he regarded the small Garda Aliens Office as particularly efficient, in contrast to some elements of Special Branch which had been penetrated by republicans).[146] The case also represented a modest success in Anglo-Irish security liaison. A further benefit was that, after de Valera's approval had been secured, the British provided advice and training on postal interception to an Irish Post Office official and later facilitated the purchase of modern equipment. This enabled the Irish gradually to build up an efficient communications censorship system which largely followed British practice. The postal censorship in particular proved an enormously valuable security tool until 1945.[147]

The second Irish encounter with German intelligence went less well. In February 1939 a German-American, Oskar Pfaus, visited Ireland. Pfaus was an official of the Fichte Bund, but he was also acting on behalf of the Abwehr. His task for them was to establish contact with the IRA. This he did with the help of Liam Walsh, an acolyte of General O'Duffy and serial embezzler who was a subscriber to Fichte Bund publications. Walsh put Pfaus in touch both with O'Duffy and, at the other end of the radical spectrum, indirectly with the IRA. On 13 February Pfaus had a successful meeting with a number of republicans, including the IRA chief of staff Seán Russell and Jim O'Donovan. O'Donovan was technically not a member of the IRA, having quit after the civil war. But he was the author of the S-plan, the recently launched IRA bombing campaign in Britain. It was agreed that the IRA would send a man to Germany to make detailed arrangements for cooperation, and O'Donovan was chosen. Although Pfaus had been under a degree of surveillance in Dublin, the Garda watchers discovered nothing either of his IRA contacts or of his meeting with O'Duffy.[148] In the year leading up to war, there were other indications

[144] Undated TS [Oct. 1938]; minute by Guy Liddell, 19 Oct.; note by Hinchley Cooke (MI5), 15 Nov. 1938, TNA, KV2/356.
[145] Hinchley Cooke to Vivian (SIS), 18 Feb. 1939; *Daily Express*, 17 Feb. 1939, TNA, KV2/356.
[146] Dan Bryan interview, 1983.
[147] O'Halpin, *Defending Ireland*, 144–5; Bryan interview, 1983.
[148] Hull, *Irish Secrets*, 56–7.

of growing German interest in Ireland as a base for intelligence operations, and reports began to reach Whitehall which suggested that German agents were seeking links with the IRA. During the war it became clear that there had been sporadic German–IRA contacts since 1936, probably initiated by the ideologically mercurial Seán MacBride—eventually to die a patron saint of the Irish left—during his brief period as IRA director of intelligence. The one-time IRA chief of staff Tom Barry told a G2 officer in 1940 that MacBride had paved the way for a visit he made to Germany in 1937. In an echo of the discussions between Clan na Gael and German diplomats which had prepared the ground for the 1916 rising, the veteran Irish-American conspirator Joseph McGarrity and the IRA's Seán Russell also put out feelers to the German embassy in Washington. Barry said that these contacts had resulted in the provision of money through Clan na Gael to Russell to fund the S-plan, and after the war Dan Bryan wrote that 'I am now satisfied that the Bombing Campaign was largely financed from German sources through America', although 'Russell did not let many of his assistants know where their money was coming from, partly because they would not approve of collaboration with the Nazis'. Germany's 'encouragement' of such activities naturally related exclusively to her own long-term aims.[149]

MI5 opened a file on IRA German contacts in June 1938. In March 1939 an MI5 man discussed the IRA bombings with a detective, and 'threw a fly over him to find out whether he thought they were financed by German money'. The officer replied that 'they had found nothing to indicate this and that with one exception the arrested men had very little cash on them'. This assessment contrasted with the conviction of Sir Robert Vansittart that Germany was financing the campaign.[150]

There was also public evidence of a shift in German attitudes towards the IRA: whereas in 1936 the German press praised de Valera's repression of it, in January 1939 it praised the Irish people's 'fight for freedom' and commended the bombings in Britain.[151] The campaign turned out to be both a political and a military debacle. Although the S-plan elaborated on the importance of industrial destruction, and was consequently a theoretical threat to defence production, what materialized were terror attacks on the softest of civilian targets. The response was led by the Special Branch at Scotland Yard, which attributed the campaign to the 'southern' IRA.[152] It damaged the republican movement's standing in Ireland, and it galvanized the British and the Irish authorities. It caused only minor disruption and the deaths of a number of civilians in England (there were thefts of explosives in Scotland, but no bombings there).[153] The Irish adopted a convoluted approach to cooperation: while the Garda would 'certainly do their best to keep the British Police informed of

---

[149] Note by O'Donoghue of his June 1940 conversation with Tom Barry, 23 Nov. 1943, MAI, G2/X/0093; Bryan to Boland, 17 May 1946 and 23 June 1947, NAI, DFA A55/1; O'Halpin, *Defending Ireland*, 128.

[150] Note by Harker, MI5, 30 Mar. 1939, TNA, KV3/120. Sir Robert Vansittart, later Lord Vansittart, had been permanent under-secretary at the Foreign Office from 1930 to 1937 before being kicked upstairs to the newly created and meaningless position of 'Chief Diplomatic Adviser'. O'Halpin, *Head of the Civil Service*, 253.

[151] Hull, *Irish Secrets*, 42

[152] Home Office secret circular 3469, 25 Jan. 1939, NAS, HH55/655.

[153] Tudor (Home Office) to Stewart (Scottish Office, 25 July 1939, NAS, HH55/655; Glasgow CID to Scottish Office, 15 May 1939, NAS, HH55/660.

anything which might be necessary to prevent the commission of any acts of violence in Great Britain', they would not 'make enquiries' about Irish people already under arrest lest 'the sympathy of the ordinary country people which is so necessary for them in the detection of ordinary crime' be jeopardized.[154] From the British point of view, this was hardly satisfactory.

Nevertheless, by the time war came, the IRA in Britain and their support networks were effectively neutralized, their potential for sabotage and intelligence gathering all but destroyed by arrests and deportations. What was also significant was that, despite some suspicions of indirect German assistance, 'the IRA and its activities' remained strictly 'a police responsibility': it was the police, and particularly the Special Branch, which defeated the campaign.[155]

In July 1939 SIS reported that 'on the 20th and 25th June a conference had taken place in Berlin between Admiral Canaris, head of the Abwehr, a representative of the German War Office, and a responsible member of the IRA who was said to have reported on the bombing campaign in Britain. Canaris was reported to have undertaken to supply him with arms and funds'.[156] This remarkable report probably came from Czech intelligence, which had an especially good source in the Abwehr and shared the product with Britain and France.[157] It was substantially accurate. Between February and August 1939 Jim O'Donovan made three trips to Germany to meet the Abwehr. Clan na Gael's Joe McGarrity attended one of these. There were significant differences between what the Irishmen wanted—an immediate supply of arms and explosives—and what the Abwehr were willing to provide to an organization which had shot its bolt prematurely with the S-plan, but O'Donovan was given coding materials and money with which to purchase a radio so that contact could be established. In July a Breton nationalist living in Ireland collected a parcel of cash for O'Donovan while on a bogus business trip to Paris. O'Donovan and his wife Monty returned from their final trip to Germany just a few days before war broke out, without arousing the suspicions of either the Irish or British authorities. Shortly afterwards, another Breton delivered a keyword for radio transmissions to London, and this duly reached O'Donovan.[158]

MI5 received information via the Foreign Office in July suggesting that German legation officials had visited a German-owned hotel in Donegal to meet both with the IRA and their one-time enemy General O'Duffy. This was supported by considerable detail, but a Garda investigation indicated that although two Germans had indeed visited, there was no evidence that they had met any republicans. It was also unlikely in the extreme that O'Duffy and the IRA would attend the same meeting. Two and two had been added to make five. The source was a Czech servant in the German legation. In August came another strange tale, passed to the Foreign Office by the Czech chargé d'affaires in London: Hempel had had discussions about forming 'an Irish Legion' to fight with Germany against Britain with two

[154] Irish high commissioner, London, to Dominions Office, 16 Feb. 1939, in Crowe *et al. DIFP* v. 407–8.
[155] *Liddell History*, 42.
[156] *Liddell History*, 43.
[157] Jackson, *France and the Nazi Menace*, 28.
[158] Hull, *Irish Secrets*, 62–3. Monty was a younger sister of my grandmother Kathy Barry.

republicans, Seán MacBride and his brother-in-law Francis Stuart. Hempel had also supposedly discussed this scheme with an unidentified member of the Irish 'Foreign Ministry' who drove 'a car bearing the number Z 6982' (this belonged to Fred Boland, the assistant secretary of External Affairs and later a key figure in Anglo-Irish security dealings). Aspects of the report—the suggestion that Boland was involved in *pour-parlers* about a possible Irish–German military alliance, the claims that Walshe had told Hempel that 'in case of war the staff of the German legation must leave Ireland', and that 'a branch of the Gestapo has been organised in Dublin'—may be doubted, but there was a germ of truth in the suggestion of sympathetic contacts between republicans and the German legation. MacBride and Stuart were strong admirers of Nazi Germany.[159] The Liddell history states that Walshe was so outraged by what he heard of this report that he informed Hempel about his unreliable employee; if true, this was an unforgivable indiscretion in security terms, because of the difficulties inherent in infiltrating a diplomatic mission (the Irish apparently never succeeded in getting inside the German legation themselves, although they had more luck with the Americans). It could also have jeopardized the developing Anglo-Irish understanding.

Stuart travelled to Germany in September to take up an academic appointment, and also acted as an IRA messenger and link for subversive purposes (his wife Iseult was the first person contacted by the key agent Herman Goertz on his arrival in Ireland in May 1940). Stuart later became a broadcaster on German English-language radio stations, delivering a peculiar mixture of apocalyptic nihilism, anti-British rants, and cryptic anti-Semitism. MacBride remained a stalwart friend of the German legation, and was most likely a key wartime source on the IRA and on Northern Ireland.

As war moved closer, other sources reported on German submarine contacts with the IRA, including a claim that U45 had landed explosives 'and a large sum in £10 notes some time in the first week of July on the south side of Belfast Bay, 16 miles from Belfast, with the aid of fishermen'.[160] Such wild tales were to become the stock in trade of MI5, SIS, and NID during the first two years of the war.

In August MI5 circulated a 'note on possible German support for the IRA'. Based on the Czech source and RUC and SIS reports, it was 'mostly in the form of allegations, lacking detail and circumstantial evidence', and its conclusions were commendably cautious: there were indications of German interest but no hard proof. At the request of the home secretary, it was shown to Chamberlain.[161] The document represented a significant development in British thinking about German engagement with Ireland, because it lent weight to the idea that the IRA might act as a fifth column—whether for espionage or for sabotage—once war came: 'it seems highly likely that the German authorities would try to support the IRA in the same way that they have the Arab Higher Committee in Palestine', and the note invoked the memory of 'Von Rintelen's successful exploits with Irish revolutionaries in the USA

---

[159] TS copy of information received by Jebb and Troutbeck of the Foreign Office from the Czech chargé d'affaires, 31 Aug. 1939, TNA, KV3/120; *Liddell History*, 43.

[160] Undated [? August 1939] MI5 memorandum on possible German IRA contacts, TNA, KV3/120.

[161] 'Note on possible German support for the IRA', undated, with ? (MI5) to Jebb (Foreign Office), and note of request from home secretary, 4 and 8 Aug. 1939, TNA, KV3/120.

during the last war . . . MI5 is inclined to regard the danger of Germany organising sabotage with IRA terrorists as a very dangerous one', although the document did not speculate on German involvement with the S-plan bombing campaign.[162]

Assessment of German clandestine activity in Ireland was complicated by the fact that GC&CS could not break the main German diplomatic cipher. In those circumstances it was natural that any story linking the legation with intrigue would be taken at face value. It is now clear from the legation's surviving communications up to September 1939 that, while its staff assiduously courted pro-German elements, under the cautious Hempel they did not become directly involved in espionage or in political intrigues. Furthermore, the legation had only limited and tangential knowledge of pre-war German clandestine arrangements concerning Ireland, including those being made through the German community and with the IRA. From a diplomatic perspective, what was potentially at stake was Irish goodwill. While de Valera clearly deprecated Hitler's domestic policies, until March 1939 Ireland was broadly supportive of German claims to contiguous territories with ethnic German populations, seeing an analogy in the alleged injustices of Versailles with the imposition and maintenance of partition. But de Valera declined to accept as legitimate Germany's absorption by *force majeure* of what was left of Czechoslovakia in March 1939, and the Irish allowed the Czechoslovak consul to remain in Dublin. Given geography and strategic realities, it was clearly in Germany's interests not to provoke Dublin into closer cooperation with Britain. Hempel's problem was that his assessment was not universally shared in Berlin.[163] On the eve of war, de Valera told him that Ireland wished to remain neutral and hoped to maintain good relations with Germany, but such neutrality could not be 'absolute': geography, economic relations, and Britain's legitimate security interests all meant that Ireland must show 'a certain consideration' for her neighbour. Neutrality would be jeopardized by attack by either Germany or Britain, and he warned against any attempt to enlist the extreme anti-British element: 'the German Legation should not allow itself to be used in any way' in 'the prosecution of the war'.[164]

De Valera took one further and overdue step in August 1939 which somewhat simplified matters. He recalled the minister in Berlin, Charles Bewley, an eccentric who had become increasingly enthusiastic about the Nazi project. Bewley was a truculent correspondent, sending reports in which naked anti-Semitism was mingled with scarcely veiled criticism of Irish policy for kowtowing to Britain. Bewley declined to return, thereby effectively dismissing himself. He spent the war in Europe, carrying out propaganda work for Germany and styling himself the former Irish minister to the Vatican—a post he had held from 1929 to 1933.[165] To have had such a representative in Berlin in wartime would have been

---

[162] 'Note on possible German support for the IRA', TNA, KV3/120; Von Rintelen, *The Dark Invader*.

[163] O'Driscoll, 'Interwar Irish–German Diplomacy', in Kennedy and Skelly (eds.), *Irish Foreign Policy*, 90–2; Smyllie, 'Unneutral Neutral Eire', 325.

[164] O'Driscoll, *Ireland, Germany and the Nazis*, 273–4; speaking notes by Walshe for de Valera, 25 Aug. 1939, in Crowe *et al.*, *DIFP* v. 495–6.

[165] Bewley to Dublin, 9 Dec. 1938, 25 Jan., 8 Feb. and 2 Aug, and Walshe to Bewley, 26 Jan., and Boland to Warnock, 1 Aug. 1939, Crowe *et al.*, *DIFP* v. 373–80, 393–5, 403–405, 479, 480–2.

disastrous. Germany accepted the Irish nomination of a successor, but war broke out before credentials could be presented. Since these bore the signature of the British monarch, presentation then became an impossibility. Consequently the legation secretary William Warnock had to act as chargé d'affaires until 1943, when he was succeeded in that role by Con Cremin. Both men were competent diplomats who successively ploughed a lonely and discreet furrow.

CONCLUSION

When war came, British intelligence knew precious little about Ireland. Despite the memory of the 1916 rising and the war of independence, despite the implications of the republican agenda both for the new Irish state and for Northern Ireland, and despite its international associations, republicanism ceased to be an object of serious intelligence interest in 1922. The IRA thereafter was primarily a police problem, to be handled respectively by the RUC and by Scotland Yard. While it occasionally came to attention because of links with communism and later with Nazism, for most of the inter-war years it was not seen as capable of posing a direct threat to wider British interests.

With the idiosyncratic exception of the Northern Ireland intelligence gatherers until 1926, British agencies were equally ignorant about Irish politics. They did not have people on the ground in either a liaising or a clandestine capacity and, apart from codebreaking, they had no reliable sources on Irish political affairs—the absence of a diplomatic presence in Dublin until September 1939 was particularly felt. Until the crucial MI5–G2 'Dublin link' was created in 1938, there were no recognized channels for systematic liaison on any aspect of security, subversion, or counter-espionage. While a good deal of intelligence material relating to Ireland accumulated in the records of SIS, MI5, GC&CS, Scotland Yard, and IPI, particularly in relation to communism, most of it came incidentally in the course of other investigations and it was not analysed primarily in terms of what it disclosed about Irish affairs. At headquarters neither MI5 nor SIS had any Irish specialist. Until 1932, and even then only briefly, Ireland was not a focus of intelligence enquiries and assessment. Thereafter until 1939 intelligence on Ireland was limited to whatever appeared in SIS's periodic QRS reports, dyspeptic mutterings rather than considered appraisals. Codebreaking provided little insight into either Irish policy or foreign diplomacy because, while GC&CS could decode at least some Italian, French, American, and Irish diplomatic cables to and from Dublin, they could not break the traffic which mattered most, German communications.

Compounding these difficulties was the fact that there were no integrating processes in inter-war Whitehall to ensure that intelligence, however and by whichever agency obtained, was assessed in the light of other information available. Such machinery only began to emerge under the stresses of war. Even then it took years to develop effective coordination so that a composite view could emerge. Whitehall's secret agencies had far greater and more obvious threats than Ireland to worry about across Europe during the approach to war. Yet Ireland was to provide

Britain with extraordinary security headaches once war came, problems accentuated by the almost complete absence of pre-war consideration of Irish affairs. In the first year of the conflict, the consequence was at first undue alarm in Whitehall, followed in the summer of 1940 by blind panic resulting in a dramatic shift in British policy on the question of partition.

2

Phoney war, phoney spies: September 1939–April 1940

THE COMELY MAIDEN SAYS NO: BRITISH POLICY AND IRISH NEUTRALITY DURING THE PHONEY WAR

When war came, de Valera reiterated that Ireland would stay neutral. This approach was widely supported across the political spectrum. His opponents as well as his adherents accepted the imperative of neutrality, although some leading figures were privately very supportive of Britain. Some were also sorry for Poland, like Ireland a predominantly Catholic state invaded by powerful neighbours. Neutrality was explicitly grounded in what de Valera regarded as Ireland's historic experience, in the failure of collective security as embodied in the League of Nations, and in the fate of small countries and nationalities drawn into the first world war. Partition as such was not adduced as a determining reason, nor the memory of British conduct during the war of independence. London might have forgotten the Black and Tans, the burning of Cork, the destruction of creameries, the killings of men shot while attempting to escape, and other excesses of Crown forces, but Irishmen had not.[1]

There was strong popular sympathy for Britain from the outset, balanced by determination to stay out of the conflict.[2] But a minority of committed republicans hoped, and some schemed, for a German victory. Amongst the latter was my mother's uncle Jim O'Donovan, the Abwehr's IRA link whom some maintain was a convinced Nazi. Other republicans, such as my Moloney grandparents, were probably not untypical. *New Statesman* readers both, they could hardly claim to be ignorant in general terms of the nastiness of the Hitler regime. Yet they longed for British humiliation. Both had been very active during the war of independence. During the civil war of 1922–3, Kathy Barry was general secretary of the Irish Republican Prisoners Dependants' Fund and a key link between de Valera and the anti-treaty military leader Liam Lynch. A strong feminist, she later became a trade-union activist. Jim Moloney had served on the staff of Liam Lynch in 1922–3. I once asked him why he and his wife had wanted a German victory. He replied that they had hoped for the destruction of the British empire, and had dismissed British reports of German atrocities during the war by reference to the Irish experience in

---

[1] The best analysis of the war of independence remains Townshend, *British Campaign in Ireland.*
[2] Wills, *That Neutral Island*, 83–111.

1914, when tales of German rape and pillage in Catholic Belgium turned out to have been largely propaganda.[3]

I should not have been surprised. Jim Moloney's first experience of repression had been at British hands. His family's home and business in Tipperary town was burnt out in an unofficial reprisal in 1920—his father was a Sinn Féin TD, and the house was headquarters for the Third Tipperary brigade at the time of the Soloheadbeg ambush in January 1919, when two RIC constables were slain, problematic killings generally regarded as the first act of the war of independence—and his brother Paddy was shot in an engagement in May 1921, his body gleefully carted through Tipperary town by police who initially believed they had got the more senior brother Con. Kathy Barry's younger brother Kevin, 'just a lad of eighteen summers' when executed in November 1920, became an enduring icon of the independence struggle. My father's father Hugh Halfpenny, an IRA officer exiled from Northern Ireland in 1922, died young in 1943 of kidney disease apparently originating in ill-treatment during internment in the war of independence. Like the Moloneys he had plenty of personal grounds—dead comrades, exile, chronic illness—to be anti-British, and his children recalled the satisfaction he took in news of every British reverse. Not all pro-Germans were republicans: Lady Fingall, in a chat with a friend, 'denounced the Jews. She wished Hitler would come here and discipline the people'. Yet most Irish people who suffered and lost during the war of independence and civil war took a different view.[4]

Government ministers and supporters had much the same kinds of personal narratives of wounds, bereavement, ill-treatment, and exile between 1916 and 1923 as those which extreme republicans used to justify supporting Germany against Britain. Gerry Boland lost his brother Harry, once Michael Collins's right-hand man, killed in controversial circumstances during the civil war; Seán Lemass's brother Noel was murdered after the fighting had ended; Tom Derrig had lost an eye during interrogation; Frank Aiken had had to leave South Armagh for good; Seán MacEntee was also exiled from Northern Ireland. Yet, despite rumours to the contrary, all of these were determinedly pro-neutrality, not pro-German (although Aiken was always suspect in British eyes), and some, including de Valera, Lemass, and MacEntee, the latter quite openly, personally favoured Britain against Nazism.

Neutrality came as no great shock in Whitehall. Most European states had indicated their desire not to be drawn into Anglo-French confrontation with Germany. While Italy was apparently only biding her time, and Romania, Hungary, and Bulgaria were in what Neville Wylie has termed the 'wait-and-see' category, most countries were firmly committed to avoiding war if they possibly could.[5] But

---

[3] Recent scholarship, including that by my Trinity colleagues, shows the extent of German atrocities and the thinking behind them. Horne and Kramer, *German Atrocities*.

[4] Todd Andrews and Dan Bryan commented to me on O'Donovan's ideological make-up; Senator Bill Quirke's evidence to pensions board, 17 Apr. 1936 (James Moloney military service pension file, in my possession); Andrews, *Dublin Made Me*, 291 (on Jim Moloney), and 279 (on Kathy Barry); on Kathy Barry's career as a republican and union activist see her papers in UCDA, P94. PRONI has security files on Hugh Halfpenny, HA32/1/360 and HA5/617, and on my grandmother's brother Dan Rice, HA5/2317. Furlong diary, 2 July 1940, UCDA, LA53/48.

[5] Wylie, 'Introduction', in Wylie (ed.), *European Neutrals and Non-Belligerents*, 15.

Ireland differed from the European norm in three significant respects: strategic defence, both because unlike the mainland European neutrals she was shielded by Britain from German attack, and because of her crucial position in the Atlantic; constitutional affairs, because Ireland, while a sovereign state, was also a dominion; and security, because she and the United Kingdom shared a common travel area, a common language, and a porous border. In that respect, as well as in terms of the threat of Axis espionage, the problems which Ireland presented for Britain were comparable less with the other European neutrals than with Afghanistan or the United States. Afghanistan shared a highly permeable border with British India, its southern tribes lived in areas which spanned the formal frontier, it had diplomatic relations with the Axis powers, and it became a centre of Axis intrigue against British interests. On 8 September the Delhi intelligence bureau warned that 'the outbreak of war has greatly enhanced the potential of Afghanistan as a base for hostile action against India', pointing to intrigues by activists such as the 'Silk Letter Conspirators', previously involved in a German scheme to stir up 'religious fanaticism amongst the Muslims' during the first world war, a plot eerily reminiscent of the storyline of John Buchan's *Greenmantle*. The United States' northern border with Canada was more or less uncontrollable, but the Americans were constrained to maintain a façade of strict regulation of movements because any decision to ease them 'would be so seriously resented not only in Mexico but elsewhere in Latin America as to actually endanger the effects of our good neighbour policy'.[6]

Among the dominions there was neither great surprise nor indignation at the Irish position. South Africa was bitterly divided: her long-serving prime minister Hertzog resigned when parliament narrowly agreed to join the conflict, with Afrikaner opinion firmly against involvement, and when his successor Smuts declared war on Italy in June 1940 Hertzog sent him 'a poisonous letter' of protest.[7] In 1942 Smuts told Dulanty that 'feeling in South Africa was not very different from that in Ireland. When the Germans invaded Holland, there was a two days' excitement . . . After that they fell back into their mood of neutrality'.[8] Australian opinion was also split on the war, with a strong minority very suspicious of British intentions, although New Zealand was more wholeheartedly committed. The Canadian prime minister Mackenzie King consulted his parliament before declaring war, but he did so apprehensively. French-Canadians were very critical, and he feared that Germany would win: on 17 September he was 'terribly afraid that neither Britain nor France will yield but will attempt to go on fighting no matter what the odds' and 'will be doomed'.[9] All the dominions were sensitive about their sovereignty, and shared memories of Britain's sometimes overbearing and patronizing attitude towards them in the League of Nations; dominions statesmen also recalled the Irish contribution towards the redefinition of dominion status embodied in the 1931 Statute of

---

[6] Hauner, *India in Axis Strategy*; Delhi Intelligence Bureau memorandum, 8 Sept. 1939, BL, L/PS/12/1760; Moffat journal, 13 Nov. 1940, Harvard MS 1407, vol. 46; Arghandawi, *British Imperialism*, 135–9; Buchan, *Greenmantle*.

[7] Smuts to M. C. Gillett, 24 June 1940, in Van den Poel (ed.), *Selections from the Smuts Papers*, vi. 239–41.

[8] Dulanty to Dublin, 18 Nov. 1942, NAI, DFA P12/14(i).

[9] Mackenzie King diary, 17 Sept. 1939.

Westminster, and had a high regard for de Valera's advocacy of the rights of small states in the League after 1932; finally, most had significant anti-war minorities with which to contend.[10]

There was one crucial development affecting Anglo-Irish relations in the early weeks of the conflict. An amiable meeting between the dominions secretary Anthony Eden and Walshe in London on 7 September produced understandings on a number of diplomatic and security issues, and two weeks later Sir John Maffey, formerly permanent under-secretary at the Colonial Office, arrived in Dublin as the 'British Representative', a compromise designation.[11] The selection of Maffey was a masterstroke. He had made his name as a political officer on the north-west frontier with Afghanistan, and had been chief political adviser to the British forces in the third Afghan war of 1919. This ended after a few months with a peace agreement, followed by a full treaty signed in November 1921 — just weeks before the Anglo-Irish treaty — whereby Britain somewhat grudgingly recognized Afghanistan's complete independence, and Afghanistan half-heartedly acknowledged the Durand line, imposed by British diktat in 1893, as her legal southern and western border (thereby accepting the loss of Baluchistan and access to the Arabian Sea). The parallels with Ireland were obvious. Maffey brought a small group of officials, who established what was in effect a high commission. Britain at last had someone in Dublin who could act as both a conduit for Anglo-Irish dialogue and an observer and adviser on political affairs, and who already had long experience of dealing with permeable borders and prickly, fractious neighbours resentful of real and imagined British wrongdoings. Maffey and his staff were to play a pivotal role in Anglo-Irish relations throughout the war, in questions of security and intelligence as well as in more conventional diplomatic business. But it inevitably took time to get the measure of the Irish government, and to win the confidence of the Dominions Office. In the first months of the war his voice carried little weight in Whitehall.

Interest in Irish affairs was spread across a number of departments and agencies. When war came, no effective coordinating mechanism existed by which their various intelligence requirements and concerns could be systematically reviewed and addressed, or incoming intelligence about Ireland coherently assessed. MI5's 'Dublin link' was the only Anglo-Irish intelligence channel, and it was at such an early stage of development and was so sensitive that almost no one in Whitehall outside MI5, the Dominions Office, and SIS knew of it. The inevitable consequence was that individual departments, agencies, and the fighting services seeking any kind of political, security, or military information were inclined to go and look for it independently and without reference either to what anyone else in Whitehall might already know or be doing, or to wider policy considerations. There was also a marked tendency to accept alarmist stories at face value.[12]

---

[10] Lloyd and James, 'The External Representation of the Dominions, 1919–1948', 500–1; Kennedy, *Ireland and the League of Nations*; Hodson, 'British Foreign Policy and the Dominions'.

[11] Walshe to de Valera, reporting on his London discussions of 6 to 10 Sept. 1939, and Chamberlain to de Valera, 19 Sept. 1939, UCDA, de Valera papers, P150/2571 and 2548.

[12] It should be noted that the Irish authorities received a comparable cascade of reports of supposed pro-German, pro-British and IRA activities. They were, however, somewhat better placed to make informed judgements because of detailed local knowledge. Canning, *British Policy Towards Ireland.*

Because of contiguity, ease of travel, trade links, a shared language, the British commercial presence, and the large numbers of Irish residents sympathetic to Britain, there was no shortage of sources of scares and surmise: Cecil Liddell later wrote of the 'flood of reports, enquiries and rumours, which poured in from every side. It was difficult, if not impossible, to avoid the fatal and futile search for spies in the "in tray", instead of visualising the situation as a whole'.[13] In the desperate weeks which followed the collapse of France in June 1940, such material was to have a profound impact on British policy.

Policy towards Ireland in the changed circumstances of war was initially formulated by much the same group of men as in peacetime. They accepted the Irish position phlegmatically; it was exactly what de Valera had told them he would do, no more and no less. Chamberlain was the same calm, measured prime minister in war as he had been in peace, when he had taken a particular interest in disposing of the major difficulties in Anglo-Irish relations. His view of de Valera remained broadly positive: he regarded him as a man sympathetic to British interests, with the crucial exception of partition (about which Chamberlain himself was fatalistic rather than convinced, viewing some form of Irish unity as potentially desirable but unachievable given prevailing attitudes in both Dublin and Belfast).

Chamberlain's policy in the first months of the war was to make sure that Irish neutrality did not jeopardize British interests, and he believed that this could most effectively be done by quiet dialogue. The dominions secretary Malcolm MacDonald was similarly well disposed: his considerable experience of negotiating with de Valera since 1936 had convinced him that the Irish leader was a reasonable and purposeful statesman. If he could not be moved on neutrality, then it was better to secure quiet cooperation than to attempt to browbeat Ireland into a more accommodating position. The home secretary Sir John Anderson, regarded as the ablest official in Whitehall before taking up politics, was an old Ireland hand. He had been installed in Dublin in 1920 with an explicit remit to reform Irish administration and to develop confidential links with the separatist movement. He had consistently urged London towards a political compromise, and was one of the architects of the eventual truce in July 1921. An unflappable man—after an attempted assassination when governor of Bengal in 1931, he had made efforts to secure lenient treatment for his young attacker—he exercised a calming influence both on his department and on his cabinet colleagues, including even the excitable Churchill. In his view Ireland presented obvious political, strategic, and security problems which were best addressed by dispassionate study and negotiation rather than by threats or precipitate action.

Anderson's voice was decisive in the cabinet's difficult decision in February 1940 not to grant clemency to two Irishmen condemned for the Coventry bombing of August 1939, which had killed five people.[14] Robert Brennan in Washington warned that 'already there was a pronounced swing amongst the younger Irish in the United States from the de Valera faction to the IRA', and he expended much of what political capital he possessed in lobbying the State Department and the White House. He even convinced the British ambassador. Roosevelt took the same

---

[13] *Liddell History*, 52.
[14] Liddell diary, 13 Feb. 1940, TNA, KV4/185; Canning, *British Policy Towards Ireland*, 259–60.

line, arguing that it would be better not to create more Irish martyrs. Brennan later wrote that Tom Barry, the former IRA chief, had 'complete evidence' showing that the two men convicted had no 'hand, act or part in the . . . explosions', but this was not the case: they had minor roles.[15] The cabinet gave the question of reprieve careful consideration—Guy Liddell heard that telephone taps disclosed that de Valera hoped to fly to London to appeal directly to King George, while 'there had been a suggestion that Dev should see the prime minister but that an intimation had been given that no useful purpose would be served'.[16] A few days later he noted that Anderson 'was adamant about the executions . . . the PM, Eden and to some extent even Winston were anxious to find a way out'—but decided not to intercede.[17] The executions did not have the calamitous effects predicted, and caused no significant change in Dublin's policy on the IRA, other perhaps than to harden it: within two months de Valera allowed two hunger-strikers to die rather than yield to their demands; within a year, three IRA men were executed for capital crimes. When discussing the death sentences passed on six IRA men for murdering an RUC constable in 1942, Anthony Eden remarked: 'I went thro' this over Coventry murder. And I will now admit I was in the wrong. There was no trouble in Eire, or America'.[18]

The cabinet's acceptance of Irish neutrality reflected other considerations. A committee of departments charged to identify means 'of inducing' Ireland 'to give fuller co-operation, especially in naval and air matters', produced a consensus that 'to push the Irish to the point of a quarrel would have worse results for us than for them. This was illustrated from all angles, both in time of war and . . . peace'.[19] The first months of the war were, if not quite a non-event, far less violent or eventful than anticipated. Once Poland had been crushed and dismembered by Germany and the Soviet Union, there appeared to be a strategic stalemate. The longer that Germany was kept hemmed in by France and Britain to the west, and neutral Italy to the south, the greater would be her difficulties as the blockade of her sea trade took hold. Nothing much happened on land. There were some aerial exchanges, but not the mass bombing which had been expected: the RAF's initial daylight operations against naval installations proved disastrous, and the first night raids against Germany entailed dropping only propaganda leaflets. Initially even experienced observers thought this prudent: a few days into the war a former military attaché in Berlin said that 'the leaflet policy is right . . . bombing might only have the effect of stiffening German resistance'.[20] Such talk reflected a general lack of enthusiasm for action which might push Germany into further violence. The thing to do was to wait until the naval stranglehold compelled Hitler to negotiate.

[15] Moffat journal, 1 Feb. 1940, Harvard, MS 1407, vol. 44; Brennan to Walsh, 23 Feb. 1940, New York Public Library (NYPL), J. C. Walsh papers, box 3.

[16] Liddell diary, 6 Feb. 1940, TNA, KV4/185.

[17] Canning, *British Policy Towards Ireland*, 258–60; Moffat journal, 1 Feb. 1940, vol. 44, Harvard, MS1407; Liddell diary, 6 and 14 Feb. 1940, TNA, KV4/185.

[18] Cabinet secretary's informal notes of war cabinet meeting, 20 Aug. 1942, TNA, WM (42) 114th, CAB195/1.

[19] Bank of England memorandum, 30 Oct. 1939, OV81/1, Bank of England archives.

[20] Liddell diary, 7 Sept. 1939, TNA, KV4/185. This was Kenneth Strong, who had been assistant military attaché in Berlin. In 1944–5 he was Eisenhower's chief of intelligence.

The sea provided the main excitement. Germany's small submarine arm achieved dramatic results in the Atlantic, the St George's Channel, and at Scapa Flow, where the battleship *Royal Oak* was sunk. On the other hand, the navy enjoyed some success against German merchant shipping, and secured an important psychological victory with the scuttling of the damaged German commerce raider *Graf Spee* off Montevideo in December. The course of events seemed scarcely to justify a more coercive policy towards Ireland, particularly in view of the need to cultivate American opinion. In any case, it was clear from all sources that there was no appetite in Ireland for joining the war. Consequently the circumstances did not exist for drastic measures such as promoting a coup by pro-British elements—an approach adopted in the rather different circumstances of Yugoslavia in March 1941—and in any case there was no secret organization or machinery in place or in contemplation to organize such an intervention. Individual ministers who thought differently about Ireland generally kept their opinions to themselves. For most, their eyes fixed firmly on the German threat to western Europe, Ireland was a minor issue. The exception, however, was a crucial and vociferous one, Winston Churchill.

THE NAVY'S IRISH CONCERNS, 1939–1940

We have seen that, despite the fact that not a shred of documentary, testamentary, or physical evidence had emerged to indicate that U-boats had received organized assistance from Irish separatists during the first world war, in September 1939 the phantasm was revived.[21] It must, however, be noted that Ireland was not the solitary locus either of submarine or of spy scares in the first months of the war: MI5 and the police forces throughout the United Kingdom were inundated with reports of mysterious strangers, apparent signalling with lights, and dark shapes seen offshore.[22] David Stafford notes that Churchill's 'U-boat anxieties finally died down' by the spring of 1940, but these were succeeded by other concerns about Irish security which were to remain with him until after D-Day in 1944.[23]

Churchill had strong though changeable views on Ireland. He had been secretary of state for war during the most violent phase of the war of independence, and was one of the signatories of the Anglo-Irish treaty. As chancellor of the exchequer in 1925, he had been involved in the hurried financial settlement which cemented the border as drawn under the Government of Ireland Act of 1920. At no stage of his career had he displayed particular sympathy for unionism, and he had rather lost interest in Ireland generally by the 1930s. He did, however, launch a strong attack in the Commons in May 1938 on the government's decision to relinquish Britain's defence rights. Churchill's attitude towards Ireland during the phoney war was framed not only by the ministerial brief which he held, but by his general conception of grand strategy and his appetite for taking the battle to the enemy.

[21] O'Halpin, *Decline of the Union*, 106–11, 159, and 'British Intelligence in Ireland, 1914–1921', 54–77; Wills, *That Neutral Island*, 116 and 136.

[22] *Curry History*, 151–3.

[23] Stafford, *Churchill and Secret Service*, 190.

While he did not personally resent the efforts of most European states to stay out of the war as he did Ireland's, he regarded their neutrality as a mere technicality rather than a moral obstacle. In the first phase of the war this was most significant in respect of Norway and of Sweden: early in 1940 he urged his colleagues to sanction what were clearly violations of those countries' sovereignty to further British interests and to damage the enemy. His views on Ireland were predictably robust.

In the first weeks of the war, the German Admiral Raeder warned the United States naval attaché that the American merchant ship *Iroquois* would shortly be sunk by the British in the Atlantic, in such a way as to make it appear that Germany was responsible. Churchill exploited this groundless claim to tell Roosevelt, in the course of what appears to have been their first telephone conversation, 'U-boat danger inconceivable in these broad waters. Only method can be time-bomb planted at Queenstown [Cobh, in Cork]. We think this not impossible'. He advised that Washington publicize Raeder's warning, which they duly did. Robert Brennan was alarmed that Raeder reportedly claimed 'that the source of his information . . . came from Ireland', although the State Department 'did not place any great reliance on this part of the story'.[24] Whether or not Churchill genuinely believed that the root of the problem lay in Ireland, the affair gave him an early opportunity, of which he availed to plant a seed in Roosevelt's mind about Irish insecurity and the problem of the ports. It was not the last time that he did so.[25]

Cabinet interest in Ireland waxed and waned. Churchill sporadically pressed for decisive action to bring the ports under British control, presenting a succession of arguments to his colleagues in September and October 1939. To what extent these were grounded as much in his personal anger at Irish neutrality as in a genuine concern for the operational needs of the navy remains a matter of opinion: the strategic arguments on which Churchill based his case were somewhat theoretical in the autumn of 1939, in that German submarine warfare, which was concentrated on the northern approaches to the British Isles, was being adequately contained by British action. There was no obvious strategic use for the southern bases which would justify coercive action to regain possession of them and counterbalance the likely damage to Britain's standing internationally, both in the United States and amongst the dominions. Just two weeks after the outbreak of war, the Canadian prime minister gave a sympathetic hearing to the new Irish high commissioner, 'a very pleasant young fellow, most attractive in many ways, typically Irish in his persuasive ways', and a few months later advised the new Canadian minister in Dublin 'to learn all he could about Ireland and say very little . . . Ireland was a very difficult country just now. Best to tell them that he had come to learn about them from them, not to talk to them'.[26]

The argument advanced by the chiefs of staff in early 1938 still held good: use of the treaty ports would be highly problematic without active Irish cooperation, and it was probable that the reintroduction of a British presence would prove a

[24] Transcript of telephone conversation, 5 Oct. 1939, in Kimball, *Churchill and Roosevelt*, i. 25; Brennan to Walsh, 12 Oct. 1939, NYPL, Joseph C. Walsh papers, box 3.

[25] Fanning, 'The Anglo-American Alliance and the Irish Question in the Twentieth Century', 192–6.

[26] Mackenzie King diaries, 20 Sept. and 21 Dec. 1939 and 12 Feb. 1940.

crucial spur for the IRA, urged on by Germany. Anthony Eden, who had made his name as an anti-appeaser politically in February 1938, albeit in somewhat confused circumstances, by resigning the post of foreign secretary because of his government's supine attitude towards Italy, was convinced that any public concession by de Valera on the ports would make the maintenance of Irish neutrality impossible. He also feared the impact of British coercion on Irish recruitment to the armed forces.[27] In cabinet he laid stress on the positive benefits of Irish security cooperation, and with the support of most of his colleagues prevailed: an official recorded that Eden 'is most disappointed with Winston's attitude . . . A[nthony] E[den] says de Valera is doing all he can for us and it would be madness to start up all the trouble again. And what would USA say? Apart from that, Eire even now is our best recruiting ground'.[28] For a time Churchill held off on the question of the ports, but he continued to declaim against the iniquity of Irish neutrality. In January 1940 he used a broadcast to castigate the supine attitude of the remaining European neutrals: 'each one hopes that if he feeds the crocodile enough, the crocodile will eat him last'. Churchill contrasted this with the courageous approach of the Finns when faced with Soviet aggression. This was a resonant but scarcely an accurate analogy: Finland was fighting Russia only because she had been invaded in November 1939, having refused to grant Soviet demands for defence rights on her territory in the approaches to Leningrad. If Finland was an exemplar for any other European neutral, the most obvious one was Ireland, another newly independent state under threat from a powerful former ruler demanding defence facilities. This was hardly the comparison which Churchill had in mind.

Churchill's vehemence in pressing the ports issue on strategic grounds suggests that at bottom it was not simply the particulars of defence facilities refused but his outrage at the doctrine of imperial solidarity repudiated, and of friendship abrogated, which motivated him. His own department had accepted the relinquishing of defence rights in 1938, while recognizing that a war with Germany was likely within a short time. It is clear that the early pressure on the ports question came down to the Admiralty from the new first lord rather than the reverse. The progress of the war at sea between September 1939 and the spring of 1940 was largely along the lines expected before hostilities commenced. What changed towards the end of that time was not the strategic situation, but British attitudes towards the conduct of the war. After six months of increasingly embarrassing inactivity, by March 1940 the mood had shifted: the negative policy of victory by blockade—ironically, primarily one grounded in theories of British naval power—now appeared inadequate when measured against Germany's unabashed success. Poland had been overwhelmed quickly and mercilessly, and there were no signs that Hitler's resolution was crumbling in the face of Anglo-French solidarity. The Allies cast around to find somewhere where positive steps could be taken. For a time they had seriously contemplated action in support of the Finns against the Soviets. But the Finns capitulated in March 1940, before the Anglo-French initiative materialized. By then the cabinet had other plans for Scandinavia. On 5 April Chamberlain assured the

[27] Canning, *British Policy Towards Ireland*, 254–6.
[28] Oliver Harvey's diary, 30 Oct. 1939, quoted in ibid. 255.

British public that 'Hitler has missed the bus', but in the following days it transpired that Germany had simply opted for rather faster forms of transport.

Churchill consistently argued that blockade of Germany could not work effectively while she was able to ship Swedish iron ore through neutral Norwegian waters. The cabinet and the French agreed to two related schemes: the mining of Norwegian waters, and the landing of an Anglo-French force at the Norwegian port of Narvik, to which ore came by rail from Sweden for shipping to Germany. The original aim was to enable Allied troops to move across Norway into Sweden to destroy the ore mines once and for all. That so cautious a cabinet as Chamberlain's could accept a scheme which involved violation of the neutrality of two European states and which would inevitably draw Germany into Scandinavia, reflected their increasing desperation. Sensing this shift in attitude towards neutrals, the naval staff added a request that Berehaven also be seized, but Churchill said that that matter should be left for another day.[29]

The planned intervention in Norway was a shambles. Just as the mine-laying began, Hitler made his move, invading Denmark with scarcely a shot fired on 6 April, and attacking Norway the next day. After a month of confused fighting ashore and along the Norwegian coast, where the navy suffered heavy losses, Allied forces were withdrawn. In other circumstances some of the public blame for this disaster might have been expected to attach to Churchill and the Admiralty. In fact, it strengthened Churchill because his instincts had been proved right: action was better than inaction. The odium for the failure in Scandinavia fell instead upon Chamberlain, whose campaign it most certainly had not been, and it was a death-knell for his leadership.

The significance of events in Scandinavia for Ireland was twofold. They underlined the fact that, even under Chamberlain, the British government's views on the inviolability of neutral states had changed radically. More ominously, they demonstrated once more that Hitler was both ruthless and efficient in his handling of inconvenient neutrals. When he felt the time was ready he simply overran them. By mid-April the strategic calculations of the autumn were redundant: what was at issue in relation to the Irish ports once the German invasions of Denmark and Norway were under way was not simply the question of whether Britain should seize them for her own use, but whether they might become a target for German action against which the Irish would be powerless. We should note that the same question arose for the French, who from early 1940 pressed their Belgian neighbours to accept Allied forces on their soil to repel a possible attack. Even after Norway, the Belgians refused to alter their position of austere neutrality, largely for fear that to do so would provoke a German assault. French officials railed against such obscurantist logic, although one British diplomat reflected that 'we cannot afford . . . proper help' if Germany did attack. The Belgians were even reluctant to enter staff talks, and this contributed to chaos when the British army moved into Belgium after Germany attacked her.[30] The possibility of a German assault on Ireland, allied to worrying intelligence reports, was to provide a stimulus for a dramatic reconsideration of how best to cope with the danger posed by Britain's undefended neutral neighbour.

[29] Ibid. 260.
[30] Jackson, *Fall of France*, 75–6.

MI5'S IRISH PROBLEMS, 1939–1940

Three weeks into the war, Churchill gave the naval staff general guidance on policy towards Ireland. This offered a more balanced and broader assessment of the official Irish position and concerns than was evident elsewhere in his private and public pronouncements. He thought that:

Dulanty is thoroughly friendly to England. He was an officer under me in the Ministry of Munitions in 1917/18, but he has no control or authority in Southern Ireland (so-called Eire). He acts as a general smoother, reporting everything Irish in the most favourable light. Three-quarters of the people of Southern Ireland are with us, but the implacable malignant minority can make so much trouble that De Valera dare not do anything to offend them. All this talk about Partition and the bitterness that would be healed by a union of Northern and Southern Ireland will amount to nothing. They will not unite at the present time, and we cannot in any circumstances sell the loyalists of Northern Ireland. Will you kindly consider these observations as the basis upon which Admiralty dealings with Southern Ireland should proceed?[31]

Yet in September 1939 Churchill and his naval advisers genuinely believed in the possibility that Germany might already be enjoying some Irish support facilities for submarine operations. Quite why remains a mystery. Guy Liddell cautioned the Admiralty against giving too much credence to 'vague allegations' about 'submarine bases', although he thought it 'highly probable that the Germans are active on the West coast . . . and that the Govt. of Eire though possibly willing are ill-equipped to deal with this matter'. A week later he noted another 'somewhat alarmist' SIS report that 'an attempt at revolution by the IRA does not appear to be out of the question'.[32]

The Admiralty were not the only service department contemplating intelligence gathering in Ireland. In January 1940 the Liddell brothers and the RUC's Inspector Gilfillan met about various issues, including somewhat ambiguous material which had reached the RUC relating to the German agent Werner Unland. They also noted the appointment to the staff of the GOC Northern Ireland of Colonel Hill-Dillon, whose experience of Irish affairs extended back to the war of independence. They agreed that, whatever else he did, 'on no account should he be allowed to dabble in S [outhern] Irish affairs or run agents into S Ireland'. Guy Liddell met Hill-Dillon the following week: he 'seems to be extremely knowledgeable . . . and seems to have great experience', but was worried:

He rather gathered that the GOC felt himself very much in the dark about Irish affairs, and unable to get any very definite information as to what was going on either in the south or the north . . . there seemed to be a possibility that Hill-Dillon might have been called upon to run some kind of a show into southern Ireland. He himself was obviously reluctant to do anything of the kind, particularly since even before his appointment had been made a neighbour told his wife that she had heard of Hill-Dillon's appointment as an intelligence officer to GOC N Ireland.

---

[31] Churchill to naval staff, 24 Sept. 1939, CCCA, CHAR19/3.
[32] Liddell diary, 24 and 30 Sept. 1939, TNA, KV4/185.

This curious form of gazetting across the garden wall was not the only thing which concerned Hill-Dillon. He 'never wanted the appointment but accepted it as a military duty', and 'realises that he is running considerable risks which he would be quite prepared to accept', but 'did not see the use of getting a bullet in his back if his appointment is not really going to be of any benefit'.[33] Hill-Dillon was, in fact, already known to G2. Among the informants whom Dan Bryan had controlled during the war of independence was a billiard marker in the Kildare Street Club, to whom Hill-Dillon, then an intelligence officer in the army's Irish Command, entrusted correspondence. This material was brought to Bryan en route to the intended destinations.[34]

Liddell's discussion with Hill-Dillon may have been significant in discouraging, if not entirely preventing, snooping south of the border by BTNI (British Troops in Northern Ireland) in the spring of 1940. After the fall of France, when invasion became a real possibility, the army's pressing need for reconnaissance appears to have produced a partial change of practice. Hill-Dillon spent almost all of the war in military intelligence. After stints in Northern Ireland and in Whitehall, where for a time he sat on the Twenty committee overseeing the running of double agents, he served in the Middle East and in Italy, and occasionally crops up in intelligence records.[35]

The flood of reports about submarines and spies in Ireland reaching London, together with more prosaic dilemmas about postal and telecommunications censorship, movement controls, and shipping, prompted a series of investigations by the lord privy seal Lord Hankey. Maurice Hankey was, at least in his own eyes, the *fons et origo* of the British system of imperial defence. One of the giants of inter-war Whitehall, he had been secretary of the CID from its foundation in 1908 until his retirement in 1938, and secretary to the cabinet from 1916 to 1938. Chamberlain brought him into the government in September 1939 because of his vast experience in defence issues. He was an obvious choice to explore intelligence and security questions which spanned a number of departments, and it was largely in such roles that he was used during his two-year ministerial career. When he became prime minister Churchill kept Hankey on, only dispensing with him a year later. Hankey had little political judgement and, having spent decades as an official listening to ministers droning on at the cabinet table, he seized the opportunity of cabinet rank to do precisely the same. Under Chamberlain, on occasion he dragged out cabinet proceedings by sending for Mahan's *The Influence of Sea Power Upon History*, from which he would read out passages to illustrate a point about grand strategy.[36]

Hankey's various investigations of intelligence concerning on Ireland in 1939–40, and his consideration of the various problems arising from the common travel area,

[33] Ibid., 7 Feb. 1940, TNA, KV4/185.

[34] Dan Bryan interview, 1983. This was probably a man named Daly. MAI, Bureau of Military History, WS476 and 477. I am grateful to Eve Morrison for this reference.

[35] Liddell diary, 5 May 1944, TNA, KV4/194; the Twenty committee minutes are in TNA, KV4/63–9.

[36] Mahan, *Influence of Sea Power Upon History*. Information from Sir John Winnifrith, 1979. Winnifrith was an assistant secretary in the Cabinet Office from 1942 to 1944 and a close friend of Sir Edward Bridges, secretary to the cabinet from 1938 to 1945. Winnifrith shared a Downing St. anteroom with other ministerial private secretaries during cabinet meetings in 1939–40.

the close economic integration of Ireland with the United Kingdom, the Irish diaspora in Britain, and the employment of large numbers of Irish people in war-related industries, led him to conclude that a clear policy was needed on security measures, particularly movement controls and communications censorship. This was required both to thwart possible German espionage mounted from Ireland, and to prevent the deliberate or inadvertent leakage of war information. It was also necessary to find some means of determining the accuracy or otherwise of the various reports of IRA plans and of submarine and other activities, as the Admiralty had already demanded. Hankey's conclusions made sense so far as they went, but they did not address a central problem which persisted for at least a year: the absence of any process for the coordinated assessment and analysis of intelligence about Ireland. That was eventually to emerge not through the cabinet committee system, but through the development of an unusually close working relationship between SIS and MI5 on Irish matters, one based as much on good interpersonal relations as on any policy edict.

The agency with the most pressing practical Irish concerns was MI5. On 27 August 1939 Guy Liddell, then deputy director of its B Division responsible for counter-espionage, made the first entry in a journal which he was to maintain more or less continuously for six years until, on 1 June 1945, he ended its twelfth volume with the weary valediction: 'I am going on leave tomorrow until June 17th'.[37] Liddell recorded various concerns as war loomed: 'Arrangements were made yesterday for the following ports between UK and Eire to be covered either by IOs [intelligence officers] or S[pecial] B[ranch] officers: Glasgow, Ardrossan, Stranraer, Heysham, Liverpool, Holyhead, Fishguard. Passengers will be interrogated'. The main worry was that aliens could move unhindered between the two islands: 'we should . . . inform the Eire Government of any doubtful aliens going there, and the general record of this traffic may be useful later on if there is any attempt by the Germans to form some sort of a base in Eire by the use of neutrals'.[38] As time went on, such concerns were augmented by difficulties in developing effective communications censorship, by the need to prevent the leakage of war information through Ireland to Britain's enemies, by the always sensitive problem of the IRA in both parts of Ireland, and by worries about German espionage. When war came, MI5's new Irish section, initially designated B9 and later B1H, consisted of one newly appointed officer, Cecil Liddell, and one clerical worker. Jo Stephenson, a barrister serving as a corporal in an anti-aircraft unit, joined in April 1940.[39] The section's main asset in addressing Irish issues was the recently forged 'Dublin link'. This was still a highly tentative relationship, but enough had been achieved before the war to provide a basis for development.

[37] Liddell diary, 1 June 1945, TNA, KV4/196.
[38] Ibid., 27 Aug. 1939, TNA, KV4/185.
[39] Ibid., 23 Apr. 1940, TNA, KV4/185; *Liddell History*, 54. After the war Sir John Stephenson (1910–97) returned to the Bar and finished his career as a lord justice of appeal. In 1989 he shared his recollections of his wartime service with me, and read me extracts dealing with Irish matters from a lengthy unpublished memoir. His father, Sir Guy Stephenson, was assistant director of public prosecutions in 1916, and had been involved in the trial of the Irish separatist and former consular service officer Sir Roger Casement, while in 1882 his great-uncle Lord Frederick Cavendish, chief secretary for Ireland, had been assassinated in Dublin's Phoenix Park by the secret society the Invincibles. On one of his liaison visits to Dublin Stephenson was shown the site of the killing by Dan Bryan.

The remit of the Irish section followed geographic rather than political logic: it was responsible for security matters affecting British interests on the entire island of Ireland. Writing in 1945, Cecil Liddell summarized his section's primary duty:

To prevent the leakage of information of military value . . . to the enemy through Eire. For this purpose the jurisdiction of the Section was:

(a) Territorial, i.e. covering all matters connected with the work of the Security Service arising in Ireland (North and South) subject to the following exceptions in Northern Ireland:

  (i) Port Control

  (ii) The security of factories engaged on war contracts . . .

  (iii) The security of Naval, Military or Air Force for which D Division of the Security Service was responsible.

(b) National, i.e. covering all matters connected with the work of the Security Service, arising outside Ireland with which persons of Irish origin (North or South) were concerned, except IRA cases in Great Britain, for which the police and Special Branch, New Scotland Yard, were responsible.[40]

He wrote with the benefit of hindsight and considerable experience. The evolution of MI5's Irish responsibilities from September 1939 was a tortuous business. Ireland was to be a major concern for MI5 throughout the war, and of intermittent interest to other agencies involved in intelligence and in clandestine warfare. At times the competing assumptions, sensitivities, and interests of the agencies and authorities involved led to considerable conflict, particularly where efforts to conduct secret operations in Ireland threatened to damage the maintenance of a cooperative security relationship. These conflicts were particularly marked in the first three years of the war.

The first test of Anglo-Irish security cooperation arose within a few days of war. On 7 September Guy Liddell noted:

the question of Dulanty's party of Germans who wish to return to their native country . . . Some of them are technicians who will be useful to the enemy but I think that we should be well-advised to let them go through. We could not have them sent over here and then arrest them without previously disclosing our intentions to the Eire Government. On the other hand if we did so the Germans would probably remain on in Eire which from our point of view would be extremely undesirable. I therefore decided that they should be allowed to pass through en bloc.[41]

On 15 September a party of about one hundred Germans resident in Ireland were allowed to travel through Britain. The group included committed Nazis, and their departure was seen both by MI5 and by the Irish as an unqualified blessing. Taken together with the fortuitous absence in Germany of about fifty Irish-based NSDAP members, including Dr Mahr, who had been attending a party rally in Nuremburg when war broke out, the voluntary exodus considerably lessened the strain on Irish security: in July 1940 only 306 Germans aged 16 or over remained in Ireland, of whom 141 were classified as refugees and a further thirty were members of religious orders. Of the remaining 135, about 100 of both sexes were thought to be active

[40] *Liddell History*, 21.
[41] Liddell diary, 7 Sept. 1939, TNA, KV4/185.

Nazis. One exception was the Austrian physicist Erwin Schrödinger. In October 1939, after representations by British scientists and possibly also de Valera, he was allowed to travel from Belgium to Dublin. He became a founding professor in de Valera's pet intellectual project, the Dublin Institute of Advanced Studies. He remained there for seventeen years, bemusing Dublin with his sexual voracity and his brilliance alike.[42]

The transit operation was important in building mutual confidence between MI5 and G2; it also drew warm thanks from Berlin.[43] It had the additional benefit of pre-empting demands for the removal of Axis civilians on the argument that their presence was a mortal threat to British interests—as was done in respect of Afghanistan and Persia in 1941, the latter being occupied by the British and the Soviets for her allegedly dilatory approach to expelling Axis civilians.[44] Had a significant number of known Nazis remained in Ireland after 1939, de Valera would certainly have been faced with a demand for their removal after the fall of France, presenting him with a nightmarish choice between refusal, which would provide a pretext for British intervention, and acceptance, which would antagonize Germany on the eve of what looked like inevitable victory.

Britain and Germany were not the only belligerents to show an interest in intelligence in Ireland in the first months of the war. A French naval officer called on Archer in Dublin, ostensibly in connection with shipping questions. He did not say a great deal or indicate his precise intentions, but remarked that 'this country was of very great strategic significance'.[45] He was probably on an intelligence mission: in October Guy Liddell noted that 'the French have been talking about running a counter-espionage organization in Eire. We have sat on this politely but heavily'.[46] The French may nevertheless have made some secret arrangements.

MI5's Irish section soon found itself swamped with business. Its first task was to put in place an effective communications and movements cordon covering the entire British Isles, which would prevent the leakage of war information and control the movement of people. Such machinery was not yet in being, although a start had been made in both jurisdictions in terms of the legislative framework. On 10 September Guy Liddell:

raised the question of Irish [communications] censorship. There is . . . nothing to prevent the Germans setting up an espionage bureau in Ireland from which they can run agents in this country. The only effective measures would be postal, telegraphic and telephonic censorship both on north and south.

External censorship has been set up in Ireland and the Eire Censor is collaborating with our Chief Censor. Censorship in Northern Ireland is on exactly parallel lines to that in force here and is run by the Chief Censor in this country.[47]

---

[42] Moore, *Schrödinger*, 351–460.

[43] Dan Bryan interview, 1983; *Liddell History*, 51. Details on German residents are in Costigan (Justice) to External Affairs, 9 July 1940, NAI, DFA, P11; Warnock (Berlin) to External Affairs, 25 Sept. 1939, NAI, DFA P24.

[44] Beaumont, 'Great Britain and the Rights of Neutral Countries', 213–38.

[45] Private information.

[46] Information from the late Commandant Peter Young, MAI; Liddell diary, 28 Oct. 1939, TNA, KV4/185.

[47] Liddell diary, 10 Sept. 1939, TNA, KV4/185.

A week later he noted that the war cabinet: 'have published a note on Eire and were anxious to get information on the possibility of espionage being run on Eire territory. I sent a note . . . setting out the whole position and giving . . . our opinion of the measures . . . in Eire to counter German activities. I also mentioned the suggestion of cooperation in wireless interception and the desirability of imposing censorship'.[48] Over the next two months Liddell recorded various exchanges on the linked problem of Irish censorship and travel controls, providing briefings, observations, and advice for Hankey, for NID, for the Home Office and for the censorship authorities.[49]

It took about a year to get the machinery of communications censorship between the two islands into effective operation. There were endless difficulties and anomalies, some created by the impossibility of controlling the border, some arising from defects in administration, and some simply unavoidable. Staff had to be recruited and trained; coverage of the mails, cables, and telephone traffic between the islands had to be given the same priority as between the United Kingdom and the outside world; and gaps and weaknesses in the emerging censorship system had to be identified and addressed. There were particular problems in relation to telephones, initially believed to be a likely source of leakages. Calls between Ireland and Britain were subject to monitoring from early September, but for some time nothing was done about cross-border calls, despite evidence of considerable indiscretion.[50] The censorship was not foolproof. It was carried out by operators listening in to each cross-channel call, who were supposed to break the connection if they heard anything suspicious. But, as was pointed out in a JIC paper, even when a conversation seemed inappropriate there could be 'a time lag of about half a minute' before a call was cut off. The JIC noted that measures were in hand to improve matters.[51]

In the decade preceding the war, postal interception under warrant had been a crucial tool in MI5's investigations generally. It had yielded useful results concerning German use of Ireland for espionage purposes, particularly in the case of Mrs Brandy. During the war it continued to be a significant source for both the Irish and the British authorities. On the outbreak of war, MI5 sought the imposition of universal postal censorship on mail passing between Britain and Ireland, but this was not sanctioned until the summer of 1940, and even then it encountered criticism from Belfast because it was applied on an all-island basis—the only logical approach, given the permeability of the border.[52] The point was raised in 'several pertinent' parliamentary questions towards the end of October by the Conservative backbencher Brendan Bracken. These were addressed not to the postmaster-general or other obvious target such as the home secretary but to the first lord of the Admiralty, presumably by quiet arrangement, since Bracken

[48] Ibid., 17 Sept. 1939, TNA, KV4/185.
[49] Ibid., 19, 22, 24, 26, and 30 Sept., 1, 2, 7, 9, 12, 16, 19, 21, 24, 25, 28, and 29 Oct., 2, 3, 6, 7, 13, 14, 16, 17, 22, 24, 26, and 27 Nov. 1939, TNA, KV4/185.
[50] Ibid., 2 and 13 Nov. 1939, TNA, KV4/185.
[51] JIC memorandum, 16 Mar. 1940, TNA, CAB 81/96, and JIC(40) 15th meeting, 21 Mar. 1940, TNA, CAB81/97.
[52] *Curry History*, 278; *Liddell History*, 54.

owed his political career to Churchill, to whom he had attached himself in the early 1930s. Guy Liddell, unconscious of the irony that Bracken, the dissimulating Tipperary-born son of a Fenian father, should press the question of Irish security, was relieved: 'Perhaps at last we may get something done'. In the event, the censorship's value proved to be negative and political: in December 1944 Liddell observed that 'it would be hard to say that Eire censorship produced any very important results'.[53]

Postal censorship was also gradually introduced in Ireland, and over time this became a very valuable security tool not only for thwarting espionage and subversion, but for gathering general information about affairs and for taking the temperature of public opinion. The Irish raised no difficulties about British censorship of Ireland's external mails, and never attempted to circumvent it.[54] In December 1939 three Irish diplomatic bags went astray in transit, and were only recovered some weeks later. Guy Liddell wrote that 'the Eire telephone checks indicate that bags . . . have been going astray. This is rather disquieting as they must often contain letters between ourselves and Archer'. He suggested to the Dominions Office that a special courier be used for such correspondence.[55]

Movement controls proved highly problematic throughout the phoney war. Initially British policy aimed primarily to regulate movements out of the United Kingdom, whether to Ireland, to the continent, or further afield. Controls were envisaged as minimizing the leakage of information, though it was also hoped that they would serve to prevent people leaving to avoid conscription. But neither the policies nor the machinery were in place in September 1939 to exercise effective control over the movement of anyone other than enemy aliens. Among people who came to Ireland were a handful of prominent individual British do-gooders, the most prominent being the Marquess of Tavistock, who sought to promote a peace-deal through making contact with staff of the German legation.[56]

The same problem arose in respect of travel from Ireland to Britain. No thought had been given to this matter before the war, and there was no system in either Irish jurisdiction to enable the operation of a travel-permit scheme for anyone wishing to go to Britain. It was only in June 1940 that a British permit office was opened in Dublin to which people wishing to travel had to apply. A similar office was opened in Belfast. Attempts to regulate the movement of people across the Irish Sea ran into various objections: Maffey reported Irish complaints about time-consuming port controls, while the Home Office and other parts of Whitehall had conflicting priorities. Departments concerned with war production did not want to be denied access to Irish labour, while Irish people in Britain resented any attempt to prevent them paying visits home. The Belfast government was very sensitive to any system of controls which placed the province on a par with neutral Ireland, yet this was the

[53] Liddell diary, 29 Oct. 1939 and 7 Dec. 1944, TNA, KV4/185 and 195; Lysaght, *Brendan Bracken*.

[54] O'Halpin, *Defending Ireland*, 144.

[55] Liddell diary, 3, 16 and 18 Jan. 1940, TNA, KV4/185.

[56] Spanish ambassador, London, to Madrid, reporting conversation with Tavistock, 17 Feb. 1942, TNA, HW37/1.

only practicable approach, because otherwise anyone who wished to evade controls placed on traffic to and from Ireland would only have to travel to Northern Ireland and take a boat from there to Britain.

The nature of the border also had a bearing on the war cabinet's decision that the Conscription Act of 1939 should not be imposed in Northern Ireland. In addition to the likely internal security complications arising from nationalist resentment, conscription would have produced a very strong reaction from de Valera. At a minimum, the Irish would have been totally uncooperative on movement controls, and would have provided sanctuary for anyone crossing the border to avoid conscription. There would also have been very serious labour-supply implications, particularly in Londonderry where thousands of dockyard workers crossed from Ireland every day. Conscription would also have acted as a recruiting sergeant for the IRA throughout the island.

Difficulties arising from contiguity were to persist. Their effective management required cooperation, compromise, and goodwill, backed up by the threat of unilateral British action if Dublin (and to an extent also Belfast) did not play the game by London's rules. From the first the British authorities involved were agreeably surprised by Dublin's willingness to accept restrictions on travel, even where these caused difficulties for Irish migrant workers. From the Irish perspective—or at least that of the handful of officials, soldiers, and policemen with knowledge of the issues—cooperation on movement controls was patently desirable both as a sop to Britain and because it enhanced Irish as well as British security. In the course of the war movement controls were more frequently deplored in Whitehall—where ministries such as Labour and Agriculture pointed to their impact on the supply of war workers, and where the fighting services complained of the threat to the morale of Irish servicemen and women if they could not easily take home leave—than in Dublin.

The movement of aliens between the United Kingdom and Ireland posed particular problems. Immediately before the war a number of Germans and other Europeans in Britain crossed to Ireland. Amongst these were people who might seek to further German interests. One of these was Werner Unland, later discovered to have been spying in Britain for some time. Interception of his post disclosed that 'he corresponds regularly with the Dansk Import & Export Co. of Copenhagen through a box number. The letters are obviously in code. Archer has given us copies of all of them'.[57] A Garda report described him as 'an elderly pagan . . . in Ireland mainly to save his own skin', who in fact never stirred from his flat despite reporting prodigious activity in his messages—in one of these he hinted that he was planning to visit Northern Ireland to meet someone from the shipbuilders Harland & Wolf, but he did not actually travel.[58] He remained at large but under watch in Dublin until April 1941, when a newly arrived agent, Gunther Schultz, was captured with documents implicating him. Unland was then interned.[59] The

---

[57] Liddell diary, 3 Jan. 1940, TNA, KV4/185.
[58] *Liddell History*, 51; Hull, *Irish Secrets*,166, quoting an undated Garda report; Liddell diary, 4 Jan. and 18, 27, and 29 Mar. 1940, TNA, KV4/186.
[59] Ibid., 51.

efficient manner in which surveillance was maintained by the Garda and G2 was a significant demonstration of Irish bona fides.

As neutrals, Irish people could move to and from the continent through Britain. Among those who attracted attention were the trade unionist John Swift, whom MI5 questioned and found unhelpfully vague about what he claimed were his links with the underground trade-union movement in Germany. Guy Liddell was inclined to doubt his veracity, as despite his left-wing background he had obtained a travel permit from the German legation in Dublin as late as 22 August. But, apart from asking Archer for a report on Swift, Liddell could do nothing to prevent him completing the journey home.[60] Another Irishman to attract interest was the writer Francis Stuart, who had featured in one of the pre-war Czech reports furnished to SIS about the activities of the German legation. He travelled through Britain on his way to take up a university post in Berlin (he was carrying messages from the IRA to German intelligence).[61] He later made propaganda broadcasts to Ireland, and was involved in one way or another in schemes to promote IRA–German cooperation. But Britain had no right to prevent his transit. Cases such as Stuart's led MI5 to press for changes to end the 'anomalous' position of Irish citizens in the United Kingdom, whether as residents or in transit. For as long as they could move freely from Britain to the continent, an MI5 officer observed to the Home Office in January 1940, 'the means of communication' of information to the enemy existed. It was galling to have to grant passage to people such as an Irish employee of Siemens who was plainly going to make a contribution to the German war effort.[62] The JIC revisited the problem in May 1940, agreeing that Irish people travelling to Germany should be watched as closely as possible.[63] There was also a danger of intelligence gathering by people in transit. These were all problems for MI5 to worry about: it must be assumed that SIS and other agencies took an interest in Irish people travelling to Europe, as they did the citizens of other neutral states, for the reciprocal reason that they could be useful for British intelligence purposes.

Two other obvious dangers arising from the easy movement of Irish people to and through the United Kingdom concerned MI5: sabotage and organized disruption. The ill-timed S-plan, while it had led to the emasculation of the IRA in Britain, had also underscored the movement's potential. An MI5 warning about a possible outbreak of IRA sabotage on 27 December caused something of an overreaction by the police, resulting in a new process for notification of such threats.[64] In the first weeks of the war, an overexcited official in Lanarkshire suggested the use of troops to break up an unofficial strike in an ironworks 'owing to the presence of an Irish element in the district'. Calmer counsels prevailed.[65] In February, MI5 received reports of suspicious behaviour by two Irish employees of a firm which had

---

[60] Liddell diary, 18 Sept. 1939, TNA, KV4/185. Swift was regarded as a communist, in practice if not in formal membership of a communist party. It is conceivable that his trip was made possible by the *rapprochement* between Germany and the Soviet Union.

[61] Ibid., 10 Feb. 1940, TNA, KV4/185; *Liddell History*, 43.

[62] Turner (MI5) to Maxwell (Home Office), 9 Nov. 1939 and 31 Jan. 1940, TNA, HO 213/1905; Liddell diary, 6 Jan. 1940, TNA, KV4/185.

[63] JIC (40) 29th meeting, 15 May 1940, TNA, CAB 81/87.

[64] Liddell diary, 20 Feb. 1940, TNA, KV4/185.

[65] Jeffery and Hennessy, *States of Emergency*, 146.

'a secret contract', a tip which led to nothing and which illustrated the prevailing jumpiness.[66] Reflecting on policy on the internment of aliens in April, Guy Liddell observed that 'acts of sabotage might equally well be committed by British subjects or neutrals and particularly by members of the IRA'.[67] In the event, it was the IRA's almost complete inactivity in Britain, either as saboteurs or as intelligence gatherers, which was to prove one of the minor puzzles of MI5's war, and the Irish community in Britain was never associated with organized disruption.

Like the republican movement with which it retained some ties, the Irish communist organization operated, albeit inadequately, on an all-island basis. Before the war it had been firmly under the thumb of the CPGB, and it was assumed that that continued to be the position. MI5 devoted a good deal of attention to the CPGB during the first months of the war. The party was known to be under instructions from Moscow to pursue an anti-war line, in terms both of public argument and of impairment of the war effort. Communists in war industries, or working in transport, might take disruptive action. It was MI5 practice to pass on the names of communist seamen to the Ministry of Shipping, 'but it has never been very clear' whether action followed. In February MI5's Roger Hollis advised that the Shipowners Association should be briefed: in addition to the problem of troublemakers, 'in time of war both communists and members of the IRA are likely to be used as couriers'.[68] There was some concern that communists within trade unions in Northern Ireland would foment unrest in shipyards and factories involved in war production. The RUC kept a watch on their activities and contacts, and sent on whatever information obtained from such surveillance to MI5.[69] In Ireland, there also appeared to be potential for coordinated activity between republicans and communists, as there were often crossovers in membership—in January 1940 six tons of stolen Irish army ammunition was found on the farm of an American communist of Irish birth, Mary McKiernan, and her stepson Francis McKiernan received a five-year sentence.[70] Until the middle of 1941 the communist line in both parts of Ireland and in Britain was consistent: the war was a struggle between two competing sets of imperialists, and it was the duty of loyal comrades everywhere to oppose it by whatever means they could (in the immediate aftermath of the German attack on the Soviet Union, Irish communists were advised not to lose contact with republicans: 'By opposing Britain and showing that by reason of Britain's treachery she cannot be relied upon as a friend of Russia it is hoped to placate those enemies of Britain in Eire who would wish for a German victory').[71]

There is no evidence that during the phoney war MI5 gave any consideration to how it would cope if the Irish ports came under British control. MI5 did, however, have some knowledge of a curious scheme which was put forward to the Dominions

---

[66] Liddell diary, 18 Feb. 1940, TNA, KV4/185.

[67] Ibid., 16 Apr. 1940, TNA, KV4/185.

[68] Ibid., 20 Feb. 1940, TNA, KV4/185.

[69] Ibid., 25 Mar. 1940, TNA, KV4/185.

[70] Mary McKiernan was a sister of the Leitrim-born Jim Gralton, a communist and an American citizen whose deportation to the USA in 1933 was a cause célèbre for the Irish left.

[71] The alleged advice of the communist organizer Tom Watters, quoted in an extract from Eastern Command monthly intelligence report, 30 June 1941, MAI, G2/X/0093.

Office early in 1940, via the Duke of Devonshire, by a retired Irish Guards officer, Conor Carrigan. In March Cecil Liddell met Carrigan, who believed that because of the memory of French assistance for the Irish rebellion of 1798, and the long tradition of Irish enlistment in the French army, de Valera could be persuaded to encourage the creation of an 'Irish Brigade' to operate in association with the French army in the defence of France. This would logically involve French naval defence of the Irish coastline: 'once the French managed to get inside the Irish ports it would not be long before the English would be able to do likewise'.[72] This implausible suggestion was kept alive for some months, more through Carrigan's enthusiasm than through any official endorsement.[73]

MI5's dealings with Ireland, initially mediated through Dulanty, were mainly routed through Maffey's office. Walshe came over for discussions on security on two occasions in April and May 1940. On 7 May Guy Liddell and Vernon Kell met Walshe, inaccurately recorded as the 'Eire Minister for External Affairs'. He pressed them on what more the Irish could do to meet British security concerns, seeking 'suggestions . . . to stop off any loop holes'.[74] This proactive approach was clearly intended to anticipate and pre-empt any British complains about Irish security deficiencies.

NAVAL INTELLIGENCE AND IRELAND, 1939–1940

MI5 did not have a clear run in attempting to address Irish security issues in the first months of the war. In keeping with its habit of independent operations, the Admiralty established a chain of informants along the southern coastline. These usually came from fairly obvious pro-British elements such as retired service personnel and their families, and employees of firms with British links, and they quickly came to Irish attention. Scare stories about German submarine activities spread like wildfire, and soon reached the United Kingdom, where they were picked up and amplified by the press. The DNI Godfrey's initial attempts to investigate such rumours ran into trouble. In October, Lieutenant Michael Mason of the Royal Naval Volunteer Reserve (RNVR) visited Ireland 'on behalf of the British Government to obtain information about German submarines using Irish waters for purposes of shelter . . . it was on my own initiative that I set foot on Irish soil'. He 'assumed for the purpose the personality of an Irish tradesman on holiday with a bicycle and an Irish accent and a vile assortment of readymade clothes'. He had almost finished his task when arrested near a coastal LOP (Look Out Post) in County Wicklow 'as a suspected republican-anarchist, or German'. He explained what he was up to, and said that the Irish peer Lord Powerscourt would vouch for him.[75] He also wrote an explanatory note to Maffey. 'Under a severe barrage of

    [72] Liddell diary, 20 Mar. 1940, TNA, KV4/185.
    [73] Morton to Churchill, 31 May 1940, TNA, PREM7/6.
    [74] Liddell diary, 7 May 1940, TNA, KV4/185.
    [75] Extract from Mason to Lord Powerscourt, undated, with Antrobus (Dublin) to Stephenson (Dominions Office), 3 Nov. 1939, TNA, DO130/4.

questions' from a Garda superintendent and Dan Bryan of G2, he let slip the fact
that he was a naval reservist.[76] His interrogators thought him an Admiralty agent,
albeit an incompetent one. In London Godfrey denied prior knowledge of Mason's
enterprise, but, although not a man accustomed to eating humble pie, took the
trouble to send a note of thanks to Maffey for his help, while stressing that 'Mason
acted, as he told you, on his own initiative'. In fact this was the second unofficial
mission which Mason had carried out at Godfrey's behest: just before the war he had
taken 'soundings off North West Africa' in his yacht *Latifa*.[77] Guy Liddell learnt
from SIS that Mason had travelled with the Admiralty's blessing: he thought 'the
incident extremely unfortunate, although NID have rather tried to make light of
it'.[78] Mason's misadventures probably hastened the appointment of a naval attaché
to Maffey's office in Dublin. On 19 October Guy Liddell discussed Ireland generally
with Commander Slade, who became NID's Irish specialist: 'I think I succeeded in
convincing him that our relations with Archer . . . were of a very frank nature and
that if any intelligence service were set up in Eire and happened to go wrong we
might lose his assistance, which was of great value to us in getting reports of the
activities of Germans in that country'.[79] Two days later Liddell noted that 'a Naval
Attaché disguised as an ex-Naval officer is to be attached to Sir John Maffey. It is
hoped that he may be able to make some progress on the submarine question'. He
met and briefed the officer chosen, Captain A. B. Greig:

I gave Greig a brief summary of our relations with Archer . . . but said that I thought it would
be better if he did not refer to our liaison in any conversation with Archer. I recommended
to Greig, although it was actually outside my province, that if it were possible for him to
arrive at a point where we could supply Eire with equipment of one kind or another and so
place them under an obligation to us, we should have much better grounds for interfering in
matters affecting German submarine activities on the West coast.[80]

Liddell's suggestion to Greig that in his discussions with Archer he should avoid
mention of MI5's existing link with G2 was rather curious. Leaving Archer under
the impression that he was dealing separately with two British agencies on related
security questions threatened to increase rather than to lessen confusion. But his
advice on how to approach the Irish, combined with the Mason debacle, may have
been responsible for a temporary change in the Admiralty's attitude.

The Admiralty kept up their demands for more information: on 28 October
Godfrey told the war cabinet committee on the leakage of information that 'in no
part of the civilised world is Great Britain less able to obtain vital information than
in Eire'.[81] On 11 November Slade of NID assured Liddell that 'NID had never
really contemplated an extensive watching service. All they wanted was to have
some check on Archer's organization. I told him that I had read his memorandum

[76] Mason to Sir John Maffey, 30 Oct. 1939, TNA, DO120/4; Dan Bryan interview, 1983.
[77] Godfey to Maffey, 9 Nov. 1939, TNA, DO120/4. Denham, *Inside the Nazi Ring*, 7.
[78] Dan Bryan interview, 1983; Liddell diary, 9 Dec. 1939, TNA, KV4/185.
[79] Liddell diary, 19 and 21 Oct. 1939, TNA, KV4/185.
[80] Ibid., 25 Oct. 1939, TNA, KV4/185. From November 1944 the post of naval attaché was left
unfilled. TNA, ADM223/257.
[81] Memorandum by Godfrey, 28 Oct. 1939, quoted in McMahon, 'Covert Operations and Official
Collaboration', 44.

for discussion with Archer and that I thought that certain things in it might give offence to the Irish. He said that the exact form in which it was to be presented to the Irish was still a matter of discussion'. Liddell recorded with some satisfaction that 'from a talk I had subsequently with Menzies' of SIS 'he evidently shares our view' on the ineptitude of the Admiralty's Irish activities and the danger which these posed to the development of constructive security cooperation with the Irish.[82] The two were soon to come under pressure to defend this point of view, when Churchill brought the Admiralty's concerns about Irish intelligence to the war cabinet.

Greig arrived in Dublin on 3 November, and took up residence in the Shelbourne Hotel, close to Maffey's office on Merrion Square. As Liddell had predicted, he found Joseph Walshe of External Affairs, and Liam Archer of G2, friendly and 'very ready to co-operate'.[83] Archer took great pains to brief Greig on the development of the coast-watching system, and invited him to inspect anything he liked. Greig, a submariner, opted for a tour of the southern coastline.[84] He sent Godfrey a 'surprisingly favourable' report of the new coast-watching service, which despite a lack of modern equipment and poor communications appeared already to be functioning well.[85] Greig also reported an exchange with Archer about the activities of would-be British informants, whose zeal in collecting rumours of suspicious activities was equalled only by their indiscretion. Amongst these was 'a Captain Stuart Pearson of the County Club, Cork', who 'had given out that he was working for DNI and has asked others to act as agents to assist him'. Greig reported that Archer 'hinted that should this man be in any way official his services would no longer be of any value . . . Archer evidently has a very good line on him, but I know does not want to have to take any serious action . . . such happenings tend to cloud the cooperation between us'. Archer made it clear that he welcomed Greig to Ireland precisely to establish a reliable professional conduit for the exchange of information and coastal intelligence, so that the Admiralty could satisfy themselves about security problems through their own man in Dublin rather than encouraging and reacting to a flood of spy or submarine stories forwarded by enthusiastic amateurs around the coastline.[86] The Admiralty's response to Greig's report indicates that Pearson was acting with official connivance:

this man has been a thorough nuisance . . . He was told that we could not authorise him . . . though we should, of course, be glad to hear . . . if he should have heard anything of interest. Thereupon he seems to have taken it upon himself to embark upon an extensive motor tour of the south of Ireland . . . making himself very conspicuous, and holding himself out to be acting for us. I had wind of his activities . . . and had already told him definitely to make no further attempts to obtain information.

This letter ended with the somewhat disingenuous remark that 'this sort of incident is not helpful, but in this case it was wholly due to misguided individualism, and not

---

82 Liddell diary, 11 Nov. 1939, TNA, KV4/185.
83 Greig to Godfrey, 9 Nov. 1939, TNA, DO 130/7.
84 External Affairs to Washington [?], 18 Dec. 1941, TNA, DFA P94.
85 Godfrey memoir, p. 201, CCCA, Godfrey 1/6.
86 Greig to Admiralty, 28 Nov. 1939, TNA, DO 130/7.

to official encouragement'.[87] Despite this embarrassment, the Admiralty continued to encourage and finance local informants for a time, and so the Irish continued to watch them. Amongst people employed by Godfrey to make enquiries was Colonel the Honourable Angus McDonnell,

an Irishman with business interests in Denmark and Sweden . . . a very good mixer, a fisherman, and [who] knew the West coast of Ireland well. When a report of an alleged U-boat sighting . . . was received, and there were many, I used to ask him to go over and investigate.

He could travel without difficulty, ostensibly to fish, could quickly establish good relations with all classes and very soon get to the bottom of the rumour which was invariably false.[88]

Such activities were an unavoidable consequence of contiguity and of British concerns about Atlantic defence. Where detected by the Irish, they were kept under observation but not uprooted, a laissez-faire policy which could not have survived had British action to take over the Irish ports been considered imminent. Irish willingness to turn a blind eye to such activities contrasts with the attitude of the Swedish, Portuguese, and Swiss governments, each of which attempted to curtail some of the clandestine activities of British officials and agents (as late as 1944, when Germany's ability to intimidate her had more or less disappeared, Sweden demanded the recall of the British naval attaché).[89] Reports produced by the NID networks in April and May 1940 were discriminating and restrained: 'the agent in charge' of the Cork coastline 'had been unable to discover any trace of U-boat activities in the harbours or inlets', while a month later it was noted that, 'now that the tourist season has opened, access has been facilitated to a number of remote bays and havens, to which our sources were hitherto somewhat chary of going'.[90] Such amateur agents, typically people with known British associations, ran some personal risks: between 1920 and 1922 a fair number of 'loyalists' had been murdered as alleged spies and informers by the Cork IRA, and as late as 1936 Admiral Somerville had been killed. It transpired that no one was killed as an alleged British spy during the war years, but this was probably a function of state repression of the IRA rather than of new-found republican forebearance.[91]

Greig's rapid establishment of a good understanding with G2, together with Archer's warning about the undesirability of running covert networks, may have contributed something to a shift in Admiralty policy. But this took time. In late November the Admiralty, in the person of the first lord, Churchill, brought 'very strong pressure' on SIS to 'provide an organization' in Ireland which could check the 'numerous reports of German submarines refuelling and landing personnel'.[92]

---

[87] Slade (Admiralty) to Greig, 1 Dec. 1939, TNA, DO130/7.

[88] Godfrey memoir, p. 112, CCCA, Godfrey 1/6.

[89] Denham, *Inside the Nazi Ring*, 69–70, 154–5, and 158. This may have been partly in response to British success in informally forcing the recall of the Swedish naval attaché in London, whose reports were reaching German hands; Mackenzie, *Secret History of SOE*, 323–4; Wylie, *Britain, Switzerland and the second world war*, 284 and 291.

[90] NID 'Irish Affairs' reports, 8 and 26 May 1940, TNA, KV4/280.

[91] Hart, *The IRA and Its Enemies*, 273–5; Borgonovo, *Spies, Informers and the 'Anti-Sinn Fein Society'*.

[92] *Liddell History*, 21.

At the inconvenient hour of 7 p.m. on 22 November, Liddell learnt that the war cabinet was to discuss this next day on foot of an Admiralty memorandum which he had not even seen. An MI5 response was required by 8.30 a.m.:

I . . . found that the memo was based on a report submitted by NID to the first lord, who had asked for its urgent consideration by his colleagues. I eventually succeeded in getting hold of Menzies [of SIS] who knew of the existence of the memo but had never been asked to put forward criticisms or been told that the matter was under discussion by the Cabinet. Since he and ourselves were the two people vitally concerned this seemed to say the least a little curious. We succeeded in getting out an answer by midnight, which was roughly on the following lines:

The question of reporting on submarine activities and setting up a secret organization . . . might vitally affect the existing relations between MI5 and the Eire Ministry of Defence. It could be done but would take at least two months and a considerably longer period if it were to be really effective. It would moreover necessitate the establishment of secret wireless stations for communication with the Admiralty. It seemed highly probable that the existence of the organization would . . . come to the notice of the Eire authorities and that the service they were now rendering to MI5 would cease in consequence. It was therefore recommended that before any drastic step was taken MI5 should get . . . Archer to come over and discuss with him the possibility of improving the coast watching service.[93]

The war cabinet remitted the question to a committee under Hankey (at this early stage of the war the JIC was not the accepted forum for interdepartmental discussion of intelligence and security issues which it eventually became). On 27 November Hankey convened a meeting 'to discuss the possible setting-up of an organization by SIS in Eire'. The chiefs of the three agencies directly affected all attended: Kell and Liddell from MI5, Godfrey and other officers from NID, and the new C, Stewart Menzies, with his deputy Valentine Vivian, from SIS. The Dominions Office was represented by John Stephenson, who was to deal with Irish affairs throughout the war. The meeting went over the ground again: Godfrey 'pressed for an organization on the lines that SIS had in other countries . . . Eire was a serious gap'. He was 'dissatisfied with the information that he was getting from the Eire government and he did not feel that any confidence could be placed in their coast watching service, even if we gave them technical assistance'. Vivian pointed out some of the pitfalls, including stereotypical weaknesses in the Irish character: an SIS network

would have to draw on indigenous material which would have all the inherent defects of the Irish, in so far as exaggerated and inaccurate gossip was concerned. It would be impossible to import British subjects. If a coast watching service was to be set up, it would have to be equipped with wireless and for it to be really effective more than 1,000 people would have to be employed . . . the matter would be bound to come to the knowledge of the Eire authorities within a few weeks.

As a compromise, Vivian suggested that the navy increase patrolling in Irish waters, while he would 'extend his own organization in a very small way', though this would only provide 'general information of the kind that he was already supplying'. This was agreed, together with further consultations between MI5, the Admiralty, and

93 Liddell diary, 22 Nov. 1939, TNA, KV4/185.

Archer and technical assistance for the Irish.[94] When Guy Liddell at NID's request asked Dulanty early in December to get Archer over for urgent consultations, he learned that the head of G2 was 'going around every inlet with the Naval Attaché and that he will not be back for 10 days'.[95]

The Admiralty moved quickly. At the end of November HMS *King Gruffydd* was sent to patrol the western seaboard in the guise of a merchantman, to determine whether German submarines might be 'using inlets on the North Western and South Western coast . . . as bases'. A number of such patrols took place over the next year.[96] The maverick pilot Sidney Cotton, who had done freelance work for SIS over Germany in 1938, flew along the west coast taking photographs useful both for hydrographic and for intelligence purposes.[97] Such clandestine patrolling and photography yielded no trace of the suspected submarines or their supposed helpers, though they provided an element of reassurance and of coastal protection, and they might have provided early warning of a German seaborne assault. In 1941 the Admiralty reported that absolutely no evidence had emerged to substantiate any of the rumours which had reached London, and after the war Godfrey wrote that 'as we now know from German records, no naval activities favourable to the Germans took place in Eireann waters, and there is no evidence of the Eireann coast being used for U-boats, or supply bases'. Nevertheless the myth persists, bolstered by fiction such as Brian Garfield's *The Paladin* and by folk memory.[98]

The Irish believed these rumours were encouraged by Britain. The newly appointed Irish high commissioner in Ottawa, John A. Hearne, conveyed Irish suspicion that British press coverage was part of a campaign to discredit Irish neutrality, complaining that through security liaison London was well aware of the true situation in Irish waters. The Canadians were not overly sympathetic: Mackenzie King thought Hearne's attitude 'typically Irish, warm towards friends, bitter towards England . . . Enough said to make clear sympathies were against Hitler but without united Ireland, not strong enough to lead to active support of British forces'.[99] There is in fact no evidence of a concerted propaganda campaign against Ireland in the first months of the war: it was only after the fall of France that she became a deliberate target of official propaganda and disinformation.

The Admiralty secured informants in the main Irish ports, as had been done during the first world war. This too could have been counter-productive, since it laid the British open to the charge that they were making preparations for possible action to seize or destroy Irish marine facilities. In practice, however, the Irish took the view that it would be impossible to attempt to prevent the passing of information to Britain. Many British companies trading with Ireland and the shipping lines

[94] Ibid., 28 Nov. 1939, TNA, KV4/185.

[95] Ibid., 6 Dec. 1939, TNA, KV4/185. Notwithstanding efforts to maintain secrecy, by the spring of 1940 pro-German elements in Dublin were aware in vague terms that Greig was being facilitated by the Irish authorities.

[96] Vice Admiral Campbell to Commander Loly, 30 Nov. 1939, ADM199/146.

[97] McMahon, 'Covert Operations and Official Collaboration', 45.

[98] Godfrey memoir, 263, CCCA, Godfrey 1/6; Garfield, *The Paladin*.

[99] Irish aide-mémoire of 22 Dec. 1939, in O'Halpin, *Defending Ireland*, 160; Mackenzie King diaries, 21 Dec. 1939.

calling at Irish ports had local representatives. In addition, Ireland's maritime trade operated entirely under British control, and she had no great shipping secrets to hide. Early in 1940 British shipping liaison officers were appointed in the main ports. Their main task was to ensure that shipping movements into and from Ireland took place under agreed protocols, including the 'NAVICERT' wartime licensing system used for all civilian shipping. They had close links with the naval attaché and they were able to pass on any rumours or suspicions they picked up in addition to doing their overt work. There were gradual improvements in the equipment and reporting procedures of the Irish coast-watchers. Observation reports were sent to Irish Air Corps patrols by radio *en clair*, thereby providing the British services with immediate access to all news of sightings.[100] In January the Admiralty asked SIS to secure 'reliable information' on whether the German legation was making use of any of the 'eight ships in all which sail between Eire and the Continent'. This did not mean that NID had eschewed intelligence gathering on their own account, but it reflected a growing willingness to work with other agencies. Not long afterwards, NID circulated information obtained from a German sailor put ashore in Montevideo after his ship the *Graf Spee* was scuttled, by an agent posing as 'a disaffected Irishman'. The sailor had worked in the German legation in Dublin, and claimed that the IRA 'were paid by Germans in dollars sent by [the] German Embassy in Washington', that contact with the IRA was maintained not through the German legation but through 58 Merrion Square (the address of Dr Carl Petersen), and spoke of plans for replenishing German submarines near Aghada in Cork harbour. Even NID treated this report with scepticism, pointing out that the sailor's list of the *Graf Spee*'s refuellings was only '30% correct', and this 'should be taken into account in assessing the reliability' of his information.[101]

SIS AND IRELAND, 1939–1940

SIS had been responsible for a crucial piece of intelligence about attempts to build links between the IRA and Germany, the report of 25 July 1939 on the meeting between Admiral Canaris of the Abwehr and an IRA representative.[102] That intelligence was supported by other material in British hands. Although inaccurate in detail, time was to show that this was true in essentials. But such material came from SIS's continental contacts—in that case, possibly from another friendly intelligence service, perhaps the Czech, the French, or the Polish—rather than from Ireland. There it had no professional intelligence machine.

Following the agreement reached on 28 November, 'SIS . . . increased their organization so as to be able to provide some check' on reports from Ireland. SIS also continued to circulate some general intelligence. One report of 30 September was 'somewhat alarmist as regards the internal situation. An attempt at revolution

---

[100] Greig to Slade, 17 Nov. and 27 Dec. 1939, TNA, DO130/7.
[101] Slade (Admiralty) to Vivian (SIS), 30 Jan., and NID note of 26 Jan. 1940 describing report from Montevideo, TNA, KV3/120.
[102] *Liddell History*, 43.

by the IRA does not appear to be out of the question'.[103] In January 1940 SIS circulated a further

disquieting report . . . A submarine base is said to exist near the mouth of the Doonbeg river in south west Clare. A submarine comes in 3 times a week and is camouflaged with a canvas screen. One of the men in charge of the local coast watching station is said to be an IRA deportee. The local Civic Guard appear to be terrorised. It was also alleged that a small tramp steamer was waylaid in Galway Bay by a submarine and made to hand over stores.[104]

The situation was equally bleak in March, showing 'a deterioration in economic conditions and a general drive towards increased support of the more extreme elements. German submarines are said to have landed on the west coast and revolutionary action in the not far distant future seems almost inevitable'.[105]

During the phoney war SIS's Irish efforts were mainly confined to harnessing the investigative energies of sympathetic individuals of much the same backgrounds as those who had been volunteering warnings to the Admiralty, such as a hotel proprietor in County Cork who had long associations with the navy. Most of these local informants were identified sooner or later by G2 through a combination of local investigation and surveillance of postal communications. Because their activities were construed as not directed primarily against Irish interests, they were regarded as fairly harmless. Some of those secretly approached for such work tipped off the Irish authorities. It was through one such contact that G2 acquired a wireless transmitter distributed as a 'stay behind' measure in the latter half of 1940, when there were real fears in London of a German attack on the Irish southern coast.[106]

SIS and MI5 had identified the clear hazards in the creation of such covert networks at a time when both the Admiralty and MI5 were seeking to improve liaison with G2, and when the RUC were strengthening their links with the Garda. There was an obvious danger that such activity, even if not seen as designed to or likely to harm Irish state interests, would distract the Irish from the investigation of German and IRA activities. On the other hand, such activities may have acted as an unintended stimulus to Irish security in 1939–40. They certainly contributed to a partial rapprochement between republicans and the state in the Munster area. The Irish army southern command intelligence officer, Florence O'Donoghue had, like Bryan and Archer, specialized in intelligence during the war of independence. Unlike them, however, he had taken no part in the civil war of 1922–3 and had been prominent in efforts to end it through intercession. He consequently remained *persona grata* in extreme republican circles in Cork and Kerry. The fact of British clandestine activity along the southern coastline, including efforts to organize pro-British residents to provide information—as had also been the case, fatally for some of those involved, during the war of independence—and the possibility of a British attack to seize the southern ports and facilities, enabled him

103 Liddell diary, 30 Sept. 1939, TNA, KV4/185.

104 Ibid., 18 Jan. 1940, TNA, KV4/185. The term 'IRA deportee' refers to suspect Irishmen and women deported from Britain during the IRA's S-plan bombing campaign.

105 Ibid., 20 Mar. 1940, TNA, KV4/185.

106 Dan Bryan interview, 1983. This set has since gone missing, although the Irish army still has a number of German agent radios.

in 1940 to persuade republicans to form the 'Supplementary Intelligence Service' (confusingly abbreviated in Irish records as SIS, but referred to hereafter for clarity as I[rish]SIS), organized on the old war of independence IRA battalion areas.[107] ISIS was designed as a surveillance organization, channelling information from localities to O'Donoghue, and carrying out local investigations on request. It was also to have a 'stay behind' intelligence role in the event of areas coming under foreign military occupation. At the time of its creation, the obvious problem for investigation was clandestine British activity; over time, however, the organization was to prove useful in respect both of American and, most crucially, of German-related intrigue. It gave G2 the capability to collect good local intelligence independently of the Garda, and it also provided O'Donoghue with a good line into the Munster IRA. So secret was ISIS, and so delicate was the fact that committed republicans cooperated with the army which had defeated them in the civil war, that its existence was never publicly acknowledged. Five years after the end of the second world war, however, the government approved the secret distribution to ISIS members of the 'Emergency Medal' awarded to those who had served in the defence forces between 1939 and 1945.

Faced with the imperative of improving on the 'limited information service' on Irish political affairs which it had provided since 1932 through QRS reports, SIS had obvious problems. SIS had already signalled concern that the Admiralty's early blunders in covert intelligence gathering in Ireland might jeopardize Anglo-Irish security cooperation, but their first major essay in the active collection of Irish information was no more convincing. Early in 1940 Valentine Vivian, who had served in the Indian police before joining SIS, turned to another old India hand for help. He recruited Sir Charles Tegart, the son of a Church of Ireland clergyman. Tegart had studied mathematics in Trinity College before joining the Indian police in 1901, where he made his name as a colourful as well as an efficient officer—he once broke both his ankles while bicycling down a set of stairs. During the first world war he had worked for IPI in Europe and the United States under Major John Wallinger, fictionalized as the reptilian spymaster 'R' in Somerset Maugham's *Ashenden* stories, probing links between Indian separatists and Germany.[108] He had been briefly involved in Irish matters, in that in July 1920 the GOC General Macready had asked that he review police intelligence in Ireland.[109] For a time in the 1920s Tegart had run IPI's office in London. In 1938 he travelled to Palestine to advise the British military authorities on how to curb the Arab revolt, recommending the erection of fixed barriers—the 'Tegart wall'—to hamper infiltration. Throughout his career Tegart had maintained contact with Ireland, returning on holidays whenever he could. An anonymous biography stated that 'an Englishman no doubt would find it difficult to understand his exact point of view for he was anything but an Orangeman; he had always detested partition and had

---

[107] Aspects of O'Donoghue's activities are discussed in O'Donoghue, *No Other Law*, Borgonovo (ed.), *Florence and Josephine O'Donoghue's War of Independence*, and Borgonovo, *Spies, Informers and the 'Anti-Sinn Fein Society'*.

[108] Maugham, *Ashenden*. I am grateful to Dr Nicholas Hiley for first pointing this out.

[109] McMahon, 'Covert Operations and Official Collaboration', 48. It is not clear whether he carried out the mooted review.

never ceased hoping for a United Ireland'.[110] This was also the view of a former Indian police colleague, Sir Patrick Kelly, who in July 1940 informed John Dulanty in London that Tegart had always been sympathetic to Irish nationalism: 'In India he had the reputation of possessing an independent mind with a bluntness of speech. He was never thought . . . to be in any sense an underhand worker. My informant's concluding words were that Tegart was always "a damned good Irishman"'.[111] The unpublished biography, evidently based largely on his diaries, states that he had hoped for

an early declaration of war . . . by Eire . . . This was the motive which Tegart and many others optimistically imagined would influence those in charge of Eire's destinies. No one thought that love of England or hate of the Germans qua Germans would come into the question. There was no reason why such considerations should do so, for so far Ireland has had little reason to love her geographic neighbour. But as . . . Eire remained neutral, Tegart became more and more disturbed in mind. Eventually he actually went over there to see if he could do any good by personal persuasion . . . . he firmly believed that friendship and co-operation with the British Empire was Ireland's only right policy. Apart from that matter he felt . . . that failure to fight on the side of justice in a war . . . left a smirch on the escutcheon of any country.

Tegart made a number of visits. He 'sought and obtained interviews with various important politicians', though his arguments were 'in vain', while his initiative 'upset the equilibrium, not to say offended the dignity of the British representatives in Eire who were little concerned with sentiment and, possibly owing to their situation, took a conventional and restricted view of such matters'.[112] But as we shall see, however high-minded his intentions, his highly coloured reports were to have a profound effect on British policy towards Ireland in the fraught weeks after the collapse of France. His activities also raised grave suspicions in Irish government circles that he was laying the ground for a British intervention.

Tegart was the most influential but probably not the only person whom SIS sent to snoop around in Ireland. In May a Captain and Mrs Price stayed in the Shelbourne Hotel, and then travelled on to Mayo and Galway, where they registered in a hotel as Captain and Mrs Higgins. Higgins drew attention to himself by making enquiries at a Garda station about the Irish army's part-time reserve. The Garda began investigating Higgins, his companion, and their various contacts. On 23 May the pair turned up in Killarney in County Kerry, and Higgins was arrested a day later and sent to Dublin after interrogation, during which 'he stated that his correct name was Higgins, but the lady with whom he was living was a Mrs Walker from Jamaica'. Papers found on him 'go to show that Higgins is a British Secret Service Agent, unless of course such papers are faked. He had in his possession a small Colt revolver with 44 rounds of ammunition'. Mrs Walker contacted him at the Garda station and suggested that she get in touch with Sir John Maffey 'in order to have matters put right'.[113] His sleeping arrangements perhaps apart, Captain Higgins

[110] Tegart memoir, 295, BL, Tegart Mss Eur C235.
[111] Dulanty to Walshe, 20 Aug. 1940, NAI, DFA A6.
[112] Tegart memoir, 295, BL, Tegart Mss Eur C235.
[113] Undated G2 report [May 1940], NAI, DFA A8.

appears a fairly typical specimen of the Anglo-Irish ex-officer type upon whom the British were prone to rely in the first year of the war for intelligence from Ireland.

It is arguable that SIS might have been better advised to bite the bullet in the autumn of 1939 and establish an Irish network under professional direction instead of adopting such a half-hearted approach to the problem of determining just what was going on. The case against such action was strong: it might jeopardize existing cooperation. Yet in April 1940 Joseph Walshe actually said that 'if the British Government cared to post intelligence agents of their own to watch the German legation no difficulty would be raised', an offer which Guy Liddell thought 'quite out of the question . . . It would be insulting to Archer and would inevitably lead to trouble'. Kell also took this line on Walshe's offer.[114] Without access to the SIS achive, it is impossible to determine whether other steps were taken during the phoney war to improve intelligence on Ireland, or to study Irish affairs in depth. Although there is one reference to a pre-war SIS 'Irish Section' in an MI5 document, MI5 records provide no trace of a functioning Irish desk at SIS headquarters until the end of 1940 or the start of 1941, when the formidable Jane Archer was recruited after her dismissal from MI5.[115]

Until the collapse of France, Ireland posed only second-order security problems, which were mainly within the remit of MI5. SIS had plenty of other pressing political and military tasks to work on in Europe and the Middle East, from the collection of intelligence to the creation of stay-behind groups in various countries likely to be or already overrun by Germany. Vivian's selection of Tegart to make enquiries in Ireland was evidently a response to pressure from the Admiralty to investigate submarine and spy stories rather than a considered preamble to the development of an Irish intelligence network geared to supply a regular stream of reports on Irish affairs.

British apprehensions about Irish stability and security were not simply the product of credulousness and poor analysis. Ireland was virtually defenceless, and Britain had no idea of what anti-invasion measures the Irish envisaged or were capable of. While most of the stories of submarine landings and of German espionage were without foundation, London already had good evidence both of German pre-war preparations for espionage in Ireland, and of some German IRA contacts. In October 1939 MI5 received additional information from their double agent *Snow*, whose account of a meeting with his German controllers in Antwerp included a fair amount of material both on German plans for *Snow* to harness Welsh nationalists as saboteurs in England, and on his controllers' rueful reflections on 'the mistakes . . . they had made with the IRA' in providing them with explosives in large amounts rather than in small consignments, and in paying them in American dollars.[116]

Actual developments in Ireland were ominous enough. In June 1939 the Irish government had introduced the draconian Offences Against the State Act (OASA). Originally drafted in the autumn of 1938 in anticipation of a European war

---

[114] Liddell diary, 26 Apr., TNA, KV4/185; Kell to Hankey, 29 Apr. 1940, TNA, KV4/280.
[115] *Liddell History*, 36.
[116] Report of *Snow* debriefing, 30 Oct. 1939, TNA, KV2/444.

in which Ireland would seek to remain neutral, by the time it became law the OASA was seen largely as a response to the IRA's English bombing campaign. It proscribed a range of activities as criminal, conferred very wide powers of arrest and detention, permitted the operation of non-jury courts, and allowed for internment without trial. There was a flurry of police activity against republicans in September, which resulted in a number of important arrests and the seizure of weapons and documents. But this was much in the nature of business as usual, rather than evidence of a realization in Dublin that with Britain at war a firmer approach to internal security was needed. When some of those captured resorted to the emotive tactic of going on hunger strike in November, the de Valera government, in what appeared to many an act of craven appeasement to republican sentiment, decided to release them. An Irish court then ruled that their internment was unlawful, necessitating an amendment to OASA. SIS reported these developments as a boost to the IRA, which 'is said to be fairly active'.[117] Amongst those eventually freed was one IRA veteran who less than a year later killed two Garda detectives in Dublin, a crime for which he was executed in the very different climate of December 1940.

The Irish government's policy of leniency towards the republican movement was completely discredited on 22 December, when the IRA brought off the astonishing coup of capturing almost all the defence forces' small-arms ammunition in a raid on the Magazine fort in Dublin's Phoenix Park. A G2 officer in Dublin had picked up a vague rumour of a planned IRA operation, but the head of the Garda security section, in Dan Bryan's words, 'pooh pooed' the report and G2 unwisely accepted his judgement.[118] This raid, 'our Pearl Harbor' as Dan Bryan afterwards recalled it, ultimately proved counter-productive for the republican movement: the army was shaken out of its lethargy, the ammunition was recovered, a large number of activists were interned, and more stringent anti-subversive legislation was introduced. But the immediate effect of the raid was, not unnaturally, to indicate that the IRA was seriously on the move and that the Irish security forces were incompetent amateurs, if not riven with disloyalty (it transpired that one of the prime movers in the raid was Thomas Doyle, a clerical worker in the Department of Defence). De Valera's protest at the sentencing to death in Britain in January 1940 of the two Irishmen convicted for the bungled coventry bombing also raised questions about his attitude towards the republican movement—Maffey thought that 'he has moved sharply to the Left. His administration is unpopular and incompetent. His eyesight is fading fast'. But the opposition leader W. T. Cosgrave, regarded as far more sympathetic to Britain—Maffey, still finding his feet in Dublin, wrote in January 'I wish he could come back to power'—also warned against the executions.[119] It is, however, possible that the very strong representations which the Irish had made in favour of clemency for the Coventry bombers contributed to the British and American perception that de Valera's government were not in full control of affairs and would be vulnerable to an IRA coup. There were well-founded as well as fanciful reasons for doubting Ireland's political stability and for fearing that de Valera was unwilling

[117] Liddell diary, 18 Dec. 1939, TNA, KV4/185.
[118] Dan Bryan transcripts, 1984.
[119] Maffey to London, 17 and 25 Jan. 1940, TNA, DO130/12.

to suppress anti-British and pro-German activists, and ran the risk of losing power if he attempted to do so.

Like the other agencies attempting to assess the validity of the mass of scare stories emanating from Ireland during the first months of the war, SIS were at a disadvantage because they did not have any experienced personnel on the ground with relevant knowledge and contacts. That problem was not addressed until after the fall of France.

THE SECURITY OF WAR INFORMATION IN THE BRITISH ISLES, 1939–1940

The presence in Ireland of Axis and pro-Axis diplomats was a constant source of anxiety, and there were also concerns about information leakages through genuinely neutral or even friendly missions. When war broke out there were some twenty diplomatic and consular missions in Dublin. Of the major powers ultimately to be involved in the conflict, only the Soviet Union and Japan had no representation in Ireland during the first phase of the war in Europe. In addition to the German legation, which could be expected to collect war information, there was anxiety about the Dublin representatives of Spain and of Italy because of their countries' close ties with Germany. Might not these attempt to collect intelligence, or to assist in German intelligence operations (as did Japanese and Spanish diplomats in London at various times during the first years of the war)? Might not these or other neutral missions obtain and relay to their capitals information of interest to Germany? The only real constraints on such activities were the risk if detected of antagonizing their Irish hosts, and the practical difficulty of communicating with the outside world.

It appears that MI5, not SIS, were the beneficiaries though not the instigators of one early intelligence coup against the German legation in the first months of the war. In December 1939 Guy Liddell recorded that material was reaching London from the German legation. The name and nationality of the informant has been excised from Liddell's diary, but it was most likely the same Czech servant who had passed on details of alleged discussions between the German minister Hempel and the Irish republicans Seán MacBride and Francis Stuart:

[EXCISED] . . . is now sending to the [EXCISED] in London torn up pieces of paper which are alleged to come from the German Minister's confidential waste. We have the originals pieced together and they are not uninteresting though somewhat inconclusive. They show connections with the IRA and give details of individuals who are dining and lunching with the Minister. These do not lead us very far but we may get something more concrete later.[120]

It is not known for how long this contact continued. It is the only evidence of successful penetration of the German legation by either the British or the Irish during the war. The latter were, of course, able both to maintain a watch on the legation and its officials, and to 'supervise' its telephone communications and its

[120] Liddell diary, 13 Dec. 1939, TNA, KV4/185.

routine postal transactions. As cooperation with MI5 increased, so much of the material gleaned from such surveillance was shared in one form or another. As early as April 1940, Liddell noted that MI5 had received 'some useful information' from Archer, who was 'somewhat bothered' about Petersen, the German press attaché. Petersen was believed to be in close touch with prominent republicans and at least indirectly with the IRA.[121]

Neutral and friendly missions in Ireland potentially had six possible means of communicating with home: by cable, by the ordinary post, by radio, by telephone, by diplomatic bag (whether carried by a courier or consigned unescorted), or by sending a member of staff with a verbal report. By convention, however, diplomatic posts were expected not to use radio transmitters for communications without the express permission of the host country, and instead to rely on the normal international telephone or cable systems. These were, like the postal service to and from Ireland, under British control. The protections accorded to neutral and friendly communications and movements of personnel did not extend to enemy correspondence, cables, or staff, nor of course to the use of the telephone, so from September 1939 the German legation in Dublin was confined to coded communications sent either by cable or by clandestine radio: the legation did have a concealed transmitter. But there were considerable risks involved in using a clandestine radio in a neutral state, because if it was detected the host country might regard it as a breach of faith and demand its removal, on the threat of the imposition of sanctions or even the severance of diplomatic links. It was clearly in Hempel's interests not to antagonize his hosts, and he was, accordingly, probably circumspect in using the radio. This may explain why the transmitter remained undetected during the first months of the war (after reviewing the question in October 1939 in the light of available intelligence and intercepted radio traffic, Hankey concluded that there was no evidence that Hempel had a radio).[122]

Early in 1940, however, the Admiralty picked up messages from Ireland in what was thought to be a German diplomatic code and working to the German diplomatic control station at Nauen. These were traced to a point somewhere between Dublin and Wicklow (about thirty miles south of the capital). Guy Liddell initially thought it best not to inform the Irish lest they should 'begin searching about for this station' before 'we had seen whether we could do anything with the signals'. Vivian of SIS, however, said that the traffic was in an 'unbreakable' diplomatic cipher, and that there was no benefit in letting it continue if it could be stopped.[123] On 21 February, after consultation with C and Slade of the Admiralty, it was agreed that Archer should be informed of these transmissions and asked to help track them down, but it is not clear exactly when this information was actually passed to the Irish—in late April Joseph Walshe, speaking of 'illicit wireless . . . doubted whether anything of the kind was going on, although he did not deny the possibility'.[124] Further such messages, and reciprocal traffic from Nauen, were picked up until June, when

[121] Dan Bryan interview, 1983.
[122] Liddell diary, 24 Oct. 1939, TNA, KV4/185.
[123] Ibid., 14 and 17 Feb. 1940, TNA, KV4/185.
[124] Ibid., 21 Feb. and 26 Apr. 1940, TNA, KV4/185. On 26 Feb. the Admiralty reported that there was an IRA broadcasting station in Drogheda. O'Halpin, *Defending Ireland*, 187.

recording and study of it was stopped 'as GC&CS had no hopes of reading it'. Nor at that stage could the Irish source of transmissions be accurately fixed.[125] As late as December 1940 MI5 informed Maffey that 'there was no reason to suspect the existence of a transmitter' in the German legation.[126] It is possible that the transmissions were weather reports, as Berlin had given Hempel instructions to provide these shortly after war broke out.[127]

Guy Liddell had quickly identified the desirability of Anglo-Irish 'cooperation in wireless interception', but it took considerable time for this to develop satisfactorily.[128] In part this was unavoidable: Britain's newly established Radio Security Service (RSS), tasked to detect clandestine traffic, was beset by organizational and policy difficulties, compounded by friction between SIS and MI5 about control of its activities. These factors greatly hampered its development and effectiveness in its first two years of operation. Initially, because the Irish traffic was linked to the Nauen diplomatic transmitter, monitoring of it was deemed to be the business of GC&CS, which carried out its own diplomatic interception using Post Office stations. The Post Office staff were less expert than RSS in interception techniques, and it was later thought that this might explain the considerable delay in pinpointing the source of the Irish transmissions. When RSS took over the work in 1941, there was rapid improvement.[129] For his part, Archer made it clear to Greig that the Irish had neither the equipment nor the personnel required for an efficient interception service (ironically, they had placed an order for good direction-finding equipment from the German firm Telefunken, but that had lapsed with the outbreak of war).[130] From November 1939 onwards some Irish officers received training in interception in Britain.[131] The creation of an interception section within G2 to track down an IRA 'pirate radio' resulted in an important early success, as in December 1939 an improvised ' "snifter" built from data supplied by the British authorities' was used to pinpoint the location of an American-manufactured transmitter which had been smuggled into Ireland and was being used for occasional IRA propaganda broadcasts.[132]

This capture was significant not only because it ended the broadcasts, but because it deprived the IRA of a high-quality set which would have been suitable for communicating with Germany. But the Irish were evidently somewhat wary of MI5's hints about more systematic cooperation on interception, concentrating instead on developing their own organization. This was not a matter simply of *amour propre* but of pragmatism: Dublin naturally did not want to have to rely on the British for information about clandestine transmissions from Ireland. There was an additional consideration: cooperation on illicit transmissions logically implied action to suppress them once detected. As the saga of the German legation transmitter

125 Liddell diary, 23 Mar. 1940, TNA, KV4/185; *Liddell History*, 62.
126 *Liddell History*, 62.
127 Berlin to Hempel, 3 Dec. 1939 (decoded 23 Jan. 1944), TNA, HW36/5.
128 Liddell diary, 17 Sept. 1939, TNA, KV4/185.
129 *Liddell History*, 65.
130 Greig to Admiralty, 15 Nov. 1939, TNA, DO 130/7.
131 Liddell diary, 17 Nov. 1939, TNA, KV4/185.
132 G2 document dated 21 Jan. 1946 on wireless detection, reproduced in *Liddell History*, 113. Dan Bryan was in the search party, but did not go into the premises as one of the IRA men operating the set, George Plunkett, had been a close friend during the war of independence.

was to show, this might present very awkward diplomatic problems for a neutral state attempting to stay on terms with both sets of belligerents. The nettle was only properly grasped in January 1942, following negotiations in London. After this, the Irish army signals corps provided 'in effect . . . an additional Y service in Eire' which was of considerable military as well as security value to Britain in respect of radio traffic generally in the British Isles, the surrounding seas and skies, and further afield.[133]

There was nothing unique in the German legation's possession and intermittent operation of a clandestine transmitter: although considered contraband, such devices were concealed in many embassies and legations in sensitive parts of the world, including, for example, the British missions in Berne, at the Vatican, and in Copenhagen, where it 'was hidden under the roof' until destroyed by the naval attaché when the Germans invaded.[134] The same was the case in London: in April 1941 Guy Liddell noted that the Hungarian military attaché was still 'blazing away' on a secret transmitter because the Foreign Office would not make a protest, despite the fact that the Hungarians were now allies of Germany.[135] This probably arose from the fact that, as C had confided a year earlier, the Hungarian minister when confronted by the Foreign Office had frankly admitted that he had a secret transmitter. It was the easiest way to communicate. He gathered that in Budapest many diplomatic missions including the British had similar arrangements. As SIS did indeed have a set in the Budapest legation, a deal had clearly been struck.[136]

The Irish had early indications that the German legation was concerned about the security of its communications. In late 1939 they politely deflected a request that German correspondence should be carried in the Irish diplomatic bag—Hempel could not use a bag because it would pass through Britain—and were similarly evasive when the Italian minister in Washington sought the same favour after Italy entered the war.[137] Both of these powers were consequently confined to relying on the impenetrability of their codes. It was just as well that the Irish refused these overtures, as the bag was not inviolable and the British would certainly have detected any such material (by 1941 the Special Operations Executive (SOE) wanted to use the American diplomatic bag to smuggle radios into countries with which Britain did not have relations, and as late as 1945 decodes disclosed that Spanish diplomats based in Turkey, and a Swedish diplomat bound for Tokyo, were carrying intelligence material for Japan).[138] There were initial suspicions that the Irish might provide such help to Britain's enemies: the British ambassador in Rome heard 'from an unimpeachable source that . . . the Irish Minister to the Holy See is acting as the intermediary for correspondence (letters and telegrams) between Dublin and Berlin and vice versa'. A fortnight later this warning was amended: the source 'is "fairly sure"' that only Irish government communications were being

---

[133] *Liddell History*, 64. This is discussed in more detail in Ch. 3 below.

[134] Denham, *Inside the Nazi Ring*, 6.

[135] Liddell diary, 12 Apr. 1941, TNA, KV4/186. The set was eventually removed on 27 Apr. 1941.

[136] Ibid., 23 June 1940, TNA, KV4/186.

[137] Warnock (Berlin) to Dublin, 25 Sept. 1939, and Brennan (Washington) to Dublin, 18 Apr. 1941, NAI, DFA, P24; *Curry History*, 259.

[138] SOE war diary, 29 April 1941, TNA, HS7/215; USNA, Magic summary, 26 Jan., and 7 Apr., citing a Japanese message from Stockholm to Tokyo, 1945, RG457, boxes 15 and 16.

relayed.[139] In October the French minister in Dublin told Maffey that he had 'good reason to believe' that the Dutch had permitted Hempel to use their bag for his correspondence, an assertion which also proved groundless.[140] There was anxiety about a report from 'a secret source that must on no account be compromised' that Hempel tried to get correspondence carried on Irish ships plying between Limerick, Antwerp and Lisbon—it was already known that intelligence reports had been carried before the war by officers on German ships calling to Ireland.[141]

This warning proved unfounded, but at least one would-be German agent, Joseph Andrews, did send messages via a ship on the Lisbon run during 1943. In February 1940, furthermore, MI5 discovered that their well-established though highly equivocal double agent *Snow*, who had smuggled an Abwehr radio into Ireland in 1938, had links with Samuel Stewart, a shipowner who 'runs several shipping lines between Belfast, Dublin, this country, and Antwerp'.[142] Irish shipping links with Europe were to command a good deal of security attention throughout the war. They became a major preoccupation of B1L, a section established in 1941 to study airline and shipping personnel, which watched 'suspicious characters and haunts in the Irish Channel and on Irish ships which plied regularly between Eire and Lisbon and only passed through a somewhat perfunctory British control'.[143]

GC&CS had one immense advantage in monitoring diplomatic cable traffic to and from Ireland. With Irish agreement, from the outbreak of war all such communications to and from Europe were routed through London.[144] This meant that all messages between Dublin and Europe could be delayed by some days even when they could not be read, and that copies of all traffic could be taken for future reference. The latter was particularly important in respect of traffic which was either unbreakable or considered not worth the trouble to break immediately, because it facilitated retrospective analysis once the material had been read. GC&CS records suggest that traffic to and from Dublin was a very low priority during the phoney war. Only ten contemporary decodes of Irish-related diplomatic traffic have been traced, none of them Irish (although an index entry in an MI5 file refers to a 'decode of telegram from Washington Ministry of Foreign Affairs Dublin', which demonstrates that the master set of diplomatic decodes now open to research is not a complete record).[145] Of these, two were French and two American. The

---

[139] Lorraine to Cadogan (Foreign Office), 18 Sept. 1939, TNA, DO130/3.

[140] Maffey to Machtig, 15 Oct. 1939, TNA, DO130/3.

[141] *Curry History*, 135; Greig's notes of talks with Walshe (External Affairs), 22 Nov. 1939, TNA, DO 130/3.

[142] Liddell diary, 13 Feb. 1940, TNA, KV4/185. On 21 Dec. 1943 Liddell wrote that Hempel was trying to dispose of 'an old Abwehr set deposited' in Ireland before the war, most probably that brought by *Snow*. On the other hand, in notes on a debriefing of *Snow* of 30 Oct. 1939 an MI5 officer wrote that 'we already know that there is a set working from Belfast'. TNA, KV2/445.

[143] *Curry History*, 263.

[144] *Liddell History*, 68.

[145] Index entry noting SIS letter of 28 Jan. covering Irish decode of 16 Jan. 1940, TNA, KV3/120. The global figures for British diplomatic decodes between 3 Sept. 1939 and 15 Aug. 1945 are given as follows: (1939) 2,288, (1940) 8,485, (1941) 13,041, (1942) 13,095, (1943) 14,050, (1945) 13,153, (1945) 8,512, making a grand total of 72,624. Report on D&R section, undated, 1945, TNA, HW12/336. The figures are based on those sent to the Foreign Office, but do not include decodes sent only to C, such as some Polish intelligence traffic.

Table 2.1. *British decodes relating to Ireland, September 1939–May 1940*

	French	Italian	USA	Totals
September		3		3
October				
November				
December	1			1
January 1940			1	1
February				
March	1		1	2
April				
May		3		3
TOTALS	2	6	2	10

remainder were Italian, and these were the only ones in any way significant (see Table 2.1).

The Italian minister Berardis had been hastily sent back from unauthorized leave in Italy just days before war broke out. If he received any specific instructions while in Italy to develop lines of contact with the IRA, or to organize or to facilitate intelligence gathering, these were not reflected in the communications decoded by GC&CS.[146] The Italians did have one potential link with the residue of the Blueshirt movement, as for a time they employed Captain Liam D. Walsh, at one time a valued sidekick of General O'Duffy, for unspecified duties before dismissing him early in 1940, probably for dishonesty. As events were to show, Walsh and his former chief were far more interested in courting the Germans.

Unlike his colleague the Italian minister in Kabul, 'a shrewd, intelligent man who . . . occupies himself by studying local politics with some care and by keeping in close touch with . . . Afghan unofficial circles', links which enabled him to promote considerable subversion once Italy came into the war, Berardis was lazy. His decoded traffic dealt mainly with Irish responses to the war, though one message of 12 September spoke of information that the British had considerable forces stationed in Northern Ireland and that they had closed the border.[147] This was no more than vague gossip, and indicated that Berardis did not have any established information-gathering network in either part of Ireland. Other Italian messages reported that both de Valera and Walshe laid great stress on Ireland's determination to remain neutral, on her necessarily close links with Britain, and on her desire to maintain good relations with Italy. At the same time, 'the internal political situation is somewhat fluid', and 'therefore . . . de Valera will have to continue to manoeuvre within a vice, constituted by the English on one side and the [extreme republicans] on the other'.[148] These decodes were circulated to the Dominions Office and the

[146] Rome cabled to tell Berardis that his leave was suspended, only to be informed that he was already in Italy. Rome to Berardis, and Malasljna to Rome, both 24 Aug. 1939, TNA, HW12/242.

[147] British minister, Kabul, to Delhi, 16 Mar. 1939, IOR, L/PS/12/1758; Berardis (Dublin) to Rome, 12 Sept. 1939, TNA, HW12/243.

[148] Berardis (Dublin) to Rome, 1 Sept. 1939 and 28 May 1940, TNA, HW12/239 and 252.

Foreign Office as a matter of routine, and as well as throwing light on the limits of Berardis's activities, they presumably had some impact on British understanding of Irish policy generally.

There are two obvious gaps in the decodes from the phoney war period. The first is Irish traffic. If GC&CS were reading Irish messages, it seems that no one bothered to circulate and store the results. It is more likely, given that GC&CS had read some Irish traffic in 1932, that the absence of Irish material up to June 1940 indicates that it was not a priority at a time when GC&CS was wrestling with far greater problems (although as late as 1944 GC&CS found some Irish cables unreadable, particularly messages in the 'Dearg' (red) system).[149] The second obvious absence in this period is German diplomatic material. This certainly does not reflect codebreaking priorities; rather, it is because, while by the autumn of 1939 GC&CS could read some German consular and naval attaché traffic, until December 1942 they were unable to make any headway with the main German diplomatic cipher, which was used for communications between Berlin and Dublin.[150] This was an especially acute problem, because of the danger of German intelligence reporting and because of the possibility of German action against Ireland as a preliminary to or as part of operations against Britain. A matter of weeks into the war, the Canadian government reported that a code telegram from the German legation in Dublin to the German embassy in Washington had passed directly from the cable station at Waterville in County Kerry to Nova Scotia. The British then secured an undertaking from the Irish that all enciphered transatlantic German cables would henceforth be routed through London. There they could be copied and delayed, even if they could not yet be read (in 1990 Sir Harry Hinsley, the official historian of British signals intelligence, pointed out that once the main German diplomatic code was eventually broken the first traffic tackled was Dublin–Berlin).[151] British inability to decode German communications contributed to wildly exaggerated estimates of German intentions and activities concerning Ireland during the summer and autumn of 1940, based mainly on rumour and surmise rather than on hard intelligence. The only pre-May 1940 messages traced in decodes made after January 1943 of intelligence significance were those of 2 and 3 December 1939, in which Berlin sent instructions on how to use code to send daily weather reports.[152]

NORTHERN IRELAND AND IRISH SECURITY, 1939–1940

Northern Ireland presented considerable challenges for MI5. Before the war contacts between Belfast and London had been sporadic and limited. The RUC's main London link was with the Special Branch at Scotland Yard, with which they had always dealt on IRA matters. While they had also faithfully reported on suspicious

---

[149] Memorandum to Denniston (head of diplomatic codebreaking) and Miss Reid, 15 May 1944, TNA, HW53/56. Irish traffic became a particular concern in the months leading up to D-Day in 1944.
[150] e.g. German naval attaché, Madrid, to Berlin, 30 Nov. 1939, TNA, HW12/245.
[151] Liddell diary, TNA, KV4/185, 29 Oct. 1939; Maffey to Dominions Office, 9 Oct. 1939, TNA, DO 130/3.
[152] Berlin to Hempel, 2 and 3 Sept. 1939, TNA, HW36/5.

foreigners and on communist activities, until 1938 to SIS and since then to MI5, this was essentially a one-way process: there was no dialogue, no liaison officers, and nothing in the nature of shared assessments of security threats. While the RUC had considerable experience in dealing with the IRA, they had no expertise in counter-espionage work, and at the beginning of hostilities had no one with 'any knowledge of German' or familiarity 'with German names'.[153] As Cecil Liddell put it in 1945, the RUC 'is jealous of its rights and responsibilities . . . and is not inclined to welcome what it calls "the amateur interference of Intelligence Officers, who lack local knowledge" '.[154] MI5's task was further complicated by the fact that Northern Ireland was an operational area for the navy and the RAF, with the former consequently claiming primacy in port and coastal security matters. In mid-November the experienced MI5 officer T. A. 'Tar' Robertson visited Northern Ireland to investigate various reports of mysterious lights seen along the coastline. Guy Liddell noted that:

TAR's impression of the local police is somewhat similar to the one I gained more than a year ago. The issue between the Orangemen and the IRA is the thing that really counts and espionage matters are of secondary importance. There is also a certain wildness in the reports which are obtained . . . We hope, through the Command Security Officer who seems intelligent and is well in with the local authorities, to get these matters sifted locally before they are passed on to us.[155]

This was probably MI5's first direct wartime encounter with the RUC; shortly afterwards, references begin to crop up in Liddell's diary indicating frequent contact by correspondence and telephone and in meetings with the RUC's inspector-general Sir Charles Wickham and the Special Branch's Inspector Gilfillan. On 12 January Gilfillan wrote direct to Cecil Liddell to tell him that he had learnt, from 'a source that is in a position to know', that IRA headquarters in Dublin had issued instructions to units that 'there will soon be a big movement made to engage Ireland's most deadly enemy both by air and sea and that being the case it is important that the men under your command be alert'.[156] These two officers constantly feature in documents relating to Northern Ireland until the end of the war. Wickham consistently downplayed reports of the IRA's supposed strength and intentions, and his views on Irish affairs on both sides of the border came to command a great deal of respect in London (and in Dublin, where G2 formed a high opinion of his common sense).[157] In April 1940 he brought in a German-speaking RNVR officer, Captain Roger Moore, to concentrate on counter-espionage—there had already been problems making sense of material from 'a good informant' on suspicious foreigners because the 'information has been transmitted through various Irish intermediaries who do not even know what a German name is'.[158] Moore became the headquarters link with the Garda, a liaison established at 'a date not exactly

---

[153] *Liddell History*, 25; Liddell diary, TNA, KV4/185,
[154] Ibid.
[155] Liddell diary, TNA, KV4/185, 14 Nov. 1939.
[156] Ibid., TNA, KV4/185, 3 and 31 Jan. 1940; Gilfillan to Cecil Liddell, 12 Jan. 1940, TNA, KV3/120.
[157] Dan Bryan interview, 1983.
[158] Liddell diary, TNA, KV4/185, 31 Jan. 1940.

known, but . . . believed to have been not long after the outbreak of war' — it seems
clear that there were also long-standing links, whether sanctioned by their respective
headquarters or not, between RUC officers and their Garda counterparts in the
border counties.[159] The RUC were not equipped, other than through liaison with the
Garda, to study German activities in Ireland. This continued to be a major concern
both for MI5 and for SIS, which sought reliable reports from other sources which
would complement what came through the MI5–G2 and the RUC–Garda links.

The RUC position on all security matters was straightforward: the force would
liaise with the armed forces and with MI5 in respect of security and counter-
espionage, but did not want anyone from any mainland agency or service conducting
enquiries independently in Northern Ireland. Both MI5 and, more surprisingly given
their activist instincts, NID seem quickly to have accepted this. It was only in 1941
that a satisfactory solution was devised, when a German-speaking BTNI officer was
employed to represent the interests both of MI5 and SIS in Northern Ireland.[160]

CONCLUSION

The quality of British intelligence on Ireland during the phoney war was not high.
Different agencies had different agendas: NID, to an extent in response to directions
from the first lord, began the war with a fixation about German submarines on
the west coast, and sought hard information which preferably would confirm that
such reports were true. MI5 were concerned mainly to build up liaison with G2,
and SIS were reluctant to spy in Ireland, partly for fear that this would jeopardize
security cooperation. In Northern Ireland the eyes of the RUC were fixed firmly
on the IRA, a threat which they continued to treat as largely a domestic and
cross-border phenomenon rather than as one which might come under German
control, although they also kept an eye on aliens, suspicious foreigners, and anything
out of the ordinary which might be linked to the war. While there was frequent
bilateral contact between most of the agencies involved, there was no coordinating
mechanism either to oversee their activities, or to settle differences and to determine
priorities. Nor was there a central process for analysing intelligence. The JIC was in
its infancy, and in the first year of the war it carried little weight. At an operational
level, until the Home Defence Security Executive (hereafter the Security Executive)
came into operation in May 1940, there was no concerted oversight of the domestic
security efforts of the various agencies involved.

Compounding these problems was the general incoherence of British security
policy when war broke out. Neither the mechanisms, the trained personnel, nor the
rules were in place to create an effective security screen around the United Kingdom.
The particular problems arising from Irish neutrality, especially in terms of the
common travel area, shipping movements, postal and telephone communications,
and counter-espionage, had not been considered in any detail beforehand. The
question of the surveillance of the Irish coastline and coastal waters to deter

---

[159] Liddell diary, TNA, KV4/185, 20 Apr. 1940 and 26 July 1941; *Liddell History*, 24.
[160] Ibid., 27 Mar. 1940; *Liddell History*, 58.

or at least to detect enemy submarine activity had not been addressed, nor had the security threat posed by enemy and neutral missions in Dublin been considered. On the military side, the armed services had only a vague idea of either the limitations or the potential of the Irish defence forces, and possessed no information about Irish defence policy (insofar as any existed). On the plus side, MI5's 'Dublin link' was already in existence and it developed quite well in the early months of war, and the appointment of a naval attaché brought a marked improvement in the quality of reporting on coastal security from Ireland (without, however, immediately diluting the near hysteria in London about supposed German submarine activities and bases).

The term 'phoney war' emerged to describe the period of relative military inaction in western Europe between September 1939 and the German offensives in Norway and the Low Countries in the spring of 1940. It applies equally to the specifics of Anglo-Irish relations during those months, for two related reasons: until late in spring 1940 Irish neutrality was a serious irritant, but it did not appear a mortal threat. The Norwegian disaster, followed by the invasion of the Low Countries and the attack on France in May, brought to a head the growing sense of unease at Westminster that under Chamberlain British military policy was going nowhere. Those pressures culminated on 9 May in Chamberlain's reluctant decision to stand down and, after Labour had signalled unwillingness to serve under Halifax, in agreement that Winston Churchill should take over. Halifax described how, after a tense discussion with both Chamberlain and Churchill in No. 10 Downing Street, when 'I said I thought Winston was a better choice . . . Winston did *not* demur'.[161]

The pressure of calamitous events during Churchill's first weeks in office, together with his own strong views on Irish neutrality, on the strategic significance of the Irish ports, and on Hitler's likely intentions, put Ireland high up on the new prime minister's agenda. They were to result not simply in a marked hardening of British policy, but in a remarkable offer of possible Irish unity. The evidence suggests that this dramatic attempt to coax Ireland into belligerency on the British side arose directly from very poor intelligence circulating in Whitehall in May and June 1940.

[161] Cadogan diary, 9 May 1940, CCCA, Cadogan papers, ACAD1/9.

3

Invasion fears: May 1940–June 1941

British policy towards Ireland in the period between the invasion of France in May 1940 and the German attack on the Soviet Union on 22 June 1941 (*Barbarossa*) was multilayered and not altogether consistent. The precipitate collapse of western Europe between April and June 1940 transformed all the calculations. Ireland suddenly became of vital importance, not for her potential role in Atlantic defence, significant though that remained, but for her vulnerability as an unarmed neutral in the middle of a war zone, a soft target which Hitler might well choose to pick off just as he had effortlessly gobbled up Denmark, Norway, and the Low Countries as a prelude to his attack on France. The likelihood of a German seizure of any part of Ireland lessened with the launch of *Barbarossa*, although it remained a credible possibility for about a year thereafter. Growing American involvement in Atlantic defence from early 1941, on the other hand, provided Britain with further opportunities to apply pressure on Ireland indirectly through the United States.

British policy both framed and was framed by the work of the intelligence agencies. These pursued parallel rather than interconnected aims. On the one hand, Britain sought Irish cooperation in a range of security and counter-intelligence activities and in planning to resist a German attack; on the other, she took steps to acquire intelligence covertly in and on Ireland, she made secret preparations for sabotage operations and for unilateral intervention in the event of such an attack, and she sought to discredit Irish neutrality through propaganda and disinformation internationally, particularly in the United States. These discrete strands of activities were largely the responsibility of different agencies and departments—MI5 and SIS, the RUC, GC&CS, MI9, SOE and the service intelligence departments, all of which had dipped into Irish affairs by June 1941—and so the study of the work of any one of these provides an inadequate understanding of British concerns and operations. It is also necessary to appreciate the changed ministerial climate in which intelligence activities took place. In temperament and in attitude towards Ireland, in his love of grand strategy, his fixation with sea power and his fascination with intelligence, and in his predisposition towards confrontation rather than conciliation, Winston Churchill was an utterly different political master to the cautious, methodical, and ailing Neville Chamberlain whom he succeeded as prime minister.

THE IMMEDIATE THREAT OF A GERMAN INVASION, MAY–JUNE 1940

British fears about Ireland's vulnerability to a German assault added a new complication to the intricacies of Anglo-Irish relations. Neutrality, previously a major political irritant and an impediment to the effective defence of shipping in the Atlantic, assumed a new strategic character. The question was no longer one of Irish bases, but of Irish defence. This occasioned a dramatic shift in British policy, in particular in respect of partition.

There were two triggers for the transformation of British policy towards Ireland. The first was Hitler's dramatic victory in western Europe. Where in March Britain and France were still contemplating how best to get at Hitler, by mid-June all of western Europe, from the northern tip of Norway to the French borders with Spain and with Switzerland, was effectively under German control, while Italy's belated entry into the war threatened British interests in the Mediterranean, the Middle East, and North and East Africa. The second reason why British policy towards Ireland changed was a reassessment of the likelihood of a German attack on Ireland, whether as a prelude to or as a diversionary move during an invasion of southern England. That possibility acquired credibility in the course of May.

On 7 May Vernon Kell and Guy Liddell visited the Irish high commission for discussions with Dulanty and with Walshe of External Affairs. They found the latter 'anxious to know whether we were satisfied with what his Gov[ernmen]t was doing and whether we had any suggestions to make which might assist in stopping up any loopholes'. They discussed various issues, including controls on the movements of enemy aliens, the surveillance of 'ships' crews and passengers' to prevent anyone slipping into Britain unnoticed, and the detection of illicit wireless traffic: Walshe did not know whether or not G2 had yet received interception apparatus promised in earlier discussions, and they agreed that technicalities should be discussed directly with Archer (in Northern Ireland arrangements were already being made to coordinate wireless interception activities between the various service departments). Walshe stated that de Valera was 'definitely very worried' about an IRA attempt to seize the British diplomatic bag in Dublin that morning, during which two detectives had been wounded: the taoiseach wondered whether all written communications between Dublin and London ought not to be in code, something which Walshe acknowledged to MI5 was 'quite impossible', and was minded to place all Anglo-Irish diplomatic mail under military guard. Walshe was 'extremely friendly and was very anxious that I go over to Dublin as soon as it was convenient', and willing 'to do anything he possibly could to help us in stopping up any loop-holes'.[1]

---

[1] O'Halpin, *Defending Ireland*, 248; Y committee minutes, 7 July 1940, TNA, HW42/5, Liddell diary, 7 May 1940, TNA, KV4/186.

On the same day de Valera used the occasion of a speech in Galway to condemn attacks on neutral European states, a clear reference to German action against Denmark, Norway, and the Low Countries. This earned a menacing rebuke from Hempel, who reported back to Berlin that Walshe had been at pains to play down the import of de Valera's remarks and to emphasize that Ireland had no quarrel with Germany. De Valera's speech was arguably intended as much for British as for German ears, lest London be minded to use force to take what Ireland would not offer voluntarily.

British fears of a German move on Ireland increased as the news from France worsened. On 15 May the Liddell brothers drove to the spa town of Droitwich to meet Archer, who was taking the cure. Their discussions, while scarcely therapeutic, were constructive. The original purpose of the meeting had been to discuss how to improve Irish capabilities in illegal wireless interception, but in the light of 'recent events in Holland' they agreed on the 'probability' of 'something similar happening in Eire'. Archer believed that 'there was nothing to prevent the Germans landing . . . and he did not see how any resistance could be maintained for more than a week'. While the government could be persuaded 'to lock up the 5th column', the Irish had virtually 'no equipment' with which to defend the state—some ministers were inclined to attribute this to British unwillingness to put weapons in Irish hands which might reach the IRA, although Archer said he had argued that, as a neutral, Ireland could not expect to be high on Britain's priorities for arms supplies. He saw 'no objection' as a soldier to the idea of Anglo-Irish staff talks in anticipation of a German landing.[2] On returning to London, the Liddells briefed Lord Hankey, who thought their information so significant that he sent them on to see the dominions secretary Caldecote.[3] Guy Liddell detected a lack of urgency: 'There seems to be little anxiety in Gov[ernmen]t departments about the present situation. Few people appear to realize the probability of an invasion of this country and of Eire'.[4] The next day a further meeting with Caldecote, also attended by Vivian and Maffey, discussed the interlinked questions of German intentions, IRA capabilities, and Irish defensive weakness. Maffey urged some concessions on arms to de Valera, who was 'thoroughly alarmed', as a preamble to asking for staff talks. He was, however, 'rather inclined to minimize the dangers of the IRA and its connections with Germany', and thought that SIS reports on Ireland 'were similar to hundreds of others . . . which had little or no foundation'. Vivian 'hotly contested this and told Maffey that he thought he was under-rating the position'.[5] In the weeks that followed, it was Vivian's fatalistic assessments which gained credibility, contributing to an astonishing shift in British policy on Irish unity.

On 22 May the Garda raided the house of Stephen Carroll Held. Held was a dealer in scrap metals who had travelled to Germany some weeks previously as

    [2] Liddell diary, 15 May 1940, TNA, KV4/186. The obituary of one of the British officers sent for discussions in the summer of 1940, Captain James Hill, *The Times*, 21 Mar. 2006, perpetuates familiar legends, stating that when he arrived in Dublin, 'the Germans were already busy on neutral territory—he discovered several staying with him at the Gresham hotel'.
    [3] *Liddell History*, 51.
    [4] Liddell diary, 16 May 1940, TNA, KV4/186.
    [5] Ibid., 17 May 1940, TNA, KV4/186.

an IRA emissary. Although MI5 had asked G2 about him as early as September 1939, he did not come under active suspicion prior to the raid.[6] He had delivered 'Plan Kathleen', an amateurish scheme for German landings in Kerry and in the north-west which would be the signal for an uprising to drive the British out of Northern Ireland.[7] Held had also sought the dispatch of a German officer to liaise with the IRA. The Garda found a parachute, insignia from a Luftwaffe uniform, a transmitter, a number of coded messages, 'a bundle of manuscript and typed notes, collectively known as . . . Plan Kathleen', and $20,000.[8] This indicated that a German agent was at large, although the Garda missed the man himself as he was out at the time of the raid.[9] Dan Bryan, in charge of G2 while Archer was in London and Belfast with Walshe for defence discussions, advised External Affairs to give copies of everything to Maffey immediately because rumours of the raid were bound to reach British ears in distorted form.[10] Included was 'an elaborate questionnaire in English but in German handwriting, which shows that preparations are being made for a landing'.[11] The agent was Herman Goertz, who had landed near Dublin by parachute on 5 May and had eventually succeeded in making contact with Irish sympathizers, including Iseult Stuart, the estranged wife of Francis Stuart, Jim O'Donovan, the Abwehr's IRA link, and the bibulous IRA chief of staff Stephen Hayes. The discovery generated shock-waves: both the Irish and the British feared that the agent had a mission to coordinate action with the IRA to coincide with a German assault, and for a time the country was awash with stories of fifth columnists lying in wait to spring to the aid of Hitler when his forces arrived.

In early May the Irish government moved against the 'Irish Friends of Germany', a congeries of former Blueshirts, extreme Catholics, Irish-language fanatics, anti-Semites, people fearful of Masonic influence, and a handful of former Fine Gael politicians obsessed with the power of international finance, arresting the group's leading lights.[12] In early June four of the most significant members were interned, leaving the organization under the control of the politically irrelevant, though poisonous, George Griffin, who continued to rail against Jews and freemasons and who went on to create the 'People's National Party' or Penapa.[13] Among the

---

[6] On 28 Sept. 1939 MI5 wrote to G2 about him. They also corresponded with the Northumberland police, which suggests that he may have made visits there in the course of his work. These communications are listed in index entries in TNA, KV3/120, but the documents themselves no longer survive.

[7] Dan Bryan observed that the plan had plainly been drawn up by someone without any grasp of military operations. In October 1941 the IRA's Liam Gaynor admitted to interrogators to being one of its authors, the others being Held and Stephen Hayes. Hull, *Irish Secrets*, 317, n. 115.

[8] Note dated 6 Aug. 1943, with Cecil Liddell to Stephenson, 24 Aug. 1943, TNA, DO121/86.

[9] Hull, *Irish Secrets*, 90–2.

[10] O'Halpin, *Defending Ireland*, 174.

[11] Liddell diary, 26 May 1940, TNA, KV4/186.

[12] Garda report on George Griffin, 14 Oct. 1940, and Garda report on Gerald Griffin, 26 May 1939, MAI, G2/X/0040A and G2/X/40.

[13] Garda reports on Irish Friends of Germany meetings of 26 June and 15 July 1940, MAI, G2/2272. Douglas, 'The Pro-Axis Underground in Ireland', 1182, makes a spirited case that these and other tin-pot groups demonstrated that 'all was far from well with the state of Irish democracy'. When considered in conjunction with the dismal wartime failures of the mainstream republican movement, they demonstrate precisely the opposite.

four men interned was the main organizer of the Irish Friends of Germany, Liam D. Walsh. Formerly a trusted aide of General O'Duffy and a one-time Fine Gael official, he had been in touch with Otto Pfaus before the war, and more recently had been employed by the Italian legation.[14] His nationality apart, Walsh could have stepped straight from the pages of Evelyn Waugh's *Vile Bodies*, a 'temporary gentleman' if ever there was one. Briefly an army officer during the civil war, he was pushed out, leaving a trail of unpaid bills and unanswered questions, when it transpired that during the truce in 1921 he had stolen funds from the IRA's Dublin Brigade. Thereafter an embezzler and con man, he had departed from his post in Fine Gael headquarters under a cloud in the late 1930s. Even the Italian legation, for whom he was employed for a time in 1939–40 to spread propaganda, eventually got rid of him. His amateurish efforts to gather information of use to the Axis aside, the Irish Friends of Germany proved to be merely a talking shop rather than either a nucleus for the revival of Irish fascism or a potentially useful auxiliary force in the event of a German landing, but this was by no means so clear to the British in the circumstances of June 1940, given O'Duffy's involvement and the presence in Ireland of an as-yet-unidentified German agent.[15]

The fates of Poland, Denmark, Norway, the Netherlands, and Belgium—all of which had more extensive and sophisticated defence forces than Ireland—suggested that Germany would have little difficulty in attacking Ireland, with or without the help of fifth columnists. In his first message as prime minister to Roosevelt, Churchill wrote on 15 May that 'we have many reports of possible German parachute or airborne descents in Ireland. The visit of a United States squadron to Irish ports, which might well be prolonged, would be invaluable'. The American president avoided a definite response, although he fully accepted the danger which Ireland was in and deplored her neutrality accordingly (following entry into the first world war, the United States navy had based destroyers and seaplanes in Ireland).[16] On 23 May the JIC concluded that, 'while the present Government . . . is sympathetic to this country and hostile to Germany, they are not able or willing to take overt measures in advance to ensure collaboration . . . in dealing with any German invasion'. The possibility of Anglo-Irish staff talks 'is being investigated, but the strictest secrecy is necessary'. Even a small German airborne force could secure suitable 'landing grounds'. Alternatively or additionally, paratroops might capture a strategic port, which could then be used to disembark reinforcements by ship. The Irish army was too small, too poorly equipped, and too dispersed to do much against such an assault (this was also the view of its recently appointed chief of staff, the forthright Dan McKenna), although it was believed that the Irish would, unlike the Danes,

---

[14] List of 'American–IRA contacts' dated '11/11 [40], which records Walsh's correspondence with Pfaus, MAI, G2/X/0825; one of the addresses under observation was 167 Strand Road, then the home of the twice-widowed Mrs Gordon, firstly the wife of an RIC inspector and then of the prominent republican Austin Stack, where over 30 Thompson sub-machine guns were discovered in 1944. From 1962 to 1978 this was my family home. When we bought the house, my father found two carefully constructed hides, in one of which was a handful of .303 ammunition.

[15] Archer (G2) to Walshe (Dublin), 29 Aug. 1940, NAI, DFA A8; McGarry, *O'Duffy*, 334–8.

[16] Churchill to Roosevelt, and reply, 15 and 16 May 1940, in Kimball, *Churchill and Roosevelt*, i. 37 and 39.

resist as best they could. Effective defence would come mainly from BTNI. Once they consolidated their grip, the Germans would probably seek to station a bomber force—'supplies of bombs and essential requirements' might already have reached Ireland 'by clandestine means'. A day later the picture painted was much the same.[17]

In London Dulanty was briefed by Norwegian officers on their experience of German tactics in landing troops from aircraft under fire.[18] On 29 May the Admiralty's assessment was that an invasion of the British Isles was probable: 'it is likely that the enemy will favour the use of the shortest sea route to his objective, but the possibility of diversionary or subsidiary operations in the Shetlands, Ireland, or North of Scotland must be borne in mind', and precautionary dispositions were made in the following days.[19] On the same day, the newly established Security Executive chaired by Lord Swinton discussed 'the state of military preparations in Eire', and Vivian spoke on 'the activities of the IRA'.[20]

Desmond Morton, the prime minister's personal link with the intelligence services, briefed Churchill on the 'serious picture' which Vivian presented:

The most urgent matter...concerns the situation in Eire...The War Office states categorically that the IRA is well armed and well organized, whereas the Eire Defence Forces are little short of derisory. There is information that a number of Germans have landed surreptitiously...and that there has been a regular communications service by wireless and other means between Eire and Germany. It is known that the Germans have plans to land troops by parachute and aircraft...but even if there was no immediate German assistance forthcoming it is probable that the IRA could overcome the Eire Forces by themselves...

The Secret Services have a great deal more detailed information, much of which has fitted into place as a result of the arrest in Eire...of an individual named Held, who had...a wireless transmitting set, and a number of papers showing that he was a German intelligence, sabotage and revolutionary agent.[21]

On 31 May Churchill was briefed on the, 'at first glance rather melodramatic and emotional', ideas of Conor Carrigan, who reprised his earlier suggestion that a call for Ireland to enter the war would come better from republican France than from monarchical Britain: 'The appeal should be made on emotional grounds recalling the Irish Brigade which fought for France against her enemies, which were then the British'. The French might return the colours of such regiments, and also dispatch officers and ships.[22] Swinton rather liked the idea, suggesting that French troops rescued from Dunkirk might be stationed in Ireland 'for retraining and re-equipment', but otherwise there was no enthusiasm for Carrigan's strange proposal.[23] A similar card had already been unsuccessfully played when, on receiving news of the German attack on France, Maffey had asked de Valera to send an 'Irish

---

[17] JIC(40) 78 and 79, 23 and 24 May 1940, TNA, CAB81/97; Denham, *Inside the Nazi Ring*, 5, describing a conversation of 8 April 1940 between the British minister to Denmark and the Danish foreign minister.

[18] Dulanty to Dublin, 28 May 1940, NAI, DFA, P12/14(i).

[19] Appreciation for commanders in chief and flag officers, 29 May 1940, TNA, ADM223/484; Canning, *British Policy Towards Ireland*, 272, n. 28.

[20] Security Executive minutes, 29 May 1940, TNA, CAB93/2.

[21] Morton to Churchill, 29 May 1940, TNA, CAB93/2 and PREM7/2.

[22] Ibid., 31 May 1940, TNA, PREM7/6.

[23] Ibid.

Brigade to France'.[24] It was instead the reports of another Irishman, the veteran Indian policeman Charles Tegart, which caught Whitehall's imagination. The apparent imminence of a German descent upon Ireland, combined with Tegart's lurid reports of widespread German and IRA activities in the state, produced a remarkable shift in British policy on the last great question in Anglo-Irish relations.

On 1 June an official in Maffey's office gave the Irish unequivocal warning that a German paratroop attack, timed to coincide with an IRA uprising, '*is imminent*', citing German plans which had fallen into Dutch hands during the invasion of the Netherlands.[25] This information was taken very seriously in Dublin, where the government had already embarked on frantic efforts to expand the defence forces. It is clear that the warning was genuine, despite the enormous practical problems which such an attack would have encountered: any German aircraft- or ship-movements towards Ireland would have to pass through the thickest British air or sea defences, resupply and reinforcement would be similarly hazardous, and British forces in Northern Ireland would certainly intervene, whether or not the Irish asked them to.[26]

It was against the backdrop of the probability of invasion that the war cabinet embarked on a new initiative. The idea of coupling Irish entry into the war with the ending of partition had been in circulation for some weeks, and Halifax had raised it in the war cabinet on 18 May. Churchill had little time for such talk, partly because he felt that Britain should not have to bargain for something to which she had a moral right, partly because he thought a German attack and an uprising in Ireland might be of benefit if it created the conditions in which Britain could occupy the ports unilaterally, and partly because he doubted whether such an initiative could succeed in the face of likely Ulster opposition.[27] But he was not in a strong enough position to dismiss the idea out of hand. As the news from France got worse in the succeeding days, so the rumours of German intentions towards Ireland intensified. Particular weight was attached to the assertions of SIS's Tegart that as many as 2,000 well-trained Irishmen ready to rise on German instructions had been successfully reinserted into Ireland since the outbreak of war, that land suitable for airstrips had been systematically bought up along the Irish coastline, that Gauleiters had already been designated for the various regions—he had met the Galway one himself—and that the IRA were poised to strike.[28] In the panicky post-Dunkirk atmosphere such reports, although very largely at variance with what Maffey's office and the Irish themselves were saying to MI5, were subject to no critical analysis at all and were instead allowed to tip the scales of high policy untested. On 4 June Guy Liddell spoke to Vivian about:

his suggestion that some effort should be made to bring the north and south together. His proposal has got to the ears of Ismay [secretary to the CID] who apparently disapproved of

---

[24] Canning, *British Policy Towards Ireland*, 266.

[25] Antrobus (BRO) to Boland, 1 June 1940, NAI, DFA, A3.

[26] Canning, *British Policy Towards Ireland*, 263–5.

[27] Ibid. 270.

[28] Fisk, *In Time of War*, 142–3. There were just 306 registered German aliens in Ireland, of whom 141 were refugees and 30 were members of religious orders. Costigan (Justice) to Dublin, 9 July 1940, NAI, DFA, P11.

the suggestion being made at the Home Defence [Security] Executive rather than at the CID. Various Cabinet Ministers then weighed in with disapproval. The facts however have now reached the P[rime] M[inister] through Desmond Morton and he is now busily knocking everybody's heads together.[29]

Some hint of this thinking seems to have leaked out: on 10 June the Apostolic Delegate in London told the Vatican of growing Irish anxiety that 'the country might be swept into the war by an invasion', and that 'many think that Churchill is better suited than his predecessor to handle the thorny question of Ireland's partition. There are hopes that a re-united Ireland may join the fight'.[30] SIS made at least one presentation on Ireland to Chamberlain, now lord president of the council, who felt that, while Tegart's reports 'might be inaccurate in some particulars . . . the general picture presented is a true one'.[31] On 12 June Liddell lunched with Morton, who:

had been astounded by the ignorance of people in high places about subjects which had been common knowledge in the intelligence services for months if not years . . . Desmond mentioned particularly the situation in Eire. Until V[alentine] V[ivian]'s people saw the Lord President, he was obviously in almost complete ignorance. He now realized what the situation is and VV's courageous suggestion . . . is being adopted, namely De V[alera] and [the Ulster leader Lord] Craigavon are being invited over to London to consult jointly with ourselves on measures for the defence of Ireland.[32]

These contemporaneous notes suggest that SIS was central to the initiative which followed under Chamberlain's direction, although with only grudging backing from Churchill. If so, it represents a spectacular intelligence failure both as regards German intentions—in June 1940 Germany still had no plans in hand for an invasion of Britain, let alone of Ireland—and, more culpably, as regards actual conditions in Ireland, where the development of efficient liaison on both naval matters and on political and security affairs provided the mechanisms for a far more measured assessment. The Irish state was undoubtedly incapable of effective independent defence against external attack, but it did have the security resources, the legal instruments, the public support, the experience, and the resolve to deal with any threat which the IRA could possibly mount. That was already clear to Maffey after less than a year in Dublin.

Despite considerable prodding from London, and an appeal from Canada to de Valera and Craigavon to 'work out a basis upon which united and effective resistance could be offered in the event of invasion or attack', it became clear within a month that neither de Valera nor Craigavon would move remotely far enough to secure an agreement which would bring about Irish participation in the war in return for a post-war ending of partition on unspecified terms and conditions.[33] On 30 June, when 'Neville [Chamberlain] made proposals that looked like coercion of N[orthern]

---

[29] Liddell diary, 4 June 1940, TNA, KV4/186.

[30] Apostolic delegate, London, to the Vatican, 10 June 1940, in Noel, *The Holy See and the War in Europe*, 453.

[31] Chamberlain to Churchill, 12 June 1941, quoted in Canning, *British Policy Towards Ireland*, 273.

[32] Liddell diary, 12 June 1940, TNA, KV4/186.

[33] Mackenzie King's message to de Valera and Craigavon, 16 June 1940, Public Archives of Canada, RG25 D1, vol. 781, file 398.

Ireland, WSC opposed in passionate speech'.[34] One minister afterwards described the Irish leaders as 'the two men who have the least appreciation that a great war was being fought . . . both were rigid and inflexible'.[35] Belfast was outraged at what it saw as Chamberlain's treachery, and Dublin could not move beyond a pledge of benevolent neutrality even if Irish unity were granted overnight—Malcolm MacDonald, who visited Dublin at the end of June to outline the offer, later told de Valera 'that I always believed that your decision was absolutely the right one—although Churchill did not agree with that when I reported to him!' This was Chamberlain's last contribution to high policy—within a few months he was dead—and like his pre-war efforts to stave off international conflict by what he saw as rational concessions, it failed. Churchill, who had never been totally convinced that a German attack on Ireland was imminent, nor that such an intervention would necessarily be a disaster, and who could not countenance 'the coercion of Ulster', was ultimately strengthened by that failure.[36] From July onwards he set his own stamp on policy towards Ireland.

The failure of Anglo-Irish political dialogue to produce constructive results occasioned shifts in defence policy in both London and Dublin. On 24 June, and despite surprisingly constructive and informative talks with the Irish military, the chiefs of staff agreed that intervention against a German attack could no longer wait upon an Irish request for assistance. As in the Far East, where plans for the defence of Malaya hinged on the violation of Thai neutrality, military logic overcame diplomatic scruples.[37] On 6 July Churchill saw what Paul Canning has termed 'his first reliable report on the situation in Ireland from British intelligence'. It suggested that there was 'complete unanimity on the viewpoint that the Irish Forces must repel the first invader, whether British or German', and stated that with the exception of a small group of republicans thought to be led by Seán Russell, the IRA were very weak in both parts of Ireland due to internment. The thousands of German-trained guerillas, the Gauleiters-in-waiting, the well-placed Quislings, and the refueling U-boats which had featured in earlier SIS assessments were conspicuous by their absence.[38]

On 10 July Churchill minuted that a sudden invasion of Britain was now unlikely, although 'of course a small raid might be made upon Ireland from Brest. But this also would be dangerous to the raiders while at sea'.[39] The twelve months from June 1940 saw sporadic recrudescence of invasion fears, and the service departments continued to plan for the contingency of a German assault on Ireland until well into 1942. In September the JIC considered two scenarios: an attack as part of an invasion of Britain, or as 'part of the plan for the extension of the blockade' of Britain. Because of the reinforcement of BTNI, either option would require more

---

[34] Entry for 30 June 1940 in Dilks, *Cadogan Diaries*, 305.

[35] Malcolm MacDonald, speaking confidentially when high commissioner to Canada, 24 May 1941, Mackenzie King diaries, 24 May 1941.

[36] Churchill to Bevin, undated but *c*.19 June 1940, quoted in Canning, *British Policy Towards Ireland*, 279; de Valera to Chamberlain, 4 July 1940, and MacDonald to de Valera, 7 July 1965, UCDA, de Valera papers, P150/2548 and 2553.

[37] Canning, *British Policy Towards Ireland*, 282; Bayly and Harper, *Forgotten Armies*, 108.

[38] Ibid., 287.

[39] Churchill to Ismay, 10 July 1940, TNA, ADM223/484.

troops but was still feasible, especially as 'the nucleus' of 2,000 to 3,000 IRA men were 'all well armed'.[40] In November the GOC in Northern Ireland, Sir Henry Pownall, attended a conference on the possibility of an invasion of the British Isles during the winter months. Pownall outlined his views that the most likely attack on Ireland would be 'on a broad front from Cork to Rosslare', possibly with a diversionary raid on Lough Swilly, and subsidiary attacks to seize aerodromes in Limerick and Dublin. The planning staff had estimated that a force of five divisions would be involved, supported by up to 8,000 airborne troops. At this 'Winston gave a jump'. Two months later, Pownall had 'little doubt that they will go for England, and probably Eire at the same time, sometime in the spring or early summer'.[41]

Even Churchill continued to admit the possibility of German action, agreeing with the Earl of Selborne in January 1941 that 'the mad policy of de Valera' meant Ireland remained a tempting target for Hitler, though he clearly did not think an attack very likely. Other indications pointed in the same direction, including an agent report which Godfrey commended as 'an example of good Secret Service work'.[42] At the strategic level, however, apprehensions about the consequences of a German invasion soon gave way to contemplation of the means by which Ireland could either be coerced into the war, or have the decision made for her by the seizure of the ports.

This was a matter close to Churchill's heart and instincts. Following a steady clear-out from the cabinet of key advocates of conciliation towards Ireland—Halifax, Hoare, MacDonald, Caldecote, all of them tainted in Churchill's eyes by their association with Chamberlain's pre-war administration—and the strengthening of his personal position, the main constraints on such an approach were less domestic than international. It was true that the other dominions were somewhat critical of Irish neutrality—the Irish high commissioner in Ottawa in June 1940 told the American minister that 'he was having a hard time . . . as Irish neutrality was even less comprehensible to the average Canadian than American neutrality'—but their views were in part influenced by the geographical fact of Anglo-Irish contiguity, and they still grasped the historical roots of Irish policy.[43] Combined, at least in the case of Australia, with the potential influence of a significant Irish immigrant bloc, these factors made the dominions less condemnatory of the Irish position than Churchill would have wished, and this had some influence on his thinking. In April 1941 the Australian prime minister Robert Menzies, who some believed saw himself as potentially 'the first Dominion Prime Minister to become Prime Minister of Great Britain', visited Ireland after he and Churchill had discussed the idea with Colonel Bill Donovan, Roosevelt's intelligence confidante who had himself just made a flying visit to Dublin. Donovan thought the heart of the problem lay in Northern Ireland, and believed de Valera's expression of personal support for Britain. Menzies

---

[40] JIC (40), 286, 18 Sept. 1940, TNA, CAB81/98.

[41] Bond (ed.), *Chief of Staff*, 8–10, 2 Nov. and 31 Dec. 1940.

[42] Churchill to Selborne, 12 Jan. 1941, CCCA, CHAR20/29 A67, Godfrey to Board of Admiralty, 8 Apr., circulating agent report of 15 Feb. 1941, TNA, ADM223/484. This was from 'a very well placed source' who had spoken to a German war ministry official.

[43] Moffat journal, 14 June 1940, Harvard, MS 1407, vol. 45.

in turn circulated a surprisingly sympathetic memorandum setting out de Valera's views—the taoiseach desperately feared a German invasion, could not understand why Britain refused to provide anti-aircraft weapons and other supplies, said that he had long believed that partition could only be solved through peaceful means, and reiterated his genuine support for the British cause. Menzies told the India secretary Leo Amery that he 'liked de Valera personally, but thought him and all Irishmen crazy'.[44]

The British government increasingly looked to their control over Ireland's seaborne trade as a means of exerting pressure on Dublin. Ireland depended overwhelmingly on Britain for her imports, particularly of strategic commodities such as oil and coal, as well as many raw materials necessary for food production and for manufacturing. Agreements made by the Chamberlain government notwithstanding—on 6 September 1939 the Irish had transferred their six oil tankers to the British flag, in return for an undertaking on security of supplies—economic pressure was now applied in earnest. Supplies were progressively attenuated in 1941–2 to a point where, while the Irish were spared the horrors of war, they were exposed to many of the associated privations. The advantage of this policy was that it did not stir up any sympathy either in the dominions or the United States, because if Ireland complained she could be shown to be living off the fruits of the courage and endurance of the British merchant marine, while refusing to take any share in the risks and the casualties which it endured (and, arguably, contributing to those casualties by refusing Britain the use of her ports and airfields for Atlantic defence). In parallel with economic pressure, an unequivocal decision was taken by Churchill, against military advice, that Ireland should not receive any weapons, not even items which the chiefs of staff thought crucial to combating a German assault in its vital initial stages, such as anti-aircraft artillery for the defence of airfields. This was a brave policy decision, grounded not at all in the need to rebuild Britain's own defences and those of the dominions—although the Canadians, having sent surplus weapons to Britain when war broke out, found themselves so denuded of arms by mid-1940 that they appealed to the United States for supplies—but based equally on Churchill's hunch about the unlikelihood of a German assault on Ireland and on his anger at Irish neutrality.[45]

THE DEVELOPMENT OF ANGLO-IRISH SECURITY LIAISON AND OF GERMAN ESPIONAGE, 1940–1941

On 17 July Dublin instructed Dulanty to protest in writing to the dominions secretary about 'certain persons' who 'have of late made rather frequent visits':

[44] Ibid., quoting Malcolm MacDonald, 2 Sept. 1941, Harvard, MS 1407, vol. 46; Donovan [in London] to secretary of the navy, 11 Mar. 1941, Roosevelt papers, Safe Files, box 3, accessed via www.fdrlibrary.marist.edu; memorandum on visit to Ireland by R. G. Menzies, undated [between 5 and 10 Apr. 1941], in Hudson and Stokes (eds.), *Documents on Australian Foreign Policy*, 552; Amery diary, 18 Apr. 1941, CCCA, Amery papers, AMEL7/35.
[45] Moffat journal, 1 July 1940, Harvard, MS 1407, vol. 45.

these people have been talking to Deputies and other Irish citizens in a manner likely to be detrimental to the interests and general well-being of the Irish state. The visits have given us the definite impression that there was interference in the internal affairs of our country . . .

The Secretary of State will realize . . . how quickly the excellent work of the British Representative . . . could be brought to naught by well-meaning British busybodies who are ignorant both of the history of Ireland and of the abiding determination of its people to work out their own destiny.[46]

Dulanty reported that Caldecote remarked on reading the phrase: '"certain persons" . . . "I know of only one person. I suppose this refers to Tegart?" I agreed and said I thought there were others. He said that he could assure me that the Government had no part in . . . Tegart's visit and I got the impression that he attached no importance to it'.[47] By the elastic standards of diplomatic discourse, this may have been true: technically Tegart was simply paying private visits to his homeland. But he had been sent there by SIS, and his alarmist reports had been lapped up in Whitehall. Dulanty's message was clear: if Britain desired an accurate picture of what was happening in Ireland, she should seek it through diplomats and attachés rather than relying on infirm ex-Indian policemen. The idea of making explicit representations arose in a curious fashion: when Walshe initially complained,

Maffey turned to me quite earnestly and said that he was in a real difficulty about these 'agents'. He would be very grateful to me if I instructed Dulanty to go to Caldecote and tell him not to send Teggart [*sic*] and any other 'agents' there in future . . . He begged me not to mention his name in this connection, as he felt his position would not allow him to object to such missions. I was naturally amazed by this sudden complete avowal of the truth.[48]

Insofar as Britain took the hint, it was in respect of MI5's activities. Their overall aim was to maintain and to increase the security of the United Kingdom, and to do this they needed Irish help. This naturally predisposed them towards cooperation, and to work to ensure that the activities of British clandestine agencies were not such as to jeopardize the security link. MI5 also dealt extensively with BTNI and with the RUC, and of all the British agencies it was consequently the one best placed to provide an informed overview of Irish issues. The thirteen months from May 1940 to June 1941 saw a steady accretion in MI5's knowledge and grasp of Irish affairs, and a marked though uneven strengthening in their links with the key Irish and Northern Irish agencies and officers responsible for security questions.

MI5's dealings with the Irish were mediated through Maffey's office, where they were handled by the principal secretary, successively Maurice Antrobus (until 1941) and Norman Archer (for two periods between 1941 and 1948). In addition to extensive dominions and colonial experience, these were both veterans of the first world war, and Archer had been a career naval officer. They consequently had direct

---

[46] Dublin to Dulanty, 17 July 1940, NAI, DFA A6.
[47] Dulanty to Dublin, 9 Aug. 1940, NAI, DFA A6.
[48] Walshe to de Valera, 15 July 1940, UCDA, de Valera papers, P150/2571l. Tegart was rejected for the post of special adviser to SOE's newly established Indian section because of chronic ill-health. SOE Delhi to SOE London, 5 Apr. 1942, TNA, HS1/200.

knowledge of military affairs as well as of civil administration, and so were well placed to advise Maffey on these aspects of his dealings with the Irish.[49]

The new Security Executive was of immediate benefit for the handling of Irish affairs. Its chairman Swinton was only of the second rank as a politician; but he was tough, he was able, and he had extensive knowledge of Whitehall, having worked in Lloyd George's secretariat between 1919 and 1922 before going into politics. As befitted a Yorkshireman, he was not afraid to tread on toes and to knock heads together in order to make progress. One early result was the decision that SIS as well as MI5 operations in Ireland should be placed under the control of the Security Executive. This unusual step united responsibility for Anglo-Irish security liaison and for covert intelligence in Ireland. The decision was evidently taken on the assumption that MI5 and SIS would be working to the same agenda—broadly speaking, the reduction of security and espionage threats. There were also rumours that Swinton attempted to wrest overall control of SIS from the Foreign Office, but this did not happen.[50]

This link between the two agencies was a determining factor in how Ireland was handled for the next five years: there is no evidence of inter-agency squabbling between MI5 and SIS on Irish matters, nor any sign that SIS pursued a different agenda to MI5's. This may partly have been a matter of personalities: the Liddell brothers worked hard at maintaining good relations with Section V of SIS, and especially with Valentine Vivian under whose wing it came. SIS also had the good sense to employ the formidable Jane Archer to handle Irish matters after she was 'sacked for insubordination' by the inept acting head of MI5, Jasper Harker, in November 1940—'a very serious blow to us all', as Guy Liddell noted, telling Swinton that she was 'far more efficient than most of the men' and had always had 'a rather privileged position as a court jester although . . . she had undoubtedly overstepped the mark'. In fact her main error was one of timing: on 27 November Desmond Morton told Churchill that it was widely believed inside and outside MI5 'that Brigadier Harker has proved quite inadequate for his task and should be replaced', and within weeks he was.[51] Jane Archer dealt with Irish matters in Section V until after the Normandy invasion in 1944, when she returned to her former specialism of international communism. She was in constant touch with the Liddells, and by the end of the war her ability was widely recognized within MI5, and by at least one SIS colleague, the Soviet agent Kim Philby, who singled her out for praise in his memoirs: 'After Guy Liddell, Jane was perhaps the ablest professional intelligence officer employed by MI5'.[52]

[49] Maurice Antrobus (1895–1985). Colonial Office, 1920; High Commission to South Africa, 1935–9; principal secretary, British Representative's Office, 1939–41; assistant secretary, Commonwealth Relations Office, 1944–55; CMG, 1943. Norman Archer (1890–1970). Royal Navy, 1908–21; Colonial Office, 1921; assistant secretary, Imperial Conference, 1930, 1932, and 1937; private secretary to dominions secretary, 1939–40; CMG, 1944; assistant under-secretary, Commonwealth Relations Office, 1949–50.

[50] Dalton diary, 11 Oct. 1940 and 17 Jan. 1941, BLPES, Dalton 1/23 and 24.

[51] Liddell diary, 18 Nov. and 6 Dec., and Morton to Churchill, 27 Nov. 1940, TNA, KV4/187 and PREM7/6.

[52] Curry to Petrie (director general of MI5), undated [1945], in O'Halpin, *MI5 and Ireland*, 16; Philby, *My Silent War*, 79.

Herman Goertz, whose presence in Ireland became known on 22 May, proved to be the most formidable but not the last German agent to arrive in Ireland in 1940. On 13 June Walter Simon was arrested at a Dublin railway station on arrival from County Kerry. Simon had landed from a submarine in Dingle Bay, and had buried his radio set before making his way to Tralee. He became intoxicated along the way, and as a result talked indiscreetly. Two detectives followed him from Tralee, and arrested him in Dublin. He claimed to be a Swedish-born naturalized Australian seaman, Karl Anderson. Despite inconsistencies in his story, and despite the fact that he was carrying a very large amount of cash in a paper bag, it was only when his fingerprints were sent to Britain that his cover collapsed completely. The British police had him on record because he had been imprisoned and then deported from England in 1938 for espionage. 'Our old friend Simon' was highly valued by his Abwehr controller, although his Irish adventure scarcely smacked of great professionalism.[53]

Three more agents were arrested in Cork city in July just a few hours after landing from a yacht in west Cork (the vessel had been spotted by a coast-watcher but, probably through inefficiency, that report was not forwarded from the local Garda station to the military authorities).[54] Two of this improbable troika, Dieter Gartner and Herbert Tributh, were ethnic Germans from South-West Africa (what is now Namibia). Their companion, Henry Obed from Lucknow in India, had first come under IPI's notice as long before as 1923, when he was said to organize 'arms smuggling through Indian seamen whom he met through the Hamburg Bolshevik Club'. He was also believed to have trafficked in drugs while operating as an importer of live animals from Asia. Obed had been in prison in Belgium on suspicion of espionage when the Germans invaded.[55] The agents were carrying incendiary bombs and other compromising equipment, and under questioning claimed to be under orders to carry out acts of sabotage in Britain. Obed was there as their guide. Guy Liddell was disappointed but not surprised to find that 'the Irish do not wish us to interview their prisoners. This is unfortunate since we might have got quite a lot of information. I imagine the grounds are purely political'. In fact, so incongruous was Obed's group that External Affairs at first suspected that it might be a British plant.[56]

On 26 August the Garda arrested another German agent, Wilhelm Preetz, in Dublin and seized a transmitter, coding materials, and copies of coded messages: they had been seeking him for a passport offence. Preetz, who had landed undetected from a submarine in Dingle Bay towards the end of June, had formerly lived in County Galway and had many contacts. He had teamed up with an old acquaintance named Joseph Donohue, and the two men spent some dissolute weeks in Dublin blowing the Abwehr's money on women and drink. Preetz did manage to make

[53] Hull, *Irish Secrets*, 111–13; Liddell diary, 19 July 1940, TNA, KV4/186; Kahn, *Hitler's Spies*, 292. Simon's MI5 file is TNA, KV2/1293.

[54] Ibid., 121.

[55] 'History Sheet' dated 26 Apr. 1934, criminal intelligence note dated 24 July 1937, and IPI to Silver (India Office), 20 July 1940, BL, L/PJ/12/477.

[56] MI5's papers on this group are in TNA, KV2/1296; Liddell diary, 17 July 1940, KV4/186; Hull, *Irish Secrets*, 125.

some transmissions, which were picked up by British intercept services and decoded. One indicated that 'a man called Donaghue [*sic*], who is presumably a German agent, is coming over here in the . . . next few days', but fortunately for him he did not travel.[57] The Irish army then also began to intercept his transmissions, but it was the Garda who independently tracked down the two men and arrested them—MI5 had expressed a hope that the transmissions might be allowed to continue, but the arrests made this impossible. Preetz had received only rudimentary radio training, and analysis of his messages by MI5 showed that he had not sent any significant information. G2 turned to the director of the National Library of Ireland, the polyglot Dr Richard Hayes, for help. As the coding material and text of messages had been captured, Hayes had no difficulty in handling the material: 'no work was necessary beyond writing a report on the system'.[58] One worrying aspect of the Preetz case was his association while in Dublin with Italian fascists, but no evidence emerged then or later that these had been involved in intelligence gathering.[59]

The Irish supplied details of what was found on these agents and on their interrogations, and pursued further lines of questioning suggested by MI5. Guy Liddell was concerned to ensure that London got the full story: 'there is still much detail that we should like to know. They have brightly told us that no useful purpose would be served by sending over an officer', a reflection of Irish caution in the delicate circumstances of the time.[60] MI5 were naturally sensitive about possible links between the agents captured in Ireland and the dozen or so under arrest in Britain, particularly as a number of the latter were being groomed to, or had already begun to, send back disinformation. In July MI5's prize double agent *Snow* received a message stating that another agent would shortly be landed either in Ireland or in Britain, and that *Snow* should obtain details of travel regulations between the islands. This message, which probably referred to Gunther Schutz, who eventually arrived in Ireland in March 1941, confirmed that German agent operations in Ireland and in Britain were to an extent interconnected.[61]

The link with Ireland was significant in terms of Britain's wider security interests. In December 1940 J. C. Masterman, an Oxford historian imported into MI5 during the first year of the war, wrote a persuasive analysis of the problems encountered in dealing with double agents. He pointed out that the ability of MI5 and SIS to keep existing double agents in play by feeding them credible material which they could relay to their German controllers was being inhibited by the understandable reluctance of the fighting services to allow genuine information to be used. There was a danger that the enemy would lose faith in the agents already under British control, and instead recruit others who might not be so easily caught. In addition, the opportunity was being lost of exploiting enemy trust in their existing agents to create notional networks of sub-agents. Finally, 'only by constant advance planning

[57] Liddell diary, 27 July 1940, TNA, KV4/186. Donohue did go to London in April 1942 to work in a pub.

[58] Valedictory report on codebreaking from 1940 to 1945 by Dr Richard Hayes, 2 Jan. 1946, National Library of Ireland, Richard Hayes MS 22984, cited hereafter as 'Hayes report'.

[59] Hull, *Irish Secrets*, 119–20. MI5 files on him are in TNA, KV2/1303–6.

[60] Liddell diary, 2 Aug. 1940, TNA, KV4/186.

[61] Ibid., 19 July 1940, TNA, KV4/186.

and by the maintenance of an adequate flow of consistent and plausible reports can the "double-agent" system be kept in being and made available for effective use' as a tool for 'large scale deception . . . at a critical moment'. There 'is a real danger that the "double-agent" system which has been built up will be allowed to collapse because no adequate use has been made of it'.[62]

Written at a time when everyone's energies were spent on securing national survival, this remarkably prescient document laid the intellectual foundations for what, as the tide of war slowly changed, became a highly sophisticated method of strategic deception. Masterman's memorandum became the founding charter of the 'Twenty (XX) Committee', representative of MI5, SIS, and the fighting services, and charged to oversee the management of double agents, which first met on 2 January 1941. The process was colloquially designated the 'Double Cross' system, the term used hereafter to describe it.[63] Besides careful planning, coordination, and the meticulous management of each double agent's relationship with Germany, the success of Double Cross lay in Britain's ability to read Abwehr codes (the decodes were known as ISOS).[64] This source was so secret that C only gave permission for all members of the Twenty Committee to be told about it in June 1942.[65] Consequently it is no surprise that in their dealings with G2 MI5 made only very limited reference to double-agent operations. Where these had an Irish angle, as with *Snow* and later with *Rainbow* and *Basket*, it was a complicating element in cooperation. Dan Bryan of G2 only learned of the eventual scale and success of Double Cross when Masterman's contraband account appeared in the United States in 1971 as *The Double-Cross System in the War of 1939 to 1945* (Masterman had been unsuccessful in earlier attempts to secure official permission to publish his 'precious (though illegal) possession').[66] Nevertheless, MI5 asked Bryan at least once to run a double agent from Ireland, and he disclosed to them that he had his own people on ships trading with Europe.[67]

On 13 March 1941 a man claiming to be a South African named Hans Marschner was arrested in County Wexford, shortly after landing by parachute. He was carrying a considerable sum of money, £1,000 in forged British banknotes, a radio, some papers, and a microscope. Under interrogation by G2, Marschner proved 'extremely evasive . . . admitting nothing unless . . . documentary evidence' supported it.[68] He acknowledged that he was an Abwehr agent, and that he had received some basic training in meteorology so that he could send weather reports. He also claimed that he was to pass on the radio to an agent who would come from Britain to collect it. Liam Archer thought this was a fabrication intended to obscure his Irish contacts, but it was true: the man concerned was in fact the long-established MI5 double

[62] Memorandum by Masterman, 27 Dec. 1940, TNA, KV4/63; Masterman, *On the Chariot Wheel*, 211–26.

[63] Minutes of 1st meeting of Twenty committee, 2 Jan. 1941, TNA, KV4/63.

[64] ISOS was an acronym for 'Intelligence Services Oliver Strachey'.

[65] Masterman to C, and reply, 5 and 11 June 1942, TNA, KV4/65.

[66] The JIC were appalled when, despite the government's best efforts, Masterman published his book beyond the grasp of the Official Secrets Act. JIC(A)(1971), 31st meeting, 12 Aug. 1971, TNA, CAB185/7; Masterman to Swinton, 20 Apr. 1961, CCCA, Swinton papers, SWIN 4/4.

[67] *Liddell History*, 67.

[68] Liddell diary, 21 May 1941, TNA, KV4/186.

agent *Rainbow*.[69] Marschner had been instructed to contact Carl Petersen at the German legation, and a Dublin-to-Berlin cable of 14 January 1941, decoded in 1943, indicates that a visitor, perhaps a courier, was expected from Europe.[70]

Marschner, whom it transpired was already known to the British from pre-war days as Gunther Schutz, concealed the fact that his key contact in Ireland was to be Werner Unland, already under Irish and British surveillance, that he was also to give money to another German named Ernstberger who had come to Ireland from Britain in May 1939, that in addition to weather reporting he was to collect economic intelligence on Northern Ireland, and that amongst his documents was a microdot containing his instructions, radio procedures, and other information. G2 found the microdot, together with sufficient clues amongst his effects to confirm the connection with Unland, against whom there was already evidence from postal interception. Investigation of Ernstberger revealed nothing save his pronounced Nazi sympathies, and he was kept under surveillance, but Unland was interned. Later interrogations and information from Britain showed that Schutz had collected intelligence there before the war while posing as a sales representative, and that while visiting Spain in 1940 he had received some correspondence from Unland at a Barcelona hotel.[71] *Rainbow* also identified him 'without hesitation' to MI5 as the man who early in 1939 had asked him in London to collect intelligence.[72] He was, in short, an agent of some experience.

On 21 May 1941 the Liddell brothers flew to Dublin for discussions with Archer, who took them to his home. Archer was 'highly interested in the identification of Marschner with Schutz'. They also discussed wireless interception, as the Irish had not yet succeeded in pinpointing the illicit transmissions which the RSS had picked up. The Liddells offered to help to expedite a fresh order for modern direction-finding sets, as the six already sent had been appropriated by the Irish signals corps and adapted for other purposes. They also sounded Archer out on the possibility of erecting RDF (radio direction finding) masts along the east coast, and concluded that he would support the proposal if the 'necessary equipment' was provided. The most significant matter discussed, however, was political: 'Before we left', Archer asked about Britain's reported plan to introduce conscription in Northern Ireland. The proposal had originated with the minister for labour Ernest Bevin, ironically a man reasonably well disposed towards Ireland and with considerable knowledge of her from his time there as a trade-union organizer before the first world war, who noted disappointingly poor recruitment figures from Northern Ireland (inflated by an unknown but substantial number of southerners). The scheme was supported by the Belfast administration. Archer said there was 'great anxiety . . . there would undoubtedly be bloodshed', and:

he could not understand what we had to gain . . . So far 150,000 had enlisted from the South and 19,000 from the North. 600 a month are crossing the Border to enlist. Our flying-boats

[69] Ibid.; *Liddell History*, 58.
[70] Hull, *Irish Secrets*, 156. The decode could not have been made before January 1943.
[71] Ibid., 148–62; Liddell diary, 27 Apr. 1941, TNA, KV4/189.
[72] Liddell diary, 20 May 1941, TNA, KV4/187; Hull, *Irish Secrets*, 152–3.

on Transatlantic patrol get up off Lough Erne every day and fly over Eire territory so low that it would be impossible . . . to say that they could not recognize their markings. Troops from the north constantly wander across the border and instead of being interned are shepherded back . . .

If conscription is enforced . . . a large number of the Catholics will refuse to register and if any attempt is made to prosecute them they will go on the run and join the IRA. Feeling in the south will be extremely bad and it seems quite likely that the Eire Gov[ernmen]t will try and enforce stricter neutrality.[73]

Archer's words made a strong impression. On returning to London, Guy Liddell showed Swinton a note of the talks. Swinton immediately arranged for Liddell and Vivian to 'go straight on' to brief Sir John Anderson, the war cabinet's home affairs expert. He in turn asked Liddell to prepare a paper for a war cabinet discussion of the question, and this he used during the meeting.[74] Its particular impact cannot be assessed, as there were many voices against conscription: the American ambassador signaled unease, and after reflecting on an approach by the Irish high commissioner in Ottawa, who warned that the measure would be disastrous and that Dublin 'has done and is doing a great many things to help the British in a very real way', Mackenzie King sent Churchill a long cable warning of the possible repercussions in Canada (where he was embroiled in a conscription controversy himself, as had also arisen during the first world war, primarily due to French Canadian resistance to compulsory service).[75]

In London Dulanty, who had known Churchill since 1908, put the Irish view in two fraught interviews. He argued that, 'owing to the highly partisan selectivity of supporters of the Six County Government to fill the ranks of the Home Guard, the B Specials, and the ARP organization, the comparatively small number available as conscripts would be men of the nationalist minority', who would go to prison rather than serve under compulsion. Churchill, who stressed his long-standing support for Irish freedom and his own hopes for a united Ireland, and declaimed against what he regarded as Irish repudiation of the treaty, said that Cranborne, the dominions secretary, had perceived an Irish threat to withdraw existing security cooperation if the measure was introduced. This was a very significant misapprehension, since such cooperation was central to Irish neutrality policy and Dulanty had no instructions to issue any such warning. He contacted Cranborne, who accepted that he had misunderstood Dulanty's arguments. On 26 May Dulanty met again with Churchill, who was in chaotic mode and

became at times emotional and would suddenly stop and say petulantly: 'But why should I go on like this?' (I should have liked to ask 'What was the good?' also). I do not think that there was any play acting because this tendency of his to emotion is the cause of some apprehension among his own supporters . . .

---

[73] Liddell diary, 11 May 1941, TNA, KV4/187; *Liddell History*, 63. The commander of the Irish army air corps made very similar remarks to the RAF's Air Commodore Carr. Report by Colonel Mulcahy, 31 Mar. 1941, NAI, DFA A3.

[74] Ibid., 23 May 1941, TNA, KV4/187; *Liddell History*, 61–2.

[75] Mackenzie King diary, 23 and 24 May 1941; Moffat journal, 12 Mar. and 29 Apr. 1941, Harvard, MS 1407, vol. 46; Hennessey, *History of Northern Ireland*, 91–2.

The atmosphere of this and the preceding interview was unfriendly. There was no exchange of views, no consideration of the position and its difficulties, but a torrent of talk . . . which seemed sometimes to overwhelm that gentleman himself . . .

His feeling of hostility was known; these conversations made crystal clear the depth and bitterness of that hostility.[76]

On the same day, and despite Churchill's passionate advocacy, the war cabinet agreed that the measure would be far more trouble than it was worth.[77] Wickham of the RUC gave Guy Liddell a pithy analysis of the crisis, in terms almost indistinguishable from Dublin's: 'the whole thing was a political ramp, by politicians in N[orthern] Ireland. They wanted to appear as great loyalists but in actual fact hoped that their suggestions would not be acceptable . . . Had it been accepted they intended to conscript the Catholics and leave the Orangemen in the factories'.[78]

The Liddells' dealings with Archer demonstrate that a high degree of mutual trust had already developed, but there were unspoken limits to Anglo-Irish security cooperation in 1940–1 in two crucial matters. The first was the activities of Goertz, whose equipment and money had been seized in May 1940. He remained at liberty for eighteen months, an almost inexplicable length of time, given the efficiency of the Garda in respect of other agents and of the IRA. Goertz was the most purposeful of the agents to reach Ireland. Sheltered by a network of republican sympathizers, amongst them a number of women who fell for him, he developed an inflated idea of himself as an unofficial emissary. This was not entirely his own fault: a number of significant Irish figures, including Major General Hugo MacNeill, made contact with him to explore the possibility of Irish–German cooperation against Britain. Such matters were well outside his original brief, which was to encourage IRA activity in Northern Ireland. Goertz soon despaired of the IRA, but he used republicans to collect intelligence in Northern Ireland which he then attempted to send to Germany. From April 1941 he had the services of a radio operator and a set provided by the IRA, and was able to send some information. He also fed some material indirectly to officers of the 2nd Northern Division along the border, including the divisional intelligence officer Major Niall MacNeill, in Dan Bryan's view a convinced 'Nazi' who was 'was inclined to act on his own' and was also in touch with the German legation.[79] He made two serious but abortive efforts to return to the continent. G2 got wind of the second of these schemes, which involved the purchase of a motor boat in Kerry in February 1941. This led to the discovery that James Crofton of the Special Branch was an IRA sympathizer who had betrayed various Garda operations and was probably responsible for identifying one minor informant, Michael Devereaux, murdered by the IRA in September 1940. Goertz, his identity still a mystery, managed to

[76] Dulanty to Dublin (by letter), 22 and 26 May 1941, NAI, DFA P12/14(i).

[77] Canning, *British Policy Towards Ireland*, 307–9. Two years later Churchill still seethed about the decision. Churchill to Attlee, 5 May 1943, TNA, DO121/84.

[78] Liddell diary, 27 May 1941, TNA, KV4/186.

[79] Hull, *Irish Secrets*, 70–5; O'Halpin, *Defending Ireland*, 245; amongst Goertz's inamoratas was Iseult Stuart, his first contact in Ireland and a close friend of the Hempels. Interview with her son Ian in the *Sunday Independent*, 18 March 2007. This interview is understandably somewhat inaccurate in details.

avoid arrest in Kerry, but Crofton was captured and jailed, a significant coup for G2 in its own squabbles with the Garda. This development caused considerable excitement in London, even though the connection with Goertz was not realized at the time.[80]

Much of the details of Goertz's activities in 1940–1 only became clear to MI5 in 1943 and 1944, after Richard Hayes broke the cipher used by Goertz and one of his Irish helpers.[81] But in 1940 and 1941 plenty of rumours about his activities and contacts reached British ears. G2 did not furnish MI5 with any information on Goertz: when Bryan visited London in November 1941 he was under clear instructions from External Affairs to say only that the Irish had a good line on the elusive agent and were confident that they would soon catch him (as they did, less than a fortnight later).[82] Although they could hardly be blamed for not recognizing it, in the same month the British were presented with one potential lead. This was when a man named Joseph Andrews approached 'the Chief Enquiry Officer, HM Customs & Excise', with a view to selling 'the names and addresses of some 1300 agents' of the Irish Hospitals Sweepstake in the United States. Andrews, who had been fired from the Sweepstake in 1938, claimed that these agents were 'providing funds for the IRA' as well as 'defrauding the US Treasury' (the latter was true). Finding the British uninterested, he sold his information to the American legation, resulting in a number of prosecutions in the United States. Andrews, 'an intelligent, plausible and unscrupulous Double Crosser . . . [whose] wife is said to be even more dangerous than he is', also got in touch with Goertz through the IRA. Incredibly, this incorrigible rogue also had a pre-war link with Guy Liddell: his father, a butcher in the north Dublin coastal village of Rush, 'buys his sheep on Lambay', the island home of Liddell's father-in-law Lord Revelstoke, and had once asked Liddell 'to find his son a job in the police'.[83]

The second area of difficulty in MI5's dialogue with G2 was rather more significant: the secret transmitter housed in the German legation. From the time, early in 1940, when the British first raised the possibility that Hempel was using a radio, the Irish reaction was extremely cautious. There were good technical reasons for hesitancy, because the British could not accurately pinpoint the source of the messages picked up from Ireland, and because G2 had to build an intercept section from scratch. On 1 January 1941, however, GC&CS decoded parts of a cable from the Italian embassy in Washington to their Dublin legation. This garbled text was sufficient to disclose a key secret: Hempel 'has obtained facilities for a connection by wireless telegraph between Dublin and Berlin', and Berardis was advised to ask his Axis colleague to permit him to send specially urgent or secret

[80] O'Halpin, *Defending Ireland*, 205; index recording various exchanges with SIS re Crofton, Mar. 1941, TNA, KV3/120. Crofton had resigned from the Garda a week before his arrest. Garda report, Tralee, 20 Feb. 1941, MAI, G2/1682.

[81] *Liddell History*, 76.

[82] Bryan's travel papers show that he was in Britain from 8 to 15 Nov. 1941. UCDA, Bryan papers, P71/408.

[83] Liddell diary, 5 Apr. 1943, TNA, KV4/191. Andrews's father James was a peace commissioner, a mark of minor civil standing. The redacted minute sheet of the MI5 general file on IRA-German contacts records a letter from Andrews about the Hospitals Sweepstake dated November 1940, and various communications with SIS relating to him. TNA, KV3/120.

communications over that link.[84] The significance of this was clear: Vivian of SIS wrote that it 'undoubtedly affords complete proof' that Hempel 'is operating a wireless set'.[85] The German legation radio was to be the single biggest issue in Anglo-Irish security relations until the problem was finally disposed of in December 1943. This concentrated minds in MI5, SIS, and the Dominions Office. The problem for the British in January 1941 was, first how to detect this transmitter in operation, and secondly how to prompt the Irish also to look for and to detect the transmitter independently: for obvious reasons, London was unwilling to tell Dublin that their information came from decoded Italian traffic.

Confirmation of the presence of a German radio can hardly have come as an enormous surprise. I have already noted that illicit radios were a feature of many diplomatic missions, both those of belligerents and of neutrals. As late as April 1944, London hesitated to act against the Swedish embassy radio, despite clear evidence that the Swedish military attaché's reports were reaching the Germans, because the Swedes knew perfectly well that there was a set in the British embassy in Stockholm, although it had never been used.[86] The British had their own sets in Dublin (where Walshe advised de Valera in July 1940 that it would be 'safer for us to make the assumption' that such supplementary communications links were intended as much to 'facilitate the British Army in its task of reoccupation', if necessary, as to provide warnings of a German attack), some of which were known to the Irish.[87]

Early in 1941 RSS succeeded in picking up a transmission 'in a diplomatic cipher . . . within a triangle around Dublin. The signals were very weak and the interception was difficult', but the traffic was to the German diplomatic wireless station at Nauen.[88] Although RSS had a presence in Northern Ireland, a precise fix on the station was likely to be achieved only through local direction-finding. The Irish were told that RSS believed the signal emanated from a point north of Dublin, although Maffey also 'mentioned in particular the possibility of the German legation having a secret wireless', but Irish signals officers could detect nothing.[89] A month later Maffey gave more details to Walshe, who was 'most perturbed and asked for further assistance in detecting and locating the German transmitter'. This was provided, but the Irish made no response, resulting in further representations by Maffey and by the Liddells during a visit in May—Cecil Liddell afterwards told Vivian that he was anxious lest too strident complaints by Maffey about Irish inaction might 'get Colonel Archer into bad odour with Walshe'. On 9 June Maffey reported that Walshe had informed Hempel that the Irish would not tolerate private wireless transmissions, but that Walshe had most probably not directly asked whether the legation possessed one. Walshe also 'assumes that we have the key to the German codes'.[90] MI5 noted that transmissions from Dublin then stopped, although those from Nauen continued.

---

[84] Rome to Berardis, 28 Dec. 1940, TNA, HW12/259.
[85] Vivian (SIS) to Stephenson (Dominions Office), 25 Jan. 1941, TNA, DO121/84.
[86] Liddell diary, 20 Apr. 1944, TNA, KV4/193.
[87] *Liddell History*, 80; Walshe to de Valera, 15 July 1940, NAI, DFA, A2.
[88] Ibid., 63; Liddell diary, 22 July 1941, TNA, KV4/188.
[89] Walshe to de Valera, 19 Feb. 1941, NAI, DFA A2.
[90] Maffey to Stephenson, 9 May 1941, TNA, DO121/84.

By then G2's new intercept unit had succeeded in tracing the transmissions to the legation. A radio watch was established in a nearby barracks while de Valera pondered this disagreeable discovery. To attempt to force the issue might provoke a diplomatic rupture at a time when Germany was in the ascendant; even if it did not, the least the Germans could demand would be that the same requirement would be set for all foreign missions, something which the British would certainly not accept, having already secured Irish acquiescence for their own secret sets. Cecil Liddell wrote to Archer to say that 'I am now in a position to give you very much more detailed information', and suggested that he and an expert travel over to Dublin.[91] This proposal was met with 'a certain coolness', the stated reasons being that Archer had been promoted out of G2, that his successor Bryan needed time to settle in, and that Walshe was on leave.[92] The Irish feared that any technical discussions would inevitably involve disclosing the source of the transmissions, resulting in an unequivocal British demand that action be taken to end them even if this caused a breach in Irish–German diplomatic relations. Dr Hayes was asked to attempt to break the traffic, while Dublin prevaricated in its response to insistent British queries. The consequence of these Irish tactics was a sharp cooling in relations between MI5 and G2.[93] That, combined with the change in control of G2, led MI5 to fear the worst. Guy Liddell considered this 'rather a serious blow as I doubt whether his [Archer's] no. two is sufficiently strong to resist pressure from above'.[94] He could scarcely have been more wrong.

MI5's dealings with the Northern Ireland authorities saw a similar pattern of increasing engagement. Sensitivities were less but were still present: the RUC remained antagonistic towards outside agencies, despite a lack of expertise in counter-espionage. In August 1940 Cecil Liddell and other MI5 officers visited Belfast to review security arrangements, noting a degree of confusion between the military, naval, and civil police authorities about the overall direction of the security effort, and identifying a range of problems in respect of the censorship of mails, telephone traffic, and telegrams between the two Irish jurisdictions. Such issues were complicated by politics and doubts about the political reliability of many Post Office employees, and by the inescapable fact that the border was 'completely open from a security intelligence point of view'.[95] In considering their report, the Security Executive noted that the 'Ulster authorities . . . were inclined to be somewhat sensitive'.[96] The dominant figure in security matters was Wickham of the RUC, who inspired great confidence and who kept his political masters largely out of the picture. Assisted by Captain Roger Moore, Superintendent Moffat, and

---

[91] Cecil Liddell to Archer, 28 June 1941, TNA, DO121/84.

[92] Bryan to Guy Liddell, 8 July 1941, and entry for 28 June 1941 in 'Dealings with the Eire Authorities in the matter of the German legation Wireless Transmitter in Dublin', with C to Cadogan (Foreign Office), 20 Apr. 1943, TNA, DO121/84.

[93] Walshe to de Valera, 18 Mar. 1941, NAI, DFA A2; O'Halpin, *Defending Ireland*, 187–9; *Liddell History*, 63–4; Vivian to Stephenson, 12 June 1941, and 'Dealings with the Eire Authorities . . .', 17 Apr. 1943; Maffey to Stephenson, 16 May 1941, TNA, DO121/84.

[94] SIS summary of dealings with the Irish on the radio question, 17 Apr. 1943, TNA, DO121/84; Liddell diary, 16 July 1941, TNA, KV4/188.

[95] Report on visit by MI5 representatives to 'North Ireland', 28–30 Aug. 1940, TNA, HO45/20570.

[96] Security Executive minutes, 6 Sept. 1940, TNA, CAB93/2.

Inspector Gilfillan of the Special Branch, he held most of the threads of security operations. He had some differences with the navy, whose anxieties about coastal security the RUC were not inclined to share and whom in general Wickham thought alarmist, and he was dismissive of local politicians.[97] He offered advice on how to deal with the IRA threat should the Germans invade and British forces cross the border to confront them:

It would be unwise to overestimate the IRA as a German ally or the amount of assistance that they could give here . . . other than starting riots in Belfast. To deal with them requires a considerable amount of experience in the country and our experience of strange intelligence officers is not very happy. In the South the Government is just as anti-IRA as in the North and should the troops enter Eire by request they would be wise to leave the IRA to the Civic Guard, giving assistance if requested rather than to try and teach the Civic Guard a job at which they are quite expert.[98]

On some key questions the approach Wickham advocated was completely at odds with the priorities of the Northern administration. He had no time for talk of sealing the border, something for which his government pressed in 1941, regarding it as completely impractical despite the views of the service departments and of Unionist ministers. Wickham also complained to MI5 that it was 'ridiculous' for the postal censorship authorities in London to 'make suggestions' about censorship controls 'without prior consultation' when they were 'entirely ignorant of local conditions'. He 'would not entertain' the proposal that 'the B Specials, who are pure Orangemen, should patrol the border between various censorship points . . . he would not entertain anything of the kind', as 'it would certainly lead to trouble if B Specials were let loose in Catholic areas'. Wickham also stressed to London Dublin's resolve to suppress the IRA and the general effectiveness of Garda operations against the IRA since the spring of 1940.[99]

Overseen by the justice minister Gerry Boland, a man with considerable personal experience of subversion and imprisonment, from April 1940 there was a marked toughening in the Irish response to IRA activities. In that month two IRA internees detained since September 1939 died on hunger strike, something which would have been unthinkable even six months before. On 3 June Boland issued over 400 internment orders, and over the next six months large numbers of IRA men and women, some significant and many small fry, were detained. What remained of the movement's leadership was bitterly split on a range of issues which were to come to a head in the autumn of 1941, with the kidnapping and court martial of the IRA chief of staff Stephen Hayes, inflicting near terminal damage.[100] When an RUC officer visited Garda headquarters in June 1940 for what was apparently the first in-depth discussion between the two police forces, he was given a list of almost 500 internees together with details of Garda operations against would-be fifth columnists. This

[97] Addendum by secretary on 'proposed special patrol of the N.E. coast of Ulster', with Security Executive minutes, 16 July 1941, TNA, CAB93/2.

[98] Extract from letter by Wickham, 11 Sept. 1940, TNA, KV4/280.

[99] Security Executive minutes, 13 Aug. 1941, TNA, CAB93/2; Liddell diary, 27 May 1941, TNA, KV4/186.

[100] O'Halpin, *Defending Ireland*, 247–50; Ó Longaigh, *Emergency Law in Independent Ireland*, 246, and tables 5a and 5b at pp. 302–3.

exchange was a harbinger of the close cooperation which was to follow.[101] In April 1941 NID reported a 'general impression . . . that . . . the Government have the IRA well in hand', a far cry from assessments of the movement's strength and standing a year earlier.[102]

Garda, RUC, and British police successes against the IRA from 1939 to 1941 were attributable very largely to three factors: the reinstatement of extraordinary powers of detention in both jurisdictions, justified not only by the specific republican threat but by the onset of European war; the age-old police practice of watching obvious places and individuals for anything out of the ordinary, which time and again produced results; and the contributions of mainly low-level informants. There is consequently a certain irony in the fact that, among the perceptive Guy Liddell's closest confidantes in the contemplation of the dangers posed by the IRA and of Axis espionage generally were Anthony Blunt of MI5, the erratic but stimulating Guy Burgess, and the perceptive and emollient Kim Philby of SIS, all of them long-term Soviet 'moles'.[103]

The Northern Ireland border, and the movements of people across the Irish Sea, were not the only travel issues which had to be addressed. Early in 1941 it became known that negotiations were under way for the development of a flying boat service between Lisbon and Foynes in the Shannon estuary. This service was to be operated by BOAC (British Overseas Airways Corporation), which was already using Foynes for transatlantic travel. There was a scramble to ensure appropriate security arrangements: BOAC in Lisbon were instructed not to permit any Irish passport holders, or anyone resident in either part of Ireland, to use the service; and the Irish agreed that all mail carried on the service would be subject to British censorship. It was also agreed that an Irish diplomatic bag could be consigned on both services, provided that assurances were forthcoming that only appropriate material would be included.[104] Foynes was to become a very important stopping-off point for transatlantic travel by civilian seaplanes, and for the Irish a crucial listening post on European and American opinion.[105]

The treatment of crashed or shipwrecked Allied servicemen, mostly aircrew, who turned up in Ireland was an irritant in Anglo-Irish relations. The Irish generally interned such arrivals, as required of a neutral state by international law, just as they did German servicemen, whereas troops who strayed across the border were simply sent back. British and German internees were housed in adjacent compounds in the defence complex at the Curragh, outside Dublin. The British were routinely allowed parole, which facilitated contact with sympathizers and with the British escape service MI9. On 26 June 1941 a carefully planned escape by nine RAF men took place—British and Irish accounts differ markedly on the crucial question of

---

[101] McMahon, 'Covert Operations and Official Collaboration', 54.

[102] Admiralty weekly intelligence report no. 59, 25 Apr. 1941, CCCA, Drax papers, 5/6.

[103] O'Halpin, 'The Guy Liddell Diaries and British Intelligence History', 670–86; Carter, *Anthony Blunt*, 249–302.

[104] *Liddell History*, 71–2. An exception to the no-travel rule could be made for Irish officials. Security Executive minutes, 20 and 27 Feb. 1941, TNA, CAB93/2. The Irish bag was, of course, subject to clandestine British inspection.

[105] See the regular G2 reports on passengers and their comments in NAI, DFA A3, A8, and A8/1.

whether this involved a breach of parole, since the scheme involved a man returning from parole feigning illness and so distracting the guards. Two of the escapers were caught at a nearby roadblock, but the other seven got clear. They were sheltered in Dublin before travelling by train to Northern Ireland.[106] The Irish traced at least some of the men through telephone taps on suspected helpers, but External Affairs told G2 to turn a blind eye.[107] The incident was a public embarrassment to the Irish—the German legation complained about Irish insecurity, and demanded the release of an equal number of German airmen—and Walshe made a strong protest to Maffey. The response was unapologetic and robust, but significantly the Irish complaint was 'so sharp' that MI9 'refrained from organizing any more escapes' in Ireland, although there was a number of further attempts by individuals.[108] There were plenty of pro-British people still willing to take a chance—financial rewards were available for anyone who helped fleeing aircrew—and consequently there were a few more escapes. Reflecting on such episodes in 1983, Dan Bryan took a fatalistic view and said that while these were a political embarrassment they did not impinge on practical security cooperation.

COVERT COUNTERESPIONAGE AND INTELLIGENCE GATHERING IN IRELAND, 1940–1941

The Irish took a measured and perhaps unduly sanguine view of British clandestine activities in the first year of the war. Reviewing developments during 1940, Bryan wrote that

there is reasonable evidence that in the panic following the collapse of France tentative measures were considered . . . by certain persons for the establishment of intelligence centres in Ireland on behalf of Great Britain. It is not certain that those measures were in the fullest degree official. There is no recent evidence of such an organization or activities and it is reasonably certain that a proposed organization for certain radio work has been discontinued. The position of Germany and Britain for the collection of information in this country is however completely different. Germany is practically completely isolated and has no contacts here. On the other hand British officers, officials and privileged members of the public generally can visit this country at will. They have friends in all parts and in all classes and meet frequently persons who are usually fully informed as to the general position . . . Further in the ultimate there are no effective restrictions on the transmission of information to Great Britain and, therefore, little need for the creation of a special organization either for collection of information or its transmission.[109]

Within a few months, however, G2 had penetrated a new SIS network, and were investigating traces of what turned out to be SOE activities.

---

[106] Foot and Langley, *MI9*, 116–17; on Irish internment of belligerents generally see Dwyer, *Guests of the Nation*.

[107] Report by officer commanding, Curragh Camp, 26 June 1941, NAI, DFA, P44; author's discussion with one of the escapers, Group Captain Hugh Verity, Cambridge, 1986; Bryan interview, 1983.

[108] Foot and Langley, *MI9*, 117; German minister to External Affairs, 25 July 1941, NAI, DFA P44.

[109] Draft G2 annual report for 1940, UCDA, Bryan papers, P71/30.

In June 1940 SIS established a professional presence in Ireland through the appointment of Captain C. S. Collinson to head the newly established British Travel Permit Office. Collinson, originally of the Royal Engineers, was a career SIS officer who had previously served in Paris, from which his family fled on 9 June: 'They just walked out of their flat and turned the key in the door'. A collector of ceramics, he also had 'some modern pictures' and was a devotee of the Russian ballet.[110] Once the 'U-boats in Irish inlets' panic had dissipated, his main covert role was a counter-intelligence one, to monitor Axis and pro-Axis activities, although even in his public persona of chief permit officer he was a conduit for the exchange of confidential material with the Irish about people wishing to travel between the two islands, some of it gleaned from police reports and some from postal censorship. Collinson reported to Section V of SIS headquarters, which from 1 August 1940 was given a curious second identity as Section B26 of MI5. This enabled greater coordination and sharing of access to records between the two organizations, and the arrangement continued throughout the war. It eventually fell victim to inter-service rivalry in 1946, as the two agencies squabbled over their respective post-war roles.[111]

Working with an official of the British Trade Commissioner's office who may also have been an SIS officer, Collinson developed networks of informants in Dublin and other major towns and along the southern and western coastlines. Amongst his principal assistants was the manager of the Dublin office of the credit control agency Stubbs Gazette, Albert Podesta. Podesta was, his Italian name notwithstanding, a Cork Protestant and a first world war veteran. He was passionately loyal to Britain. An enthusiast by nature, before the war he had been involved in the 'Safety First Association', and had even made a radio broadcast on safety. Collinson first met him at a social function, and eventually asked him to help. Stubbs provided good cover for low-level intelligence gathering because the firm routinely investigated the financial affairs of individuals and enterprises, often employing enquiry agents on a casual basis (although Stubbs had been suggested, along with the travel agency Thomas Cook, as a possible international cover organization for SIS immediately after the first world war, Stubbs headquarters evidently did not know anything about the Dublin operation: when the general manager was due to visit from London in 1942, Collinson 'gave orders that all work by P[odesta]'s group should stop for the week').[112]

There was no shortage of people willing to aid the British cause. Many amateur sleuths came to Garda attention, sometimes resulting in warnings to desist and even threats of internment, or occasionally arrest: one Englishwoman was deported in 1941 after arousing suspicion through making frequent trips to coastal areas, while an ex-navy officer was briefly detained in Cork when spotted 'taking notes, while viewing Leap Harbour'. He produced the time-honoured excuse that he was

[110] McMahon, 'Covert Operations and Official Collaboration', 48; Furlong diary, 30 July and 13 Aug. 1940, UCDA, Furlong papers, LA53/48. Furlong was director of the National Gallery of Ireland.

[111] Cowgill (SIS) to Wood (MI5), 28 July 1940, and minutes by ? and by Guy Liddell, 1 and 8 Aug. 1946, TNA, KV4/205.

[112] Report by Commandant Hayes, 24 Feb. 1942, MAI, G2/X/1091; Bryan interview, 1983.

a keen yachtsman.[113] Podesta recruited various helpers and informants, including the groundsman of a Dublin rugby club, a nurse whose brother was a prisoner of war, a bookie, and former members of the defunct Dublin Metropolitan Police and of the Garda. Pro-British sentiment was reinforced in some cases with modest regular payments. Through Podesta and other helpers Collinson acquired contacts throughout Ireland.[114]

Amongst Podesta's early recruits was a fellow Stubbs employee named Moore. Moore had taken the anti-treaty side in the civil war, and he had no intention of spying for Britain. He happened to know Dan Bryan by sight, and he approached him near his home. Moore agreed to keep G2 briefed on the work of Collinson's secret organization. This he did until its dissolution in the spring of 1945, and he was probably the agent whom Bryan once described as 'worth a hundred men to me'.[115] Through Moore, G2 were able not only to monitor much SIS and other British clandestine activity and to identify sources and informants, but to profit from their work: a great deal of SIS material on pro-Axis activities and individuals appears unattributed in G2 reports to their customers.

The first dated documents relating to Collinson's network are from June 1941, and identify people on whom he wanted information. Hundreds of such unsigned directives were recorded by G2, the last, no. 1882, dated 25 April 1945. They generally sought enquiries about people said to be sympathetic to the Axis, or to be directly in touch with one of the Axis legations, though many others were targeted simply because they had foreign names. A retired doctor staying in Buswell's Hotel 'was "more than friendly"' with a woman who had 'acted (small roles) at Gate Theatre', and he 'paid some of her bills at hotel'. A Dublin family included a woman 'aged 25 years, a blonde and fairly attractive. She also drinks a good deal and is said to have a knack of "picking up men with money". She frequents several public houses in the company of her sister-in-law and they are described as "Good time girls"... Locally the family are regarded as "tough" and without morals or scruples'. Charles Chenevix Trench, a prominent radical, 'is described as an intellectual and has a large number of friends, including Patrick O'Connor (the bearded artist)'. While Podesta's man could obtain 'no definite information as to his political activities and there is no record of his connection with "Breton Nationalist Movement" and this organization is unknown in Dublin', his brother 'is stated to be very pro-Nazi'. On this Dan Bryan noted: 'Wrong. Communist'. Alan Graves, a wealthy former British consular official with a German wife of Jewish extraction, was investigated because of his social contacts with the decidedly louche Carl Petersen. Petersen himself became an object of fascination for the Irish as well as the British authorities because of his propensity to play the Nazi

---

[113] Bryan (G2) to Duff (Justice), 5 Apr. 1945, MAI, G2/X/0244, re Ms Stella Jackson, who was deported on 19 Apr. 1941; superintendent, Skibbereen, to Garda headquarters, 16 Mar. 1943, NAI, JUS8/908.

[114] Interview with Dorothy and Evelyn Podesta, Bangor, Co. Down, 2000. I am grateful to David Truesdale for putting me in touch with the Podestas.

[115] Information from Douglas Gageby (1912–2004), who joined the defence forces after graduating from Trinity College Dublin and was posted to G2 because of his language skills. He later became a distinguished editor of the *Irish Times*. Bryan made the remark late one night after seeing a mysterious visitor out of G2 headquarters, where Gageby was duty officer.

in public: in December Walshe complained about his conduct to Hempel, after a drunken contretemps with three Gardai when he told their superior, 'if any of them are alive at Christmas, congratulate them'.[116] His drinking companion Graves was, it transpired, emphatically pro-British, but 'in certain quarters . . . is regarded as "sex-mad" and has occasionally entertained certain theatrical ladies' in a flat which he maintained for such liaisons, a conclusion reached independently by the Irish.[117] Sexual licence was a running theme in these reports, particularly in respect of Petersen and his circle. One woman, investigated because she 'allegedly cohabits' with the attaché, was found to be 'actually very respectable . . . a weekly communicant', but she shared accommodation with Petersen's mistress.[118]

Amidst such tittle-tattle was a good deal of very valuable material. Access both to Collinson's requests for information and to the results produced by Podesta's group gave G2 a crucial insight into British intelligence priorities. Moore also provided G2 with details on the development and activities of Collinson's networks across Ireland, including one '"Ace" agent in Cork', an 'ex-officer of the British Army, a well known Mason and a popular social figure. He is secretary of a well known Cork Golf Club'.[119] This man was identified as Captain W. M. Reidy.[120] Moore also reported the involvement of Lieutenant-Commander Clarke of the British Trade Commissioner's office, who used his official post as cover to 'act as paymaster and contact man for . . . some of the country groups'.[121] Clarke and Collinson did not always see eye to eye, and through Moore G2 were able to follow their relationship in some detail. Moore provided the names of many people said to have offered help or actually to have been recruited, as well as unwitting informants, such as 'several members of the Garda' who told 'one of our helpers in Limerick . . . that they (the police) have received secret instructions to be on the watch out for British agents'.[122] Moore picked up a good deal of information on intelligence operations, some of it bordering on the farcical. He passed on whatever he could discover about other British agencies, some of which was borne out by other intelligence.

The British and Irish records contain absolutely nothing to indicate that Collinson was attempting to secure information on Irish policy or to suborn senior officials: his operations were directed against pro-Axis elements and the Axis and other legations. Thus the Irish penetration of his networks was an unintended boon all round: SIS were able to satisfy themselves with a diet of detail which largely supplemented and supported what came through the G2–MI5 liaison, while G2 were content to observe Collinson's networks and to feed off their enquiries because these were not directed against the Irish state or against neutrality.[123] G2 did not disclose any knowledge of Collinson's activities to MI5, and both MI5 and SIS prided themselves on their discretion: the Irish Section history commented that, had the

---

[116] Garda report by Inspector Flynn, 29 Nov. 1940, NAI, DFA P41.
[117] Various reports from June 1941, MAI, G2/X/1091.
[118] Unsigned TS note of report by Moore, 19 Nov. 1941, MAI, G2/X/1091.
[119] Unsigned TS note of report by Moore, 30 Dec. 1941, MAI, G2/X/1091.
[120] McMahon, 'Clandestine Operations and Official Collaboration', 51.
[121] Unsigned TS note of report by Moore, 13 July 1944, MAI, G2/X/1091.
[122] Unsigned MS note of report by Moore, 12 Feb. 1942, MAI, G2/X/1091.
[123] Bryan interview, 1983.

Irish discovered the SIS presence, 'the effect on our political relations . . . would have been very serious and irreparable harm would have been done to the general security cooperation which had been built up both by the Security Service and by the RUC'. Whereas in neutral Switzerland the security authorities waxed and waned in their attitude towards British clandestine activities—despite generally good relations between various British operatives and the Swiss security service, partly sweetened by the 'timely release' of strategic raw materials for the Swiss army, in 1943 Berne cracked down on British industrial intelligence gathering because this was aimed at detecting Swiss breaches of the economic blockade of Germany—in Ireland G2 generally preferred to observe rather than to deter British snooping.[124]

G2 penetrated other British networks in the first years of the war which may have been the responsibility either of SIS or of NID. Dan Bryan described these as being concentrated in southern coastal areas, and so thought that they were most likely elements of naval intelligence arrangements, but recent scholarship indicates that they were an SIS responsibility.[125] G2's Southern Command intelligence officer Florence O'Donoghue, who like Bryan and Archer had cut his intelligence teeth in the war of independence, had considerable and sustained success in monitoring such activities.[126] Postal interception and the postal censorship were obvious but very valuable means of doing so: Bryan afterwards remarked that these produced material 'of the highest quality' on espionage and other security problems, as well as yielding a great deal of information on opinion and conditions in Ireland and in the outside world.[127]

In March 1941 MI5 arranged for Captain V. B. Caroe of BTNI, who had 'a thorough knowledge of German', to be seconded to work for them in Northern Ireland. In the event of a German attack he would act as the link between BTNI and MI5. SIS, who 'had been asked by GOC BTNI what arrangements they had made in the event of the invasion of Eire', then requested that Caroe also represent them in Northern Ireland and maintain contact with SIS's Irish organization.[128] This joint appointment worked well, further evidence of the generally good relations which prevailed between MI5 and SIS regarding Ireland throughout the war years. SIS appear also to have been involved in early efforts to develop clandestine communications links for use in the event of a sudden German attack. On 7 July 1940 two radio operators arrived in Dublin in the guise of servants of the newly appointed air attaché, Group Captain D. G. Lywood, who was himself working under civilian cover by agreement with the Irish. Based in his west Dublin home, these were to assemble and operate a transmitter which would be used to send word of an invasion. The arrangement was cleared in advance with the Irish.[129]

The scheme, however, quickly ran into trouble with Lywood, who, unlike the other attachés, came to be regarded by the Irish as a fusspot. On 12 July he

[124] O'Halpin, *MI5 and Ireland*, 21; Wylie, *Britain, Switzerland and the second world war*, 291.
[125] McMahon, 'Covert Operations and Official Collaboration', 49.
[126] On O'Donoghue see Borgonovo (ed.), *Florence and Josephine O'Donoghue's War of Independence*.
[127] Quoted in *Defending Ireland*, 215.
[128] Liddell diary, 7 Mar. 1941, TNA, KV4/186; *Liddell History*, 58.
[129] Maffey to London, 4 July 1940, TNA, DO120/14.

complained to London of the demeanour and conduct of one of the operators, Martin, notionally his secretary. Martin had 'left W/T [wireless telegraphy] equipment about not properly safeguarded' and 'proceeded to sleep out in Dublin for the night'. He also 'lacks initiative and imagination', and should be replaced by someone more suitable.[130] There was better news of the other operator, Austin, who 'in contrast . . . has endeavoured to carry out his duties in the guise allotted him. He has worked hard as butler in my house' and so managed 'to allay any local suspicion', enabling Martin to carry out the necessary technical work on the hidden transmitter.[131] On 24 July the Air Ministry passed on to Lywood a request to 'be friendly and kind and helpful to the operators, whose activities may not be clear to him at present but who have proved in the past to be very useful to us'.[132] The next day the Dominions Office weighed in, telling Lywood that 'the technical people here' advised that two operators were definitely needed, though they conceded that Martin and Austin 'are rather a problem. In their own circles they are exceptionally highly paid and apt to "throw their weight about". It is therefore bound to be a difficult problem how to keep such people doing nothing as members of the domestic staff without occasional trouble'.[133] These clear hints failed in their aim: Martin left Dublin on 26 July, leaving Austin in sole charge of the radio. A month later came more bad news, after a wireless expert visited Lywood's house. He found Austin 'vague in his replies', while his claim that 'he receives consistently loud reports' was 'difficult to believe as the aerial is inefficient in every respect . . . if we have to rely in any way' on Austin's set 'to get messages to London, I consider it most unlikely that we should succeed'.[134] A month later, after the two men had a further talk, Austin wrote in the dignified tone befitting his cover job of butler: 'With reference your remarks . . . in connection with schedules will you please communicate with Major Maltby, c/o Passport Control Office, 54 Broadway . . . He . . . will I feel sure do something in this connection. I am as I have already explained only carrying out my instructions. In the meantime I am communicating with Broadway'.[135] Broadway was SIS headquarters, and Maltby, of whom Guy Liddell once observed that 'whatever his merits may be, [he] never fails to radiate dishonesty', was an SIS communications specialist who was also controller of the RSS.[136] The Dominions Office suspected that SIS had their own uses for the Lywood set. The saga rumbled on: a compromise was arranged, whereby Austin departed in February 1941 and the set was handled by an RAF operator. But, perhaps predictably, Lywood was displeased: 'I am unable to establish satisfactory cover for this man. His appearance daily at my house at a fixed time' was 'not an easy matter to account for in a small house'. He wanted 'a *keen* and competent man . . . given about a week or ten days instructions in order to effect his cover as a valet or butler'. SIS responded that, whereas 'when we had our own operator [Austin] every schedule was met without

[130] Report on Martin by Lywood, 12 July 1940, TNA, DO120/14.
[131] Lywood to Antrobus (BRO), 23 July 1940, TNA, DO120/14.
[132] Hylton-Foster to Lywood, 24 July 1940, TNA, DO120/14.
[133] Stephenson to Antrobus, 25 July 1940, TNA, DO120/14.
[134] Report by H. A. Whyte, 26 Aug. 1940, TNA, DO120/14.
[135] Austen to Whyte, 8 Oct. 1940, TNA, DO120/14.
[136] Liddell diary, 7 Feb. 1944, TNA, KV4/193.

fail or difficulty', the RAF operator clearly needed to be 'gingered up into attending to his business'.[137]

Additional steps were taken to enable the rapid communication of news of a German attack. Two radios were installed in Maffey's office, operated by RAF personnel as Station AA.[138] A direct telephone link to Belfast was established, users being warned that the Irish would certainly be listening in; and the radios of two merchant ships moored in the Dublin docks were, through NID, also available to transmit a warning.[139] After some confusion at the London end, a dedicated teleprinter link between Maffey's office and the Admiralty was opened in April 1941; in return, the British undertook to end the constant interruption of calls between the Irish high commission in London and External Affairs.[140] The most intricate arrangements, however, were those surrounding the installation in Lywood's establishment of a clutch of carrier pigeons. Pigeons were a recognized means of military and intelligence communication: indeed, the Air Ministry's imposingly titled 'chief pigeons officer' had been 'employed on pigeons duty in Ireland during the last war', and the birds were considered sufficiently valuable an intelligence resource to warrant the lifting of a ban on the shooting of peregrine falcons because 'they apparently prey on homing pigeons coming in from the Continent'.[141]

This scheme was Lywood's brainchild, and after securing Irish assent to their covert importation he initially envisaged placing the birds with a trustworthy pigeon-fancier in Dublin. In the end, however, it was agreed that they should be accommodated in his house, under the care of a Cambridge land economy graduate selected by the Air Ministry.[142] It is not known how often the birds flew, or when they were finally removed from the air attaché's residence. By the spring of 1942 concerns had shifted: MI5 decided to spend £200 sending 'expert falconers to the Scilly Isles to see if we can get some of the pigeons said to be passing . . . en route from Eire to the continent'.[143]

SIS continued to circulate 'QRS' reports. Those covering the first years of the war have not been traced, but there is an almost complete run from May 1942 to December 1944 in Dominions Office records. From other evidence, it is likely that the quality, content, and frequency of these reports rose once Collinson began to operate. He was possibly the source of an interesting SIS report of March 1941, which stated that Wendell Wilkie, the defeated American presidential candidate whom Roosevelt had then sent around the world to stress the importance of international solidarity against Hitler, had

---

[137] Stephenson to Antrobus, 15 Aug. 1940, and Antrobus to Stephenson, 10 Feb. 1941; Lywood to Maffey, 25 Mar., and Stephenson to Antrobus, 1 Apr. 1941, TNA, DO121/16.

[138] Memorandum by Pryce (BRO), 1 and 9 Oct. 1940, TNA, DO120/16.

[139] Note by Pryce (BRO), 31 Aug.; copy of NID to Swinton, 27 Aug. 1940, TNA, DO120/14. On 25 November 1941 the Admiralty told Greig that the two operators on cargo ships in Dublin port were being withdrawn. TNA, DO130/16.

[140] Note by Boland (Dublin) of talk with Antrobus (BRO), 26 Nov. 1940, and Boland to Department of Post and Telegraphs, 20 Apr. 1941, NAI, DFA P42.

[141] Liddell diary, 31 Aug. 1940, TNA, KV4/186; note by Lywood, 1 July 1940, TNA, DO120/14.

[142] Note by Lywood, 1 July 1940, TNA, DO120/14. When I was a student at Cambridge land economy was universally regarded as much the least-challenging course on offer.

[143] Liddell diary, 28 Apr. 1942, TNA, KV4/187.

told Dev[alera] that the U[nited] S[tates] considered that . . . the Irish insistence on the partition question was disproportionate and hardly worthy of consideration. This remark appears to have made a deep impression on all those present who were careful not to take up the challenge. Wilkie laid great stress on British courage and powers of endurance and said that he thought that if they held out another 5 months victory would be assured. He tried to impress upon the Eire government that their present neutrality policy was unreasonable and a false position from the American standpoint.[144]

This unusually detailed piece of political intelligence was perhaps based on nothing more than gossip, although it might also have come from a decoded Irish or American cable. Summary descriptions of other SIS reports indicate predictable concerns and subjects: suspect individuals, rumours of networks in various places, possible IRA–German links in Ireland and Britain, subversives within the civil service, the capture of the German parachutist Marschner/Schutz in Wexford, and pro-Nazi Irishmen such as the one-time IRA man and solicitor Con Lehane, and Seán MacBride.

There is no evidence that SIS were asked to interfere in Irish affairs in order to bring about a change of regime in this time of acute crisis. To an extent this was in contrast to the situation in 1932–3, when British policy towards Ireland and her management of growing economic and political disputes with de Valera had been largely influenced by a longing to see the back of him and to facilitate the return to power of the supposedly more malleable Cosgrave.[145] By July 1940, and even in the midst of U-boat and IRA scares, there was considerable realism in the assessment of Irish political conditions. It was obvious both from Maffey's reports, and from soundings taken by journalists and others, such as the Anglo-Irish writer Elizabeth Bowen, that Cosgrave and his colleagues in opposition were as committed to neutrality as was de Valera.

In July Cosgrave told Maffey that it was 'a great pity that the problem of partition could not be tackled now. It could only be solved in a crisis. If left to hang over there would be bloodshed', and in December he and his colleague General Mulcahy signalled sympathy on the issue of ports and airfields but argued that progress could only be made by educating public opinion, not by lectures or threats.[146] The only significant figure who might have been willing to participate in a seizure of power was General O'Duffy, once Cosgrave's party leader but now completely beyond the political pale. His heart was firmly with the Axis, and he was already deeply involved in a flirtation with the German legation. Of mainstream politicians, only James Dillon was willing consistently to make the case for joining Britain. In July 1940 he appears to have been very indiscreet, telling Maffey that 'recently on the Defence Board he has been conscious of a tendency on de Valera's part to recede somewhat from the former position which was that Eire should call in British help as soon as an invasion had taken place', but although a brilliant orator and Dáil performer, he

---

[144] Ibid., 3 Mar. 1941, TNA, KV4/189.
[145] Canning, *British Policy Towards Ireland*, 131–52.
[146] Ibid. 294–5; Maffey to Machtig (Dominions Office), 12 July and 23 Dec. 1940, TNA, DO130/12.

had no following on the neutrality question, and in 1942 he was pushed out of the Fine Gael party on that issue.[147]

THE FADING OF THE IRA THREAT

The almost complete cessation of organized IRA activity in Britain after the spring of 1940 was unexpected, although as Sir Frank Newsam of the Home Office pointed out to a nervous general in early May, 'it was fair to say that the IRA Organization had been almost entirely suppressed'.[148] In June what appeared to be an IRA document was found on a railway line near Manchester: 'Its contents ring fairly true, and indicate that the Germans, in conjunction with the IRA, are planning some kind of action on the West Coast rather than on the East. They seem to have established wireless communication between Arklow [a small port south of Dublin] and the Pennines'. The document also indicated that weapons and individuals might be concealed in caravans around the country, prompting talk of a general search.[149] This turned out to be a complete red herring. On 13 July Guy Liddell reflected on conflicting indications about German plans: 'As regards sabotage . . . it may be that the Germans are holding their hands until the day of invasion, when we may see things going up, either through the agency of the IRA, or of some elements of the BUF [British Union of Fascists]'.[150] The JIC and the Security Executive also fretted about the number of Irishmen employed on building aerodromes and in special military areas, fearing that among these might be IRA men who would act as saboteurs or spies.[151]

The IRA in Britain were conspicuous by their complete inactivity once the S-plan fizzled out, and even in Northern Ireland they attempted little and achieved far less despite the abundance of targets and opportunities. This was attributable to a number of factors. The first, already noted, were the vigorous police and legal measures taken by the British authorities from the spring of 1939 onwards. Many activists had been jailed, and others deported to Ireland, where a number ended up in internment. There was also the grim example of the executions of the Coventry bombers in February 1940—arguably, the fact that these were locally recruited sympathizers, not ringleaders or trained assassins, had a salutary impact in émigré circles. In addition, the IRA were under intense pressure in both parts of Ireland. Emergency legislation both created new offences and provided new legal frameworks which made convictions much easier to secure. Internment without trial was applied throughout the British Isles. With the outbreak of war there was also an enormous increase in surveillance and control generally. To eat, to buy clothes, to work, to be considered for national service or to be exempted from it, everyone had to register

---

[147] Report by Maffey, 17 July 1940, TNA, DO130/12; Manning, *Dillon*, 161–2.
[148] JIC(40), 1 May 1940, TNA, CAB81/87.
[149] Liddell diary, 8 June 1940, TNA, KV4/186; *Liddell History*, 34. G2 were supplied with a copy of this document 'found on 7/6/40 on the railway near Manchester', which they in turn passed to External Affairs, undated, NAI, DFA 8.
[150] Liddell diary, 13 July 1940, TNA, KV4/186.
[151] JIC(40) 26 and 29, 1 and 15 May 1940, reflect such concerns. TNA, CAB81/87.

with relevant ministries or authorities. This was not simply a matter of securing benefits and entitlements; rather, failure to register became an offence in itself. Men of military age were particularly likely to be asked for papers constantly, since they might be evading conscription, or be deserters. For non-British residents and for Irish migrant workers there were additional controls. Travel permits were required for movement between Britain and Ireland, and non-possession was an offence. Moving from one employment region to another required permission, and even switching jobs without official sanction was prohibited.

Churchill fretted about transient Irish saboteurs—in July 1941 he minuted that it was 'a most important point'—but he need scarcely have worried.[152] Movement into and out of areas of military significance involved special passes, checks, and explanations, and every traveller was liable to encounter one kind of official check or another. These factors, as much as increased police surveillance—in October 1940 the Special Branch complained that they were 'very hard up for informants in IRA circles'—explained IRA inactivity in Britain. The police remained on the alert, particularly in areas with large Irish populations. In April 1941 a Special Branch superintendent in Liverpool told Cecil Liddell that the IRA still possessed 'a magnificent intelligence service . . . the women were especially dangerous and very well trained'. But 'unlike Scotland Yard', the Liverpool force 'had not blown all their informants . . . and . . . had contacts in Eire itself'. Liddell and Vivian agreed that the Liverpool police could send someone across to Ireland, provided that 'if he is rumbled' he should be clearly on police business: 'It would be fatal . . . if there was the least suggestion that his contact had been sent to Eire at the instigation of any "Intelligence" authority'. An officer duly travelled over and provided a somewhat lurid report emphasizing IRA readiness to act in Britain should an invasion come, claiming that Dulanty and his staff were involved in the smuggling of people wishing to evade travel controls, and stating that the IRA were not currently collecting intelligence in Britain for transmission to the German legation. MI5 met the £30 cost of this adventure, although it was scarcely worth the outlay.[153]

On top of the effectiveness of police action was the fact of communications censorship. While never absolutely foolproof, postal censorship between Britain and Ireland gradually became highly efficient. MI5 regarded this as crucial: asked to rank the most important countries for postal censorship in July 1940, 'we have said that we place Eire first, Spain and Portugal second, and America third'.[154] Telephone traffic was subject to considerable restriction, strict supervision, and the intervention of operators: on 15 December 1940 a travelling salesman referred to bomb damage and troop movements in a call to Londonderry, resulting in a rapid prosecution, and in March 1941 two young cinema projectionists in Dundee received three months imprisonment 'for telephoning the German legation in Dublin'.[155] The

---

[152] Morton to Churchill, 9 July, and note of Churchill's minute to home secretary, undated, TNA, PREM7/4.

[153] Liddell diary, 13 Oct. 1940, TNA, KV4/186; O'Halpin, *Defending Ireland*, 231–2; report by Cecil Liddell of visit to Liverpool, 10 Apr., Vivian to Liddell, 12 Apr., and Baxter (MI5, Manchester) to Liddell, 26 Apr. and 21 June 1941, TNA, KV3/120.

[154] Liddell diary, 30 July 1940, TNA, KV4/186.

[155] Summary of Special Branch monthly reports, Jan.-June 1941, NAS, HH55/51.

Customs service was ordered to be especially thorough in inspections of ships and boats moving between Ireland and Britain, often resulting in the detection of unauthorized mail consigned to crew members or passengers for posting to avoid censorship between the jurisdictions. Travelling without a permit between the two islands was also a common practice, particularly in fishing boats and other small vessels, and the crews of ships regularly plying between Ireland and Britain were regarded as likely couriers. These concerns eventually led to a decision in 1942 to place MI5 agents 'on the Irish boats'.[156]

The relative ease with which people could move freely between the two islands and within Britain even after the introduction of travel regulations is reflected in British records.[157] Irish people travelling in Britain frequently feature for offences such as landing without a valid permit, moving from one kind of employment to another without permission, and altering permits in order to obtain better-paid jobs. Many minor breaches of rules and regulations were the subject of prosecutions solemnly noted in Special Branch reports.

In Aberdeen, 'John O'Donnell McDonald (71), a tramp . . . on being arrested for lighting a fire on the sea front during the black-out, proved to have neither Identity Card nor Ration Book': the hapless Roscommon man was, however, 'quite harmless'.[158] Irish deserters from the armed forces often turned up under borrowed or fictitious identities, whether attempting to get home to Ireland or working in Britain. Michael Kirk was charged with making false statements on job applications. He proved to be a deserter from HMS *Repulse*, who had returned to Ireland before travelling over to Scotland to find work. Given his ship's eventual fate in the South China Sea, perhaps he made the right choice.[159] On occasion deserters from the Irish army were arrested, such as one man caught in Northern Ireland and sent back to Scotland carrying papers identifying him as James Kinahan, on the run from the British army. There it transpired that he was actually Bernard Carpenter of the Irish army, who 'owing to certain grievances wished to join the British Army': two deserters had met by chance and had simply swapped papers.[160] Few miscreants were as adventurous as Patrick Gerard Starrs, an 18-year-old from Limerick. He used an out-of-date permit to enter an aerodrome where he had previously worked, and then boarded an unguarded aircraft. He 'was not discovered until the aircraft was over [the] Atlantic'. The police decided he had not had 'any subversive reason', and he escaped with a 10 shilling fine.[161]

The one area where the IRA did manage to do anything at all to hamper the war effort was in Northern Ireland. In 1941 BTNI still assumed for planning purposes that in the event of a German invasion the IRA would rise, but this was unsupported by available intelligence on IRA capabilities, organization, and

---

[156] Liddell diary, 31 July 1942, TNA, KV4/190. The section history of MI5's merchant shipping security section B1L is at TNA, KV4/26.

[157] Air Ministry memorandum on the problem of Irish workers and the dangers of information leakage, 29 Oct., discussed on 6 Nov. 1940, JIC(40) 355, TNA, CAB81/98.

[158] Summary of Special Branch reports, Jan.–June 1941, NAS, HH55/51.

[159] Ibid.

[160] Summary of Special Branch reports, Sept. 1942, NAS, HH55/54.

[161] Summary of Special Branch reports, Feb. 1944, NAS, HH55/58.

weapons.[162] The IRA's performance was in fact derisory, despite German interest in receiving information on shipping and on British forces in Northern Ireland, and despite the opportunities offered by an open border and by the presence of the Axis legations in Dublin. Cecil Liddell was guilty of only a slight overstatement when he wrote that 'no single case of espionage or sabotage by the IRA or by the Germans through the IRA is known to have occurred': such efforts as were made by the IRA and associated groups to collect war information in either Britain or Northern Ireland for the Axis powers were generally extremely amateurish in execution and in content.[163]

A partial exception was a fourteen-page survey of the damage wrought by the German air raids on Belfast of April–May 1941. This typescript document, proudly titled 'Comprehensive Military Report on Belfast', and 'issued by THE DIRECTOR OF INTELLIGENCE, in co-operation with the MILITARY INTELLIGENCE OFFICER of NORTHERN COMMAND', gave a detailed account of damage, and also identified industrial targets which had escaped destruction. Appended was a map on which were marked 'the remaining and most outstanding objects of military significance, as yet unblitzed by the Luftwaffe. The Police Barracks are marked because, in this occupied area, they are really a military rather than a civil force'. A 'Special Note' explained: 'Re the symbol coloured light blue, it may be noted that the road thus marked, is the Fall's [*sic*] Road, the chief site of Nationalism, while the square is the Prison, where some 300 to 400 Irish Republican Soldiers are imprisoned'.[164] The message was clear if not explicitly stated: please come back and finish off Belfast, but refrain from bombing our people and our prisoners. The document was found when a courier was arrested in Dublin in October 1941. It appears not to have reached German hands, and it is not clear whether G2 showed it to MI5. However, MI5 did have sight of the contents of a number of enciphered messages obtained by the Garda early in 1942, which once broken a year later disclosed attempts by the Northern IRA to pass on information about 'the arrival of Americans at Derry' and the 'construction by the Eire authorities of an aerodrome at Limerick'.[165]

Fears that the IRA were poised to mount a *coup d'état*, which had been such a feature of British assessments at the high point of panic in May and June 1940, evaporated very quickly. Vigorous police action in the wake of the IRA's attempt to seize the British diplomatic bag in May caused the cumulative erosion of the IRA's organization in Dublin. In August two detectives were murdered during a raid on an IRA house. One of the two men quickly convicted and executed was a distinguished IRA veteran, Patrick McGrath, who had been freed through public pressure the previous December.[166] In November an IRA party en route to assassinate a leading detective, Michael Gill, crashed their vehicle and were captured by a passing army

---

[162] Fisk, *In Time of War*, 276–7.

[163] *Liddell History*, 56; Bryan interview, 1983; Hull, *Irish Secrets*, 145–7.

[164] Undated [1941] IRA bomb damage survey of Belfast, MAI, G2/X/1722.

[165] SIS analysis of Pandora material, 6 Aug., with Cecil Liddell to Stephenson, 24 Aug. 1943, TNA, DO121/86.

[166] His case was raised on 6 Nov. 1939 at a meeting of the Fianna Fáil national executive by Mrs Tom Clarke and Mrs Margaret Pearse, respectively the widow and the mother of executed leaders of the 1916 rising. UCDA, Fianna Fáil party records, FF/342.

patrol. Garda raids saw the arrest of most of the IRA headquarters staff, and of the production team of the pro-Axis IRA propaganda sheet *War News*. All this, together with the widespread use of internment against the IRA and its helpers, soon produced a British reappraisal of the relative strengths of the republican movement and of the Irish state.

One question which remained unanswered, however, was the extent of IRA links with Germany and their potential for disruption in Ireland. The key to this lay not in Ireland but in Europe. In July 1940 Frank Ryan, the leading IRA left-winger sentenced to death during the Spanish civil war, was allowed to escape from jail and was driven to the French border, where he was handed over to the Abwehr. This contrived escape was partly the work of the Irish minister in Madrid, Leopold Kerney, whose conduct over the next few years showed him to be a serious menace to Irish interests.[167] Ryan was brought to Berlin in the care of Jupp Hoven and Helmut Clissmann, whom he had known in Ireland before the war. Two months earlier the Abwehr had succeeded in bringing to Berlin another key IRA man, the former chief of staff Seán Russell, whose secret departure from the United States they arranged. Russell received training in modern sabotage methods with a view to returning to Ireland in June to galvanize the IRA. Those arrangements fell through. When Ryan arrived in Berlin, he agreed to join Russell in a return to Ireland.

On 8 August the two men embarked on a U-boat. The parallels with the voyage of Roger Casement from Germany to Ireland on the eve of the 1916 rising are obvious, although Casement's personal mission was to dissuade his co-conspirators in Ireland from pressing on with rebellion because Germany would not send military aid as envisaged. Had Russell and Ryan landed and their presence become known, this would most likely have been construed both by the British and the Irish as the preamble to a German assault. In those circumstances, Britain would have had either to insist that the Irish immediately permit British forces to strengthen Irish defences, or occupy key positions in Ireland unilaterally whatever the consequences. In the event, Russell fell ill during the voyage, and he eventually died when about 100 miles off the Irish coast. Ryan, who had received no specialist training and who may not have had full knowledge of Russell's mission, made the puzzling decision to go back to Germany rather than to land alone. He was not to get another chance to return to Ireland. Ryan disclosed Russell's fate in a letter to Kerney in 1942, although rumours persisted of murder by the Germans, by the British, even by Ryan himself. From all that is known about the inability of British agencies to operate in Germany after 1939, it is very difficult to believe that they would have been able to position anyone close enough to Russell to bump him off.

This is not to say that London was hampered by any ethical doubts about assassination as an unavowed tool of warfare: in March 1941 SOE's Gardyne de Chastelain, a specialist on Romania based in Turkey, and whose son John was to play a central a role in the Irish Good Friday Agreement of 1998, received instructions from London to intercept and kill the leading Indian nationalist Subhas Chandra Bose, thought likely to pass through Turkey en route from Kabul to Berlin. The plan fell through because Bose travelled via Moscow, and during an uncomfortable

---

[167] O'Halpin, *Defending Ireland*, 194–6; Hull, *Irish Secrets*, 126–7.

two-year sojourn in Germany coincidentally met Ryan on the street.[168] In March 1941 SOE were told to kill a number of German officials in the Middle East who were engaged in the manipulation of Islamic opinion.[169] SOE also planned to kill the Grand Mufti of Jerusalem as he made his way through Turkey to Berlin, together with the ousted Iraqi dictator Rashid Ali—in order to overcome Foreign Office objections to such actions on neutral Turkish soil, Colin Gubbins of SOE suggested that the prime minister should be asked personally 'to wire the ambassador in Ankara'.[170] It is, therefore, clear that London regarded assassination of individuals on neutral territory, whether enemy citizens or not, as a legitimate tool of warfare. The fact that such killings were apparently not considered in respect of Ireland, particularly in the desperate months after the fall of France, is explained largely by political and diplomatic calculations, and also by the fact that the Irish got on top of German espionage and of the IRA so quickly.

G2 and MI5 both made considerable efforts to ascertain Russell's fate after 1940, and they continued to seek news of Ryan.[171] The Germans made desultory use of him in succeeding years, and schemes were developed in outline in 1941 and 1942 which envisaged getting him back to Ireland to serve German ends, but once the likelihood of an invasion of the British Isles had disappeared he did not have very much to offer. He died in Dresden in 1944, thereby escaping the embarrassment for a socialist of having to explain his years under Nazi patronage.

Russell's death put an end to any realistic prospect of effectively harnessing the IRA for German war aims. Had he landed, he would have found the organization in a pitiful state, vitiated by infighting and under the hammer in both parts of Ireland. He might have imparted a greater sense of purpose to one or another faction, but it is unlikely that he could have pulled the organization together. Even if he had, the fading of German interest once the possibility of invading the British Isles disappeared in the autumn of 1940 would surely have left him high and dry. Just at the moment when Afghanistan became doubly interesting to Germany because of her borders with British India, with Persia, and with the Soviet Union in the summer of 1941, so Ireland disappeared from Berlin's list of useful places from which Britain might be threatened. Henceforth Germany's main interest in Ireland was in keeping her neutral, and in securing whatever war information as could be collected and communicated back to the continent.

THE FIGHTING SERVICES AND INTELLIGENCE ON IRELAND, 1940–1941

The Irish intelligence requirements of the fighting services varied considerably and they changed over time. The efforts of individual services caused some

---

[168] Hull, *Irish Secrets*, 136–8; SOE war diary, 7 Mar., 16, 17 and 18 June 1941, TNA, HS7/214, 215, and 217.
[169] SOE war diary, 7 Mar. and 18 Apr. 1941, TNA, HS7/214 and 215.
[170] SOE war diary, 1/2 July 1941, TNA, HS7/218.
[171] Liddell diary, 2 Oct. 1942, TNA, KV4/190.

confusion and friction with other agencies in the first year of the war, but in each case the appointment of attachés in Dublin and the development of good links with the Irish resulted in a more orderly and discreet approach to the hunt for intelligence.

We have already seen that the Admiralty had been first in the field where Irish matters were concerned. Notwithstanding Archer's well-taken warnings to Captain Greig on the futility of encouraging networks of amateur informants, NID continued to solicit reports from well-disposed people along the southern and western coasts and in the significant ports. In the last weeks of the war in Europe, G2's man inside the SIS organization in Dublin reported Podesta's statement that NID 'had a naval intelligence man in each port and at Foynes' and that 'reports on all outgoing ships are/were sent to the Admiral commanding western approaches', a claim which seems credible.[172] By the spring of 1940, Godfrey had concluded that most of the reports which continued to flood in about submarine movements along the west coast were unfounded. He was influenced in this by Greig, whose liaison with G2 on coastal surveillance was already close and productive. The Admiralty also pressed SIS to improve their Irish intelligence gathering, a demand which influenced the creation of Collinson's organization in June 1940.[173]

In September Godfrey visited Ireland to assess matters for himself.[174] He took a further significant step when he appointed Commander C. B. Slade, his Irish expert, as his representative in Belfast. In addition to liaising with the attachés in Dublin, Slade's task was to develop covert 'contacts with those who travel regularly between North and South Ireland . . . This arrangement worked extremely well'.[175] With radio reports from the Irish coast-watching service available to the Admiralty at the same time as to Irish defence headquarters, with Captain Greig so effective in liaison, and with British routing officers who could control Irish shipping movements as well as keep an eye on marine matters generally in the major ports, by the summer of 1940 Godfrey had every reason to be confident in his Irish intelligence.[176] The Irish, whose maritime lifeline existed entirely on British sufferance, were assiduous in maintaining liaison: in May 1941 Walshe received a request through Maffey from 'Godfrey of the Admiralty' for 'large scale commercial plans' of seventeen Irish ports. He consulted de Valera, who 'thinks it would be just as well to supply the plans, since, if they wanted to go to the trouble, the British could get all the information without recourse to us'.[177]

The RAF's requirements in relation to Ireland were largely technical and specialized. In the immediate aftermath of the fall of France, two officers were sent to Ireland, ostensibly on a fishing holiday, in order to reconnoitre possible sites for airfields.[178] Once Lywood got into his stride and the Irish proved very cooperative,

[172] Report by M[oore], 27 Apr. 1945, MAI, G2/X/1091.

[173] *Liddell History*, 20.

[174] Liddell diary, 20 Oct.1940, TNA, KV4/186; Godfrey memoir, 203, CCCA, Godfrey papers 1/6.

[175] Godfrey memoir, 204, CCCA, Godfrey papers 1/6.

[176] The G2 files on submarine sightings 1940–5 include correspondence with Greig. MAI, G2/X/0152.

[177] Walshe to Archer, 14 May 1941, NAI, DFA A8.

[178] McMahon, 'Covert Operations and Official Collaboration', 48.

reliance on such amateur espionage decreased considerably, although the air attaché was prone to snoop on his own account: in April 1941 this 'Englishman, public school, Officer, type, age about 38, smooth easy manner, dark moustache, dark hair receding from forehead, medium height and build', drew considerable attention to himself while making enquiries about a recently crashed Focke Wolfe aircraft in Cork. He told a G2 informant that 'Jimmie Flynn . . . is one of ours . . . Jimmie wants money', a remark duly reported to Archer: 'I consider Lywood very indiscreet, criminally so . . . We are aware for some time that Flynn . . . is operating for Maffey's office but have been unable to obtain proof'.[179] Weather reporting from Irish meteorological stations continued along the same lines as had operated in peacetime; this was particularly significant in respect of weather over the Atlantic.

An efficient Irish air movements reporting system took time to develop. Early in 1940 a basic scheme for the air defence of the Dublin region came into operation, but the need for a country-wide system was also recognized both for air defence purposes and to keep track of violations of Irish air space. The network which emerged drew largely on the coast-watching service and on their reporting system. The eventual provision of radios at command centres greatly increased the speed of reporting *en clair* to headquarters on frequencies known to the British, along the lines agreed for submarine sightings, and the Irish air observation service soon developed close links with the RAF in Northern Ireland (in March 1941 two Irish air corps officers visiting Belfast found discussions with their RAF counterparts surprisingly sticky, until it transpired that the British had not succeeded in picking up Irish air movements reports by radio and were sceptical that such were being broadcast. Archer immediately arranged a demonstration transmission which the RAF did pick up, and the atmosphere improved markedly).[180]

There are plenty of indications that the RAF recognized that the Irish were supplying them with all the information they acquired on air movements, and were taking a very constructive and accommodating approach to the myriad of problems arising from air operations. Lywood and his successors became advocates for the provision of equipment and machines to the Irish, the general embargo on arms supplies notwithstanding, on the basis partly of reciprocation for cooperation and partly of enhancing Irish capabilities in aerial surveillance of coastal waters.[181] The RAF took a keen interest in all air crashes, and secured access to whatever remained of crashed enemy aircraft and equipment. In the summer of 1941 the RAF advanced plans for a chain of 'RDF masts on the East coast of Eire', as 'there is a definite gap in our defences on the Welsh coast'. The plan envisaged using the same process as with the coast-watching service: the Irish operators would radio their reports to headquarters, and the British would intercept these transmissions. MI5 thought they could convince the Irish to accept this, particularly as Dublin had recently been bombed without warning from the air, but there was pessimism about whether Churchill could be persuaded to support the provision of modern

179 Archer to Walshe, 30 Apr., enclosing report by O'Donoghue, 28 Apr. 1941, NAI, DFA A8.
180 Archer to chief of staff, 27 Mar. 1941, NAI, DFA A3.
181 Begg (air attaché) to Air Ministry, 26 Nov. 1942, TNA, DO35/1109/14.

air defence equipment.[182] For whatever reason, the initiative never materialized, although the Irish did permit the discreet erection in County Donegal of a radio beacon for aircraft using the seaplane base at Lough Erne in Fermanagh. Early in 1945 the Irish agreed to the erection of a marine radar station at Malin Head, again in County Donegal, but the ending of the war in Europe stopped that project.[183]

The army's intelligence requirements on Ireland arose from BTNI's mission to move across the border if required, whether to counter a German attack or to seize one or more of the Irish ports. In the first year of the war there was a certain amount of local snooping by officers supposedly on leave. One case, that of Major Byass, proved a particular irritant in July 1940, when he was detected while engaged in a clumsy reconnaissance of routes and airfields. The Irish army and BTNI were already engaged in detailed discussions, so Byass's activities caused concern as possible evidence of British designs to operate independently on Irish territory—de Valera brought up the cases both of Byass and of Tegart in a discussion with Maffey, in which he also pleaded for 'a few anti-aircraft guns' to defend Dublin and 'begged us to grant' a 'small amount of equipment'.[184] The rapid development of efficient liaison after the Anglo-Irish defence discussions in the last week of May 1940, including the stationing of a signals detachment in army headquarters in Dublin to provide a radio link to BTNI, more or less put an end to covert military intelligence gathering. In May 1941 the DMI noted that BTNI 'now covered Eire well', mainly through liaison rather than through snooping, although at unit level individual officers undoubtedly continued to try their luck (in 1942 G2 discovered that a signals corporal working in the 2nd Northern Division intelligence office had been suborned both by the IRA and by British officers. G2 helped him to flee the country before either of his secret paymasters turned nasty).[185]

On 10 March 1941 Maffey hosted a lunch at his home for Joseph Walshe, the Irish chief of staff McKenna and Liam Archer, incorrectly reported by Maffey to be 'his No. 2' rather than director of intelligence, the military attaché in Dublin Major Norman ap Rees Pryce, and Brigadier Gregson-Ellis of BTNI. After Walshe departed, an 'extremely cordial' meeting took place. McKenna 'could not have been more frank, and invited any questions that we liked to put. He even divulged the proposed location of his Battle Headquarters', and invited Gregson-Ellis 'to visit any defence work at any time, and promised that he should be shown anything that he liked to see'. The one difficulty in Anglo-Irish military liaison remained that of equipment: McKenna 'was particularly anxious to have concrete assistance in the form of material, whose arrival he could point to as being the direct result' of the meeting. Maffey thought it 'absolutely essential to release some further supplies . . . *quickly*'. Gregson-Ellis emphasized that the GOC BTNI had written to London and would again press on these lines, but had 'no *powers* in the matter';

[182] Liddell diary, 4 June and 14 July 1941, TNA, KV4/188.
[183] Early in 1945 work began on an anti-submarine radar station at Malin Head in Co. Donegal, which was to be notionally under Irish control.
[184] Maffey to London, enclosing note of talk with de Valera, 16 July 1940, TNA, DO130/12.
[185] F. N. Davidson diary, 14 Mar. 1941, Davidson papers, Liddell Hart Centre for Military Archives, Kings's College London; O'Halpin, *Defending Ireland*, 175; information from the late Commandant Peter Young, 1998.

in any event, material was desperately needed elsewhere. McKenna, seizing on this, 'pointed out that the cessation of supplies to Eire obviously implied that no invasion was anticipated'.

The discussion turned to what might happen if the Germans did attack, where the main assault might be expected—Gregson-Ellis was particularly concerned about a possible parachute attack on Collinstown and Baldonnel aerodromes, and also warned that the Germans might drop troops in British battle-dress and put it about that this was an operation to seize the ports—and issues which would arise once BTNI responded to a request for aid: due to supply problems some Irish troops still wore coal-scuttle helmets of the German pattern, and it was essential that these be replaced if fatal confusion was to be avoided. The Irish were also insistent that the British military should consult the local Garda before taking any drastic action against suspected spies. Both sides agreed that Cork was the most likely area for a seaborne invasion, and McKenna explained his dispositions to counter that threat. Commenting on the possibility of an attack in the Limerick area—via the Shannon estuary—McKenna expressed satisfaction with the defences in place, and added wherever an assault came, 'all the inhabitants would fight, women included; and that the greatest ruthlessness would be displayed by the Eire forces'. While Maffey took this in the context of a German assault, McKenna may also have intended to give Britain further food for thought. McKenna 'several times deprecated the waste of effort which was thrust upon him by his present instructions to look Northward as well'. While neither BTNI, the War Office, nor the Dominions Office thought there was the slightest chance of obtaining political sanction for a renewal of military supplies, at however exiguous a rate, all argued that such a decision would make considerable sense. The March meeting, of which de Valera received a full report, was significant for another reason: it convinced Gregson-Ellis of McKenna's sincerity, and this in turn guided BTNI's advice to SOE about planned Irish operations.[186]

SOE AND IRELAND, 1940–1941

The speed of Germany's victories in western Europe meant that there was little planned destruction of installations, transport infrastructure, and fuel and supply dumps other than as an incidental consequence of the fighting, although the British managed localized destruction of port facilities and the removal of some strategic materials in the Netherlands. When MI(R) began planning for sabotage and other 'stay-behind' activities in the event of a German invasion, they initially concentrated on preparations in Britain itself, with the creation of a network of 'auxiliary units' of civilians tasked to collect intelligence and to carry out acts of resistance in areas overrun by the invader.[187] The question of what to do about Ireland only came

[186] Maffey to London, 18 Mar., enclosing minutes of meeting of 10 Mar.; minute by ?, 26 Mar. 1941, TNA, DO35/1109/14; army memorandum for taoiseach, 16 Mar. 1941, UCDA, de Valera papers, P150/2616.
[187] Anglim, 'MI(R), G(R) and British Covert Operations, 1939–42', 635.

under consideration late in 1940, after MI(R)'s absorption into SOE, as a result of pressure from BTNI.[188] Significantly, there was no suggestion that such plans should include measures directed against Irish interests, for example to hamper the Irish army should Britain decide to seize the ports by force. Thinking was predicated on the need to address the threat of invasion by Germany.

Responsibility for implementing sabotage schemes and establishing stay-behind networks in neutral and enemy territory passed in July 1940 to the newly established SOE, which operated under the control of the Minister of Economic Warfare. This secret agency assumed control both of SO1 (underground propaganda) and SO2 (sabotage and subversion), in the process assimilating SIS's Section D, and MI(R) of the War Office. At the time of this amalgamation, the JIC noted that MI(R) had already begun 'considering Fifth Column and sabotage activities in the Dominions, the Colonies and India . . . the execution of such activities was as yet very much in the future'—an MI(R) paper of 24 May had raised possibilities for 'counter-action . . . by the clandestine mobilization of subject populations and those which become subject to German occupation (e.g. Belgians, French, Spanish, Irish and even English)'. Of the dominions, Ireland was the most urgent case because of the likelihood of a rapid German invasion, and it is in this context that SOE's Irish interests have to be considered.[189] There was initially talk of sending the displaced head of Section D, Colonel Grand, 'who has been completely disloyal', to Ireland, but he went instead to India. SOE faced a host of daunting challenges, and it was not until January 1941 that 'the possibilities of establishing an SO2 organization in Eire were discussed'.[190] This was also the month in which operations 'Shrapnel' and 'Brick' were devised to establish stocks of weapons in the Portuguese Cape Verde islands and in the Azores, in anticipation of British seizure of these neutral territories in order to prompt 'enemy action' against them.[191]

The Irish plan elicited a sharp response from SIS: C told SOE's Frank Nelson that 'the whole question of Secret Service interpretation of Cabinet instructions is at issue . . . I gather that . . . the question of recruitment has already arisen . . . I do not, of course, know in the least what is in your mind or how far things have gone, but a discussion with Vivian seems to me to be imperative'.[192] Nelson replied in conciliatory vein: 'if we should finally decide to send anyone he would be primarily concerned with spreading whispers and making a survey of points which should be destroyed in the event of enemy invasion'.[193] C remained hostile, pointing to the danger that discovery of SOE activities would jeopardize Anglo-Irish security cooperation. His objections caused SOE 'some embarrassment', as BTNI had

---

[188] Outline plans were made for Kenya, Aden, and New Zealand, but there was no mention of Ireland. MI(R) war diary, 3 Sept. 1939–2 Oct. 1940, TNA, HS8/263.

[189] JIC (40) 34, 24 May; JIC(40)52, 22 July 1940, TNA, CAB81/87.

[190] Hugh Dalton's note of talk with Grand, 22 Aug., TNA, HS8/367, and Dalton diary, 18 and 26 Sept. 1940, BLPES, Dalton I/23. Dalton was the minister responsible for SOE from July 1940 to February 1942; Seaman, ' "A New Instrument of War" ', 19; SOE war diary, 30 Jan. 1941, TNA, HS7/212.

[191] SOE war diary, 22 Jan. 1941, TNA, HS7/212.

[192] Menzies to Nelson (SOE), 15 Feb. 1941, TNA, HS6/305.

[193] Nelson to Menzies, 17 Feb. 1941, HS6/305.

repeatedly asked about planning for sabotage operations in Ireland—or '16-land', as it was also termed in SOE documents—in the event of a German attack.[194] But SOE had secured the backing of the chiefs of staff, and on 3 March unveiled a proposed 'programme' of action. This was approved for transmission to BTNI, with the covername 'CLARIBEL II'.[195] The detailed plan has not been traced, but its general thrust can be inferred. The original 'CLARIBEL' was a series of schemes also prepared early in 1941 for selective destruction of transport and communications infrastructure in France, Belgium, and Denmark, intended to 'hamper the enemy invasion effort and disorganize its timing programme'.[196] *Claribel II* would have required the goodwill of local employees of British companies, supplemented by demolition teams sent across from Britain or down from Northern Ireland. The extent of sabotage which could have been achieved in the limited time available, especially if the Irish forces were vigilant, remains a matter of opinion. A scheme was certainly worked out for the destruction of facilities at Dublin airport, probably relying on employees of British firms based there.[197] Plans were made for the destruction of Irish fuel stocks to prevent them falling into German hands. Fuel imports and storage were largely in the hands of British firms, and in December the JIC were reassured to learn that 'an arrangement has been made . . . with the three principal Companies . . . that the stocks there . . . should be kept down'. Plan 'Vista', for the destruction of the fuel stocks of BOAC at Foynes by an employee named Munro, who 'might even consent to stay behind after the Germans had overrun the area', was agreed in June 1941. One SOE officer suggested having 'a light aircraft available for this man after he had done the job', and BOAC were also advised to contact the aptly named 'Mr Bird of the Air Ministry'.[198] If patriotism was not a sufficient incentive—in other countries British as well as local employees sometimes baulked at assisting in the destruction of company assets—compensation might have been offered, as in Yugoslavia, where SOE paid a company to adulterate its stock of locomotive oil, and in Portugal, where Shell cooperated in drawing up plans to destroy oil stocks in the event of a German invasion.[199]

As in other neutral countries, the desirability of making such preparations for destruction had to be weighed against the danger of discovery. In that respect, Britain's Romanian experience in 1939–40 was not an encouraging portent: there, ambitious schemes to disrupt German commerce by blocking the Danube at the Iron Gates, and to sabotage oil fields, failed partly because of the understandable reluctance of patriotic Romanians to destroy their own economic infrastructure, despite frantic overtures and inducements. This was, as the minister responsible observed, 'a bitter disappointment' which probably contributed to the demise

---

[194] SOE war diary, 28 Apr. 1941, TNA, HS7/215.
[195] Ibid., 25 Mar. 1941, TNA, HS7/214.
[196] SOE appreciation, 25 Mar. 1941, TNA, HS6/217.
[197] Private information.
[198] JIC(40), 396, 5 Dec. 1940, TNA, CAB81/99; SOE war diary, 1/2 July 1941, TNA, HS7/218.
[199] SOE war diary, 4 Apr. 1941, TNA, HS7/215. The Portuguese arrangements were discussed on 13 Jan. 1941, TNA, HS7/212.

of Section D.[200] As was disclosed to the Admiralty in December 1942, the Irish themselves made extensive plans for the destruction of key port facilities and airfields, although shortages of explosives and other materials made the likely effectiveness of these dispositions problematic, and from a British point of view there was always the consideration that the Irish might just as likely put them into effect to hamper a British invasion as a German one.[201] The SOE plan did not envisage preparatory measures such as suborning of local officials or covert subsidy of Irish opposition groups, methods which were features of British schemes in other parts of the world at the time (for example, as relations with the Vichy administration in Damascus deteriorated early in 1941, it was decided to 'undertake the bribery' of one or more Syrian political parties).[202]

On 31 March the chiefs of staff instructed SOE, in cooperation with BTNI, to take 'such steps as may be necessary with or without the knowledge of the military authorities in Southern Ireland' to 'lay the foundations for an organization to undertake subversive warfare . . . in the event of the Germans occupying part of Ireland'.[203] This unequivocal directive cleared the way for SOE to start planning in earnest. Within a week a scheme for stay-behind operations emerged. Initially, 'dumps of materials', 'toys'—explosive devices—and 'wireless sets' should be moved to Northern Ireland, and a 'senior agent' appointed who 'should be . . . in communication with England via Northern Ireland. This agent [is] to take no further action except in perfecting his communications with England and Northern Ireland and deciding on suitable persons to be appointed for suitable jobs when permission is given'. The plan also envisaged the 'recruitment and training at one of our schools of 50 stout hearted Irish men from different districts, including wireless operators, who would be willing to go into Ireland to organize opposition behind the German lines as and when required'. If BTNI agreed, equipment and weapons could be smuggled in 'and stored at points'.[204]

This scheme certainly caused explosions, but in Whitehall rather than in Ireland. The chiefs of staff decision of 31 March had taken account of the possibility of obtaining Irish help for such operations. Given the extent of Anglo-Irish counter-invasion planning already in train through the British military mission in Dublin, C warned that any attempt to establish a stay-behind organization would be 'definitely dangerous and open to the strongest objection, unless the arrangements were made with the full knowledge and co-operation of the Eire Defence Authorities. I would not, however, feel that it is very likely that they would favour such a scheme if sponsored by or controlled in any way from England or Northern Ireland'. He also warned that 'the American attitude might be very detrimentally altered by any

[200] Porter, *Operation Anonymous*. SOE's Romanian specialist Gardyne de Chastelain left Romania in February 1941 after completing plans for a sabotage campaign due to begin on 1 March. It did not materialize. See also Maurice Pearton, 'SOE in Romania', in Seaman (ed.), *Special Operations Executive*, 123–36; Hugh Dalton to Churchill, 1 Oct. 1940, TNA, HS8/367.
[201] Fisk, *In Time of War*, 274–5.
[202] SOE war diary, 19 Mar. 1941, TNA, HS7/215.
[203] Quoted in 'Note on SOE Eire', 24 Dec. 1941, TNA, HS6/305.
[204] Unsigned memorandum for Nelson, 5 Apr. 1941, TNA, HS6/305.

such clumsy interference in Irish affairs'.[205] After receiving 'a very urgent reply by telephone on the Final Draft' of the plan, he responded in icy terms: 'I feel that it would save any possible telephonic misunderstanding, if I write'. He warned SOE of the perils of 'any action which, if it leaked out, would be interpreted as clumsy interference', and added that MI5, 'whose valuable liaison with the Eire Defence Ministry depends entirely upon mutual good feeling, have even stronger views than expressed here'.[206]

A compromise was agreed: an SIS officer would accompany the SOE party to meet BTNI about the plan. On 30 April SOE's Colin Gubbins and Major Sheridan visited Northern Ireland to discuss the possibility of establishing stay-behind and sabotage groups 'and in particular... the initiation of a whispering campaign in Dublin'.[207] Gubbins had spent the last year of peace writing manuals on irregular warfare in MI(R), was head of the British military mission in Poland when war broke out, and had distinguished himself in the fighting in Norway, before becoming head of the military side of SOE. He was surprised to find BTNI quite as adamant as C that only with Irish help could stay-behind parties be formed. BTNI specifically advised that McKenna and Archer should be privately approached. They were to be asked to identify and recruit not members of the Irish defence forces, who if Germany attacked would be fully engaged, but unspecified civilians who would be both trustworthy and capable of waging irregular warfare. BTNI's Gregson-Ellis, fresh from his meeting with McKenna, argued that

no scheme could be agreed that entailed the taking into Eire of anything in the nature of explosives, arms, etc unless the Eire Army Authorities, with whom he and his people were in close touch, were first informed. To introduce such stores without first informing the Eire Army leaders (or some of them)... would wreck... good relations... and would lead to further concentration of Eire forces on the border, with the result that BTNI forces would be hampered, and the Germans left greater freedom of movement if they landed.

He emphasized 'one other aspect of the situation', the Irish argument that 'you don't really expect invasion, otherwise you would give us arms', stated that 'the Prime Minister absolutely refuses to allow any arms to be sent to Eire, and up to now will scarcely discuss it'—Churchill had already overruled the chiefs of staff on the issue—and asserted that 'anyone who offered arms to the Eire Army leaders, and was able to implement his offer, could expect to obtain anything within reason for which he asked'.[208]

Gubbins stressed the need for speed, as 'in a number of countries we had not been allowed to introduce wireless sets while opportunity offered, and... when the Germans marched in, it was impossible to introduce them. We did not wish to be in the same position in Eire'. The question was how to do this. There was general agreement that the stay-behind organization should if at all possible be established

---

[205] Menzies to Jebb (SOE), 15 Apr. 1941, TNA, HS6/307.
[206] Menzies to Jebb, 24 Apr. 1941, TNA, HS6/307.
[207] SOE war diary, 28 and 30 Apr. 1941, TNA, HS7/215.
[208] Note of a meeting with BTNI, 30 Apr. 1941, TNA, HS6/305.

with Irish blessing. The alternative, 'a separate secret organization, which if exposed would be repudiated by HMG [His Majesty's Government] and of which the chief organizers would never admit having any associations with HMG', was not ruled out: it was thought 'not impossible that a number of tough people could be found and organized; though not without considerable risk; this view is, of course, absolutely contrary to that' of Vivian of SIS, who wished to protect both his own clandestine operations in Ireland and MI5's crucial liaison with G2. 'After long discussion', it was agreed that Gubbins should 'write a letter on War Office paper' to Pryce, the military attaché, 'which Pryce can show to Archer'. This would be 'couched in terms as impressive as possible (since Irishmen probably regard themselves as expert saboteurs without anything to learn)', while not disclosing anything which 'would help the Germans if it got into wrong hands'. It would describe training facilities, 'be accompanied by an appendix showing the nature of our toys', and include an offer either to train Irishmen in Britain or to send two SOE trainers to Ireland. The 'toys were now ready . . . and could be moved to Northern Ireland ready for transfer to Eire when and if required'. McKenna and Archer should be advised to rely on the part-time Local Security Force in building up a stay-behind organization, as the 'regular army, probably the most suitable and trustworthy, are useless, since in war they will either be fighting or prisoners'.[209]

Gubbins was entirely persuaded: the only way to establish a stay-behind organization 'within a reasonable time' was 'by taking the Irish into our complete confidence . . . providing them with the training and the stores and leaving them responsibility for the organization and the execution'. Such proposals would be 'swallowed avidly' by McKenna, 'an honest to God soldier with no political bias who is solely concerned with trying to carry out his Government's policy of resisting invasion from whatever direction it may come', and who had 'admitted . . . the folly of building defences . . . on the approaches from Ulster, but said that political considerations compelled him to waste time and money on these'. It would be an understanding strictly between military men: some of 'the Eireann ministers are almost self-confessedly pro-German, others are indiscreet and one or two, but not more, may be trustworthy'.[210] SIS proved surprisingly receptive to the plan. On 8 May C 'gave his approval . . . subject to the agreement of other departments'. The proposed letter to the Irish went through several drafts, with one being rejected as smacking of 'codology' in its effusive references to Irish martial traditions, and the final version was typed up for signature on 4 June.[211]

The *Claribel* plan as agreed with BTNI reflected the extraordinary confidence which Gregson-Ellis reposed in both McKenna and Archer following their meeting in Maffey's house. However understanding of British strategic concerns, it was wishful thinking to suppose that these officers would not merely countenance the discreet creation of British stay-behind parties, but actually take the lead in their establishment behind the back of their own government—the meeting at which

---

[209] Ibid.
[210] Memo by 'M' (Gubbins), 1 May 1941, TNA, HS6/305.
[211] Comments by Pryce on draft, 29 May, and final text, 4 June 1941, TNA, HS6/305.

Gregson-Ellis had formed such a favourable impression of the two officers, after all, had taken place with the certain knowledge of de Valera's foreign-policy *eminence grise* Joseph Walshe.

The plan strongly suggests that the British were still unaware of the pro-German intrigues of another senior Irish officer, Major-General Hugo MacNeill, who had long talked of expelling the British from Northern Ireland by force.[212] He had made unofficial contact with the German legation in December 1940 to raise the possibility of German assistance in the event of an expected British invasion, and had suggested that a military specialist should be sent over. This was absolutely contrary to Irish policy, as the government had just refused a German request to send more officials to Ireland. This became clear to the British in 1944, when Jane Archer of SIS analysed hitherto unbroken German diplomatic traffic from Dublin dating back to 1940. MacNeill also made contact with the German agent Goertz, again to promote his idea of an Irish-German military alliance, a matter on which hard evidence first emerged through a successful Anglo-Irish operation to break the code used by Goertz in 1943.[213] From 1941 to the end of the war MacNeill was GOC of the 2nd (Northern) Division, tasked with protecting the northern half of the state.[214]

The revised *Claribel II* ran into further trouble in Whitehall. On 23 May SOE's Gladwyn Jebb was reminded that in the past few months the chiefs of staff had seen three proposals to give the Irish some weapons turned down flat by Churchill. He would certainly veto *Claribel II* if he learnt of it. If, however, SOE decided 'to introduce your "devices" without sounding [out] the Eire authorities, I suggest you should do so on your own authority'.[215] A week later the chiefs of staff 'definitely turned down' the scheme. In reaction to these setbacks, Jebb made one last effort in the name of his minister Hugh Dalton. He wrote to Desmond Morton to stress that the plan had been developed in close consultation with BTNI: it had been agreed that 'the best organization—although not the only one—which could be built up quickly would be composed of people in the Éire Local Defence Force, selected by those officers in the Eire Army whom we trust'. Dalton had asked Jebb, 'in the very exceptional circumstances of our case', to obtain 'some slight relaxation' of the rule that 'supplies of war material of any kind should not be sent to Eire'. A week later came a very dusty reply which put an end to the scheme once and for all: the prime minister believed that to give the Irish arms would only encourage them in their intransigence, and thought it more likely that such weapons would be used against Britain than against a German invader. SOE took this as a command to cease planning an Irish stay-behind organization, and nothing further on these lines was done.[216]

There are some parallels with SOE's experience elsewhere. In the spring of 1941 Churchill remarked that 'the capacity of Spain and Portugal to resist the increasing

[212] O'Halpin, *Defending Ireland*, 136–7.

[213] Hull, *Irish Secrets*, 145–6 and 333, n. 212; *Liddell History*, 76; Cecil Liddell to Stephenson (Dominions Office), 24 Aug., enclosing unsigned analysis by Jane Archer of SIS of decoded German 1940 traffic in which MacNeill featured as 'L', dated 6 Aug. 1943, TNA, DO121/84.

[214] Dan Bryan, quoted in O'Halpin, *Defending Ireland*, 245.

[215] Major-General L. C. Hollis (secretary, chiefs of staff subcommittee) to Jebb, 23 May 1941, TNA, HS6/305.

[216] Jebb to Morton, and reply, 6 and 13 June 1941, TNA, HS6/305.

German pressure may at any time collapse', but attempts to establish stay-behind organizations to operate in that eventuality were hampered by the strong opposition of the respective British ambassadors.[217] These argued that if 'British intrigues with their domestic Oppositions' were to be uncovered, Franco and Salazar would interpret these as preparations for a coup, and seek German help (when the pro-Axis government of Yugoslavia was overthrown in March 1941, the minister responsible for SOE noted: 'What a day! . . . it is clear that our chaps have done their part well'). It took a further year before the ambassador in Madrid would allow the importation of radio sets, by which time the strategic situation had so changed that Spanish wrath could be safely risked. In Portugal SOE made greater progress, but were seriously embarrassed in May 1942 when the police uncovered a scheme to train two local radio operators. This led to the withdrawal of a key operative, although Salazar was eventually persuaded to tolerate limited British clandestine activity on the basis that it was directed solely against German interests and was not a threat to his regime.[218] In Turkey stay-behind preparations were also initiated 'against the possibility of the Turkish Government collapsing', despite the acknowledged danger of discovery, while London sanctioned payments in Sweden to 'a director of a reputable steel business under cover of which finance could be provided for the preparation of S[pecial] O[perations] cells' throughout the country.[219]

Churchill's reported response raises the question of whether he still seriously envisaged circumstances in which Britain might take Irish ports and airfields by force. This seems unlikely. At his behest, Britain had some months before embarked on an undeclared economic blockade of Ireland. Dulanty was assured by Malcolm MacDonald that it was 'a complete mistake' to think that Britain was using 'subtle means to force us into participation in the war', but the evidence is clear: in February Churchill stressed to colleagues that 'the intention was to make Southern Ireland realize how great a wrong they were doing to the cause of freedom by the denial of the ports'.[220] The blockade proved to be politically ineffective: so far from weakening de Valera domestically, it strengthened his position, and it created severe trade difficulties for Britain, particularly in South Wales, where Ireland was a significant customer for the variety of coal produced, as well as economic problems for Ireland. But in the summer of 1941 it was believed that it still held out some promise of eventual success.

Whatever ambitions the prime minister may have continued to entertain to resolve the ports question by force, at no point did either BTNI or SOE prepare their Irish stay-behind schemes along lines designed to hamper Irish defensive arrangements. The plans were constructed entirely in terms of a possible German attack on Ireland, not a British one. The vicissitudes which SOE endured in attempting to secure approval in London for their preferred procedure of relying on the Irish military were not unique: as Neville Wylie has shown, their early plans in the Balkan neutrals had also been predicated on the cooperation of the

---

[217] Churchill to Roosevelt, 23 Apr. 1941, in Kimball, *Churchill and Roosevelt*, i. 173.
[218] Mackenzie, *Secret History of SOE*, 323–4; Dalton diary, 27 Mar., and report on 'certain activities in Yugoslavia', 24 May 1941, BLPES, Dalton 1/24 and II/11/3.
[219] SOE war diaries, 1/2 July and 11/12 Aug. 1941, TNA, HS7/218 and 219.
[220] Dulanty letter to Dublin, 1 Mar. 1941, NAI, DFA P12/14(i); Churchill to Wood and Cranborne, 17 Feb. 1941, quoted in Canning, *British Policy Towards Ireland*, 306–7.

various national armies, and in those cases they had largely fallen apart when that cooperation was withdrawn.[221]

BRITISH PROPAGANDA AND IRELAND, 1940–1941

In parallel with its planning for stay-behind operations in Ireland, SOE became involved in another significant strand of clandestine activity. There were major developments in overt propaganda directed against Ireland, in the introduction of Irish themes into black propaganda and disinformation directed towards the Axis powers, and in the use of neutral Ireland as a locale in which misleading war news could be planted which might then find its way to Axis ears and so eventually influence enemy policy.

Such activities must be seen within the broader framework of British efforts to use techniques of overt and black propaganda effectively against the Axis. Propaganda policy was initially characterized by what one historian has termed 'two years of chaos'.[222] Driven by exaggerated estimates of the contribution of propaganda, both overt and clandestine, to German victory in western Europe in 1940, SOE and other British agencies placed a premium on 'political warfare' as a means of resistance to the Axis. Tools to be used included, naturally, the unadorned truth—the BBC's international reputation for impartiality, at least as compared with that of most state broadcasters, was recognized as a pearl beyond price. But truth was a finite asset, and other approaches were also employed. These ranged from the insertion of chosen lines of argument and analysis in the national and international press to the dissemination of 'sibs' or 'whispers'—manufactured rumours—designed to confuse or mislead, to the production of fake publications and to 'black' broadcasting, where programmes were broadcast on the frequencies of genuine enemy stations or from notional stations under British control. In Turkey, like Ireland a strategically significant neutral, 'a whispering campaign' was initiated in the summer of 1940.[223]

Just how ruthless the British approach could be in the realm of black propaganda is reflected in an SOE document from late 1941. An officer about to return to the United States remarked that 'existing photographs' of real German atrocities 'available from occupied territories...are indifferent in quality, owing to over-reproduction'. What was now needed was 'a regular supply...manufactured by us in Canada...the most obvious setting for atrocity photographs at the moment is Russia...we should get to work while there is still snow in Canada'.[224]

Where Ireland was concerned, the British media seldom needed to be fed any lines. In the first year of the war columnists and cartoonists amplified the rumours of German submarines along the west coast, and generally pilloried de Valera for

---

[221] Wylie, 'SOE and the Neutrals', 163.

[222] Taylor, *British Propaganda in the Twentieth Century*, 151.

[223] SOE war diary, Oct.–Dec. 1940, TNA, HS7/211 (the 1940 diary was not organized on a day-by-day basis). For intelligence operations relating to Turkey, see Denniston, *Churchill's Secret War*.

[224] G106 to A/D, 26 Nov. 1941, TNA, HS1/333.

his short-sighted folly in not standing by Britain—in July 1940 he complained that 'there was such a wave of this that it suggested permission or connivance', and as early as April Maffey hoped that London 'will do their best to hold the Press in check'. While there is no direct evidence of this, in that month the JIC did consider and approve a rumour that de Valera, while opposed to British occupation of the treaty ports, would welcome an American offer to defend them.[225] In the autumn and winter of 1940 press attacks on Ireland sometimes exceeded what the government thought useful, and at one point the dominions secretary asked the Ministry of Information to attempt to curb Fleet Street's zeal. The British legation in Kabul made similar representations in 1942 in respect of alarmist press coverage from Reuters about the activities of the Axis legations: the argument was that such material made it harder for the Afghans to take steps against Axis intrigue for fear of appearing to be Churchill's lapdogs. London was not entirely persuaded: 'presence of Axis legations . . . is not matter which can be entirely' discounted, and 'an occasional jab' might be no bad thing. A few months later, the Foreign Office did write reprovingly to the Sheffield *Weekly Telegraph* for publishing an alarmist story, partly so that the correspondence could be solemnly produced when the Afghans duly complained.[226]

In January 1941 the poet John Betjeman was appointed as press attaché in Dublin. The Irish felt they could not object—the Germans already had Carl Petersen—although it was clear that Betjeman's main task would be to attempt to influence Irish opinion by all possible means. The Irish aimed to counter foreign influences on the media by the operation of a very severe press and cinema censorship (the controller of censorship from 1941, Thomas Coyne, had served in the Royal Flying Corps during the first world war, but this did not render him amenable to pro-British material). Censorship left the national press, in Godfrey's words, 'dull and insipid', although Clair Wills has demonstrated that local newspapers were less closely policed.[227] Betjeman soon became an object of widespread rumour and of official suspicion that he was pursuing a covert as well as an overt role. Betjeman's main tasks were twofold: to cultivate the Irish media and attempt to infuse a sympathetic attitude to Britain into Irish commentary on the war; and to counter Axis propaganda in Ireland.[228] The latter task involved the analysis of pro-Axis publications and the discreet investigation of their origins, work which brought him into contact with the Ministry of Economic Warfare as well as with the Dominions Office and the Ministry of Information (where one of his correspondents was the historian Nicholas Mansergh, already a shrewd academic commentator on

225 Maffey to London, 19 Apr., and 16 July 1940 (enclosing note of talk with de Valera), TNA, KV4/280 and TNA, DO130/12.

226 Canning, *British Policy Towards Ireland*, 303. The minister for information at the time was Churchill's confidant Brendan Bracken. Kabul to London, and Delhi to Kabul, 17 and 20 May, and [illegible] to Peel, India Office, 21 Oct. 1942, 10R L/PS/12/1783.

227 Walshe to de Valera, 13 Nov. 1940, UCDA, TNA, de Valera papers, P150/2571; Godfrey memoir, 193, CCCA, Godfrey papers, 1/6; on censorship policy see esp. O'Drisceoil, *Censorship in Ireland*; Wills, *That Neutral Island*, 430; Ó Longaigh, *Emergency Law*, 23.

228 Washe to de Valera, 13 Nov. 1940, NAI, DFA A2. Material on the German requests is in NAI, DFA A21. The Germans increased the number of locally employed staff in 1941, drawing on the German community. Bryan to Walshe (Dublin), 16 Jan. 1942, NAI, DFA A8.

independent Ireland).[229] While Robert Fisk rightly dismisses the allegation that Betjeman was a spy, in 1942 he did agree to participate in the dissemination of whispers.[230]

Another distinguished writer, Elizabeth Bowen, moved back to her family home in Cork with official encouragement to work on behalf of the Ministry of Information, talking to politicians and opinion-formers as well as to members of the public. She submitted a number of critical but perceptive reports on the emotions and calculations underpinning Irish policy. One, which concluded that in existing circumstances neutrality was the only feasible policy for de Valera, was commended to Churchill by the dominions secretary Cranborne in November 1940, a chance which later contributed to the accusation that she had been a British intelligence agent as distinct from a well-informed observer.[231]

The theme of Ireland as a haven for U-boats and Nazi spies was taken up by various British newspapers and cartoonists, reinforcing widespread myths about the extent of German penetration and the threat presented to Britain by Irish neutrality in 1940–1 (after which the cartoonists largely lost interest in Ireland).[232] One of the more curious examples was the thriller *Dark Duet*, published in 1942. Its author, Peter Cheney, of Irish descent and formerly a Fascist, was already a successful writer. *Dark Duet* features two British counter-intelligence officers who are in Ireland to track down German agents. These they eliminate with gusto: the book describes how they use 'Process 5' (assassination) on one suspect, as 'there is nothing official on the woman . . . You can't *prove* anything'. The book is devoid of Irish characters, being populated entirely by the British protagonists and their German prey, one of whom complains about the difficulties of infiltration into Britain: 'the damned English get more cautious every day, and the Irish are a sick headache'. While unflattering about the damp Irish climate and the potholed roads, *Dark Duet* made no political critique of Irish neutrality—while it offered a picture of an Ireland awash with German intrigue, it assumed that England was also crawling with German spies (something also suggested in Margery Allingham's *Traitor's Purse* and Agatha Christie's *N or M?*, pieces of patriotic crime-writing produced by two queens of the genre during the darkest days of the war).[233] It is hard to believe that Cheney's brutal text was officially inspired in hopes of discrediting neutral Ireland.

The dangers posed by irish neutrality and axis intrigue are taken up in post-war popular fiction and film, notably in David Grant's *Emerald Decision* (1980) and Brian Garfield's *The Paladin* (1980), a purportedly true story which centres on

[229] Ó Drisceoil, *Censorship in Ireland*, 147. Conversation with Professor Mansergh, Cambridge, Sept. 1986.

[230] Fisk, *In Time of War*, 441; Cole, *Propaganda, Censorship and Irish Neutrality*, 69–72, 131–7, deals extensively with Betjeman's overt activities but does not discuss whispering.

[231] Canning, *British Policy Towards Ireland*, 294–5; Fisk, *In Time of War*, 411–13, 422–4, 439–40; Wills, *That Neutral Island*, 116–17. See also Wills's discussion at p. 169 of the coastal activities of the eccentric author T. H. White, remembered mainly for *The Sword and the Stone*, part of the novel sequence *The Once and Future King*.

[232] This is borne out by the database of images in the British Cartoon Archive at the University of Kent, where references to Ireland by wartime cartoonists such as David Low disappear after 1940.

[233] Cheney, *Dark Duet*, 134 and 136; Allingham, *Traitor's Purse*; Christie, *N or M?*.

the hero's discovery of a secret U-boat base in Donegal obligingly maintained for the Germans by the Irish army, while Jack Higgins's *The Eagle Has Landed* (1976: director John Sturges) has a strong anti-hero in the resourceful IRA man turned German agent Liam Devlin, whose life story appears to be an amalgalm of those of Francis Stuart and Frank Ryan. Ken Follett's *The Eye of the Needle* (1981: director Richard Marquand) also features an IRA man working for the Germans—confusingly, the same actor, Donald Sutherland, plays the Irishman in the film versions of the two books. The film of Ewan Montagu's *The Man Who Never Was* (1955: director Ronald Neame), which, like the book on which it was based, purported to be factual, also has an Irish spy based in London, Patrick O'Reilly, who radios Germany with important information.[234] *I See a Dark Stranger* (1946: director Frank Launder) uses the theme of a passionately anti-British Irishwoman who spies for the Germans before seeing the error of her ways just in time.

British propaganda about Ireland internationally was subject to fewer constraints, because so much could be disseminated on an unavowable basis. Rumours could be planted and reports inspired which put Ireland in a poor light without Britain appearing to play a part. The United States was the most significant market for such black propaganda in 1940–1, both because of the American government's hostility to Irish neutrality and of the assumed political strength of the Irish-American diaspora, whose isolationism and Anglophobia had to be combated by all possible means. De Valera had spent much of the war of independence in the United States, raising funds, generating public support, and attempting—although he met with no success at all—to influence the Wilson administration to endorse separatist Ireland's cause. After 1939 the abject failure of Irish separatist diplomacy in 1919–21 in terms of influencing the American government was ignored or forgotten, for very different reasons, both by Dublin and by London. The State Department was also mindful of domestic 'political considerations' in public comment on Irish neutrality, despite the president's personal hostility to the Irish position.[235]

Roosevelt's unequivocal support for Britain's war, and his appointment of the passionate Anglophile David Gray to represent the United States in Dublin in February 1940, were clear signals that the administration had no sympathy for Ireland's position. Yet British policy-makers continued to fret about the political influence of Irish-Americans and their capacity to damage British interests. Of particular concern, until his departure in October 1940, was the rabidly isolationist American ambassador in London, the Irish-American Joseph Kennedy, some of whose pessimistic communications they could decode. In British eyes, about the only thing in Kennedy's favour was his utter lack of interest in Irish issues—'I never understood this but I could see he was whipping himself up into his campaign for US', he remarked dismissively in his diary after de Valera buttonholed him about

---

[234] Montagu oversaw Operation *Mincemeat*, whereby fake plans for the invasion of Greece were planted on the Germans in 1943. When Duff Cooper, who as a minister had knowledge of this, wrote a fictionalized account as *Operation Heartbreak* in 1951, Montagu was prevailed on by the Admiralty rapidly to write what purported to be a full account, *The Man Who Never Was* (London, 1953). The aim of his literary efforts was to obscure the fact that the key to the deception lay in British ability to decode Abwehr radio traffic.

[235] Moffat journal, 3 Sept. 1939, Harvard, MS 1407, vol. 43.

partition during ceremonies marking the installation of Pope Pius XII in Rome in March 1939.[236] On a visit to Washington in December 1939 Kennedy used language 'picturesque in the extreme' to inform State Department officials that 'no one in England . . . wants to fight' except the 'ruthless and scheming' Churchill, who 'wants us in' and 'is in touch with groups in America who have the same idea, notably strong Jewish leaders'. Of Ireland he said nothing. His friend Montagu Norman noted that Kennedy left his London post 'slighted by Downing Street and Washington', his withdrawal unmourned: one minister described him as 'a defeatist and a crook'. His successor, John Winant, had some knowledge of Ireland and of Irish officials from his service in Geneva with the International Labour Organization, but was also a strong Anglophile.[237]

As an adjunct to diplomatic advocacy of her cause, Britain developed more subtle means of discrediting Irish neutrality. The challenge was to neutralize Irish-American hostility to the war, and incidentally also to encourage Irish participation in it, without appearing to do so. In July 1940, less than two months after Churchill had suggested to Roosevelt that he station elements of the United States navy in Irish ports, the JIC approved a rumour that the United States was about to send troops to defend Ireland, 'this assistance being acceptable to Mr de Valera whereas British assistance is still discouraged'.[238] In February 1941 the head of SOE's American operations discussed the 'possibility of reversing Irish Catholic influence' in supporting American isolationism.[239] He also reported on discussions with SIS's New York representative: 'The principal subject discussed . . . was the influencing of the policy of the Irish government from the USA. This matter had already been explored but was for the moment held up', but as regarded the 'combatting [of] hostile activities operated from America' an 'Irish project was being closely studied'.[240]

The British controlled one significant propaganda vehicle in the United States, the American Irish Defense Association (AIDA). This was established late in 1940 or early in 1941, and after Hitler's attack on Russia SOE in New York told London that 'there was a chance now of obtaining the active support of Irish Communists in America'.[241] AIDA's membership came mainly from respectable Irish-American East Coast society—priests, academics, lawyers, congressmen, local politicians, journalists, and trade unionists—and it had a distinctly Democratic political ethos. The officer board of AIDA included as treasurer Christopher Addis Emmet, described as a 'grand nephew' of the Irish patriot Robert Emmet.[242] As well as making a public case for Ireland to stand by Britain in her hour of need, and indirectly influencing Irish-American opinion in favour of increased support for

[236] Kennedy's diary, 12 Mar. 1939, in Smith, *Hostage to Fortune*, 316–17. De Valera planned to visit the USA on the occasion of the opening of the New York World Fair, but due to the international situation did not do so.

[237] Moffat journal, 8 and 15 Sept. 1939, Harvard, MS 1407, vol. 43; Montagu Norman diary, 17 Oct. 1940, Bank of England archives; Dalton diary, 15 Oct. 1940, BLPES, Dalton 1/23.

[238] JIC(40) 154, 5 July 1940, TNA, CAB81/97.

[239] SOE war diary, 24 Feb. 1941, TNA, HS7/213.

[240] Ibid., 24 Feb. and 19 Mar. 1941, TNA, HS7/213 and 214.

[241] Ibid., 24–6 July 1941, TNA, HS7/218.

[242] Robert Emmet was executed in 1803. It seems more likely that Christopher Emmet was a great-grandnephew.

Britain, AIDA encouraged the publication of articles, letters to the press, statements by key churchmen, public lectures on aspects of the challenges to democracy presented by the Axis, and similar activities. AIDA also advised Bill Donovan's Office of the Coordinator of Information (an umbrella propaganda and intelligence organization which later became the Office of Strategic Services or OSS) on a series of short-wave broadcasts to Ireland by prominent Irish-Americans—among names put forward in January 1942 were Al Smith, the first Catholic to run for the White House, the boxer Gene Tunney, and the film stars Maureen O'Hara, Burgess Meredith, and Errol Flynn.[243]

The arguments advanced by AIDA were generally constructive rather than directly critical of the Irish government, stressing that as a new democracy which had enjoyed considerable public support in the United States during its legitimate struggle for freedom, Ireland naturally now belonged with Britain and the United States aligned against the European dictators. In March 1941 the association sent a telegram to de Valera setting out the case for allowing the use of the ports. Robert Brennan was alarmed at AIDA's activities: he reported to Dublin that none of the people linked to it were 'ever connected with Irish [independence] movement', although in his memoirs he states that its chairman was 'a friend of mine, a man who had given good service to Ireland'.[244] AIDA was denounced by isolationist politicians as a genteel front for British propaganda. Although the charge could not be proven, it was true.[245] It is clear from the detailed SOE records that from its early days AIDA was under its indirect control, through a member of its officer board.[246]

Brennan suspected British manipulation of the American media against Ireland. A political appointee who had been a journalist, a leading republican propagandist, and a diplomat *manqué* during the war of independence, he was ill-equipped to counter it. Whereas the East Coast press had been vaguely sympathetic towards independent Ireland before the war, the same elements became increasingly critical of Irish neutrality on both moral and pragmatic grounds. The American government regarded the Irish position as illogical and absurd, an impression probably reinforced since September 1939: in the first year of the war J.P. Moffat, the head of the State Department's Division of European Affairs, whose brief included Ireland, was constantly besieged by the representatives of one hapless European neutral or another about to be or already gobbled up by Hitler or by Stalin.[247] The official American view was that Ireland would surely share the same fate at German hands

---

[243] Note of AIDA meeting with CIO and Office of Facts and Figures, 5 Jan. 1941, and list of suggested speakers, 7 Jan. 1942, TNA, HS8/60.

[244] Wills, *That Neutral Island*, 120–1; Brennan (Washington) to Dublin, 15 Sept. 1941, NAI, DFA P.52; Brennan, *Ireland Standing Firm*, 23. This material was originally published as a series of articles in the *Irish Press* in 1958.

[245] On 10 Nov. 1941 Senator Wheeler claimed that the association was the warmongering Donovan's creation and called for his dismissal. *Congressional Record*, vol. 87, no. 201. Although published as recently as 2006, Cole, *Propaganda, Censorship and Irish Neutrality*, 89, dismisses charges of British control of AIDA despite the ample evidence in SOE records.

[246] The records from January 1941 to January 1942 are in TNA, HS8/56–60.

[247] Moffat had served at the League of Nations from 1933 to 1937. He knew the Irish official Seán Lester, who became acting secretary-general of the League in 1940, and was on close terms with another Irishman, E. J. Phelan of the International Labour Organization (which in 1940 moved from Geneva to Montreal).

unless she joined with Britain in the defence of the British Isles and of the Atlantic. Sympathy for Britain in Washington was also strengthened by her resolution in the face of German air attack after June 1940.

Brennan had few senior contacts within the administration, his only significant Congressional friends were sworn isolationists, and, as was clear from his disastrous mishandling of the question of a new American minister to Dublin, he was prone to blunders. In any event, his preference for working the isolationist side of Capitol Hill and for associating with the most anti-British Irish-Americans was scarcely calculated to commend him to Roosevelt's administration. He was 'pleased at my reception' at the funeral in Philadelphia of the Clan na Gael leader Joe McGarrity, who had travelled to Berlin in June 1939 to copperfasten arrangements between the IRA and the Abwehr (although Brennan was unaware of the latter links), yet seems not to have exploited this renewed cordiality to find out whether the Clan were up to their old tricks.[248] Brennan was also hamstrung in combating American press criticism of Ireland, particularly on the crucial question of the ports, which had particular resonance in the United States, by his very limited access to significant opinion-formers. Irritated by a hortatory poem of Christmas greetings in the *New Yorker*, which concluded by urging Ireland affectionately but firmly, 'Come on, Eire, be good sports! Give J Bull the use of your ports!', he missed midnight mass in order to write a riposte. This ended:

> Cynics then may say in glee
> 'Of all the Goddam fools there be
> The Irish surely lead the drove.
> For many a century they strove
> To get the English out; and then
> Why they just asked them back again'.

He sought to have this dubious composition published anonymously.[249] In reflecting on Brennan's somewhat lame performance, we should note that other small states had their own difficulties getting their message across in Washington as the Roosevelt administration inched America towards war: Malcolm MacDonald, the former dominions secretary reportedly regarded as 'rat poison' by Churchill because of his role in the 1938 Anglo-Irish negotiations, and now British high commissioner in Ottawa, remarked that Canadian publicity in the United States 'was so bad that words could not describe it'. With one exception, 'there was nobody in the Canadian Government establishment who knew his way around Washington and the Canadian legation just didn't count. Even socially, it was a dead loss'.[250]

March 1941 brought a new low in Irish–American relations. Frank Aiken visited Washington to ask for American defence, food, and shipping aid. This proved a policy and publicity disaster, where Dublin had expected to make

---

[248] Brennan to Walsh, 12 Aug. 1940, NYPL, Joseph C. Walsh papers, box 3. For Brennan's Blunder, see p. 152 below.

[249] Frank Sullivan, 'Greetings, Friends!', *New Yorker*, 21 Dec. 1940; Brennan to Walsh, 26 Dec. 1940, NYPL, Joseph C. Walsh papers, box 3.

[250] Entry for 18 Dec. 1940, in Dilks, *Cadogan Diareis*, 341; Moffat journal, 16 Aug. 1941, Harvard, MS 1407, vol. 46.

headway. The imperturbable and taciturn Aiken, described by Bill Donovan as 'of the extreme Left Wing' but nevertheless a man whom the president should see, was believed, correctly or not, to be amongst the most pro-German of Irish politicians.[251] Roosevelt left Aiken to kick his heels for a fortnight before granting an interview: he then took the opportunity during an ill-tempered meeting to berate the folly of Irish neutrality, and the press generally took their lead from the administration's manifest hostility.[252] The Irish request for arms was not met, although Roosevelt, responding to press comment on reported shortages in Ireland, did afterwards grudgingly undertake to secure two ships for the Irish for grain imports.

It would be wrong to attribute Aiken's tribulations mainly to British machinations: Roosevelt had long-standing and coherent policy reasons for trying to push Ireland into an accommodation with Britain instead of reassuring her in her neutrality. But it seems likely that the clandestine influence which Britain exercised in the American media played some part in the public discrediting of the Irish position in 1940–1. Britain was not the only belligerent seeking to manipulate Irish-American opinion: in January 1941 the German ambassador in Washington was instructed 'to cultivate your relations with Irish leaders' to ascertain how they would react to a British occupation of Ireland. The necessary 'pecuniary means' would be made available immediately, and 'I also request that this message be kept secret so far as the other members of your staff are concerned'. Whether or not much was achieved by such means is unknown.[253]

While the White House and the State Department were implacably hostile to the Irish position and supportive of Britain's arguments about Atlantic defence, even Roosevelt, already constrained by the strength of isolationist sentiment generally, had to take some heed of Irish-American opinion. To some extent Irish-America was a dog which neither barked nor bit in active support of Irish neutrality between 1939 and 1941, a few growlings in Congress aside, but that in turn may have been attributable to the relative circumspection with which Roosevelt proceeded as he sought to pressure de Valera into supporting Britain.

The management of covert propaganda and other forms of 'political warfare' proved difficult in relation to Ireland as it did to almost every country, particularly where the matters at issue crossed interdepartmental boundaries. By the autumn of 1940 the situation was Byzantine, as individual agencies manufactured and circulated sibs, whispers, and 'false rumours'—they could not agree even on the terminology to be used—some of which were now coming back through MI5-controlled double agents for further investigation. Two coordinating mechanisms were agreed to tackle this problem: the 'W' board, which would vet all information being offered to the enemy via double agents, and the Inter Services Security Board (ISSB). This provided a clearing-house through which all rumours, whispers, and sibs had to be approved by a committee representative of the intelligence agencies,

---

251 Donovan [in London] to secretary of the navy, 11 Mar. 1941, Roosevelt papers, Safe Files, box 3, accessed via www.fdrlibrary.marist.edu.

252 Rosenberg, 'The 1941 Mission of Frank Aiken to the United States', 162–77.

253 Berlin to German ambassador, Washington, 26 Jan. 1941, quoted in Magic summary, 30 June 1943, NARA, RG457, box 5.

the fighting services, and the Foreign Office.[254] The idea was to ensure that whispers originating in one section of the British war machine did not inadvertently damage the interests of other parts. But, to quote the official history of deception, the ISSB was responsible 'neither for formulating nor for implementing any overall deception "policy". In the early years of the war no such policy existed'.[255]

The spreading of whispers was complicated by jurisdictional disputes. There were constant arguments about which department or agency was entitled to initiate what kind of whisper, a good deal of bickering about the appropriate channels through which such whispers could be disseminated, and friction about the planting of whispers in neutral countries: in June 1941 the JIC chairman warned that the Foreign Office 'were very nervous lest it become known in America that we were spreading rumours. He referred to rumours concerning America and . . . all such rumours this week were cancelled . . . We should at least be extra careful', since even the Roosevelt administration would not take kindly to evidence of covert interference.[256] The spreading of rumours in Turkey, initiated in late summer 1940, was completely stopped in 1941, evidently because of the objections of the British ambassador, and although later resumed, 'it must be clearly understood that Istanbul should be used only as a source for whispers to the Balkans and that the ban on whispers about Turkey or for consumption in Turkey still held good'.[257] The issue of whispering in Ireland was also to become a contentious matter, not because anyone feared antagonizing de Valera—he was fair game—but because of an inter-agency dispute.

The use of Dublin as a centre for the spreading of whispers became entangled with the separate question of SOE's plans for stay-behind groups. In January 1941 SOE had selected as their Irish agent James Roderick Keith. 'Roddy' Keith was the Dublin-born son of a British army officer, and of 'a family more English than Irish. Their views were definitely pro-British'. Keith was an employee of the advertising agency J. Walter Thomson and also co-proprietor of a firm 'which is about to commence exporting razor blades to England'. He had recently returned from 'several months' in Latin America working for the Ministry of Information, 'who wrote him an excellent reference'. Keith sought an army commission, but an SOE interviewer thought he would be 'an excellent man as our chief whisperer in Dublin'. Keith assured SOE that 'it would not be hard for him through his friends to get information to the German and Italian legations. He said that he could ensure the publication of practically any report we desired in the *Cork Examiner* and that he certainly had influence with the *Irish Independent*'.[258] There spoke an advertising man. The reality was that, in the name of maintaining unblemished neutrality, the press censorship regime was far stricter than any which applied in other neutral

[254] Liddell diary, 1 and 9 Oct. 1940, TNA, KV4/187.

[255] Howard, *British Intelligence in the second world war*, v. 22; O'Halpin, 'Hitler's Irish Hideout', in Seaman, *Special Operations Executive*, 201–16, discusses SOE's Irish propaganda activities in more depth.

[256] D/Q9 to AD/AD1, 3 June 1941, TNA, HS1/333.

[257] Foreign Office to Cairo, 10 June 1943, TNA, FO898/69; SOE war diary, 26 May 1942, TNA, HS7/233.

[258] Undated extracts from Keith's SOE personal file, in Stuart (SOE adviser) to the author, 18 June 1999.

democracies. Irish censorship has been criticized by historians for its dampening impact on political discourse as well as for its role in suppressing war news and comment.[259] It is worth noting that one of the principal justifications advanced by the government was the fear that foreign powers might seek to influence Irish public opinion by infiltrating appropriate material into the public domain. This is precisely what SOE set out to do, among other things, in Ireland.

SOE obtained an ungazetted commission for Keith, with effect from 21 March 1941. They also began discussions with BTNI on whether he 'should do further work', most likely the identification of targets for destruction in the event of a German attack. On 15 March he returned to Dublin to begin his work as 'D/Q10'. His communications with SOE were handled by the military attaché, Pryce. On SOE instructions Keith applied for an Irish passport, as this would enable him to travel abroad in neutral guise. He did not stay very long in Ireland, and his impact as a whisperer is impossible to judge. While many whispers approved by the ISSB reflected sexual or supernatural themes—Mussolini's insatiable appetite for his nurses, venereal disease among German soldiers, 'condoms de plaisir' in Bordeaux dosed with itching powder, Baldur von Schirach leaving a Budapest hotel dressed as a woman, as well as ghouls giving birth to children, strange stars seen in the firmament, and other portents of disaster designed to influence Muslim opinion in the Vichy French empire—those with a bearing on Ireland were disappointingly prosaic: in the autumn of 1941 'R/427' simply stated that 'de Valera is going to allow the Americans to use Irish naval bases', and 'R/456' claimed that 'during the last six weeks, 1,200 American "technicians" have arrived in Eire'.[260] These were presumably intended partly to embarrass de Valera and perhaps to tempt him into a denial which would further damage him in American eyes.[261]

Only a few whispers can be directly associated with Keith: 'S/535' had a military theme related to Atlantic defence, stating that 'the USA has just handed over to Britain, under Lend and Lease, one of the three fortified floating islands equipped with electrical defence apparatus, which is to be used as a base for anti-U boat aircraft . . . It has already accounted for three submarines in the past ten days'. S/599 was more closely tailored to Irish religious sensibilities: 'the Pope has excommunicated Hitler but the excommunication has not been made public'.[262]

A handful of Irish-related whispers have been identified amongst the hundreds approved by the ISSB in 1941/2. The most interesting, however, seems to have been developed without reference to the ISSB. Following the astonishing arrival of Hitler's deputy Rudolf Hess in Scotland in May, the Ministry of Economic Warfare prepared an elaborate circumstantial account of his interrogation. The intention was to sow discord between Mussolini and Hitler, who were scheduled to meet shortly to discuss strategic issues. The key implication of this account, artfully

[259] Ó Drisceóil, *Censorship in Ireland*.

[260] Undated list of sibs presented to the ISSB [late 1941], TNA, FO898/69. This file also contains the condom sib, in Adams to Crossman (Richard Crossman, the peppery political journalist attached to PWE. He later served in the Labour government between 1964 and 1970, provoking a crisis when he decided to publish his cabinet diaries), 22 Aug. 1941, TNA, FO868/69.

[261] Reynolds, *Rich Relations*, 117–18.

[262] Unsigned note to Pryce, enclosing whispers 'for my friend Roddy', 8 May 1941, TNA, HS6/305.

tucked away towards the end of the story, was that as part of a potential peace offer carried by Hess, Hitler was minded to let the British retain the Italian colonies in Africa which they had already captured, and to accept British naval primacy in the Mediterranean. This carefully contrived yarn was to be planted on an unsuspecting Italian in Dublin—whether a resident or a diplomat is not clear—in hopes that it would be faithfully relayed to Rome so as to reach Mussolini's ears before the planned meeting with Hitler at the Brenner Pass. That meeting took place before the story could be put into circulation. In any event, it is hard to imagine how any listener, unless accompanied by a stenographer, would have been able to absorb so subtle and lengthy a whisper in sufficient detail accurately to report it to Rome in all its nuanced glory.[263]

Keith was already in difficulties by May, when 'it was agreed not to mention' his whispering work to the JIC.[264] SOE privately maintained that they had a monopoly on the distribution of whispers outside the United Kingdom, but they were evidently uncertain that other agencies agreed. Keith had already earned the hostility both of the military attaché and of SIS in Dublin, who complained that his indiscretion jeopardized other British interests. Early in June BTNI told SOE that 'Keith, your tame Irishman (or is it Englishman living in Ireland?) has been exploded and urgently asks that he be recalled at once'.[265] SOE brought him back to England, although 'we do not accept as well founded the complaints about him' in 'reports which C's department may have'.[266] Keith had further plans. He offered to return to Dublin to set up a 'scheme for monitoring the [German legation's clandestine] wireless; this could then be handed over to any future agent we may have in 16-land. The proposal after discussion I rejected because I feel sure that [Vivian of SIS] would say that any future agent must have nothing to do with Keith, Keith's friends or Keith's business'.[267] Keith accepted a proposal by SOE to let him 'go back to 16-land temporarily on salary' and to meet 'reasonable expenses incurred in winding up his affairs in Dublin undertaken at our request'. He would then be placed in the ' "pool" [of undeployed SOE agents] with a recommendation that he is fit for employment'.[268] In July there was a change of plan, and SOE initiated efforts to obtain him a conventional military posting, but the following month came another twist. Despite a 'disturbing report' about his comments while on a training course, Keith was prepared for a propaganda mission in Africa. On 27 August, by now bearing the codename 'W/KQ', he returned to Dublin to assemble elements of his cover as a promoter of Irish exports and occasional foreign correspondent for Irish newspapers.[269]

G2 had already opened a file on Keith, possibly on foot of a distinctly odd letter to his Dublin-based wife 'Angel Pie' sent earlier that month. In language liable to catch the eye of even the slackest postal censor, he had written: 'I have two

263 Undated document, and Murray to Leeper (PWE), 3 June 1941, TNA, FO898/30.
264 D/G to ADA, 19 May 1941, and unsigned note, TNA, HS6/305.
265 Unsigned minute, 31 May 1941, TNA, HS6/305.
266 'Note on SOE Eire', 24 Dec. 1941, TNA, HS6/305.
267 AD/A1 to AD/A, 17 June 1941, with Stuart to the author, 18 June 1999.
268 Ibid.
269 Information in Stuart to the author, 18 June 1999.

highly important messages for you to deliver. Will you say to Ulick: "How sad it is about poor Pierce", & will you also say if he appreciated the first appearance of the ringmaster. The latter is so important that if you leave without seeing him, I would like you to leave a message'.[270] G2's interest in Keith was probably heightened by his claim on returning to Dublin to have lost a briefcase containing his Irish passport—he 'made enquiries in various Left Luggage and Lost Property offices' to sustain this deception before reporting the matter to the Garda—and he succeeded in obtaining a replacement, 'but only one valid for USA, Canada and UK . . . After rather lengthy negotiations it was also made valid for British, French, Spanish and Belgian Colonial possessions; also Spain and Portugal'. Keith then travelled to Cork, where he obtained a letter of introduction from members of a Catholic missionary order active in Africa: 'armed with this and a letter from the *Tablet* [the English Catholic journal] called on the Editor of the [*Catholic*] *Standard*. Was appointed their African correspondent and obtained a letter to this effect. Arrangements £4.4.0 per article plus certain travel expenses'. Keith ran into further delay in obtaining visas for various colonial territories in west Africa, but he secured a sympathetic hearing from 'Mr Fay, Minister for External Affairs', who 'has instructed the Irish representatives to Vichy and to Madrid to use their influence on my behalf'. Here again was evidence of an advertising man's propensity to talk things up: Fay was only a middle-ranking official, a point which an Irish agent might have been expected to grasp. His relentlessly optimistic progress report continued:

As the visa delay was a disappointment, spent nearly a week 'cultivating' the FIM [Federation of Irish Manufacturers]. The result were good, and have produced a letter from the Secretary appointing me to report on the postwar trade outlook. The FIM is keen for the Government to sponsor this appointment thus obtaining diplomatic privileges and has sent a memorandum to the Minister to this effect.

(One member said that I should take trade samples with me and suggested a pedigree bull and seed potatoes!)[271]

These plans later fell through, perhaps because Keith's cover was wearing very thin. In October his name cropped up through postal surveillance of another Anglo-Irishman, and further enquiries added to Irish doubts about him. He reportedly claimed to acquaintances that he had been appointed a special correspondent for the unashamedly pro-British *Irish Times*, whereas G2 enquiries—some, perhaps not coincidentally, carried out by an officer of Anglo-Irish background—indicated that no one in the newspaper knew of him. Early in 1942 Dan Bryan told Walshe that 'we have not succeeded in getting anyone who can really vouch for him', and that 'neighbours with whom he is friendly have come to the conclusion that he is engaged on a "hush-hush" job. What reliance can be placed on this . . . we cannot say'.[272] The problem resolved itself, as postal intercepts revealed that Keith had joined the King's Royal Rifle Corps. Two months later he was 'congratulating'

---

[270] Keith to 'Angel Pie', 13 Aug. 1941, MAI, G2/3916.
[271] Keith to 'Caesar' (SOE's Julius Hanau), 18 Sept. 1941, with Stuart to the author, 18 June 1999. The FIM was also something of a hotbed of anti-British and anti-Semitic opinion.
[272] Report by Captain Hewett, G2, 16 Jan. 1942, and Bryan to Walshe, 21 Feb. 1942, MAI, G2/3916.

himself for 'joining at the right time', and G2 ceased surveillance of his Irish correspondence shortly afterwards.[273]

Jo Stephenson recalled that SOE had received 'a bloody nose' and had ceased to operate in Ireland by 1942.[274] But documents now available indicate that SOE never entirely lost interest in Ireland either as the location for or as a target of whispers. It is also clear that somebody—quite possibly the service attachés, if not Keith—did make outline plans for the sabotage of key facilities, and that in the last weeks of the war SOE planned a *coup de main* to seize the records of the German legation before Hempel could destroy them.[275] Neither SIS nor MI5 approved of Keith's activities, and urged his recall lest he compromise SIS's operations or jeopardize MI5's liaison with G2. Yet the SIS networks which C and Vivian sought to protect in demanding Keith's withdrawal had already been penetrated by G2. Roddy Keith may not have been the most effective or discreet of secret agents, but despite SIS's complaints he seems to have come under Irish suspicion only after his initial withdrawal. This contrasts with the experience of SOE in Portugal, where the ambassador insisted on the withdrawal of their representative in 1942 after Salazar complained about his activities.[276]

Roddy Keith's story is also significant for the use which SOE attempted to make of his Irish background in his planned work in Africa. Irish citizens, in common with those of other neutral states, were highly prized as couriers and intelligence gatherers in neutral and enemy territory. One example is that of a report on morale and general political conditions forwarded by SOE in Berne in July 1941 prepared by 'Miss Darina Laracy, an Irish journalist who has just come out of Italy'.[277]

INTELLIGENCE ON THE ACTIVITIES OF FOREIGN DIPLOMATS IN IRELAND, MAY 1940–JUNE 1941

Early in July a JIC subcommittee considered the question of German and Italian cable traffic. Transatlantic cables were routed through London and delayed for ninety-six hours, before proceeding via Washington. Cables to Ireland were, similarly, delayed in London (the process was not foolproof: in December 1941 G2 noted that a German cable from Berlin sent via Berne 'was *not* held up in London').[278] The question was whether the delay mechanism provided sufficient protection of British interests, or whether some more draconian control should be imposed. The service departments were naturally fearful that careless talk by

[273] Undated notes of contents of letters from Keith to his wife, and Bryan to Walshe, 11 Mar. 1942, MAI, G2/3916.

[274] Interview with Sir John Stephenson, 1989.

[275] Unfortunately, the Foreign and Commonwealth Office have repeatedly declined to permit access to the SOE file 'Sabotage in Eire', TNA, HS6/306; Eden (foreign secretary) to Churchill, 6 Apr. 1945, TNA, DO35/1229.

[276] Wylie, ' "An Amateur Learns His Job"?', 452–7.

[277] SOE war diary, 26 July 1941, TNA, HS7/218. Darina Laracy (d. 2003) was married to Ignazio Silone, the exiled Italian socialist writer. I owe this information to Deirdre McMahon.

[278] JIC(40) 150, 2 July 1940, covering report by the ISSB, TNA, CAB81/97; G2 document on German diplomatic cables, with Bryan to Walshe, 9 Jan. 1942, NAI, DFA A/8.

servicemen on leave in Ireland, or news picked up in Northern Ireland, was a real problem: 'There is reason to believe that the Germans, through sources in Eire, have been collecting scraps of news and gossip which may not in themselves seem very important but which pieced together may give the Germans a fairly clear picture'.[279] Despite their fears about such communications, the JIC concluded that on balance the existing regime should continue, for three reasons: if the enemy legations were barred from sending cables, neutrals such as Spain might let them use their facilities; consequently, it would 'not be possible to differentiate' between enemy and neutral cables in imposing a ban; and finally, 'information is now being obtained from certain telegrams, notably in the case of Italy and certain neutrals such as Japan'.[280] In other words, the risk of information flowing from the legations was already outweighed by the intelligence benefits derived from reading some of that traffic. This tension between potential leakage and intelligence yield from enemy communications was to be a continuous theme in debates about Irish security throughout the war. In May 1941 the Canadians, who could track Italian and German transatlantic cables passing through Nova Scotia and who were not then aware of British codebreaking capacity, were much disconcerted by extensive traffic which 'would seem to indicate great activity of some sort between the German and Italian ministers at Dublin, and their colleagues in Washington'.[281] Canada only began to work systematically on illegal wireless interception and on decoding of diplomatic traffic in the course of 1941, initially employing the controversial American Herbert O. Yardley in May. Choosing to specialize 'in . . . two fields (French and Japanese) . . . we have pulled our own weight and made many worthwhile contributions to the common pool of knowledge'. The cable companies also supplied Ottawa with copies of Irish diplomatic messages *en clair*, not that these contained any great secrets. When Alastair Denniston of GC&CS discovered a year later that Yardley was involved in Ottawa, he insisted on his removal because of his alleged unreliability.[282]

Decodes of diplomatic traffic yielded a certain amount of useful intelligence, in particular about Irish economic difficulties and about Italian efforts to garner and to pass on war information to Rome. The decodes also provided intelligence on what neutral diplomats were up to: whether by accident or design, these too could stumble on and report home material of value to an enemy. It is important to stress that the problem of information leakage through diplomatic missions in Ireland, while it was to play such a central part in Anglo-Irish relations until after the invasion of Europe in June 1944, arose also in London. In addition to deliberate

---

[279] JIC(41) 124, 28 Mar. 1941, TNA, CAB81/98.

[280] JIC(40), 150, 2 July 1940, TNA, CAB81/97.

[281] Department of National Defence to director of military operations and intelligence, 21 May 1941, PAC, RG24/C1, C5258. As well as examples of encoded Axis cables between Dublin and Washington, the accompanying material includes an *en clair* telegram from de Valera to Dr Mannix, the powerful Irish Catholic archbishop of Melbourne. On the development of Canadian codebreaking see Wark, 'Cryptographic Innocence', 639–65, and Kahn, *The Reader of Gentlemen's Mail*, 213–14.

[282] 'A History of the Examination Unit, 1941–1945 by members of the staff and others associated with the work', edited by G. de B. Robinson, July 1945, ii, 5, 12 and 13 (I am grateful to Professor David Stafford, then director general of the Canadian Institute of International Affairs, for allowing me to consult a Xerox of this document in Toronto in 1987); Moffat journal, 28 May 1942, Harvard, MS 1407, vol. 46; Kahn, *The Reader of Gentlemen's Mail*, 213–14.

Table 3.1. *British decodes relating to Ireland, June 1940–June 1941*

	French	Irish	Italian	Japanese	USA	Others	Totals
June 1940			12				12
July		2	9		1	1	13
August			5	3		1	9
September		2	3				5
October	2	1	2	1			6
November	15	3	1	2			21
December			2		1		3
January 1941	4	2	16		1	1	24
February	2	4	6	1		2	15
March		1	5	2	1		9
April		3	3	1	1		8
May	1	1	5			1	8
June		2	3	1		1	7
TOTALS	24	21	72	11	5	7	140

intelligence activity on behalf of Germany by Japanese, Spanish, and Hungarian diplomats in London in 1940 and 1941, and thereafter by Spaniards (unbeknownst to their ambassador, but with the blessing of Madrid), there was always a danger that a well-disposed neutral or even an ally would send out sensitive material which the enemy might get his hands on, whether through espionage or decoding. This happened in the cases of reports by the Swedish military attaché in 1943, and of cables detailing shipping construction and movements sent by the Chinese naval attaché in 1944 and 1945.[283]

Table 3.1 gives some indication of British priorities as inferred from the volume of decodes traced from May 1940 to June 1941. As with comparable data in the previous chapter, it should be remembered that not every anodyne decode was necessarily stored and circulated. It is likely that the large number of French decodes found for November 1940, as compared with the handful for other months, reflects a deliberate study to ascertain what the new attachés in Dublin were doing rather than an exceptional volume of messages.

The Irish decodes—July 1940 produced the first surviving decode of an Irish diplomatic cable since the summer of 1932—mainly revealed efforts to obtain cargo ships and armaments in North America, and underlined the desperate supply problems which Ireland faced and which Britain took a strategic decision to exploit in December 1940. The material may have had some confirmatory value. The Irish traffic casts very little light on Irish diplomacy, beyond Dublin's reiteration of its neutrality policy and injunctions to all missions to avoid antagonizing anyone. Only twenty-one such decodes have been traced for the year to June 1941, when Irish codes were first reported to be under special study by GC&CS's Research Section. Perhaps the most interesting decode concerning Irish diplomacy in the United

---

[283] Liddell diary, 12 and 17 Apr. 1941, 3, 13, and 20 July 1943, and 22 Feb. and 27 Mar. 1945, TNA, KV4/187, 192 and 196. The fault lay not with the attaché but with his defective codes. For examples see his telegrams to Chungking, 9 and 12 Dec. 1944, TNA, HW12/307. Japanese decodes of his messages are disclosed in Magic summary, 18 Oct. 1944, USNA, RG457, box 13.

States was an Italian one: in May 1941 the Italian ambassador in Washington reported that Brennan had told him he was lobbying 'members of Congress and political personalities. . . of Irish origin to press the President to ask Churchill for a declaration that the British will not invade Eire'.[284]

There are no decodes of traffic between Dublin and Warnock in Berlin, whereas the Irish records include over thirty exchanges, including his explanation of his apparent inactivity by reference to 'eye trouble' which made it difficult for him to encode and decode messages effectively. The absence of Irish Berlin decodes may simply mean that Warnock was using a system which GC&CS could not read.[285] The most significant Irish decodes were probably those of 2 and 13 June 1941, when the minister at the Vatican reported on an inappropriate initiative by a 'German Archbishop in the Holy Office', who used the pretext of discussion of the pastoral needs of Irish prisoners of war to introduce an Irish monsignor to 'a representative of the German General Staff with an amazing knowledge' of Irish affairs, who asked if the monsignor knew Frank Ryan, showed 'no interest in the spiritual needs of prisoners', and displayed 'a disquieting interest. . . in getting a man of anti-British sympathies and in maintaining secrecy'.[286] Irish decodes were generally anodyne; the British undoubtedly secured far more useful material through monitoring Dulanty's telephone conversations with Dublin and probably also through bugging his office and perhaps suborning staff (responsibility for 'miking' or otherwise penetrating foreign missions lay from March 1941 with MI5's Anthony Blunt, a close friend of Guy Liddell and, as was revealed many years later, a dedicated Soviet agent).[287]

Of the Irish-related decodes of other states, perhaps the most exotic were a Saudi telegram from London of July 1940 which spoke of the likelihood of the invasion of both Britain and Ireland, and a January 1941 request from the Turkish ambassador in London for permission to visit Ireland because, like Spain, she was 'gradually assuming a new importance. . . in addition to feelings not too friendly to the British which persist. . . the Germans are conducting the most dangerous propaganda'.[288] The Belgian minister in Dublin was instructed to prevent the sale of a vessel in Wexford which his government in exile had requisitioned.[289] A Mexican cable from Lisbon of April 1941 reported the Irish minister to Spain, Leopold Kerney, as saying 'he personally would. . . prefer British arrogance to Nazi absorption', an interesting comment in view of Kerney's republican links, his involvement with Frank Ryan, and his reputation in both Dublin and London as a republican intriguer.[290]

There was little of interest in the handful of American decodes: in November 1940 David Gray reported that members of the opposition had warned de Valera against any thought of declaring war on Britain. Gray was to be a thorn in de Valera's side,

---

[284] Gannon, *Colossus*, 86; Italian ambassador, Washington, to Rome, 5 May 1941, TNA, HW12/264.

[285] Warnock to Dublin, 5 Nov. 1940, NAI, DFA P12/3; minute on 'unbroken Irish ciphers' to Denniston and Miss Reid, 15 May 1944, TNA, HW53/56.

[286] Irish minister, the Vatican, to Dublin, 2 and 13 June 1941, TNA, HW12/254.

[287] Liddell diary, 7 June 1940, TNA, KV4/186. On Blunt see Boyle, *The Climate of Treason*. Curry, *The Security Service*, 259–60.

[288] Saudi minister, London, to Riyadh, 1 July 1940, and Turkish ambassador, London, to Angora, 9 Jan. 1941, TNA, HW12/254 and 260.

[289] Belgian minister, London, to Belgian legation, Dublin, 11 Aug. 1940, TNA, HW12/255.

[290] Mexican minister, Lisbon, to Mexico City, 29 Apr. 1941, TNA, HW12/264.

and an occasional nuisance to Maffey, throughout the war. An elderly man whose wife was an aunt of Mrs Eleanor Roosevelt, he had been a surprise appointment in February—not least to Robert Brennan, who some weeks previously had cheerfully presented Ireland's *agrément* to the appointment of Governor Earle of Pennsylvania as minister in Dublin. He had taken this step on the basis of press reports and gossip, only for an indignant White House to point out that no decision had been taken on who was to get the post. It is quite possible that the selection of Gray was the result of White House indignation at this egregious *faux pas*.[291] A State Department official noted that Gray 'knows a great deal about Ireland, and is friends with "all the right people"—the degree of rightness nowadays depending upon the length of time they stayed in jail' during the war of independence, but in fact the new minister had little grasp of the dynamics of Irish politics.[292] This was not simply a matter of his understandable hostility to Irish neutrality generally and especially to policy on the ports, his star-struck courtship of the Anglo-Irish, and his constant colloguing with de Valera's Fine Gael opponents; rather, it was a combination of his alarmist and gullible attitude towards security matters, his booming indiscretion, and his unusually good lines of communication with the White House (through his wife).

All this was clear to the Irish within a few months of Gray's arrival: a G2 report on events during the year 1940 complained that the American legation 'is probably a greater centre of pro-British influence . . . than the office of the United Kingdom Representative, who evidently feels himself restricted in a way that the American Minister does not'.[293] All this was also clear to London through decodes: in March 1941 the State Department sought Gray's advice on British views about Aiken's efforts to buy arms in the United States—he naturally took Whitehall's line that to provide weapons would only encourage the Irish to stay out of the war—and a month later an American offer to negotiate the provision of two cargo ships for Ireland was couched, from Britain's point of view, in suitably minatory terms about the need for a 'more cooperative attitude' towards Britain if further aid was to be obtained.[294] Shortly before Pearl Harbor, Churchill saw a decode of a message to Gray containing a very firm response to Irish complaints about the presence of American technicians in Northern Ireland.[295] It suited Britain to have a fervent Anglophile representing the United States in Dublin at such a time rather than some green-eyed Irish-American, yet Gray was to prove a complicating factor second only to Churchill in the management of Irish–Allied security relations because he never grasped the issues involved.[296]

The traffic of the Japanese, the Vichy French, and particularly the Italian missions in Dublin was potentially of great interest to Britain. The Japanese only established

[291] Moffat journal, 9 and 10 Jan. 1940, Harvard, MS 1407, vol. 44.
[292] Moffat journal, 12 Feb. 1940, Harvard, MS 1407, vol. 44. Brennan made no mention of this incident in *Ireland Standing Firm*.
[293] Gray to Washington, 24 Nov. 1940, TNA, HW12/259; draft of G2 annual report for 1940, UCDA, Bryan papers, P71/33.
[294] Hull to London embassy, 11 Mar., and Hull to Dublin, 25 Apr. 1941, TNA, HW12/262 and 263.
[295] Washington to Gray, 18 Nov. 1941, with C to Churchill, 23 Nov. 1941, TNA, HW1/251.
[296] Girvin, *The Emergency*, 181–215, offers a markedly more sympathetic assessment of Gray's first year in Ireland.

a presence in July 1940, when Beppu, consul in Liverpool, was transferred to open a consulate. The immediate purpose was probably to make arrangements for the departure through the western port of Galway of about 300 Japanese civilians resident in Britain, an exercise accomplished without incident in November 1940 when they were picked up by a Japanese liner. Guy Liddell thought it 'fairly clear that Beppu will now be acting as a courier between this country and Eire for the Axis powers', and also that the Japanese might be 'intermediaries between the IRA in Liverpool and Dublin'. Beppu's Liverpool housekeeper, an Irishwoman, was also suspected.[297] Decodes of his cables in 1940 and 1941 gave no indication of such activity, nor of espionage. In his first message he said Dublin was 'tranquil', remarked on the 'extreme censorship' imposed on the press, said that talk of U-boat bases on the west coast appeared untrue, and observed that the main constraint on a British invasion from Northern Ireland, where she had half-a-million troops, was American opinion.[298] He reported that apart from some of the 'business caste', '95% are determined on neutrality and the non-return of the harbours'.[299] He passed on what war news he could, for example on the likelihood of trouble if conscription were imposed in Northern Ireland, but he had few means of collecting information—there was no community of Japanese nationals to draw on—and the main topics of his communications throughout the first two years of Japan's war were the travails of Irish missionaries in the Far East.

The most significant Japanese decodes in 1940–1 were Beppu's account of discussions with de Valera and with Walshe not long after his arrival. In August de Valera spoke of 'British resolve to fight to the finish' and 'the strength of their moral[e]', and in October Walshe stressed that, while Britain had suffered 'considerable damage from . . . air raids . . . the spirit of the citizens was vigorous and the defensive measures had exceeded expectations'. The Irish expected a long war.[300] In January 1941 Tokyo told him they wished 'to establish a Legation in Dublin', and that 'you are to act temporarily as chargé d'affaires'. He was to ascertain the Irish view and report back. While his reply has not been traced, it appears that the proposal was unwelcome—the Irish probably saw it as provocative for the British and Americans.[301] Beppu's mission was instead designated a consulate general, but received no increase in staff.

Vichy French traffic cast some light on Vichy policy and activities, and provided an insight on the Dublin legation which supplemented information discreetly passed to Maffey and his officials by two members of the staff, Saffroy and Roché.[302] The new French regime moved to increase the size of the mission by the appointment of no less than three service attachés. This was a puzzling development, unwelcome to both the Irish and the British governments—hitherto the French service attachés

[297] Liddell diary, 6 July 1940 and 29 May 1941, TNA, KV4/187 and 188.
[298] Beppu to Tokyo (via London embassy), 7 Aug. 1940, TNA, HW12/255. At the time Britain had one under-strength division—perhaps 15,000 men—in Northern Ireland. Canning, *British Policy Towards Ireland*, 282.
[299] Beppu to Tokyo, 18 Feb. 1941, TNA, HW12/262.
[300] Ibid., 7 Aug. and 1 Oct. 1940, TNA, HW12/255 and 257.
[301] Tokyo to Beppu, 11 Jan. 1941, TNA, HW12/261.
[302] Antrobus (BRO) and Maffey to Stephenson, 3 Dec. 1940 and 7 Feb. 1941, TNA, DO35/1109/16.

in London had also been non-resident attachés in Dublin—as there was scarcely enough legitimate business to be done in Ireland to occupy one defence specialist, let alone three. The obvious inference was that these would have clandestine roles. It may be, however, that the postings were intended largely to rescue officers marooned in Britain, where they were well treated but were effectively prisoners. The first to arrive, in January 1941, was a military attaché, Commandant Lachevre. He was well known and liked in London. En route to Dublin he called to the War Office and had a lengthy discussion with an old contact, during which he expressed the belief that Britain would eventually prevail, although he was critical of de Gaulle—'a good soldier but he has put himself on a pedestal . . . and will not be forgiven by the French for insulting their beloved Marechal'. Lachevre 'is undoubtedly pro-Ally . . . and can be looked upon as friendly to England . . . in Dublin'.[303]

In November 1940 Vichy suppressed the new post of naval attaché—one enigmatic decode indicates that the incumbent may have had instructions to establish a coastal intelligence network along the lines planned the previous autumn, but he explained apparent inaction in producing a promised report on the coastline by the necessity for a 'hurried return' to London 'to save personal belongings and my family'.[304] In January 1941, however, Vichy had a change of heart, and sent over Capitaine Albertas, who had been in limbo in Britain since escaping from France with British forces in June 1940. A naval aviation specialist, he had served as air attaché in London from 1932 to 1937. The RAF director of intelligence Archie Boyle knew him as 'a man singularly heavy in speech and movement for a Frenchman, of rather ordinary stock and upbringing, with a very pretentious and common little wife'. He was 'thoroughly disgruntled at the time of Oran' in July 1940—when the royal navy sank French ships at anchor lest they eventually come under German control—but 'basically there is good soil on which to sow seed, provided one can make the right approaches to him'. After taking Albertas to lunch, Boyle judged him still 'a firm friend of this country and convinced that we should win eventually. He will be useful to us in Dublin, I think'.[305] Antrobus of Maffey's office was not so sure: 'the impression we gather is that he is a good deal more pro-Vichy and anti-British than one might have expected from the reports which you have sent us'. Boyle was nettled: 'It is possible that Antrobus knows more about Albertas than I do, but I gave you my impressions after meeting Albertas, and with three years close acquaintanceship, if not friendship, with him. Without any doubt at all I would back my opinion to be the right one, and if he is properly handled Albertas will prove to be a good friend to this country, as he was in former days'. This crisp judgement was completely wrong: Albertas was a passionate Vichyiste and Hempel's favourite Frenchman, and the Admiralty soon reported

---

[303] Vichy to French minister, Dublin, 18 Sept. 1940, TNA, HW12/257; War Office to Dominions Office, 15 Jan. 1941, enclosing memorandum of discussion with Lachèvre, TNA, DO35/1109/16.

[304] Naval attaché, Dublin, to Vichy, 11 Nov.; French minister, Dublin, to Vichy, 25 Oct., enclosing message from naval attaché, and Vichy Admiralty to naval attaché, 31 Oct. 1940, TNA, HW12/257.

[305] Vichy to French minister, Dublin, 25 Jan. 1941, TNA, HW12/261. Albertas arrived on 16 Apr. 1941. G2 memorandum on French legation, 25 Oct., with Bryan to Boland (Dublin), 2 Nov. 1943, NAI, DFA P75; Boyle to Dominions Office, 7 Mar. and 5 Apr. 1941, TNA, DO35/1109/16.

that he was under instructions from Admiral Darlan to enquire into the 'political views of certain French residents in Eire'.[306] It is worth noting that the Vichy naval attachés in Stockholm displayed similar loyalty to Darlan despite considerable British efforts to woo them. The assistant naval attaché, Bedin, who had avoided internment through Admiral Godfrey's unofficial good offices in June 1940, was secretly pro-British.[307]

Decodes suggest that in reality Vichy diplomats were mainly concerned with ascertaining how Britain was coping with sustained aerial bombardment, although they also submitted a handful of reports on Irish policy and on defensive capacity and preparations, emphasizing Irish resolve to fight any invader using guerrilla tactics. Their traffic yielded no indication that Vichy was using Dublin actively to spy on Britain, or that her diplomats were working in concert with the Axis missions. The presence of service attachés, nevertheless, gave serious grounds for both British and Irish concern about the possible leakage of military and naval information (as early as January 1941 G2 furnished External Affairs with a note on the political allegiances of members of the Vichy legation, already something of a bear pit, together with 'copies of, and extracts from, various French correspondence' which had been obtained 'through very special channels').[308] In the parallel case of Afghanistan, the Vichy legation was also riven by factions, with individual officials maintaining contact with the British.[309] The Dublin legation circulated a newsletter, *Nouvelle de France*, but never engaged much with the Irish public despite the potential appeal to Catholics of the Vichy experiment.[310]

Britain did not complain to Dublin about the Vichy presence in Dublin. It would have been rather difficult to do so, since Canada and the United States also maintained relations with Vichy until the autumn of 1942.[311] The London-based Canadian chargé d'affaires at Vichy, Dupuy, became 'a key diplomatic intermediary' between Britain and Vichy, albeit not a very farsighted one, laying the groundwork for a system of direct communication between Churchill and Pétain, of whom he was an ardent admirer. This ill-judged arrangement was vetoed by the foreign secretary Anthony Eden and SIS.[312] The fact that Vichy cables could be decoded in transit in London provided insurance on the security side. It is also likely that the Dublin legation was viewed as a potential channel of communication, as was also the case in Canada. In September 1941 Churchill urged Mackenzie King to maintain

---

[306] Boyle to Dominions Office, 21 Apr. 1941, and undated document supplied by MO8, TNA, DO35/1109/16. MO8 was a department of the War Office dealing with service attachés.

[307] Denham, *Inside the Nazi Ring*, 28; Godfrey memoir, 171, CCCA, Godfrey papers 1/6.

[308] Archer (G2) to Walshe (Dublin), 30 Jan. 1941, NAI, DFA A8.

[309] British Legation, Kabul, to India Office, 11 June 1942, BL, L/PS/12/1933.

[310] Copies of this newsletter are in MAI, G2/X/0593; Wills, *That Neutral Island*, 275, cites the approving attitude of the *Standard*, the main Catholic newspaper, towards Pétain.

[311] South Africa also had a minister accredited to Vichy until April 1942, but this London-based official never visited Vichy and was maintained in London simply as a sop to the South African nationalist opposition. Hammer, 'Insight on Vichy', 179.

[312] Thomas, 'France in British Signals Intelligence', 59; Moffat journal, 9 and 11 May 1942, Harvard, MS 1407, vol. 46; Thomas, *Britain and Vichy*, 80–2, 132; Dalton diary, 18 Dec. 1940 and 19 Mar. 1941, BLPES, Dalton 1/23 and 24.

relations with Vichy: 'You can never tell when this contact may be useful', and the prime minister clung to this line into 1942, despite Foreign Office misgivings.[313]

GC&CS were also able to read some Spanish diplomatic traffic to and from Dublin. This was potentially significant, because Spanish diplomats often acted as intelligence bagmen for the Axis powers. No evidence was found to indicate that the Spanish mission was involved in anything untoward, although the minister was thought to be strongly pro-Axis. His legation was to remain an object of interest both to the British, who had the advantage of reading its traffic, and the Irish, who could not, but who had good local sources of information.[314]

The Italian minister Berardis was a regular reporter both on his dealings with Walshe and on his occasional talks with de Valera. He soon realized that his cables, addressed to the Italian embassy in Washington, were being routed via London, complaining about a message of 12 June which the British had 'held . . . up and mutilated the ciphered text' (ironically, GC&CS had not received a copy of that cable). The day after Italy entered the war a group of Trinity College students demonstrated outside his legation, 'shouting "Up Trinity College", "Down with Mussolini" and "Up de Valera"' and singing, surprisingly enough, the Irish national anthem. Berardis expressed irritation at the stationing of a Garda at the front door. He discussed the matter with a Garda inspector 'in broken English, and carried on most of his conversation with me in Italian, through his Secretary', which indicates that he was not particularly well equipped to absorb information and observations offered to him in discussion.[315] His political reporting reflected the prevailing flux in Dublin—on 28 May Irish ministers thought a German assault 'probable', yet a day later 'the view . . . is that Germany lays her plans too well to commit the political error of a landing'.[316] He initially predicted that the British offer of eventual Irish unity would fail, but in July warned that 'the possibility' of its succeeding 'cannot be excluded'.[317] De Valera told him that an invasion by either belligerent 'would inevitably provoke the immediate intervention of the other' and 'a bitter and confused struggle' which 'would not . . . facilitate the offensive operations of any belligerent'. He gave 'significant hints . . . en passant', evidently intended to reach 'my German colleague', that Ireland would remain neutral even if national unity was achieved.[318] A sceptical employee told a friend that Berardis 'loves to display and wanted to show off how much superior his entertainment is to the German and French legations. To achieve this he has got himself into debt for which his wife has to pay. He loves working all night which makes him ill the next day'.

---

[313] Moffat journal, recording Mackenzie King's account of a talk with Churchill, 18 Sept. 1941, Harvard, MS 1407, vol. 46; Thomas, *Britain and Vichy*, 131–2.

[314] In June 1943 spare parts for Petersen's Hellschreiber were sent from Berlin to Madrid, presumably for transmission via the Spanish bag to Dublin, although on 4 Dec. 1943 Hempel had still not received them. SIS analysis of Hempel's communications, 20 Nov. to 11 Dec. 1943, TNA, DO121/86.

[315] Berardis to Rome, 17 June 1940, TNA, HW12/253; reports by Sergeant Lynch and Inspector Breen, 10 and 18 June 1940, NAI, JUS8/821.

[316] Berardis to Rome, 28 and 29 May 1940, TNA, HW12/253.

[317] Berardis to Italian embassy, Washington (for Rome), 2 July 1940, TNA, HW12/254.

[318] Berardis to Italian embassy, Washington (for Rome), 23 June 1940, TNA, HW12/253; Furlong diary, 8, 20, 25, and 29 July, 9 and 12 Aug., and 7 Nov. 1940, UCDA, Furlong papers, LA53/48.

A few weeks later Walshe expounded on 'how difficult it was for a country geographically and economically linked with Britain' to maintain absolute neutrality, and stressed that Ireland 'hopes not to remain remote from the reconstruction of Europe, from which in the past she has been debarred', and 'intends to resume her place amongst the Catholic nations'.[319] July saw the first demonstration of keenness to relay war information, when Berardis reported in vague terms on civilian and naval shipping movements off the Irish coast.[320] In October he passed on what he could glean about morale and political feeling in Britain, although in 'an island of internees' it was difficult to get 'trustworthy reports and concrete judgements'.[321] In January 1941 he reported de Valera as saying that the British remained menacing on the issue of the ports, while Walshe predicted early American entry into the war: 'He added that a decisive Axis attack on the British island should not be too long delayed', but two months later 'emphasized Britain's formidable capacity to resist'.[322]

Berardis 'often reported' that, 'owing to the isolation of this post, it is difficult to obtain' information on war matters, but he did his best: in February he reported that a Norwegian ship had just left Dublin carrying scrap iron to Britain, and that some Greek vessels were berthed and awaiting sailing orders, and in April, May, and June he stated that the aircraft carrier *Illustrious* and other warships had been attacked and damaged during the air raids which had left Belfast 'a vast [ruin]'.[323] In May he said that Britain had recently reduced her forces in Northern Ireland: 'the same information, without any more detail, reached the German minister here', a remark which suggests a degree of cooperation on war information between the Axis legations (something which Berardis vehemently denied after the Italian surrender). For three years he was to send a considerable number of such reports, particularly about Northern Ireland. Cumulatively these demonstrated that he was relying entirely on hearsay, and had no organization or funding to collect intelligence, although, as we shall see, one of his messages in 1942 caused Churchill to throw a tantrum.[324] What Rome made of his reports is uncertain: in November one of his staff claimed that 'all his telegrams about Ireland have so far remained unanswered without exception', an impression borne out by his decoded traffic.

Berardis was in touch with members of the Italian community around Ireland. Their political leader, Count Eduaro Tomacelli, was appointed as an honorary attaché shortly after Italy entered the war. There was particular alarm when he bought, 'under conditions of some secrecy, an estate of 190 acres in the immediate vicinity' of an army airfield at Gormanstown. Garda and G2 inquiries indicated that the purchase was simply the fulfillment of a long-held ambition, although rumours persisted about his real objectives.[325] In later years there was also concern about a

319 Berardis to Italian embassy, Washington (for Rome), 14 July 1940, TNA, HW12/254.
320 Berardis to Italian embassy, Washington (for Rome), 9 July 1940, TNA, HW12/254.
321 Berardis to Italian embassy, Washington (for Rome), 30 Oct. 1940, TNA, HW12/257.
322 Berardis to Rome, 30 Jan. and 25 Mar. 1941, TNA, HW12/260 and 263.
323 Ibid., 8 Feb., 28 Apr., 10 May and 4 June 1941, HW12/261, 264 and 265.
324 Ibid., 7 May 1941, TNA, HW12/264; Furlong diary, 7 Nov. 1940, UCDA, Furlong papers, LA53/48; Liddell diary, 22 Oct. 1942, TNA, KV4/189.
325 Ibid., 25 Mar. and 15 June 1941, TNA, HW12/262 and 264; note by Bryan, 9 May 1939, and Bryan to Chief Superintendent Carroll, 26 Nov. 1941, MAI, G2/0222; O'Halpin, *Defending Ireland*, 145.

small kernel of Italian fascists in Dublin after the Italian collapse in 1943, although these do not seem to have done much more than meet semi-secretly to bemoan the Duce's bad luck.

Decodes demonstrated that Berardis's relative inactivity contrasted with that of other Italian envoys stationed on the edges of the British empire: the traffic of Quaroni in Kabul, and of Gabrielli in Baghdad, was replete with intrigues against British interests, emphasizing particularly themes of Islamic identity and of Arab nationalism. Rome vigorously encouraged such enterprises, and authorized large subsidies for significant regional figures such as the fugitive Grand Mufti of Jerusalem. He had fled to Lebanon from Jerusalem in 1937 to evade detention by the British, moved to Baghdad in autumn 1939, and eventually went to Berlin, where he helped in the formation of an 'Arab legion' and of Bosnian Muslim SS units, and schemed to destroy the Jews of Palestine. The Italian legation in Kabul for years channelled money to the mercurial Faqir of Ipi in remote Waziristan, in hopes that he would one day deliver on his promise to persuade the tribal peoples of the north-west frontier to rise against British rule (in fact he contented himself with ritualized raids on isolated outposts of British rule, drawing an equally ritualized response from local levees assisted by the RAF).[326]

Compared with such Kiplingesque villainy, Berardis's efforts to damage British interests from Dublin appear lame, although there is no indication that Rome expected him to do any more. His greatest indiscretion was probably his account of a warm conversation with Cardinal MacRory, the Catholic archbishop of Armagh and primate of All Ireland, and much the closest thing to a Grand Mufti which the Irish church was to produce: according to Berardis, not a man prone to understatement, in October 1940 this nationalist zealot 'expressed his admiration for our country, a nation . . . renewing its strength under our great Captain, the Duce', and 'augured for the arms of Italy "a most brilliant victory which . . . he hoped would see the collapse of the age old policy of . . . intransigence pursued by John Bull"'.[327] This evidence of MacRory's anti-British attitude may have come as an irritation in Whitehall, but certainly not as a surprise.

The glaring gap in British codebreaking in 1940–1 was German diplomatic communications. The high-grade cipher used was not broken until December 1942. GC&CS had records of most but not of all German cables between Dublin and Berlin since September 1939, and of only some of the clandestine radio traffic. In addition, for whatever technical reasons some messages were never fully broken. Consequently no complete record of Berlin's communications with its Dublin mission up to December 1942, and the legation's reports, could be constructed even when the available messages were studied in 1943 and 1944. It was only after the war that the capture of German records allowed a comprehensive picture to be

---

[326] Large numbers of decodes of traffic between Rome and Baghdad (up to June 1941), and Kabul (up to the spring of 1943), dealing with such intrigues, can be found in the monthly collections in TNA, HW12. See Chenevix Trench, *The Frontier Scouts*, 221–60, for a colourful account of British clashes with the Faqir during the war, and Hauner, 'One Man Against the Empire', 183–212.

[327] Berardis to Italian embassy, Washington (for Rome), 6 Oct. 1940, TNA, HW12/257. It is worth noting that the most powerful Catholic prelate in Ireland, the archbishop of Dublin Dr McQuaid, was anti-Axis.

obtained, although even then some problems remained due to Hempel's caution in disguising the names of some of his most significant Irish contacts. It is an open question whether, if Britain had been able to read Hempel's traffic in 1940–1, this would have had a significant influence on policy. It would certainly have disclosed that de Valera and Walshe were emollience personified towards Hempel in 1940. This would have been understandable, if distasteful, to British eyes, although perhaps as likely to enrage Churchill as to enlighten him. Decodes of German traffic would also have shown the tentative development of clandestine links between Hempel, an unnamed army officer (Hugo MacNeill), and General O'Duffy. In the circumstances of 1940–1 this intrigue might well have been interpreted as the precursor either to a pro-German coup, or to a shift in Irish policy towards collaboration with Germany. If so, its discovery might well have provoked a British military reaction.

It is worth noting that at much the same time decodes of Italian traffic to and from Iraq, an even younger state than Ireland and also a neutral, although with British forces *in situ* under a treaty of 1930, provided London with a good deal of advance warning of the Rashid Ali takeover of power at the end of March 1941. This nationalist revolt was fomented by the Axis powers, with vague promises of military support—in February the Italian minister in Baghdad reported that the Iraqi prime minister needed a consignment of weapons to 'prove to the army chiefs how well founded [is his reliance] on the assistance of the Axis Governments'. Italy should 'reinforce the present resistance to British demands'—and such timely intelligence enabled the deployment of Indian troops who landed unopposed in Basra in mid-April. Leopold Amery noted that 'it looks as though Rashid Ali is afraid'.[328] After staging his coup, the hapless Rashid Ali waited in vain for the promised Axis assistance: he became 'very much vexed by the fact that at this delicate moment . . . we have as yet given him no reply about support by Axis air forces', which never materialized to any significant extent because Hitler needed his aircraft for the forthcoming attack on Russia. The superior British forces duly ousted Rashid Ali, despite the objections of General Wavell, the GOC in the Middle East, to the diversion of forces to what he saw as a sideshow, who proposed instead seeing if a deal could be struck. Despite SOE's hopes of killing him, Rashid Ali got away: the Italian foreign minister found him still 'a vivacious and resolute man, who has great influence upon his people'. He and the Grand Mufti, these 'useful pawns', as the Italian minister in Kabul described them, sat out the remainder of the war in Europe.[329]

While the parallels with Irish circumstances are not exact, the Iraq case illustrates the significance of diplomatic decodes, in that case Italian, for British policy,

---

[328] Italian minister, Baghdad, to Rome, 22 and 30 Jan., 5, 14 Feb., 5 and 12 Mar. 1941, TNA, HW12/260, 261, and 262. Rashid Ali is referred to in these messages as 'Gailiani', an Italianized version of the suffix. Amery diary, 18 Apr. 1941, CCCA, Amery papers, AMEL7/35.

[329] Italian minister, Baghdad, to Rome, and replies, 3, 4, 8, 14, 17 and 23 Apr., TNA, HW12/263; Dalton diary, 16 and 20 June 1941, BLPES, Dalton papers 1/24; Muggeridge (ed.), *Ciano's Diaries*, 432, entry for 10 Feb. 1942; British minister, Kabul, to London, citing confidential source on Italian minister, 14 Aug. 1942, BL, L/PS/12/1933.

including the decision to use force to restore an amenable Iraqi administration. It also demonstrates how the Axis made a strategic misjudgement in encouraging the Rashid Ali coup: it might have been far wiser simply to adopt a policy of encouraging the Iraqis to keep enforced cooperation with Britain to a minimum, just as was done with Ireland. This would have presented London with an awkward diplomatic and strategic dilemma, whereas the coup gave a legitimate reason to intervene.

German material retrospectively decoded as Pandora in 1943 and 1944 also showed that Hempel had been in indirect touch with Goertz in the months after his arrival in Ireland: on 29 September 1940 he radioed details of the agent's plan to 'reach France by motorboat', although it remained unclear whether he had had advance knowledge of the dispatch to Ireland of any German agents other than Schutz in 1941.[330] Pandora revealed Berlin's instructions to offer the Irish military aid in the event of a British attack. On the other hand, the traffic also showed that the Irish had firmly resisted very considerable German pressure to accept additional legation staff: on 18 December Berlin told Hempel they were sending two military officers and a radio operator, purporting to be diplomats and a clerical worker respectively, in view of the 'increasing importance of Dublin as an observation post to keep watch on English military measures, and the results of raids upon England'. Berlin even forwarded the registration number of the civilian Junkers aircraft—'D-AGAK'—which would arrive at Rineanna airfield in Limerick at dawn on 21 December.

The Irish refused to grant landing permission, despite a strong warning from Hempel that diplomatic relations might be in jeopardy. It is said that a German aircraft was heard over Rineanna, where the runway had been blocked, on 21 December, although this cannot be confirmed. Dublin later conceded that Germany had the technical right to increase her diplomatic representation if she wished. The only Irish stipulation was that such staff must arrive 'by the ordinary means of transport'. Since this would have involved going through British-controlled territory, the Germans withdrew the request. The British only became aware of this German–Irish contretemps, significant not only because it showed that Hempel was prepared to allow his mission to be used for intelligence purposes, but also because it demonstrated Irish resolution in the face of a clear German threat, through retrospective decoding of Dublin–Berlin traffic in January 1944.[331] Had London been able to read the messages at the time, they would have had to act. As their decisions to assassinate German officials in the Middle East showed, the problem facing them would not have been ethical but practical: how to intercept and destroy the aircraft, and how to pressure the Irish, while disguising their main source of information.

[330] 'Special interrogation report on Major General Erwin Lahousen and Sdf (Z) Kurt Haller', 19 June 1946, p. 7, TNA, KV2/769.
[331] Reports by Walshe of discussions with Hempel, 19 Dec. 1940 and 6 Jan. 1941, NAI, DFA A21; Fisk, *In Time of War*, 251; undated extract from decode of Berlin to Hempel, and extract from decode of Berlin to Hempel, 18 Dec. 1940, given under 'Researches into earlier material' in 'Summary of most secret information from Dublin 8th–22nd January 1944', TNA, DO121/87; Walshe to de Valera, 6 Jan. 1941, UCDA, de Valera papers, P150/2571.

CONCLUSION

Operation *Barbarossa*, the German attack on the Soviet Union on 22 June 1941, in retrospect appears decisive as the moment when an invasion of any part of the British Isles ceased to be a possibility. That is not quite how it was viewed at the time: most British observers shared the opinion of the vice-chief of staff, who wondered gloomily if the Russians would last 'three weeks, or three months?', and that was also broadly the view in Washington and Ottawa.[332] The British Isles remained a possible target for invasion, and Ireland remained a conspicuously weak link. The issue of the ports remained a very sore one, although the strategic argument for British use was not pressed within Whitehall with the same gusto as in the first year of the war. This was largely because the calamities of May and June 1940 had necessitated the routing of all convoys around the north of the island, beyond the reach of German aircraft operating from western France.

Yet the year since the collapse of France had seen significant positive developments. Anglo-Irish security liaison had developed well in most respects, with the Irish willing not only to capture German agents but to share information about them. SIS had established a professional presence in Ireland, SIS and MI5 had a joint representative working with BTNI, and the quality of intelligence on Irish affairs had improved markedly. Robust processes for the reporting of sea and air movements had been put in place and were working well, and communications censorship was increasingly effective. The fighting services were meeting their intelligence needs through cooperation and through the work of their attachés, and the two Irish police forces had established a satisfactory headquarters link in addition to informal contacts along the border. The British military mission was working effectively with the Irish army on counter-invasion planning. SOE's plans for Irish operations had been thwarted by their enemies in Whitehall, to the unconfined relief of SIS and MI5. The Irish government had proved to be far more stable and more resolute, and the IRA far weaker, than had appeared possible in the summer of 1940, and with the significant exception of the elusive Goertz, Irish security had proved surprisingly efficient. Internationally, the drive to discredit Irish neutrality was in hand, and Irish-American isolationism was under covert attack. The great unresolved problem was that of the Axis diplomatic presence. This was compounded by two factors: the issue of the German legation radio, and British inability to break the German diplomatic cipher. The radio was to dominate Anglo-Irish security relations for the next two years.

---

[332] Pownall diary, 29 June 1941, in Bond, *Chief of Staff*, 29; Moffat journal, 23 June 1941, in conversation with Norman Robertson of the Canadian Department of External Affairs, Harvard, MS 1407, vol. 46.

4

From *Barbarossa* to *Torch*: July 1941–December 1942

The eighteen months between July 1941 and December 1942 saw momentous changes in Britain's fortunes of war. Humiliation in the Far East at the hands of Japan was followed by catastrophic reverses in North Africa. For a time in the summer and early autumn of 1942 India became almost ungovernable during the Quit India campaign. But even then there were two positives: the Americans had begun to fight hard in the Pacific, and in the battle of Midway had inflicted a decisive defeat on Japan's carrier fleet, the backbone of her earlier successes; and contrary to predictions Russia had continued to resist, battering the German armies even when yielding ground. Britain, her dominions and colonial armies, and her European ally Greece inflicted a decisive regional defeat on Germany in the second battle of El Alamein in October. By December the Anglo-American invasion of French North Africa had succeeded, and in the east the battle of Stalingrad had turned decisively in Russian favour. In the same month GC&CS finally broke the German diplomatic cipher, enabling Britain to study communications between Berlin and the German legation in Dublin. This meant that for the remainder of the war the bulk of the most secret German diplomatic communications could be read by the Allies as Pandora. Sir Harry Hinsley pointed out to this writer that the first German diplomatic traffic targeted by GC&CS was Berlin–Dublin, a reflection of the significance which Whitehall attached to those messages. The breakthrough transformed British policy, making Whitehall at once more confident and more circumspect in its dealings with Dublin.

By July 1941 Ireland was far down the list of British strategic concerns. What is surprising is not that she received little prime-ministerial attention, but that she got any at all. Yet Churchill never lost his interest in the errant dominion, and this factor continued to complicate the management of intelligence and security operations. So too did a new element in the equation, the entry of the United States into the war after Pearl Harbor. The Americans already had personnel in Northern Ireland—Irish protests about this in Washington in the autumn of 1941 were dismissed, as was clear from a decoded cable to Gray seen by Churchill.[1] Now the province was to become a holding camp and training ground for large numbers of American troops, who would soon assume responsibility for its defence and for countering a German attack anywhere on the island. Fears that they would become the targets of IRA attacks never materialized, although their demeanour

---

[1] Washington to Gray, 18 Nov. 1941, TNA, HW1/251.

and indiscipline sometimes caused friction with the local population.[2] America's entry into the war upped the ante for Irish neutrality, which was now seen in Washington as threatening not merely British and Canadian but American interests and lives in the Atlantic, and the security of future Allied operations in Europe and the Mediterranean. The Irish refusal to fight on Britain's side or even to make concessions on bases stood in stark contrast to the manner in which Mexico, Cuba, Haiti, and the Central American states dutifully declared their solidarity with the United States immediately after Pearl Harbor by severing relations first with Japan and then with Germany.[3] These developments, while they added what London viewed as welcome additional pressures on Ireland, had one awkward consequence: they increased American interest in the details of Irish security and in the problem of the Axis legations. In particular, they gave David Gray in Dublin legitimate grounds for becoming involved. A meddler by nature, Gray's initiatives in security questions and his often alarmist reports to Washington cut across the work of British agencies and threatened their best-laid schemes.

Early in August the DNI John Godfrey made a four-day visit to Belfast and Dublin. His conclusions, circulated to the JIC on his return, reflected considerable development in British understanding of Irish security issues. Godfrey began by stating that 'the best source of intelligence as regards both Ulster and Eire is Sir Charles Wickham', whose 'officers collaborate closely with the Civil Guard in Eire . . . he is thus able to keep close watch on German and IRA activities on both sides of the Border'. Wickham described the IRA as 'a spent force . . . their activity is confined almost entirely to occasional acts of sabotage or hooliganism in Northern Ireland'. The Dublin authorities 'are keeping a careful watch on all German activities . . . and curbing the activities of the German Minister and his staff', and Wickham convinced Godfrey that 'further control of movements or communications across the Border is both impracticable and politically undesirable'. Godfrey noted an apparent difference of opinion between Wickham and the admiral commanding in Belfast on 'protection against theft and sabotage', although he took no clear position on this himself.[4]

In Dublin, Godfrey met with Maffey, with Walshe, and with Gray. He recorded their key observations in turn: Maffey detected growing respect for Britain because of her resilience in the face of air raids, but increased Irish apprehension about the likely consequences of such attacks on them: in May thirty-four Dubliners were killed when a single German aircraft bombed the city, perhaps inadvertently; there was also the bloody example of Belfast, which was devastated by German raids in April and May, with 900 fatalities and 50,000 houses damaged or destroyed. Belfast was poorly defended, being considered too remote from France for the Germans to mount heavy raids, but compared to Dublin it was a fortress. Maffey advised that, should 'we contemplate seizing bases . . . we should give Ireland prior help to defend her towns . . . against air attack'. Gray wanted 'a much stiffer attitude' and 'is all for

---

[2] Report by county inspector, Londonderry, on conduct of American troops, 12 Sept. 1941, TNA, CJ4/30.

[3] Knight, 'Mexico, *c.*1930–1946', in Bethell (ed.), *Cambridge History of Latin America*, vii. 64–5.

[4] Note by Godfrey, 16 Aug. 1941, JIC (41) 335, TNA, CAB81/104.

combined Anglo-American action regarding ports'. Walshe was 'very interested in the bases question, but is ignorant of the strategical as distinct from the political aspect . . . would welcome more information on strategical issues . . . would like to think need of bases was lessened by recent events', and welcomed American proposals to use 'Shannon for [a] Civil Aviation terminus'. Godfrey added parenthetically that, at about the time of his visit, Walshe had been at pains to stress to the Italian minister that there was 'no prospect of joint British–American action to obtain Eire bases. This information is graded A1' (it clearly came from a decoded Italian cable of 9 August).[5]

Godfrey described a dinner party where, 'as always in Ireland, there was a good deal of political talk'. After 'a long and somewhat exhausting evening', he concluded that 'the Irish cannot or will not understand the *geographical* factors which make . . . bases imperative. They cannot see that they and ourselves are like two houses on the edge of a cliff, which will both fall into the sea unless something is done to stop coast erosion'. They found this argument 'too realistic . . . and invariably slide off into politics'. While they 'hammer away incessantly at the Partition grievance . . . they have no clear idea of what they would do with the Six Counties if they got them . . . Their conceit is impenetrable and they cannot bear to be ignored', and they 'cling passionately to their neutrality and are prepared to put up any argument, however futile, to justify their attitude'. While they identified partition as the main grounds for neutrality, 'I believe . . . that the real fear . . . is fear of air attack, which the Germans cleverly keep alive by their occasional raids'. The one point on which Godfrey felt slightly at a disadvantage was 'our refusal to give them arms. They think . . . we are inconsistent in urging them to stand up against the aggressor and giving them nothing to do it with. This is the usual complaint of a small neutral, and is never an easy one to answer'. Godfrey concluded that 'Eire still clings to neutrality', largely due to fear: 'practical evidence of our ability to give them immediate protection against air attack would reduce their fear and greatly increase the chances of a favourable reaction if we were compelled to demand bases'.[6]

This sober dissection of both the security and the wider political issues arising from Irish neutrality was worlds away from what had been on offer in Whitehall only a few months before. It set a tone for professional analysis and discussion of Irish affairs which was by and large maintained for the rest of the war, occasional bouts of Churchillian apoplexy apart.

THE ISSUE OF THE GERMAN LEGATION RADIO IN 1941–1942

The problem of the mysterious transmissions from 'Station AM' assumed more serious proportions as time went on. Notwithstanding the Italian decode which indicated that Hempel had a secret transmitter, it was not certain that this was the

---

[5] Ibid. On the Belfast blitz and Ireland's reaction see Wills, *That Neutral Island*, 212–18. The 'A1' source is clearly Berardis to Rome, 9 Aug. 1941 (decoded on 13 Aug.), TNA, HW12/267.

[6] Note by Godfrey, 16 Aug. 1941, JIC (41) 335, TNA, CAB81/104.

'Station AM' which the Post Office interceptors at Sandridge occasionally picked up. Because of doubts about their expertise, responsibility for monitoring Station AM passed to RSS in the autumn. Direction-finding indicated that 'Station AM' was definitely in the Dublin area. A review towards the end of October showed that until 10 August 'traffic was passed fairly regularly in both directions', but that afterwards the traffic had all been from Nauen, apart from one Dublin message on 4 October.[7] On 2 September Walshe assured Maffey that 'they had definitely disposed of the matter', and that the radio would never be used again—the previous month de Valera had warned Hempel about it, pointing out that the British 'might know the German code'—but it was heard less than a month later. In November Dan Bryan visited London for discussions. Vivian told C that

Our plan is that Colonel Bryan should be asked to bring a technical advisor . . . and that Maltby should have a preliminary talk with them to find out . . . (1) what has actually been done in the way of D[irection]/F[ind]-ing and picking up the German diplomatic wireless transmissions . . . and (2) whether the Eire authorities have been able to detect any other enemy wireless station transmitting from Eire . . . We propose to tell Colonel Bryan that in spite of Walshe's confidence, the German . . . station has been transmitting since the Eire authorities believed they had disposed of it and, under due safeguards, it will probably be necessary . . . to put certain technical data before Colonel Bryan . . . to convince him of this point.

C minuted that 'the Irish delegate must not know too much of what we do over here'.[8]

There was parallel reticence on the Irish side: Bryan was under strict orders from External Affairs not to disclose the fact that the transmissions had been traced to the legation, nor that a codebreaking unit had been established to attempt to break the traffic.[9] Following Bryan's visit, arrangements were made for an RSS officer to visit Dublin, and there was

a good deal of discussion as to what he might or might not tell the Eire experts . . . Commander Denniston [then head of GC&CS] ruled that the table of call signs . . . by means of which Mr Dawson [of RSS] was able to pick up the German station and listen to the AM station in Dublin, *should not be given to the Eire Government*. In fact, no information whatever was to be given as to our investigation into the German system of call signs . . . Mr Dawson was going to get over that difficulty by memorizing the future call signs and 'being very clever when he heard the station he wanted'.

Dawson would also have to produce a plausible story if he was 'asked to explain how we were able to pick up the Dublin station on 4th October'.[10]

---

[7] Kenworthy (GC&CS) to Maltby (RSS), 25 Oct. 1941, TNA, HW14/21. This, and Irish records, indicate that the official history is incorrect in stating that transmissions from Dublin ceased 'in the middle of 1941'. Hinsley and Simkins, *British Intelligence*, 205. For further references see O'Halpin, *Defending Ireland*, 189, n. 115.

[8] Hempel to Berlin, 12 Aug. 1941, quoted in 'Summary of most secret information from Dublin', 19 Sept.–2 Oct. 1943, TNA, DO121/87; Vivian to C and reply, 22 and 23 Oct. 1941, TNA, HW14/21.

[9] O'Halpin, *Defending Ireland*, 188.

[10] ? to Maltby (RSS), 27 Oct. 1941, TNA, HW14/21. Denniston was replaced as head of GC&CS in January 1942 by Commander Edward Travis, and was put in charge of commercial and diplomatic codebreaking in Berkeley Street, London. Denniston, 'The Professional Career of A. G. Denniston', in Robertson, *British and American Perspectives*, 121.

The reluctance of both the British and the Irish to disclose to each other the extent of their knowledge of the illicit transmissions should not be construed simply in terms of wider political tension. GC&CS were of necessity always extremely circumspect in dealings even with other British agencies. Furthermore, C kept very tight control of the product of the codebreakers' labours. For reasons which are not always apparent but which probably relate to SIS's particular interests, some series and some individual decodes were not circulated at all to other agencies, or were supplied only in heavily redacted form: thus a Spanish consular cable of October 1943 was completely withheld from circulation, while only the first paragraph of a Japanese message from Lisbon to Tokyo was circulated 'to DNI, DMI, and MI5', although 'I do not see how we can stop DNI, DMI and MI5 asking what it is all about, as their own paragraph is comparatively innocuous, but we can only refer them to C'.[11] What is remarkable is not that C was so guarded about sanctioning discussion of anything relating to German transmissions with officials of a neutral state, but that force of circumstances dictated that there should be some dialogue even though that inevitably involved some indication of British knowledge and interest.

On 15 December Hempel responded to a protest by Walshe about Goertz by saying that 'things happened without his knowledge, and then he was asked to put out the fire'. Walshe also handed over 'the full text of . . . three messages sent out', thereby demonstrating that the Irish maintained a radio watch on the legation, and warned that the radio issue 'was fraught with the gravest consequences'.[12] Around the same time, the Irish received a visit from Colonel Stratton of the RSS, in his civilian guise of professor of astrophysics at Cambridge. Stratton afterwards reported that he was 'confident' that the radio was in the legation, that the Irish knew this, and that they had extended 'willing cooperation'. Stratton also managed 'to arrange, in effect, that the Eire Signals Corps should provide RSS with an additional Y [intercept] service in Eire, sending reports of all transmissions'. In return RSS would pass on any intercepts picked up from Ireland, and generally provide comment and advice. Dan Bryan secured External Affairs' approval for these arrangements, which operated from the beginning of January 1942 until the end of the war.[13] It is not clear whether any of the various British radios in Dublin—the two in Maffey's office and that in Lywood's house operated by the RAF, and those attached to the British military mission—were ever utilized to attempt to monitor illicit traffic. The Irish radio stations at Malin Head and Valentia also became relay stations for encoded British Atlantic traffic which was sent on by cable to London and Devonport—'the contents are of course not known to the operators'—although this was arranged separately.[14]

On 2 February 1942 Station AM sent a brief message. Cecil Liddell visited Dublin: 'once again the atmosphere was cordial', and the Irish raised the question

---

[11] Note by DJ[?], 19 Feb., with decode of Lisbon to Tokyo, 4 Mar., and Cecil to Jenkins, 16 Oct., with decode of Spanish cable from Casablanca to Tetuan, 11 Aug. 1943, and note by TNA, HW37/2 and 3.

[12] Note by Walshe for de Valera, 15 Dec. 1941, NAI, DFA A34.

[13] SIS summary of dealings with the Irish on the radio question, 17 Apr. 1943, TNA, DO121/84; Bryan to Walshe, enclosing British proposals, 15 Dec. 1941, NAI, DFA A25; *Liddell History*, 64.

[14] Walshe to de Valera, 16 Feb. 1945, UCDA, de Valera papers, P150/2571.

of jamming the set. Within a few days, however, the problem acquired wholly different proportions. On 11 and 12 February the German capital ships *Scharnhorst* and *Gneisenau* fought their way up through the English Channel to their home port. Visibility was poor due to a snowstorm. Despite extensive efforts, neither the navy nor the RAF was able to prevent this. Coming just as disaster struck in the Far East, this humiliation on her own coastline was a considerable blow to Britain. In a clear reference to the sinking of the *Prince of Wales* and the *Repulse* in the South China Sea, Churchill remarked that 'the Japanese seem to destroy our battleships at 400 miles range, while we can do nothing to theirs spending a whole day even a few miles off our coast'—and Guy Liddell noted 'a growing feeling in the House [of Commons] that all these disasters are due to incompetence both in ministerial and in service ranks'.[15]

The British press carried stories that Germany benefited in planning this coup from weather reports radioed from the Dublin legation, a claim which the Irish assumed was most likely officially inspired; on the other hand, the first lord of the Admiralty told Dulanty in confidence that he considered the movement of the ships to Germany a great relief, because they could now be bombed mercilessly whereas the RAF had had to be mindful of French casualties in attacking them in Brest. Another of Dulanty's contacts, Sir Arthur Street of the Air Ministry, also offered his view that Germany had 'plenty' of sources of weather information and that any report from Dublin would not have been of any account.[16] The issue nevertheless caused the Irish great concern, because their own radio watch indicated that there had been a transmission from the legation early on the afternoon of 11 February. As luck would have it, RSS had not taken a copy of that transmission. In February 1943 GC&CS began work on previously unreadable Pandora traffic between Dublin and Berlin. SIS concluded that Hempel had indeed sent a weather report at the time of the English Channel action, although the RAF pointed out 'that it seemed certain that the Germans got full weather reports on the night in question from reconnaissance planes . . . in the Atlantic north and west of Ireland from as early as 7 a.m. on 11 February'.[17]

In retirement Godfrey was dismissive of the claim that the legation's message had played any part.[18] At the time the question was not so clear, and the press stories brought the issue of the legation radio into the public domain, giving it further salience in Anglo-Irish dialogue.

As a result of the furore, Walshe spoke to Hempel 'in the most formal manner possible', telling him that the Irish were aware that after a 'silence of one or two months' Hempel had sent three messages on 10, 11 and 12 February: ' "nothing would bring disaster to Irish neutrality more swiftly or easily than another German wireless transmission" '. The set was not used for months thereafter. However, in

---

[15] SIS summary of dealings with the Irish on the radio question; Amery diary, 12 Feb. 1942, CCCA, AMEL7/36; Liddell diary, 13 Feb. 1942, TNA, KV4/189.

[16] Dulanty to Dublin, 16 Feb. 1942, NAI, DFA P14(i).

[17] Vivian to Stephenson, 13 Apr. 1943, TNA, DO121/84.

[18] O'Halpin, *Defending Ireland*, 190; Ellison (BRO) to Dublin, 11 Mar. 1942, passing on an Air Ministry request. NAI, DFA A14. In February 1943 'automated meteorological transmitters' were washed ashore on the west coast. The Irish and British were unable to determine whether or when these had functioned. G2 memorandum, 21 Jan. 1946, reproduced in *Liddell History*, 114.

1943 Pandora revealed that in September 1942 an interned Luftwaffe radio operator had been selected ostensibly as an occasional clerical worker in the legation, but in fact to operate the set if required, and that Hempel had sought ways by which such transmissions might be disguised.[19] On 28 October Walshe telephoned Hempel to say he was aware that in the past couple of days Berlin had made several transmissions to Dublin, and warned him not to reply: 'je vous prie instamment, doctor, de ne pas le faire. Parce que—hum—c'est . . . très . . . fatale'. To this Hempel replied 'Oui'. He then advised Berlin that he would only use the transmitter again if the Allies invaded Ireland.[20]

Bryan told Liddell that the Irish still hoped to deal with the transmitter by 'technical means', that is, by jamming, and sought British advice. RSS were doubtful if this could be done effectively, and feared it would cause 'immense dislocation to our own wireless traffic here', but it was not thought wise to stress this lest the Irish 'might subsequently say "Well, we could have dealt with the legation wireless . . . but at the special request of the British, who feared that our attempts would interfere with their transmissions, we refrained from doing so"'.[21] A week later Dick White and Guy Liddell visited GC&CS to discuss various problems. GC&CS thought 'that there was only a very remote chance' of their ever breaking the German diplomatic cipher, and asked MI5 if the Irish might be able to obtain copies of the legation's reciphering tables, obviously by subterfuge, a somewhat indelicate idea which was not put to G2 at that time.[22]

In the immediate aftermath of the English Channel action, Godfrey demanded that the legation be shut by one means or another. Cecil Liddell sent him a memorandum concluding that on balance it appeared that the mission was not directly involved in espionage.[23] This rather courageous conclusion was broadly vindicated once Pandora became available. But the problem remained that, in certain circumstances, Hempel and his staff might radio vital intelligence even at the risk of a rupture in diplomatic relations. The issue of information leakage through the Axis legations arose again in the autumn, as preparations for the Anglo-American landings in French North Africa, Operation *Torch*, intensified. Maffey advised against pressing the Irish to demand the handover of the radio, because the presence of the radio strengthened the argument that the legation was a threat to British security. MI5, on the other hand, were keen to have the radio dealt with, arguing that it might be used to send crucial operational intelligence. An additional question was what to do about Axis cables in the weeks leading up to *Torch*: to cut them off completely might prompt Hempel to radio crucial information whatever the diplomatic consequences, and it was also thought possible that a complete ban on cables might enable the legation to secure Irish permission to use the radio

---

[19] Quotations from Hempel to Berlin, 19 Feb. and 11 Sept. 1942, in 'Summary of German Cable and Wireless Messages . . .', 17 Apr. 1943, TNA, DO121/84; Walshe to de Valera reporting interview with Hempel, 17 Feb. 1942, UCDA, de Valera papers, P150/2571.

[20] Transcript of Walshe Hempel telephone conversation of 28 Oct., with Bryan to Walshe, 3 Nov. 1942, NAI, DFA A 25; Hempel to Berlin, 29 Oct., quoted in 'Summary of German Cable and Wireless Messages . . .', TNA, DO121/84.

[21] Cecil Liddell to Stephenson, 14 Mar. 1942, TNA, DO121/84.

[22] *Liddell History*, 65; Liddell diary, 20 Mar. 1942, TNA, KV4/189.

[23] Liddell diary, 18 and 19 Feb. 1942, TNA, KV4/189.

since they would have no other means of communication with Berlin. David Petrie concluded that, given the uncertainties, a cautious approach was required: it was decided to subject Axis cables to 'varying and increasing delays' so as to leave the enemy and the Irish unsure whether the changed pattern was significant.[24]

On 16 October Berardis sent Rome a message touching on Irish press reports of an 'imminent British offensive in Egypt'.[25] This run-of-the-mill decode was one of two selected for Churchill to see on 22 October. Perhaps failing to note that Berardis cited newspapers as his main sources, Churchill referred it to the foreign secretary Anthony Eden, who in turn asked: 'Have we any evidence recently of activities of Axis legations in Dublin? With the extension of the war the continuation of these anomalies becomes increasingly absurd'.[26] C was asked to give SIS's views, and Jane Archer duly produced a document. Guy Liddell recorded his reaction:

> Viv[ian] telephoned about a report on Ireland which is being sent to the F[oreign] Minister [*sic*] for transmission to the PM. The latter has become alarmed by one of the telegrams by the Italian representative in Dublin which appeared to him to indicate leakage of information. In actial [*sic*] fact the information that has been obtained by Berardis . . . is of little consequence. Much of it has been inaccurate.
>
> I told Viv that I thought the report which had been put up by Jane gave away too much about our relations with Dan [Bryan of G2] and SIS agents. I thought this could be said verbally to the Foreign Secretary.[27]

On 31 October it was agreed to hold up all Axis cable traffic 'from Dublin until after TORCH has started', a matter of a few days.[28]

From a subsequent decode it appears that Rome attached value to the Berardis message but queried the length of time involved in sending it (they eventually received it on the afternoon of 22 October).[29] It later transpired that Hempel too had sent a cable about 'the movement of ships from Belfast', which 'was accurate as far as it went' although the information had been 'obtained at third hand and was not very clear'. Berlin radioed repeated requests to Hempel for further information, to be sent back by the same means. Hempel declined to use his radio, but eventually cabled that he had no further details (his message of 17 October had stated that 'six small and speedy convoys of troops were said to have left England and Northern Ireland that week for destination East'). Guy Liddell surmised that 'the Germans have got wind of TORCH and are anxious about the move of convoys from N[orthern] Ireland'.[30] Rumours of a forthcoming major operation were already doing the rounds in Britain: Churchill was 'hopping mad' when he saw a decode to that effect from the Spanish ambassador Alba, although as Liddell observed 'it is his duty to report to his Government what he sees, hears and thinks . . . The fault

[24] *Liddell History*, 69.

[25] Berardis to Rome, 16 Oct. 1942, TNA, HW12/281.

[26] C to Churchill, 22 Oct., attaching a copy of the Berardis decode, and Eden to Cadogan (permanent under secretary of the Foreign Office), 23 Oct. 1942, TNA, HW1/1996.

[27] Liddell diary, 25 Oct. 1942, TNA, KV4/190.

[28] Ibid., 31 Oct. 1942, TNA, KV4/190.

[29] Rome to Berardis, 9 Nov. 1942, TNA, HW12/282.

[30] *Liddell History*, 70; Liddell diary, 31 Oct. 1942, TNA, KV4/190; précis of Hempel to Berlin, 17 Oct. 1942, in SIS summary of German communications relating to use of the Legation radio, 17 April 1943, TNA, DO121/84.

lies with those who confide in him' (a comparable problem arose the following July, when the Swedish military attaché got wind of the Allied plans to invade Sicily and duly cabled this to Stockholm).[31]

The events of October 1942 presented the Axis legations in an altered light: whereas in 1940 and 1941 they had appeared largely as a kind of advance guard helping to prepare the ground for a German attack, henceforth they would be studied in Whitehall in terms of the danger which they posed to Allied offensive operations. As Pandora was to make clear, Hempel was very conscious that in the altered circumstances of the war the policy which he had earlier pursued of steering as far clear as possible of anything to do with intelligence, lest he be compromised and his mission closed, was no longer tenable. By 1943 he accepted that circumstances might arise in which he would have to risk his mission in order to send vital war information. Pandora ensured that the British were able to keep track both of his thinking and of Berlin's instructions to him.

SIS AND IRELAND, 1941–1942

Information on SIS activities in Ireland is sadly incomplete, and what little we have comes largely from Irish records. Nevertheless, the main lines of the story are clear enough. The volume of passenger traffic across the Irish Sea ensured that Collinson was under constant pressure in his overt role of head of the permit office, where by mid-1942 there were thirty-eight staff.[32] His secret activities were also extensive, as he developed and superintended the work of secret networks around Ireland: he 'wants a man in Ennis [in County Clare] at a starting salary of £10 per month. He has the rest of the county covered'. Most of this activity involved the investigation of suspicious individuals, groups, or organizations thought to be engaged in pro-Axis activities including espionage and propaganda. In October G2's informant Moore reported that Podesta had introduced a Ms Gladys Harben to Collinson 'as a possible maid to be planted' on the Vichy French naval attaché Albertas, although 'her French is not fluent enough to be able to listen to telephone conversations'. Soon she was ' "installed" and doing her stuff', reporting daily to Podesta, but within a month was 'trying to get out of her job'.[33] Amongst those investigated by SIS was Dr T. G. Wilson, 'said to be physician to Hempel and to German internees'. SIS need not have worried: Wilson was already working for another British secret agency, the escape service MI9, and in 1942 was convicted for helping a British serviceman who had escaped from the Curragh internment camp (Guy Liddell noted that the Irish appeared to know about 'the whole of the MI9 set up').[34] There was no evidence of attempts to penetrate the IRA directly: the

[31] Liddell diary, 30 Oct. 1942 and 5 July 1943, TNA, KV4/190 and 191.

[32] Collinson to Passport Control Department, 18 June 1942, FO366/1287.

[33] Unsigned MS reports, 5 Oct. 1941, and undated, MAI, G2/X/1091.

[34] Maffey to Walshe, 21 Oct. 1942, protesting at the proceedings being taken against Wilson: 'there will clearly be something lost for Eire in the goodwill of the Allied countries'. DFA, P44; *Irish Press*, 29 Oct. 1942; Liddell diary, 30 Oct. 1942, TNA, KV4/190. Wilson received a fine and a suspended sentence. Because he had transported an internee in his car, his petrol permit was withdrawn for a time, causing him considerable hardship as it meant he had to cycle between hospitals.

names of some of those who sheltered Goertz did crop up, but only after these had become public knowledge through police raids. A Rathmines boot-mender was 'a dangerous Communist and pro-German', a Miss Sutton of Leeson Street was 'said to be distributing anti-British propaganda', and the landlady of a well-heeled man deported from Britain the previous year, whose letters had been noted in censorship, 'states that she believes he was a British S[ecret] S[ervice] Agent, although she spoke highly of him. Pod[esta] believes this correct'.[35] Dan Breen, the maverick Fianna Fáil TD and passionate pro-German, was 'a frequent caller after dark' to the home of Thomsen of the German legation: 'B[reen] seems to be trying to hide his identity by turning up his collar'. An ex-Garda 'has been put on it as a special job to watch the house'.[36] Such material, in tone and content not dissimilar to reports produced by the Garda and by G2, was mainly of negative value. Moore also reported that Collinson 'states that he has an indirect contact in D[epartment of] Justice who is third from top'. This was probably E. C. 'Ned' Powell, who reportedly often played golf with two British officials and who might have let slip pieces of gossip.[37] Moore's reports also indicated that other intelligence operations were ongoing: when Podesta asked about 'sending a man to cover the Sinn Fein Wolfe Tone Commemoration lecture', Collinson replied that 'he was covering it with "a good man from another team" . . . M[oore] gathers . . . that the "good man" is a civil servant employed in Income Tax, but got no further details'.[38] Given the range of departments and agencies with interests in Ireland, it is highly likely that there were other British networks in existence: we have already seen how MI9 and SOE became involved in 1941, and the latter organization continued to nurse ambitions for Ireland.[39]

One of the great mysteries of these days was the so-called 'Hayes confession' which emerged in Dublin in the autumn of 1941. This document, purportedly a factual explanation of the IRA's various failures since 1939, was allegedly written by the IRA chief of staff Stephen Hayes, after he had been kidnapped and interrogated over a period of two months by disgruntled IRA men from Northern Ireland. Hayes had become chief of staff by default when Seán Russell left Ireland in 1939. He was a heavy drinker and had never inspired much confidence, and was believed to be indiscreet when in his cups. He managed to escape from his captors in Dublin in early September, and extracts from his supposed confession were circulated by the IRA two days later. To some extent this publicity coup distracted attention from the real lesson of the Hayes kidnap, which was that the IRA were in desperate straits and that there was a marked divide between Dublin and northern republicans. The confession made the sensational claim that two ministers were in league with the IRA and had had talks with the elusive German agent known to be at large about German military aid. This was Goertz, who was under Hayes's protection. There were internal contradictions which suggested that, if not a complete fabrication, the confession was a mélange of fact and surmise which would not have been out

---

[35] Note dated 19 Oct. 1941, MAI, G2/X/1091.
[36] Note dated 13 May 1942, MAI, G2/X/1091.
[37] Archer to Bryan, 12 Jan. 1942, MAI, G2/X/1091.
[38] Note dated 15 June 1942, MAI, G2/X/1091.
[39] Captain Hayes to Bryan, 17 Feb. 1942, MAI, G2/X/1091.

of place in a Moscow show trial, elicited under prolonged coercion by a coterie of embittered northerners who sought to find the explanation for dismal failure on both sides of the border and in Britain in the comforting theory that everything had been betrayed by a single traitor. Maffey's staff were, like everyone else, bemused by the confession, which 'has somewhat fluttered the dovecots here', but were sensibly sceptical.[40]

SIS presumably made their own enquiries and came to some conclusion about the confession's reliability, but the only forensic analysis of it traced dates from 1943, when it had become possible to test some of its claims through Pandora. From these it emerged that, from his own knowledge of the ministers whom Hayes denounced, Hempel thought their involvement in a pro-German intrigue highly unlikely; on the other hand, he felt there might be something in the confession's premise that Goertz was regarded as a significant emissary. He also speculated that the reason Goertz had remained at liberty was that the police could watch him through Hayes; overall, however, although its claims were 'not entirely rejected' by trusted sources 'who are in close touch with the IRA', Hempel thought the confession an elaborate fabrication which might even be the work of British intelligence.[41]

Sixteen out of eighteen QRS reports from spring 1942 to December 1944 have been traced. They were circulated fairly widely in Whitehall, to the Treasury, the Dominions Office, the three service departments, the Home Office, and the Metropolitan Police. They contain only SIS material from Ireland, and have not been qualified, amended, corrected, or amplified by reference to intelligence from other sources such as decodes. The report covering March and April 1942 and the succeeding bi-monthly surveys reflect considerable sophistication as compared with the panic-stricken stories produced by SIS in the spring and summer of 1940. It was stated that the Irish were preoccupied with economic matters, and that 'opinion continues to harden in favour of neutrality', although 'the overwhelming majority . . . are clearly pro-British'; the 'severe Allied reverses in the Far East' had led to 'a heavy crop of defeatist talk, much of it clearly based upon exaggerated stories . . . by travellers from England'; the conviction and execution of the IRA gunman George Plant 'demonstrated afresh' the government's determination to 'suppress the Extremist IRA'; and the German legation continued to distribute propaganda.[42]

The succeeding report remarked on 'a deepening of apathy . . . The people no longer fear an invasion'. The only political question that mattered was supplies, where the government had blundered badly on clothes rationing: 'the influence of the Drapery Trade is widespread'. The crackdown on the IRA continued, as did the circulation of German propaganda: copies of speeches by Hitler and Ribbentrop had been 'sent to every Roman Catholic priest in Co. Galway and to National School teachers throughout Eire', and there were suspicions of a German whispering campaign about the 'bad behaviour' of American troops in Northern

[40] Archer (BRO) to Costar (Dominions Office, 4 Oct. 1941) TNA, DO130/23.
[41] Undated [1943] SIS analysis of allegations of Irish government intrigues with Herman Goertz, and Hempel to Berlin, 20 Oct. 1941, TNA, DO121/86.
[42] QRS 196, 1 May 1942, TNA, DO121/85.

Ireland. 'Loyalists' complained of the negative impact of damaging rumours. The best news, from an SIS perspective, came with the appointment of the 'strongly pro-British' Dr Ernest Alton as provost of Trinity College, despite calls for someone of 'advanced nationalist views' (among whom there would have been precious few amongst the fellows of Trinity). De Valera 'received Dr Alton with great cordiality and informed him that the cabinet were unanimous in approving his election'.

The next report again spoke of 'the prevailing apathy', of the increased activity of the newly formed republican party Córas na Poblacha and other fringe groups, of the success of the government's policy of releasing IRA internees on parole, of the imprisonment of the adventurer Charles McGuinness for espionage (which 'has still been kept out of the press'), of rumours that 'Italian elements are becoming more active in Dublin', encouraged by their legation, and of the openly anti-Axis views of Michael MacWhite, the Irish minister in Rome home on leave. The report for the last months of 1942 predicted that a general election was unavoidable, that neutrality 'will not be an . . . issue', that although some in Fine Gael were optimistic, the smaller Labour party were 'outpacing' the others 'in intensive organization', and, rather curiously, that Colonel P. A. Mulcahy attributed his transfer from command of the air corps to the artillery corps to 'the intrigues of the Jewish TD Robert Briscoe, who took advantage of manifest resentment in Government circles when Mulcahy's son joined the RAF'. The execution of the IRA man Maurice O'Neill for killing a detective demonstrated the government's continued resolve and the IRA's relative weakness, and links were emerging between the German legation and the new fascist party Ailtirí na hAiséirghe ('architects of the resurrection'). Hempel was rumoured to 'have made fairly large purchases of diamonds', and to be contemplating 'putting out peace feelers', and the Japanese mission 'continue their social activities'. The spectres which had haunted SIS in 1939 and 1940 had been succeeded by duller if more credible stories of economic hardship, political ennui, and widespread fear of bombing, leavened only with the occasional piece of gossip.[43]

The impact of SIS's Irish activities on London's analysis of Irish security and political affairs in this period is unascertainable without access to SIS headquarters records. Much of the detailed material which Collinson's organization provided was scrappy, inconsistent, incomplete, and contradictory. That was in the nature of the operations he was running, where the emphasis was primarily on the accumulation of a mass of low-level material through investigation of individuals, observation, and the harvesting of talk and opinion rather than on the penetration of the inner circles of the Irish government. It was the job of the Irish section at SIS headquarters to make sense of such material in the context of the many other sources available—decodes, information from other agencies, press reports, postal censorship, the observations of people travelling between Ireland and the United Kingdom, and so forth. Furthermore, anyone in Whitehall who wanted

---

[43] QRS reports nos. 197, 198 and 200, 4 July and 1 Sept. 1942 and 1 Jan. 1943, TNA, DO121/85. It is hard to believe that Briscoe, who was very active in international Jewish affairs and who knew more than most about the Nazis, would have held a grudge against anyone fighting for Britain. Mulcahy ultimately became chief of staff of the defence forces, which scarcely suggests that his career had been blighted.

to see how things stood in Ireland could visit at their will. This cornucopia of access and information—which contrasted with the inevitable dearth of material on countries in Axis-controlled Europe—required careful marshalling and sifting in London where, as Guy Liddell's diary shows, Jane Archer, Valentine Vivian, and occasionally even C himself were closely involved in the analysis of Irish affairs. But SIS documents, for example that of June 1941 on 'Quislings in Eire', have largely disappeared from the records.[44]

The Garda and G2 mounted many enquiries themselves into the activities of people who were believed to be, or who reportedly aspired to be, British agents or informants. Postal censorship threw up a good deal of amateur intrigue, and inquisitive Englishmen who took an interest in military dispositions were frequently reported to the Garda. These were sometimes arrested and interrogated. Many investigated for clandestine pro-British activities of one sort or another were warned off with the threat of prosecution or even internment: one man who was arrested and taken to Arbor Hill prison in May 1942 was 'very frightened and vowed to P[odesta] that he would not touch any similar matters in future'.[45] Information gathering was not the only clandestine activity detected: Cedric Tilson, a first world war veteran and stalwart of the Royal British Legion in Cavan, was duped into providing letters of recommendation for two supposed Irish army deserters who said they wished to enlist in the British army in Armagh. He was sentenced to six months' imprisonment in October 1941.[46] The German legation had a certain fascination for British servicemen and women, occasionally resulting in complications. A Royal Artillery soldier from Westmeath, seen visiting the German legation while home on leave in July 1941, was temporarily interned while the Garda checked out his story that, being formerly a journalist, he had tried to obtain an interview with Hempel for his regimental newspaper. The man was allowed to return to Britain after a couple of weeks, presumably with some explaining to do to his commanding officer. In June 1942 another man, evidently an MI5 stooge, was arrested for questioning by the Garda after approaching the legation. He was found to be carrying a piece of paper bearing the names 'of TAR and Marriott, the address room 055 and the W[ar] O[ffice] telephone number with our extension and a note to get in touch with them in any emergency', hardly the mark of a well-prepared double agent.[47] Decodes later showed that Hempel had been asked about the possibilities of recruiting Irish workers in British armaments industries as informants, but there is no evidence that he succeeded in doing so.[48]

In the early months of 1941 the newly created Twenty committee did contemplate Irish operations. In February it was invited to consider 'the movement of coffins out of this country to Ireland and the possibilities of this channel'. Quite what these possibilities might have been is not clear, but by a nice irony the remark came from

---

[44] Listed on 10 June 1941 in the contents of Frank Ryan's MI5 file, TNA, KV2/1991.

[45] Report by M, 13 May 1942, MAI, G2/X/1091.

[46] *Irish Independent*, 3 Oct. 1941. Tilson was released after six weeks.

[47] Liddell diary, 4 June 1942, TNA, KV4/190. T. A. Robertson and John Marriott were senior MI5 officers.

[48] 'Summary of most secret information from Dublin 22nd March–3rd April 1943', citing a message of September 1942, TNA, DO121/87.

Ewan Montagu, who was to achieve fame in the 1950s through his account of a later deception operation involving a dead body.[49] The committee agreed on 'Plan IV', a scheme which involved a fictitious office worker in the Security Executive, 'James Sullivan', who was to write to the German legation enclosing misleading information about bomb damage which might encourage a switch in German targeting from cities to airfields.[50] After careful drafting, SIS's Felix Cowgill announced that the material could not after all be dropped into the legation letter-box because of tight 'Irish control', and an alternative plan of enclosing it within a sealed envelope was adopted. This was predicated partly on the Irish not opening German legation mail in the ordinary post, a problematic assumption. There was no consideration of possible Irish reaction to such a scheme if it was uncovered. By one means or another the letter was eventually delivered, but there was no response. The trick was then tried on the Japanese embassy in London, again without results. Finally MI5 used their established double agent *GW* to pass the material to the Spanish press attaché, known to be working for the Axis, and the scheme was judged a success.[51] At the end of August it was decided that Sullivan should inform *GW* that he could purloin documents for twelve hours at a time, so that *GW* could tell 'his Spanish friends'. Here the trail runs cold, but given British mastery of Spanish espionage in Britain, it is quite possible that Sullivan continued to pass on material.[52]

I have already noted SOE's problems securing sanction for whispers in Ireland, largely because of SIS opposition. SIS evidently attempted to develop their own lines for deceiving the enemy through Ireland: early in October 1942 an officer told the Twenty committee that he was 'in a position to provide a channel for deceptive information to the Italians in Dublin', and it may be that this was used for the remainder of Italy's war—Berardis was an indefatigable relayer of whatever war gossip he came across.[53]

COUNTER-ESPIONAGE AND SECURITY: GERMAN AND IRA ACTIVITIES

The greatest problem for both the British and the Irish security agencies, the legation radio aside, continued to be the threat of German espionage. Of the agents sent to Ireland, only Goertz was still at large in June 1941, but the Garda were on his trail. A breakthrough came in September, when they raided the Shankhill home of his principal IRA contact Jim O'Donovan, who had only recently come under suspicion. He was interned. The Garda for the first time came up with the name Goertz, asking the RUC if the British authorities had any information on him. This aroused intense interest in MI5: Cecil Liddell reported the matter direct to David

[49] Twenty committee minutes, 27 Feb. 1941, TNA, KV4/63; Montagu, *The Man Who Never Was*.
[50] This 'Dublin plan' was also discussed at the W Board, to which the Twenty committee was subordinate, on 5 Apr. 1941, TNA, KV3/70.
[51] Twenty committee minutes, 6, 13, 20, 27 Mar., 3, 10, 17, 24 Apr., 1, 8, 15, 22, 29 May, 5, 12, 19, 26 June, and 10, 24, and 31 July 1941, TNA, KV4/63.
[52] Ibid. 21 Aug. 1941, TNA, KV4/63.
[53] Ibid., 8 Oct. 1942, TNA, KV4/65.

Petrie, who noted that 'this is a very interesting minute which has been seen by Lord Swinton. The cropping up of the name of Dr Goertz is very suggestive'.[54] The details of Goertz's pre-war conviction in England for espionage, and photographs, were duly supplied through the RUC. In the same month Maffey provided the Irish with what should have been a crucial lead, after Joseph Andrews visited the American legation on 10 September to say that he had been asked by the IRA to hide a radio in his house. The Garda were reportedly unimpressed with this story, possibly on account of Andrews's known character, and beyond keeping observation on his house for a week did not pursue the lead as assiduously as they might have done.[55]

Sheltered by republican sympathizers, amongst them his clutch of adoring women, Goertz was eventually captured in Dublin on 27 November 1941, probably due to the treachery of Joseph Andrews; this rogue *sans pareil* was to resurface in 1943.[56] MI5 learnt of the Goertz arrest not from official Irish sources but through the press: 'so far the Irish tell us very little. They probably fear that we should use this case as a pretext for pressing the Eire Gov[ernmen]t to forego its neutrality and turn the Germans out. There is fairly conclusive proof that Goertz was working in close conjunction with the IRA'. Cecil Liddell visited Dublin, and as expected found that the Irish would not allow him to question Goertz, but he was able to give them some pointers for 'further interrogation'. Prior to his trip he had advised the Dominions Office that, while 'it can be said that we have received extremely good co-operation and I am very anxious not to give the impression that we have made any complaint', there were 'limitations'. Most significantly, the Irish would not give anything 'which would give us a handle for saying that the Germans . . . must all be interned or kicked out, or which would strengthen our hand in asking for the use of the Eire ports as bases'. In addition, the Irish would not let British officers interrogate captured agents, and would not ask those agents any questions based on British information, for fear that the Germans would accuse them of breaching neutrality.[57] Liddell was conscious that he was walking a tightrope in, on the one hand, assuring Bryan that MI5 'were not in any way complaining of lack of co-operation on his part', and not 'losing the opportunity of increasing that co-operation'.[58]

There were particularly strong reasons for Irish reticence about Goertz. This became clear to MI5 in 1943 from Pandora decodes dating from 1941. These showed that, through the agency of O'Donovan, Goertz had had meetings with the ailing General O'Duffy—'this personality, who stood close to National Socialism'—in

[54] Petrie to Guy Liddell, 20 Sept. 1941, TNA, KV3/120.

[55] Chief Superintendent Carroll (Garda security section) to Walshe (Dublin), 18 Sept. 1941, attaching detailed TS report on Goertz's pre-war activities in Britain. This is plainly a British Special Branch or MI5 document. NAI, DFA A34; note dated 6 Aug. 1943, with Cecil Liddell to Stephenson, 24 Aug. 1943, TNA, DO121/86.

[56] Hull, *Irish Secrets*, 196–9.

[57] Liddell diary, 4 Dec. 1941 and 6 Jan. 1942, TNA, KV4/189; Cecil Liddell to Dominions Office, 29 Jan. 1941, TNA, KV4/280. The Iraqis proved more obliging when they captured a group of German saboteurs in June 1943, allowing the British to interrogate them extensively on the condition that they were then returned. Details of this are in TNA, WO208/1575.

[58] Cecil Liddell to Vivian, 1 Feb. 1942, TNA, KV4/280.

November 1940, and with Major General Hugo MacNeill.[59] He apparently hoped to promote a concordat between the IRA and MacNeill's followers in the army. The Irish were naturally not anxious to apprise the British of these developments. In April 1941 Goertz had secured the help of a competent radio operator, Anthony Deery, who was on the run following an IRA raid. Goertz composed various messages detailing schemes for escaping Ireland, but Deery did not acquire a transmitter capable of raising Germany until July. Goertz then apparently did manage to send some messages dealing with his plans to escape to France by boat, which are recorded in an Abwehr war diary, although it is curious that none of these transmissions were picked up by either RSS or the Irish.[60] In April 1942 the Garda finally caught up with Deery, and also seized his transmitter.[61] Yet this was not the end of the Goertz problem: in succeeding years his own efforts to communicate from prison, and the use of his code by the egregious Joseph Andrews to sell intelligence to the Germans in Lisbon, were to cause further difficulties.

In February 1942 Gunther Schutz escaped from Mountjoy Jail, and was sheltered in Dublin by the strongly republican Brugha family. MI5 informed their double agent *Rainbow* of the escape lest Schutz contact him, as Schutz had been involved in his initial recruitment in late 1939: *Rainbow* 'has taken the line that as Schutz is an old school friend . . . it would be extremely difficult to hand him over to the police'. Accordingly, with David Petrie's blessing, *Rainbow* was given 'a guarantee' that if he provided information leading to an arrest, Schutz 'will not be executed', although Liddell concluded that in any case 'there is obviously nothing to be gained by executing Schutz. On the contrary it may be possible to obtain a great deal of useful information', although it seemed 'extremely unlikely' that he would come to Britain.[62] Schutz in fact lay low in Dublin, where he met members of the Northern IRA and prepared a coded message to the Abwehr to be smuggled to the German legation for transmission. Despite reservations about involvement in an espionage case, the legation provided Schutz with some money and relayed the message, together with Hempel's observations on the matter. Berlin replied suggesting that Schutz should remain in Ireland, offering to send him another radio, and directing Hempel to give him more money. Hempel did not act on this. On 30 April, just hours before he was due to be brought south to County Wicklow to board a boat which would bring him to France, Schutz was captured in a Garda raid on the Brugha home, and his encoded message was later broken by Richard Hayes.[63]

Schutz's escape and recapture had ramifications in a suprising number of directions. In addition to his sensitive links to *Rainbow*, the manner of his escape,

[59] Translation of Goertz's account of his mission, smuggled out of prison addressed to the German legation but intercepted by G2, undated [Dec. 1944], National Library of Ireland, Hayes MS 22983; various Dublin Berlin decodes dating from 1941, appended to MI5 note of 8 Aug. 1943, with Cecil Liddell to Stephenson, 24 Aug. 1943, TNA, DO121/86.

[60] Hull, *Irish Secrets*, 172–5.

[61] Ibid. 170. After the war Deery was released and, like other IRA detainees, was allowed to resume his civil-service post.

[62] Liddell diary, 23 Feb. and 6 Mar. 1942, TNA, KV4/189. Hull, *Irish Secrets*, 152, identifies *Rainbow* as a Portuguese named Pierce, whereas both Liddell's diary and Hinsley and Simkins, *British Intelligence*, 43, indicate that *Rainbow* was British-born but had been raised in Germany.

[63] Hull, *Irish Secrets*, 232–4.

his intrigues with the Northern IRA, the German legation's admittedly reluctant support for him, and his succouring by the Brughas reflected the tangled interplay of Irish, British, and German interests and preoccupations. Cathal Brugha had died a hero's death in the first week of the civil war—when he received news of it de Valera asked my grandmother to tell Caitlín Brugha that 'I feel that robbed of Cathal we are all robbed of the one man who could have made victory possible—I cannot write to her whose loss is the greatest of all. Oh cruel cruel that it is by Irish men he should be killed'—and so she and her children were treated with a certain degree of consideration, despite their known involvement in subversion. Mrs Brugha was very active in the circulation of IRA and German propaganda, her son Ruairi was interned for IRA membership, and her daughters were key players in the IRA's support networks. The Garda raids on the Brugha home and business in which Schutz was discovered were mounted as the result of the arrest in Belfast of a courier, Henry Lundborg, who 'had quite an elaborate questionnaire relating to disposition of troops etc in Northern Ireland' for the Northern IRA. Lundborg admitted bringing documents from Belfast to the Brugha family's outfitting business, where he delivered them to Noinín Brugha. She was already known to the Garda as a significant figure in the IRA's communications system, and she was duly interned. MI5 concluded, not unreasonably, that there was 'at least a strong inference' that the IRA were collecting such material for the Germans, whether or not the latter had actually sought it. The case illustrated the crossover between anti-British, anti-state, and pro-German activities and interests, as well as the political sensitivity of acting against such a prominent republican family.[64]

IRISH AGENTS AND DOUBLE CROSS: THE BASKET CASE

A separate Irish espionage case provided British agencies with a different set of issues. On 18 July a parachutist landed undetected at Summerhill, County Meath. Three days later his parachute was discovered by a farmer, and witnesses spoke of a man seen attempting to hitch a lift. The Irish aircraft plotting system showed that an unidentified aircraft had flown over the area on 18 July. By the time that this material had been collated, however, the British were, unusually, well ahead of the Irish in respect of what had happened, because on 23 July, at a railway halt just north of the border, a man had told an RUC man that he needed to speak to an intelligence officer. This was Joseph Lenihan, the black sheep of a prominent Athlone family—his nephew Brian rose to be a Fianna Fáil foreign minister and *tanaiste* (deputy prime minister) in the early 1990s, his niece Mary (O'Rourke) became a long-serving cabinet minister, and his grandnephews Brian and Conor are now ministers, and he was to prove one of the most perplexing agents to come into MI5's hands. Possessed of 'a phenomenal memory for facts and faces', he gave 'more fresh and accurate information' about German intelligence in the Netherlands and

---

[64] De Valera to Kathy Barry, 8 July 1922, UCDA, Kathleen Barry Moloney papers, P94/28; Liddell diary, 18 Feb., 11 and 20 Apr. 1942, TNA, KV4/189.

France than had any other agent. He was also independent minded to a fault, making him very difficult to handle.[65]

Lenihan had gone to Jersey to work as a farm labourer just before the Germans occupied the island. Some of his interrogators, and post-war research, suggested that he was recruited there as an agent. He offered an alternative story, saying that he had overpowered a German sentry—'I batted him, you see'—before singlehandedly stealing a 22-foot boat. Contrary winds blew him not to England but to France, where he said he was arrested and eventually recruited as an agent. A former IRA man, he had refused payment from the Germans. Whatever the facts, it was certain that he received radio and some meteorological training in France, before being dispatched to Ireland from the Netherlands in January 1941. His aircraft ran into difficulties and returned without dropping him.[66] He was eventually dropped in Ireland in July, with the mission of broadcasting weather reports from Sligo in the north-west, and was supposed later to travel to England to report on air raid damage.

On 23 July Guy Liddell noted that 'a message has come through from Banham the RSS man in Ulster that a man called Joseph LENIHAN . . . was sitting in his office drinking a cup of tea. The story is that Lenihan came down . . . on Sunday, made his way across the border and gave himself up . . . He has left his two-way wireless set in Eire but has with him an auxiliary one-way set. We have arranged that Cecil and TAR shall . . . fetch him back to this country'.[67] Robertson received 'outstanding' cooperation from the RUC, and Lenihan was flown to Hendon, and then interrogated in MI5's Camp 020 at Latchmere House at Ham in Surrey. It was 'absolutely essential that as few people as possible should know and that if possible the Irish authorities should not be informed as we were afraid of leakage to the German Legation . . . This would have jeopardized the case in the event of our wishing to run the case as a double cross'.[68]

The Irish nevertheless came into the picture on 24 July, when a branch manager of the Ulster Bank in Dublin informed the Irish Department of Finance that a curious character had deposited £370 five days previously. Dan Bryan of G2 afterwards surmised that the branch had already been in touch with its Belfast headquarters. When G2 contacted the Garda, they already 'knew all about Lenihan', because an RUC officer had arrived to brief them on the case. On 25 July MI5:

had a conference about Lenihan. We came to the conclusion that the only use we could make of his set would be by impersonation. Lenihan was dropped . . . with instructions to send weather reports . . . and to proceed to England in order to obtain information about air raid damage. He had given himself up in Northern Ireland because he had a criminal record in the south. He is wanted for unlawful assembly, presumably in connection with an IRA meeting, and has also done time for fraud. The Irish have already discovered his parachute, and his set, which has not so far been taken, is left . . . on the Eire side of the border.[69]

---

[65] *Liddell History*, 60; Captain Goodacre's comments on Lenihan, 9 Aug. 1941, TNA, KV4/PF60920. I am particulary grateful to David Suckling for directing me to this source.

[66] Transcript of Lenihan interrogation, 26 July 1941, TNA, KV4/PF60920.

[67] Liddell diary, 23 July 1941, TNA, KV4/188.

[68] Aide-mémoire by T. A. Robertson, 25 July 1941, TNA, KV4/PF60920.

[69] Dan Bryan interview, 1983; Liddell diary, 25 July 1941, TNA, KV4/188.

Lenihan had left most of his secret ink and his main radio in a Dundalk hotel, bringing his auxiliary set across the border to prove his story.

Lenihan, born in 1906, initially told MI5 that, after briefly studying medicine, he had worked four years in the civil service until 'I got fed up, and went to Canada . . . then . . . to America . . . For a short period I was in China'. After three years in Ireland from 1932 to 1935, during which 'I did a spot of wandering . . . I did not do much work', he arrived in Britain in 1936. But the Garda reported that he had been jailed for a year and had lost his post as a Customs official for involvement in an IRA car-smuggling racket. An SIS operative in Dublin picked up this item separately after a tip-off: 'the [bank] Manager merely passed the matter on to me as being something in which I might be interested . . . the records here show' that Lenihan was convicted in February 1935.[70]

After release Lenihan left Ireland. He claimed to have fought in the Spanish civil war, to have spent two years in the American army, and to have soldiered in China against the Japanese. Garda enquiries revealed that he had long had the name of an accomplished dissimulator, effortlessly mixing fact and fiction. He had left his own family in the dark about his whereabouts for years, and various acquaintances testified to his ability to spin a yarn. There were gaps in his account of his pre-war activities, but more pertinently his narrative of his arrival was plainly false: whereas he claimed that he had travelled to Northern Ireland within a day of landing, the bank lodgement and the Irish aircraft plot indicated that he had landed no later than 19 May. Garda investigations revealed that after reaching Dublin he had spent a good deal of time drinking with an old acquaintance, a former bank clerk turned firewood salesman whom the Garda regarded as harmless. Another drinking companion, Charles McGuinness, was in an altogether different category. A petty officer in the newly established Irish marine service, McGuiness too had had a picaresque life, smuggling weapons for the IRA during the war of independence, serving in Byrd's expedition to the South Pole, acting (or so he claimed) as president of a Central American republic, and taking some part in the Spanish civil war; his name was amongst a list of contacts supplied to the German agent Walter Simon in June 1940, and he had been involved in the abortive scheme to help Goertz escape by boat in early 1941. G2 did not wish the Garda to question him about Lenihan, presumably lest this tip him off that he was under suspicion, and nor were MI5 informed about McGuinness. In 1942 McGuinness was jailed after contacting the German legation to offer a mass of information he had accumulated on Atlantic convoys.[71]

After no fewer than nine interrogations, MI5 officers were divided on what to do with Lenihan. The OC of Camp 020 believed that 'the great danger . . . is German infiltration'. Lenihan's very openness stood against him: 'He . . . admits with engaging candour that he disapproves of the British Government . . . I am therefore quite at a loss to understand why he should wish to assist'. A colleague

[70] Transcript of first Lenihan interrogation, 24 July 1941, and SIS report from Dublin of 28 July, with SIS to Cecil Liddell, 5 Aug. 1941, TNA, KV4/PF60920.

[71] Hull, *Irish Secrets*, 174, 181 and 232; Bryan to Walshe, 17 Apr. 1942, attaching documents on McGuinness. NAI, DFA A8.

took the opposite view: 'From beginning to end Lenihan has recounted his story with the utmost frankness and honesty . . . those parts of it which can be checked from other sources have been proved to be absolutely true. He is an exceptionally observant and intelligent type with a gift for shrewd inference', and his 'moral courage' was demonstrated 'by his gratuitous statement . . . that he had no love for the British Government, an opinion he could easily have withheld'.[72]

The RUC and Garda agreed to a temporary swap of Lenihan's two radios. Guy Liddell noted that this 'matter was referred to Dev', although there is no other evidence of this. Despite the extent of Irish knowledge of Lenihan and his mission, and the RUC's reservations about his truthfulness, there remained a temptation to use him as a double agent. MI5 initially discarded the idea of operating his radio, after the RAF vetoed the sending of any meteorological material, but decided he should 'send a message in secret ink indicating that he has managed to get over here and has established contact with an IRA friend in Liverpool. We will ask for instructions . . . we may be able to work him through a cut out'.[73] In the Twenty committee 'it was suggested that *Basket*', the cover name assigned to Lenihan, 'be run as a "fool"-agent'. This eventually happened, but only after considerable debate within MI5 on what to do with him.[74]

Lenihan sent two coded letters to the Madrid address provided by the Abwehr, but drew no response. In January 1942 the unimaginatively titled 'Plan Shamrock' saw MI5 attempt to contact Germany on his radio, which was installed in a house in Ham. The operator transmitted 'with his left hand, and rather shakily, making a number of mistakes, in an endeavour to imitate Lenihan's style'. The aim was not to pass any traffic, but 'to see whether after six months the German Organization still listens for their radio agents'. If contact was established the transmission 'should be broken off and not resumed'. In fact no response was picked up, and after the war interrogation of a German intelligence officer indicated that 'no message was ever received'.[75]

Lenihan's health was a continuing difficulty. His hands had been very badly affected by frostbite during his flight to Ireland, and required months of treatment. In October it was decided that, once in good physical shape, he would be placed as an agent on a boat sailing to South America. In the meantime, Robertson suggested that he be employed as a 'loafer' in 'public houses and other places, where interesting information and gossip might be picked up. This suggestion has the obvious merit that it would give him something to do'.[76] Shortly afterwards MI5 decided to pay Lenihan off. In January 1942 David Petrie agreed that he be allowed to take a job, and to pay him £50 immediately with '£200 to be placed in an account and released to him after the war, provided he behaves himself. He is to be warned against going

[72] Memorandum by Lieutenant Colonel Stephens, 9 Aug. 1941, TNA, KV2/PF60920.

[73] Liddell diary, 26, 28 and 30 July, and note by Robertson, 7 Aug. 1941, TNA, KV4/188 and KV2/PF60920. Hinsley and Simkins, *British Intelligence*, 92 and 195, give an inaccurate summary of his case, saying that after landing he 'at once' went to Northern Ireland and 'gave a full account of himself'.

[74] Twenty committee minutes, 21 Aug. 1941, TNA, KV4/63.

[75] Hull, *Irish Secrets*, 182; memorandum on Basket, 22 Jan. 1942, and extract from interrogation report, 2 Mar. 1946, TNA, KV2/PF60920; Liddell diary, 27 Jan. 1942, TNA, KV4/190.

[76] Robertson to Liddell, 27 Oct. 1941, TNA, KV4/PF60920.

back to Eire and will be told to report his movements'. A couple of days later, Lenihan 'handed back the £50 and tore up the agreement. Characteristically he had a good deal to say about us and our methods . . . What he obviously resented was any sort of restriction on his liberty and the fact that we obviously did not trust him entirely'.[77] Although he continued to provide information and observations on German intelligence, he became very restless, and in July was 'caught trying to get out of the country by joining the crew of a fishing boat leaving Fleetwood . . . to fish off . . . Donegal'.[78]

The *Basket* case is interesting not only for its Irish angle but because it shows how, contrary to the impression created by Masterman's *The Double-Cross System*, MI5 hoped to use him as a double agent even though knowledge of his arrival was widespread. His case failed to develop not because of security calculations, but because the Germans did not respond. By February 1943 MI5 were prepared to let him pay a visit home: Belfast 'think we are crazy . . . [but] I cannot see that there is any harm to be done', a conclusion endorsed by Petrie, although G2 said that given his 'habits and character' they 'hesitate to guarantee a 100%, fool-proof, check on his doings'.[79]

Lenihan's case saw the introduction of stricter scrutiny of correspondence from Irish people resident in Europe, and this, in combination with enquiries by G2, led to the identification of three Irish civilians who had received agent training.[80] These were James O'Neill, a seaman who turned himself in upon arrival in Britain in November 1942, John Francis O'Reilly, who was captured shortly after landing by parachute in County Clare in December 1943, and Jack Vickers, a seaman interned in Holland who freely admitted to British officials in Lisbon that he had been recruited as an agent before being permitted to leave for Ireland in 1944.[81]

Lenihan's case raises the wider question of the running of double agents either actually or notionally based in Ireland. A scheme was developed to entrap one Gunner Jackson, who had written to the Spanish embassy in London offering military information, by having him meet a supposed German agent who would make arrangements for him to travel to Ireland. Jackson was arrested in England, and Guy Liddell, who gave evidence at his trial, was 'rather appalled' at the death sentence quickly passed.[82] More significantly, in the spring of 1942 SIS reported that German intelligence in Lisbon were seeking an informant amongst Irish seamen, hoping to gather intelligence on Allied forces in Northern Ireland. MI5 asked Dan Bryan whether he would run 'a reliable man as a double agent, but it is not thought' that this happened. This was a considerable gesture of confidence in G2 and in

---

[77] Liddell diary, 19 and 21 Jan. 1942, TNA, KV4/189. Early in 1943 the Irish government remitted to his London bank account the £370 seized in May 1941.

[78] Liddell diary, 8 Feb. and 4 July 1942, TNA, KV4/190.

[79] Liddell diary, 9 Feb., TNA, KV4/191; minute by Petrie, 1 Feb., TNA, KV2/PF 60920; Masterman, *The Double-Cross System*, 99–100; Hankinson (BRO) to Boland (Dublin), conveying message for Bryan from Cecil Liddell, 30 Jan., and Boland's reply, 4 Feb. 1943, NAI, DFA A60.

[80] *Curry History*, 280.

[81] Ibid.; *Liddell History*, 61 and 70. Irish files on O'Neill and on O'Reilly are in MAI, G2/4174 and 3824. On Vickers, see Guilfoyle, G2, to Boland (External Affairs), and reply, 25 Feb. and 5 Mar. 1943, NAI, DFA A8/1, and Liddell diary, 27 Apr. 1944, TNA, KV4/193.

[82] Liddell diary, 22 Dec. 1941 and 5 Feb. 1942, TNA, KV4/189.

Bryan.[83] He responded that, 'while he would shut his eyes to anything that we might do on Eire soil, of course with his knowledge, he could not . . . run a double agent outside Eire', although 'on more than one occasion he, as he called it, "ran a line" on Germans or those working with them in Eire itself'. This qualified refusal to cooperate meant that 'unfortunately double agents based on Eire could not be used owing to the difficulty of running them from this side'.[84]

The next Irishman to turn up under German sponsorship was James O'Neill, about whom MI5 and G2 knew in advance through postal censorship. O'Neill had been approached in Germany by

our old friend JUPP HOVEN . . . O'Neill agreed to work for the Germans. After instructing him in various means of communication they gave him work in a firm . . . which had a sub-contract in France. While in France he was allowed to escape. This was to be his cover story. He was to go to Donegal and to transmit from there weather reports, and reports about the armed forces in Northern Ireland. He was to construct his own transmitter. Before departure he was to be given £1,000 and crystals for his wireless set. Unfortunately however he elected to cross the Franco-Spanish border before he had received either the money or the crystals. His excuse was that the man failed to keep the rendezvous. He notified the Germans of what he had done before leaving . . . he . . . was eventually repatriated. We have considered the possibility of using him but in all the circumstances we are inclined to turn down the proposition.

On his return to Ireland O'Neill was also interrogated by G2. The code he had been trained in was very primitive, and from this it was inferred that the Germans had never invested much hope in him.[85]

Ireland sometimes cropped up incidentally in the activities of other double agents: thus *Springbok*, based in Canada, mentioned an Irishman whom he had met while training with the Abwehr in Germany, who was 'apparently assisting [in] the formation of a Casement Brigade'. He 'had been interned by the Falangists and was subsequently released at the request of the Germans'. He 'was deaf and wore a microphone; he had crisp, reddish-brown hair, red face, freckles and was cleanshaven. Aged about 45, always wore tweeds', he had 'worked for the Spanish Republicans during the Civil War'. This was clearly Frank Ryan.[86] Ryan's whereabouts and activities were of considerable concern both to London and to Dublin. It is curious, given that he first came to MI5's attention in 1929, that it was not until October 1941 that he was placed on the visa blacklist: it was thought that he might arrive in Britain 'as seaman or under false name from Lisbon'.[87] From early 1942 there were frequent exchanges between MI5 and G2 on the matter; MI5 were also in regular touch with SIS about Ryan in the spring of 1942, suggesting that there were indications that Ryan might embark on a mission for Germany. It is most likely that such indications were spotted in ISOS. MI5 also acquired a

[83] *Liddell History*, 67.

[84] O'Halpin, *Defending Ireland*, 19 and 60–1; *Liddell History*, 67.

[85] Liddell diary, 7 and 17 Dec. 1942, TNA, KV4/191; *Liddell History*, 70–1; MAI, G2/4174; Hayes report, p. 3.

[86] Liddell diary, 9 June 1942, TNA, KV4/189; Marriott to Liddell, 19 July 1942, TNA, KV2/769; Hull, *Irish Secrets*, 217–8.

[87] OB1H/P to D4b, 10 Nov., and note of MI5 letter to SIS conveying information obtained from G2, 11 Nov. 1941, TNA, KV2/1991.

number of elliptical references to Ryan through postal censorship. These indicated that he had managed to smuggle a letter to Gerald O'Reilly, another republican leftist living in New York. O'Reilly's correspondence with his Irish communist and republican contacts were also under Irish surveillance, while a certain amount about Ryan emerged from interception of the post and from publications of British communists involved with the International Brigade Association of Spanish civil war veterans.[88]

One of the great puzzles of Ryan's time in Berlin is why, even after *Barbarossa*, communists in Britain and Ireland continued to campaign for his safe return. Given the nature of communist discipline, which in India saw the communist party turn overnight from being key instigators of subversion to acting as the Raj's most potent intelligence source on Indian nationalism, the continued interest in Ryan among Irish and British communists suggests that Moscow had reason to believe that he remained loyal to their cause.[89] Alternatively, they may have calculated that he could do less damage if returned to Ireland: by 1942 the Soviets would have been at least as well informed as were the British about the fact of his release from jail and of his involvement with German intelligence. An International Brigade Association flyer stated that Ryan's 'presence in Ireland would help enormously to unify and strengthen the forces for freedom there', and that he 'would lead the Irish people in the path of solidarity with the British people'. The association was undoubtedly under the control of the CPGB, which in turn was a loyal and highly disciplined instrument of Moscow's will. Such language raises the possibility, however fantastic it may seem, that Moscow seriously believed that Ryan might be capable of swinging opinion in Ireland towards support for Britain's—and therefore also Stalin's—war.[90] There is a more cynical explanation for the continued communist championing of Ryan's cause: Moscow may have wished to discredit him in German eyes by appearing still to have faith in him.

Since leaving Spain, Ryan had been in occasional touch with Leopold Kerney, the Irish minister in Madrid who had helped to free him in 1940. Kerney did not tell Dublin this, despite very clear warnings given during a visit home in 1941 to tread carefully after he admitted to Dan Bryan that he had agreed to Ryan's escape on his own authority because he had no means of securing Dublin's approval.[91] Nor did Kerney mention that he allowed various people to use his diplomatic bag to avoid censorship (External Affairs extended such a facility to the powerful archbishop of Dublin, Dr McQuaid, in 1942 after he complained that his correspondence was opened in censorship, but he was regarded as highly trustworthy). Most seriously, even after being warned about his conduct, Kerney continued to facilitate correspondence to and from Budge Mulcahy, wife of Helmut Clissmann, the Abwehr man, pre-war German agent

---

[88] The first reference in the lengthy chronological list of contents of Ryan's MI5 file to correspondence with Dublin is on 21 Jan. 1942, TNA, KV2/1999.

[89] Report by Stirling police of International Brigade Association pamphlet on Ryan, 1 Mar. 1941, NAS, HH55/51; for material on dealings between the Communist Party of India and SOE, see TNA, HS1/190 and 199.

[90] Undated [1942?] International Brigade Association flyer, TNA, KV2/1999.

[91] Bryan's note of interview with Kerney, 20 Oct. 1941, MAI, G2/0257.

and friend of Frank Ryan, and also family letters to the maverick former minister in Berlin Charles Bewley, working as a journalist and propagandist in Italy under German patronage. Kerney only acknowledged that he had been in touch with Ryan after a suggestive reference to this was noted in a private letter to his daughter.[92]

In August 1942 MI5 received information, probably through ISOS, which led them to conclude that Ryan and Clissmann had flown from Berlin to Madrid on the same aircraft, the first occasion on which the two men were connected in British records.[93] This visit was presumably in order to facilitate a meeting between Kerney and Dr Edmund Veesenmayer, the German ambassador to Yugoslavia who had previously specialized in the manipulation of nationalist minorities and who had taken an intermittent interest in Ireland. The Germans chose to approach Kerney because they could 'get nothing out of the then [Irish] Chargé d'Affaires in Berlin', William Warnock. In the course of two meetings with Kerney, Veesenmayer apparently asked about Irish policy in the event of German victory against Russia, which he observed would inevitably be followed by the defeat of Britain. Kerney afterwards claimed that he remained entirely non-committal, but the very fact of secret meetings with a senior German official, arranged through the agency of Ryan, was both contrary to established practice—it was for the Irish representative in Berlin, who had his orders from Dublin, to deal with the German government—and deeply compromising. It is also clear that the British got wind of this contact, what Walshe later termed 'the Madrid betrayal', long before Dublin did.[94] On 2 October Guy Liddell, presumably relying on ISOS, noted that 'Clissmann has arrived in Madrid and has been accompanied by, we believe, Frank Ryan'.[95] After the war the British supplied G2 with further information on the Veesenmayer–Kerney discussions.[96]

The wider question of Irish citizens under Axis control, whether prisoners or willing helpers, continued to attract interest. A handful of Irish people were involved in propaganda broadcasting to Ireland; one or two, such as Francis Stuart, were easily identifiable, while others operated under aliases. Stuart apart, the broadcasters were a congeries of drunks, nobodies, and ne'er-do-wells.[97] MI5 found G2 somewhat reticent about such people, who as neutrals were breaking no laws, yet their broadcasting activities were obviously an embarrassment to Dublin. Stuart and perhaps others had IRA links, and there was always a likelihood that the Germans would attempt to use them more actively.

---

[92] Ó Drisceoil, *Censorship in Ireland*, 72–3; McQuaid to Walshe, 2 Feb., and Walshe to McQuaid, 11 Nov. 1942, Dublin Diocesan Archives, folder marked 'Department of Dublin, 1941–1971'; copy of Dr Bewley to Kerney, 18 Sept. 1941, asking him to forward the enclosed to Charles, MAI, G2/3666. The file contains further such material.

[93] Cecil Liddell to Hart (MI5), 28 Sept. 1942, TNA, KV2/1999.

[94] Walshe (at the Vatican) to Nunan, 6 July 1953, NAI, DFA A47.

[95] Liddell diary, 2 Oct. 1942, TNA, KV4/190.

[96] Bryan to Boland, 18 June 1946, NAI, DFA A47.

[97] On these see O'Donoghue, *Hitler's Irish Voices*; the first document on O'Reilly's MI5 file is a note to port-control officers of 20 Jan. 1942, TNA, KV4/119. Bryan to Walshe, 24 Feb. 1942, attaches note saying O'Reilly 'does the Irish broadcasts from Germany'. NAI, DFA A 8.

There were also concerns about a second and much larger set of Irish people, those who were prisoners of war. Decoded Irish telegrams from the Vatican of June 1941 had spoken of possible German designs on Irish prisoners, and this and other material in prisoners' correspondence contributed to MI5's conclusion that 'the Germans are trying to get some representative of the Vatican to send anti-British priests ostensibly to look after the spiritual welfare' of Irish prisoners, but in fact to help to recruit for 'a brigade on Casement lines'. When the escape service MI9 were consulted, it transpired that they already had a good deal of information through secret correspondence with Irish officers imprisoned in Germany, and arrangements were made to watch the matter jointly.[98] The main threat from this initiative was neither military nor political, unlike the position in 1915, when Roger Casement made his forlorn rounds of prisoner-of-war camps seeking to suborn Irishmen from their allegiance in order to join an 'Irish Brigade' to fight for Irish freedom. In 1941 there was not even a clear notional use for such a unit, since a sovereign Ireland already existed. The main danger was that it might become a reservoir from which secret agents could be recruited and trained.[99] This was to prove the only practical use which Germany made of the Casement brigade, unlike the rather more substantial Indian Legion formed from Indian prisoners in Germany and Italy (not that the Indian Legion achieved much in political terms, as it fought only in Europe and never captured Indian nationalists' imaginations as did Subhas Chandra Bose's Indian National Army (INA) in the Far East).[100]

Between July 1941 and December 1942 the problem of enemy agents in Ireland, as in the United Kingdom, transformed from one where these were primarily to be regarded as adjuncts to a future attack, to one where the main danger which they posed was to the security of Allied offensive operations. In July 'MI5 ventured to claim for the first time' that they 'controlled "the main portion of the German [espionage] system in this country" '.[101] By the end of the year, all the German agents sent to the United Kingdom were in British hands, and a number were being run with increasing confidence as double agents. In addition, intelligence gathering for the Germans and Japanese by proxies in the United Kingdom, mainly Spanish, was well understood and under control. In Ireland the situation was almost equally satisfactory, in that all the Axis agents were under lock and key. They were not available to the British for interrogation or Double Cross purposes, but nor were they able to do any harm to Allied interests. Furthermore, relations between the

---

[98] Liddell diary, 7 Aug. 1941, TNA, KV4/188, and *Liddell History*, 57. Three of the eight officer prisoners selected for the unit were in clandestine communication with London using codes smuggled to them by MI9. Hull, *Irish Secrets*, 217–18.

[99] MI5 were somewhat suspicious of an escaped prisoner of war, Flight Sergeant William Joyce, who on return to Britain explained that he was a first cousin of 'Lord Haw Haw by whom [he was] visited at prison camp'. They asked G2 to keep an eye on him during a visit home to County Mayo. Hankinson (BRO) to Boland (Dublin), conveying a message 'from London' for Bryan, 10 Nov. 1942, NAI, DFA A60.

[100] On the Indian legion see Hartog, *Sign of the Tiger*. Hartog, who was the legion's last interpreter, argues that its history and record have been unfairly overshadowed by that of Bose's Indian National Army (INA) in the Far East. On the INA, see Ward Fay, *Forgotten Army*, a somewhat mawkish account, and the rather more dispassionate, though briefer, treatment in Bayly and Harris, *Forgotten Armies*.

[101] Hinsley and Simkins, *British Intelligence*, 99.

Garda and RUC, and between G2 and MI5, were by now so close that not only could information on espionage be freely exchanged, but what amounted to joint investigations of some of the more abstruse aspects were being quietly undertaken. These explorations were to bear fruit in the course of 1943.

ANGLO-IRISH COOPERATION ON WIDER SECURITY QUESTIONS

The deepening of Anglo-Irish security cooperation was not without its drawbacks. In January 1942 Guy Liddell was alarmed to discover that

Maffey . . . has made a suggestion that we were not altogether satisfied that Ireland was not being made a base for espionage . . . Walshe has suggested that somebody should go over and discuss the matter. I have no idea what prompted Maffey. The fact is that our opposite numbers are doing us very well but there are certain limiting factors. Firstly they do not wish to give us an excuse for occupying ports. Secondly they do not want to run the risk of being accused by the Germans of a violation of neutrality owing to their having transmitted to us certain information about Germans detained in Eire.[102]

This pragmatic analysis of the motivations of Irish cooperation linked de Valera's pre-war commitment to prevent Ireland being used to harm British interests with the pressing issue of the ports. Throughout the war years there was an element of tension between the pursuit and maintenance of good security relations at a professional level, and the higher policy of the Allies. Whatever the practical benefits of security cooperation, to Churchill and other ministers it seemed that the Irish were simply doing the minimum necessary to keep Britain and later also the United States from unilateral action to seize Irish facilities. Irish reticence on the matter of the German legation radio in 1941–2 heightened this impression.

Britain's dilemma in dealing with Ireland was not unique: she had encountered much the same problems elsewhere. In August 1941 she and her new Soviet ally issued an ultimatum to the Persian government to reduce the number of resident Axis citizens, both civilians and diplomats, because these were viewed as a threat to Allied interests in the region: 'the slowness of the Persians in handing over the Germans' provided at most a flimsy pretext for the completion of the Anglo-Soviet military occupation which followed. The disobliging Shah went into exile and the occupation was not resisted—'the Persians have given way all along the line so far as the legations and German nationals are concerned', and what transpired to be extremely limited and ineffective German espionage and sabotage networks, largely created in haste after the occupation, were detected and dismantled by British, Russian, and Persian action.[103] The Irish chargé in Berlin reported press

---

[102] Liddell diary, 29 Jan. 1942, TNA, KV4/189.

[103] Beaumont, 'Great Britain and the Rights of Neutral Countries', 217; British minister, Tehran, to Foreign Office, 22 Apr. 1942, L/PS/12/656; Magan, *Middle Eastern Approaches*, 34–70; Amery diary, 10 Sept. 1941, CCCA, AMEL7/35; interview with Brigadier Magan, Tipperary, 2000.
During the first world war Britain and Tsarist Russia had had a limited understanding on Persia. Busch, *Britain, India and the Arabs*, 135.

commentary on the occupation, which stressed 'British hypocrisy. The small number of Germans in Iran could not have threatened . . . Britain or Russia'. For whatever reason, this was one of only two diplomatic decodes shown to Churchill on 5 September.[104]

Barbarossa reshaped the politics of the Near East. In July, the British succeeded in furious representations in Kabul against the proposed replacement of the German minister Pilger by Otto von Hentig, an Islamic specialist who had played a key role in the unsuccessful Niedermayer mission to Afghanistan in 1915–16 by which Germany had attempted to persuade the Afghans to help drive the British out of India. Such exercises in imperial subversion have been airily dismissed as being 'as laughable as they were fruitless', but the attempt cost Germany almost nothing and might well have succeeded in lighting a fire along the north-west frontier. The obvious comparison is with Ireland, where the German-backed 1916 rebellion—a piece of cut-price subversion which cost Berlin only a converted trawler, a few sailors captured, and 20,000 second-hand rifles—unarguably changed the course of British imperial history.[105] In Afghanistan, as in Ireland, London was acutely aware that Germany might promise the restoration of lost lands—Baluchistan and the port city of Karachi—in return for help in beating Britain. So threatening a figure was Hentig, who by January 1941 was operating in the Levant, that SOE had several times been instructed to kill him and his assistants: after repeated failures to do so, arising partly from fears of antagonizing the Vichy authorities in Syria, SOE Cairo were told that 'the high authorities were most disappointed' at the delay. Hentig survived the war, publishing a memoir in the 1960s and visiting Afghanistan as a guest of the king.[106] Pilger had to carry the burden of intelligence gathering and subversion in Kabul, work for which he had neither the training nor the aptitude, and was fortunate to survive Soviet custody in 1945–6.

British success in forcing the Afghans to withdraw their agreement to Hentig was shortly followed by a sensational incident in which two armed German civilians disguised as tribesmen were shot in a confrontation with police outside Kabul, an episode which infuriated the Afghan government. In the wake of the occupation of Persia, there was considerable debate about the wisdom of a joint Anglo-Soviet démarche about Axis civilians in Afghanistan. Quaroni in Kabul warned Rome that, while the Afghans would resist occupation or the passage of British or Soviet troops, they might accept a rupture in relations with the Axis. On this Churchill minuted: 'The door is open so we may PUSH. Now's the time'. But Sir Francis Wylie, the minister in Kabul, warned against appearing to threaten the Afghans, and he found some support in Delhi and London. The India secretary Leo Amery argued that 'we should be very careful of over-calling our hand with the Afghans for no larger result than interning 100 Germans', and was irritated to find that 'Winston had sent a curt note urging us to brush aside Wylie's more cautious suggestions and push the

[104] Berlin to External Affairs, 1 Sept. 1941, TNA, HW1/46.

[105] Nicosia, '"Drang nach Osten" Continued?', 238–9; Fergusson, *War of the World*, 115; Arghandawi, *British Imperialism*, 92–106.

[106] SOE war diary, 9, 17, 22, 24, 26, and 29 Jan., 4 and 5 Feb., 19 Mar., 4 Apr. 1941, TNA, HS7/212, 213, 214, and 215; Ludwig W. Adamec, *Historical Dictionary of Afghanistan* (Metuchen, NJ, 1991), 108–9.

Afghans hard at once' despite Amery's and the foreign secretary's concerns about issuing threats 'for so small an object', particularly when London had decided to rule out the use of force as a sanction (the Soviets would undoubtedly have insisted in participating in any military occupation as they had in Persia, a development which would have turned one hundred years of British policy in the region on its head).[107]

A few weeks later Churchill, who thought Wylie 'worthy but weak', personally directed the minister to apply strong pressure about the Axis presence. The India Office and Delhi supported Wylie in his reservations, and only the expulsion of civilians was achieved. Churchill sent Wylie lukewarm congratulations, tempered with a reproof about 'the labour and cost of . . . profuse telegraphing . . . Clarity and cogency can I am sure be reconciled with a greater brevity'. The Soviets cooperated in the exercise: within days of *Barbarossa* their Kabul embassy offered to share intelligence on the issue, as 'they have a good deal of information about Germans employed by the Afghan Government, [but] they know little of German activities generally as there is very little contact between Germans and Russians'.[108]

Previous British representations in March, before the Soviet Union came into the war, had been brushed away by the Afghan government. At the time, as Italian decodes revealed, an Afghan minister visiting Berlin 'for the purpose of a cure' had outlined his country's 'territorial claims' to the foreign office, while more moderate elements within the Afghan government were adamant that they would not break their valuable commercial agreements with Germany.[109] Mindful of the fate of their Persian neighbours, the Afghans had no choice but to comply with the ensuing Anglo-Soviet démarche: in October, and after a widespread consultation process, the government mournfully announced in a radio broadcast that they had agreed to expel all German and Italian civilians 'to avoid any misunderstandings with their neighbours', although 'departure . . . will retard . . . educational and industrial programmes'. The British and Soviet representatives 'have given assurances that their respective governments have no further demands to make inconsistent with [the] freedom and neutrality of Afghanistan', a spectacularly empty pledge. Just over 200 Axis civilians left under British safe conduct.[110]

In February 1942 it was Egypt's turn to feel the heat: when the government resigned in protest after reluctantly complying with British demands to break off relations with Vichy, the ambassador, Lord Killearn, surrounded the royal palace with armoured cars and dictated the appointment of a compliant prime minister. This 'national humiliation and disaster' poisoned Anglo-Egyptian relations thereafter, although Killearn, a bully by disposition, crowed: 'I confess I could not have more enjoyed' the crisis.[111] Such successes for his personal policy of blunt confrontation with uncooperative neutrals contiguous to British-controlled territory

---

[107] Amery diary, 8 Sept. 1941, CCCA, AMEL7/35.

[108] Ibid., 15 Sept. 1941,CCCA, AMEL7/35; diary of British military attaché, Kabul, 27 June 1941, IOR, L/PS/12/1844.

[109] Rome to Italian minister, Kabul, and reply, 16 and 17 Mar. 1941, TNA, HW12/262.

[110] Hauner, 'Afghanistan Between the Great Powers', 488–9; British minister, Kabul, to London, paraphrasing Afghan broadcast, 19 Oct. 1941, IOR, L/PS/12/1783.

[111] Stephens, *Nasser*, 55; entry for 4 Feb. 1942 in Evans, *Killearn Diaries*, 215.

probably reinforced Churchill's natural inclination to bring Ireland to heel. It also bore out the pre-war predictions of the Irish Department of External Affairs, which in November 1937 had advised de Valera that due to defence rights ceded to Britain, both Egypt and Iraq were merely 'satellite states . . . they are obliged to take part in some manner in all British wars, no matter how small the extent to which their own interests are involved'.[112]

German agents, and the legation radio, were the most serious but not the only problems on which the British required Irish help. Control of communications and of the movements of people between the two jurisdictions became more rather than less complicated as the war progressed. The understanding reached by Colonel Stratton in December 1941 on the sharing of intercept data between RSS and the Irish signals corps meant that for the rest of the war transmissions in the British Isles were monitored by what was almost a unitary system. For technical reasons beyond the scope of this study, the arrangement with the Irish improved coverage from Britain and vice versa.[113] Effective control of the movement of people proved harder to achieve. The introduction of a travel-permit system brought an element of control over individuals moving between Britain and Ireland. Between 1940 and 1945 over 198,000 permits were issued to Irish men and women, but the actual number of people who migrated was higher.[114] As Wickham of the RUC and others had consistently pointed out, it remained impossible to prevent people moving between the two Irish jurisdictions. In April 1942, when the Security Executive considered representations to strengthen border security, the RUC recommended that on the contrary, the existing group of 'Travellers Censorship Officers' should be disbanded because it was 'of no practical use . . . there is nothing to prevent anyone crossing on foot across the fields', and any 'increase in the security measures . . . which fell short of effective control might well be prejudicial to real security . . . any control which gave apparent but not real security would at once give rise' to calls for the censorship of communications between Northern Ireland and Great Britain to be lessened: 'the intensification of . . . [overt] control' might result 'on balance, in a decrease in security'.[115] It was also very difficult to prevent the illicit passage of communications and the smuggling of people by ship, both between Ireland and Britain, and Ireland and the Iberian peninsula. Efforts to ensure security sometimes caused friction: twenty-nine Irish priests and three nuns en route from Rome to Ireland were closely questioned and strip-searched, as permitted by regulations for people coming from enemy territory, prompting vigorous protests from Dublin but no lasting repercussions.[116]

Most of the infractions detected were of no direct security significance—Teresa Monaghan, a Belfast hairdresser, was discovered on a Dutch vessel posing as the captain's sister-in-law while 'taking a holiday trip' to Scotland, and the following

[112] Hauner, 'Afghanistan Between the Great Powers', 490–2; External Affairs memorandum, 23 Nov. 1937, quoted in Kennedy, "A Voyage of Exploration', 10–11 and n. 19.

[113] A British document setting out the technical arguments for cooperation can be found with Bryan to Walshe, 15 Dec. 1941, NAI, DFA A25. Direction-finding was not a precise science: in January 1942 RSS reported picking up German weather transmissions from Dundalk, Cork, and Tyneside. Liddell diary, 12 Jan. 1942, TNA, KV4/189. This appears to have been a false alarm.

[114] Connolly, 'Irish Workers in Britain', 122.

[115] Security Executive minutes, 29 Apr. 1942, TNA, HO45/21985.

[116] Liddell diary, 6 Aug. 1942, TNA, KV4/190.

month an Irish labourer returning home was found to be carrying letters from friends 'which indicated a widespread scheme' to have relatives send telegrams about family illness so that men would be allowed back to Ireland on compassionate grounds—but such minor transgressions underlined the ease with which the control regime might be evaded by the enemy's agents.[117] Reviewing the question after the war, Cecil Liddell noted that many Irish travellers gave false particulars, usually either 'women who wished to join their husbands . . . contrary to the regulations that Irish workers were not allowed to have their wives and children here, and (b) young men or women' who lied about their age to escape the tedium of their neutral home. In such cases, 'vetting had not been properly carried out by the Civic Guard . . . the most important check on Irish workers coming to this country'. In Northern Ireland the problem was more acute because the permit regulations were enforced only erratically: in 1944 a leading Catholic layman in Belfast wrote that 'a large number of men and girls arrive here regularly in search of work and many of them get stranded' without papers.[118]

In September 1942 the Security Executive commissioned a document from MI5 on the possibilities of information leakage, possibly as a result of indications from ISOS that a crew member of the Irish ship *Kyle Clare* 'has been reporting to the German I[ntelligence] S[ervice] in Lisbon'.[119] The first draft report to the Security Executive was considered 'somewhat complacent' in pointing out that no evidence at all of leakage had emerged from censorship and from port controls, and it had been revised before circulation.[120] During the discussion which followed, an Admiralty man 'got rather excited about what he described as the lack of security measures at the ports. This aroused the D[irector] G[eneral of MI5], who gave him a raspberry', and asked him for 'any evidence of leakage but clearly he had none'. Guy Liddell 'talked to him afterwards and explained more or less what we were doing with regard to placing agents on ships. He seemed fairly satisfied. The general feeling of the meeting was that the present measures were in all the circumstances as adequate as could be expected'.[121]

MI5's information was that the Irish were already keeping 'a strict watch' on shipping—in February 1942 Bryan had told them that G2 had informants on some ships sailing from Ireland.[122] In the same month an Irishman in Glasgow was arrested for 'sending messages by a seaman . . . to his brother in Eire about convoys', a discovery which may have contributed to MI5's decision to place their own 'seaman agents' on boats plying between Ireland and Britain, South America, and the Iberian peninsula. These were to 'discover whether any . . . crew are acting as couriers', and 'the obvious man to employ is someone who goes regularly and has a specific job which will not arouse suspicion'.[123]

[117] Scottish Special Branch monthly summaries, May and June 1942, NAS, HH55/53.
[118] Note by Cecil Liddell, 14 Dec. 1945, TNA, KV4/258; Walshe to Archbishop McQuaid, 1 June, and Owen Kelly to McQuaid, 29 May 1944, Dublin Diocesan Archives, folder marked 'Department of External Affairs, 1941–1971'.
[119] Liddell diary, 25 Aug. 1942, TNA, KV4/190.
[120] Ibid., 16 Sept. 1942, TNA, KV4/190.
[121] Ibid., 21 Sept. 1942, TNA, KV4/190.
[122] *Liddell History*, 66–7.
[123] Liddell diary, 18 Feb., 31 July and 4 Aug. 1942, TNA, KV4/189 and 190.

This innovation was the responsibility of MI5's B1L section, already mired in confusion due to a failure to identify the precise role of such agents: were they there simply to observe and report on suspicious transactions, or were they to be used actively as channels for disinformation? By August 1942, when no fewer than 350 seamen had been enrolled as agents, a new head of the section decided instead to 'concentrate on a small number'. Through the work of the section 'letter smuggling to and from Eire' was 'largely suppressed', a worthwhile if modest achievement, while it may have been responsible for the detection in February 1943 of one 'Moriarty, an Irish seaman', who 'arrived at Liverpool from USA. He was in possession of details of convoy routes, and was reported to be anti-British'.[124] The conclusions of the official historians were less generous: 'the work of B1L proved unrewarding—it did not lead to the detention of any agents—and it was greatly reduced during 1943', but that is perhaps too stark a finding, since it did contribute to the control of letter smuggling.[125] The section itself claimed another success:

One of our intended double agents, GWLADYS, was in touch with the Pan-Celtic Union in Dublin . . . [and?] the German-controlled Breton autonomist organization . . . This [excised] provided GWLADYS with a very good motive for getting in touch with the Germans, which he later succeeded in doing. We had given GWLADYS considerable training . . . and we arranged with him to join the Welsh nationalists . . . in order to acquire the right background . . . He was introduced by them to the Scottish nationalists, and was able to talk intelligently about their work to the Pan-Celtic Union in Dublin. Our reason for preparing GWLADYS with this background was that we knew from Special Sources [ISOS] that the enemy were interested in the Breton autonomist organization, which was connected with the Pan-Celtic Union.[126]

Despite the seaman-agent initiative, it was clear that without local cooperation in the various ports involved outside the United Kingdom, observation of suspicious individuals or transactions could only take place on the ships themselves. This inevitably led the British to seek local help, which in the Irish case was readily forthcoming through G2 and the Garda, and in North America from the Canadian and American authorities (where the main concern was the smuggling of weapons for the IRA).[127] In more exotic locales, such as Lisbon, where the quaysides teemed with touts, informers, and agents of every hue, and where the police, customs, and security agencies were heavily penetrated by various foreign intelligence services, it was impossible to reach a comparable reliable arrangement.

The subversive and sabotage potential of the Irish in Britain continued to exercise the Security Executive, MI5, and the police. The MI5 regional security officer in the north-west was surprised when a Special Branch man assured him that, 'with two or three exceptions, there are no IRA people in Liverpool'. The difficulty was

---

[124] Guy Liddell to Curry, 28 May 1945, TNA, KV4/26; *Curry History*, 263; Liddell diary, 18 Feb. 1943, TNA, KV4/191.
[125] Hinsley and Simkins, *British Intelligence*, 179.
[126] B1L section history, undated, TNA, KV4/26; Hinsley and Simkins, *British Intelligence*, 44. German intelligence agencies used a variety of codes and ciphers, some of which were vulnerable to decoders from early in the war. The term ISOS was applied generally to such decoded traffic, whatever the originating German organization or code or cipher system used.
[127] *Liddell History*, 67.

that the police saw only 'an IRA problem, not . . . a problem of Irishmen who might be connected with the German Intelligence Service'. Fear of industrial and military sabotage remained, and after Victor Rothschild of MI5 expressed concern about the IRA's potential 'in respect to sabotage at time of invasion', a conference of chief constables, officials, and MI5 officers was convened. The star of the show was the RUC's Roger Moore, who was 'able to give . . . information "straight from the horse's mouth"'. He outlined the recent Lundborg case while stressing that the IRA were a spent force incapable of serious mischief in either jurisdiction.[128] Moore repeated these points at a meeting of regional security officers a fortnight later, where Cecil Liddell also described the 'imperfect but improving' vetting of Irish workers by both the Garda and British authorities. As a result of these discussions, it was agreed that MI5 should provide some funds for chief constables to use in securing informants—Moore said the RUC spent about £1,500 a year on such activities—although the results were meagre in the extreme.[129]

In truth, there was little enough to worry about. No evidence ever emerged of organized IRA sabotage in Britain after 1940, and this was not for the want of vigilance and investigation. Charles Corey, a deserter from the Irish Guards who set fire to buildings on the Scottish farm where he worked, was initially suspected of sabotage. It proved to be a 'case of wanton destruction by a drunken, lawless Irishman', although when arrested Corey shouted: 'To Hell with this country. I will never fight for Britain. Good old Germany is the best country in the world. I wish they would come over now and bomb you bastards'. On St Patrick's Day 1942, 'the slogan "Up Dublin we are still neutral" was found painted on a noticeboard in a labourers' camp' on Tiree in the Inner Hebrides: the very fact that this far-flung graffito was solemnly recorded in a Special Branch monthly summary rather suggests a dearth of worthwhile subversive activity on which to report.[130] Over the course of the war, the Irish feature as objects of suspicion in such police summaries far less often than either communists or Jehovah's Witnesses. The communists, whose activities in building up 'Connolly clubs' to forge a link between Irish republicans and the communist movement in Britain, and in advocating immediate Indian freedom, were sometimes the subjects of police reports, changed tack after *Barbarossa* with a speed and zeal of which even Stalin might have approved. Ireland and India disappeared from the CPGB agenda, and British imperialism was forgotten as the spotlight turned on the Trotskyites: 'Hitler's Agents! . . . a greater menace than enemy paratroops'.[131]

Postal censorship and movement controls, while they could be evaded, continued to prove both a generally effective bar to the casual disclosure of war information and a reasonable barometer of Irish émigré opinion—regular analytical summaries of Irish and of Northern Irish as of other regional traffic were prepared and circulated by the censorship authorities, with comments on the underlying political

---

[128] Regional security officer to MI5, 3 Mar.; minutes of meeting, 10 Apr., Cecil Liddell to Wickham, 13 Apr., and to Petrie, 29 Apr. 1942, TNA, KV4/233.

[129] Minutes of meeting, 21 Apr., and Cecil Liddell to Petrie, 29 Apr. 1942, TNA, KV4/233.

[130] Scottish Special Branch summaries, October 1941 and March 1942, NAS, HH55/52 and 53.

[131] Scottish Special Branch summaries, Dec. 1940 and Oct. 1942, NAS, HH55/50 and 54.

sentiments, attitudes towards the war, and state of morale disclosed.[132] Evidence from postal censorship of the dissatisfaction of many Irish at what they saw as British failure to acknowledge the contribution of Irish people individually to the war effort prompted Churchill to a characteristically idiosyncratic suggestion in October 1941: drawing attention to 'the passage marked "A" in red' on a postal censorship report, he said that 'now the time is right to form an Irish brigade also an Irish wing or squadron of the RAF . . . The pilot Finucane might be a great figure. Pray let me have proposals. The movement might have important political reactions later on'. The service departments eventually managed to kill off the proposal on grounds of impracticality; a few months later the Germans took care of Finucane.[133]

Although not attributable to British action—apart from exchanges between the RUC and the Garda—the process of subduing the IRA continued with considerable effect in Ireland. There was still violence—three detectives were killed during 1942, two during raids on safe houses and one, Sergeant Denis O'Brien, in a planned assassination, and the IRA's George Plant was executed for the murder of an informer—but the IRA, now under the nominal leadership of the Belfast-based Hugh McAteer, were no longer capable of organized disruption or of intelligence gathering. Only a few activists such as Harry White, involved in all three Garda killings, kept the flag flying. By the end of 1942 almost all the senior officers and the most committed volunteers in both parts of Ireland were either in prison after conviction or in internment, together with a considerable number of women responsible for much of the staff and intelligence work. The organization was left in the hands of inexperienced youths (Charlie Kerins, nominally chief of staff when captured in 1944, was only 26 years of age when executed for his part in the O'Brien murder).

There was, however, a flurry of minor and inept IRA cross-border raids in September 1942 which took Belfast by surprise. G2 had received a tip-off that something was in the air, but according to Dan Bryan the Garda 'pooh-poohed' this (G2 and the Garda security section under Patrick Carroll had a sometimes fraught relationship). Consequently Bryan said nothing to MI5—'If I told them this thing was pending my credit was up'—and when next in London he was brought up 'formally to meet the boss of MI5', David Petrie, 'who challenged me about these raids'. Bryan offered no excuse: 'You have to keep your own rows between yourselves at times', a sentiment with which most of the British officers with whom he dealt would undoubtedly have concurred.[134]

The initiation by two American airlines and by BOAC of services to and from North America passing through the seaplane terminal at Foynes in 1942 threw up a number of new problems.[135] The British government initially put forward Lough

[132] Examples of such periodic summaries for Ireland and Northern Ireland between 1940 and 1943 can be found in TNA, CJ4/30.

[133] Churchill to secretaries of state for war and air, 8 Oct. 1941, TNA, DO35/1109/14. Wing Commander Brendan 'Paddy' Finucane, DSO, DFC (1920–42), from Dublin died when his plane crashed in the English Channel in July 1942. He was credited with destroying 32 enemy aircraft.

[134] Dan Bryan transcripts, 38, 48–9 (in my possession).

[135] Liddell diary, 3 Mar. 1942, TNA, KV4/189.

Erne as an alternative transit point, but the Americans were not to be dissuaded from using the more attractive Shannon estuary: in any case, Lough Erne had been developed merely 'as a base for minor repairs' and 'any further extension would take months to complete'. Furthermore, its use depended 'on the goodwill of the Eire Government' in allowing aircraft to use Irish airspace, and this would scarcely continue since they would regard 'the abandonment of Foynes as a breach of the spirit of our agreements with them'.[136] The Security Executive agreed that it would be disastrous if the Americans went ahead with their proposal to censor airmail to and from Ireland in the United States, having no faith in their new ally's understanding of this abstruse art (when war broke out there had been a minor spat with the Americans because the British unilaterally imposed censorship on mails carried by the Pan American clippers using Bermuda en route to or returning from Lisbon).[137] The Irish were simply informed that all eastbound post for Ireland would have first to be sent to Liverpool for censorship. The Irish agreed to this, maintaining the decencies by insisting that such mail must then be returned from Liverpool to Foynes for transfer rather than the far quicker solution of having it simply sent across the Irish Sea to Dublin.[138] In 1941 MI5 posted a man to Foynes in the guise of a BOAC passenger welfare officer, to keep an eye out for any breaches of security while people were on the ground; this was Conor Carrigan, whose madcap scheme for a Franco-Irish alliance had received serious consideration in Downing Street in May 1940. He was due to be posted to BOAC in Lisbon, and in preparation was sent to Foynes to familiarize himself with airport procedures. He spoke openly of his many Whitehall contacts, and informed the G2 officer at Foynes that he had been 'asked unofficially by his friends in MI5 to report unofficially on this Airport'.[139]

In June 1942, on an Irish initiative, a Home Office official was stationed at Foynes as an immigration officer. He liaised with Collinson in his overt role of head of the British permit office in Dublin, and also provided 'valuable reports' on passenger traffic to London. In addition to his Home Office salary, this official received substantial allowances from both MI5 and SIS, a reflection of the importance attached to his covert reporting role.[140] Foynes was also an important listening post for the Irish: G2's representative reported whatever news and views he could pick up relating to the war, including useful material on the approach of other neutrals towards the Allies (in the autumn of 1942 the attitude of Turkish officers en route for training in Britain 'is aptly summed up in "With Germany—Friendship. With the UK—Alliance"', while British and American aircrew who had crashed in Portugal remarked on the generous treatment they received).[141] In October 1942 Roosevelt's wife Eleanor, travelling as 'Mrs Smith', was held up for two days en

---

[136] Liddell diary, 31 Mar. 1942, TNA, KV4/189; appendix to item 3 of Security Executive minutes, 1 Apr. 1942, TNA, CAB93/2.

[137] Moffat journal, 26 Dec. 1939 and 19 Jan. 1940, Harvard, MS 1407, vols. 43 and 44.

[138] Liddell diary, 3 Apr. 1942, TNA, KV4/189; *Liddell History*, 72.

[139] *Liddell History*, 73; Bryan to Walshe (Dublin), 21 Oct. 1941, enclosing summary of report on Carrigan, NAI, DFA A8.

[140] *Liddell History*, 73–4; G2 report by Hewett, Foynes, G2, 27 July 1942, NAI, DFA A60.

[141] Weekly reports by Hewett, 14 Sept. and 22 Nov. 1942, NAI, DFA A8/1.

route to England (the American representative at Foynes had the good grace to thank his Irish counterpart for his help in smoothing the way).[142]

Guy Liddell used Foynes himself in May 1942. He arrived on the BOAC service from Southampton and spent a night in the picturesque village of Adare—'it looked as if there were some quite good fishing to be got . . . and the country is . . . characteristically beautiful'—before travelling on to the United States. Even he proved susceptible to the virus of suspicion of hotel staff which infected so many British wartime visitors: 'the proprietress' of the Dunraven Arms hotel 'struck me as being a little odd. I rather thought she had a German accent . . . it would be quite easy to pick up some interesting information' from transit passengers.[143]

Irish cooperation in military aviation was also considerable: in November 1942 the air attaché wrote that their attitude to British aircraft and crews which made emergency landings or crashed 'does rather stretch their interpretation of neutrality to breaking point'. Almost all air crew were quietly let go, and the Irish 'are undertaking the salvaging of aircraft on our behalf'. All 'secret equipment [is] handed over to me without delay', and the 'regular army have been put to guard the aircraft, often for a considerable length of time under extremely uncomfortable conditions'.[144] This accommodating attitude became ever more significant as Allied air traffic increased, ensuring that the British and American air forces, like the intelligence agencies, took an increasingly forgiving view of neutrality.

America's entry into the war presented a number of problems for Britain in dealing with Ireland. Responsibility for responding to a German invasion, still regarded as a possibility—in January the chief of the Imperial General Staff, Sir Alan Brooke, took part in discussions with General Franklin, the GOC of BTNI, and the RAF about a revised counter-invasion plan—was to be passed to the Americans, whose troops were pouring in to the province.[145] There was an obvious likelihood that American forces would seek to gather intelligence independently, a danger only partly addressed by good Anglo-American liaison and a firm agreement that even when an American general took command of all forces in Northern Ireland in May 1942, BTNI should continue to be the sole provider of Irish intelligence.[146] MI5's dilemma was clear:

A great deal of valuable and delicate information concerning Eire was being passed to BTNI by the Security Service and SIS, and BTNI had agreed that they would not themselves attempt to run any intelligence organization. It was feared that if the Americans took over this very delicate and complicated machinery or attempted to run their own intelligence in Eire, the results might be disastrous. Lord Swinton . . . saw the American Ambassador in London, who agreed that the American forces should rely on us for all information about Ireland (North and South). He was informed about the Security Service link with the

[142] Churchill to Roosevelt, 24 Oct. 1942, in Kimball (ed.), *Churchill and Roosevelt*, i. 636; Bryan to Walshe, 1 Nov. 1942, enclosing copy of letter of thanks to Hewett from the American vice-consul at Foynes, NAI, DFA A8/1.

[143] Liddell diary, 26 May 1942, TNA, KV4/189; Archer (BRO) to Boland, 22 May 1942, passed on a message for Bryan from Cecil Liddell about Guy's impending stopover. NAI, DFA A8.

[144] Begg (air attaché) to Air Ministry, 26 Nov. 1942, TNA, DO35/1109/1.

[145] Danchev and Todman (eds.), *Alanbrooke Diaries*, 271, entry for 17 Jan. 1942.

[146] Minutes by Stephenson and Costar, 7 and 21 May 1942, TNA, DO35/1109/14.

Department of Defence, but not about the SIS organization, and was advised that as far as conditions in Northern Ireland were concerned the American Commander should be guided by Sir Charles Wickham . . . The Security Service liaison with BTNI was continued and they remained the recipients of all Security Service and SIS information, with the responsibility of passing on to the American GOC such information as he required.[147]

This arrangement held good in respect of the American forces in Northern Ireland; almost immediately upon entry into the war other American agencies began to collect intelligence independently in and about Ireland (eight months after Pearl Harbor, one OSS survey of sentiments at Notre Dame, the elite Irish-American college, found most faculty members to be pro-IRA, anti-British, anti-communist, and anti-Semitic, although also strongly in favour of American involvement in the war).[148]

American determination to gather Irish intelligence, initially without informing the British of their activities, was scarcely surprising given both their Atlantic interests and the arrival of their forces in Northern Ireland. In addition, in 1940–1 Britain had been at pains to portray neutral Ireland to Washington as a nest of spies and pro-Nazis, an exercise in which they were joined by David Gray, whose passionate opposition to Irish neutrality and appetite for outlandish rumours were clear to the Irish within months of his arrival in the summer of 1940. His military attaché, Colonel Reynolds, was no better, sending reports which, while they rightly stressed the weakness of the Irish army, wildly overstated the strength and potential of the IRA—in September 1942 he described it as 'a powerful organization . . . It has the sympathy of a considerable part of the population . . . and to some extent, of the Government of Eire', and 'will try to foment trouble with British and American troops . . . and is, or will become a strong Axis agent'. He did, however, quote Wickham as dismissing the organization 'with contempt . . . He regards them as a pack of lawless "corner boys" and "crack pot conspirators" incapable of serious mischief'.[149] In 1948 Dan Bryan described the wartime American legation as 'hypersensitive' to German and 'even alleged Japanese activity', in contrast to the generally phlegmatic outlook of the British after 1940 as Anglo-Irish security relations deepened.[150]

It is of course the duty of a diplomat to represent the government which sends him, not to make himself agreeable to the state in which he is stationed, and it is certainly true that Gray reflected rather than formed the administration's attitude towards Irish neutrality.[151] But, just as Robert Brennan in Washington failed to engage with and to understand the Roosevelt administration, instead concentrating on Irish-American churchmen and politicos, so Gray, instead of studying the Dublin government closely, spent most of his time talking to its domestic critics. His antagonism towards neutrality, when combined with his alarmist streak, caused considerable difficulties as the war went on, not only to the Irish but to the British

---

[147] *Liddell History*, 75.
[148] Report by Freidiger on opinion at Notre Dame, 24 Aug. 1942, USNA, RG226, entry 142, box 2.
[149] Reynolds, *Rich Relations*, 119; O'Halpin, *Defending Ireland*, 229; Gray to Welles, 8 Sept., and enclosed summary sheet with report by Reynolds, 7 Sept. 1942, USNA, 841D.00/1351.
[150] O'Halpin, *Defending Ireland*, 280.
[151] Fanning, 'The Anglo-American Alliance', 193–4.

agencies dealing with Irish affairs. As early as January 1942 he warned Washington that 'anyone who wishes to can observe American-built bases in Ulster . . . Eire would be a good field for high class Irish-American agents with inside knowledge of IRA activities in America. Inclined to doubt efficiency of British secret service here'.[152]

In the same month, G2 noted the arrival of a former American vice-consul in Cork, R. B. Patterson: 'within a few days it was learned from an authoritative source that he was on a mission from the office of the Co-ordinator of Intelligence (Colonel Donovan) . . . it implies immediately' that he 'was no mere press agent'. 'Wild Bill' Donovan had visited Ireland in March 1941 and had raised the question of the ports with de Valera; he remained convinced that, with appropriate pressure at the right moment, the Irish could be forced to change their policy.[153] When the United States entered the war, he obtained Roosevelt's 'permission to play an aggressive hand' on the ports issue, as America's vital interests were more clearly at stake. He had initially contemplated sending Errol Flynn and other film stars with Irish connections, both for propaganda purposes and to collect intelligence, but discretion of a kind had evidently intervened.[154] He instead dispatched Patterson, under press cover. Patterson recruited a Kerry cattle-dealer to set up information-gathering networks along the south-west coast, and these reported to the American legation. These intrigues were quickly penetrated by G2's southern command representative Florence O'Donoghue, enabling the Irish to watch them closely thereafter.[155] In the United States OSS, perhaps taking over where AIDA had left off, considered how to address the 'problems presented by the present orientation of the papers upon which' the Irish population of New York 'depend for their information'.[156]

By the autumn Donovan reportedly had no fewer than five officers in London waiting to go into Ireland, three SO (special operations) specialists—who would presumably have been tasked to help pave the way for Anglo-American action to seize the Irish ports by force—and two SI (secret intelligence) men.[157] One of the latter, the former Trinity College student Ervin 'Spike' Marlin, arrived in Dublin in September as 'Special Assistant' to Gray both to conduct independent enquiries and to establish a link with Irish security. Things began auspiciously enough—Gray told Washington that 'my fears about him were not well founded. We will try to make him useful'—but the honeymoon was brief. The problem was that Marlin soon got on very good terms with G2, and through that link and through his own enquiries came to broadly the same conclusions about security conditions in Ireland as did MI5. Gray, on the other hand, was convinced that the IRA remained a credible

[152] Gray to Washington, 18 Jan. 1942, USNA, RG84/841D.00/1325.
[153] Winant (London) to Washington, 11 Mar. 1941, conveying Donovan's report, USNA, 740.0011, European War, 1959/8944; reports on Patterson by Hewett, G2, Foynes, and Birthwhistle, G2, Athlone, 22 and 30 Jan. 1942, NAI, DFA A8.
[154] Smith, *Shadow Warriors*, 101.
[155] G2 report, with MS additions dated 9 Feb., and O'Donoghue to Bryan, 6 Nov. 1942, MAI, G2/X/0902 and G2/X/1122; O'Halpin, *Defending Ireland*, 239.
[156] Spencer Phoenix to David Bruce, 26 Mar. 1942, enclosing memorandum by Allen Dulles on Irish American opinion, USNA, RG226, entry 142, Box 2.
[157] Smith, *Shadow Warriors*, 184.

fifth column in Northern Ireland, and that Ireland was awash with Axis spies, and also argued that these factors should be stressed in order to compel de Valera to cooperate by granting access to the ports. He consequently disputed both Marlin's conclusions and his right to report to OSS independently of him. In December he forced Marlin's withdrawal from Dublin. Marlin henceforth dealt with Irish matters from the OSS office in London, reporting to the head of OSS in Europe, Colonel David Bruce. Gray continued to rely on his military attaché Colonel Reynolds, who warned that 'sooner rather than later' the 'British and American soldiers in Northern Ireland will find themselves in the role of the "Black and Tans" of 1942, bloody fighting will ensue, and Ireland will be ripe for a German invasion'.[158]

MI5 remained unaware of Marlin's original appointment to Dublin for over a year, although in March 1943, by which time Marlin had left, Guy Liddell noted that a contact in the American embassy had told him that there 'are already two OSS men' in Ireland.[159] The Liddell history incorrectly records Marlin's arrival as occurring 'as early as February or March 1944', a year-and-a-half later than in actuality, and states that MI5 only learnt of it in late April during security planning for *Overlord* (the invasion of France).[160]

In Ireland, as in the Middle East and the Balkans, the British were to find that initially little could be done to prevent the Americans from operating independently.[161] The question of Irish security assumed far greater salience in Anglo-American planning in 1943, as serious preparations began for the liberation of Europe; at the professional level, this provided the momentum for the development of genuine Anglo-American security cooperation on Ireland. That Gray remained an alarmist on security questions broadly suited British interests, and it may, in combination with the minister's habitual indiscretion, explain why Maffey never sought to disabuse him of his fixation by reference to the practicalities of Anglo-Irish cooperation. This ensured that the State Department continued to take a very jaundiced view of Irish security, and that the Irish remained under pressure from Washington to eject the Axis legations. That was Maffey's number-one priority by the autumn of 1942, and the succeeding year was to see a major breakthrough.

INTELLIGENCE ON DIPLOMATIC ACTIVITIES, JULY 1941–DECEMBER 1942

Decodes yielded a great deal of information on a range of issues and concerns, from sustained Irish efforts to secure shipping space and supplies, to American reservations about the adequacy of their 'Brown' code, to Vatican concerns about Irish missionaries, and to Irish–Turkish trade. More significantly, they produced good material on Irish dealings with foreign diplomats in Dublin, together with

---

[158] Gray to Welles (State Department), 8 Sept., enclosing memorandum by Reynolds, 7 Sept. 1942, USNA, RG84, 841D.00/1351; O'Halpin, *Defending Ireland*, 230–1.
[159] Liddell diary, 9 Mar. 1943, TNA, KV4/191.
[160] *Liddell History*, 89–90.
[161] Smith, *Shadow Warriors*, 183–4.

Table 4.1. *British decodes relating to Ireland, July 1941–December 1942*

	French	Irish	Italian	Japanese	USA	Others	Totals
July 1941	2	56	2	1	3	1	65
August	2	48	2				52
September	2	21	1				24
October	3	43	7			4	57
November	2	41	7		1		51
December	2	16	1	1		1	21
January 1942	1	12				2	15
February	5	4	3				12
March	2		4	1		4	11
April	3			2		2	7
May	1	2	1	6		1	11
June		2	5	6			13
July		7		2			9
August	1	5	1	4			11
September	2	6	4	2		3	17
October		11	5	1			17
November	2	4	2	1			9
December	2	1	7	5			15
TOTALS	32	279	52	32	4	18	417

insights into the activities of two of the three Axis missions, the Italian and the Japanese. Irish cables from occupied Europe also provided a window into the course of affairs as seen by Irish diplomats from their general observations and from their occasional interactions with German, French, Italian, Spanish, Swiss, and Vatican officials.

The unanswerable question relating to the bulk of such material is a simple one: did it have any influence on British policy towards Ireland? As already noted, many of the relevant policy files were weeded of intelligence papers before release, making it impossible to assess the impact of such material on officials and ministers. Even where Churchill saw Irish-related decodes, their impact cannot be measured other than in the small minority of instances where he was moved to do more than simply acknowledge sight of them.[162]

What is most striking about the surviving set of decodes distributed by GC&CS between July 1941 and December 1942 is the pattern (some Irish cables, such as one about 'material for a new suit', were so innocuous that they were not circulated and no copies have survived).[163] Irish traffic, from being evidently an object of intense interest in the latter half of 1941, faded away virtually to nothing from December 1941 onwards (see Table 4.1). This marked change was probably a result of American entry into the war, and perhaps also of the fact that there was no evidence of Irish efforts to reach secret understandings with the Axis powers, either directly or through intermediaries.

[162] This material is in a separate series as TNA, HW1.
[163] Parenthetical explanation by GC&CS in decode of Berlin to Dublin, 1 Nov. 1941, TNA, HW12/270.

Decodes nevertheless yielded some useful material: the sheer banality of traffic between Madrid and Ontiveros, the Spanish minister in Dublin, indicated that he was not involved with the Japanese intelligence-gathering organization which used the Spanish foreign service for espionage purposes throughout the war.[164] This was an important negative finding, particularly as SIS termed the minister 'pro-Axis'.[165] Irish traffic similarly provided no evidence of bad faith, but some indications of priorities. Decodes did reveal Irish interest in the modalities of neutrality internationally. In October 1941 the minister in Berne supplied details on request on the Swiss rationale for returning a German aircraft: it was unarmed and on a training flight, and the Germans had occasionally done the same for Swiss aircraft which had strayed. Dublin continued to solicit information on Swiss practice regarding such incursions.[166] One unexceptional Irish report from Berlin of September 1941, which spoke of German press reaction to the Anglo-Soviet occupation of Persia in August, was selected for Churchill to see (the occupation had been preceded by a demand that the Persians expel a significant number of German industrialists and technicians, which the Germans warned would be a breach of neutrality).[167] Dublin was clearly anxious to get news of Seán Russell, asking Kerney to investigate a rumour that he had been killed in Lisbon.[168] After Pearl Harbor, Dublin sought details of the protocols surrounding the departure and safe conduct of Axis diplomats from America, presumably in anticipation of a similar scenario in Ireland.[169] Dublin's cables seldom had much political content, but the sentencing to death of six IRA men in Belfast for killing an RUC man evoked a strong response: the minister in Vichy was instructed to observe that the disturbances in Northern Ireland were 'neither widespread nor serious', that the root cause was partition, and that the Allies should apply to Ireland 'the principles' they invoked 'for other small nations'. The high commissioner in Ottawa was advised to argue that 'the British advice on the BBC European Services to people in occupied countries has had a share in these developments'.[170] The Holy See's intention to intercede was also disclosed in decodes of Vatican traffic.[171]

Cables between External Affairs and Dulanty are conspicuous by their absence. Dublin preferred to maintain contact with Dulanty by courier, by frequent visits, and by telephone (despite the fact that such calls were clearly subject to British interception). MI5 did obtain a certain amount of useful information by such

[164] In October 1942 the Japanese ambassador in Madrid reported that the new Spanish foreign minister Jordana agreed that Japan could continue to use the Spanish diplomatic service and facilities for espionage, but asked for greater discretion, TNA, HW12/281.

[165] QRS report, 1 Mar. 1944, TNA, DO121/85.

[166] Dublin to Berne, and reply, 1 and 3 Oct. 1941, and Dublin to Berne, 6 Aug. 1942, TNA, HW12/269 and 279.

[167] Berlin to Dublin, 1 Sept. 1941, with C to Churchill, 5 Sept. 1941, TNA, HW1/46. Beaumont, 'Great Britain and the Rights of Neutral Countries', 217.

[168] Dublin to Kerney (Madrid), 6 Aug. 1941, TNA, HW12/267. The Irish mission in Lisbon was only opened in 1942.

[169] Dublin to Washington, 5 Jan. 1942, TNA, HW12/272.

[170] Dublin to Vichy and to Ottawa, 5 Aug. and 8 Sept. 1942, TNA, HW12/280.

[171] Vatican to apostolic delegate, London, and reply, 29 and 31 Aug. 1942, TNA, HW12/280. In the event five of the men were reprieved, amongst them Joe Cahill, later to become chief of staff of the Provisional IRA in the 1970s.

eavesdropping (Jo Stephenson of MI5 recalled Dulanty as very talkative on the telephone).[172]

The energies of Irish diplomats as reflected in these decodes were largely concentrated on securing supplies and ships to transport them: Guy Liddell noted in July 1941 that 'reports indicate that there is a shortage of essential products in Ireland'.[173] One message stands out: in October 1941 the legation in Berne reported representations from James Joyce's son Giorgio in respect of his late father's secretary Paul Leon, a Russian Jew under arrest in Paris who was likely to be executed. This was the first of what after 1942 became a fairly frequent theme of Irish decodes, reports on or action following requests to intercede to succour individual Jews or groups of Jews.[174] There was some decent political reporting from Vichy, from the Vatican, and especially from Rome. Among Vatican material was an assurance from the Pope that he 'appreciated highly the Taoiseach's offer of help' in launching a peace initiative at an appropriate time, though he was very 'pessimistic' about the war's likely duration.[175]

In Rome the Irish minister Michael MacWhite had good contacts among the diplomatic corps and a talent for concise reportage. He was an old European hand, a French Foreign Legion veteran who was three times awarded the Croix de Guerre during the first world war. He represented Ireland at the League of Nations in the 1920s before being posted as minister to Washington and ultimately to Italy in 1938 (from where he soon reported his suspicion that his office was being spied on and his diplomatic bag opened by the Italians).[176] His cable and written reports were distinguished by his efforts to provide a broad assessment of Italian policy and public opinion—often, as he made clear, acutely at odds with each other—and it is not surprising that a good number were selected by SIS for Churchill to see, particularly during the summer and autumn of 1943 as Italy tottered and surrendered. After MacWhite reported rumours that the Italians had decoded the traffic of some neutral diplomats, Dublin cabled: 'Better not send further reports about military matters'.[177] His informative written reports went by diplomatic bag, and it must be assumed that these too were copied en route.

William Warnock in Berlin did his best, although he was clearly constrained in his range of contacts and relied mainly on press reports and on occasional bilateral discussions with middle-level German functionaries and with fellow neutral diplomats. From the British perspective, his reports were significant in that they showed no Irish engagement with Germany beyond purely functional exchanges, largely concerning sporadic bombing of Irish territory and attacks on Irish ships: in June 1942 he relayed Dublin's 'profound resentment' at the sinking of a clearly marked Irish ship, 'a flagrant disregard of Irish neutrality and sovereign rights'. The

---

[172] Interview with Sir John Stephenson, 1989; Liddell diary, 6 Aug. 1941, TNA, KV4/188.
[173] Liddell diary, 29 July 1941, TNA, KV4/187.
[174] Berne to Dublin, 31 Oct. 1941, TNA, HW12/270.
[175] Vatican to Dublin, 30 Dec. 1941, TNA, HW12/272.
[176] MacWhite to Dublin, 17 Dec. 1938, in Crowe *et al.*, *DIFP* v. 382–3.
[177] Dublin to Rome, 17 Feb. 1942, NAI, DFA P12/8.

Germans quickly acknowledged responsibility, but refused to pay compensation.[178] In October 1941 Warnock reported that two Irishmen had begun broadcasting propaganda for the Germans. Blair, broadcasting as 'Pat O'Brien', was head of the Irish section; another was John O'Reilly, 'once clerk in Customs, Rosslare, who was . . . in the Channel Islands at the time of German occupation. Both have assured me that they will say nothing endangering Irish neutrality'.[179] O'Reilly, whose presence in Berlin had already been noted by G2 through his broadcasts, was to provide a great many headaches in the winter of 1943–4 after returning to Ireland as a German agent.[180] One Irish cable from Berlin did carry a personal message for Hempel: 'your sister and Schwarb visited farm and saw Moser 25th July. Decided to keep managers'.[181] This appeared a completely innocent private communication, but it lent itself to a more hostile construction. Given that Hempel's official communications contained very sensitive material, however, it seems reasonable to conclude that Warnock was simply doing Hempel's family a favour, and that the concession was not abused in this case. There is nothing in British records to indicate otherwise, although the suspicion arises that the Germans might have been deliberately softening up the Irish chargé by sending a harmless personal message so that he might subsequently accept others which had hidden meanings.

Warnock reported not only on the press but on wider or alternative public opinion, describing general disappointment at the slowness of the Russian campaign and at increased shortages of food and clothing. Irish reports from Berlin were to attract considerable British and American interest in the last year of the war, not for what they disclosed about Irish policy but for their account of conditions in the capital of the Reich.

Irish traffic to and from the United States was mainly concerned not with high policy but with supplies and shipping. Brennan continued to report on growing American hostility towards Ireland, even before the United States entered the war. This was exacerbated by Irish protests at American involvement in the construction of naval facilities at Londonderry. Even people Brennan regarded as well disposed, such as the mayor of New York, Fiorello LaGuardia, who believed that due to Gray's hostile reportage Roosevelt 'is misinformed as to Ireland . . . begged me for some encouragement for his hope that solution reconciling Irish rights with American interests can be found'. The Australian minister noted that when Brennan protested that the arrival of American troops in Northern Ireland 'condoned partition . . . he was told that this was fantastic and not worth discussing'.[182] Traffic with Canada was mainly about supplies, although one enigmatic cable emerged from Ottawa at the end of December 1941 following the governor-general's reception for the visiting Churchill. The prime minister had spoken warmly to the Irish high commissioner, John Hearne, of his 'great appreciation of "the very nice message indeed" which he said he had received' from de Valera, an interesting remark given Ireland's renewed

[178] Dublin to Berlin, 15 June, and reply, 17 July 1942, TNA, HW12/277 and 278.

[179] Berlin to Dublin, 26 Oct. 1941, TNA, HW12/269.

[180] Bryan (MAI, G2) to IO, Southern Command, 15 Dec. 1941, MAI, G2/3824.

[181] Berlin to Dublin, 9 Aug. 1941, TNA, HW12/267.

[182] Washington to Dublin, 31 Jan. 1942, TNA, HW12/273; diary entry, 12 Feb. 1942, in Casey, *Personal Experience*, 87.

refusal to join the war following American entry, despite Churchill's dramatic message: 'Now is your chance. Now or never. "A nation once again"', sent to de Valera on 8 December.[183]

Japanese traffic yielded nothing of significance save reassuring evidence that Beppu was not systematically gathering intelligence, as London had feared he would. Most of his work concerned the welfare of Irish missionaries in the Far East, about whom Dublin was very concerned. Despite various discussions and assurances, by the autumn of 1942 many were in 'concentration camps', partly because those who had left Ireland before independence had British rather than Irish papers.[184] Decodes also showed that Japan viewed this question in the wider context of relations with the Holy See, to which a minister was appointed in the spring of 1942. This was linked to the fact that Japan had occupied Asian territories such as the Phillipines with large Catholic populations. In October Tokyo said Irish missionaries without Irish papers would have to be treated as 'enemy aliens' for the time being.[185]

In May 1942 Japanese traffic between Madrid and Tokyo included intelligence purportedly received a day previously from Northern Ireland detailing the arrival of American troops by ship at Belfast, Londonderry, and Warrenpoint, who were believed to be joining a Capetown-bound convoy. This material had been garnered by Spaniards in Britain (who were being fed deception material). Churchill saw that decode, together with Beppu's sober assessment of British opinion and advice to Tokyo not to read too much into two by-election victories for independents.[186] Further reports from Madrid gave details of ships under construction in Belfast, while messages from Dublin speculated on the propaganda possibilities arising from ill feeling between American troops and the British public.[187] Beppu also reported that the Irish were 'lost in admiration of [*sic*] the very rapid progress of the imperial army' in the Far East.[188] There is nothing in the Japanese decodes or in British records to indicate that London ever considered using the Dublin mission as a back channel to Tokyo, either before Pearl Harbor or as the war drew to its close, although, as with Vichy, Churchill was always mindful of opportunities for contact: in September 1941, at a time when relations with Japan were fast deteriorating, he urged the Canadians to appoint a minister to Tokyo without delay.[189]

The Vichy minister de Lafourcade, according to G2 in October 1943, 'has never been "collaborationist"...and...always moved socially in British, Allied and De Gaullist circles...Never had any Axis social contacts'.[190] His intercepted reports consistently stressed British resolve, buoyed up by American support and

---

[183] Ottawa to Dublin, 30 Dec. 1941, TNA, HW12/272; Canning, *British Policy Towards Ireland*, 312–13.

[184] Beppu to Tokyo, 2 July, and Vatican to Dublin, 12 Oct. 1942, TNA, HW12/278 and 281.

[185] Tokyo to Japanese minister, the Vatican, 28 June 1942, TNA, HW12/278; Tokyo to Japanese ambassador, Rome, 10 Oct. 1942, USNA, RG457, box 2.

[186] Magic summary, 18 May 1942, USNA, RG457 box 1; Beppu to Tokyo, 5 May 1942, TNA, HW1/558; Hinsley and Simkins, *British Intelligence*, 107–10; *Curry History*, 275.

[187] Magic summaries, 12 July and 31 Aug. 1942, USNA, RG457, box 1.

[188] Beppu to Tokyo, 10 Mar. 1942, TNA, HW12/275.

[189] Moffat journal, 18 Sept. 1941, reporting a conversation with Norman Robertson, Harvard, MS 1407, vol. 46.

[190] G2 report on personnel of the French legation, 25 Oct. 1943, NAI, DFA P75. This drew extensively on intercepted correspondence.

by Soviet resilience. In April 1942 he argued that, notwithstanding disaster in the Far East and the failure of the Cripps mission to India, Britain remained determined and pugnacious.[191] A number of surveys of the British economy, prepared from published data, were remitted by the commercial attaché. Such French reports were generally distinguished by an absence of bombast and by efforts at a cold appraisal of Britain's situation, although the growing influence of the labour movement and enthusiasm for Russia, reflected in the widespread display of 'drapeaux rouges' during visits by Soviet representatives, were noted disapprovingly.[192]

Britain also had information from inside the legation, as one of the attachés, Louis Roché, was in touch with Maffey's office (he wrote in the warmest terms congratulating Jack Balfour of the Foreign Office on the award of an honour, a letter which the Irish duly opened en route). Another Vichy official was observed by the Irish to lunch frequently with Collinson of SIS.[193] Overall it was clear that Vichy diplomats in Dublin were not acting in Axis interests (although an SIS 'QRS' report of September 1942 stated that one made 'clumsy attempts to pump possible sources . . . on the subject of impending operations on a Second Front'). This was a significant negative, as was the absence of any marked shift in their approach after Darlan intensified cooperation with the Axis in May 1941. They did not, for example, do much to broadcast the virtues of the new Vichy social order, some aspects of which might have been expected to appeal to conservative Catholic opinion (although the country's key prelate, the Francophile Archbishop McQuaid of Dublin, was personally sympathetic towards the Allies, and was not anti-Semitic).[194] On the other hand, proposals such as that of September 1941 to arrange the transfer by seaplane of stranded French citizens to France and of Irish citizens to Ireland, which apparently were considered 'more than satisfactory' by the Irish, must have caused concern in London.[195]

The traffic also produced evidence of discord in the mission: in November 1941 one official refused to sign a pledge of loyalty to Pétain.[196] Such friction was, of course, not peculiar to the Dublin mission: Vichy representation in Canada was similarly split, with an anxious and quiescent minister in Ottawa and a pushy consul-general in Montreal who devoted considerable energies to portraying the Pétain regime to French-Canadian opinion as the embodiment of pastoral Catholic values, to the discomfiture of the Canadian government. A number of Vichy radio stations also broadcast propaganda to Quebec aimed at Catholic opinion (on much the same lines as Vichy courted Catholics in her own overseas possessions).[197] In responding to American warnings about possible 'dirty work' by Vichy diplomats, a Canadian official gave 'a clean bill of health' to the minister Ristelhueber, but

[191] De Lafourcade to Vichy, 21 Aug. 1941 and 15 Apr. 1942, TNA, HW12/266 and 275.
[192] Ibid., 21 Feb. 1942, TNA, HW12/273.
[193] Photostat of Roché to Balfour, 6 Jan., and Archer (G2) to Walshe, 30 Jan. 1941, NAI, DFA A8.
[194] QRS report, 1 Sept., 1942, TNA, DO121/85; Clarke, 'Higher Ranking Women and the Vichy Regime', 333–4.
[195] Albertas (naval attaché, Dublin) to Vichy, 2 Sept. 1941, TNA, HW12/267.
[196] De Lafourcade to Vichy, 3 Nov. 1941, TNA, HW12/270.
[197] Moffat journal, 22 Nov. 1941, Harvard, MS1407, vol. 45; Jennings, *Vichy in the Tropics*, 96–7.

'was not so sure' about representatives in Montreal and Halifax. In Kabul, Vichy diplomats' attempts to establish clandestine contact with the British legation in the autumn of 1942 were treated with suspicion, as they were suspected of playing 'a very double game'.[198]

In December 1941 Vichy agreed to permit R. M. Smyllie, the Anglophile editor of the *Irish Times*, to visit unoccupied France to assess conditions for himself.[199] Apart from further economic surveys, the only material of significance came in the wake of the Anglo-American invasion of French North Africa (the Irish minister in Vichy reported that the French government could no longer communicate with missions abroad in code, but it is impossible to confirm this from British records).[200] While the naval attaché Albertas pledged his continued loyalty to Vichy, his assistant Bernier, a Deuxième Bureau officer in Dublin since May 1941, declared for Darlan and asked permission to rejoin the French forces in Algiers.[201]

The Italian minister's traffic continued to be of interest and most was decoded: in October 1941 GC&CS noted that 'of his last 87 messages' sent via Washington, '85 were read by us'.[202] This material disclosed one significant Irish–Italian understanding which developed after Japan entered the war. In April 1942 de Valera thanked Berardis 'warmly' for the interest which the Italian government was taking in the fate of Irish missionaries in the Far East.[203] The Japanese surmised that there must be a 'very secret agreement' between Ireland and Italy, although the Italians firmly denied this when asked by the Japanese ambassador in Rome, and the Americans explained Japanese willingness to treat missionaries well by reference to the policy of 'deference to the Catholic Church'.[204] In June 1942 Berardis said de Valera 'hoped to avoid trouble for his country, apart from such as inevitably arose from the economic situation'. Churchill's annotation runs: 'Keep handy. I may want it'.[205]

Berardis relayed what scraps came to him from Northern Ireland, especially about naval matters. In July 1941 he passed on word of the arrival of Americans in Londonderry, remarking that the British wished to suppress news of 'the new military collaboration between [Northern] Ireland and the United States'.[206] A report of a cordial conversation between Berardis and de Valera, unfortunately slightly corrupted, portrayed the taoiseach as angered by the 'meagre' outcome of the Aiken

---

[198] Moffat journal, 14 Mar. and 28 May 1942, Harvard, MS 1407, vol. 46; Foreign Office to British minister, Kabul, 19 Oct. 1942, TNA, FO 371/31331.

[199] La Fourcade to Vichy, and reply, 5 Nov. and 15 Dec. 1941, TNA, HW12/271.

[200] Murphy (Vichy) to Dublin, 19 Dec. 1942, NAI, DFA P12/1.

[201] Albertas to Vichy, and Bernier to Rabat, both 8 Dec. 1942, TNA, HW12/283. After he reached Casablanca, Bernier remained in friendly correspondence with de Lafourcade. G2 report on personnel of the French legation, 25 Oct. 1943, NAI, DFA P75. In May 1942 the French premier Pierre Laval expressed his admiration for Irish neutrality and his hope that this could be maintained despite the arrival of American troops in Northern Ireland. Murphy (Vichy) to Dublin, 11 May 1942, NAI, DFA P12/1.

[202] GC&CS note on Berardis to Rome, 31 Oct. 1941, TNA, HW12/270.

[203] Berardis to Rome, 15 April 1942, TNA, HW12/276.

[204] Magic summaries, 25 Oct. (quoting Japanese ambassador, Rome, to Tokyo, 13 Oct.) and 13 July 1942, USNA, RG457, box 1 and box 2.

[205] Berardis to Rome, 16 June 1942, and undated annotation by Churchill, TNA, HW1/654.

[206] Ibid., 8 July 1941, TNA, HW12/265.

mission, which he said had been launched at the behest of the American minister. When asked whether the 'Anglo-American' build-up in Northern Ireland did not threaten Ireland, he gave only a 'vague answer', emphasizing the state's determination to defend her neutrality, while Walshe remarked that the development related solely to 'the bare military necessities for the protection of the Atlantic convoys'.[207]

Berardis also found Walshe bullish about Britain's capacity to defend herself from invasion.[208] In November 1941 he dismissed Rome's suggestion that the Italian community in Ireland might advance him sterling, with the equivalent amount to be credited to them in Italy: Italians in Ireland were 'mostly miserable dealers in provisions and ice-cream . . . hard hit' by economic conditions and without any cash to spare.[209] He advised Rome that propaganda broadcasts in Irish would be ineffective because so few people understood the language, and suggested instead bilingual broadcasts featuring a combination of cultural, religious, and political themes.[210] In June 1942 he reported that Walshe had stressed the negative impact on Irish opinion of German air attacks. Even the bombing of Belfast 'seemed an act scarcely worthwhile' in terms of Germany's war aims, and lent itself to Allied propaganda.[211]

Cardinal MacRory continued to express his 'lively sympathy for our country'. As the war turned against Italy in 1942, the cardinal 'did not hesitate to come to a reception given in his honour at this Legation', and subsequently spent 'a whole afternoon' with Berardis, while there were other Northern Ireland contacts, including a Dr Ryan of Queen's University who was 'friendly' towards Italy.[212] Following the arrival in Northern Ireland of American troops, of 'bad quality' and indisciplined, Berardis predicted renewed pressure on Ireland to concede air facilities.[213] In September 1942, perhaps in response to a request from Rome, he sent two lengthy reports on neutrality and on British economic pressure on Ireland: in the same month Guy Liddell noted that 'we have seen signs of a little information of no great importance going out through Italian BJs [diplomatic decodes]'.[214] As already discussed, Berardis's October comments based on newspaper speculation about imminent operations in North Africa provoked a storm when Churchill saw them.[215]

Berardis's traffic showed that he had the will but not the means to collect useful war intelligence. Because his cables went through London, and because GC&CS could read his traffic, however, his activities did not cause MI5 too much anxiety. The great concern remained the German legation, in terms both of its unreadable traffic and of its clandestine radio. Once Pandora became available in 1943, a study was initiated of such hitherto unreadable Dublin-Berlin cable and radio traffic as

---

[207] Berardis to Rome, 7 and 9 Aug. 1941, TNA, HW12/267.
[208] Ibid., 13 Sept. 1941, TNA, HW12/267.
[209] Ibid., 1 Nov. 1941, TNA, HW12/270.
[210] Ibid., 25 Jan. 1942, TNA, HW12/273.
[211] Ibid., 8 and 9 June 1942, TNA, HW12/277.
[212] Ibid., 10, 25 and 31 Oct. 1941 and 30 Sept. and 5 Dec. 1942, TNA, HW12/269, 281, and 283.
[213] Ibid., 17 Jan., 9 and 10 Feb. 1942, TNA, HW12/273 and 274.
[214] Liddell diary, 16 Dec. 1942, TNA, KV4/190.
[215] Berardis to Rome, 12 Aug., 1 and 9 Sept. 1942, TNA, HW12/279 and 280.

had been intercepted and stored. Only portions of this material have been traced, mainly in SIS précis concentrating on three central concerns: Berlin's efforts to get Hempel to use his radio to send urgent intelligence; Hempel's efforts to retain an arm's-length relationship with Goertz before and after his capture; and Hempel's advocacy of German encouragement of the Northern IRA, 'provided ensuing action is directed exclusively against England'. Hempel had a trusted intermediary with links to the Northern IRA—the British assumed this to be Seán MacBride, which seems likely—who convinced him that the 'Irish National Revolutionary Movement cannot be repressed . . . it should not be repelled by open indifference' in Berlin, lest that strengthen 'elements . . . who are accessible to Communist influence'. He sought 'urgent instructions', which were not forthcoming.[216]

One Irish reference in Portuguese traffic was sufficiently interesting to be shown to Churchill. A foreign ministry account of the first remarks of the new Irish chargé d'affaires in March 1942 said he conveyed Irish admiration for Portugal and her constitution, and explained that his government had 'convinced England of the impossibility of entering the war on her side without provoking civil war'.[217]

BRITISH PROPAGANDA AND IRELAND, 1941–1942

The Irish were acutely aware that the policy of neutrality was likely to be the subject not only of open but of covert attack, and not only by Britain: in 1941 G2 reported indications that Gray was confidentially floating the possibility of a scheme whereby, 'following the example of Iceland', the Irish would invite the United States 'to occupy this state for mutual protection', a line which was also being disseminated in British 'whispers'. It was thought that such talk was intended not to persuade the Irish into cooperation, but rather to embarrass and discredit them for their refusal to compromise on the question of the ports and airfields.[218] In reality, whatever steam there had been in covert propaganda against Ireland evaporated with the entry of the United States into the war. Thereafter the United States government and people could be expected to regard Irish neutrality as a threat to their own interests and the need secretly to reinforce such views disappeared.

Even when not the object of 'whispers' and other forms of clandestine propaganda, Ireland remained a tempting locale for dissemination of material. In August SOE's Gladwyn Jebb brought up another Irish whispering scheme, this one originating with the Admiralty. They wanted to feed whispers to Albertas, still thought in London to be latently anti-Vichy despite the assessments of Maffey's staff to the contrary, in the hope that the material would eventually reach the ears of the deputy and de facto head of the Vichy government, Admiral Darlan.[219] SOE liked the idea, as it had long 'realised . . . what an excellent centre Dublin was for planting

[216] 'Summary of most secret information from Dublin, 22nd March–3rd April 1943', citing messages of November 1942 and January 1943, TNA, DO121/87.
[217] Lisbon to ambassador, London, 1 Mar. 1942, TNA, HW1/386.
[218] Bryan to Walshe, 19 July 1941, NAI, DFA P6.
[219] In fact the Albertas scheme was not put into operation. Memorandum on 'Whispering in Eire', 13 Oct. 1942, TNA, HS6/307.

rumours to get back to official quarters in Germany, Italy and France' through their legations. There was, nevertheless, a difficulty: following the removal of Roddy Keith and the abandonment of the 'CLARIBEL II' stay-behind scheme, 'we have no one . . . to whom we can send whispers, and even if we appointed somebody, we have no channel of communication', as the military attaché had washed his hands of such activity as a result of Keith's performance. Furthermore, it was likely that Vivian of SIS, 'owing to his very natural desire to protect his own organization' in Ireland, 'might find himself unable to put more than a few into circulation'.[220] Jebb unilaterally ruled that the 'ban on SOE action in Eire did not include a ban on whispering', a convenient though somewhat questionable finding which meant that higher authority need not be consulted, but the plan foundered on the twin problems of communication and distribution. C unhelpfully adduced 'security grounds' for refusing the use of the SIS Dublin bag, while the military attaché was unwilling to help in the light of his experience with Keith. BTNI did offer to post on 'apparently harmless letters in Belfast . . . a veiled Playfair code should be easy to use', but enthusiasm for the project petered out despite Admiralty support and the identification of a possible whisperer in Dublin—an Anglo-Irish barrister who had served during the first world war.[221]

SOE's continued interest in whispering was complicated by the creation in August 1941 of the Political Warfare Executive (PWE). This was formed largely through taking over SOE's black propaganda responsibilities. SOE claimed residual whispering rights in themes relating to strategy and military operations, together with a monopoly on the distribution of all whispers outside the United Kingdom, but these claims were by no means universally accepted in Whitehall. Such jurisdictional uncertainties provided fertile grounds for interdepartmental friction, of a kind for which only historians are properly grateful because of the rich documentary sources generated by such rows. The issues came to light in February 1942, when PWE raised the possibility of Irish whispering. SOE were apprehensive lest this resurrect the question of whether they had had authority for their earlier whispering activities: as one official delicately put it, 'there is no record in our files' that C 'ever gave direct consent to our whispering in Eire', and the question 'was never discussed' with him 'on his own merits'. But 'Dublin is an ideal whispering centre, and we are very keen to get started there again'.[222]

What followed veered into the realm of comic opera—indeed, PWE's chosen instrument in Dublin, the press attaché and poet John Betjeman, has been brilliantly caricatured in a musical farce, *Improbable Frequency*.[223] An inveterate gossip and *ex officio* a propagandist, he was an obvious though perhaps too conspicuous choice for the clandestine task of whispering. Fragmentary evidence suggests that as well

[220] AD/A1 to AD/A, 2 Aug. 1941, TNA, HS6/307.
[221] Slade (NID) to Brooks (SOE), 19 July, and D/QA to D/Q8, 6 Aug. 1941, TNA, HS6/305; note on 'Eire whispering', 21 July 1942, TNA, HS6/307.
[222] D/Q8 to AD/P, 27 Feb. 1942, TNA, HS6/307.
[223] Arthur Riordan's *Improbable Frequency* was first performed in Dublin in 2004. In the Abbey Theatre production of 2005, Betjeman was pink-socked, mincing, and generally fantastically camp. The musical, set in Dublin during the Emergency and involving mysterious radio transmissions, also features the libidinous physicist Erwin Schrödinger.

as investigating the production and distribution of German propaganda, including the legation's weekly news-sheet, information on which he passed to Collinson of SIS, Betjeman was involved in the drafting of a supposed German propaganda directive on themes to be followed in material circulated in Ireland.[224] Nicholas Mansergh, who worked on Ireland in the Ministry of Information, was adamant that Betjeman was never involved in intelligence activities per se: he recalled him as adept at demolishing silly stories which did the rounds, and as a proponent of a more vigorous British information policy. Mansergh also argued that it would have been impossible for Betjeman to do his overt press job effectively if simultaneously involved in covert propaganda.[225] Yet the record does indicate that, even though Betjeman scarcely deserves the title of 'spy' sometimes bestowed upon him, he certainly dipped his toe in the murky waters of clandestine propaganda.[226]

PWE's plans for Irish whispers alarmed one SOE official on grounds of principle: it would be 'most dangerous for us to allow [John] Rayner [of PWE] to go ahead with his private arrangement with Betjeman on the grounds that whispers are PWE's responsibility and not SOE's . . . Responsibility for choosing and using channels for rumours is the responsibility of SOE'. It followed that PWE's initiative should be under the umbrella of SOE: 'We have always wanted to whisper in Eire', and it might be 'worth our while to make contact ourselves with Betjeman and instruct him in our experience of operational whispering'.[227] Quite what distinguished 'operational whispering' from the more usual artifices by which good stories are put into circulation—'Did you hear that', 'I promised not to repeat this', and so on—was left unstated. The official concluded that 'we shall get farther in the long run, and avoid many pitfalls, by reopening the whole question' with C rather than going behind his back: 'We should not be complicated this time by the larger issue of SOE sabotage organizations. It is also clear that after our last experience we must safeguard ourselves by giving "C" information about Betjeman, his methods and agents'.[228] SOE eventually summoned up the courage to clarify the matter by consulting C, who rather surprisingly agreed. SOE officers were pleased: 'I can imagine no better centre from which to start rumours provided we make it clear that no other subversive activity will be undertaken', that SOE would use a PWE agent 'for the purposes in question', and that SIS and MI5, 'who have a kind of combined section to deal with Eire', were consulted appropriately.[229]

In July Rayner of PWE briefed Betjeman and showed him 'certain of our sibs [whispers]. Betjeman . . . has already made three contacts amongst pro-British

---

[224] Memorandum by Betjeman, 23 Mar., and undated [Apr. 1942] draft German propaganda directive, with Betjeman to Mansergh (Ministry of Information), 18 May 1942, TNA, DO130/4.

[225] Conversation with Professor Nicholas Mansergh, Cambridge, 1986.

[226] 'How Verse Saved Poet Laureate from the IRA', *Guardian*, 22 Apr. 2000. This article maintains that, because he sent insightful reports on Irish politics and on divisions within the IRA (and because the IRA reportedly contemplated shooting him), Betjeman was a spy. This is to equate the job of press attaché, which naturally involved both promoting the British point of view and ascertaining as much as possible, with covert intelligence gathering. With the limited exception of his PWE work discussed here, there is no evidence that Betjeman exceeded his overt role.

[227] Note on 'Eire whispering', 21 July 1942, TNA, HS6/307.

[228] Ibid.

[229] Ibid.; AD/P to D/CO(A), and D/Q to A/DP, both 27 Feb. 1942, TNA, HS6/305.

Eireanns as proposed disseminators', but was not given any whispers for distribution. Two months later came disappointing news: Betjeman 'is not now able to undertake' whispering, but he had 'recommended a man for the job'.[230] Betjeman's recruit was Dr George Furlong, the director of the National Gallery of Ireland, who knew Collinson and who had strong social links with the Italian legation. After 'vettings' by SOE and SIS—who presumably noted his years of postgraduate study in Germany, and probably also his homosexuality—Furlong was interviewed by Rayner. He was to be used 'solely for propaganda sibs, and . . . no sibs in any way connected with strategic deceit shall be sent (PWE are not allowed to draft sibs dealing with strategy, but sometimes they submit to ISSB sibs which are on the borderline. Such sibs I will not permit for Furlong)':

Our plan for the immediate future should be:

   a) Each week Rayner and I earmark suitable sibs for Furlong.

   b) That, at present, these particular sibs should go to no SOE people abroad.

   c) That I should, each week, ask Rayner to pass the selected sibs to Furlong (thereby retaining SOE's function as disseminators, and using Rayner as a cut-out).

   d) That Rayner shall pass them to Furlong by word of mouth during Furlong's frequent visits to London; or via Betjeman . . . ; and possibly, later on, by C's bag.[231]

No further evidence of this whispering scheme has been traced. If Furlong did indeed engage in clandestine activities, it would have been the norm rather than the exception for the heads of the troika of Irish national cultural institutions. We have seen that Dr Adolf Mahr of the National Museum was unavoidably absent from his desk for the entire war—providentially from the point of view of the Irish government, since they did not have to take a view of his political connections—because when hostilities broke out he was visiting Germany.[232] Richard Hayes of the National Library, by contrast with his museum and gallery analogues, remained loyal exclusively to the state which employed him. Yet even then he was drawn into the intelligence world, because of his prodigious facility both for languages and for codebreaking.[233] He became G2's main port of call on everything to do with codes and ciphers.

The tortuous logic which SOE applied to their whispering ambitions in Dublin reflect the organization's wider difficulties in Whitehall in developing a distinct role in the face of the hostility of other agencies and services, rather than factors particular to Ireland. The issues which delayed their Irish whispering campaign were not ones of principle but of jurisdiction: PWE saw themselves as the appropriate originator and disseminator in Ireland, and SOE were by no means confident that their claims to be the designated whisperer in Ireland would withstand scrutiny

---

[230] D/Q to AD/P, 27 July and 20 Sept., and note of talk with Rayner, 15 Sept. 1942, TNA, HS6/305.

[231] D/Q10 to AD/P, 13 Oct. 1942, TNA, HS6/307; Furlong diary, 13 Aug. 1940, UCDA, Furlong Paper, LA53/48; C had already told SOE that his Dublin bag was insecure. Hale (SOE) to Rayner, 4 Aug. 1942, TNA, HS6/305.

[232] *Liddell History*, 38, 40 and 46; Hull, *Irish Secrets*, 30–2, 107 and 295, nn. 10 and 11.

[233] O'Halpin, *Defending Ireland*, 187.

by SIS or the JIC. The compromise reached may have satisfied honour all round, but with so many opponents in Whitehall it is perhaps not surprising that SOE's whispering plans generated at least as much friction and confusion in London as they did discord and uncertainty amongst Britain's enemies.

Despite these setbacks, SOE were not left entirely out of the picture, in that their political head, Lord Selborne of the Ministry of Economic Warfare, was pleased to accept membership of a war cabinet committee established in 1942 to consider economic policy on Ireland.[234] But by then the steam had rather gone out of the idea of starving Ireland into the war, and the question of non-military supplies for Ireland had become one primarily of acknowledged interdependence: unless the Irish received a certain amount of locomotive coal, for example, they could not transport the agricultural goods which Britain desperately needed.

CONCLUSION

In June 1941 an invasion of the British Isles was still a possibility. A year later Churchill remarked that the 'situation had changed . . . no risk now of invasion of Ireland: at least th[at] danger has receded'.[235] By December 1942 the question was not if but when and where the Allies would seek a foothold in mainland Europe. This decisive shift in the fortunes of the war in the west between June 1941 and December 1942 occasioned parallel changes in British intelligence involvement in Ireland. The main problem arising from Irish neutrality by the end of 1942 was no longer a strategic one—Irish defencelessness, and the denial of port and air facilities to Britain and her new and somewhat overbearing ally the United States—but a security issue: how could the leakage of war information through Ireland be minimized? The problem increasingly presented itself not only in a defensive but in an offensive sense: by the end of 1942 it was clear that Double Cross was growing in effectiveness not simply in respect of counter-espionage and counter-intelligence, but as an instrument of strategic deception. This complicated the question of leakage through Ireland, which became a matter not simply of preventing accurate war information reaching the Axis, but ensuring also that Axis confidence in the deception material increasingly being planted on them was not undermined by any uncontrolled stories, however wild, inaccurate, or misleading.

Managing this complex process was essentially a matter for the intelligence professionals, with occasional reference to the Security Executive, and was not something which could usefully be addressed by ministers in private or in public. As the lead agency on Irish matters, MI5 had achieved a good deal by the end of 1942. Relations with G2 were close and constructive, while the RUC were also working well with the Garda. On the clandestine side, SIS's counter-intelligence networks appeared to be doing a reasonable job (albeit under G2's prying eyes), and the quality

---

[234] Selbourne to Attlee, who as deputy prime minister chaired the committee, 1 June 1942, TNA, HS8/900.

[235] Cabinet secretary's informal notes of war cabinet meeting, WM (42) 96th, 27 July 1942, TNA, CAB195/1.

of intelligence on Irish affairs had improved immeasurably. The Americans had begun to take an independent hand in Irish affairs, but there were good prospects for cooperation through OSS's London office. The great gap remaining in British knowledge was that of German diplomatic communications. This was about to be closed by GC&CS.

5

Preparation for *Overlord*: January–December 1943

The year 1943 began and ended with intelligence breakthroughs of the first rank. GC&CS's success in producing Pandora meant that from January German diplomatic communications could generally be read as rapidly in London as in Berlin; that achievement in turn had a decisive impact on British management of the problem of the German legation transmitter, a process which culminated in the German handover of the set to the Irish in December. For the rest of the war the British had full control of Berlin–Dublin communications.

These developments took place against a shifting strategic backdrop. By 1943 it was clear that the British Isles were no longer a likely invasion target, and that American war production and Soviet resilience were shifting the strategic balance in Europe. In the Pacific, furthermore, Japan had lost the strategic initiative, although on land she still appeared almost invincible. The great question was not if, but when and where the Allies would go on the offensive: the Russians were already calling for a 'Second Front' in western Europe, and despite their war with Japan the Americans were also keen to bring the fight to Hitler. In the course of the year the north-east of the island of Ireland, from being a possible soft spot in the defences of the British Isles, became primarily a staging post for American troops and war supplies, while the danger which neutral Ireland posed to Allied interests was redefined. Irish unpreparedness to resist a German attack, and even the question of the ports, became non-issues for the Allies; what increasingly mattered, as they prepared for the invasion of Europe, was Irish security. This involved a host of considerations of policy and of practice, largely of matters of detail which only specialists could properly evaluate and address; but those matters in turn hinged on a question of the highest political sensitivity, Irish maintenance of diplomatic relations with the Axis powers. Management of these intersecting and sometimes conflicting strands of Anglo-Irish relations was further complicated by increased American interest in the question of Irish security. This interest was itself reflected in two discordant streams: Gray's reportage to Washington on the German espionage threat, and the more considered activities of OSS through its London office. The year was to see a high degree of collaboration amongst the various British departments and agencies with Irish concerns; it was also to show how even so passionate an Anglophile as Gray could be an encumbrance because of his lack of understanding of security issues and, paradoxically, because of his unusually good lines of communication to the White House.

COUNTER-INTELLIGENCE COOPERATION: THE
EASTWOOD CASE

In February GC&CS learned through an ISOS message from Portugal to Berlin that a cipher message from Ireland had reached the Germans in Lisbon. Almost simultaneously, SIS reported that one of their informants, Granja Tomas, 'who is a kind of hanger-on at the docks at Lisbon, was given a letter in code' by a crewman from the Irish tramp steamer *Edenvale* to deliver to the German embassy. He had first gone to his SIS paymasters and they copied it.[1] The Irishman involved was a ship's cook named Christopher Eastwood, who made regular trips to the Iberian peninsula (he had been 'wounded in a brawl with Portuguese police in Lisbon', and jailed for a time in 1942).[2] The message, which the British could not decode, had been sent by Joseph Andrews, using Goertz's cipher. Andrews, who represented himself as Goertz's chosen successor but was in fact operating independently of him and of the IRA, sought to extract money from the Germans in return for intelligence supplied.

G2 were told about Eastwood, and were supplied with the cipher text of the messages—a second had been obtained in Lisbon in March.[3] A week later, one of these 'appeared in ISOS. It indicates that consideration is being given to the formation of an anti-Communist army in Eire under [General] O'Duffy. It is not clear whether the intention is to get this army out to the Russian front or whether the scheme is likely to act as a cover for a revolutionary body in Eire itself'.[4] G2's codebreaker Richard Hayes now came into his own. He intensified his investigations of the cipher text captured with other material in Stephen Held's house in May 1940, and eventually broke it, showing it to be a journal which Goertz had kept from the time of his landing to when he finally made contact with the IRA. The news caused a stir in MI5:

Dan has just telegraphed to say that the. . . HELD cypher has been broken and it may be identical with the one being used by GOERTZ. Messages that we have obtained in Lisbon have been examined and appear to be in the handwriting of ANDREWS. Andrews met Eastwood on arrival [in Ireland] and there was an exchange of notes. A cypher had been found in Goertz's cell, probably through the assistance of his servant who is in Dan's employ. Dan has asked us to send over an expert to look at the cypher.[5]

In fact, news of this discovery should have reached London somewhat sooner than it did: Bryan only learned of it incidentally in discussion with Hayes, who had broken the cipher some time before and had then provided the key and the German text to Bryan's deputy, de Buitléir. De Buitléir, who had been foisted upon Bryan because of his knowledge of German, had a limited understanding of intelligence matters and was reflexively anti-British. He also lacked the mental agility for intelligence

[1] Liddell diary, 10 Feb. 1943, TNA, KV4/191.
[2] Report by Lieutenant Eager, G2, 31 July 1942, DFA A8/1.
[3] Liddell diary, 10 Mar. 1943, TNA, KV4/191.
[4] Ibid., 16 Mar. 1943, TNA, KV4/191.
[5] Ibid., 25 Mar. 1943, TNA, KV4/191.

liaison, once giving away far more than he was supposed to in a meeting with MI5—when Bryan taxed him with this, he replied that he could not keep five or six balls in the air at the one time. He defended his withholding of the news of Hayes's discovery by remarking that he did not think a few weeks would make any difference since the material dated from 1940, and that he assumed that Bryan would only pass it to the British anyway.[6]

Cecil Liddell and Denys Page, an expert on Abwehr ciphers who later became Regius Professor of Classics at Cambridge, duly visited Dublin, although only after C's assent had been secured. Through ISOS they already knew the key words necessary to read the Eastwood material, though they could not disclose this to the Irish; once Hayes explained how the cipher worked, Page was able to read the messages.[7] This proved a significant breakthrough: Hayes wrote that the Goertz cipher was 'the best . . . in our experience used by the Germans during the war . . . British cryptographers have described it as "in the very first class, and amongst the best three or four used in the war" ' (although in 1985 the official historian Harry Hinsley told Deirdre McMahon that it was 'of no importance'). MI5 and G2 agreed that for the moment the Eastwood link should continue to operate, under appropriate surveillance at both ends, to see how it might develop. The risks in this were limited: it was desirable for G2 to know as much as possible about the material being sent from Ireland, so as to determine whether Andrews was operating on Goertz's behalf and perhaps using the residue of his networks to collect intelligence; the requests which the Germans in Lisbon made for additional material were also significant, since they indicated priorities regarding Ireland. For the British, the fact that they could read the ISOS traffic between Lisbon and Berlin meant that, even if messages were not intercepted en route by their Lisbon agent, they would soon learn their contents.

Analysis of the Eastwood material showed that two-way communication with the Iberian peninsula using shipborne messages was a very lengthy business: it took anything from a month to six weeks for Andrews to obtain replies, something about which he complained bitterly, requesting funds to buy a transmitter instead.[8] The messages bore out suspicions about Hempel's intrigues in 1940–1 with General O'Duffy and, more alarmingly, with General Hugo MacNeill. The messages continued until August, when the Germans discovered, whether through indiscretion or treachery, that Eastwood's Portuguese intermediary was an SIS agent: they 'are aware that Eastwood is blown and they are trying to get him off the ship . . . We do not know whether he is prepared to fall in with their wishes . . . Cecil is going over to Dublin'. Fortunately for Eastwood, he stayed on board. He, Andrews, and two associates were arrested on 17 and 18 August after the *Edenvale* docked at Drogheda. Copies of the messages in code and *en clair* were found in a search of Andrews's house.[9]

MI5's management of this case reflects the high degree of trust which had developed between the Liddells and G2 (although in January MI5 had been somewhat miffed to learn from a former employee of the Irish Department of

[6] Bryan interview, 1983; Bryan transcripts, p. 52.
[7] Liddell diary, 5 Apr. 1943, TNA, KV4/191.
[8] Hayes report; *Liddell History*, 75–6; information from Dr Deirdre McMahon, Mar. 2007.
[9] Liddell diary, 20 Aug. 1943, TNA, KV4/192.

Defence that he had seen documents relating to British forces in Northern Ireland: 'While we do not mind Dan having this information . . . we are rather worried about its passing through a number of offices in Eire').[10] In his Irish section history Cecil Liddell was at pains to point out that 'the breaking of the cipher was chiefly due to the Irish', and that Hayes's codebreaking gifts 'amounted almost to genius'. He was, however, perhaps overstating personal factors when he wrote that 'there is no doubt that this co-operation was largely due to Colonel Bryan's enthusiasm as an intelligence officer and to Dr Hayes' cryptographic zeal. It is very doubtful if his military superiors agreed to the passing of the ciphers to the British and certainly his political superiors would not have done so'.[11] As was probably the case elsewhere—in early 1942, when Turkish 'confidence' in Britain's prospects 'ha[d] been greatly shaken', the 'Turkish Secret Intelligence ha[d] in many circumstances shown itself most cooperative to ours'—it is more likely that de Valera sanctioned cooperation precisely because it could be kept secret and could act to mitigate the acrimony of diplomatic exchanges.[12] The Irish evidence suggests that by 1943 Bryan had a free hand, rather than that he and Hayes were exceeding instructions. Given his close relations with Walshe and Boland of External Affairs, furthermore, he probably consulted one or other on the question. The material about O'Duffy and MacNeill was something of an embarrassment, but G2 knew that the British had long been watching both men.

The Eastwood case is also significant because it reflects the working out of a perennial British dilemma during the war, whether and if so how to engage in sigint (signals intelligence) cooperation with other powers, particularly small neutral states with limited technical capacity but with vital local knowledge and access. There were clear dangers, as even an expression of interest in a particular question could indicate a gap in existing knowledge, or a sudden shift in priorities: throughout the war C was very cautious about sharing sigint expertise and the product of sigint activities not merely with foreign neutrals, but with allies and even with other British agencies—MI5 themselves had grievances where C was discovered to have preventing them even learning about decodes with a bearing on their interests. Yet there were occasions when the game of limited cooperation with neutrals was judged worthy of the risk, even though it inevitably involved some disclosure of British concerns and, potentially, of knowledge and capacity. As late as June 1941, when German troops were known already to be in Finland, C had personally approved the provision of additional intercept equipment to the Finns, with whom Britain had been cooperating on Russian codes and ciphers since mid-1940. The day after the Finns joined with Germany in *Barbarossa*, Guy Liddell saw C: 'He said that the Finns had for some time been decoding the Russian cyphers and passing the information to the Germans. I gather that we also have had the benefit of this service. We have now been obliged to inform the Russians'.[13]

---

[10] Liddell diary, 4 Jan. 1943, TNA, KV4/191. The Irishman concerned was named Peter Corcoran.

[11] *Liddell History*, 75–6; Girvin, *The Emergency*, 306, offers a very different interpretation of the significance of the case, although based on a somewhat cursory narrative.

[12] Note on Turkey, 27 Feb. 1942, TNA, HS3/235.

[13] The Finns were also cooperating with the Japaneese. O'Halpin, 'Small States and Big Secrets', 11–14; Liddell diary, 23 June 1941, TNA, KV4/188.

The risks were perhaps less in the Irish case. But neither Bryan nor Hayes was an intelligence ingénue, and in the course of his liaison on Abwehr ciphers Hayes unavoidably accumulated considerable knowledge of British codebreaking generally. For their part, the British came to realize that Hayes was exceptionally able. Early in 1944 Maffey warned Gray to be discreet in his cables to Washington: the Irish had 'a very skilled cryptographer' who had already 'broken his [Maffey's] code messages from London'.[14] In fact Hayes never attempted a serious study of British traffic, although on one occasion Bryan forwarded him a telephone intercept of a London–Dublin call in which reference was made to a cable already sent (this could have provided a 'crib' into an otherwise unreadable communication). Hayes's valedictory report of January 1946 makes clear that the *raison d'être* of his work was German communications, both diplomatic, which proved beyond his resources, and agent traffic, where his achievements were considerable.[15]

The nuances and qualifications surrounding liaison on counter-espionage with the Irish were also to be seen within Whitehall. In August Guy Liddell noted that the head of Section V, the always difficult Felix Cowgill, 'has . . . had a raspberry' from his subordinate Jane Archer: 'He told her that she should not on any account tell MI5 about the Josephine messages and the Goertz message', and 'still less' should she tell Denniston of GC&CS without 'the Chief's [C] approval. She replied that she had already told MI5 and that as regards the chief she was quite capable of looking after her own affairs'. Liddell added that 'some people think that Felix is going off his rocker', although this was probably unfair as Cowgill had always been obstructive and secretive. The generally good relations between Section V and MI5 owed a great deal to Jane Archer, who was willing to circumvent Cowgill in her dealings with her former colleagues.[16]

The Eastwood case is also notable for MI5's willingness to let it run for so long. This is clearly linked to the fact that the messages did not seriously threaten security, giving only low-grade information of doubtful authenticity, and that through ISOS they could monitor German responses. In the course of 1943 Lisbon became an important centre for the provision of disinformation, both through Double Cross agents and through whispers, and some of these may have had incidental Irish themes: 'D/8', a two-part sib sent out from London in November 1943, stated that 'Soldiers returning from leave in Northern Ireland report US troops arriving there with divisional sign of red diamond. Believed to have come from Iceland'.[17] It may have been thought possible that the Eastwood channel could eventually be used for disinformation, presumably by deceiving or suborning its moving spirit Joseph Andrews, already recognized to be an eminently bribeable rogue.

---

[14] Gray to Washington, 22 Feb. 1944, USNA, State Department, 841D.01/240.

[15] Hayes memorandum; his papers also contain one London–Dublin telephone transcript dating from 1944: a reference to a coded cable was circled in Bryan's hand and passed on to Hayes. Hayes MSS 22984. As is discussed in Ch. 6, Hayes did break an intercepted transmission to a possible resistance group in Germany in 1945.

[16] Liddell diary, 28 Aug. 1943, TNA, KV4/192. 'Josephine' was an underground network in France. What linked its activities with Goertz and Ireland is not known.

[17] Whisper sent to Lisbon, 27 Nov. 1943, TNA, HS8/948.

MOVEMENT CONTROLS AND PREPARATIONS
FOR THE INVASION OF EUROPE

The prosaic problems of movement controls within the British Isles continued to command MI5's attention. The dilemmas were now familiar: while security concerns were paramount, Britain needed Irish labour. Ministries concerned with war production screamed out for Irish workers; the fighting services, while in theory the greatest opponents of easy movement between the two islands because of the danger of the leakage of war information, in fact wanted easy access to potential recruits and for morale reasons were in favour of allowing Irish servicemen to visit home on leave. In December 1943 David Petrie chaired a meeting devoted to the problem of 'Irish labour' in the run-up to *Overlord*, at which it became plain that those most insistent on tighter controls and greater security were simultaneously the greatest offenders, because they continued to allow Irish servicemen to return home on leave.[18] This was to be a recurrent theme over the next six months.

The question of what to do about Ireland's transport links with neutral Europe and with North America also continued to present problems. The Eastwood case highlighted the problem of ships' crews carrying letters and other contraband, a practice which remained widespread despite various efforts to stamp it out. Guy Liddell noted that Belgian refugees in Britain had succeeded in communicating with relatives in occupied territory 'by means of a courier and postbox via Eire'.[19] The fishing industry was a particular concern, since it was virtually impossible to monitor the movements of trawlers and, even if prohibited from doing so, British, Spanish, and French boats might call into Irish ports on the plea of bad weather or mechanical difficulties.[20]

Such difficulties as arose with air travel came not from the Irish, but from Britain's American allies. There were tight British controls on the BOAC service between Foynes and Lisbon, and between Foynes and the United States, but London never had unqualified confidence in the effectiveness of American security measures for Pan American flights, although the Americans did station a security officer at Foynes to keep an eye on transit passengers. For their part, the Americans appeared to construe British concerns partly as reflecting an anxiety to assert hegemony over the operation and development of North Atlantic civil aviation, one of those areas of policy where it was already clear that the post-war ambitions of the two allies were unlikely to coincide.

The effectiveness of movement controls between Ireland and Britain was another potential source of Anglo-American disagreement, as the build-up of American forces in the United Kingdom intensified. In March the Liddell brothers dined with

Col[onel David] Bruce, head of OSS in this country. Bruce is a very charming, cultured American. I had heard from Thurston [an FBI liaison officer in London] that he intended

---

[18] Liddell diary, 21 Dec. 1943, TNA, KV4/193.
[19] Ibid., 9 Mar. 1943, TNA, KV4/191.
[20] Ibid., 27 Apr., 22 June and 25 Sept. 1943, TNA, KV4/191 and 192.

to operate in Ireland and in fact had already two agents there. By way of throwing a fly over him I turned to [*sic*] conversation to Eire generally, but he did not rise. I told him that though there were of course many opportunities for leakage of information, we had no evidence that the Germans had a collecting centre for reports that they might receive from labourers and others returning to Eire once every 6 months on leave. I pointed out that if there were any organization of this kind it would have to be on a very large scale if there was to be any continuity to the information received. It would therefore be difficult to organize anything of the kind without its existence becoming known.[21]

This was a significant meeting. Bruce was to play an important role during the debates about Irish security in the months before *Overlord*, when his voice was a counterweight to the warnings emanating from the American legation. Bruce also had constructive discussions with the Garda and G2 during a visit to Dublin, and was supplied with information on the interned German agents and their cipher systems.[22] It is clear that in the wake of the unexplained withdrawal of Spike Marlin in December 1942, the Irish set out to win the confidence of OSS in London, since they regarded Gray as incapable of setting aside his antagonism towards neutrality when considering security questions. In this they were undoubtedly correct. Gray's reportage on security issues contrasted markedly in tone and insight with what Maffey was telling London at the same time. Both men were anxious above all to prevent the leakage of war information to the Axis, but whereas Maffey took a dispassionate approach and left the details to the professionals, Gray gorged on rumour, wallowed in suspicion, and took upon himself a role of evaluator of intelligence for which he had neither the training nor the temperament. He regarded all Irish concessions to the Allies as window-dressing, and doubted both their willingness and their capacity to prevent the Axis powers from collecting information. In contrast, the Canadian minister in Dublin, whose country had a direct interest in shipping security because of the Canadian navy's major role in Atlantic convoy protection, in November gave his prime minister 'an interesting account of de Valera's attitude of benevolent neutrality'.[23]

SIS IN IRELAND, 1943

In discussing SIS activities regarding Ireland in 1943, it is essential to distinguish between, on the one hand, intelligence and observations garnered in Ireland by Collinson and others, and on the other, the analytical and policy activities of SIS in London. Whereas Collinson was left to collect material without knowledge of the broader picture, the Irish section in London had access to a range of material of which he probably knew nothing, including Pandora, ISOS, and the reports and views of MI5.

QRS reports from Ireland continued to provide a generally balanced, if unavoidably dull, assessment of political affairs. Their main subjects were the Axis legations,

[21] Ibid., 9 Mar. 1943, TNA, KV4/191.
[22] O'Halpin, *Defending Ireland*, 230.
[23] Mackenzie King diary, 25 Nov. 1943.

the activities of extremist political organizations and of the IRA, and party politics. The reports were evidently compiled from a variety of sources—one spoke of 'our observers'—possibly including Collinson's networks.[24] If they devoted more attention to Córas na Poblachta and Ailtirí na hAiséirighe than their electoral weight merited, this was hardly surprising as both were militant republican groups and the latter was also unashamedly fascist.[25] Furthermore, in the course of 1943 some indications emerged which suggested efforts to build up links between Ailtirí na hAiséirighe and General O'Duffy's former followers now in the even more extreme 'Peoples National Party', although by then the great man himself was rumoured to be suffering 'from acute alcoholic poisoning'.[26] The expected alliance between Ailtirí na hAiséirighe and the other fringe parties did not materialize. Apathy was widespread and there was no visible appetite for the general election due in June, in which Labour were predicted to do well. In March the appointment to the high court of A. K. Overend KC, 'a Protestant loyalist', gave increased confidence to the Protestant community, who 'also feel that de Valera has dealt fairly with religious minorities and is not influenced by the Roman Catholic Hierarchy to the same extent as Mr Cosgrave'. More interest 'is centred on the proposals of the Beveridge report' than any other issue, and candidates 'have been obliged to take notice . . . in their electioneering'. Gearóid Ó Cuinneagáin, the leader of Ailtirí na hAiséirghe, had founded 'a Pan Celtic Union as a rallying point for Irish, Scottish, Welsh and Breton nationalists'. It was believed that he 'is "run" by Ernest Blythe and J. J. Walsh . . . ex-politicians [who] are potential Irish Quislings'.[27] These two were later reported to be behind the establishment of '23 clubs for school children . . . Lectures are given to the youths on Nazi lines', but the initiative had run into clerical opposition.[28]

The June election saw de Valera suffer somewhat at the polls—Fianna Fáil lost ten seats and its share of the vote fell by 10 per cent—but Cosgrave's Fine Gael, so far from enjoying a renaissance, 'suffered a severe eclipse'. Its vote also fell by 10 per cent, and it lost thirteen seats. 'IRA and Fascist groups did badly', and Labour's expected surge did not materialize (the party was in turmoil as organizers tried to thwart communist entryism: after visiting Ireland in the autumn, the CPGB leader Harry Pollitt remarked that 'comrades . . . seem to be doing a good job of work in the Labour Party'). A later QRS report gloomily observed that if there were to be a further election soon, as some pundits expected, 'the Cosgrave Party could be written off'.[29] The great surprise of the election was the strong performance of the newly formed Clann na Talmhan, a party of protest representing mainly small farmers which was at least as anti-British as Fianna Fáil. As a populist agrarian party

[24] QRS report, 1 Nov. 1943, TNA, DO121/85.
[25] See the discussion of this curious party in Ní Lochlainn, 'Ailtirí na hAiséirighe: A Party of its Time?', 187–210. Douglas, 'The Pro-Axis Underground', 1179, argues that the party has been too easily dismissed. See Hamilton, *The Speckled People*, 116–19, for an interesting portrait of Ó Cuinneagáin.
[26] QRS report, 1 Sept. 1943, TNA, DO121/85; Wills, *That Neutral Island*, 363–7.
[27] QRS report, 1 Mar. 1943, TNA, DO121/85; Wills, *That Neutral Island*, 366, on Blythe's help for Aiséirí.
[28] QRS report, 1 May 1943, TNA, DO121/85.
[29] Pollitt to Stewart, 5 Oct. 1943, quoted in Puirséil, *Irish Labour Party*, 103; QRS report, 1 Jan. 1944, TNA, DO121/85.

it adopted some lines of argument which had Nazi resonances and which echoed the eccentricities of the Axis-influenced and spectacularly unsuccessful fringe parties which so worried the British—its spokesmen claimed the financial system was in the grip of malevolent, alien, and un-Christian forces—but it was equally hostile to metropolitan Ireland, to civil servants, to taxation, and to all non-rural public expenditure. As shall be seen, in predicting trouble for Cosgrave the QRS reports were rather more perceptive than was Collinson himself.

In the wake of the election, reports detected nuances in the government's approach to potential subversives:

the Government is taking no apparent action against subversive and pro-Fascist organizations which openly advocate the abolition of the Border by force. Yet another such organization has come into existence. 'The Green Front' was launched on 12 September with the advertised mission to abolish the Border. Its supporters and organizers appear to be a hotch potch. . . from 'Ailtirí na hAiseirghe', the 'Young Ireland Association' and 'Coras na Poblachta'.[30]

A handful of republicans recur in these reports. Dan Breen was one; another was Seán MacBride, 'the prominent Dublin barrister and counsel for members of the Extremist IRA. . . [who] has always been regarded as a potential Quisling'. SIS reported that in June he had travelled some distance to dine with Hempel during the German minister's holiday stay in County Mayo.[31] Whether accurate in detail or not, these reports pointed in the right direction: Breen and MacBride were close associates of the legation to the bitter end, and through his links with the republican movement in Northern Ireland the latter was most probably a conduit of such scraps of war information as reached Hempel. The German minister himself was reportedly 'still investing money in moveable assets. Frau Hempel recently paid £70 for an antique table'.[32] Cumulatively, such QRS material at least provided a flavour of Irish affairs as seen through the eyes of pro-British observers.

Much of this material was, of course, also available to G2 through their man Moore. He also kept them abreast of the activities of Collinson's networks, at least as disclosed by the indiscreet Podesta, who complained that his chief had given him a dressing down for writing a letter to the *Evening Mail*. Moore also reported that London had asked about two Italian cafés: 'one or both of these establishments is being used as a clearing house for espionage for the Axis Legations. This comes from a very delicate source, and HQ points out that (1) at least may already be under police observation'. Enquiries should be 'conducted by a helper whose caution and discretion can be relied on completely', and presumably Moore got the task. The results were almost certainly negative.[33]

QRS reports are not the only SIS documents which have come to light for 1943. On 18 June Jane Archer sent Cecil Liddell 'three studies of de Valera' volunteered by SIS's 'representative' in Ireland. She had already 'explained. . . verbally the circumstances' in which this material had been prepared. The first document was by

[30] QRS report, 1 Nov. 1943, TNA, DO121/85.
[31] Ibid., 1 July 1943, TNA, DO121/85.
[32] Ibid., 1 Nov. 1943, TNA, DO121/85.
[33] G2 interviews with Moore, 10 Feb. and 27 Apr. 1943, G2/X/1091.

'a friendly and well informed University Lecturer', the second 'consists of notes sent to our representative by the Editor of an Irish evening paper', and the third 'is the work of our representative' himself. The three documents 'are avowedly intended "to act as an antidote" to "very dangerous views" our representative has heard expressed in London'. Jane Archer's estimate of the material was suggested in her remark that, 'unless you think otherwise, I am not proposing to send them to the Dominions Office', and they do not appear to have reached that or any other policy department.[34]

The blocking by headquarters of inconvenient reports from the field is almost a cliché of writing about intelligence. The unceremonious spiking of Collinson's vigorous counterblast to what he regarded as London's complacency fits that familiar pattern. The lecturer wrote of de Valera's

mediaeval intolerant strain in his now tortured mentality . . . recent changes in his features show a definite deterioration in his moral fibre and a definite loss of that conviction which was formerly his most compelling asset . . . From 1940 on de Valera would at a number of times have had a much better chance than Smuts to have led a nation into the conflict with little internal opposition . . .

Never a word of thanks is offered for the goods and services still supplied by the British and the Americans. They, like neutrality, are God's free gift to Eire through the hands of his servant de Valera . . .

Any examination of his party will stress its essentially one-man nature . . . Mr de Valera has . . . different moral standards and offers no more than lip service to democracy . . . The fundamental picture . . . is of a man always pursuing a dual policy, and never making a stand from which he cannot wriggle out.

Quite how this assessment lay with the author's argument that de Valera would never abandon neutrality was not spelt out.[35]

The editor's contribution similarly concentrated on de Valera's shortcomings. For Britain, his defeat in the forthcoming election 'is desirable . . . Any estimate of de Valera's feelings and intentions must take into consideration the influence of his Spanish blood on his father's side', from which he inherited his 'early hostility to Britain'. He had used press censorship to prevent 'any wave of anti-German or pro-British feeling', as instanced by the censor's refusal to allow 'publication of US press comments in favour . . . of Mr Churchill's speech to US Congress', and 'refusal to allow publication of photograph of Sir John Maffey at [a] Boys Brigade inspection'. Fine Gael offered a 'better understanding and closer friendship with Britain . . . backed by the best elements in the country, including most of the former Unionists. The Party's strength is growing, and its moderate, sound policy should win many additional votes'. While reluctant to make a forecast, the editor claimed that 'shrewd observers agree that the Government will not hold its ground'. Fine Gael and Labour

are almost certain to gain . . . On that reckoning de Valera would lose his majority and a likely result would be Fine Gael–Labour Government.

---

[34] Blanked-out signature, but clearly Jane Archer to Cecil Liddell, 18 June 1943, TNA, KV2/515. The full text of all three TNA documents can be found in O'Halpin, 'Long Fellow, Long Story', 194–203.

[35] 'Report No. 1: Eamon de Valera', with Archer to Liddell, as in n. 34 above.

Taking a long view, and provided that the post-war situation as affecting Eire were sternly handled by Britain, and provided also that economic reality were brought home to the people of Eire, we might yet see a South African parallel here—with General Mulcahy as the Smuts and de Valera as the Hertzog of Eire.[36]

This analysis had echoes of the policy of confrontation urged on the British government by Cumann na nGaedheal emissaries when de Valera came to power in 1932.

Collinson's own contribution was more resonant still. It must be borne in mind that his main job was not to gather political intelligence or to mount covert operations against the government, but to monitor foreign activities in Ireland, to keep a close watch on the Axis and other diplomatic missions and their Irish friends, and to manage the travel permit system. Because his intelligence role was an undercover one, he had no involvement in Anglo-Irish security liaison. It is also unlikely that he was privy to all of SIS's Irish intelligence, in particular decodes.

Collinson set out to dispel

an impression in many responsible quarters . . . that de Valera is alone capable of governing Eire with sufficient firmness to maintain order . . . that his policy of neutrality is less likely to harm our interests than would that of any other . . . leader, and that if he is returned to power . . . he can be relied on to go still further in the direction of friendship . . . and to guide post-war Ireland towards friendly relations with her principal neighbour.

He continued in spirited vein:

The contention that de Valera's policy of neutrality is less susceptible of harm to our interests than would be that of any other Irish government is not only begging the question but suggests that hitherto our grievances . . . have not been substantial. That we have at times benefited by attempts to apply neutrality with impartiality, while admitting concessions in return for indispensable concessions, is undeniable, but the debit balance is represented by the refusal to hand over the Ports, the toleration of dangerous Axis activities under diplomatic immunity, and an Intelligence liaison stopping short at any information which might justify its suspicion against Axis diplomat . . .

The Fine Gael Party has many faults which it would be absurd to attempt to pass over. They have not been opposed to . . . neutrality . . . They still have some unsatisfactory elements . . . and their attitude to such problems as the [Irish] language one is undoubtedly ambiguous . . .

If it is objected that this note of alarm concerns the far too distant future and that the vital present problem is the successful termination of the war, then it is necessary to consider carefully whether dealings with the Eire Government are destined still to play an important part in our strategical plans. It cannot be ruled out entirely that the development of the Battle of the Atlantic might yet bring the Irish Ports into prominence. If they are to be obtained without bloodshed, would it not be better to see an Eire Government with whom negotiations could be carried on rather than one dominated by a man incapable of any form of compromise?[37]

---

[36] 'Report No. II: notes on the general election position in Eire', with Archer to Liddell. General Smuts backed South African participation in the war in 1939; Hertzog argued against it, and left the government.

[37] 'Report No. III: Eamon de Valera', with Archer to Liddell, 18 June 1943.

This lengthy essay reflected better on Collinson's literary abilities than on his grasp of Irish politics. G2 got to hear of his observations with almost indecent speed:

a report was sent to the British Intelligence HQ by their chief agent . . . on the prospects of Fine Gael victory . . . This report was based apparently on information supplied which left the agent under the impression that Fine Gael would be well disposed to the British authorities. Subsequently it was pointed out . . . that Fine Gael opposed sanctions on Italy [in 1935 following the invasion of Abyssinia], a fact of which he was unaware. Furthermore it was suggested to him that the prospects for a Fine Gael victory were not so good as he was led to believe. He was perturbed . . . as it belied his report.

The matter is of interest as an indication of external interest in our domestic politics which we know to be under continuous observation by the chief British Intelligence agent here.[38]

Jane Archer's treatment of Collinson's documents suggests that his stock as an analyst of Irish affairs was not high at SIS headquarters, where both C and Vivian consistently endorsed the argument of the Irish section and of MI5 that cooperation with de Valera was the only sensible approach. Collinson's standing in Whitehall would presumably have suffered further had SIS been aware that the Irish had such intimate and rapid knowledge of his operations and reportage.

Collinson arguably went beyond his remit in advocating a firmer policy. He did not suggest specific changes in approach, beyond urging London to hope for a Fine Gael government, nor indicate how London might help to secure such an outcome, and gave no hint that he had any scheme in view. In truth, his arguments came far too late to get a hearing: in 1940, when the invasion threat was at its height and the IRA appeared a credible fifth column, a proposal to organize a coup to produce a more sympathetic government might have been considered. Such action at any stage in the war would have required the cooperation of significant opposition figures; of these, the only likely candidate was General O'Duffy, the last vestiges of whose Blueshirt organization might have offered some organizational support and muscle. But O'Duffy was largely discredited and, as Pandora had confirmed during 1943, by 1940 he was far closer to the IRA than to his former followers in Fine Gael.

In August, Stephenson of the Dominions Office commended a study of the Goertz case provided by MI5 but probably prepared in consultation with SIS: 'the conclusion is that there is no adequate evidence of any Irish Government implication with [*sic*] German activities. On the contrary, the Irish authorities appear with reasonable success to have been able to check German intrigues with the extremist IRA element'.[39] The study drew extensively on Pandora from 1940 onwards. Whatever comfort the British could draw from evidence that the Irish had not been in cahoots with the Germans at any time, and that the cautious Hempel had been mainly a passive relayer of war information which came to him incidentally and sporadically, was offset by two factors: Germany's deteriorating war position, which rendered continued Irish neutrality far less significant in Berlin's eyes as against the possibility of acquiring significant intelligence on Allied plans for the invasion of Europe; and Hempel's possession of his clandestine transmitter,

---

[38] Note dated 20 Jan. 1943, MAI, G2/X/1091.

[39] Stephenson to Machtig, 25 Aug., with MI5 document forwarded by Cecil Liddell, 24 Aug. 1943, TNA, DO121/84.

which might enable him to send a vital warning even at the cost of a rupture of diplomatic relations. The second of these two problems was finally disposed of just as the year neared its end.

DIPLOMATIC INTELLIGENCE IN 1943

Despite GC&CS's success with Pandora, there remained some limitations: while German cables could be copied while passing through London, for technical reasons and even with Irish cooperation not all radio messages could be intercepted. Furthermore, as already noted, GC&CS had records only of some pre-1943 German communications with Dublin, partly because earlier in the war, when intercept resources and personnel were limited and the demands on them enormous, unreadable radio traffic from the diplomatic station at Nauen was not recorded. On 2 February 1943 Alastair Denniston of GC&CS set out a programme for the retrospective study of Germany–Ireland traffic, directing that 'at least one decoder' should 'give this Dublin work first priority'.[40] The study continued for the remainder of the war.

The year 1943 saw a marked shift in the interest taken in Irish diplomatic messages. Traffic with North America continued to concentrate largely on shipping and supplies, with very occasional flashes of political material: in April the high commissioner in Ottawa gave an account of a difficult conversation with the visiting foreign secretary Anthony Eden, who 'was aloof and hardly courteous', and indignant that Walshe had visited him in London ' "to talk, if you please, about post-war cooperation. This is a club, and if you are in it, you play by the rules and play the game or you do not. That is all" '. The British high commissioner, Malcolm MacDonald, was 'rather embarrassed' by such a broadside at a social function, though he loyally reiterated Eden's argument that Ireland should come into the war.[41] Repeated instructions to the Irish minister in Vichy to persuade the French not to do anything about the now openly pro-Algiers de Lafourcade in Dublin — 'the situation may turn against us at any time if you take no action' — indicated Irish anxiety not to be caught on the wrong diplomatic foot. When Vichy finally replaced him in November, their nominee as chargé d'affaires promptly declared for Algiers himself.[42] In May an American visitor to GC&CS reported that 'much the largest item in Irish Government traffic was to and from Vichy', although it is not clear whether this was a long-term pattern because it is impossible to determine how many decodes were made (as distinct from stored and circulated).[43]

Irish messages from the Vatican and Rome reflected the gradual collapse of Fascist authority. In January Dublin heard of rumours of an increased German military and security presence around Rome, and of growing Italian bitterness

---

[40] Note by Denniston for Turner, 2 Feb. 1943, TNA, HW36/5.
[41] Hearne (Ottawa) to Dublin, 2 Apr. 1943, TNA, HW12/287.
[42] Dublin to Vichy, 13 and 23 Sept. and 5 and 19 Oct., and de Lafourcade to Algiers, 18 Nov. 1943, TNA, HW12/292, 293 and 294.
[43] Denniston, *Thirty Secret Years*, 131.

towards Mussolini, as well as talk that Turkey might soon abandon neutrality in order to pre-empt Soviet expansion towards the Dardanelles. Despair and disunity were growing, encapsulated in one Italian's fatalistic observation that the country would have to 'drain the bitter cup of defeat' (Churchill saw this decode).[44] On 29 July MacWhite reported how Mussolini, after tendering his resignation, 'found that all his cars had disappeared' and had to leave Rome 'in a Red Cross ambulance'; the minister to the Vatican naively predicted that, if given sufficient weapons, the Italians 'will adhere to the Axis, and fight stubbornly'. In August a letter from MacWhite passed on an Italian warning that 'the Germans have a very expert decoding service who are working overtime'. This contact begged MacWhite for that reason never to quote him by name in a cable: 'Our code must be very well known to them by now'.[45] In the succeeding months the two ministers reported on the continuing political uncertainty, on the depredations of the Germans and the arrest of all Jews, 'including women and children', on German efforts to lure neutral missions into recognizing the Italian Fascist government at Salo, on fears that Rome would become a battleground, and on the Vatican's resentment and mistrust of the German occupation forces. By mid-November Ireland, Afghanistan, Switzerland, and Sweden were the only neutrals still represented in the chaotic Italian capital, from where MacWhite continued to report in quietly ironic tones: his cables also featured prominently in Magic summaries, which carried material supplied by GC&CS. Churchill made particular reference to one of MacWhite's messages on the Italian political situation in December, although he inaccurately attributed the decode to the Irish minister at the Vatican: 'this squares very much with what I have heard from other source'.[46]

The Allies also took increased interest in Irish reports from Berlin, where the new chargé d'affaires Con Cremin noted how 'the Mussolini affair has had a profound effect . . . and in private conversations the obvious parallel is being drawn'. Early in October Dublin asked if the German leadership was still 'capable . . . of keeping the people in the war, with so many key factors to discourage any hope of military victory?' Cremin was also instructed to take a tough line on German refusal to recognize an Italian ship recently reflagged as Irish, and to warn that unless Berlin changed its tune 'the whole question of our relations' might arise.[47] He sought Swedish advice on the question of issuing Irish visas to Jews in the Netherlands, a reflection of a marked increase in Irish interest in the fate of individual groups of Jews in the latter half of 1943. This probably arose from three causes: de Valera's close personal links with the Irish Jewish community, particularly through the Fianna

[44] Vatican and Rome to Dublin, 14 and 29 Jan., and Rome to Dublin, 11 Feb. 1943, TNA, HW12/284 and 285, and HW1/1370.

[45] Rome to Dublin, 29 July, and the Vatican to Dublin, 8 Aug. 1943, TNA, HW12/290 and 291; MacWhite letter to Dublin, 14 Aug. 1943, NAI, DFA P12/8. If MacWhite's letter went by diplomatic bag it was probably seen by the British.

[46] Rome to Dublin, 29 July and 4, 11 and 27 Oct, and 14 Nov. 1943, and the Vatican to Dublin, 6 Aug., 18 and 26 Oct. and 9 and 11 Nov. 1943, TNA, HW12/290, 291, 293, and 294. There was a misunderstanding, genuine or not, about German traffic to and from Dublin. GC&CS would send only the decodes: 'If the originals were sent over there would be real difficulties in production of duplicate copies'. Denniston to GC&CS representative, Washington, 4 Jan. 1944, TNA, HW53/17. C to ?, 3 Jan. 1944, quoting the prime minister, TNA, HW1/2314.

[47] Berlin to Dublin, 29 July, and Dublin to Berlin, 1 and 5 Oct. 1943, TNA, HW12/291 and 293.

Fáil deputy Bob Briscoe, who was very active in Jewish affairs internationally; the Allied declaration on the fate of European Jewry in December 1942; and subsequent Vatican prompting (this trend was also apparent in decodes of the traffic of other neutrals such as Spain, Portugal, and Argentina, while Turkey, Persia, and Bulgaria made some efforts to succour their Jewish nationals in German hands). The British were not very enthusiastic about such Irish efforts, whether because they might mitigate international indignation about neutrality, or because, as a cabinet committee concluded, Ireland could only feed such refugees with British help, 'which it would be undesirable to give'.[48] On 27 November Cremin sent word that the legation and all its records had been destroyed in an air raid, making his job even harder in the violent times to come.[49] A few weeks later he reported that 'we have had such devastation . . . it is doubtful whether any return to normal conditions can be expected for some time', yet the public attitude remained 'a mixture of fortitude and apathy. There is magnificent discipline'.[50] Civilian resilience under sustained aerial bombardment was not an exclusively British characteristic.

The year 1943 also produced one transcript of an intercepted Irish phone-call. Dulanty rang Walshe in November, mainly to discuss a speech in the Dáil the previous day by James Dillon, the maverick TD who had left Fine Gael over neutrality. Dillon lauded Britain and the United States, although he antagonized left-wing deputies by emphasizing his detestation of Russia. British newspapers had reported his remarks selectively, but not the fury with which they had been greeted. Dillon was a powerful, if theatrical, orator, but Walshe was distinctly unimpressed:

Of course, it is most extraordinary—now I haven't heard Dillon talk for quite a long while and I was aghast myself, at the egotism of the man . . .

He used to put two hands together on his chest, you see, and the 'I'm not ashamed of anything in my time', attitude 'Since I came into public life I have never swerved . . . from definite principles . . .'

London: I thought, Joe, that he had grown out of that . . .

Dublin: You known what he does John, he puts himself on the stage of the Dáil. He goes in for histrionics in a most incredible way. His gestures are just asinine . . .

London: . . . But Joe . . . couldn't there be some means of letting us have over here something, you know, that we could, I mean something—when the T[aoiseach] makes his rejoinder, couldn't we get something that we could give the P[ress] A[ssociation] . . . If you could Joe, let us have something.

Dublin: Sure, we'll try John.[51]

This is the only such transcript found, although hundreds must have been produced during the course of the war.[52] Some transcripts of Irish taps on diplomatic missions have also survived.

---

[48] Herzog, *Living History*, 12; Dublin to Berlin, and Berlin to Dublin, 1 and 18 Nov., and the Vatican to Dublin, 5 Dec. 1943, Dublin to Berlin, 5 Jan. and 28 May 1944, TNA, HW12/294, 295, 296, and 301; Wasserstein, *Britain and the Jews*, 155, and 165 quoting minutes of a meeting of 7 Jan. 1943. For contrasting recent views on the role of the Vatican during the war, in terms both of moral leadership and of succouring of the Jews, see Cornwell, *Hitler's Pope* and Burleigh, *Sacred Causes*.

[49] Irish minister, Berne, conveying message from Berlin, 27 Nov. 1943, TNA, HW12/294.

[50] Berlin to Dublin, 23 Dec. 1943, TNA, HW12/297.

[51] Transcript of Dulanty telephone conversation with Walshe, 12 Nov. 1943, TNA, DO121/87.

[52] Interview with Sir John Stephenson, 1989.

Table 5.1. *British decodes relating to Ireland, January–December 1943*

	French	Irish	Italian	Japanese	Others	Total
January	2	2	3	2		9
February		5	13	1	2	21
March	3	1	2	6		12
April	3	1	1	1	3	9
May	3		3			6
June	1		2	1	1	5
July		2	9	1		12
August		2	3	3	1	9
September	1	4	1	2		8
October		11	2	2	1	16
November	3	21				24
December	4	6	2	1		13
TOTALS	20	55	41	20	8	144

Ireland occasionally featured incidentally in non-Irish-related diplomatic traffic (see Table 5.1). In February 1943 the Spanish ambassador in London reported that Dulanty had conveyed to him Irish eagerness to respond to Vatican requests to succour 'non-Aryan' children believed to be refugees in Spain.[53] In October the Persian minister reported on talk of a possible British decision to remove Ireland from their list of recognized neutral states.[54] But it is safe to conclude that the rest of the neutral world was not much interested in Ireland one way or the other. The Allies were flexing their muscles to make neutrals collaborate across the world. Portugal ceded bases in the Azores, enabling the Allies to extend their sea and air coverage in the Atlantic, a concession which Germany complained about but could not deter: Berlin reserved the right to attack Allied forces, but the Portuguese ambassador responded courteously that if such attacks resulted in Portuguese casualties they would 'present a danger to the continuation of friendly relations'. G2 believed the Portuguese concession, partly motivated by Lisbon's concern to protect her colonial interests in Africa and Asia in the shakeout which would follow an Allied victory, would reopen the issue of the Irish ports.[55] Even Sweden, which had developed a remarkably successful Janus-like relationship with both sets of belligerents since 1939, found herself obliged to respond to increased pressure to reduce concessions to Germany, particularly in respect of trading in strategic materials and of the use by the Germans of the Swedish railway system for military purposes: in July Churchill saw a decode concerning the shipment of munitions through Sweden to Finland. On the other hand, in the same month the Foreign Office were pleased when Sweden refused to accept a successor to the Vichy minister in Stockholm.[56] If *force*

[53] Spanish ambassador, London, to Madrid, 12 and 25 Feb. 1943, TNA, HW12/285.

[54] Persian minister, London, to Tehran, 23 Oct. 1943, TNA, HW12/293.

[55] G2 note on the Azores, 14 Oct. 1943, NAI, DFA A8/1; Portuguese ambassador, Berlin, to Lisbon, quoted in Magic summary, 2 Nov. 1943, USNA, RG457, box 7.

[56] C to prime minister, 3 July, attaching Luftwaffe decode of 2 July 1943, TNA, HW1/1876; Carlgren, *Swedish Foreign Policy*, 142–68; Foreign Office to British representative, Algiers, 17 July 1944, TNA, FO660/117.

majeure was applied to seize bases or to bring Ireland into the war, there would be no great international outcry from any states outside Axis control.

Berardis's cables to Rome initially reflected a certain determination to keep the flag flying despite the dismal progress of Italy's war. On 3 January he wrote that in 1942 he had sent 177 cipher cables and had received 104, a figure which GC&CS approvingly noted tallied with their records. He complained about the supply of news from Rome and said he had had to produce a newsletter at his 'personal expense' (this had generated Irish complaints about its violent and anti-Semitic language). On political affairs, he reported disillusionment in Britain about progress in North Africa, and added an optimistic gloss: 'time is . . . not on the side of the Allies'.[57] The Allies' meeting at Casablanca had not produced clear agreements on strategy, although it was rumoured that Britain would launch an attack on Norway to coincide with further operations in North Africa (for which, it was believed, many British and American troops had just been moved from Northern Ireland).[58] Only a couple of his March messages have been traced, one on food shortages and fears of air raids in Britain, the other giving Irish press opinions on Allied strategy in Tunisia.[59]

As defeat for Italy loomed, Berardis's communications took on a somewhat surreal tone. In April he solemnly assured the Ministry of Popular Culture that their broadcasts to Ireland could usually be heard very well: 'the male and female announcers . . . are generally good. The female voices are more distinct . . . in broadcasts to England it is preferable . . . not to have announcers with American accents'.[60] In June he relayed Walshe's prediction that the Allies would not dare to attack the Italian mainland, 'having already had much experience of the tenacious pugnacity of the Italians', and passed on encouraging rumours of American cowardice and incompetence in the Tunisian campaign. As the invasion of Sicily unfolded, he found solace in press comments on the hazards posed by the Straits of Messina, while news of the bombing of Rome, and the accompanying Irish protests—on 19 March de Valera appealed to the belligerents to spare the city—brought him to fever pitch: de Valera told him the bombing represented 'the blackest page of history', and said he would press for international intercession. On 28 July Berardis abruptly changed sides, reporting that the entire Italian community 'are united in their devotion and faithfulness' to King Victor Emmanuel, who had assumed national leadership following Mussolini's departure from Rome, and stated that de Valera had told him that the Allies 'will be responsible before humanity for the destruction of the [eternal?] city . . . the English will go down in history . . . for the barbarous way in which they have waged this war', a conclusion which Churchill marked in red ink.[61]

[57] Berardis to Rome, 8 and 27 Jan. 1943, TNA, HW12/284 and 285.

[58] Ibid., 29 Jan. 1943, TNA, HW12/285; there is Irish material on Berardis in UCDA, MacWhite papers, P194/548 and 9.

[59] Ibid., 5 and 10 Mar. 1943, TNA, HW12/286.

[60] Rome to Berardis, and reply, 27 Feb. and 20 Apr. 1943, TNA, HW12/288.

[61] Keogh, *Ireland and the Vatican*, 178–9; Berardis to Rome, 26 and 30 June, and 15, 20, and 24 July, and 28 July 1943, TNA, HW12/289 and 290, and HW1/1876. Although the stated targets were the Roman railway marshalling yards, the American bombing on 19 July caused about 1,500 deaths as well as considerable destruction. Conway, 'Myron C. Taylor's Mission to the Vatican', 96.

Thereafter Berardis had little to say until December, when he complained of German broadcasts claiming that the Italian community was still pro-fascist. There was in fact only 'a small group . . . tied up with the German espionage organization . . . individuals whom . . . I have asked to have repatriated'. SIS estimated that there were about 165 Italians in Ireland, of whom perhaps thirty were fascists. For his part, Hempel told External Affairs that he found frequent visits by Italian fascists 'rather embarrassing . . . he would prefer to have nothing to do with them'. Walshe thought this attitude 'very wise', although he had cause to doubt Hempel's sincerity since he had to bring up the question again two months later. Hempel in fact reported on these Italian contacts in very positive terms to Berlin.[62] Berardis attributed the misleading German claims about continued fascist activity to Hempel, 'with whom I have never been in effective cooperation. He is engaged here in all kinds of spying'.[63] This was a bit rich coming from someone who had sent whatever war information he could collect while Italy was still in the fight, and who according to Hempel had 'at the beginning of the war . . . made "the most fantastic proposals" . . . about the use' which could be made of the Italian and German communities in Ireland. SIS reported that Berardis was much disliked by his staff, who viewed this one-time 'ardent Fascist's' efforts to ingratiate himself with his new masters with a combination of amusement and contempt.[64] The decodes reinforce the impression of a shameless turncoat. The same was true of his Kabul colleague Quaroni, who denounced the German legation and sought to minimize his involvement in intrigues against British interests, despite the fact that decodes showed him to have been heavily involved in subversive operations against India and the Soviet Union well before the Germans.[65]

Decodes disclosed a significant shift in the interests and activities of the two-man Japanese consulate in the course of 1943, despite inherent difficulties in securing war information. Traffic to and from Tokyo was, according to Denniston of GC&CS, in a 'low-grade' code 'which we rarely take the trouble to read' as it 'appears to have no intelligence value'.[66] In January Beppu reported Irish representations about one John MacDermott, a Shanghai municipal official held on suspicion of espionage. Surprisingly, these bore fruit: early in March he was 'immediately taken back to his residence'.[67] Tokyo reminded Beppu that, since the closure of the London embassy, 'we have been relying on . . . your consulate . . . for an estimate of the general situation'. He was to report in detail on British affairs under a number of

[62] Berardis to Italian ambassador, Madrid, 18 Dec. 1943, TNA, HW12/296; 'Summary of most secret information from Dublin', 22 Mar.–3 April 1943, TNA, DO121/87; Walshe to de Valera, 6 Nov. 1943 and 25 Mar. 1944, NAI, DFA A2 and A55 1; Hempel to Berlin, undated, quoted in 'Summary of most secret information from Dublin, 19 Sept.–2 Oct. 1943,TNA, DO121/87.

[63] Berardis to Italian ambassador, Madrid, 24 Dec. 1943, TNA, HW12/295.

[64] Walshe to de Valera, 25 Mar. 1944, NAI, DFA A55 1, reporting Hempel; QRS report, 1 Sept. 1943, TNA, DO121/85.

[65] Axis intrigues in Afghanistan were analysed in some detail in 1943 in L/PS/12/1798. See also the record of Quaroni's discussions with Connor-Green of SOE in November and December 1943. These took a long time because of his 'uncontrollable garrulity'. British minister, Kabul, to India Office, 3 Dec. 1943, IOR, L/PS/12/1805.

[66] Denniston to Corderman (US War Dept.), 5 Nov. 1943, TNA, HW53/16.

[67] Beppu to Tokyo, and replies, 9 and 30 Jan. and 26 Mar. 1943, TNA, HW12/286.

headings.[68] Beppu replied that he would do what he could, adding a cautionary note: 'One naturally supposes that all telegrams are read in the British "Black Chamber" '.[69] In June he was told that, while the Lisbon mission could provide a good survey of the British press, 'there are gaps in authentic information about domestic conditions in England'; he should provide 'collated reports on currents of public opinion etc and tendencies'. He should also inform Tokyo 'if there are any activities of Irishmen towards England that would serve for propaganda purposes'. Tokyo also enquired whether Beppu could purchase copies of *Hansard* and forward them to Lisbon.[70]

This pressure for material on Britain had some results: the consulate began to develop links with republican elements, as is reflected in an unusual message from Beppu of 1 July which stated that 'a member of my staff' had heard from a Northern IRA man in Dublin at the end of May that an Anglo-American assault on Dieppe was planned for the end of July: 'As the IRA have a scheme for creating disturbances in Northern Ireland in rear of British Army after the latter becomes involved in Europe', he believed that the Dieppe information was offered 'in good faith'. In order to protect his source Beppu did not say anything to 'the Legations of our Allies'.[71] These IRA links may have been facilitated by an employee of the consulate, Sheila McInerney, who had been interned for republican activities in 1940. G2 also believed that Beppu's colleague Ichihashi had links with a group of Basque exiles, though the purpose of this never became clear. Beppu was reported by SIS to have been rebuffed in his own efforts to ingratiate himself with the press through 'recent visits to the Pearl Bar, the haunt of Irish journalists', an indication of efforts to be more active in gathering information.[72] In September Guy Liddell told colleagues, in the course of a long debate on when, after the defeat of Germany, it would be appropriate to lift restrictions on travel from Ireland, that 'we had good reason to think that the Japs were attempting to build up their espionage organization' in Ireland and 'would probably make use of the remnants of any German organization'. Consequently the existing travel control system should remain in force until Japan too was defeated.[73]

When Japanese-controlled Burma declared its independence on 1 August, Beppu made the reasonable suggestion to Tokyo that the new Ba Maw regime in Rangoon should announce itself to Ireland by telegraphing Irish missions in Europe asking them to inform Dublin, rather than relying on Japanese diplomatic channels which might lend colour to British charges that the new government was merely a puppet regime. He also sought additional staff, asking that Tokyo should consider sending these in a 'special aeroplane', although he did not think that the Irish would allow one to land, as 'results would increase a hundred-fold' if reporting was done by people with 'an intimate knowledge of the new situation in Japan and East Asia'.

[68] Tokyo to Beppu, 19 Feb. 1943, TNA, HW12/285.
[69] Beppu to Tokyo, 21 Jan. 1943 , TNA, HW12/286.
[70] Tokyo to Beppu, 10 June, and to Lisbon, 26 July 1943, TNA, HW12/289 and 291.
[71] Beppu to Tokyo, 1 July 1943, TNA, HW12/290.
[72] QRS report, 1 Sept. 1943, TNA, DO121/85.
[73] Liddell diary, 7 Sept. 1943, TNA, KV4/192; G2 to External Affairs, 2 June 1943, NAI, DFA A8/1.

Tokyo did not think this feasible, and advised: 'take good care of your health and do your best to carry on'.[74] He did what he could, reporting speculation about an imminent Second Front by Irishmen home on Christmas leave, which he termed 'mere gossip'.[75]

The consulate continued to nurture links with republicans, and with Indian nationalists based in Ireland. In November Beppu reported on the establishment of a 'National Anti-Partition Movement', which claimed to have nearly 3,000 members in both parts of Ireland, and on a meeting of the 'Green Front' held to commemorate the execution for mutiny in India in 1920 of Private James Daly of the Connaught Rangers. The meeting passed a resolution saluting the Indian Provisional Government of Subhas Chandra Bose, newly established under Japanese patronage in Singapore, drawing parallels between the Irish and Indian freedom struggles, and stating that the fight would go on 'until the British and American invaders had been chased out of the whole of Ireland'.[76] On 17 November Beppu gave External Affairs the text of a message from Bose, to which Walshe sent a brief and entirely non-committal acknowledgement of receipt. Bose later broadcast that this minimal exchange constituted Irish recognition of his government, a claim still widely accepted despite de Valera's clear statement in the Dáil setting out the reasons why recognition was impossible (Afghanistan used much the same arguments for refusing to recognize the new Burmese government).[77] On 8 December Beppu relayed a further message from Bose to de Valera (whom Bose had met before the war): he thanked Ireland for her 'tremendous help' to 'the oppressed peoples of India' (Ireland had recently donated £200,000 towards famine relief in Bengal, a catastrophe in which over 3 million people died, and one exacerbated by security restrictions on farming and fishing in coastal areas and by the British cabinet's initial callous suspicion that pleas for assistance were 'a bluff on India's part': when the India secretary Amery proposed a broadcast outlining the extent of Britain's response, Churchill objected 'that to do so is making too much of the famine and sounding apologetic').[78] During the Red Fort trials in 1945–6 of Indian soldiers who had joined Bose's Indian National Army to fight alongside the Japanese for Indian independence, some defendants sought copies of any correspondence between Bose and the Irish government. There was none, other than Walshe's brief acknowledgement of Beppu's letters.[79]

---

[74] Beppu to Tokyo, 8 and 24 Aug., and Tokyo to Beppu, 8 Oct. 1943, TNA, HW12/291, 292, and 293.

[75] Ibid., 29 Dec. 1943, TNA, HW12/296.

[76] Ibid., 19 Nov. 1943, TNA, HW12/295. The Green Front appears to have been a *nom de guerre* of the IRA and its supporters for the purposes of public meetings.

[77] Copies of Tokyo to Dublin attaching message from Bose, 17 Nov., and of Walshe to Beppu, 24 Nov., and BBC digest of Bose broadcast of 2 Dec. 1943, TNA, DO35/2059; Gordon, *Brothers Against the Raj*, 502; Das, *Subhas*, 571; *Dáil Debates*, 16 Feb. 1944, vol. 92, accessed via http://www.oireachtas-debates.gov.ie. I am grateful to Dr Kate O'Malley for this reference. German legation, Kabul, to Berlin, 4 Aug. 1943, TNA, HW12/291.

[78] Tokyo to Beppu, 8 Dec. 1943, TNA, HW12/296. There were obvious parallels with the Great Famine of 1845–7. Amery diary, 12 Jan., 4 Aug., 22 Sept. and 12 Oct. 1943, CCCA, AMEL7/37. Bayly and Harper, *Forgotten Armies*, 282–91; O'Malley, 'Ireland, India and Empire', 198–203.

[79] Bose, *The Lost Hero*, 730–5; Maffey to London, 26 Nov. 1945, enclosing copies of Beppu to Walshe, and reply, 17 and 24 Nov. 1943, TNA, DO35/2059.

Further decodes indicated limited contact with republicans and people who passed on news from Northern Ireland.[80] There were also very occasional references to Irish affairs in other Japanese traffic. From Berlin, the Japanese ambassador reported a far-fetched German plan to initiate a propaganda campaign directed at Australia. As well as emphasizing that British incompetence had seen thousands of Australians killed or captured far from home, and stressing the perils inherent in a Soviet victory, it suggested that as 'two thirds of the people of Australia are of Irish origin we shall encourage them' to take 'the same neutral stand as Eire'. In December Tokyo ruminated on the 'delicate' issues surrounding the wishes of the new Japanese-backed Laurel government in the Philippines to replace the serving Catholic archbishop, an Irishman thought insufficiently cooperative in their plans to utilize Catholicism to 'obtain a hold on popular sentiment'. Replacement by a Philippino would help Catholics somewhat 'oppressed' by European control of their church.[81]

Beppu's mission was the only factual basis for the rumour which persisted in the United States that Ireland housed a substantial and militant Japanese community. A Chinese military party which passed through Foynes in transit to Britain in 1943 was initially 'suspicious of everyone', because they had been told in the United States that Ireland was awash with Japanese.[82]

The French minister de Lafourcade submitted a few observations on the forth-coming election early in 1943, but his most significant communication was not to Vichy but to Algiers: on 27 February he wrote that his British and American colleagues were in agreement that he should not break with Vichy for the moment lest this create a vacancy which might be filled by Albertas, who with Lachèvre continued to express 'les sentiments collaborationistes'. If Vichy sacked him, he understood that the Irish would regard him him and colleagues as representing the Free French administration in Algiers.[83] On occasion he reported in almost identical terms to Vichy and to Algiers, whereas Albertas sent a review of British debates on maritime strategy only to Vichy.[84] In April de Lafourcade complained to Vichy that the attaché had sent him 'plusieurs lettres pleines d'insolence et d'imputations fausse et ridicules', but by June he was reporting solely to Algiers, assuring them that the Irish had always been very pro-French: although they admired the Free French and disliked Vichy's anti-Semitism, Pétain was still respected as 'the hero of Verdun'.[85] De Lafourcade's manoeuvres were followed with some interest not only in London but in Washington, where it was also noted in October that Hempel had advised Berlin to tell Vichy to replace the minister with Albertas, 'the only one who remains faithful to the French policy of collaborating with Germany', rather than with the legation secretary Cauvet-Duhamel, whom he rightly depicted as a secret adherent

[80] O'Halpin, *Defending Ireland*, 240.

[81] Japanese ambassador, Berlin, to Tokyo, 6 Sept., and Tokyo to Manila, 29 Dec. 1943, TNA, HW12/292 and 296.

[82] Monthly report for November 1943 by Hewett, G2, Foynes, NAI, DFA A8/1.

[83] De Lafourcade to Vichy, 22 and 25 Jan., and 21 Feb. 1943, TNA, HW12/284 and 286.

[84] De Lafourcade to Vichy and to Algiers, 23 and 24 Apr., and Albertas to Vichy, 24 Apr. 1943, TNA, HW12/287. Albertas was later banned from travelling to North Africa. Algiers to London, 9 Nov. 1943, TNA, HW12/294.

[85] De Lafourcade to Vichy, 10 Apr. and to Algiers, 12 June 1943, TNA, HW12/288 and 289.

of Algiers. The warning fell on deaf ears: Cauvet-Duhamel was appointed, only to declare for Algiers within days.[86] Decodes of Irish traffic confirmed External Affairs' dread of having to choose between rival French representatives, and a warning was sent to Vichy that if de Lafourcade was dismissed Ireland would not recognize a replacement—a position which may have been influenced by a G2 report that Albertas would be Vichy's choice.[87]

THE GERMAN LEGATION RADIO

Pandora now enabled London and Washington to determine both Berlin's instructions to Hempel, and what he was actually up to in Ireland. As already seen, analysis of previously unreadable traffic was in some respects encouraging: Hempel had generally steered clear of active espionage and had been embarrassed by the capture of German agents in 1940–1. Nevertheless, he clearly had, however reluctantly, given some of them limited support. The decodes also disclosed his intrigues with O'Duffy and MacNeill (the latter not identified by name), and his somewhat faulty interpretation of the Hayes confession, but that material was rather old hat and on balance did not discredit the Irish government, since Hempel's contacts were plainly unofficial. As SIS concluded in April, the retrospective evidence of Pandora bore out the view that de Valera had played straight with Britain in 1940 and 1941.

The acquisition of Pandora had two consequences: it meant that current communications between Dublin and Berlin could be read, subject to occasional technical limitations, particularly with respect to radio transmissions; and it enabled the study of hitherto unreadable messages for the years 1939–42, although as already noted, not all such traffic had been stored. For whatever reason, however, copies of German traffic to and from Ireland after January 1943 almost never appear in GC&CS's master record of diplomatic decodes in the National Archives series HW12. This presumably reflects a policy decision at the time. It appears that copies of many if not all Irish-related decodes, including German messages, were grouped together by SIS and numbered with an IR prefix by date of decoding, and from this it may be inferred that the closed SIS archives may hold a full run of decodes of German traffic relating to Ireland in association with all other Irish-related diplomatic decodes.[88] But individual German messages do turn up in other British series, and many more are summarized or referred to in SIS reports available in Dominions Office records and in the Magic summaries. But the latter were prepared as précis for American policy-makers, and unlike the comparable British series do not provide the full text of every decode.

Taking the Magic summaries and two British sources together—Dominions Office files, and the daily selections of decodes provided for the prime minister—about

[86] Precis of Hempel to Berlin, undated, in Magic summary, 28 Nov. 1943, USNA, RG457, box 8.

[87] Precis of Dublin to Vichy, 13 and 23 Sept. 1943, in Magic summary, 29 Nov. 1943, USNA, RG457, box 7; Dublin to Vichy, 13 and 23 Sept. 1943, TNA, HW12/292; G2 report on the French legation, 25 Oct. 1943, NAI, DFA P75.

[88] IR 0001 is Hempel to Berlin, 29 Oct. 1941, TNA, DO121/86. I am grateful to Gill Bennett, formerly of the Foreign Office Historical Section, who attempted without success to trace this IR series.

sixty German messages to and from Ireland in 1943 can be identified. This figure is clearly only a fraction of the total volume of traffic. The material is nevertheless significant: included in it are plenty of indications, as the year went on and Germany's overall position deteriorated, that Hempel was torn between his core task of maintaining diplomatic relations, and Berlin's growing demands for war information even if its collection might compromise the legation. Thus a decode of 29 January disclosed further details of the plan to use an interned German airman to operate the radio in a crisis, since his transmission style would be unknown to Irish and British interceptors.[89] Hempel also reported steady pressure from the Irish about his radio.

In June Hempel was instructed to analyse the Irish press for material which could be used in planned 'open or disguised' propaganda broadcasts aimed at Irish-America. Berlin wanted 'convincing new themes over and above the well-known anti-Communist and anti-Jewish attitude of the Irish'.[90] In October he reported fatalistically on the likely outcome of his representations to the Irish about their lax treatment of crashed Allied aircraft and aircrew, and in the same month he told Berlin that he had thought it wisest not to ask the Irish to recognize Mussolini's new Salo government.[91] His message of 16 October, numbered 'IR 5524' by SIS, which recounted a discussion with Walshe about the implications for Portugal's neutrality of her decision to allow the Allies to use the Azores, was drawn to Churchill's attention by C: 'although I do not usually send you German messages from Dublin . . . the attached . . . is worth your notice, as it gives a plain statement of Irish policy'.[92] German irritation at the purchase by the Irish of two Italian ships marooned in Ireland since 1940 was also tempered by a disinclination to antagonize Dublin.[93] In November Berlin directed Hempel to collect the 'fullest possible reports on everything you can learn concerning England', and authorized him to 'spend additional funds to expand your news-gathering machinery and bring about a substantial expansion in your reporting'. A further message stated that 'there is particular interest here in all reports concerning English war preparations of every sort', on Anglo-American air losses, on 'internal conditions (with particular reference to the attitude of Fascist circles) . . . and finally Great Britain's attitude towards Russia'.[94] These instructions were decoded by GC&CS almost immediately, and they added impetus to the British drive to force the issue of the legation radio.

By April it was clear from Pandora that, notwithstanding the Irish warnings and Hempel's own arguments of the previous autumn against using the radio,

[89] Hempel to Berlin, 29 Jan., cited in MI5 analysis of German legation traffic, undated, with Vivian to Stephenson, 14 Mar. 1943, TNA, DO121/84.
[90] Berlin to Hempel, 17 June 1943, quoted in Magic summary, 30 June 1943, USNA, RG457, box 5.
[91] Magic Summary, 21 Oct. 1943, USNA, RG457, box 7.
[92] C to Churchill, 21 Oct., with Hempel to Berlin, 16 Oct. 1943, TNA, HW1/2138. Decodes in the IR series are not organized chronologically: e.g. those of 2 and 9 Apr. 1943 are numbered respectively 5062 and 0055. TNA, DO121/84.
[93] Magic summaries, 22 and 29 Oct. 1943, USNA, RG457, box 7.
[94] Ibid., 7 and 29 Dec. 1943, quoting Berlin to Dublin, 29 Nov. and 17 Dec. 1943, USNA, RG457, box 8.

the legation was following Berlin's orders to make serious preparations to resume transmissions should an urgent need arise: decodes of December 1942 traffic showed that Hempel was contemplating arrangements for a hiding place for the radio somewhere in Dublin, and he also sought technical advice on ways of disguising future transmissions.[95] Decodes of some of the backlog of German messages from 1939 onwards also helped London to form a clearer view of the radio issue, of Hempel's attitude towards intelligence gathering, and of his contacts with the IRA and with a coterie of former Blueshirts and army officers who saw General O'Duffy as a potential saviour of Ireland.[96] On 12 April the question was reviewed in the Dominions Office. It was decided to summons Maffey from Dublin, and to draft a report for submission to the prime minister suggesting that a move might now be made to persuade the Irish to impound all diplomatic radios (this appears to have been Jane Archer's idea). C noted that 'our own [radio in Dublin] would also have to be surrendered, but this does not now matter'.[97]

On 29 April, after C agreed that he 'should be put in the picture but he alone should have the facts', Maffey was briefed on Pandora.[98] This unusual privilege for a British representative serving abroad enabled him to see the problem for the first time in the round; it also somewhat complicated his relations with Gray, who was not similarly informed. Even Washington was not fully informed on Dublin–Berlin traffic: in December an American official sent an assurance to Denniston that 'he perfectly understands your not wishing to pass certain traffic for reasons of policy. He knows that you have a restricted series and does not wish to question it'. There would be 'no hard feelings . . . by your simply regretting' inability to send certain material. To this Denniston replied, honestly or otherwise, that his reasons were technical, not political.[99]

The Dominions Office meeting elicited some disagreement between Maffey, whose strategic aim was to use the radio issue as a lever to force the closure of the German legation, and MI5, who argued that the two questions should be kept separate and that the radio should be tackled first. Arising from the meeting, the dominions secretary Clement Attlee, also deputy prime minister and Labour party leader, sent a lengthy memorandum to Churchill on the legation radio question. Despite his lack of ministerial experience before 1940, Attlee already had a high reputation in Whitehall as an effective minister and chairman, whereas Churchill's genius lay elsewhere. Quite apart from their conflicting ideologies, the two men could scarcely have been more different in personality: where Churchill was emotional and impetuous, Attlee was deliberate and measured. Their experience of the first world war had been rather different: Churchill had been one of the architects of the Dardanelles disaster, whereas Attlee had fought in it (he served in

---

[95] Hempel to Berlin, 7 Dec. 1942, decoded 9 Apr. 1943, TNA, DO121/84.

[96] Ibid., 29 Jan., and 'Summary of German Cable and Wireless messages between Dublin and Berlin', 17 Apr. 1943, TNA, DO121/84.

[97] *Liddell History*, 77; C to Sir Alexander Cadogan, permanent under-secretary of the Foreign Office, 20 Apr. 1943, TNA, DO121/84.

[98] Vivian to Stephenson, 13 Apr. 1943, TNA, DO121/84; *Liddell History*, 77.

[99] O'Connor (British liaison officer with American codebreaking organization) to Denniston, 21 Dec. 1943, and Denniston to O'Connor, 4 Jan. 1944, TNA, HW53/16 and 17.

the same regiment as the DMI, General Davidson, whom he approvingly termed 'a dour Scot').[100]

Drawing on Pandora, Attlee's memorandum pointed out that the radio had transmitted only once since 1941—when the *Scharnhorst* and *Gneisenau* slipped through the Channel—but noted that Berlin had asked Hempel to broadcast in October 1942 during the build-up to *Torch*, although after 'strong representations' by the Irish he had refrained from doing so. Since that time, Berlin had sent advice on technical means of disguising transmissions should these become necessary 'on any matter of "vital importance"'. The obvious solution would be to insist that the Irish confiscate the set, but 'this course is open to certain objections'. First,

there is a risk that if action . . . is taken now when the transmitter has been silent for 18 months, it might suggest to the Germans that we have succeeded in reading their cable messages about the wireless transmitter. Clearly we must not risk disclosing that we have this valuable source of information . . . which covers not only Dublin but also German Legations elsewhere in the world.

(b) To make this demand now might make it more difficult later to press a further demand for the removal of the German Legation altogether. It would surely be much better . . . to get rid of the German Legation entirely if and when we can. If the Germans were to use the transmitter again this might afford a sufficient lever for the purpose.

It was also possible, if the set was surrendered, that 'they or the IRA might succeed in setting up another transmitter'. Furthermore, pressure now would undoubtedly be regarded as a signal that major operations were imminent. In addition,

the actual information which the German Minister has so far been able to collect and telegraph does not suggest that hitherto he has been able to obtain any information seriously likely to hamper or injure our operations. The close watch which the Irish Security authorities keep on his movements and contacts, in co-operation with our Security authorities, can go some way to prevent his having much greater success in the future.

The risk of the Germans 'being able to . . . send over in time of emergency, e.g. at the beginning of active operations from this country, some piece of vital information' not obtainable by other means, had to be weighed against 'the risk of compromising our knowledge of the German cipher and the value' of that source: 'I consider that our interests would be better served by taking this risk'.[101]

This characteristically measured assessment drew a pettish response:

your minute . . . referring as it does to the most secret sources, ought not to have come to me other than in a locked box.

I think we must endure this abominable state of things for the present. The entry of the United States into the war has changed the picture, and it may be possible to take stronger

[100] Information from Sir John Winnifrith, Sir Thomas Padmore, and Sir Edward Playfair, 1979 and 1981. In addition to his own observations, Winnifrith knew of Churchill's cabinet style through Sir Edward Bridges.xs Examples of Churchill's indiscipline in cabinet and committee work are too numerous to cite. In the 1960s Bridges encouraged the publication of Wheeler Bennett, *Action This Day*, a collection of sanitized vignettes which are belied by contemporary evidence in sources such as the Alanbrooke and Colville diaries. On Davidson, see Dalton diaries, 13 Dec. 1940 and 25 Mar. 1941, BLPES, Dalton 1/23 and 24.
[101] Attlee to Churchill, 3 May 1943, TNA, DO121/84; *Liddell History*, 78.

action against Southern Ireland and to force them to dismiss the enemy representatives they harbour. Their conduct in this war will never be forgiven by the British nation unless it is amended before the end. This in itself would be a great disaster. It is our duty to try to save these people from themselves. Any proposals that you may make to terminate the enemy representation in Dublin will be immediately considered by me. We ought not to shirk the difficulties unduly for the sake of a quiet life.

Churchill then inexplicably switched to another hobby horse quite unconnected with the radio issue:

Much of the above also applies to the fact that there is no conscription in Northern Ireland. I think it likely that Sir Basil Brooke's Government will submit fresh proposals. The situation is vastly different than it was before America came into the war and when we last considered the matter. This might be quite a good line on which to bring things to a head with de Valera, and the Cabinet will have in due course to decide upon the matter . . . There seems to be a very strong case in favour of doing what is right and just and facing the usual caterwaul from the disloyal Irish elements in various parts of the Dominions. I shall take advantage of my visit to Washington to discuss the matter again with the President. I am quite sure that opinion in the House of Commons would be overwhelmingly favourable.[102]

(Roosevelt had recently assured Churchill that 'I frankly doubt whether it would create much of an issue in this country' if conscription were to be introduced in Northern Ireland.)[103]

There the matter rested for some months. In August Churchill discussed Ireland with Mackenzie King, telling the Canadian leader that Roosevelt planned to send a letter to de Valera, 'in which he had recited all that America had done to help Ireland through the years. He was asking de Valera . . . to now assist the Allies'. Mackenzie King noted approvingly that Roosevelt would then publish the letter, vindicating an approach which 'I made a year ago'. This proposal was greeted with alarm in London, where Leo Amery noted that the cabinet were 'unanimously against it', as was Maffey in Dublin, 'for the very obvious reason that de Valera would raise his old grievance over "partition" and in a manner that would both damage Anglo-American relations and . . . also defeat the President's main object . . . to secure the Irish vote for next year's election'. Churchill, still in the United States, 'reacted violently in a long telegram'. On his return he 'reopened the subject . . . to the surprise of all of us by announcing not only that he wanted the message sent, but that he proposed now, during the war, to solve the Irish problem'. Attlee, Cranborne, and other ministers spoke strongly against this, and Churchill had to give ground:

Winston, with not too good a grace, postponed the matter for another discussion. But I am afraid that unless he draws in his horns over this we shall be in for trouble both in Ireland and internally in the Cabinet. Ulster will bitterly resent any idea of trying to persuade her to come in under de Valera even if the latter should at the last moment lend a base or two to America. I have always been afraid that at some point Winston might lose his balance and it may be that this is the one.[104]

---

[102] Churchill to Attlee, 5 May 1943, TNA, DO121/84.
[103] Roosevelt to Churchill, 19 Apr. 1943, in Kimball (ed.), *Churchill and Roosevelt*, ii. 192.
[104] Mackenzie King diary, 15 Aug. 1943; Amery diary, 22 Sept. 1943, CCCA, AMEL7/37.

Pandora continued to yield useful material on Berlin–Dublin exchanges, and Jane Archer's continuing research into pre-1943 traffic also cast a good deal of fresh light on Hempel's reportage and on Berlin's thinking. In November Guy Liddell was gratified to learn that 'a very good anonymous letter' concocted by Tómas Harris of MI5 'posted in Eire to the German Minister' and containing 'some quite good information . . . has been duly passed on to Berlin'. MI5 'intend to use this channel for deception'.[105] Less welcome was news which had reached him in August: 'an informant of OSS in Berne has picked up 3 messages from Dublin to the Germans relating to GOERTZ'. This generated a considerable problem: having secured these, OSS could scarcely refuse more such offerings, lest an apparent lack of interest indicate that the Allies already had access to such material through other means. That increased the risk of discovery and potentially might prompt the Germans in turn to change their diplomatic cipher. In the event, the Berne source—which came to OSS only because a British legation official had refused approaches from a disaffected German—continued to provide material until the end of the war, and the Germans appear never to have detected the breach of security.[106]

The Irish dilemma with which MI5 were faced—that to force the closure of Axis legations would be to cut off Britain's ability to study and to police their intrigues—was not dissimilar to the problems arising from the Axis presence in Afghanistan. There the Allies—in this case the British and the Soviets—had to deal with greater threats. As with Dublin, the British could read Italian but not German traffic to and from Kabul until 1943, and it was perfectly clear that both Axis powers were extensively engaged in clandestine activities relating both to the north-west frontier and to the southern Soviet Union, and to an extent also to eastern Persia. In the autumn of 1942 the British and the Soviets jointly presented a very strongly worded démarche to the Afghan government, following the discovery of a German-supported plot to fan up trouble amongst the tribes along Afghanistan's border with the Soviet Union: this Buchanesque plan was to culminate in a drive by 10,000 horsemen into Uzbekistan. Discovery of the scheme left the German legation in a 'peculiarly delicate' situation which might have led to its closure.[107] When the plot was uncovered, according to the Italian minister in Kabul (who claimed to have warned his German colleague that the scheme was 'not only dangerous but futile'), the Afghans were 'furious', but 'our greatest ally in this matter was Sir Francis Wylie [the British minister]. The terms and method of the Joint Demarche with the Soviets so angered the Afghan Government as almost to neutralize their fury against the Germans . . . In this affair you made a great mistake in not taking into account the touchiness of the Afghans about their independence'.[108] Yet the bullying may have unwittingly served another purpose: although the Afghans insisted on a drastic reduction in the staffs of the German and Italian legations in the course of 1943, they

[105] Liddell diary, 29 Nov. 1943, TNA, KV4/192.

[106] Ibid., 27 Aug. 1943, TNA, KV4/192; Grosse, *Gentleman Spy*, 184–92.

[107] Vickery (IPI) to Silver (India Office), 16 Nov. 1943, (IOR), L/PS/12/1805. Buchan, *Greenmantle* (Penguin edn.), 13–15, 143–5.

[108] British minister, Kabul, to Foreign Office and to Government of India, 2 Oct. 1943, enclosing notes of Signor Quaroni's statements to himself and to W. R. Connor-Green, the SOE representative in Kabul. (IOR), L/PS/12/1805.

refused to shut them down. As matters developed, this suited the British—because from January 1943 Pandora included Kabul–Berlin traffic—and the British and the Soviets jointly, because from November 1942 they shared a key double agent, Bhaghat Ram Talwar, against the Japanese-supported Indian separatist movement of Subhas Chandra Bose. Baghat Ram was the Germans' star agent in India, and he was controlled from the Kabul legation and relied on them for his communications with Bose (although from September 1943 he also had a direct radio link from Delhi to Berlin, which he operated under the co-supervision of an Irish officer, William Magan). His German cover name was 'RK', while the British assigned him the Double Cross cover name *Silver*.[109] If the German legation had been closed, it would have cut off a vital channel through which the British and Soviets were able both to penetrate and manipulate Bose's underground organization in India, and to pass strategic disinformation to the Germans and Japanese.

Axis activities in Ireland were on a far less ambitious scale than in Afghanistan, but they remained of enormous concern. On 25 October Guy Liddell dined with Liam Archer, now assistant chief of staff, who was 'in very good form. He has come over visiting Air Force training centres etc.' It seems likely that they discussed security issues.[110] As preparations for *Overlord* intensified, the calculations surrounding the legation radio changed. On 29 October Cecil Liddell sent the Dominions Office a document arguing that it was now essential to secure the removal of the radio: 'We feel strongly that this is a risk which we must take every possible step to eliminate'. Pandora showed that Hempel was responding to pressure from Berlin to secure as much information as possible, particularly from the many Irish people, both civilians and servicemen, visiting from the United Kingdom. He then had about £3,500 in his 'special secret service account', and was unaware that a further £1,500 transferred from Berne to a fictitious 'William Green' account in Dublin had been blocked. There was always a danger that the legation might uncover some vital secret.[111] Pandora also showed that as early as September 1941, after the occupation of Persia, Berlin had advised Hempel on the terms of the Anglo-Soviet démarche to the Tehran government to withdraw code facilities from the Axis and Vichy missions there.[112] Similar demands had been made of the Iraqis and Egyptians in 1941.[113]

Maffey attended a meeting in the Dominions Office to discuss the radio in the light of an overall review of security surrounding *Overlord*. An interception specialist

---

[109] Magan, *Middle Eastern Approaches*, 18–19. Bhagat Ram Talwar was a committed communist. His story is extraordinarily complex. He accompanied Subhas Bose on his escape to Kabul in 1941, and was recruited by the Germans. From November 1942, on Soviet orders, he also worked for the British, ensuring that they indirectly controlled Bose's underground organization in India. He omitted this salient detail from his memoir *The Talwars of Pathan Land*, written with the assistance of the Communist Party of India, and until that fact emerged in the 1970s he was closely associated with efforts to keep Bose's memory alive, even contributing to a commemorative volume edited by Sugata Bose, *Netaji and Indian Freedom*. He was by far Britain's most successful double agent in the Far East, and this is reflected in the large SOE, India Office, and MI5 files on his case.

[110] Liddell diary, 25 Oct. 1943, TNA, KV4/193.

[111] Cecil Liddell to Stephenson, 29 Oct. 1943, and enclosed undated memorandum, TNA, DO121/84; 'Summary of most secret information from Dublin', 28 Nov.–11 Dec. 1943, TNA, DO121/87.

[112] Berlin to Hempel, 17 Sept. 1941, TNA, DO121/84.

[113] Irish minister, Vichy, to Dublin, 6 Jan. 1942, NAI, DFA P12/1.

explained that, 'although there was a double check on Dublin from London and Gib[raltar], no absolute guarantee of picking up a message could be given'. On the other hand, it was almost certain that if he wished to transmit after so long an interval, Hempel's operator would have to show 'some signs on air' in course of preparing the set. It was agreed that the Irish must be pressured into confiscating the radio: if necessary they could save face by taking possession of all diplomatic sets. But an unexpected complication arose which delayed implementation of the change of policy by some weeks: the Foreign Office were worried that a successful démarche might provoke the Germans into demanding reciprocal action against clandestine British sets in Berne and the Vatican (we have seen that when it emerged in April 1944 that the Swedes had an illicit radio in their London legation, the fact that SIS had one in Stockholm served to stay any action, despite the fact that some Swedish diplomats were known to assist in German espionage). It was hoped that the Vatican radio would shortly cease to be significant, as it was 'expected that Rome would be captured'. It was agreed not to take any action in Dublin for at least a month.[114] After reviewing the position with Captain Caroe (the MI5/SIS representative in Northern Ireland), Guy Liddell suggested that the push to get rid of the radio should be postponed until '4–5 weeks before the operation. It would not give the Germans much time to get a new set going and would not . . . pinpoint *Overlord* since aerial reconnaissance would by that time have made it clear that operations were impending'. This sophisticated argument was, however, overtaken by events.[115]

Late in November Liddell noted what was to become a complicating factor in the saga of the German legation: at the war cabinet

there was a lively discussion about Ireland's neutrality. Gray . . . drafted rather a good letter to Dev, urging Eire to join the Allies. When on leave he showed it to the President who showed it to Winston at the time of the Quebec Conference [in April]. Winston referred it back to the Cabinet who pronounced against any move of the kind. The case was very ably argued by Cranborne. The PM was not however satisfied. He takes the view that if Eire does not come in with us during the war, the prospect of a solution as between north and south will recede even further than it is already. Everyone will argue that had it not been for our hold upon the North the Germans might well have invaded Ireland with disastrous results for ourselves. If on the other hand Eire joined in with us and became a real part of the Commonwealth, some kind of solution might be possible. In the present state of the game the naval authorities do not regard the Irish bases as of any great importance. Maffey and the D[ominions] O[ffice] I believe opposed the move as they thought it better to let Ireland stew in her own juice and discover for herself how she alienated opinion both here and in the USA.

I gather that there has been some tentative approach by both the Scandinavians and the Low Countries to Gen[era]l Smuts to be brought within the orbit of the British Empire. This is an extremely interesting move and one which, if the Irish only knew, might make them think quite a lot.[116]

---

[114] Liddell diary, 7 Nov. 1943, TNA, KV4/192; *Liddell History*, 78; Liddell diary, 20 Apr. 1944, TNA, KV4/193.

[115] Ibid., 17 Nov. 1943, TNA, KV4/192.

[116] Ibid., composite entry for 23–7 Nov. 1943, TNA, KV4/192. Smuts had played some part in laying the ground for the Anglo-Irish treaty of 1921.

What is significant about this entry is not the strange concept of Scandinavian and even Balkan wings of the British empire—C told Liddell he had heard that Romania and Bulgaria might also be interested—but the fact that Gray had succeeded with his personal lobbying of the two leaders at Quebec, far beyond the moderating influence of their security advisers. Gray's intention was to place de Valera in a position where either he would have to make major concessions on the Axis legations and the ports, or be seen to value neutrality above the legitimate security interests of the Allies.[117]

In November Cecil Liddell visited Dublin, and was invited to stay overnight as the guest of General McKenna. During a lengthy conversation, he committed a calculated indiscretion. McKenna 'asked him what we were really anxious about. Cecil said that in connection with the Second Front we were clearly anxious about leakage of information which might take place by wireless . . . and said that possibly some *démarche* might be made' requesting the surrender of all diplomatic radios. The general 'was very sympathetic', and Guy Liddell thought 'the probability is that he reported the matter and that Dev thought it better to take action before receiving a peremptory request'. In a curious penitential twist, Cecil Liddell later criticized himself in the third person: taking McKenna into his confidence 'was improper, and . . . a grave risk was incurred'.[118]

Pandora showed that shortly afterwards the Irish warned Hempel that they would most likely soon be confiscating all diplomatic radios. Guy Liddell thought that 'this has probably come' through his brother's talk with McKenna. Pandora also disclosed that Berlin was casting around for a solution: 'The Germans have no alternative means of communication and are wondering whether it would be possible to get wireless parts by submarine. They will be left without a receiving set as well as a transmitter'. Just a week before the climax of the crisis, Hempel was instructed that if at all possible he should track down an Abwehr set believed to be stored in Dublin since before the war, and represent that to the Irish as the one which he had been using. Alternatively, he could attempt to use the Abwehr set if he had to yield his own radio.[119]

On 15 December came another twist, when Maffey warned London that Gray had precipitately told Washington that the Axis legations and the radio were unacceptable security risks, that the IRA remained a potent danger to the Allied cause, and that vital information could easily be smuggled out from Britain to the west coast of Ireland, where 'there are thousands of fishermen, many of them members of the IRA, whose business takes them into waters where a rendezvous with a German submarine is a simple matter'. Gray recommended that the Allies demand that the German and Japanese missions be closed on security grounds.[120] This communication reflected not only Gray's ingrained prejudices and fixation about espionage, but his ignorance of the workings of the Anglo-Irish security relationship. Gray, who 'received numerous reports and rumours, nearly all of them

---

[117] Liddell diary, 8 Dec. 1943, TNA, KV4/192; Girvin, *The Emergency*, 298–301.

[118] *Liddell History*, 79–80; Liddell diary, 3 Dec. 1943, TNA, KV4/195.

[119] Liddell diary, 3 Dec. 1943, TNA, KV4/195; Berlin to Hempel, 16 Dec. 1943, quoted in Magic summary, 7 Jan. 1944, USNA, RG457, box 9.

[120] Gray to Washington, 13 Dec. 1943, USNA, RG84, 841D.00/1358A.

without foundation', had had no one to advise him on intelligence matters since the enforced departure the previous December of Spike Marlin. Marlin had reported positively on Irish security, and Gray regarded him as too close to the Irish, who had 'hoped to make use' of him 'as a channel for rehabilitating themselves in the USA'. The Federal Bureau of Investigation (FBI) had also circulated a lengthy and detailed study of the IRA which had been 'received from a highly confidential source', most likely MI5 or Scotland Yard Special Branch, which accurately portrayed the organization as weak, divided, and directionless. If Gray knew of these exchanges he discounted them, and in issuing his call for action he simply bypassed both OSS and the London embassy.[121]

In light of this complication, Maffey was instructed to make his own démarche about the radio immediately and to ask Gray to put his planned representations on hold. On the same day Walshe spoke to Hempel about the radio, pointing out that it was the biggest single issue in Irish–Allied relations and also that any attempt to use it would probably result in a rupture in diplomatic relations. It is impossible to say whether this pressure alone might have yielded results, because within days there came a dramatic development which forced Dublin's hand. This was the arrival in County Clare of two parachutists, John Francis O'Reilly and James Kenny, on the night of 16–17 December. The Irish air movements system had plotted the flights of their aircraft accurately, and both men were detained almost immediately. They were agents of the Sicherheitsdienst (SD), under orders to make their way to Britain to collect and radio back intelligence (although their sets, while 'of a very high grade', had 'voltages . . . not . . . suitable for . . . this country or Eire . . . but . . . for the USA').[122] O'Reilly, already on British and Irish watch lists because he had made some propaganda broadcasts, was a rogue and dissimulator who gave G2 much trouble, although at first he was frank about his task and his training. Kenny, who was injured on landing, was a dim nonentity unsuited to espionage.[123] Neither the German foreign ministry nor Hempel, for whom this was a catastrophe, had been forewarned.

On 20 December Walshe told Hempel that these events 'filled us with alarm about Germany's intentions . . . I asked him to warn his Government once more about the folly of thinking that parachutists could be landed here without escaping arrest. It was a very small country where everybody knew everybody else's business and no stranger could escape notice for long'. He asked Hempel formally either to hand over the radio or to destroy it to Irish satisfaction 'at once'. Hempel was evidently 'very worried indeed' about the agents, 'about whom, I feel sure, he has not been given notice'. He suggested that the radio be placed for safekeeping in a bank. On the same day Maffey saw de Valera, and later reported that the removal

---

[121] OSS 'Report on the present state of Eire', 27 Jan. 1943, USNA, State Department, 841D.00/358A; *Liddell History*, 89–90; O'Halpin, *Defending Ireland*, 230; J. Edgar Hoover (FBI) to Berle (State Department), 30 Sept. 1943, USNA, RG84, 841D.00/1421.

[122] Liddell diary, 26 Apr. 1944, TNA, KV4/193.

[123] The MI5 file on these agents includes correspondence and documents from G2, the RUC, the Garda, the Irish army signals corps, BTNI, and SIS, reflecting both a high level of interest and a high degree of cooperation between all parties involved in their cases. TNA, KV4/119. The G2 file on O'Reilly was created in October 1941. MAI, G2/3824.

of the set from the legation was imminent.[124] The radio was duly collected by Fred Boland of External Affairs and the signals officer Commandant Neligan, who first examined it to confirm that it was intact and capable of working to Germany, and it was placed in a bank vault. Maffey reported this to London on 24 December. Hempel did not inform Berlin of what had happened until 7 January, and in the meantime received a series of somewhat contradictory messages suggesting ploys he might use to deflect the Irish demand (Jane Archer surmised that the confusion in Berlin was partly the result of intense air raids, as some messages indicated that the sender had no access to recent files).[125]

The outcome of the radio saga was satisfactory from the point of view of the British security authorities. Hempel now had to rely exclusively on cables to communicate with and to receive instructions from Berlin, and Britain both controlled the flow of that traffic and could read it. The issue of the Axis missions remained, and on this there was shortly to be a clash between the higher political objectives of the Allies and their own best interests as seen by their security advisers.

CONCLUSION

The very considerable intelligence and security breakthroughs achieved during 1943—Pandora, the removal of Hempel's radio, the Eastwood case—were at times overshadowed by continuing ministerial anger and concern with Ireland, now focussed less on the issue of ports and bases, and far more on the matter of the Axis missions. As the number of American troops in the United Kingdom increased dramatically during the year in preparation for *Overlord*, so did American concerns about the security of the planned operation and the potential for leakage of information through Ireland. Despite the development of good MI5–OSS liaison in London on Irish matters, and the positive outcome of David Bruce's March visit to Dublin, the fine details of Anglo-Irish, Irish–American, and Anglo-American security cooperation were either not studied or were discounted at the policy level in Washington, where Gray's reports and ideas continued to tip the scales.

The challenge for British intelligence as 1944 began was to secure as many additional concessions as desirable from the Irish without jeopardizing existing cooperation. In these circumstances, ministerial involvement could often be far more of a hindrance than a help. At the political level, however, there remained considerable disquiet at the continuation of Axis representation in Ireland. That was to find expression within a few weeks in the 'American note' crisis.

---

[124] Minutes by Walshe for de Valera, 15, 20 and 22 Dec. 1943, NAI, DFA A25; *Liddell History*, 81.

[125] 'Summary of most secret information from Dublin, 25th December 1943–7th January 1944', TNA, DO121/87. Girvin, *The Emergency*, 307, downplays the significance of the radio and its handover, but as indicated by the many documents cited, it was absolutely central to British concerns about Ireland.

6

Anomalous, benighted backwater: January 1944 to the late 1940s

THE AMERICAN NOTE CRISIS

In the first five months of 1944 Irish security remained a major preoccupation for British intelligence. Management of the issue was complicated by the increased interest of the United States in the question, in terms both of the attitude of OSS, and the rather different opinion of the remorseless David Gray. Gray's reportage led to what became known as the 'American note' crisis, a very public dispute between the Allies and Ireland hinging on the issue of the Axis legations.[1] This row threatened to upset MI5's carefully arranged applecart of security measures agreed with the Irish, and it illustrates the familiar problem of amateur alarmists in the policy system.

On 2 February Churchill wrote in approving terms of Gray's advice to Washington to demand the closure of the Axis legations. He said that the two Allies should each issue a démarche: 'the German and enemy Embassies [*sic*] should be sent away forthwith . . . We ought not to be behind when the United States themselves were pressing in a matter of this kind against the hostile gang in Dublin'. The planned demand caused something approaching consternation in both MI5 and SIS. Churchill asked the chiefs of staff for their views, and the matter was referred to the JIC, and on to Guy Liddell, who

> had frequent conversations with Jane and C [while preparing] a note giving the pros and cons in favour of the expulsion of hostile legations from Eire. It was thought desirable to have this short note for presentation to the PM if . . . he wished to consult C and the D[irector]G[eneral of MI5] before meeting the Cabinet . . .
>
> C tells me that the PM has withdrawn all copies of the JIC memorandum on the expulsion of hostile legations from Dublin. He does not know the reason but is trying to find out.[2]

The JIC memorandum based on Liddell's note did eventually reach the cabinet, despite Churchill's disapproval. It advanced a pragmatic argument against forcing the closure. This was the real possibility that the Irish would lessen or end security cooperation just as *Overlord* loomed, particularly if news of an Allied démarche leaked out:

> there would be very little, if any, security advantage in the removal of the German Legation, whose communications we . . . controlled, but which, if removed, might be replaced at the critical moment by enemy agents with means of communication which it would take time

---

[1] Gray to Washington, 13 Dec. 1943, USNA, RG84, 841D.00/1358A.
[2] Liddell diary, 4 Feb. 1944, TNA, KV4/193.

to discover, all the more so as our relations with Eire would be so strained that it was at least doubtful whether we should continue to receive the assistance we had hitherto received in matters of this kind.

The war cabinet concluded that, while 'there would be no security advantage in the removal of the German Legation', Britain should support an American démarche through verbal representations from Maffey after the Irish had had time to digest the American message.[3] Liddell afterwards learned more from the Dominions Office, who explained that the genesis of the initiative lay in Gray's proposed letter to de Valera of the previous spring, which both Roosevelt and Churchill had approved at Quebec but which the war cabinet had vetoed. Despite British success in forcing the surrender of the legation radio, the prime minister 'feels himself in a rather weak position vis-à-vis the USA' on the question of the security of *Overlord* 'and is anxious to meet their wishes'.[4]

Liddell's own view was that 'it would be disastrous if the Eire Govt. broke off their relations at our instigation since they would then come to us and ask for armaments for their protection'. After the war, such weapons 'would . . . probably . . . be used against us in a battle between north and south'.[5] A few days later Liddell recorded that 'C told me that the PM had tackled him about the Irish question . . . and accused him of putting a spoke in his wheel. C replied that he was only concerned with the diplomatic cable side of the business, not with the security angle. This rather confirms that the PM was considerably irritated' by Liddell's document and the JIC memorandum to which it gave rise. MI5 continued to have 'great misgivings' lest, 'at a most critical moment, the intelligence cooperation with the Irish might be seriously prejudiced' by the démarche.[6]

There are both parallels and contrasts with Allied deliberations on the issue of the Axis legations in Kabul. In the spring of 1943 Wylie, the British minister, had renewed pressure on the Afghans to stamp out continuing intrigues against India and the Soviet Union. The Soviets were advised to protest independently as a joint démarche might be 'too heavy a weapon'.[7] The response of the American minister in Kabul and of the State Department to this plan could scarcely have contrasted more with their attitude to Ireland: 'any attempt to force Afghan Government to expel Axis Legations or even forcing them to compel Legations to reduce their staff drastically would be inexpedient'. The American embassy in London conveyed a similar view to the Foreign Office: 'any show of compulsion by the British and the Russians would cause so much bitterness throughout Afghanistan that any benefits that might otherwise accrue would be outweighed'. If the Afghans bowed to such pressure, 'the very stability of the . . . regime might be endangered'. Such meddling in Britain's traditional sphere of influence was too much for Anthony Eden, who presented a sharp aide-mémoire telling Washington to mind its own business.[8] Wylie claimed

---

  3 *Liddell History*, 82–3.
  4 Liddell diary, 7 Feb. 1944, TNA, KV4/193.
  5 Ibid., 8 Feb. 1944, TNA, KV4/193.
  6 Ibid., 11 Feb. 1944, TNA, KV4/193; *Liddell History*, 83.
  7 Foreign Office to British embassy, Moscow, 12 May 1943, BL, L/PS/12/1798.
  8 British minister, Kabul, to Delhi, 8 June, and Eden to Halifax (ambassador in Washington), 11 June 1943, IOR, L/PS/12/1798.

his American counterpart had misrepresented him as wanting the Axis legations closed: 'for almost two years I have held strong personal view that except in extreme last resort it would be madness to confront Afghan Government with demand to expel the Legations'.[9] As in Dublin, there were considerable intelligence reasons for leaving the legations alone: 'if there are no Japanese embassies there will be no channels through which to pass deception . . . we might therefore leave the one in Afghanistan which from the deception point of view was the most important'.[10]

By the spring of 1944 there was apprehension in Delhi because the Soviets seemed keen on forcing the expulsion of the Japanese: 'intelligence authorities here . . . regard continued presence of Japanese Legation . . . as most desirable for reasons which will probably occur to you', although IPI concluded that there was 'no alternative' if the Afghans offered to act.[11] In October the Japanese minister reported that the Afghans had given 'a strong refutation' of British charges that his legation was operating 'a spy ring on a considerable scale', describing him as 'very cautious'. The Afghans realized that the Japanese mission was 'extremely irritating for the British, and they were seeking to find some pretext for driving it out'. It is of course possible that these representations were a bluff, intended to mask British ease with the mission's clandestine activities.[12] In the event, the Japanese and German legations remained until the war's end, and the Allies continued to read their communications and to control the informants on whom they depended, particularly the star double agent *Silver*.[13] In stark contrast to his colleague in Dublin, after Tokyo capitulated the American minister in Kabul, whose attitude had long irritated London, expressed 'his sympathy' to the Japanese minister, and 'asked me if there were any requests . . . I would like to present'. He obligingly delayed the freezing of the legation's funds so that debts due to the Afghan government could be paid.[14]

Another obvious comparator was Persia, where the Tehran government's reluctant acquiescence in Anglo-Soviet demands to expel all Germans 'engaged in undesirable activities' in 1941 had been insufficient to prevent occupation a matter of weeks afterwards. Within a month this had led to the effective abandonment of Persian neutrality at the point of British and Soviet guns, and it had soon become clear that the stated reasons for intervention, concerns about a possible German coup, were not the real ones. The British and the Soviets constantly hectored the Persians about their, perhaps understandable, lack of enthusiasm during the occupation—in August 1943 the British minister told the Iranian prime minister that he had 'allowed the Tehran police to become more and more corrupt, inefficient and hostile', and provided him with Anglo-Soviet lists of suspects to be interrogated and detained—demeaning treatment which Tehran had no choice but to bear until the

[9] Wylie to Delhi, 26 July 1943, IOR, L/PS/12/1798.

[10] SOE London to Hill (SOE representative in Moscow), 14 May 1943, TNA, HS1/191; Delhi to London, 16 May 1944, IOR L/PS/12/1798; Liddell dairy, 26 Sept. 1944, TNA, KV4/195.

[11] IPI to India Office, 20 May 1944, BL, L/PS/12/1798.

[12] Delhi to Kabul, 16 May, and IPI to India Office, 20 May 1944, IOR, L/PS/12/1798; Japanese minister, Kabul, to Tokyo, 24 Oct. 1944, TNA, HW12/306.

[13] Magan, *Middle Eastern Approaches*, 17–18; interviews with Brigadier·Magan, 2000 and 2001; Howard, *British Intelligence*, v. 209–11.

[14] Japanese minister, Kabul, to Tokyo, 29 Aug. 1945, TNA, HW12/331.

Allies left in 1946 (as late as July 1945, the Persian minister in London advised against reinstating recently released internees in their railway jobs lest this jeopardize negotiations for an end to the occupation).[15]

The eventual presentation of the American note on 21 February, with its declaration that the Axis legations were 'a danger to the lives of American soldiers and to the success of Allied military operations', produced a furious Irish reaction. The Irish got wind that something unpleasant was coming, and when Gray met de Valera 'he got a rocket. He was followed shortly by Maffey who was not at all well received. Dev got very excited and said that if necessary Ireland would fight'.[16] Gray told Washington that judging by the immediate Irish reaction he thought it possible that his cable traffic was being read. Washington were unperturbed: they had used the 'Brown' code, 'in which we no longer place great reliance . . . it was believed that no great harm would come should they [the Irish] obtain a copy in advance'. Alastair Denniston of GC&CS observed that there was evidence the Germans had been reading that system for some time, and that 'the breaking of the Brown book does not test the abilities of the Irish cryptographers, but tests the competence of the Irish intercept authorities'.[17] In reality Hayes never attempted to break American traffic, though the fact that the Allies thought him capable of it was indicative of the impression he had already made on GC&CS in his dealings with them.[18]

On 7 March the Irish government issued a public statement disclosing the terms of the American demand, and placed their defence forces on high alert in anticipation of a possible Allied incursion. The American press had a field day: *Time* hailed the 'staid, though strong, language of the US note', speculating that 'gaunt, US born "Dev" . . . hopped good and mad from his chair, sputtering more sparks than the fire on his hearth'.[19] Gray had proposed the note almost entirely by reference to *Overlord*, but the initiative owed little to the practicalities of security and a great deal to the long-standing American grievance about Irish neutrality and to his alarmist mindset. The Magic summaries available to the State Department in the preceding months did include Berlin's directions to Hempel to collect more war information, but had almost no Dublin–Tokyo traffic. This is a clear indication that Beppu's mission was not thought capable of obtaining and speedily transmitting useful war information to Tokyo. The Germans were so regarded at the time that the note was agreed, but the surrender of Hempel's radio completely changed that calculation.

The note and Gray's part in it have recently been robustly defended by Brian Girvin, on the grounds that Ireland should have been pushed into abandoning neutrality in the light of the hideous nature of the Nazi regime as disclosed by its conduct since 1939. This essentially moral argument is beside the point, because the

[15] Beaumont, 'Great Britain and the Rights of Neutral Countries', 217–18; British minister to the prime minister, Tehran, 29 Aug. 1943, IOR, L/PS/12/656; Persian minister, London, to Tehran, 11 July 1945, TNA, HW12/323.

[16] Liddell diary, 28 Feb. 1944, TNA, KV4/193.

[17] Gray to Washington, and reply, 22 Feb., and Washington to Gray, 21 Apr. 1944, quoted in O'Halpin, *Defending Ireland*, 186; Denniston to SIS, 24 Feb. 1944, TNA, HW53/22.

[18] Gray to Washington, 22 Feb., and Washington to Gray, 2 Apr. 1944, USNA, RG59, 841D.01/240 and 342. There is no evidence that Hayes ever attempted to break American traffic.

[19] Wills, *That Neutral Island*, 387; *Time*, 20 Mar. 1944.

note related to security, not to the Holocaust. Gray plainly had no grasp either of the extent and limits of the actual threat of leakage through the legations, or of what was at risk in presenting the note, should the Irish react by reducing security and other forms of cooperation crucial to Allied operations. His Belgian counterpart remarked that he had spoken 'with the boldness which has often served him badly . . . about 72 years old but preserves his youthful aggressiveness. The rather crude sincerity which characterises him in common with most of his countrymen is . . . out of place in Ireland'. Responding to queries from Madrid about the nature of the American demands, the Spanish minister reported that in the Dáil 'the tone was elevated because opposition orators applauded' the taoiseach.[20]

De Valera told the Canadian minister that 'there was no evidence which, even if he desired to do so, would justify ordering the withdrawal of the Axis representatives . . . he based himself on information which he received from the Irish Secret Service working in conjunction with the British Secret Service', and sought Canadian intervention to have the note withdrawn.[21] In Ottawa Norman Robertson, the secretary of the Department of External Affairs, advised Mackenzie King that, whereas in the comparable case of Argentina the Americans had provided hard evidence of espionage by German diplomats, in Dublin 'they did not go out of their way to give Mr de Valera a plausible public occasion for modifying his policy'. It was 'a mistake in judgement' for the British and American governments to make formal representations in the manner which they had, although he did not think Canada should intervene. Mackenzie King, who had no great reason to defend Irish neutrality in light of the Canadian navy's major role in the war in the Atlantic, then gave an unusually sympathetic hearing to the Irish high commissioner. Afterwards he 'dictated a long memo' critical of the démarche.[22]

This intervention was based partly on Mackenzie King's attachment to the ideal of dominion independence and interdependence, sentiments which de Valera professed to share, together with anger that Canada, whose forces would also be involved in *Overlord*, had not been consulted by Britain. A few weeks later, amid rumours of a proposed second note, Robertson advised 'protesting pretty sharply to the United Kingdom, first, about the complete lack of consultation on a question of this importance, and secondly, about the unwisdom in the common interest of the action that had actually been taken', and the Canadian government agreed to send a message 'drawing attention to the need for Commonwealth consultation in matters of this kind', and expressing 'misgiving about the action that had been taken'.[23] Canadian resentment at what appeared yet another manifestation of the habitually overbearing approach of the United States to smaller states, an attitude which Canada had had to endure for decades, also played some part in Ottawa's

[20] Text of Goor to Spaak (in London), 25 Mar. 1944, NAI, DFA A8/1; Madrid to Spanish minister, Dublin, 13 Mar., and reply, 16 Mar. 1944, TNA, HW12/298.

[21] Canadian minister, Dublin, to Ottawa, and minute by Robertson for prime minister, 22 and 25 Apr. 1944, PAC, RG25 D1, vol. 781, file 398.

[22] Cunningham, 'Ireland, Canada and the American Note', in Keogh and O'Driscoll (eds.), *Ireland in the second world war*, 149, 153–5; Mackenzie King diary, 27 Feb. 1944.

[23] Robertson to prime minister, and extract from cabinet war committee, both 15 Mar. 1944, PAC, RG76, vol. 821, file 552–1–541.

reaction to the crisis. In the following weeks Gray resiled from much of his earlier far-fetched estimates of German espionage on which the note had been largely based.[24]

The American note caused acute alarm in Dublin. It appeared to de Valera to indicate that, notwithstanding the extent of security cooperation, America and Britain were bent on creating circumstances in which Ireland would either break off relations with the Axis powers completely, or be subject to punitive action, ostensibly in the name of *Overlord*'s security but in reality to bring an end to neutrality by the threat of force. On 26 February Smale, the American consul in Cork, telephoned the GOC of Southern Command to report a rumour that on the night of 21–22 February a German submarine had landed a party of 'four or five Irishmen and four Germans, together with a lot of radio equipment'. Interviewed about this by G2's O'Donoghue, Smale 'professed to be convinced that information was going out of this country to Germany', although he 'appeared to be in a nervous and excited condition, and not too sure of his ground'. The Irish might reasonably have construed this exchange as a conscious follow-up to the American note, perhaps to put them on their toes. Dan Bryan dismissed the consul as a 'busybody' who had probably paid for this fabricated information—the consul had denied this, but admitted that the military attaché was inclined to such practices—although O'Donoghue and the GOC could 'exercise . . . discretion as to the information you give him as a courtesy, not as a right, while allowing for his "busybody" activities'.[25]

MI5 afterwards surmised that the real purpose of the American note was to create circumstances where 'it could be put on record . . . that the Irish Government had refused a request which might have removed a danger to the lives of American soldiers'.[26] In this it probably succeeded: the public reaction of the Irish undoubtedly further antagonized American officials, contributing to difficulties in the immediate post-war years when Ireland sought to ease her diplomatic isolation. But given what was at stake as the invasion deadline neared, February 1944 was scarcely the time for political point-scoring by a great and ascendant power against a minor neutral state. After the note and the Irish response were made public on 9 March, SIS reported that 'de Valera has added considerably to his political stature' by his handling of the affair, and 'even the *Irish Times* published a laudatory leader'. SIS also reported general public acceptance of the justification on security grounds of the travel and other restrictions imposed by Britain.[27]

The American note should not be analysed in isolation, because it fitted the pattern of Washington's approach to the world's remaining neutrals. On 2 May, 'after protracted negotiations' with the Allies, the Spanish agreed to expel 'designated

[24] Girvin, *The Emergency*, 306–14; Gray to Washington, 17 Apr. 1944, USNA, RG84, 841D.01/328 and 342.

[25] O'Donoghue to Bryan, 28 Feb., and Bryan to assistant chief of staff, 21 Feb.; Bryan MS note on formal instructions to O'Donoghue, 4 Mar. 1944, MAI, G2/X/1122. Smale, the American consul, had some experience of coastal investigations from his time as a consul in Havana, where smuggling was a significant problem. I am grateful to David Spearman for this information. Smale to Washington, 12 Feb. 1945, NARA, RG59, Decimal File 1945–1945, Box 5989, argued that recent evidence of smuggling indicated continuing inadequacy of Irish security measures.

[26] Liddell diary, 22 Feb. 1944, TNA, KV4/193; *Liddell History*, 83.

[27] QRS report, 1 May 1944, TNA, DO121/85.

Axis agents', to close the German consulate in Tangier, to reduce exports of the strategic mineral wolfram to Germany, and to withdraw their troops from the eastern front. Despite these concessions, the Spanish continued, and in some respects intensified, covert cooperation with the Germans through increased smuggling, protection of German intelligence personnel, and other measures completely at odds with the May agreement. The Spanish also continued to pass intelligence for the Japanese, as did the Finns material gathered by their military attaché in Washington.[28] In August, and again despite considerable British reservations about the advisability of an all-or-nothing approach, the United States insisted on issuing Sweden with what was viewed in Stockholm as a unilateral demand to cease trading with Germany, which in effect would have amounted to an abandonment of neutrality. The Swedes, sensing British and even Soviet unease at this 'violent' approach, managed to avoid a confrontation through a combination of prevarication and sophistry, and maintained diplomatic relations with Germany to the end while progressively attenuating trade and political links. Curiously, a decode in April 1945 indicated that a Swedish diplomat en route to Tokyo was carrying intelligence from the Japanese naval attaché in Stockholm (of course this may have been a private arrangement).[29]

In South America, by 1944 most countries had cut their links with Germany and Japan and were dancing to Washington's tune: Bolivia, which contrived to stay neutral, agreed to send Japanese and German residents to be interned in the United States despite the Axis sympathies of the ruling junta. When the Perón government in Argentina was detected in an ill-judged and eccentric scheme to purchase weapons from Germany in December 1943, the United States took this as 'concrete proof of Argentina's collusion with the Axis', and forced Buenos Aires to break with Germany and Japan in January 1944. Relations with the United States remained very strained, and an American economic blockade continued, but Argentina at least finished the war on the side of the angels, having spent much of it cheering on the Axis devils.[30]

What the American note put at risk, as MI5 observed, was the intricate Anglo-Irish security understanding which had been built up over four years. It also threatened the considerable operational assistance which the Irish provided to the Allied air forces, which went well beyond passive tolerance of technical breaches of sovereignty such as overflights. Bill Donovan of OSS took a somewhat similar view in respect of security, telling Roosevelt at the end of March that 'the cooperation in intelligence matters offered and given by the Irish [since David Bruce's visit to

---

[28] Appendix B of Magic summary, 3 Nov. 1944, and Japanese ambassador, Ankara, to Tokyo, 26 Jan. 1945, USNA, RG457, boxes 14 and 15; Magic summary, 17 Apr. 1944, NARA, RG457, box 10.

[29] Carlgren, *Swedish Foreign Policy*, 200–3; Levine, 'Swedish Neutrality During the second world war: Tactical Success or Moral Compromise?', in Wylie (ed.), *European Neutrals*, 328–9; Magic summary, 7 Apr. 1945, USNA, RG457, box 16.

[30] Venezuela broke off relations with the Axis powers after Pearl Harbor, while remaining technically neutral until 1945. Chile reluctantly did the same in January 1943, but again did not declare war. Uruguay broke off relations with the Axis in December 1941 and, while she remained neutral, was consistently pro-American. Whitehead, 'Bolivia Since 1930', 533; Rock, 'Argentina 1930–46', 60–1; Ewell, 'Venezuela Since 1930', 739; Drake, 'Chile 1930–58', 298; Finch, 'Uruguay Since 1930', 201, in Bethell, *Cambridge History of Latin America*, viii.

Dublin in March 1943] has been very full. It should be pointed out that we did not offer the Irish information in return and have given them little'.[31] Robert Brennan briefed the State Department on the realities of Anglo-Irish security cooperation, pointed to G2's good links with OSS, and suggested that the Americans appoint a security attaché in Dublin. Gray's response to a report of this meeting was rather lame, probably reflecting his previous ignorance of the depth of the Anglo-Irish security understanding: 'The general line . . . is that the British were kept informed of everything. This of course is probably true and publicity would embarrass the British and possibly reduce present efficiency of joint security measures', although he maintained that the key point remained that 'Eire is geographically situated so as to favour espionage and . . . Axis representatives presumably take advantage of the opportunities'.[32]

The response both of MI5 and of OSS to the American note indicates that in terms of security—the ostensible focus of the démarche—the initiative was regarded as potentially catastrophic. On 15 April, when talk of a further note was in the air, Ambassador Winant cabled Washington to say that 'I have talked with Sir David Petrie . . . and Colonel Russell Forgan, who is acting for the OSS in Colonel Bruce's absence. They both agree that the Eire Government is making every effort to cooperate on security measures. They feel a second note might disturb this situation'.[33] These high-level representations followed an Irish proposal, put forward by Walshe at the Dominions Office a fortnight earlier, for a tripartite conference on security. Walshe also sought the appointment of British and American security liaison officers in Dublin, a proposal which neither OSS nor MI5 liked. Cecil Liddell thought the Irish initiative 'an attempt to shelf [*sic*] responsibility. If we refuse to meet them they may say they had made an effort to cooperate . . . if we met them and something goes wrong about *Overlord* security they would say that they did everything they were asked to do'. MI5 advised that the conference should take place only on the firm understanding that responsibility for security would continue to lie squarely with the Irish.[34] The British and Americans eventually accepted the idea of a conference, subject to the reservation that the continued presence of Axis legations in Ireland would still constitute an uncontrollable security risk. This was, as MI5 had previously argued, a rather problematic assumption: now that the Allies could control and read all the communications of these missions, there was a very strong case for letting them operate. In the analogous case of the Japanese embassy in Berne in December 1944, the JIC accepted precisely that logic, and we have already seen that the same reasoning applied in respect of the Japanese legation in Kabul.[35]

Maffey conveyed British willingness to attend the proposed conference, whereas American acceptance was communicated by Marlin to Dulanty in London. This

[31] Donovan memorandum for President, 30 Mar. 1944, USNA, RG84, 844.008.

[32] Note of meeting between Hickerson and Stewart (both State Department) and Brennan, 11 Apr., and Gray to Washington, 17 Apr. 1944, USNA, RG84, 841D.01/328 and 342.

[33] Winant (London) to Washington, 15 Apr. 1944, USNA, RG84/841D.01/333.

[34] Liddell diary, 22 Apr. 1944, TNA, KV4/193; *Liddell History*, 88–9.

[35] Wylie, *Britain, Switzerland and the second world war*, 270, n. 7; Delhi to London, 16 May 1944, IOR, L/PS/12/1798.

curious procedure, which meant that Gray had no advance notice of so important a development in his own backyard, and arising largely from his initiative, indicates OSS's lack of confidence in his judgement and discretion.[36] A few days later the Liddells dined with Walter Bell of British Security Cooperation in New York, who brought Marlin along. The dinner went well, although, whether by accident or not, the MI5 officers were given the wrong impression about when Marlin had first gone to Dublin:

Marlin . . . was sent over . . . by OSS some 6 months ago, ostensibly as one of Ambassador Gray's attachés. He seems to have gone down very well with the Irish who always refer to him in glowing terms, particularly Joe Walshe. Marlin however does not think very much of Joe nor does he much like the general set up . . . as compared with 1932 when he was at Trinity. He regrets the passage of the Anglo-Irish and rather dislikes the little counter-jumpers who have established themselves in office, many of whom have only a thin veneer of culture. One is inclined to wonder whether Marlin says one thing to us and another to the Irish, but . . . I am inclined to think that he is straight. He is certainly a very pleasant individual. He is going to act as the American representative in the Security talks which we are to have . . . with Dan.[37]

In advance of the conference, the Americans indicated that they wished to ask the Irish for a guarantee that they would not grant the Germans wireless facilities. Cecil Liddell ducked a definite response to this idea, claiming that it had already been the subject of a cabinet decision, but the proposal indicated a level of misunderstanding of the security situation—MI5 had already advised that cable facilities for all legations should not be withdrawn until shortly before *Overlord*, precisely for fear that otherwise the Irish might feel obliged to grant wireless facilities, however limited, to foreign missions.[38]

The security conference eventually took place in Dublin on 1 May. David Petrie had expected to attend, but a decision was taken to keep the Allied representation at middle level so as to ensure that the Irish could not overplay the significance of whatever was agreed.[39] The OSS representatives Marlin and Hubert Will prudently paid a visit to Gray immediately beforehand to put him in the picture in general terms. They, and Cecil Liddell, then had detailed discussions with Dan Bryan and Chief Superintendent Carroll. The meeting was essentially technical, because there was no disagreement about the underlying policy of completely isolating Ireland until the invasion of Europe had successfully started. Discussion ranged over a large number of issues, including surveillance on the Axis legations and Axis nationals, internees, and pro-Axis groups; the IRA, 'described as being at a very low ebb . . . its members so divided among themselves that it could scarcely be described as an organization'; increased postal censorship; increased monitoring of cross-border traffic; coast-watching and air-movements reporting; the detection of illicit wireless transmissions; extra security for Irish government wireless and broadcasting stations; restrictions on Irish fishing boats (which were anyway hampered by shortales of fuel);

[36] *Liddell History*, 89.
[37] Liddell diary, 24 Feb. 1944, TNA, KV4/193.
[38] Ibid., 21 Feb. and 28 Apr. 1944, TNA, KV4/193.
[39] Petrie to Cecil Liddell, 23 Apr. 1944, TNA, KV4/280.

increased controls on passengers passing through Foynes; and even fuel restrictions on Irish military aircraft, to ensure that none capable of flying to France would be allowed to carry sufficient fuel to do so.

Most of these measures represented a tightening-up of existing controls rather than the imposition of new ones, although one innovation did emerge on the margins of the conference: MI5 and OSS agreed for the first time to swap intelligence on Ireland, an elementary measure which might with profit have been adopted years earlier, although at Churchill's personal direction such exchanges were to be confined to 'special lines of mutual interest'. Marlin soon fell foul of this injunction: on 25 May the Liddells complained that he 'seemed to be going outside his sphere by seeking for information of a political kind both here and in Ireland'. Walter Bell said 'that MARLIN was considered to be rather a joke in his own organization and we all agreed that it would be a mistake to get at loggerheads with OSS. We decided therefore to pursue the line that in view of the PM's directive we could not give purely political information. If MARLIN persisted, we would take up the question with Bruce'.[40] Marlin was withdrawn to the United States soon afterwards.

THE ISOLATION OF IRELAND BEFORE *OVERLORD*

In January MI5 learned that Dr Little, an Ulster Unionist MP, wished to raise the issue of Irish security in the Commons, on foot of a circumspect answer to a parliamentary question on the capture of the Clare parachutists. It was thought he might call for a debate on Irish security to be held in a secret session, a prospect which caused MI5 much alarm. The home secretary was asked to explain to Sir Basil Brooke 'that we are in close touch with the Eire authorities in this matter and they are proving extremely cooperative'. It was hoped that Brooke would then persuade his party colleague not to press the matter further.[41]

In February and March the question of imposing complete isolation on Ireland was discussed extensively. Churchill, as usual, was bullish on the question. The Security Executive, which had to consider the practicalities of operating a quarantine system, were more careful. MI5's 'chief concern . . . was to prevent such drastic measures being taken as would antagonize the Irish and terminate their cooperation in intelligence matters at the very time when it was most needed'. Guy Liddell advised Sir Findlater Stewart 'not to interfere in any way with the German cables from Dublin', for fear that the Germans might devise an alternative method of communication in advance of *Overlord*. At Stewart's suggestion, MI5 drew up a list of 'the services and assistance given by the Eire Government which might be jeopardised'. In addition to Irish movement controls and the G2–MI5 link, the document stated that the RUC were particularly concerned about their liaison with the Garda on IRA matters. It also pointed out that Irish labour engaged on vital war work in Britain might react adversely if relations with Ireland deteriorated

---

[40] A detailed summary of the Dublin security conference is reproduced in *Liddell History*, 103–9.
[41] Liddell diary, 21 Jan. 1944, TNA, KV4/193; MI5 minutes on the issue, 19, 20, 22, and 24 Jan. 1944, TNA, KV4/280.

as a result of arbitrary British action. This cautionary note may have had some influence, since the measures announced by Churchill in the Commons on 14 March,
while rigorous, were not presented as punitive: he assured Roosevelt that 'motives
of self-preservation and not spite dictate our actions'. The Irish responded to this
British decision to isolate the island by banning the recruitment in Ireland of workers
for Britain: 'The excuse is that, as the Eire Govt do not know what sanctions we
are going to impose they may have to keep men for cutting peat if they cannot get
coal'. Maffey wanted to make some 'reassuring statement', whereas Churchill 'seems
to take pleasure in keeping Dev on tenter hooks. The whole effect of this . . . is to
damage ourselves. The Americans, having started the trouble are now easing off,
giving Ireland certain commodities . . . and leaving us to hold the security baby'.[42]

The tight travel restrictions imposed were less effective than had been hoped.
The border remained porous: in May, Walshe remarked to Archbishop McQuaid
that 'even now, notwithstanding the emergency ban on movements, the passengers
going north are frequently not asked for their permits or whether they have any
documents'. While civilian traffic across the Irish Sea virtually ceased, the problem of
servicemen taking leave in Ireland continued much as before: on 18 May 'people are
said to be leaving the country for Eire [on compassionate grounds] and on discharge',
and two weeks later Cecil Liddell was 'very worried about the continuous flow of
troops to Eire on either compassionate leave, or embarkation or disembarkation
leave. Some 5000 a week have been going. This of course drives a coach and four
through all the restrictions that have been placed on travel to Eire . . . Findlater
Stewart has written a note on the subject urging the Services', who had demanded
extra restrictions in the first place, 'to cut down as far as possible'.[43] Noting the
casual attitude of the armed services to the ban, the Home Office also refused to
'cancel compassionate leave for civilians'.[44]

MI5 were also faced with the problem of how to handle Irish citizens wishing
to return home from Europe. On 7 May a particularly strange case emerged, when
telegrams arrived from Madrid from both SIS and the ambassador. These concerned
an Irish priest, 'the holder of a British passport and head of some local British
education institute', who 'had three charges up against him of homosexuality. In
one case a Spanish soldier was under arrest'. The priest was 'said to be anti-British
and a great personal friend of the Archbishop of Madrid. Apart from this there are
allegations' that he had supplied 'a certain amount of American press information'
to a German diplomat. In a response which could have come straight out of the
Catholic church's own well-thumbed, if unwritten, handbook for dealing with such
embarrassments, the ambassador concluded that the obvious solution was to get the
priest out of Spain before he was prosecuted or, worse still, succumbed to further
temptation: 'It is suggested that Cadogan [of the Foreign Office] might say a word to
the Apostolic delegate. On arrival we shall house him and interrogate him. If we are

[42] *Liddell History*, 84–6; Churchill to Roosevelt, 19 Mar., USNA, 841D.01/319; Liddell diary,
17 Feb. and 27 Mar. 1944, TNA, KV4/19

[43] Walshe to McQuaid, 1 June 1944, Dublin Diocesan Archives, folder marked 'Department of
External Affairs, 1941–71'; Liddell diary, 18 and 28 May 1944, TNA, KV4/193. Hinsley and Simkins,
British Intelligence, 254.

[44] *Curry History*, 284.

satisfied about his German connections, he will have to run loose, at any rate until after *Overlord*.[45] The Spanish soldier, presumably, was left to his fate in Franco's jails.

The British government hesitated over the question of the banning of diplomatic communications with the outside world. The Foreign Office were worried about possible retaliation by other states, and there was also an issue of timing: if this was done too far in advance of *Overlord*, some missions might find ways of circumventing the ban. On the other hand, it was abundantly clear from decodes of both Allied and neutral diplomatic traffic from London that even the most innocent reportage could provide indications of military significance. Furthermore, even an utterly erroneous report might cause the Germans to lose confidence in the elaborate deceptions fed to them through Double Cross. The ban was introduced at midnight on 17 April, and was only lifted on 19 June, almost two weeks after *Overlord* had begun. Soviet and American government communications were the only ones exempted.[46]

The success of *Overlord* occasioned a rapid revision of many of the temporary travel restrictions. Within a month, Whitehall committees were contemplating the resumption of civil air flights between the two islands, together with some liberalization of controls on shipping to and from the Iberian peninsula. There was a clear, though unspoken, assumption that Ireland no longer represented a serious source of leakage of war information. The 'Irish Channel agents' of MI5's B1L shipping security section 'were discarded', not that they had been of much positive use, and there was a general easing off in policy and in practice.[47]

By now the IRA presented little threat in Ireland, north or south. In what may be a reflection of a general collapse in republican morale, a former IRA officer, who had been indirectly involved in the murder of the alleged informer Michael Devereaux in Tipperary in 1940, turned up in Belfast seeking to enlist in either the Royal Marines or the Commandos—he was not fussy about which of the two elite units he joined. He was sent back across the border. The IRA and their supporters could raise scarcely a whisper of defiance even when their chief of staff, Charlie Kerins, was executed in December 1944 after conviction for the Sergeant O'Brien murder of 1942, making him the last Irish republican put to death after sentence for a political crime.[48] On the other hand, a large number of IRA detainees and prisoners were freed, even without giving undertakings as to their future behaviour and associations. In the first five months of 1944 about 130 were released, and by the end of the year the state held only 240 republican men (the last of the women had been freed late in 1943). This policy of accelerated release was largely the personal decision of the justice minister Gerry Boland, who took the view that by and large internees would be more interested in resuming their normal lives than in continuing in republican conspiracy. With a handful of exceptions, this proved an accurate assessment. By March 1945 only 115 remained in custody.[49]

[45] Liddell diary, 7 May 1944, TNA, KV4/193.
[46] Hinsley and Simkins, *British Intelligence*, 255.
[47] B1L section history, p. 10, TNA, KV4/26.
[48] My grandmother was involved in reprieve agitation. UCDA, Kathleen Barry Moloney papers, P94/46.
[49] Ó Longaigh, *Emergency Law in Independent Ireland*, 302.

SECURITY COOPERATION AFTER *OVERLORD*

Ireland remained a concern in the immediate aftermath of *Overlord*. On 9 June an RSS officer travelled to Dublin to see G2 about an anonymous letter which suggested that German internees in the Curragh were operating a radio: 'RSS have no trace but it is not altogether impossible as 3 German [internees] are attending Trinity College'. There turned out to be nothing in the scare.[50] On 11 June, according to Guy Liddell, Churchill 'seems to have three bad bees in his bonnet. Firstly de Gaulle, secondly Ireland, and thirdly the visitors ban. His good bee is the President, and anything that is contrary to the latter's wishes is liable to be swept aside'.[51] At the professional level, relations remained excellent. On 16 July Liddell humorously noted:

Dan has picked up a pigeon sent from the Resistance Movement in France. He has sent over the message but Walker apparently wants to have the pigeon as well. This raises a question of Eire's neutrality. I have suggested to Cecil that he should write a letter to Dan stating that it cannot... be denied that the pigeon was on an operational flight and should therefore, according to international law, be interned for the duration of the war. On the other hand, if he could see his way to assisting us we should be very grateful.[52]

Cordial relations between MI5 and G2 were unaffected by the political tensions over security which had dominated Anglo-Irish relations in the months leading up to *Overlord*. In August Bryan appealed to External Affairs to help obtain an exit permit for a Miss Kelly, who wished to return from Britain to deal with family matters. He was concerned that if she was not permitted to leave, her sister, who handled all G2's confidential correspondence, would have to give up her job. Cecil Liddell eased his mind: 'Permit issued 22nd August'.[53] At the political level, there was also evidence of a desire to please: in February Liddell noted that 'Dev has agreed to the establishment of Radar at Malin Head. The apparatus to be used to enable our Air Force to locate their position when dealing with U-Boats'. It would be 'run notionally by the Irish ostensibly for the guidance of aircraft', but the RAF would be in de facto control until peacetime.[54] A month later the Irish passed over cipher and other material which, insecurely stored in a wooden box, had drifted in from a scuttled U-boat off Cork unbeknownst to the crew, who were later rescued: 'It appears that [General] McKenna on his own initiative had decided to transmit the contents of this box to us'. This created potential difficulties, as 'his act was obviously unneutral and had been carried out without the knowledge of External Affairs'. It had been 'necessary to get the documents photographed as soon as possible and returned to Ireland in case any questions should be asked'. They included 'details

---

[50] Liddell diary, 9 June 1944, TNA, KV4/194.

[51] Ibid., 11 June 1944, TNA, KV4/194.

[52] Ibid., 16 July 1944, TNA, KV4/194.

[53] Bryan to Boland, 18 Aug., and Archer to Boland, with message for Bryan from Liddell, 28 Aug. 1944, NAI, DFA A8/1.

[54] Liddell diary, 21 Feb. 1945, TNA, KV4/196.

of the latest type of torpedo, which are of great interest to the Admiralty, and also charts of our minefields'.[55]

The lifting of the Irish travel ban was considered as early as July, but in the event it was not removed until May 1945. There had been talk of easing restrictions on travel to and from Northern Ireland in January, but MI5 argued that this would make it almost impossible for the Irish to maintain their controls and would result in a general degradation of security.[56] In practice, the travel restrictions were interpreted so liberally from the autumn of 1944 as to be meaningless for British and Irish people, provided that they had the requisite documentation. The evidence indicates the travel ban was formally maintained so long for two reasons: in the immediate aftermath of *Overlord* there might be a risk of accidentally providing the Germans with a 'clear indication that the landing in Normandy was a major offensive . . . and not a feint'; and at the political level there was no disposition to make life easier for Ireland. The system of travel permits remained in place until the early 1950s, not for security reasons but to provide some control over the British labour market. The theory was that Irish citizens holding travel permits could if necessary be evicted from Britain if unemployment rose.[57] There is nothing to suggest that this residual control was in any way effective.

The ban on Irish ships trading with the Iberian peninsula was not lifted until after the end of the war in Europe. Modification was considered as early as 22 June 1944, but action was thought unnecessary: the Irish were not complaining, as they 'derived considerable benefits from the new arrangement which gives them greater tonnage'. MI5 viewed this as a collusive arrangement which suited both countries. The British ships assigned to carry cargoes between Ireland and the Iberian peninsula charged lower rates, while the small Irish ships taken over on hire by Britain for the duration of the ban were particularly useful for short cross-channel journeys. Within a month of *Overlord* the possibility of permitting civil flights to and from Ireland was under discussion, and the ban was lifted two months later (despite significant Anglo-Irish tensions over the future of transatlantic civil aviation).[58] As late as January 1945 the Security Executive fretted about whether to recommend that 'local passengers and mails' could be carried between Foynes and Lisbon on the Pan American service. David Petrie warned that 'the enemy were still very anxious to obtain information as to the order of battle of the United Nations forces in Great Britain, and also as to the effects of their V.1 and V.2 bombardment'. The 'security objections' were 'overwhelming', and it was agreed not to support the proposal. There was a hint in the discussion of two peripheral themes—irritation at American disregard for security, and suspicion that the United States was seeking to secure a post-war advantage over British airlines by commencing a passenger service to Europe.[59] MI5 prevailed in a minor scuffle with the postal censorship authorities, who wished to reduce their scrutiny of Irish mail: 'we have always been in a difficulty in dealing with

---

[55] Liddell diary, 26 Mar. 1945, TNA, KV4/196. This salvaged material was collected and brought to Dublin by the German-speaking Douglas Gageby of G2. Information from Douglas Gageby.
[56] Liddell diary, 17 Jan. 1945, TNA, KV4/196.
[57] *Liddell History*, 91–2.
[58] Liddell diary, 22 and 30 June 1944, TNA, KV4/194; *Liddell History*, 93.
[59] Security Executive minutes, 10 Jan. 1945, TNA, CAB 93/2.

a question of this kind because of the very confidential nature of the real control, namely those exercised through the good offices of Dan and co and Pandora which cannot be revealed'. If the postal controls were eased, the Irish would take this as confirmation that the Axis missions were no longer considered a security threat.[60]

MI5 and GC&CS continued to talk with G2 on code matters. O'Reilly, the Clare parachutist, had a close understanding of the cipher he had been provided with. Initially he appeared willing to explain its workings and was supplied with materials to prepare examples, but after a time it was suspected that he had no intention of doing so, and intended instead to smuggle out messages to the German legation.[61] G2 preempted this by suddenly seizing his working papers, including material which he had thrown on the fire in his cell but which was salvaged and treated to recover the text (Hayes's codebreaking records include a box containing fragments of burnt paper treated with chemicals and pressed between glass slides). Hayes's examination of this material disclosed 'a hitherto unknown method of turning letters into figures on [a] keyword in such a way that some letters were represented by a single figure and others by . . . two digits'. This intriguing discovery seemed of 'quite minor significance at the time', but GC&CS were excited at the news, as was reflected in a telegram from Cecil Liddell: 'Page and self delighted come over when you think suitable stage of interrogation reached . . . Information about ciphers and device of great interest'.[62] So it proved: in the final year of the war the German army adopted the technique in 'an entirely new system of substitution and transposition ciphers', and Hayes was told that 'this whole set of ciphers would never have been solved without this vital piece of information culled from O'Reilly's work'. Hayes made one other breakthrough of minor interest: in March 1945 the Irish picked up what appeared to be transmissions to a resistance group inside Germany, the only 'British cipher' of which he had experience. These were probably fakes intended to be easily broken and read by the Germans, adding to their demoralization. Guy Liddell certainly thought so.[63]

Overlord greatly reduced concerns about Northern Ireland. In October Guy Liddell noted that Wickham was: 'heartily sick of the Northern Ireland politicians. Partition has now become the battle cry that keeps both Dev and Sir Basil Brooke in office. If they had not got the border they would probably lose their jobs. He would like to see a united Ireland and thinks that if there had been one Irish Gov[ernment]t it would have joined us in the war'.[64]

A good deal of retrospective investigation and analysis was carried out jointly by MI5 and G2, particularly on the case of Frank Ryan, while the remaining movement controls and other residual measures threw up occasional problems, but the main subjects of Anglo-Irish security dealings going forward related to awkward issues such as the possible movement of alleged war criminals through Ireland: in April 1945 Dan Bryan wrote that 'the use of South American passports by Germans

[60] Liddell diary, 7 Dec. 1944 and 6 Jan. 1945, TNA, KV4/195 and 196.
[61] On 18 Jan. 1944 G2 noted that O'Reilly had changed his story but would not elaborate on it. MAI, G2/3824.
[62] 'Hayes report'.
[63] Ibid.; Liddell diary, 26 Mar. 1945, TNA, KV4/196; Wilkinson and Bright Astley, *Gubbins*, 210–11.
[64] Liddell diary, 4 Oct. 1944, TNA, KV4/194.

is engaging the attention of the authorities in other countries', and the question remained sensitive for a couple of years.[65] These were matters where professional goodwill might sometimes alleviate but could never disperse the awkward political climate in which dealings took place. MI5 and G2 also cooperated closely in investigating the activities of the Breton Guy Vissault de Coetlogon, arrested for treason in October 1944. Displaying more courage than sense, de Coetlogon had assisted in German efforts to establish stay-behind groups after *Overlord*. He was brought to Britain for questioning. From this it emerged that he had visited Ireland in 1938, when only a teenager. The purpose of that visit was not espionage, but rather the exploration of shared Celtic roots and culture. During it de Coetlogon had met Helmut Clissmann and Jupp Hoven, who worked on such sentiments among Irish republicans and encouraged exchanges with like-minded Celts. He also met Bretons resident in Ireland, most notably Erwin Mill Arden, and the Fianna Fáil TD Dan Breen. When questioned by G2 and the Garda in January 1945, Mill Arden denied all knowledge of de Coetlogon, but admitted that in July 1939 he had collected money in Paris for the IRA's Jim O'Donovan; in 1941 he also allowed O'Donovan to write a message in secret ink on an anodyne letter which he sent to the Spanish lawyer Jaime Champourcin, the middle-man in the release of Frank Ryan from jail, who was in close touch with the Abwehr.[66]

De Coetlogon had also known the Mulcahy family into which Clissmann had married, and had met other republican notables including, most likely, Moss Twomey, the former IRA chief of staff. His interrogation disclosed that in 1941 he had been recruited by two men styling themselves the 'Owens brothers'—Jupp Hoven and his brother—who were then attached to the Abwehr in Paris. From these he got a general picture of the Irish missions of the agents Goertz and Schutz. In the course of seeking a Breton fisherman capable of transporting agents to the British Isles in 1941, he also met Frank Ryan in Paris, possibly to discuss a return to Ireland by sea. De Coetlogon also stated that for a time in 1943 he had been employed by the SD on the analysis of intelligence from Ireland, mainly from Belfast, Cork, Dublin, and Galway. He 'insisted after considerable pressure' that these 'were sent by agents working in Ireland with W/T sets', 'Albert, René and Pierre', to whom he had given briefings on Irish political affairs prior to their departure to carry out 'sabotage [presumably in Northern Ireland] and to obtain political information'.

This sensational claim puzzled both MI5 and G2 considerably, because so far as they were aware the only Irish agent reports to reach the Germans in 1943 were those carried by Eastwood to Lisbon. Furthermore, as de Coetlogon was working for the SD in 1943 it seemed unlikely that he would have seen the handful of messages sent by Goertz's wireless operator Anthony Deery up to his capture in March 1942, as these were in the possession of the SD's rivals in the Abwehr. The Irish material he recalled seemed to be primarily political and of no intelligence value, and MI5 reasoned that it derived from 'political and general

<hr />

[65] Bryan to Duff (Department of Justice), 24 Apr. 1945, MAI, G2/X/0244.
[66] Year-by-year analysis of de Coetlogon interrogation, undated, Oct. 1944, TNA, KV2/303; Hull, *Irish Secrets*, 46–7.

situation reports from newspapers and possibly other sources' prepared by the German foreign office—O'Reilly, the Clare parachutist, had also described working on such material in Berlin—rather than from clandestine sources. The two agencies came to the unsatisfactory conclusion that de Coetlogon's narrative was somewhat jumbled and inaccurate in specifics, but not false. After the war some Breton and Flemish nationalists who had collaborated with the Germans managed to make their way to Ireland, where they became part of what might be termed the broad republican anti-establishment. De Coetlogon, who MI5 informed G2 had been willing to 'go to Dublin and Sligo with a W/T set' to 'open up a "double cross" service', was not so fortunate, being executed by the French in April 1945.[67]

There is a ghoulish symmetry in the fact that counter-espionage cooperation with the Irish against Germany began and ended with the execution of Frenchmen—in 1939 the mercenary traitor Sous-Lieutenant Aubert in Toulon, in 1945 the Breton nationalist and collaborator Vissault de Coetlogon. Their cases also illustrate two strands of German intrigue involving Ireland, the one purely opportunistic—Aubert addressed his messages to Dublin simply because the reliable Mrs Brandy, widow of a part-time agent, lived there—and the other based around the deliberate exploitation of Pan-Celticism against British interests.

Despite the extent and success of Anglo-Irish security cooperation, old myths died hard: in December 1944 a Garda officer reported an approach by a British naval intelligence officer, who asked 'whether I had heard of any unusual happenings on the North Donegal Coast . . . he said they were worried lest a German submarine had been recently sheltering or getting supplies such as vegetables especially in Sheephaven Bay'.[68] Nevertheless, it is clear that Whitehall's assessment both of the historic and the future security problems posed by Ireland was considerably influenced by the liaison built up since September 1939. Even at the political level, there was quiet recognition that Ireland had not let Britain down in security terms. A few years after the war the Labour foreign secretary Ernest Bevin, who as minister for labour from 1940 had been closely acquainted with the question of Irish migration, went out of his way at a reception in Brussels to praise the Irish contribution to the success of *Overlord*. He stressed the war cabinet's acute anxiety about the secrecy of the invasion preparations: 'we had to take the top Irish officials into our confidence . . . they gave . . . co-operation unstintingly, and (he repeated this with emphasis) not one single leak occurred. This is a great tribute to the Irish government and the Irish officials concerned'.[69]

DIPLOMATIC INTELLIGENCE 1944–1945

The satisfactory resolution of the German legation radio issue did not leave British minds entirely at rest. Pandora revealed that Berlin had continued to urge Hempel

[67] Transcript of de Coetlogon interrogation, and analysis of his responses, 18 Oct., and Cecil Liddell to Moore (RUC) and to Bryan, 3 and 24 Nov. 1944, TNA, KV2/303. By February 1945, Jupp Hoven was a prisoner of war in the United States. Liddell diary, 8 Feb. 1945, TNA, KV4/196.

[68] Chief Superintendent, Letterkenny, to Garda Headquarters, 4 Dec. 1944, NAI, DFA P94.

[69] Quoted in O'Halpin, *Defending Ireland*, 234.

Table 6.1. *British decodes relating to Ireland, January 1944–May 1945*

	French	Irish	Italian	Japanese	Others	Total
January 1944		6	2	6		14
February		6	2	3		11
March		9	1	3		13
April	2	4		1		7
May		21				21
June	2	18		3		23
July	2	13		5		20
August		17		4		21
September	4	12	1	6	1	24
October	2		1		1	4
November	1	13		2		16
December	7	26		1		34
January 1945		12		1	1	14
February		9		3		12
March		8		2	2	12
April		6		1		7
May	4	15	1	1		21
TOTALS	24	195	8	42	5	274

to find a solution which would not involve losing the set. In January there were fears that a Spanish diplomat returning to Dublin might bring in another transmitter for the Germans: 'we shall try to get a look at this and if possible put it out of order', although there is no evidence that any attempt was made to import such a radio. American codebreakers remained concerned that Berlin continued to transmit to the German legation call-sign, indicating that Hempel might have a second set.[70]

There was no great shift in emphasis in British decodes relating to Ireland in the six months running up to *Overlord*, but a marked change thereafter. Where material circulated up to June reflected considerable Axis anticipation of an Allied invasion, that after the blow fell indicated greater Allied interest in Irish diplomatic reporting from Axis Europe. This is not altogether reflected in the bald summary in Table 6.1. As in previous chapters, the missing dimension is German diplomatic traffic between Dublin and Berlin; this is partly offset by individual German decodes available in other British records and in the Magic summaries.

These decodes cast some light both on Axis activities concerning Ireland, and on the development of Irish policy as the war in Europe moved towards its climax. They reflect the gradual development of consultation between neutral diplomats in Rome and in Berlin on humanitarian questions, which in turn increased neutrals' awareness of the nature and scale of Germany's forced labour and extermination policies.

The contents of Irish traffic were subjected to considerable analysis in the months leading up to *Overlord*. GC&CS continued to experience difficulties with some cables—on 1 May a meeting at GC&CS heard that 'the Irish . . . had recently introduced more complicated methods which embarrassed our authorities as they

---

[70] Liddell diary, 8 Jan. 1944, TNA, KV4/193; O'Halpin, *Defending Ireland*, 190.

are no longer fully aware of what was being discussed'.[71] Two experienced decoders 'were concentrating on this' (a year previously, it appears that Irish material was handled by a single officer whose main business was Siamese traffic).[72] Progress was slow: 'the Irish are now using a cipher we can rarely read', particularly messages in the highest-grade Dearg system, which on 15 May was termed 'unbreakable'.[73] Returns of Irish traffic between March and June identified a number of potentially significant messages to and from Washington, Madrid, and Berlin which could not be decoded. Furthermore, through human error in the cable censorship there were 'occasional missing cables' which 'were never sent here. It is of the utmost importance that all cables in and out of Dublin should be available to us'.[74] Although redacted, the records also show that for two months GC&CS were supplied with photographs of recent original Irish messages, in code and *en clair*, some bearing the stamp of the Irish legation in Berlin. They also received a photograph of a signed original file copy of a note by Cremin addressed to External Affairs. Given the nature of the redactions, it is probable that the material was secured by SIS. How did they come by it? It seems highly unlikely that, at the height of the war, they managed not merely to penetrate the Irish legation in their enemy's tightly guarded capital, but to smuggle out the results of their espionage in an extraordinarily timely fashion; it is far more likely that Cremin, mindful of the destruction of the legation and all its records the previous November, routinely sent material for safe keeping to the Irish legation in Berne. If so, either the documents were intercepted and photographed in transit, presumably in Switzerland, or an intruder or insider in the Berne mission provided the original material to be photographed. In either case, it was a timely piece of espionage.[75]

Dublin's instructions to missions abroad, hitherto generally characterized by brevity and banality, reflected the impact of the American note. When a second démarche was in the air in April, Walshe sent two furious messages to Brennan in Washington, declaiming against the idiocy of American claims about gaps in Irish security: 'we are convinced that the American Government does not fear serious espionage from here . . . Their real object is to force us to abandon neutrality and enter the war'. While the 'British are proceeding on the basis of friendly cooperation' and 'Maffey leaves such matters to British and Irish security experts', Gray 'sends home rumours and stories' and on his advice the State Department 'are wrong not only in their estimate of extent of danger but in thinking that anything can be gained by getting tough'. GC&CS were unable to read some of Brennan's messages home, not that this hapless diplomat had much useful to tell Dublin.[76]

MacWhite's reports from Rome on the shifting sands of Italian politics, on food shortages, on German military attitudes, on growing Allied air superiority, and the

---

[71] 26th meeting of heads of Diplomatic and Research sections, 1 May 1944, TNA, HW53/17.

[72] Denniston, *Thirty Secret Years*, 124, quoting a report by an American code expert visiting GC&CS, 21 May 1943.

[73] Minute by ? [possibly Jane Archer of SIS], 17 May 1944, TNA, HW53/56. The letterhead on the document has been redacted.

[74] Unsigned note to Mr Rees, 30 May 1944, TNA, HW53/56.

[75] Photograph of Cremin to Dublin re Mr Rooney, 1 June 1944, TNA, HW53/56.

[76] Dublin to Brennan, 17 and 19 Apr. 1944, TNA, HW12/300 and 301.

efforts of German and Italian fascist representatives to lure the neutral missions into moving north into the area controlled by Mussolini's Salo government featured extensively not only in British decodes but in the Magic summaries. In February he reported a consensus amongst the diplomatic corps that 'the loss of Rome would mean a serious loss of morale for the Axis and would very likely precipitate a Balkan crisis'. Shortly afterwards he observed that 'no one wants to hold office under the Fascist Republic, but those who refuse are as likely to be shot as those who accept'. During the first days of the Anzio operation the Germans 'sent groups of soldiers through the principal streets singing songs of victory', but two days later they 'appear to be less optimistic now'.[77] In June he offered the uncharacteristically alarmist assessment that the inevitable political turmoil which would follow Germany's departure would see 'either Fascism or Boshevism triumphant'.[78]

The fall of Rome to the Allies on 5 June greatly reduced the intrinsic value of MacWhite's reports, but interest in those of Con Cremin intensified. This is reflected not only in the number of Irish decodes shown to Churchill, but in the considerable attention they received in the Magic summaries. While they shed some light on the nuances of Irish–German relations, their main value to the Allies was undoubtedly as reportage of the ebb and flow of opinion and morale in Germany. In May 1944 Cremin reported on his surprise at the unusual degree of confidence displayed by an 'ordinarily rather skeptical and objective' German official that the impending Allied assault on Europe's Atlantic coast, wherever it came, would be decisively beaten. Others expressed the hope that the attack would come soon.[79]

Cremin's work increasingly involved interventions and representations in respect of people whom the Germans wished to kill: as well as various groups of Jews across Europe, these included in May 1944 an Irish passport-holder sentenced to death for sheltering American airmen in France.[80] His most significant task in 1944, however, was probably to deliver an aide-mémoire which stated that the Irish government attributed the recent American démarche on Irish security to 'German infringements of our sovereignty and neutrality, such as parachute landings . . . recurrence of acts compromising to us would definitely [entail] most serious consequences'. The German under-secretary of state replied that 'neither German Government, any Official Authority including Military Authority nor German Legation know of or had anything to do with this landing . . . his opinion was that [the two] men wanted to go home and persuaded some pilot to take them'. This 'quite friendly' if somewhat surreal exchange echoed what Hempel had reported: an unequivocal Irish threat of drastic repercussions if any more agents arrived.[81]

---

[77] MacWhite to Dublin, 3, 5 and 13 Feb. 1944, TNA, HW12/298.

[78] Ibid., 29 July and 4, 11 and 27 Oct. and 14 Nov. 1943, and 17 Jan. and 19 June 1944, and the Vatican to Dublin, 6 Aug., 18 and 26 Oct. and 9 and 11 Nov. 1943, TNA, HW12/290, 291, 293, 294, 296, and 301.

[79] Magic summary, 15 May, quoting Cremin to Dublin, 8 May 1944, USNA, RG457, box 11.

[80] Dublin to Cremin, 11 and 22 May, and Cremin to Dublin, 19 June 1944, TNA, HW12/300 and 301. The man concerned was Robert Armstrong, originally of Edgeworthstown, Co. Longford, and 'well known to General MacKeon', the war of independence hero and Fine Gael TD. His execution was postponed in June and the Irish were advised to make a plea for mercy. On 29 July 1944, Cremin told Dublin that his sentence had been commuted to eight years' servitude. TNA, HW12/303.

[81] Cremin to Dublin, 17 Mar. 1944, TNA, HW12/300.

As the bombs fell thicker and thicker on Germany in the autumn, Dublin and Berlin found time to conclude a financial agreement covering commercial debts, although even this technical exercise fell foul of Nazi madness—the German official involved was married to a Turkish woman, and was one of many sent 'on prolonged leave' as a result of an edict removing people with spouses of enemy nationality from state service. This delayed completion of the negotiations. Hempel attempted to have the Irish recognize the protectorate of Bohemia and Moravia as part of the Reich for the purposes of the agreement, but the Irish would recognize only the Sudetenland. That point settled, the agreement was eventually signed by Cremin in Berlin. Within months, however, Dublin had second thoughts. In late April Cremin reported from Bregenz on his efforts to get the Germans to pay some of their debts by transferring funds in Switzerland or Portugal—the official concerned had turned up only 'by a coincidence . . . I think he is well disposed and will do his utmost to arrange the transfer of the sum mentioned', although he had neither the authority nor the records necessary, and probably had other plans for any funds he could get his hands on. Dublin seems belatedly to have got cold feet about transacting such business with the crumbling Reich: 'Please destroy Debt agreement . . . and relevant papers'. There were also conversations about a possible swap of interned civilian seamen, an enterprise which might have provoked difficulties with Britain had a definite arrangement been made.[82]

Cremin had more success in rescuing Mary Cummins, an Irish woman imprisoned since February 1941 for resistance activities in France, 'working with the British Intelligence Service and French Second Bureau . . . her motives for so acting were fundamentally charitable and to some extent financial. I intend to take her with us if possible', and he managed to bring her with his family to safety in Switzerland in April 1945.[83] In the last months of the Reich's existence, he doggedly reported on civilian morale, on the growing fear of Russia—'although there are stories of arrivals of Russians in some towns which are in strong contrast to the official version, there is no doubt that most people are terrified of what the Russians will do if they get here'—and on rumours that Himmler would succeed Hitler and seek peace with the western Allies. As conditions deteriorated in the capital he moved first to Salzburg, and then to Bregenz, cutting himself off from access to the German government. By then, as Walshe put it to the new Italian minister in Dublin, the 'only business' which Ireland had with the Reich concerned 'bombs dropped on our territory by German bombers'.[84]

Irish decodes, in common with those of other neutrals—Spain, Portugal, the Holy See, Sweden, and even predominantly Muslim states such as Turkey and Persia—reflected continued fragmentary efforts to do something for groups of

[82] Cremin to Dublin, and Dublin to Cremin, 21 Dec. 1944, TNA, HW12/307. The man concerned, Dumont, had a Turkish wife. Magic summary, 16 Jan., USNA, RG457, box 9, Cremin to Dublin, 20 Jan. and 24 Apr., and Dublin to Cremin, 17 May 1945, TNA, HW12/308, 315 and 316.

[83] Frank Cremins (Berne) to Dublin, 7 July 1941, TNA, HW12/266; Cremin to Dublin, 1 Feb. 1945, TNA, HW12/309. Ms Cummins's name is redacted in some British documents. Keogh, *Con Cremin*, 83–5. She is listed as 'Lucy Cummins' in Walshe to de Valera, 28 Nov. 1941, UCDA, de Valera papers, P150/2571.

[84] Cremin to Dublin, 1 and 2 Feb. 1945, TNA, HW12/309; Confalonieri (Dublin) to Rome, 15 Feb. 1945, TNA, HW12/311.

Jews across Europe. German refusal generally to recognize foreign citizenship as a legal protection against persecution, while a minor technicality in terms of the Holocaust, was an affront to neutral states like Ireland attempting to play by the conventional rules of international diplomacy in their treatment of the belligerents. This clear breach of international law provided reassuringly procedural and technical grounds for seeking discourse with Germany and her satellites which might possibly have humanitarian benefits. The catastrophe which befell Hungarian Jewry in October 1944 was an unusually public event which unfolded before the eyes of the international community of neutrals, amongst whom there was no longer any doubt about Germany's genocidal policy. The Vatican encouraged Ireland to associate herself with representations to the Slovak and Hungarian governments about the deportation of Jews, a fruitless intervention: 'all Jews except those in hiding have been deported to Germany'.[85]

Irish efforts, however diffident, to raise such matters were inevitably rebuffed. An official told Cremin in October that 'rumours of intention to exterminate Jews were being spread by . . . enemy sources' and were quite untrue; when Dublin enquired about Jews from Kaunas in Lithuania a few weeks later, Cremin was brushed off: 'while they were anxious to help us in every way . . . affecting our interests directly or indirectly, they would find it difficult to understand how the question of Lithuanian Jews could affect us particularly'. Cremin sought guidance on whether 'the matter is important to us because of possible hostile propaganda if we were to seem to be indifferent', a cable selected for Churchill to see. A later Irish aide-mémoire about another group of Jews was refused by the German foreign office on the grounds of 'the persons concerned not being Irish and having no Irish connections etc'., and immediately afterwards Cremin was told, apropos of earlier enquiries about Jews in Vittel in France, that 'no further possible representations could be received from us in connection with the persons concerned'.[86]

The strangest Irish message was one from Lisbon in October 1944. This discussed the 'highly complicated' matter of a child entitled to Irish diplomatic protection: it 'appeared to be a case of seduction of a girl of twelve by a married man of 50', a German who 'is thought to be an important secret agent', and who had made over property to her. The Irish chargé suspected that the 'mother is a British secret agent and that contact with German has resulted in daughter becoming German agent or tool'. The chargé approached the British minister, who said that 'their security people' would like to see both mother and daughter return to Britain. At C's direction this enigmatic decode was not circulated in the usual fashion, instead being copied only to Section V of SIS.[87]

The only other theme of concern to Britain in Irish traffic in the last phase of the war was the question of post-war transatlantic civil aviation. Britain and the United States had somewhat differing views on this: for strategic as well as commercial

[85] Irish minister, the Vatican, to Dublin, 9 and 21 Dec. 1944, TNA, HW12/307.

[86] Dublin to Cremin about Jews in Vittel in France, 5 Jan.; Cremin to Dublin, 28 Oct., 29 Nov., 15, 18, and 24 Dec. 1944, TNA, HW12/296, 305 and 307.

[87] Irish chargé, Lisbon, to Dublin, 2 Oct. 1944, and undated note by Robert Cecil, personal assistant to C, TNA, HW37/3. The Irish chargé was a brother of the IRA's Jim O'Donovan, but there is no suggestion that he was in any way disloyal to the Irish state.

reasons, Britain favoured the establishment of a major hub in Scotland, whereas the Americans seemed fatally attracted by Shannon, where the Irish intended to develop their existing airfield into one capable of handling transatlantic traffic. Through Irish decodes from Chicago, following an unsuccessful conference on international post-war civil aviation, the British were able to observe the unwelcome progress of an Irish–American understanding which copperfastened Shannon's position as America's post-war European hub (two of these cables were selected for Churchill to see).[88] He wrote censoriously to Roosevelt on the question: 'Naturally everyone here is astonished that this should have been started without our being told beforehand. We already complained when they were invited to the Chicago conference without a word to us'. Roosevelt's reply was unusually peremptory: the deal did not imply forgiveness for Ireland's neutrality, any more than did a comparable arrangement with Spain, and 'any feeling of complacence [*sic*] . . . on the part of the Irish has now been somewhat deflated by their being left out of the San Francisco Conference'. 'There can of course be no question of annulling the agreement. I am sorry but there it is'.[89]

If it yielded no worthwhile positive intelligence, Italian traffic at least provided some light relief. In May G2 told MI5 that, 'with one or two exceptions, there had been very little indication of pro-Axis activities by the Italians', while in January Berardis, revelling in a new guise of anti-fascist crusader, had provided a list of Italians—mainly café proprietors, but also including my prep-school art teacher Signor Volpi—who continued to worship Mussolini. The group had been interrogated, and 'appeared to be very frightened and for the most part stated that their attitude was attributable rather to their dislike' of the turncoat Berardis 'than to loyalty to Mussolini'. Of Berardis, a QRS report observed that, 'previously a noisy Fascist, [he] is now lavish in his entertainment of Allied sympathisers', while another stated that he 'has been singularly unhelpful in response to attempts to obtain . . . details of Axis activities in Dublin' before the Italian defeat. He 'admitted that at one time Hempel induced him to mobilize the Italian Fascist colony . . . for active work . . . but . . . he and Hempel quarreled before anything could be accomplished'. He 'complained that Hempel treated him "as a vassal" '.[90]

Berardis's nominated successor arrived in Dublin at the end of September, yet to Rome's mystification he was still signing cables over a fortnight later. He indulged in more foot-dragging before returning home. In January 1945 MacWhite reported from Rome that 'Berardis is still hanging around here . . . He thinks he is the best fitted for either the Vatican or the Moscow Embassy but nobody here seems to take him seriously. He called in a couple of days ago and asked if I would not tell the Foreign Ministry what a clever fellow he is'.[91] When placed on the retired list in

---

[88] These November 1944 Irish cables from Chicago to Dublin are in TNA, HW1/3362 and 3375.

[89] Churchill to Roosevelt, 27 Jan., and Roosevelt 's reply, 15 Mar. 1945, in Kimball (ed.), *Churchill and Roosevelt*, iii. 520 and 566–7. The San Francisco conference of June 1945 established the United Nations organization.

[90] *Liddell History*, 104; QRS reports, 1 Mar. and 31 Aug. 1944, TNA, DO121/85.

[91] Foreign Ministry (in Naples) to Berardis, 18 Sept., and précis of Rome to Berardis, 13 Oct. 1944, TNA, HW12/304 and 305; MacWhite letter to Dublin, 17 Jan. 1945, NAI, DFA P12/8.

1947, he mounted a spirited campaign for reinstatement, circulating a memorial setting out his case. He was not to be compared with the ambassadors to Spain and Japan, who had accepted enforced retirement: his memorial quoted David Gray as saying he knew Berardis had never been in favour of Italy joining the war, claimed his relations with Hempel were restricted to 'purely outward formalities', and pointed out that he was the first Italian representative abroad to 'take on the representation of the legitimate government'. He had occupied a 'special moral position at home and abroad'. It would be 'diabolical to judge men and events by the results of the war and to make scapegoats of worthy and honest officials'. It is not known whether his government yielded to these characteristically overblown entreaties.[92]

The long-running saga of divisions and backbiting within the French legation continued during 1944, even after the final collapse of the Vichy regime in August. In October Paris recalled Lachèvre and Albertas, both of whom had been in administrative limbo and without pay since the spring, only to learn that both first wanted their debts cleared and their fares paid. Lachèvre left in December, shortly after the death of his wife in France. Albertas received a further instruction to return, but continued to raise difficulties: he demanded £700 to meet the cost of moving himself, his wife, his daughter, and his secretary. The French minister was close to despair, imploring Paris to reiterate the order in categorical terms so as to put an end to 'toute tergiversation'.[93] French and Irish decodes also disclosed some hiccups arising from the change of regime following the liberation of Paris: much to Walshe's indignation, Irish recognition of de Lafourcade as the representative of de Gaulle's new government did not secure reciprocal acceptance of Murphy. Walshe suspected that de Lafourcade's cables explaining the position might have been discounted, as 'we fear they regard him as useless'. The rift was eventually smoothed over. Murphy finally met de Gaulle informally in March 1945. He found the general 'rather cold. His voice is rather harsh, and he speaks very deliberately. He rarely looks at you'. De Gaulle declared himself 'very touched' by de Valera's message of goodwill, and responded: 'Ireland and France . . . had always been friendly. There was no reason for quarrels between them'. Murphy was not yet formally recognized as minister, and de Gaulle surprised his departing guest by nevertheless laying on a guard of honour.[94] The British may have missed that report, which went by post. There is nothing to suggest any great irritation in London at the time it took for the Irish to withdraw recognition from Vichy, although by July 1944 the Foreign Office were nettled by the Swiss attitude, despite Berne's particular need to stay in touch with whatever functioning authorities there were in those areas of France adjacent to their borders.[95] De Gaulle's apparent acceptance of Irish neutrality was not shared by the

---

[92] Berardis to Boland, 12 Dec. 1947, enclosing an English translation of the memorial, NAI, DFA P166. In 1950 he prepared a lengthy private memoir, 'Missione Nell Eire (21 Novembre 1938–23 Octobre 1944)', a copy of which is in UCDA, de Valera papers, P150/2705. Quaroni, Berardis's counterpart in Kabul, by 1945 was ambassador in Moscow.

[93] De Lafourcade to Paris, 22 Oct., 4 and 8 Dec. 1944, TNA, HW12/305 and 307.

[94] De Lafourcade to Paris, 27 Sept., and Walshe to Murphy (via Berne), 9 Oct. 1944, TNA, HW12/305; Murphy letter to Dublin, 26 Mar. 1945, NAI, DFA P12/1.

[95] Foreign Office to British representative, Algiers, 17 July 1944, TNA, FO660/117.

new French minister, who in May suggested that Paris stimulate press criticism of Ireland: 'Venant de la France, cette constatation aurait ici du poids'.[96]

Decodes indicated that by the start of 1944 Japan's demands on Beppu were growing. Tokyo wanted hard information on the British economy: in January they reiterated their need for material on war production, on commodity prices, on labour questions—'natures of industry, classification of unemployment, and its causes'—on 'post-war questions', and on 'any items which can be concluded as British weaknesses', a list which suggested efforts to construct a sophisticated picture of Britain's long-term capacity to wage war, albeit material which was scarcely within Beppu's competence to deliver.[97] Other cables conveyed the same message: Beppu was to step up his information gathering, whatever the risk to Japanese–Irish relations. Tokyo sent him a new cipher keyword, consigned via the ambassador in Berlin, who was asked to request the Germans to include it in one of their messages to Hempel.[98] This exercise in inter-Axis solidarity would have worked very well until Pandora came on stream; in 1944 it simply allowed GC&CS to confirm their parallel mastery of Japanese and German diplomatic traffic.

Of the 116 cables Beppu sent in 1944, thirty-four have been traced. These show that he ran into acute problems as he attempted to discharge an expanded remit. In February he sought and obtained permission to rent a large house to serve as a combined office and residence. It was 'unsatisfactory' that 'the listener to British broadcasts is actually carrying out his duties in his own flat', and it made sense to consolidate in one premises.[99] The Garda and G2 had been paying particular care to his mission for over a year, after the first indications of links with republican circles and with a 'Friends of India Society' (FOIS) emerged through observation of the movements and associations of Beppu's subordinate Ichihashi. Ichihashi had taken up with a coterie of Northern IRA men to whom he was giving money in return for war news, and had encouraged the FOIS (ironically, G2 obtained evidence which suggested that this organization, established quite suddenly in Dublin in 1943, was most likely a British front to facilitate the study of links between Indians and Axis sympathizers).[100]

Less than a fortnight before *Overlord*, Beppu was summonsed to External Affairs, where Walshe 'spoke to him without concealment about the incorrect behaviour of . . . Mr Ichihashi', who 'had for a long time been causing us some worry' because he was in touch with 'Irish subversive elements' and 'was also interested in the activities of a group of Indians in Dublin'. Walshe also asked whether the Japanese possessed a transmitter. A few days later Beppu 'quite cheerfully' presented a cock-and-bull story explaining Ichihashi's activities, and Walshe then 'felt obliged to dot the i's and cross the t's' of the accusations. Beppu 'became perturbed . . . He got as pale as a Japanese can, and he looked both astonished and very guilty'. Walshe suggested that 'Security officials should interview Mr Ichihashi', a proposition which 'convinced Beppu that we were very sure of our ground': Beppu then 'became full of

[96] French minister, Dublin, to Paris, 14 May 1945, TNA, HW12/317.
[97] Tokyo to Beppu, 24 Jan. 1944, TNA, HW12/296.
[98] Tokyo to Berlin, 19 Jan. 1944, TNA, HW12/297.
[99] Beppu to Tokyo, 18 Feb. 1944, TNA, HW12/297.
[100] All material on FOIS comes from O'Malley, 'Ireland, India and Empire', 203–9.

smiles and explained that . . . when certain people came to them and were enemies of their enemies, they felt they had to be kind to them, and anything that had been done by Ichihashi was certainly not intended in the remotest way to injure the interests of Ireland'.[101]

This was a delicate moment. Beppu had conceded that Ichihashi had been in touch with the IRA, whose chief of staff was still being sought for the murder of Sergeant O'Brien, plainly to obtain war information. In comparable circumstances neutrals such as Sweden, Portugal, and Afghanistan had demanded the withdrawal of offending officials of both sets of belligerents. Because of its land border with India, Afghanistan is the best comparator. There, the British military attaché in Kabul was forced out in 1941 for unacceptable activities, which included allowing young Afghan men to drink in his house. While the British legation made a show of rejecting such allegations, it is clear that they were aware of his 'personal foibles' and that he was regarded as a dodgy character. He was succeeded by a better-behaved officer, and in the summer of 1942 a Russian-speaking SOE agent arrived as first secretary in the legation and took over intelligence gathering, doing an excellent job while maintaining good relations with the Afghans.[102] In the autumn of 1943 and early 1944 three of the staff of the German legation and one Italian involved in espionage and subversion against India and the Soviet Union were withdrawn—the British happily gave the Germans safe conduct across India to the Arabian Sea, and they eventually reached Germany via Persia, Iraq, and Turkey.[103]

The Irish would not have known of the Afghan case, but they probably heard in general terms of comparable steps quietly taken by European neutrals and would have known that these need not have led to a diplomatic rupture. On the other hand, action against Ichihashi might have had implications for Irish missionaries under Japanese control in the Far East. There were additional and perhaps decisive considerations: his departure, however diplomatically disguised, would have required a British safe conduct, and this was unlikely so close to *Overlord*. His case could also have been seized on by the Allies as confirmation that the Axis legations were actively engaged in espionage. That would utterly discredit Dublin's position on the American note, which was that the Axis missions were not a threat to Allied security, and would make it almost impossible not to take comparable action against the German legation.

The Allies seem not to have got wind of the affair—there is no mention of it in Guy Liddell's diary, or in decodes of Beppu's messages to Tokyo—and the Irish action probably put an end to Ichihashi's intrigues. Nevertheless Beppu continued to send on whatever war news he could, including 'chit-chat . . . picked up' from 'Irishmen who had been to the Belfast district on a summer holiday'. They spoke of the rumoured effectiveness of the V1 flying bombs, of the open belief of most

[101] Walshe to taoiseach, 27 May and 1 June 1944, NAI, DFA A2.
[102] O'Halpin, 'Britain's Neutral Neighbours', 35–7.
[103] Berlin to Kabul, 18 Dec. 1943; German minister, Kabul, to Berlin, 16 Feb. 1944 and 13 and 14 Apr. 1945, TNA, HW12/295, 297 and 318. In 1971, at a conference in Calcutta on Subhas Chandra Bose, Professor Milan Hauner met one of the Germans involved in espionage in Kabul, Herr Witzel. The latter was very discomfited to find that Hauner had been reading his reports to Berlin in the German archives. Information from Professor Hauner, 2006.

American troops stationed in Northern Ireland that they were bound for France, and of American reports of the dogged resistance of Japanese forces in the Pacific. A few weeks later, people who had visited Belfast reported that three or four newly built medium aircraft-carriers were on sea trials, and that almost all American troops had departed.[104]

These were the last decodes with any intelligence content: most of Beppu's communications thereafter dealt with shortages of money and with missionary questions. In February 1945 SIS reported that Beppu had stopped 'payment of Ichihashi's salary to defray debts. There was said to be one debt of £80 for presents to a lady friend' (Beppu's own eminently respectable passion was golf: before Pearl Harbor he had been elected a member of a club, although only after 'considerable pressure' on the committee from External Affairs, and 'could find nobody willing to play with him'). In February Tokyo sent Beppu a mild reprimand about the length of his cables, on grounds both of expense and of the time involved in decoding them, insisting that he be more concise. In March Tokyo cabled Shanghai with a query about an imprisoned Irish doctor and his wife whose case Beppu had raised. In April came news of the disappearance, while in Japanese navy custody in Manila on 10 February, of four Irish priests, whose bodies were never found. Beppu warned it was 'most important to give . . . the facts' lest the issue lead to a severing of relations, something which Maffey thought possible: de Valera might use the issue of 'the assassination of Catholic priests . . . it would be easy, would cost nothing, and might gain much', particularly in the United States. Beppu, reporting on a talk with Walshe, believed that Ireland would stay neutral although the Allies might bring further pressure about the 'running sore' of the Japanese mission. He may have been right: plans were afoot to force neutrals generally to break off relations with Japan. The treatment of European missionaries had become a difficult issue for Tokyo, 'in view of the special importance which we attach to our relations with the Catholics'.[105]

Beppu reported Walshe as saying that the battle for Okinawa had made the British realize that 'Japan is a tougher enemy than Germany', but that Allied power must eventually prevail. Just a week before Hiroshima, he reported indiscreet remarks made by Robert Brennan, on leave from Washington, 'to a member of my staff' (presumably a local employee, since even Brennan would scarcely have been so foolish as to talk freely to a Japanese official) at a party: 'American sentiment . . . was strongly in favour of forcing Japan to her knees because of Pearl Harbor . . . but how Japan was to be occupied no one had the foggiest idea' and, surprisingly presciently, 'America had no scruples about using cruel and inhuman weapons and methods of warfare as long as Japan was powerless to retaliate'. Brennan also recounted the story of how, when Roosevelt died, the Soviet ambassador had demanded to be allowed

---

[104] Beppu to Tokyo, 2 and 31 Aug. 1944, TNA, HW12/303 and 304;.

[105] G2 interview with M, 21 Feb. 1945, MAI, G2/X/1091; Smyllie, 'Unneutral Neutral Eire', 325; Tokyo to Beppu, 27 Feb.; Tokyo to Shanghai, 11 Mar.; Maffey to London, 21 May., Beppu to Tokyo, 1 May and 20 July, TNA, HW12/310, 312, 315, and 326; DO35/1229; Liddell diary, 17 Apr. and 5 May, TNA, KV4/196; Tokyo to Japanese minister, the Vatican, 9 May 1945, TNA, HW12/316. Two of the four priests were posthumously honoured for their aid to American civilian internees and prisoners of war. Crowley, *Those Who Journeyed With Us*, 21–2.

to view the body.[106] When Beppu's mission was inspected by the Allies after Japan's surrender they found precious little of interest. Beppu ignored a general order for all Japanese diplomats abroad to return without delay, staying in Ireland until 1948.[107]

The decoded traffic of greatest interest to the Allies was, naturally, German. It is also the hardest to track in British records, although the Magic summaries partly compensate for this. The fact that Hempel had surrendered his transmitter did not prevent Berlin from pressuring him to produce more intelligence. Espionage, however, was effectively ruled out in February 1944, when the German foreign ministry convened a conference, because of 'recent events in certain neutral countries'—presumably including the captures of Kenny and O'Reilly—to consider 'whether the achievements of . . . intelligence organizations . . . justify our running the risk of political attacks' where these were detected.[108] The success of *Overlord* rendered the German legation very much less significant in security terms. Hempel had neither the means nor the will to do much more than report dutifully to Berlin on dealings with the Irish, and furnish vague accounts of the impact of the war on Britain. One message sent in early January 1945 spoke of 'the very depressed morale and notorious war weariness reported on all sides to exist in England', described the fall of V-weapons in London and Manchester, and predicted the failure of Britain's 'entire potato crop' due to 'incessant rain'. It also relayed a suggestion from 'an informant who has a thorough knowledge both of the British and of the North American population . . . that a bombardment of the great United States cities, particularly New York, might produce absolutely decisive results', given the 'hysterical impressibility prevalent among the American population'. The cable ended with a rumour of Roosevelt's deteriorating health, and a claim that Churchill, 'whose popularity . . . had sunk . . . to a very low level, had recently declared in an intimate circle that he had always regarded the Bolshevists as Brutes . . . but they were even worse than he had thought'. This was one of the last Dublin cables selected for Churchill to see, and he doubtless enjoyed it.[109]

As the war neared its end, Hempel was the recipient of a 4,000-word 'speech directive' from Ribbentrop. This delusional tract, which must have taken Hempel's cipher clerk many hours to decode, set out points which he should propound so as to reach 'important English and American personalities'. The line of argument was straightforward: 'the moment will come when Germany will have to choose between the East and the West'. In the former case, which many of her people appeared to prefer, all of Europe would become communist and Russia would become by far the most powerful state in the world. Britain would inevitably be engulfed by Bolshevism, leaving the United States isolated: 'If the West misses the psychological moment, then Germany will be forced to choose the East irrevocably'. The directive attempted some conciliatory notes: Germany had been 'slandered' for her treatment

---

[106] Beppu to Tokyo, 6 July and 8 Aug. 1945, TNA, HW12/323 and 329.
[107] The *Evening Herald*, 14 Aug. 1948, reported that he was prosecuted for failing to return earlier. Nothing more is known of him.
[108] Berlin to missions in neutral countries, 9 Feb., in Magic summary, 20 Feb. 1944, USNA, RG457, box 9.
[109] C to Churchill, and Churchill's annotation, 17 and 18 Jan., enclosing decode of Hempel to Berlin, 12 Jan. 1945, TNA, HW1/3449.

of organized religion, whereas 'practically every church . . . is more filled than ever before'; while the treatment of German Jews was 'a domestic . . . affair . . . the Jewish question in other countries does not interest Germany . . . we are even of the view that we can cooperate with the other countries in the solution of the world's Jewish problem'. Having floated the possibility of a peace agreeable to the western powers, the directive ended rather oddly with a paean of praise for 'National Socialism, the very doctrine which the British and Americans want to exterminate'. They should instead 'wish only that nothing should happen to Adolf Hitler'. Four days later, and doubtless to the despair of his cipher clerk, Hempel was told not to use the material pending further instructions. This elephantine decode was shown to Churchill, although he can hardly have bothered to read the whole thing.[110]

Hempel replied at length, remarking that people capable of influencing Allied opinion 'do not exist in Ireland', while since the American note 'this Legation has been virtually isolated from all circles that have relations with England and the United States'.[111] Dublin never became a centre for peace soundings—Stockholm, Madrid, and Berne were far better placed, with the Swedes particularly favoured by Himmler and other German leaders—although there was some unease in Whitehall lest de Valera attempt to don the mantle of honest broker, perhaps in tandem with the Holy See. In March Guy Liddell noted that 'de Valera has been making some peace feelers, both in his conversations with Hempel and with Maffey. He evidently wants to pose as a mediator. This would certainly suit his vanity'.[112]

The remainder of the war passed largely without incident for Hempel. Unknown to him, the Irish achieved a significant success which threw light on his legation's links with Goertz. Following his incarceration in November 1941, Goertz contrived to smuggle out a number of letters to Irish sympathizers. Many of these messages came into G2 hands—one of Goertz's guards was encouraged by G2 to act as a courier, but another, whom Goertz had also bribed, did manage to deliver a number to the intended recipients between 1941 and 1943. This was only discovered in 1944, when the corporal concerned was interrogated and then used to pass false messages back to Goertz. In October Goertz changed his keywords and 'tried to get in direct touch with the German Legation. After some weeks intensive study, the new keywords were discovered and the ciphers read without difficulty until March 1945 when this series ended'. Richard Hayes sent in a request, supposedly from Hempel, asking Goertz to supply a full account of his mission. This the imprisoned agent did, in a long series of messages which greatly added to Irish knowledge of his activities, his range of contacts, and his evasions during his original interrogations. In the course of this deception, G2 even told Goertz that he had been promoted to major in recognition of his achievements before his arrest.[113] G2 evidently kept this coup to themselves, presumably because of the delicacy of Goertz's disclosures of his contacts, as there is no mention of it in British documents.

[110] Ribbentrop to Hempel, 16 and 20 Feb., in Magic summaries, 23 and 26 Feb. 1945, USNA, RG457, box 15, and in TNA, HW1/3539. German ambassador, Madrid, to Berlin, 11 Mar. 1945, TNA, HW12/313, confirms the circulation of the Ribbentrop message.
[111] Hempel to Berlin, 10 Mar. 1945, in Magic summary, USNA, RG457, box 16.
[112] Liddell diary, 27 Mar. 1945, TNA, KV4/196, Carlgren, *Swedish Foreign Policy*, 214–20.
[113] Hayes report; Hull, *Irish Secrets*, 244–9.

G2 also uncovered the text of a message for Goertz from Berlin sent via the German legation in the summer of 1944. This led Hayes to mount a sustained investigation of stored German traffic 'in an attempt to relate' this message 'to three telegrams which seemed with high probability to be the cipher text', which was assumed to be 'based on a machine'. He devised 'an interesting mathematical system', and 'the theoretical value of the work done was of great interest', but he could not crack the cipher.[114] For their part, the British naturally protected the Pandora secret. Hayes, who by the end of the war had a good idea of the scale and complexity of British codebreaking, was led to believe that GC&CS never broke the German diplomatic cipher. He was instead told that in the course of 1943 a well-placed agent in the foreign ministry, with whom 'the British refused to deal' whereas the Americans did, had begun to supply copies of German diplomatic communications, primarily relating to the Far East. He assumed it was possible that some Dublin–Berlin traffic had come to hand.[115]

Although the Irish did not know about Pandora, their own work provided plenty of evidence that the German legation had been involved in some clandestine activities. Goertz's inadvertent disclosures in his account of his mission, in tandem with other material in G2's hands, could undoubtedly have been used as a reason either to expel the German legation, or at a minimum to withdraw permission for them to send coded cables. Reciprocal steps would have been taken in Berlin, but Ireland had very little to lose. The outcome of the war was no longer in doubt, and nor was the nature of the Nazi regime. It was also now clear that Hempel's protestations of ignorance about espionage were untrue, and that his mission was to an extent implicated both in the agents' activities and in interference in Irish political affairs through encouragement of pro-Nazi fringe groups and individuals.

The question of why Ireland did not force a break can be answered only by reference to de Valera's long-established and clearly articulated views on neutrality. If he was not prepared to abandon this at the hour of maximum danger in 1940, at a time when Britain believed her very survival was at stake, when an offer to facilitate Irish unity was on the table, and when a clear link had emerged between Germany and the IRA, why should he do so when the Allies were on the brink of victory? Again, having faced down what he regarded as a direct threat in the bombastic American note, de Valera was unlikely to act in a way consonant with what the Allies were demanding. Furthermore, to break with Germany on the basis of her limited clandestine activities might appear an admission that the Americans had been right, whereas the thrust of Irish policy since 1940 was to repress all activities inimical to British interests, and they believed that they had been extremely successful in doing so as regards both espionage and the legation radio. It remains an open question whether, had the American note not been presented and endorsed by the British, de Valera might have chosen to break off relations with Germany on his own terms in 1944 in the light of Goertz's disclosures in combination with what was already known about agent activity.

When the war in Europe ended the Irish allowed Hempel to remain, despite Allied pressure to force his return to Germany. The same approach was initially

---

[114] Hayes report.
[115] Ibid.

taken with German agents, who were allowed out on parole. Because of the nature of their activities, however, their case for special treatment was weaker. A number returned voluntarily to Germany in 1946 and 1947, while Goertz, theatrical to the last, committed suicide in a Garda office rather than accept deportation. Three remained in Ireland, while the most exotic, Henry Obed, went back to India.[116] Hempel's comfortable post-war fate contrasts with that of Hans Pilger, appointed to Kabul at the same time as Hempel was to Dublin. Through force of circumstances Pilger's legation had become primarily an espionage bureau after *Barbarossa*, with Pilger remaining in charge throughout because in 1941 Britain forced the Afghans not to accept his nominated replacement. Although he lost the three staff mainly involved in intelligence in the autumn of 1943, and later handed over some contacts to the Japanese mission, Pilger continued to do what he could. His last intelligence report from Kabul was sent on 14 April 1945, by which time there was probably no one left in Berlin to read it. When Berlin ceased communicating with him, he asked his Japanese colleague for help, and Tokyo reported that Hitler had died 'in action'.[117] A couple of days later he told the Japanese minister he was closing the legation and intended to live as a private citizen in Kabul. He lamented Germany's sad fate, having been led twice into catastrophic war: 'having. . . cooperated with me as a comrade in arms for some years he was today once and for all bidding farewell as Minister'.[118]

When the Allies took possession of the German legation in Kabul, it was agreed that the staff could be interrogated in Moscow during their repatriation—the Indian authorities saw only trouble if the group came to India, because their presence might jeopardize ongoing deception operations against Japan. The State Department and the Afghans were concerned to extract a guarantee that the party would be sent on to Germany.[119] Pilger gave the Afghans some Swiss francs to be transferred to Switzerland 'for the maintenance of his wife and daughter', though this transaction was blocked: 'If the. . . family run out of funds they have the alternative of returning to Germany and living in the same way as other Germans', although in fact their Berlin home and all its contents had been lost in the massive air raids of November 1943 which had also destroyed the Irish legation.[120] He and his party left on 14 August. Five months later the Afghans politely pointed out that 'no news of these gentlemen's arrival at their destination has been received'. A British official applauded this query, so 'in accord with the Pathan notion of the sanctity of safe-conduct'. London, however, were concerned lest the Soviets prove awkward about German officials in British and American hands. Despite British reservations, the Americans 'feel they are under a moral obligation' and persuaded the French to raise the matter, and in April 1946 the Soviet member of the Allied

[116] Hull, *Irish Secrets*, 251–60; Obed's repatriation caused the India Office some technical problems. IPI to Mr Silver, India Office, 27 July 1945, IOR, L/PJ/12/477.

[117] Pilger to Berlin, 14 Apr.; Tokyo to Kabul, 6 May 1945, TNA, HW12/318 and 316.

[118] Japanese minister, Kabul, to Tokyo, 8 and 10 May 1945, TNA, HW12/315 and 317.

[119] British minister, Kabul, to London, 11 May, TNA, FO371/45212; London to Kabul, 1 June, TNA, FO371/45212; Delhi intelligence bureau to India Office, 22 May, IOR, L/PS/12/1878; Afghan minister, Washington, to Kabul, and reply, 22 and 26 June 1945, TNA, HW12/322 and 323.

[120] Foreign Office to India Office, 6 Aug. 1945, IOR, L/PS/12/1878; Berlin to Kabul, 29 Nov. 1943, TNA, HW12/295.

Control Commission in Berlin suddenly announced that Pilger's party 'had been found in Russia, was in good health, and would be sent back soon to Germany'. A year later one of the group was selected for interrogation in Berlin.[121] Like Hempel, and largely thanks to the persistence of his former hosts in Kabul, Pilger eventually made it home.

AXIS INTELLIGENCE GATHERING, 1944–1945

German espionage in Ireland ended with the capture of O'Reilly and Kenny in December 1943. No further cases were detected either of agents being sent, or of war information being successfully collected by any means other than gossip. By March 1944 ISOS showed that that the Abwehr in Madrid and Lisbon, 'presumably as a result of the publicity given to the arrest of O'Reilly and Kenny . . . have been given instructions that no further operations are to be undertaken in Eire'.[122] As their decoded traffic indicated, the Japanese mission, isolated, short of money, and under threat of closure if there were any further transgressions, fell more or less completely silent after *Overlord*.

There was, nevertheless, some concern in Whitehall at the speed with which the Irish authorities were willing to forgive the wrongdoings of their own people who had been involved with German intelligence. Even before *Overlord*, Dublin had been sufficiently confident to parole the hapless Christopher Eastwood, as his family was in desperate straits: the minister responsible, Gerry Boland, observed laconically that all seamen smuggled letters. This was despite concerns expressed by G2 and External Affairs, who wished to be able to say that he remained under supervision. The captured German agents stayed where they were, with the exception of the elderly Ernst Weber Drohl, who was paroled on health grounds because he was clearly incapable of presenting a security threat. Joseph Andrews, whom G2 regarded as by far the most dangerous of the remaining Irishmen detained for dealings with Germany, remained in custody until May 1945, despite representations from politicians of various parties. Also released at that time were most of the IRA men not already freed under parole or unconditionally, although a handful serving sentences stayed in jail.

Matters touching on Ireland occasionally arose in the management of deception operations. In October 1944 the Admiralty's representative on the Twenty committee, the barrister Ewan Montagu, complained that a new notional sub-agent at Londonderry, recently acquired by the German agent *Ostro*, was reporting 'naval information which was substantially correct'. *Ostro* had been a worry to the Twenty committee since the autumn of 1942. A Czech based in Portugal, he was an ingenious producer of intelligence reports based on published sources, gossip, and

---

[121] Afghan minister, London, to Foreign Office, 23 Nov.; British legation, Kabul, to London, 23 Nov. 1945, TNA, FO371/45212; note by Baker (India Office), 16 Apr., and extract from Control Commission Political Directorate minutes, 11 Apr. 1946, and IPI to India Office, 28 Apr. 1947, IOR, L/PS/12/1878.
[122] Liddell diary, 1 Mar. 1944, TNA, KV4/193.

shrewd guesswork which his German paymasters accepted as genuine. The Twenty committee had suggested in 1943 that he be either suborned or eliminated, lest his fabricated reports lessen German confidence in those supplied through Double Cross.[123] This extreme measure was still under consideration when one of his reports at the start of June 1944 suggested, 'among much erroneous detail', that the Allies' main invasion objective was the Cherbourg peninsula—Allied deception schemes and the work of Double Cross were intended to convince the Germans that the main landings would be in the Pas de Calais, and that the Normandy operations were essentially a feint designed to suck in defenders.[124] *Ostro*'s guesses about the invasion target, together with his new Londonderry agent and some alarming reports on the pattern of fall of V1 and V2 weapons in southern England, reignited the Twenty committee's ire. Even as the war in Europe drew to its inevitable close, the committee bayed for blood. The chairman, J. C. Masterman, stated that given 'this agent's threat to deception and security', the majority view was that *Ostro* should be 'eliminated', if necessary by 'physical liquidation'. *Ostro* was sent 'a blackmailing letter', but did not respond. Masterman told his committee colleagues that after further discussions it had been 'unanimously agreed . . . that serious consideration ought to be given to the most direct method of all', and C was approached to plan and carry out the operation.[125] To the evident disappointment of some committee members, including Masterman and Montagu, C thought that *Ostro* should instead be invited to work as a double agent. By then the Portuguese police were hunting for him, creating the possibility that he would be arrested before the Twenty committee could have him killed.[126]

Notwithstanding the issues involved, there is something rather chilling in the way that Masterman, who had spent the first world war as a civilian internee in Germany, and whose personal experience of conflict was confined to the playing fields, common rooms, and committee tables of Oxford, should press so hard for the death of a fraudster who was simply making up stories to sell to a gullible enemy.[127] Neither SIS nor SOE shared his enthusiasm for so drastic a solution, while the head of deception planning concluded in March that *Ostro* was 'no longer a danger to deception, even though he might still be a danger to security'. Faced with this further disappointment, the Twenty committee, evidently convinced that there must be someone in Whitehall who shared their blood-lust, turned to the service departments to produce 'a formal request' for *Ostro*'s assassination. On 12 April an SIS representative warned that he 'had not yet approached C, and added that in

[123] Masterman, *The Double-Cross System*, 151.

[124] Hinsley and Simkins, *British Intelligence*, 199–200; Seaman, *Garbo: The Spy Who Saved D-Day*, 73–4.

[125] Twenty committee minutes, 15 Feb. and 22 Mar., and Liddell diary, 20 Mar. 1945, TNA, KV3/69 and KV4/196.

[126] Twenty committee minutes, 1 and 8 Mar. 1945, TNA, KV3/69.

[127] Masterman was an accomplished sportsman who represented England in hockey and tennis, and rose to serve as vice-chancellor of the University of Oxford. He bore a sense of guilt about inadvertently missing military service during the first world war, when so many of his generation fought and died. Masterman, *On the Chariot Wheel*. Sir John Winnifrith, an undergraduate at Christ Church in the early 1930s, during a stint in the Cabinet Office bumped into Masterman, improbably resplendent in a military's uniform. Masterman, perhaps conscious that he appeared a warrior *manqué*, greeted his former student brusquely: 'What are you doing here?'.

any event SOE might not be in a position to assist'. This was unwelcome news for Montagu, perhaps anxious for a scalp before returning to civilian life (where he sat on the bench from time to time as a recorder, but never had the opportunity to sentence anyone to death), who again 'stressed the menace to security'. But, thanks largely to C's tergiversations, *Ostro* escaped the axe.[128]

One other Double Cross matter with an Irish bearing arose in March 1945: the Twenty committee noted clear evidence that the Germans attached great value to false information on minefields in the Irish Sea provided by *Tate*, resulting in routeing orders for U-boats which might well bring them into genuine minefields.[129]

SIS AND IRELAND, 1944–1945

The surviving SIS reportage from Ireland in the months leading up to *Overlord* dealt with general political conditions. One report spoke of 'the quite remarkable political apathy', while another praised the local-government minister Séan MacEntee, who 'has never lacked moral courage . . . he is said now to be the most pro-British member of the Eire Government and has throughout the war spoken openly of his hopes of an Allied victory'.[130] The fringe pro-Axis and nativist parties still received some attention, but QRS reports conveyed a sense that pro-Axis opinion had diminished almost to nothing, while the IRA were a disparate group of directionless desperadoes, where four years before they had appeared a disciplined secret army in waiting. There really was not much more to say. The snap general election held on 30 May produced the result which everyone expected and de Valera desired, with Fianna Fáil regaining an overall majority. All seven of Ailtirí na hAiséirighe's candidates lost their deposits, postponing to infinity the reemergence of a serious Irish fascist movement just at the moment when the one effective Irish fascist, General O'Duffy, succumbed to chronic illness. While invasion preparations intensified in Britain, Hempel 'was out of Dublin for three weeks during May taking a cure', and 'it was noticed that the minister for the coordination of defence measures Frank Aiken was present' during a Spanish legation reception 'for the Axis diplomats'.[131]

In the aftermath of the American note crisis, SIS headquarters decided to rein in Collinson's operations for fear of further antagonizing the Irish. Collinson visited London 'for special instructions regarding the organization and its enquiries', and on his return spent 'nearly four hours' with Podesta. Collinson 'appeared nervous that our people might suspect him. He was not to worry about the Garda and said he had a number of policemen who were very reliable but he did not want M[ilitary] I[ntelligence] to know that he was the hub of the organization'. While Podesta's group had performed discreetly,

certain other members on the permanent staff throughout the country were frequenting hotels and flashing money and openly boasting that they were British Secret Service agents.

---

[128] Twenty committee minutes, 29 Mar., 12 and 19 Apr. 1945, TNA, KV3/69.
[129] Ibid., 22 Mar. 1945, TNA, KV3/69; Masterman, *The Double-Cross System*, 183.
[130] QRS reports, 1 Mar and 1 May 1944, TNA, DO121/85.
[131] QRS report, 1 July 1944, TNA, DO121/85.

C[ollinson] states that these people are responsible for the Irish authorities knowing of the organization's activities but implied that the authorities do not know that C was directing the activities. HQ had stated that all this had to stop and hence his previous instructions that all enquiries were to cease until further notice. Existing staff would be paid to the end of June but without expenses . . .

P[odesta] gathered that after the American Note had been delivered de Valera said something about the activities of the British Secret Service in Ireland . . .

C said that he thought the whole organization would be reorganized and he had recommended that P's group be included as part of it. They were going to weed out the undesirables. C would see P again, meanwhile P was to keep his ears to the ground and M[oore] was to keep in touch with his police friends. If anything of particular urgency was to crop up P was to ring C but other than this all their enquiries were to cease.[132]

News of this outbreak of discretion must have caused G2 both satisfaction and amusement.

In the run-up to *Overlord*, both C and Petrie took a close interest in the problem of Irish security. From July 1944 they are conspicuous by their absence from the records concerning Ireland. Once the Normandy invasion had been accomplished, Ireland became a counter-intelligence and security backwater. This was reflected, *inter alia*, in a lunchtime conversation in early September between Guy Liddell and Jane Archer, who 'had practically nothing to do' and who longed for a more active role, whether in SIS or her former service MI5. She and Liddell

agreed that for the time being . . . we were far more likely to get information by overt means than by underground means, and also that whereas in wartime the Eire Government might be prepared to wink an eye at SIS activities about which they were aware, they would probably take strong exception to them in peacetime. At the same time we felt that there was a risk that at some future date things might boil up again . . . our liaison might come to an end or at any rate cease to be profitable.

The succeeding paragraph, which is excised, possibly related to the details of SIS organization. They then went on to discuss Jane Archer's employment prospects, as she had forfeited her MI5 pension when dismissed in 1940 and wished to go on working for a few years. Liddell undertook to see what he could do. Someone suggested that she would be suitable for SIS's restructured counter-intelligence Section IX, now under Kim Philby. This gave the Soviet mole 'a nasty shock, particularly as I could think of no plausible reason for resisting it'. He was wary of Jane Archer because of her formidable brain and determination, her extensive knowledge of pre-war communism internationally, and because during her debriefing of the defector Krivitsky in 1940 she had 'elicited a tantalizing scrap about a young English journalist whom the Soviet intelligence had sent to Spain during the Civil War' (Philby knew that this referred to him, and feared that it might eventually prove his undoing).[133] Jane Archer did feature briefly again in Irish affairs: in January 1945 she told Guy Liddell that she had been asked by Vivian, 'rather mysteriously some time ago whether she knew anything about a man called

---

[132] G2 note of interview with Moore, 17 Apr. 1944, MAI, G2/X/1091.
[133] Liddell diary, 6 Sept. 1944, TNA, KV4/194; Cecil, 'The Cambridge Comintern', 178–9; Philby, *My Silent War*, 78–9.

Clissmann, which was as good as asking her whether she had heard of the PM and also whether she knew about an enterprise known as SEEHUND'. She then discovered a reference to this in ISOS decodes, and found a report which 'is very interesting but is surrounded with a veil of secrecy and mystery which we are endeavouring to penetrate'.[134] The succeeding sentences are redacted, but most likely relate to a scheme involving Ireland (perhaps, given the cover name, the dispatch of agents by sea).

In Whitehall, the ground was being prepared for battle between MI5 and SIS for post-war responsibility for counter-intelligence and security. In advance of formal deliberations on the question, Liddell pointed to the 'Cicero' disaster in Ankara, where the British ambassador's valet had sold many secret documents to the Germans, to argue that MI5 should deal with security questions abroad, and argued that his service should also have some foreign representation. He was gratified by the fact that the Foreign Office man to whom he put these preliminary arguments 'was not apparently shocked'. In the event, it fell to Sir Findlater Stewart to adjudicate on the big questions of post-war intelligence organization in the autumn of 1945, as is discussed below.[135]

After *Overlord* very little of substance appeared in the QRS reports circulated around Whitehall by SIS: the IRA were a spent force; politics remained cripplingly dull, with Fine Gael rudderless and Labour disheartened by their failure to capitalize on economic stagnation and widespread privation; and the most contentious matter expected to arise during the 1945 local elections was 'the subject of the County Managers. The system is not popular although it does produce more efficiency in the hands of local affairs'. This prediction, while of interest to connoisseurs of public administration, in intelligence terms was insignificant.[136] SIS determined to wind up their Irish operations, because with the success of *Overlord* Axis activities in Ireland no longer presented a serious threat to British interests, and MI5's good links with G2 should be sufficient for the remainder of the war and on into peacetime. The news was received with resignation amongst Collinson's group in Dublin, where members, including G2's informant Moore, contemplated the disagreeable prospect of being paid off for good. A G2 report in mid-July noted 'a general tightening up in . . . expenditure'. Podesta 'is now practically in complete control. He is to get a good man to take charge of five centres—Cork, Limerick, Galway, Clare and Donegal', although there were doubts whether the Cork nominee would take the job on the terms of £10 a month offered. A 'peace-time organization' under Podesta 'has been mentioned . . . Money would be much more restricted . . . than . . . heretofore', but a number of people, including an ex-policeman in Dun Laoghaire, would be 'kept on'. Podesta had obtained 'a very full report on the Kerins–Dr O'Farrell affair'—Kerins had been captured

[134] Liddell diary, 25 Jan. 1945, TNA, KV4/196.
[135] Ibid., 9 Sept. 1944, TNA, KV4/194. This was Neville Bland, who had been secretary to the 1927 secret service committee which looked at intelligence organization in the wake of the fiasco of the Arcos Raid. TNA, F01093/71.
[136] QRS reports, 31 Oct. and 31 Dec. 1944, TNA, DO121/85; the management system had been introduced nationally in 1941. County and City Managers Association, *City and County Management*, 1–19.

in Dr O'Farrell's house in Dublin on 17 June—'so full in fact that it could hardly have been compiled except by, or with assistance from, some official source'.[137]

In October 'C[ollinson] expects to be going at end of week', but his work would be continued for the time being by the assistant passport control officer Savage. 'C hopes to come back in a few months to look at things. He complimented P[odesta] and staff for the careful way things had been handled, especially their having avoided police contact'. Most of the helpers were gradually paid off. In December Moore found Podesta 'very alarmed' about an errant Stubbs man, who was 'drinking, helping himself to cash, and staying away from work. P would like to get rid of him', but he 'has been in on the C[ollinson] end and P is afraid to sack him on that account', lest the man go to the Irish authorities. Moore understandably 'feels that there is no need for worry on that score but he cannot tell P[odesta] why he feels that way'. Podesta also said that 'about a year ago', when discussing Churchill with Collinson, the latter 'said that MI5 had held back certain information regarding Ireland as Churchill was so impetuous they were afraid of rash action being taken', an observation which, while correct, was hardly one which should have been shared with a local agent. Podesta eventually found the courage to sack his problematic employee, and he continued to seek information. Amongst enquiries opened was one about 'Desmond FitzGerald, architecture student', who was rather improbably alleged to have offered his services to the German minister 'and wished to go to Germany to fight'.[138]

The SIS operation finally came to an end in the spring of 1945, about a month later than stated by the Liddell history. One of the last enquiries concerned 'T. L. Mullins', the newly appointed general secretary of Fianna Fáil (this was not so inappropriate as it might appear, because Mullins, a former TD, had figured in Garda reports as an associate of German diplomats in the early years of the war). As late as the last week in March, SIS supplied London with a report on a meeting of a Frank Ryan memorial committee in Dublin, possibly obtained from an informant, and the last enquiry recorded by G2 was issued on 25 April. On 4 April Podesta returned 'very dissatisfied' from a meeting in the British Permit Office: 'It appears that P did not see S[avage] in person. Miss H informed him that the organization was being closed down at the end of a month . . . Both P and M feel somewhat aggrieved at the abrupt closing down of the work'. A fortnight later the decision was confirmed by Miss H, as 'both the Government and the people here had swung round in their attitude towards the British . . . the only body which were causing worry was Ailtirí na hAiseirighe'. There was no mention of further work, and 'all the files had gone to London', but 'a recommendation had been made and would be backed strongly by the Dublin Office for a handsome present for P and M. There was a suggestion that P's organization would keep their ears to the ground and pass on any information of interest but there would be no pay—any expenses

[137] G2 note of interview with Moore, 13 July 1944, MAI, G2/X/1091.

[138] G2 notes of interviews with Moore, 17 Oct. and 27 Dec. 1944, and 16 Jan. 1945, MAI, G2/X/1091. Desmond FitzGerald, later to become Professor of Architecture at UCD, was the son of a former minister in the Cosgrave governments of 1922–32, and the brother of the future taoiseach and markedly pro-Allied Garret FitzGerald.

incurred would be repaid'. Podesta 'had a few drinks with Clarke', the paymaster for Collinson's country networks. He was 'in turn in an expansive, boastful and re C a malicious frame of mind', spoke of naval intelligence men 'in each port and at Foynes', and suggested that Collinson had been transferred at Maffey's behest (this was possibly a fiction planted on Clarke, as Collinson had stated the previous October that his move was to be depicted as a demotion).[139]

Albert Podesta, for four years Collinson's faithful though indiscreet Sancho Panza, continued to work in Stubbs for a time, but he missed the intrigue and the money of the war years. His is a poignant though hardly unique tale of someone who gave more to his country than he ever received. After quitting his job and making a disastrous investment in a confectionary enterprise at the behest of two British ex-officers, a caste for which he always had a fatal reverence, he took to drink and the family endured very hard times. In the early 1950s, and then only with the assistance of the British Legion, they moved to Brighton. There they lived in poverty, alleviated by a kindly Irish landlord. Podesta eventually found employment in Glasgow. He wrote to Collinson on a number of occasions, seeking help in securing a better job and recalling the excitements of Dublin. Collinson, who had retired to Paris after leaving SIS in 1957, replied in polite but cautious terms. During a holiday in Scotland in August 1962 the two men met briefly. It was 'indeed a pleasure to see you again, after so many years, for I remember my stay in Dublin with some pleasure, particularly as I had dealings there with so many pleasant people and made so many good friends'. Collinson continued in civil though guarded vein, saying that since retirement he 'deliberately avoided contact with my former employers . . . you would do well to put your case' to Sir Fitzroy Maclean MP, whom Collinson knew slightly from the pre-war Paris embassy, 'although of course the nature of the work you did for me . . . should not be referred to' (which was of course the only element of Podesta's hard-luck story likely to commend him to Maclean).[140] Collinson was intrigued by newspaper cuttings which Podesta had sent relating to German espionage in Ireland, most probably extracts from Enno Stephan's *Spies in Ireland*. He

read with interest the batch of newspapers and was able to follow the articles . . . they do not give much information that we did not possess at the time, apart from the main workings of the services in the enemy country. There were, you will recall, a number of similar activities which are not recorded, but they possibly originated from a different service [than that] of which the author of the articles examined the records. On the whole, the most consoling impression from a reading of these 'revelations' is that however many trips, blunders and stupid failures we ourselves were responsible for, the other side produced far greater and far graver ones and, in fact, lost a host of golden opportunities by crass ignorance and sheer incompetence.[141]

---

[139] *Liddell History*, 98; enquiry docket no. 1860, 26 Feb.; SIS to Cecil Liddell, 29 Mar. 1945, TNA, KV2/1991; G2 notes of interviews with Moore, 5, 21, and 27 Apr., and enquiry docket No. 1882 re Mullins, 25 Apr. 1945, and 17 Oct. 1944, MAI, G2/X/1091. Miss H was possibly Miss Gladys Harben, the French speaker who had briefly infiltrated Albertas's home in 1941.

[140] Fitzroy Maclean had been head of the British military mission attached to Tito's partisans in Yugoslavia from 1943 to 1945.

[141] Collinson to Podesta, 28 July and 3 Sept. 1962 (letters in the possession of the Podesta family); Stephan, *Spies in Ireland*. It is not clear how Podesta obtained Collinson's Paris address.

BRINGING IRELAND TO BOOK IN THE COURT
OF WORLD OPINION? SOE'S FINAL IRISH FLING

In the autumn of 1944 SOE were instructed that the main strategic objective of
their operations in Europe henceforth was to destroy the will of the German people
to continue the conflict. This directive tied in with the western Allies' bombing
strategy, now focused unashamedly on the wholesale destruction of German centres
of population. Major-General Gerald Templer, an old friend of Colin Gubbins
temporarily attached to SOE headquarters while recovering from wounds bizarrely
inflicted in Italy by a flying piano, antagonized the Foreign Office with a scheme
based on the unlikely premise that it would be possible to foment an uprising in
Austria using disillusioned Nazi deserters, and generally he had little impact on
SOE's campaign against Germany.[142] But it was not for the want of trying. He
mounted a ferocious attack in December 1944 on a PWE paper on 'Methods of
breaking the German will to resist'. Templer, a fiery Ulsterman, thought PWE's
plans 'inadequate to meet the urgent requirement' of the chiefs of staff, because 'the
time-lag would be too long for the schemes to be effective in the immediate future',
and because the 'schemes . . . make too little provision for reaching and subverting
the mass targets—the German armed forces . . . plus the civilian population in their
immediate rear, whose will to resist' presented the Allied armies' 'most pressing
problems'. As an alternative he put forward a scheme which 'is simple . . . can start
within a few days', 'will be known to succeed or not within a few weeks', and cannot
'lay H[is] M[ajesty's] G[overnment] open to charges of complicity'. A newcomer to
black propaganda, he complained that, 'unless HMG agrees to jettison former ideas
about the ethics of deceiving friends, and adopts the general principle that "the
end justifies the means"—even to the extent of involving (by unacknowledgeable
means) the government of a neutral state—no scheme for breaking the enemy's
will to resist can be adopted with the rapidity now necessary'. Templer's nostrum
was 'the . . . "Casement" plan'—a clear reference to Sir Roger Casement and his
ill-fated dalliance with Germany during the first world war. Devised by Major
Wintle of the Iberian section of SOE, this was posited on Dublin's well-publicized
response to an American demand for an undertaking to hand over any alleged
Axis war criminals who might turn up in Ireland. This de Valera regarded as a
snare, and he furnished an equivocal answer (although Maffey said his government
regarded it as 'favourable').[143] The Irish line was consistent with the public position
on neutrality adopted since the outbreak of the war, but it left the state in an
embarrassing position in the court of world opinion, by now conscious not only
of Hitler's territorial depredations but of his treatment of the Jews (although the

---

[142] Wilkinson and Bright Astley, *Gubbins and SOE*, 209.
[143] Minutes of a PWE/SOE meeting, 11 Jan. 1945, at which Wintle explained his ideas. TNA,
FO898/357; Garnett, *The Secret History of PWE*; Walshe to de Valera, 14 Nov. 1944, UCDA, de Valera
papers, P150/2571. Garnett is better known as a second-generation member of the Bloomsbury group.
De Valera twice refused to answer parliamentary questions about the Allied request. *Dáil Debates*,
vol. 95, 18 Oct. and 9 Nov. 1944.

term 'war criminals' was not yet associated particularly with the Nazi campaign to exterminate the Jewish race, and none of those executed in the Far East for war crimes was accused of involvement in the Holocaust).

There was an element of hypocrisy in the Allies' demands about alleged war criminals: even before the war ended, it was obvious that their own approach would be highly contingent. A case in point is that of the Grand Mufti of Jerusalem, whose assassination London had vainly ordered in 1941. Despite the pleas of Jewish leaders and unequivocal evidence of his involvement in the creation of a Bosnian Muslim SS division which perpetrated major atrocities against Jews, Serbs, and communists, the French decided that it would be against their Middle Eastern interests to hand him over to the British, instead holding him 'in a suburban "villa" . . . treated with all the consideration due to a prominent personality of the Islamic world'. French policy was clear at the time through decodes—in July 1945 the Mufti 'was anxious to express his gratitude for the welcome which the French Government was according him . . . he volunteered to extend to us his complete cooperation in our policy with regard to the Arab States and the Muslim world'—but London and Washington chose not to pursue the matter vigorously for fear of antagonizing Arab opinion (although a decode showed that the equally anti-Semitic Ibn Saud of Saudi Arabia had no sympathy for the Mufti or for the Iraqi nationalist Rashid Ali, because 'they not only betrayed the English, but they betrayed me . . . and the Arabs in general' by seeking to bring the Germans into the Middle East).[144] After a year's respectful incarceration in France the Mufti was allowed to escape to Egypt.

Even before SOE's scheme was hatched, the Irish were aware of rumours that the state would become a safe haven for Nazis: in October a G2 officer recorded an American passenger who commented on construction work at Foynes 'half jokingly . . . "I see you are getting ready for the Axis Chiefs when they arrive", and supplemented this by saying that as Eire was the only country that had not decided to bar War Criminals, this would be the natural haven for them to flee to'. While 'none of the other passengers in the launch openly supported' this, 'by the whispering among them, they seemed to be of the same opinion'.[145] It is of course quite possible that American intelligence, inclined to act unilaterally where Ireland was concerned, had already put such a rumour into circulation. By January 1945 'stories backing up the general line of the "Casement" Plan' were 'already being "planted" both in Germany and neutral countries' by SOE, although without an explicitly Irish angle.[146]

The declared objective of the plan was to disclose to the German armed forces and people that

their leaders have made all arrangements . . . for escape to safety in EIRE, some by submarine, some by aircraft . . . There have already been numerous rumours—some inspired by us—that

---

[144] Magic summaries, 31 May and 10 July 1945, USNA, RG457, boxes 17 and 18. Ibn Saud to Imam Yahya, Yemen, 24 May 1945, TNA, HW12/317.

[145] G2 report from Foynes, 17 Oct. 1944, NAI, DFA A8/1.

[146] Minutes of a PWE/SOE meeting, 11 Jan. 1945, TNA, FO898/357. The plan is briefly discussed in Taylor, *British Propaganda*, 209–10, but not at all in the more recent Cole, *Propaganda, Censorship and Irish Neutrality*.

the Nazis are 'getting away', though EIRE has not been mentioned. On each occasion the enemy Press and Radio have re-acted [*sic*] sharply; newspapers have emphasized the 'impossibility' of such a manoeuvre and have reaffirmed the unity of Leaders and People.

This plan would necessitate '"planted" stories in certain newspapers of neutral countries'; 'rumours circulating along all possible channels, interpreting and exaggerating the published stories'; a 'Parliamentary question, inspired if it does not come naturally', asking if the government had any information about Nazi plans to use Ireland as a bolt-hole, and parliamentary complaints that the government should demand 'a categorical denial from the Eire Government' that Ireland would extend sanctuary. All this would be reported dispassionately 'by the BBC, in all languages (white [propaganda])'. PWE's clandestine German stations, which purported to represent a variety of political viewpoints within Germany, would also take up the question:

Once German home propaganda has been forced into a denial (or even an airy dismissal) of the escape plot, black radio, rumours, cryptic statements by ambassadors and others in official Allied positions, and 'intelligence' sent . . . by double agents can have free play. *The German armed forces and our people are reached, initially, by the Germans themselves, through their own Propaganda Ministry.* The enemy is forced to act as Allied agents for dissemination and the Allied propaganda (black and white) is in the strong position of using genuine German sources as a peg on which to hang their propaganda.[147]

It may be that Templer's enthusiasm for this bizarre plan was simply the personal folly of a bluff warrior unfamiliar with the Whitehall labyrinth. The Cabinet Office official to whom it was submitted remarked dryly that 'I am not myself attracted by the selection of Eire for this venture'. But the scheme was considered at very high levels in SOE, in PWE, and in the Foreign Office before being rejected on explicitly 'political grounds'—the view outside SOE was that Ireland was an inappropriate as well as a somewhat implausible Nazi haven, and that Argentina seemed a much more credible destination. Just before Christmas the SOE council was told that the plan would go ahead, but that 'another country would probably be substituted for Eire'.[148]

There the matter might have rested, had not there been an intervention by Professor Douglas Savory, the MP for Queens University Belfast, who, with suspiciously apposite timing, put down a parliamentary question on the Irish attitude towards war criminals. Savory, a constant critic of Irish neutrality, had an intelligence background: a linguist, he had served during the first world war under the celebrated '"Blinker" Hall of NID, who had been centrally involved in the gratuitous denigration of Roger Casement through disclosure of his homosexuality while he was awaiting execution'.[149]

---

[147] Undated SOE memorandum submitted by Templer, with Capel-Dunn (Cabinet Office) to Bruce Lockhart (PWE), 20 Dec. 1944, TNA, FO898/357.

[148] Capel-Dunn to Bruce Lockhart, 20 Dec., and SOE council minutes, 22 Dec. 1944, TNA, FO898/357 and HS8/201.

[149] O'Halpin, *The Decline of the Union*, 112–15, and 'British Intelligence and Ireland, 1914–1921', 56–67; TS of Savory's unpublished memoir 'From the Haven into the Storm', PRONI, D/3015/2/141A, and Bracken to Savory, 30 May 1941, conveying the prime minister's congratulations on his 'remarkable speech', D3015/1A/10/3/1.

Templer seized on his fellow Ulsterman's question, claiming that, 'although not inspired by us', it had had the desired effect of bringing the notion of Ireland as a refuge for the Nazi leadership into the public mind: 'It would seem that policy objections . . . to involving Eire can now be waived since any damage on this score has presumably already been done. Under these circumstances, we feel it might be advisable to continue with the next step of the Casement Plan in order to benefit from the flying start which fortuitously we have been given'.[150] At a subsequent meeting SOE's Major Wintle offered what was surely one of the more ludicrous arguments ever advanced in a whitehall committee: there would be 'no difficulty in convincing the German public of the plausibility of the Eire plan, since criminals are known to hide near the scene of their crimes', and 'the German reaction would be much more violent in the case of Eire . . . He thought the Germans would exploit the idea of a small, powerless country being brow-beaten by the United Kingdom, and this strong reaction would be much in our favour'. PWE's Robert Bruce Lockhart disagreed:

One of the many arguments against Eire was the difficulty of making the idea plausible to the German people; he did not see that the parliamentary question had in any way eased this difficulty. Another important argument . . . was the political complications involved, which was likewise unaffected . . . [Furthermore] the idea of the German war criminals' plans for escape had been much used in the past and . . . there was danger of the whole thing becoming ridiculous if too many countries were referred to as asylums.

PWE's Selfton Delmer concurred: 'once the idea became ridiculous it would spoil the effect of other stories now in circulation, some of which were producing very satisfactory come-backs'. Bruce Lockhart added that any decision to reinstate Ireland would have to be referred to the war cabinet, who would most likely reject it on political grounds.[151] Official approval was instead given to Argentina. History was to show that this destination was clearly also the personal preference of a large number of German war criminals. To add verisimilitude to the rumours, it was envisaged that a suitable German would be 'framed' in either Spain or Portugal. When arrested by the local police, he would be carrying papers dealing with the alleged escape plan.[152]

In February Templer wrote that 'for various reasons, it is not possible to produce in Iberia an "incident" which will have the desired effect . . . I am afraid it seems that there is very little that this organization can contribute towards the plan'. Because of his 'keen interest in the Casement plan', he sought PWE's views and news of 'the line of action you propose to adopt'. Bruce Lockhart's marginal note on this distinctly sniffy letter ran: 'I have explained to General Templer that we shall do and are doing our best to implement this plan without concentrating on Eire or on the creation of . . . [illegible] incidents'.[153] It is hard to escape the conclusion that in persistently calling for the Irish option Templer was bent on damaging Ireland's

---

[150] Templer to Bruce Lockhart, 19 Jan. 1945, TNA, FO898/357.
[151] Minutes of a PWE/SOE meeting, 25 Jan. 1945, TNA, FO898/357.
[152] Minutes of a PWE/SOE meeting, 11 Jan. 1945, TNA, FO898/357.
[153] Templer to Bruce Lockhart, 5 Feb., and Bruce Lockhart's note, 9 Feb. 1945, TNA, FO898/ 357.

international standing. Other criticisms were levelled at the plan: the PWE historian David Garnett pointed out in 1947 that rumours about the Nazi leadership's plans to flee were already in circulation. These 'contradicted a major theme of our political warfare to Germany', which was that Hitler's determination to fight to the end would bring ruin all round, 'which had the advantage of being true'. Templer moved on to championing another 'wild scheme' involving Germany which again ran into intense opposition.[154]

What Templer failed to do with his *Casement* plan, de Valera temporarily achieved when on 2 May he called to a dumbfounded Hempel to convey his formal condolences on the death of Hitler. To world opinion, this was at best a piece of pedantry extraordinary even by de Valera's exalted standards of hair-splitting, at worst a confirmation that Ireland had been secretly pro-Axis. Brian Girvin has recently argued that by his action de Valera 'dramatically signalled his distance from democratic Europe in a most uncompromising fashion', a claim which rests on the fragile theory that de Valera was a crypto-Falangist at heart, while almost equally implausibly Conor Cruise O'Brien argues that it was a gesture calculated to garner support for the Fianna Fáil candidate in the upcoming presidential election.[155] To critics of Irish neutrality, the action was (and remains) a God-sent propaganda coup, all the better for being entirely of de Valera's own doing. Portugal had boxed clever over the death, lowering her flag in respect but choosing not to offer official condolences to the German embassy. It was, said Salazar, 'the least that could be done. We have not only the right but the obligation to do it for the sake of international courtesy in an apparently insane world'. Nevertheless, his ambassador in Washington told Lisbon that 'I have proof that our gesture of international courtesy has . . . offended and pained the American people . . . it has had wider repercussions than any other incident . . . within my memory . . . there is nothing to be done to remedy or mitigate this effect'.[156] American criticism of Ireland was even stronger, the more so as she had failed to follow the Portuguese example in 1943 by making bases available while remaining neutral.

Yet Churchill was to overplay his hand in response in his VE (Victory in Europe) Day address, in which he lambasted Ireland for her neutrality and for maintaining diplomatic relations with the Axis. The prime minister could command any audience, but he seldom paused to consider whether loose rhetoric might not offer his opponents a trick (as with his outlandish prediction of Gestapo methods should Labour win power in the forthcoming general election). His VE Day attack on Ireland was, in Nicholas Mansergh's words, 'out of proportion and out of place', yet his greatest error was not one of language but of tactics: as Maffey ruefully pointed out, instead of de Valera being left to stew in his own juice, with his obsequies to the departed Führer remaining the dominant motif of Irish neutrality internationally,

---

[154] Internal history of PWE by David Garnett, 1947, TNA, CAB 102/610; Liddell diary, 25 Jan. 1945, TNA, KV4/196.

[155] Girvin, *The Emergency*, 1; O'Brien, *Memoir*, 105.

[156] Salazar to Portuguese ambassador, Washington, and reply, 4 and 7 May, USNA, Magic summary, 5 May 1945, RG459, box 17, and TNA, HW12/316.

'it is indeed sad that Dev should have got the limelight...But how are you to control Ministerial incursions into your china shop? Phrases make history here'.[157]

By attacking de Valera instead of ignoring him, and advancing what was essentially a brutal realist analysis of the folly of Irish neutrality, Churchill handed de Valera the opportunity of taking the high moral ground in a contemporary version of Thucydides' Melian dialogue. In a meticulously crafted and carefully delivered broadcast response, de Valera excused Churchill for understandably overblown talk in his hour of victory, and complimented him on the restraint which the prime minister had—by his own account—displayed in not forcing Ireland into the war. Those courteously patronizing words delivered, de Valera proceeded to set out unassailable reasons why great powers could scarcely simultaneously claim to be the champions of freedom and justice, and act as though it were part of the natural moral order to push around small countries simply on the basis of might equals right. This struck a chord which resonated not only in Ireland and among the Irish diaspora, but with small states across the world. As Maffey observed, 'his speech is acclaimed in all quarters, even in T[rinity] C[ollege] D[ublin] and by the *Irish Times*'. The Canadian minister Kearney remarked that, after de Valera's visit to Hempel, 'We had him on a plate. We had him where we wanted him. But look at the papers this morning!'[158] A week later Joseph Walshe telephoned Archbishop McQuaid's secretary to say that leaflets and messages had been circulated—including some in the Irish Insurance Company, always a hotbed of republican opinion despite its staid line of business—announcing a memorial mass 'for the repose of the soul of Herr Hitler...Buses 20 and 21 pass the church'. Walshe was sure that the prospective celebrants had been misled into believing this would be a purely private affair. McQuaid's secretary's typed note ended with a sentence in red: 'All this activity could easily be the work of American or British *agents prov[ocateurs]*'. The mass did not go ahead.[159]

One other Irish proposal emerged involving SOE, this one rather more firmly grounded in *Realpolitik*. The issue of how to handle German diplomatic missions in neutral states was debated in Whitehall as the end of the war drew near. As in other security questions, the Allies were not of one mind on the best way to proceed. It was clearly desirable to obtain as much evidence as possible of secret Axis activities in neutral countries, for purposes of retrospective analysis, to help in locating Axis assets, to uncover escape lines, and to have the option of showing neutrals just how underhand Axis diplomats had been. The key to obtaining such material was, self-evidently, to take Axis missions by surprise before everything incriminating could be destroyed. There was, consequently, considerable alarm when Maffey telegraphed that Gray had been instructed by Washington to demand that once Germany surrendered the Irish should admit the Allied powers to the German legation (given Gray's outlook, it is likely that this was his idea in the first place).

---

[157] Mansergh, *The Unresolved Question*, 313–14; Maffey to Machtig (Dominions Office), 21 May 1945, TNA, DO35/1229.

[158] Memorandum by Maffey, with Maffey to Machtig, both 21 May 1945, TNA, DO35/1229. For an interesting critique of de Valera's speech see Roberts, 'Three Narratives of Neutrality', 170.

[159] Note of telephone message from Walshe for McQuaid, 30 May, and McQuaid's MS note, 31 May 1945, Dublin Dioscesan Archives, folder marked 'Department of External Affairs, 1941–1971'.

This galled Anthony Eden. He feared it would result in a tip-off to Hempel, who 'will no doubt inform Berlin who would immediately send a warning to all their diplomatic posts in neutral territory', resulting in bonfires of valuable documents in German missions across the world: 'we have as a matter of fact been working out ourselves a plan for securing possession of these archives in conjunction with SOE'. He suggested consulting Washington to produce 'a joint plan . . . and meanwhile ask them to stay their hand in Dublin and in any other neutral capitals where action may have been contemplated'. The plan was for *coups de main* in the neutral states, probably to be executed simultaneously, although serious objections might well have arisen due to the diplomatic implications, since force would have to be used and local police guarding the missions might well have been drawn in. Nor was Maffey impressed by Gray's proposal. In an evident reference to the American note crisis, he wrote that 'this case furnishes another example of the State Department acting unilaterally in Eire in a matter in which we should have been consulted'.[160] For whatever reason, the route eventually chosen for gaining access to the German and later to the Japanese missions in Dublin was the conventional one of requiring the Axis representatives to hand over possession. In each case this gave the diplomats time to destroy all sensitive material.

ASSESSING IRELAND'S IMPACT ON BRITAIN'S WAR

In the immediate aftermath of the war, Maffey asked whether de Valera should be shown some of Hempel's decoded communications. These would demonstrate that, contrary to his repeated protestations, the German minister had often attempted to pass war information, had been in touch with Goertz and other agents, and had responded energetically to instructions from Berlin about increased information gathering from 1943 onwards. The material should then be given 'the fullest publicity', which would 'shatter the local complacency'.[161]

Vivian, not unnaturally, was very much against this. Disclosure 'of our material would not produce a very convincing story', because it showed that, while Hempel passed on whatever 'military and naval espionage material as he was able to obtain', its 'generally poor quality . . . might well add weight to de Valera's contention that the restrictions and supervision exercised over the Legation staff gave them little opportunity of collecting really valuable espionage material'. Vivian's second argument was one of principle: 'the revelation . . . of our ability to read the very high-grade type of cipher employed by our late enemies is . . . out of the question; and it is a little disturbing that Maffey should have imagined that the obvious necessity of concealing from the world in general the extent to which we have succeeded in this particularly delicate and secret form of Intelligence should be altered by the cessation of hostilities'.[162] On this basis the proposal was dropped, although it would surely have been possible for London to say that they had obtained

---

[160] Eden to Churchill, and Maffey to Machtig, 6 and 19 Apr. 1945, TNA, DO35/1229.
[161] Maffey to Dominions Office, 2 Aug. 1945, TNA, DO121/89.
[162] Vivian to Dominions Office, 16 Aug. 1945, TNA, DO121/89.

copies of Hempel's communications by other means, such as the seizure of foreign ministry records in Berlin. A year later Vivian wrote that analysis of such captured material did 'show Hempel's complicity in the Goertz case and anxiety to assist his Government by all means in his power. But they also showed how his efforts were circumvented and largely thwarted by our own security arrangements and by de Valera's determination to avoid any complications'.[163] When such seized material gradually became available to scholars in the 1950s, it cast considerable light on German–Irish relations, including the knavery or stupidity of Leopold Kerney in Madrid. In 1950 Professor Desmond Williams of University College Dublin, who had for a time worked on the British *Documents on German Foreign Policy* series, gave Dan Bryan a guarded hint that the series would put some Irish officials in a very poor light. Bryan asked Guy Liddell for a general indication of what this might mean, so that his government would be forewarned. Liddell wrote to the Cabinet Office, who assured him that the publication schedule for the next couple of years would only bring the story up to the time of the Munich crisis. He informed Bryan accordingly, adding that he hoped a recently posted copy of *Animal Farm* 'will amuse you'. Three years later Williams lost a libel case taken by Kerney on foot of one of a number of *Irish Press* articles which provided a picture of German–Irish relations. Williams had paraphrased, without identifying Kerney or the locale, the reports of Veesenmayer of his clandestine discussions with an Irish diplomat in 1942—'the Madrid betrayal', as Joseph Walshe termed it—but, as often happens in Irish libel cases, an undeserving plaintiff won out.[164]

There was widespread recognition in Whitehall that, like it or not, Ireland had proved a surprisingly willing and efficient security partner. As Maffey wrote in October 1945, 'in this underground of intelligence and intrigue . . . a British authority in Ireland could never achieve what was achieved by a native authority. "The dog of the country hunts the hare of the country" '.[165] This opinion was undoubtedly shared by most of the officials who dealt with Irish issues during the war, including men such as Godfrey who had initially been sceptical of Irish goodwill, competence, and commitment: of all those who reflected on Irish security, he alone linked Irish effectiveness in security and counter-espionage with previous experience, pointing out that the Garda, 'having only recently emerged from a state of civil war', were 'particularly good at detecting underground conspiracies'. A similar argument was advanced shortly after the war ended in the influential American journal *Foreign Affairs* by the strongly pro-British editor of the *Irish Times*, R. M. Smyllie.[166]

---

[163] Vivian to Dominions Office, 2 Aug. 1946, TNA, DO121/89.

[164] Note by Liddell of visit to Dublin, 5 and 6 Sept., and Liddell to Bryan, 1 Nov. 1950, TNA, KV4/281; Walshe (at the Vatican) to Nunan (Dublin), 6 July 1953, NAI, DFA A47. Kerney's family have created an interesting website, www.leopoldhkerney.com. I am grateful to Manus O'Riordan for drawing this to my attention. The evidence remains overwhelming that Kerney repeatedly acted without orders, was in touch with Frank Ryan for two years without informing Dublin, allowed republicans, including Mrs Clissmann, to use his diplomatic bag even after being warned by G2 and by de Valera during a visit in 1941, and met Veesenmayer without consulting Dublin.

[165] Report by Maffey, 5 Oct. 1945, quoted in Fanning, *Independent Ireland*, 124.

[166] Godfrey memoir, 202, CCCA, Godfrey papers 1/6; Smyllie, 'Unneutral Neutral Eire', 325.

Godfrey, who as DNI had pressed vigorously for intelligence gathering in Ireland in the first year of the war, afterwards wrote about the Irish problem in surprisingly upbeat terms:

The endearing qualities of the Irish . . . were never so apparent as when they met an Englishman, whose leg they enjoyed pulling. I was to learn this during my visits to Dublin, where I received the most charming hospitality from redoubtable Sinn Feiners who had been 'out' in the 'troubles'.

As Mr Walshe, the foreign minister, told me, they were not really neutral as the police made life a burden for the few hundred Germans in Eire, and left the thousands of English people to travel as they liked. We made unlimited use of Shannon Airport. Whenever a report (invariably false) of a U-boat using an Irish port was received I was able to send an emissary in plain clothes to investigate . . .

As we now know from German records, no naval activities favourable to the Germans took place in Irish waters, and there is no evidence of the Eireann coast being used for U-boats, or supply bases.

Perhaps because he ceased to be DNI before Pandora became available, Godfrey was even charitable about Hempel, who 'was determined to remain quite neutral in spite of proddings from Berlin. He never meant to return to Germany'.[167]

The in-house history of MI5's Irish section prepared by Cecil Liddell advanced a startling and courageous analysis of the likely consequences had Ireland joined the war:

It is at least arguable that, as things turned out, Eire neutral was of more value . . . than Eire belligerent would have been. Had Eire come into the war . . . her people would almost certainly have been conscripted and with almost equal certainty as long as there was any threat of invasion, would have been held in Eire. Equally, the Conscription Act of 1939 would have been made applicable to Northern Ireland . . . [conscription] would have produced 300,000 in Eire, and 100,000 in Northern Ireland . . . the 300,000 in Eire would, for the greater part of the war, have been sitting about . . . waiting for an invasion which never materialized. They would have had to have been supplied with arms . . . to resist attacks by air and land . . . when supplies were practically non-existent, particularly at the period of greatest danger after the fall of France; all this to the accompaniment of minor guerrilla warfare by the IRA and their sympathizers.

The Liddell history then reflected on the voluntary contribution of Irish people to the war effort, as compared with what might have been obtained through belligerence and conscription: 'A conservative estimate of neutral Eire's contribution to the British war effort (armed forces and labour) is . . . about 165,000. While this is just over half of the 300,000 men which conscription in Eire could have been expected to produce, and includes women as well as men, it is at least extremely doubtful whether this valuable labour reserve would have been available had Eire entered the war'.[168] Commending the history to David Petrie, Jack Curry, the MI5 officer overseeing the production of all the section histories, thought it

[167] Godfrey memoir, 205, CCCA, Godfrey papers, 1/6.
[168] *Liddell History*, 31–3.

one of the three or four most impressive records. It stands out by virtue of its high quality and the way in which it is presented. Even more important is the evidence which it furnishes . . . of the high quality of the work which it reflects . . .

. . . the special nature of the problem of Eire brought the officers concerned directly into contact with the ultimate issues of policy on a high level . . . On the level of high policy—in the long history of the relations between the British Government and the Irish—they have assisted in making a contribution which . . . deserves to be remembered as one wholly to the credit of everyone who has had a part in it.

Curry suggested that a note from Petrie expressing particular thanks for the work of Jane Archer would be 'a gesture which might help to build up the good relations with SIS in other directions, which are very much to be desired in the immediate future'.[169]

Petrie, while 'all in favour of what you say about the merits of this chronicle', and who had 'been kept in pretty close touch all along, particularly in the anxious months preceding *Overlord*', felt that 'adequate acknowledgement has already been paid to the valuable collaboration' of Jane Archer. The 'one factor indispensable to success was the good-will of the Eire Officers, and it is not the least part of the credit due both to [Jane Archer] and Mr [Cecil] Liddell that they were able to keep and even increase their confidence as time went on. The retention of this good-will represents our best hope for an adequate knowledge in the time to come of all intelligence and security matters having a common interest to Ireland and ourselves'.[170] Curry was perhaps naive in thinking that the minor success in counter-espionage cooperation between MI5 and SIS which Ireland represented would carry much weight with Sir Findlater Stewart's review of post-war intelligence organization.

Stewart's long-anticipated inquiry took place in the autumn of 1945. Stewart was nobody's catspaw. A former head of the India Office, he had long exposure to problems of security and external subversion; as chairman of the Security Executive from 1943 on he had been well placed to observe the operation of Double Cross and strategic deception, and to assess the relative and joint performances of SIS and MI5 and customers' expectations of each agency.[171] His findings fell very much SIS's way. The rational case which Guy Liddell, Dick White, and other senior MI5 officers had advanced around Whitehall since 1943—quietly supported by the enduringly collegiate Kim Philby of SIS, though not by his chief C—for an integrated worldwide counter-intelligence organization incorporating the relevant arms of MI5 and SIS was pushed aside (such a unitary organization would have suited Philby and his Soviet masters, particularly as he might well have become head of it). This was the kind of tussle in which C, who 'no one in his right mind would have accused . . . of being outgunned in Whitehall', excelled. As Philby put it, 'his real strength lay in a sensitive perception of the currents of Whitehall politics, in an ability to feel his way through the mazy corridors of power'.[172] Petrie, on the other hand, was a relative outsider, an India specialist brought into Whitehall from retirement in 1941 when MI5 appeared on the point of implosion. While he and

[169] Curry to Petrie, undated [early 1946], in O'Halpin, *MI5 and Ireland*, 16.
[170] Petrie to Curry, undated [early 1946], in ibid., 17.
[171] This was the view of Sir John Winnifrith.
[172] Nigel Clive, *A Greek Experience 1943–1948* (London, 1985), 30; Philby, *My Silent War* 82.

his service had done well, he did not carry much weight with the mandarins, and in any case he was thought to be worn out and was about to step down.

C swept the board.[173] Despite MI5's considerable wartime achievements across the globe, not only in counter-espionage but in penetrating the enemies' intelligence services and manipulating them through Double Cross, Stewart came out decisively in favour of SIS, which secured unequivocal responsibility for counter-intelligence and deception outside the United Kingdom, and which also absorbed those parts and functions of SOE deemed still useful in post-war circumstances—SOE itself was wound up on 31 March 1946. MI5's consolation prize was an enhanced role in colonial and commonwealth security as Britain prepared to face the post-war challenges and dangers of decolonization and the return to centre stage of the pre-war threat of international communism, now immeasurably more powerful because of the Soviet Union's victory. The spirit of cooperation which had developed during the war did not survive the shake-up: in August 1946 MI5 were almost apoplectic to discover that Section V of SIS was still using the MI5 cover name B26 to solicit favours across and outside Whitehall concerning the affairs of former agents who needed papers, ration books, and the like: Guy Liddell believed there was a danger of SIS 'spoiling our markets', while Dick White thought that B26 was 'a necessary war-time measure which it would be unwise to continue further into peace', and another officer wrote that 'SIS are concerned with foreign countries & if they want to do anything in the UK that might affect security we should know about it & deal with it'.[174]

The question of Ireland arose. MI5 were very conscious that relations with SIS had been very good there—we have seen that Curry had suggested to Petrie that the relevant sections of his history should be sent to Stewart to bolster MI5's case for an expanded overseas counter-intelligence role in tandem with SIS. But there remained the question of which agency should take responsibility for Ireland in the future. On 20 November 1945 Stewart ruled that there could be no guarantee that MI5's close understanding with G2, which relied entirely on goodwill, would continue indefinitely, particularly if the issue of partition again reared its head. In such a situation, 'there would be no flow of intelligence from Eire until the Dominion Office again laid the task of getting it upon SIS'. Consequently, SIS were instructed to develop a small peacetime Irish organization as a safeguard, which in times of crisis could be mobilized and expanded as necessary.[175] It is said that, in discharging that duty, they reactivated some of their wartime operatives, to the great convenience of G2.

Whatever exiguous arrangements were made do not seem to have lasted very long. In January 1948 Guy Liddell suggested that SIS might need to reactivate an Irish network should a dynamic new force in Irish politics, Clann na Poblachta, headed by Seán MacBride, defeat de Valera in the forthcoming Irish election. SIS did not expect such an outcome, but de Valera was ousted by an extraordinary congeries of five parties from across the political spectrum, ranging from Fine Gael to two Labour factions

---

[173] Liddell diary, 12 Nov. 1943 and 17 May 1944, TNA, KV4/192 and 193.
[174] Minutes by Liddell, White and ?, 8, 12 and 19 Aug. 1946, TNA, KV4/205.
[175] *Liddell History*, 99.

and to MacBride's ultra-republican group. This 'Interparty Government' was headed by John A. Costello of Fine Gael.[176] MacBride, formerly a key IRA man and more recently Hempel's trusted confidante, became minister for external affairs: Liddell minuted that 'the new Minister for Defence (O'Higgins) . . . should be alright but MacBride . . . may be a bore'. Eight months later, in circumstances of considerable confusion which took not only London but de Valera, now in the unaccustomed role of opposition leader, entirely by surprise, Costello announced in Ottawa that Ireland intended to declare herself a republic and to leave the commonwealth.[177] This strange decision threw up the question of how Ireland should be treated in intelligence terms, particularly in view of the heat being generated on the partition issue. MI5 were clear that liaison on counter-espionage should continue: 'it is a fair assumption to make that if the Soviet espionage attack on this country is based outside our borders, then Eire is at least as likely a base' as any other western European state: a liaison . . . would be unlikely in the foreseeable future to become embarrassing'. On the other hand, the DMI told the JIC that while maintaining liaison on espionage, 'we should take steps to increase the flow of intelligence . . . and endeavour to obtain a Ministerial ruling that Eire should be treated as an intelligence target'. Colleagues downplayed this. The DMI was given leave to bring the matter up again if the situation warranted it, although one MI5 officer thought his fears 'exceptionally silly'.[178] A year later Liddell told the former DMI Paddy Beaumont-Nesbitt, who had been asked by RUC inspector-general Richard Pim to sound out MI5 and SIS about intelligence arrangements in the light of agitation on the partition issue, that 'we had no clandestine contacts in the south and were, therefore, not in a position to help'.[179]

British and Irish officials who worked on security and counter-espionage questions during the war became very close. In addition to the warm tributes paid in the Irish section history and in the accompanying minutes, there is plenty of evidence in private papers, including passages in Jo Stephenson's unpublished memoirs. This is also borne out in Irish sources, in particular in Dan Bryan's papers. This correspondence shows how strong were the personal links built up between intelligence officers of the two unequal and, at least in public, mutually dissatisfied states. Most of Cecil Liddell's letters begin with a ritual sentence of thanks to Bryan and his wife for sending 'a most delicious round of spiced beef', a Christmas turkey, 'a most delicious tongue', and supplies of butter, all commodities still severely rationed in Britain; they also convey warm greetings to Liam Archer, 'the Doc' [Hayes], and various G2 officers.[180] In thanking Bryan for a joint of lamb, Cecil wrote that

I have been & still am working on a note of the work of the past six years. As I am by myself & also working in my City office it is rather a formidable task; but I am always coming across instances of your kind 'help & cooperation' & realize more than ever how much I owed to you & your staff . . . War is certainly unpleasant but it has its compensations & for

[176] Vivian to Liddell, 23 Jan. 1948, TNA, KV4/281.
[177] Minute by Liddell, 24 Feb. 1948, TNA, KV4/281; Mackenzie King diary, 7 Sept. 1948.
[178] Minute by J. H. Marriott (MI5), 8 Apr.; extract from minutes of JIC meeting of 17 June 1949, TNA, KV4/281.
[179] Liddell to Vivian, 12 July 1950, TNA, KV4/281.
[180] Cecil Liddell to Bryan, 25 Aug. and 9 Sept. 1944 and 16 Mar. 1945, UCDA, Bryan papers, P71/415, 416, and 420.

me one of the happiest has been the friends made on your side on the visits to Dublin. Please remember me to Joe [Guilfoyle] & Liam [Archer] . . . One day, hook or crook, we must get you all over here. Stephenson is still in Germany.[181]

Cecil remained in regular touch until his death in 1952.

Jo Stephenson, whose professional link with Ireland ended in 1942, visited Bryan while holidaying in Ireland in 1950, and in an unpublished memoir wrote warmly of the professionalism of the Irish intelligence officers with whom he had dealt.[182] Guy Liddell also met up with Bryan and others on occasional private visits, on one of which the two men went off with each others' coats. When Cecil died, Guy wrote to Bryan thanking him for his condolences:

I should like to thank you for your message of sympathy about Cecil. Please convey, too, my thanks to Joe Guilfoyle for his message. I know how much importance Cecil attached to the friendships that he made in Ireland, He always enjoyed his visits and the warm welcome that was always accorded to him by you and his other friends.

I expect by now that you will have had a letter from the office with the proposal that we should come over on a visit sometime next month . . . I need not tell you how much we value the association, which Liam and you have done so much to promote, and how anxious we are that it should continue with your successor.

I cannot say how much I regret your departure [from G2 to become commandant of the Military College], but for you it looks like a substantial and well-deserved promotion and I should like to wish you the very best of luck in your new job and to thank you for your wholehearted co-operation and many kindnesses in the past. I hope you feel, as I do and as I know Cecil did, that Liam and you have laid the foundations of something really worth while.

Looking forward to seeing you next month.[183]

Such friendships did not rely on complete openness and transparency. One of the marks of professionalism in intelligence cooperation is the mutual recognition that sharing of material and knowledge is a limited and contingent business, dependent not simply on mutual esteem, trust, and goodwill but on particular circumstances and conditions which could easily change. This was what happened after *Barbarossa*, when C had to disclose to the Soviets what the Finns had told London about Russian ciphers in 1940–1. MI5 never disclosed all their Irish information and concerns to G2, any more than G2 were entirely frank—it is clear from the Liddell history that no one in MI5 realized that the Irish had penetrated Collinson's SIS networks, or London would scarcely have revived these in November 1945 against the day when partition might become a major complicating issue (as Guy Liddell and Jane Archer had warned). Again, while there developed a high degree of mutual esteem and cordiality between Richard Hayes and British codebreakers, GC&CS never told him about Pandora and he would probably have been shocked at their indiscretion if they had.

Evidence of north–south security links is harder to find, but there continued to be exchanges between RUC and Garda headquarters, as there certainly were at

[181] Cecil Liddell to Bryan, 9 Dec. 1945, UCDA, Bryan papers, P71/425.
[182] Stephenson to Bryan, 24 Aug. and 27 Dec. 1949, and 8 Apr. and 28 Dec. 1950, UCDA, Bryan papers, P71/456.
[183] Guy Liddell to Bryan, 4 Apr. 1952, UCDA, Bryan papers, P71/455(8).

local level in border areas: when the RUC in Belfast heard rumours in 1948 that an IRA faction were planning to assassinate a leading republican in Donegal, the county inspector for Londonderry called to the home of the Garda superintendent in Letterkenny to brief him (the intended target refused Garda protection). A year later Roger Moore of the RUC assured MI5 'that he has an effective unofficial liaison on police matters with the Eire police', but there was trouble ahead.[184] In 1950, when Anglo-Irish relations were in a difficult phase because of Irish departure from the commonwealth, Commander Len Burt of the Scotland Yard Special Branch 'received a warning from Paddy Carroll', the Garda's security specialist,

that drilling was going on quite openly in Phoenix Park by irregular troops, and that although certain members of the Government did not wholly approve of this they would not do anything to stop it. Carroll said further that Roger Moore's life was in considerable danger and that he thought the latter would do well to take his pension as soon as he could and clear out. He had in fact said the same thing to Roger Moore himself, though not quite so positively. He then went on to say that he did not know how his liaison could be conducted with the North after Roger Moore's departure, since he had no real confidence in Moore's successor . . . As regards his liaison with Burt, he thought it could continue but it would be preferable if Burt's presence in Dublin were avoided, since his visits had become known to a number of people. If they met in future he thought it had better be in Wexford, where I think Carroll has his home.

I suggested to Burt that possibly Carroll might have two motives in his approach. Firstly, he might be acting under instructions with the intention of exerting pressure on the Government here to find a solution of [*sic*] the partition issue. This seemed on the whole most unlikely. Secondly, Carroll, who over a period of years had collaborated closely with the RUC, might have certain fears about his own safety and feel that the moment had come for him to detach himself from the North . . . and to take greater precautions in regard to his liaison with Burt. Burt thought that this was possible, although unlikely.[185]

Despite Carroll's pessimism, security relations appear to have remained on an even keel in the years following Irish departure from the commonwealth. MI5's view that their liaison with G2, and the RUC and Scotland Yard link with the Garda, rather than covert intelligence gathering, were the best means of keeping abreast of security affairs in Ireland appears to have prevailed. In January 1955 Dick White, now director-general of MI5, met the DMI to discuss a War Office proposal that 'political agreement should be sought for secret service work to be undertaken in Eire' by SIS. White doubted whether such sanction would be obtained, and added that 'even if it were, I should still think it appropriate to try to secure Eire Government approval for a closer liaison between the Garda and the RUC. I added that no secret service coming in from the outside could possibly compete with the coverage secured by the Garda and I thought it would, in any case, run into grave danger of crossing Garda lines'.[186] The matter was taken up by the British ambassador. An Irish official responded that 'liaison would continue to be

---

[184] Minute by Scherr (MI5), 21 Apr. 1949, TNA, KV4/281.

[185] Guy Liddell to Vivian, 12 July 1950, TNA, KV4/281. Carroll was Garda commissioner from 1967 to 1968.

[186] Note by White, 24 Jan. 1955, TNA, KV4/258. White moved to SIS as C in 1956, and may have taken a similar line there.

of the personal and informal character that he thought at present existed between individuals in the two Police forces and that the more informal it was and the less that was known about it the better'.[187] It was on that furtive basis that liaison continued until the outbreak of the Northern Ireland troubles in 1969.[188]

CONCLUSION

The five months leading up to *Overlord* were difficult and tense for British agencies dealing with Irish security. They were made more so by Churchill's petulant streak; despite the advice of his ministers, of the JIC, of C, and of MI5, he insisted on supporting an ill-thought-out and ill-informed American démarche which could only increase the instability of Irish–Allied security relations and put existing cooperation, not only on *Overlord* security but on operational matters, in jeopardy. While it had the benefit for him of making the Irish jumpy, this approach threatened Britain's best hope of maintaining the secrecy of the invasion preparations.

Once *Overlord* took place, Ireland virtually disappeared from London's intelligence agenda. It continued to have some significance for air and sea operations, where arrangements and understandings continued, but the danger of serious leakage of war information had gone, and with it the attention of ministers and senior officials. The *Casement* plan apart—and that was an aberration championed at senior level only by a partisan amateur—there was no interest either in punishing Ireland for neutrality or for wasting any more time persuading her to change tack. From being the gap through which key secrets might leak, after June 1944 Ireland became what it had been for most of Whitehall before the war, an anomalous, benighted backwater.

In the post-war era the Anglo-Irish security relationship built up at professional level came under some strain, not because of the Cold War, but as predicted in 1944 by Guy Liddell and Jane Archer because of the Northern Ireland issue. This caused particular problems when Ireland left the commonwealth, because that step was feared to presage a more proactive approach on partition by Dublin, possibly including support for armed action. From the available evidence, it appears that it was only after some deliberation that London decided in 1949 to continue to rely on existing channels of police and security liaison and on conventional diplomacy to ascertain what was happening and what was likely to happen in Ireland.

[187] Quoted in Reeves, ' "Let Us Stand By Our Friends" ', 101; O'Halpin, *Defending Ireland*, 244.
[188] O'Halpin, 'The British Joint Intelligence Committee and Ireland', 8–9.

Conclusion

Intelligence activities concerning Ireland during the second world war belong at different points on a spectrum running from what became almost a full alliance—in terms of security and counter-espionage, and aspects of wireless interception and codebreaking—to aggressive black propaganda against Irish neutrality and to the operation of covert networks of agents and informants throughout Ireland.

The initial problems which Ireland presented in 1939 arose from historical circumstances. Despite, or perhaps because of, the war of independence and the continuing sensitivity of partition, with the limited exception of the short-lived Northern Ireland 'secret service', no arrangements were put in place either to liaise with the new state on security matters of mutual interest, or to study Irish political affairs closely. This was also so where diplomacy is concerned; Irish representation in London was not matched by a British presence in Dublin until after war broke out. The very limited steps which were taken to obtain political intelligence once de Valera came to power in 1932 were of little consequence and yielded no benefits for British policy-makers.

There was also a failure of analysis in Whitehall about Ireland's likely attitude in a future war involving Britain. This seems a remarkable oversight, even in the fraught years of the late 1930s when Britain had so many other worries to contend with. The decision in 1938 to cede the defence rights guaranteed by the 1921 treaty was taken in a miasma of vague optimism that in time of war Britain would somehow not be damaged by the concession. There were good practical reasons for not holding on to the ports and other facilities and defence rights, not least the difficulty of operating them effectively in the absence of Irish cooperation, but that consideration should have led logically to reflection on why Ireland might very well not wish to join a British war. The answer lay first in recent Anglo-Irish history: why should a state whose entire political elite had risen to prominence through participation in the independence struggle, and whose only direct experience of conflict and oppression was at British hands, voluntarily choose to join with Britain in what, in 1939, appeared to many simply a rerun of the great conflict for hegemony in Europe of 1914–18. But secondly and perhaps decisively, the explanation lay in the mindset of small neutrals generally as the great powers moved towards war. This was reflected in the attitude expressed by such states at the League of Nations, and in the domestic pressures on their governments to avoid involvement at all costs—Belgium, which repudiated its alliance with France in 1936, being a case in point.

Britain had every right to be disappointed at Irish neutrality; she cannot have been surprised. What followed from likely Irish neutrality were two sets of concerns which the intelligence agencies were slow to address: the danger that Ireland might be used by foreign powers as a base from which to spy on the United Kingdom, and the likelihood that any enemy of Britain would seek an understanding with the IRA. The crucial preparatory breakthrough to address these problems came from an unexpected Irish initiative just as the Munich crisis came to a head; this laid the foundations for the eventually highly effective counter-espionage and security cooperation which developed, but it did little to increase the flow of information to London on political affairs or on the intentions of the Irish government. These were matters which required both diplomatic and intelligence activity on the ground in Ireland, but none was forthcoming until after war broke out.

It is ironic that, as during the first world war, the initial intelligence concerns of British policy-makers were with a security threat which simply did not exist: just as in 1914, in 1939 there were no U-boats sheltering in Irish inlets, and no obliging subversives with barrels of diesel to refuel them. It is remarkable that such an implausible fear was allowed to dominate Irish intelligence gathering for the first eight months of the war, long after the arrival of an energetic naval attaché should have dispelled any such nonsense.

De Valera stuck by the security aspect of the commitment which he had long offered, that Ireland would not allow herself to become a base for hostile activities directed against Britain. At a professional level, Irish cooperation was generally willing and over time became very effective—in respect of coast-watching, observation and reporting of air movements, access to enemy equipment found in crashed aircraft or washed up along the coast, meteorological reporting, communications censorship, shipping and air controls, and travel permits—and in respect of counter-espionage, of thwarting the IRA, and of German agent communications reached a pitch of high efficiency. This met the specific interests of Allied security, probably, as Cecil Liddell's Irish section history argued, to a greater extent than could have been achieved had Ireland been coaxed or forced into the war on Britain's side.

The problem of German agents in Ireland proved to be linked to the wider issue of the control of espionage generally. *Basket* provides the most spectacular, but not the only, instance of interconnection of Irish and Double Cross issues: there were also significant Irish dimensions to the cases of *Snow*, the foundation stone of the system, and *Rainbow*. These were matters where, despite the strength of their links with G2, MI5 had to tread carefully for fear of disclosing the wider secret of Double Cross.

Where de Valera signally failed to deliver on his commitment to have regard for Britain's legitimate defence concerns, partly for complex domestic reasons relating to fear of maintaining an over-powerful army, but partly simply because of a refusal to spend money, was in the matter of defence. Ireland, like many European neutrals and her fellow dominions Canada and South Africa, was virtually unarmed in 1939. This made neutrality not merely galling but threatening to Britain's strategic interests, because Ireland was wide open to a sudden attack of precisely the kind which Germany mounted against the Low Countries, Denmark, and Norway in 1940. Yet, as Churchill constantly pointed out, to provide Ireland with sufficient weapons to resist such a German attack would only reinforce her in her determination to remain neutral, besides diverting scarce supplies from other petitioners who were already in the war against the Axis. This conundrum was never satisfactorily resolved, and the wisdom of not providing weapons in 1940–1, particularly for airfield defence, was never put to the test because Germany never attempted to gain a foothold in Ireland. SOE's plans to prepare the ground for stay-behind activities in the event of a German attack were stymied both by the prime minister's personal arms embargo and by the warnings of MI5 and SIS that such preparations, if discovered by the Irish, would jeopardize security cooperation. As the war progressed, the intelligence agencies grew less sympathetic towards Irish pleas for weapons, reasoning that there was a danger that these would be turned against Northern Ireland in a future campaign to end partition.

British policy was considerably influenced by diplomatic codebreaking. Italian and Japanese traffic gave an accurate view of the intentions and activities of their Dublin representatives. It became clear that neither were actively engaged in collecting and relaying intelligence, but that both passed on whatever material came their way opportunistically. Decodes also disclosed increased Japanese interest in Ireland as a source of intelligence on Britain in 1943, although practical problems meant that their Dublin consulate could not fulfil such a role effectively. Decodes revealed that the Vichy French legation was not bent on intelligence gathering and, perhaps more surprisingly given the close relationship between the Spanish diplomatic service and the Japanese elsewhere, that the Spanish minister did not act as an Axis spy. Decodes also indicated that Ireland did not do favours for other countries by disguising their messages within Irish traffic and diplomatic mail, despite requests from the Germans and the Italians. This was an important negative.

Once Pandora became available, close study of available German traffic between Berlin and Dublin since 1939 provided all the material necessary to assess Hempel's activities and the changing requirements which Berlin placed upon him. It may seem a strange argument, but British policy was probably better served by not having contemporaneous access to Hempel's 1940 traffic, because that might have precipitated pre-emptive diplomatic and even military action which could have brought a clash with Ireland which would have damaged British interests in the United States. This is particularly so in respect of Berlin's demand in December 1940 that the Irish immediately accept additional legation staff whose role, as explicitly stated to Hempel, would be to gather intelligence. Irish diplomatic traffic, on the other hand, was of interest primarily because of the light it shed on conditions in Europe as the tide turned against the Axis. It also yielded material of value in relation to Irish trade and shipping difficulties, where British policy in 1941–2 was to maintain what amounted almost to an economic blockade of Ireland, and in the autumn of 1944 disclosed the unwelcome emergence of an Irish–American entente on post-war Atlantic civil aviation. Churchill's complaints about this occasioned a rebuke from Roosevelt.

While the relative involvements of the different intelligence agencies varied somewhat over time, MI5 and SIS were consistently engaged with Irish questions. After the crisis of May–June 1940, they worked increasingly closely with the Dominions Office. Sir John Maffey was also crucial. His experience in India, and in Britain's scuffles with Afghanistan along the north-west frontier, as well as his time in Whitehall had left him an equable and perceptive observer of political affairs.

Unlike some British representatives in neutral states, he made sure that he was closely involved in discussion of security issues. The result was that by the autumn of 1940 there was considerable integration of analysis of the problems encountered and of the possible ways ahead between the intelligence agencies, the policy department responsible for Ireland, and Britain's man in Dublin.

The policy decision taken in 1938 to help the Irish out with their concerns about German espionage proved a wise one. That initial contact became the conduit through which not only security but broader military cooperation was initiated in the crisis months of May and June 1940. Apart from a difficult period in the summer of 1941 because of tension about the German legation radio, MI5 and G2 worked closely throughout the war. The professional and personal relationships built up were predicated on a high degree of mutual respect and trust, though naturally not on complete disclosure. The people involved in this secret rapport remained loyal and discriminating servants of their respective states. It is important to note the evident efficiency of the Irish against the IRA, and against German espionage, as indicated not only in post-war studies but in the observations of Sir Charles Wickham as early as 1940. The Eastwood case of 1943 reflected the very high degree of trust which developed between MI5 and G2, and brought GC&CS the bonus of Richard Hayes's discoveries about the workings of the Goertz cipher which were to have a wider application in the last year of the war. The finesse with which G2 deceived Herman Goertz into furnishing a detailed report of his mission reflected their sophisticated approach to counter-intelligence and counter-espionage. So too did the early and undetected penetration of SIS's Dublin activities, a coup of which London seems to have remained blissfully unaware. In addition, the Irish coastal and air observation systems provided a mass of operational intelligence to the Allies on the Atlantic theatre, while the prosaic matter of weather reporting was also crucial for air and sea operations. Cooperation on wireless interception from December 1941 greatly benefited British radio security, and must have been of considerable operational value.

British covert activities in Ireland after June 1940 were directed almost entirely against the perceived threat of Axis espionage. There was no attempt to interfere in Irish domestic politics, apart from encouragement for the handful of public figures willing to argue for Irish participation in the war at Britain's side. There is no evidence that, apart from outline plans for the sabotage or destruction of key facilities in the event of a German attack in 1940–1, Britain made any secret arrangements potentially inimical to Irish interests. The fact that SOE were forced out of Ireland in 1941 within months of sending in an agent underlines Whitehall's apprehension that any secret preparations made behind Irish backs would provoke a crisis in security relations if discovered. SOE's difficulties in fending off that criticism were compounded by the prime minister's adamantine refusal to let the Irish have weapons even when the chiefs of staff recommended otherwise.

Deliberate targeting of Ireland for black propaganda purposes was limited: the U-boat scare was one in which the Admiralty itself had implicit faith in 1939, although it is likely that its continued currency in the United States, which was the key theatre for British propaganda against Irish neutrality until Pearl Harbor, owed something to British activities. The activities of AIDA, and fragmentary traces of other schemes to influence American opinion against Ireland, as well as targeting Catholic and Irish-American circles, are clear evidence of a policy of discrediting Irish neutrality, whether as a prelude to possible armed action or simply as a means of reinforcing the Roosevelt administration's hostility. After Pearl Harbor there was no need covertly to play up the folly of Irish neutrality in American minds. The firm refusal in the last months of the war to accept the *Casement* plan so passionately advocated by General Templer reflects Whitehall's lack of interest in punishing Ireland. What was the point?

At two moments of crisis—June 1940 and December 1941—Churchill set aside his resentment to sanction dramatic though undeliverable suggestions of eventual Irish unification in return for immediate Irish participation in the war against the Axis. The first and most significant offer arose from an SIS initiative, itself the product of a panicky assessment of lurid and far-fetched intelligence on the relative strength and resolution of the Irish government and the pro-German IRA, and on German intentions towards Ireland.

Intelligence operations had a generally positive and moderating influence on British policy. Cooperation on security, both between London and Dublin and, what is much harder to measure, between Belfast and Dublin, was the necessary cornerstone. For the Irish, of course, cooperation was a means not so much of providing covert support for the Allies, as of minimizing opportunities for the Allies to claim that neutral Ireland was a mortal danger to Allied operations. The deeper that cooperation became, the more the Allied armed forces and intelligence agencies feared its possible loss. So far as was possible—and for much of the war they succeeded because Ireland was generally very small beer—MI5 and SIS strove to keep Irish matters well away from 10 Downing Street. When they were unable to do so, they held their breath lest the prime minister's interventions lead to a collapse in security and military cooperation.

Churchill's treatment of wartime intelligence concerning Ireland does not add much lustre to his reputation as a politician with a particular understanding of the secret world and its secret sources. He can scarcely be criticized for his personal resentment of Irish neutrality, of the way in which de Valera publicly nursed the partition grievance, and of the taoiseach's tendency to moralize about the plight of small peaceful states in a world at war; but his occasional interventions were petulant rather than considered. They generally went against what the intelligence agencies were attempting and against their direct advice. The unusual unity of purpose between MI5 and SIS saw them speak with a single voice on Ireland in Whitehall, where C took a marked interest in the issue of Irish security and acted as an important counterweight to Churchill's wilder enthusiasms, prejudices, and outbursts, sometimes receiving a dressing-down for his pains.

Neville Wylie observes of Anglo-Swiss relations that 'no policy decision was taken during the war without the intelligence community's say, and most crucial junctures in Anglo-Swiss relations before the summer of 1943 were stamped with the indelible mark of Britain's intelligence services'.[1] The same could scarcely be said of Ireland. Ireland was quite unlike the other long-term European neutrals with

---

[1] Wylie, *Britain, Switzerland and the second world war*, 299.

which Britain dealt during the war, both because of contiguity and because of recent history. This was reflected not only in the intricacies of the Anglo-Irish security understanding, but in the attitude taken at the political level. Churchill nursed a personal grievance against Ireland, as a back-stabbing dominion and former British possession, which he did not have against any other European neutral, despite the fact that Switzerland, Sweden, the two Iberian dictatorships, and Turkey all maintained close economic relations with the Axis powers until very late in the day, and that Sweden, Switzerland, and Spain all provided significant military and intelligence assistance and concessions to Germany. Ireland he regarded, like Iraq, Persia, Egypt, and Afghanistan, as scarcely a sovereign state at all but a begrudging former colony or protectorate, which should be browbeaten into cooperation. It is in the intelligence, security, and wider strategic problems posed by those states for British interests, and their wartime experience at British hands, that the closest parallels with Ireland can be found.

Bibliography

OFFICIAL RECORDS AND PRIVATE PAPERS HELD IN PUBLIC
REPOSITORIES

Bank of England, London

Norman diaries (ADM34)
Overseas Eire 1927–March 1940 (OV81/1)

British Library (BL), London

India Office records (LP/J, and LP/S)
Rich MSS
Saklatvala MSS
Tegart MSS

British Library of Political and Economic Science (BLPES), London

Dalton papers

Military Archives of Ireland (MAI), Dublin

Bureau of Military History
G2 records (G2 and G2X)

National Archives of Ireland (NAI), Dublin

Department of Foreign Affairs (DFA)
Department of Justice (JUS)
Department of the Taoiseach (DT)

National Archives (TNA), London

Admiralty (ADM)
Air Ministry (AIR)
Cabinet committee papers, memoranda, and war cabinet papers (CAB)
Dominions Office (DO)
Foreign Office (FO)
German Foreign Office (GFM)
Government Code and Cipher School (HW)
Home Office (HO)
Morton papers (PREM 7)
Northern Ireland Office (CJ4)
Political Warfare Executive (FO898)
Security Service (KV)
Special Operations Executive (HS)
War Office (WO)

National Archives and Records Administration of the United States (NARA), Washington, DC

National Security Agency (RG457)
Office of Strategic Services (RG226)
State Department (RG59)

National Archives of Scotland (NAS), Edinburgh

Scottish Special Branch reports (HH)

Public Archives of Canada (PAC), Ottawa

Department of National Defence
Mackenzie King diaries (accessed via http:king.collectionscanada.ca/EN)

Public Record Office of Northern Ireland (PRONI), Belfast

Home Affairs (HA)
Savory papers

PRIVATE PAPERS IN ARCHIVES AND REPOSITORIES

Bodleian Library, Oxford

Curtis papers
Sankey papers

Churchill College Cambridge Archives (CCCA)

Amery papers
Cadogan papers
Churchill papers
Drax papers
Gilchrist papers
Godfrey papers
Swinton papers

Dublin Diocesan Archives

McQuaid papers

Houghton Library, Harvard

J. P. Moffat papers

Liddell Hart Centre for Military Archives, Kings College London

Davidson papers

Marist College, New York

Franklin Roosevelt papers (accessed via http://www.fdrlibrary.marist.edu)

New York Public Library (NYPL)

Joseph C. Walsh papers

University College Dublin Archives (UCDA)

Bryan papers
de Valera papers
Fianna Fáil party papers
Furlong papers
MacEntee papers
Moloney (Kathleen Barry) papers

PAPERS IN PRIVATE HANDS

Podesta papers

PARLIAMENTARY AND OFFICIAL PUBLICATIONS

Congressional Record
Dáil debates
House of Commons debates

NEWSPAPERS AND MAGAZINES

Evening Herald
Guardian
Irish Independent
Irish Times
New Yorker
The Times

THESES

O'MALLEY, KATE, 'Ireland, India and Empire, 1919–1949', Ph.D. thesis, Trinity College Dublin (2006).

O'NEILL, MICHAEL, 'The Irish Army in the War Years: Manpower, Equipment and Organization, 1940–45', Ph.D. thesis, University College Dublin (2006).

BOOKS, CHAPTERS, AND ARTICLES

ADAMEC, LUDWIG W., *Historical Dictionary of Afghanistan* (Metuchen, NJ, 1991).

ALLINGHAM, MARGERY, *Traitor's Purse* (London, 1941).

ANDREW, CHRISTOPHER, *Secret Service: The Making of the British Intelligence Community* (London, 1985).

—— and DAVID DILKS (eds.), *The Missing Dimension: Governments and Intelligence Communities in the Twentieth Century* (London, 1984).

ANGLIM, SIMON, 'MI(R), G(R) and British Covert Operations, 1939–42', *Intelligence and National Security*, 20: 4 (Dec. 2005), 631–53.

ANNAN, NOEL, *Changing Enemies: The Defeat and Regeneration of Germany* (London, 1995).

ARCHANDAWI, ABDUL ALI, *British Imperialism and the Struggle for Independence, 1914–21* (New Delhi, 1989).

BAYLY, CHRISTOPHER, and TIM HARPER, *Forgotten Armies: Britain's Asian Empire and the War with Japan* (London, 2004).

BEAUMONT, JOAN, 'Great Britain and the Rights of Neutral Countries: The Case of Iran, 1941', *Journal of Contemporary History*, 6 (1981), 213–28.

BECKETT, IAN (ed.), *The Roots of Counter-Insurgency: Armies and Guerilla Warfare, 1900–1945* (London, 1988).

BEESLY, PATRICK, *Very Special Admiral: The Life of Admiral J. H. Godfrey CB* (London, 1980).

—— *Room 40: British Naval Intelligence, 1914–1918* (London, 1982).

BENNETT, GILL, *Churchill's Man of Mystery: Desmond Morton and the World of Intelligence* (London, 2006).

BETHELL, LESLIE (ed.), *The Cambridge History of Latin America*, vol. vii: *Latin America Since 1930*, vii: *Mexico, Central America and the Caribbean* (Cambridge, 1990).

—— *The Cambridge History of Latin America*, vol. viii: *Spanish South America* (Cambridge, 1991).

BEW, PAUL, PETER GIBBON, and HENRY PATTERSON, *Northern Ireland 1921/2001: Political Forces and Social Class* (London, 2002).

BOND, BRIAN, *British Military Policy Between the Wars* (London, 1980).

—— (ed.), *Chief of Staff: The Diaries of Lieutenant General Sir Henry Pownall*, vol. ii: *1940–1944* (London, 1974).

BORGONOVO, JOHN, *Spies, Informers and the 'Anti-Sinn Fein Society': The Intelligence War in Cork City* (Dublin, 2006).

—— (ed.), *Florence and Josephine O'Donoghue's War of Independence: A Destiny that shapes our ends* (Dublin, 2006).

BOWMAN, JOHN, *De Valera and the Ulster Question, 1917–1973* (Oxford, 1982).

BOSE, MIHIR, *The Lost Hero: A Biography of Subhas Chandra Bose* (1st edn., London, 1982; revised edn., London, 2004).

BOSE, SUGATA (ed.), *Netaji and Indian Freedom: Proceedings of the International Netaji Seminar 1973* (Calcutta, 1975).

BOYLE, ANDREW, *The Climate of Treason: Five Who Spied for Stalin* (London, 1979).

BRENNAN, ROBERT, *Ireland Standing Firm: My Wartime Mission in Washington* (Dublin, 1958; Cork, 2002).

BUCHAN, JOHN, *Greenmantle* (1916; Harmondsworth, 1956).

BURLEIGH, MICHAEL, *Sacred Causes: Religion and Politics from the European Dictators to Al Qaeda* (London, 2006).

BUSCH, B. M., *Britain, India and the Arabs, 1914–1921* (Los Angeles, 1971).

CANNING, PAUL, *British Policy Towards Ireland, 1921–1941* (Oxford, 1985).

CARLGREN, W. M., *Swedish Foreign Policy During the second world war* (London, 1977).

CARTER, MIRANDA, *Anthony Blunt: His Lives* (London, 2001).

CASEY, R. G., *Personal Experience 1939–1946* (London, 1962).

CECIL, ROBERT, 'The Cambridge Comintern', in Andrew and Dilks, *The Missing Dimension*, 169–98.

—— 'The Assessment and Acceptance of Intelligence: A Case Study', in Robertson, *British and American Perspectives*, 166–83.

CHEYNEY, PETER, *Dark Duet* (London, 1943).

CHRISTIE, AGATHA, *N or M?* (London, 1941).

CLARKE, LINDA, 'Higher Ranking Women and the Vichy Regime: Firings and Hirings, Collaboration and Resistance', *French History*, 13: 3 (1999), 333–4.

CLIVE, NIGEL, *A Greek Experience, 1943–1948* (London, 1985).

COLE, ROBERT, *Propaganda, Censorship and Irish Neutrality in the second world war* (Edinburgh, 2006).

CONNOLLY, TRACEY, 'Irish Workers in Britain During World War Two', in Girvin and Roberts, *Ireland and the second world war*, 120–32.

CONWAY, J. S., 'Myron C. Taylor's Mission to the Vatican, 1940–1950', *Church History*, 44: 1 (1975), 96.

COOPER, ALFRED DUFF, *Operation Heartbreak* (London, 1951).

CORNWELL, JOHN, *Hitler's Pope: The Secret History of Pius XII* (London, 1999).

CORSE, EDWARD, 'British Propaganda in Neutral Eire After the Fall of France, 1940', *Contemporary British History*, 1 (Jan. 2007), 1–18.

COUNTY AND CITY MANAGERS ASSOCIATION, *City and County Management, 1929–1990: A Retrospective* (Dublin, 1991).

CRADOCK, PERCY, *Know Your Enemy: How the Joint Intelligence Committee Saw the World* (London, 2003).

CROSSMAN, RICHARD, *The Diaries of a Cabinet Minister* (London, 1976).

CROWE, CATRIONA, with RONAN FANNING, MICHAEL KENNEDY, DERMOT KEOGH, and EUNAN O'HALPIN (eds.), *Documents on Irish Foreign Policy*, vol. V: *1937–1939* (Dublin, 2006).

CROWLEY, PATRICK (ed.), *Those Who Journeyed With Us: Deceased Colombans, 1918–2006* (Navan, 2007).

CUNNINGHAM, EMMA, 'Ireland, Canada and the American Note', in Keogh and O'Driscoll, *Ireland in the second world war*, 149, 153–5.

CURRY, J. G., *The Security Service 1908–1945: The Official History* (London, 1999).

DANCHEV, ALEX, and DAN TODMAN (eds.), *War Diaries 1939–1945: Field-Marshal Lord Alanbrooke* (London, 2001).

DAS, SITANSHU, *Subhas: A Political Biography* (New Delhi, 2001; pbk. edn., 2006).

DEAN, EDWARD PACKARD, 'Canada at War', *Foreign Affairs*, 18: 2 (Jan. 1940), 292–304.

DENHAM, PETER, *Inside the Nazi Ring: A Naval Attaché in Sweden 1940–1945* (London, 1984).

DENNISTON, RALPH, 'The Professional Career of A. G. Denniston', in Robertson, *British and American Perspectives*, 104–29.

—— *Churchill's Secret War: Diplomatic Decrypts, the Foreign Office and Turkey, 1942–44* (Stroud, 1997).

—— *Thirty Secret Years: A. G. Denniston's Work in Signals Intelligence 1914–1944* (Clifton-upon-Teme, 2007).

DEVLIN, JUDITH, and HOWARD CLARKE (eds.), *European Encounters: Essays in Memory of Albert Lovett* (Dublin, 2003).

DILKS, DAVID (ed.), *The Diaries of Sir Alexander Cadogan OM, 1938–1945* (London, 1971).

DONAHUE, LAURA K., 'Regulating Northern Ireland: The Special Powers Act, 1922–1972', *Historical Journal*, 41: 4 (1998), 1089–120.

DOUGLAS, R. M., 'The Pro-Axis Underground in Ireland, 1939–1942', *Historical Journal*, 49: 4 (2006), 1155–83.

DRAKE, PAUL, 'Chile, 1930–58', in Bethell, *Cambridge History of Latin America*, viii. 269–310.

DUGGAN, J. P., *Herr Hempel at the German Legation in Dublin* (Dublin, 2002).

DWYER, T. RYLE, *Irish Neutrality and the USA, 1939–1947* (Dublin, 1977).

—— *Guests of the Nation: The Story of Allied and Axis Servicemen Interned in Ireland During World War Two* (Dingle, 1994).

ENGLISH, RICHARD, *Radicals and the Republic: Socialist Republicans in the Irish Free State, 1925–37* (Oxford, 1994).

EVANS, TREFOR (ed.), *The Killearn Diaries 1934–1946: The Diplomatic and Personal Record of Lord Killearn (Sir Miles Lampson) High Commissioner and Ambassador, Egypt* (London, 1972).

EWELL, JUDITH, 'Venezuela Since 1930', in Bethell, *Cambridge History of Latin America*, viii. 727–90.

FANNING, RONAN, *Independent Ireland* (Dublin, 1983).

Ibid., *The Irish Department of Finance, 1922–1958* (Dublin, 1978).

____ 'The Anglo-American Alliance and the Irish Question in the Twentieth Century', in Devlin and Clarke, *European Encounters*, 185–220.

____ with MICHAEL KENNEDY, DERMOT KEOGH, and EUNAN O'HALPIN (eds.), *Documents on Irish Foreign Policy*, vol. I: *1919–1922* (Dublin, 1998).

FAY, PETER WARD, *The Forgotten Army: India's Armed Struggle for Independence, 1942–1945* (Ann Arbor, Mich., 1995).

FERGUSSON, NIALL, *The War of the World: History's Age of Hatred* (London, 2006; pbk. edn. 2007).

FINCH, HENRY, 'Uruguay Since 1930', in Bethell, *Cambridge History of Latin America*, viii. 195–232.

FISK, ROBERT, *In Time of War: Ireland, Ulster and the Price of Neutrality, 1939–45* (London, 1983).

FOLLIS, BRIAN, *A State Under Siege: The Establishment of Northern Ireland, 1920–1925* (Oxford, 1995).

FOOT, M. R. D., 'Foreword', in MacKenzie, *Secret History of SOE*, pp. i–ix.

____ 'Michael Collins and the Origins of SOE', in M. R. D. Foot (ed.), *War and Society: Essays in Honour of J. R. Western* (London, 1973), 57–69.

____ and J. LANGLEY, *MI9: Escape and Evasion, 1939–1945* (London, 1979).

GANNON, PAUL, *Colossus: Bletchley Park's Greatest Secret* (London, 2006).

GARFIELD, BRIAN, *The Paladin* (London, 1980).

GARNETT, DAVID, *The Secret History of PWE: The Political Warfare Executive, 1939–1945* (London, 2002).

GIRVIN, BRIAN, *The Emergency: Neutral Ireland 1939–1945* (London, 2005).

____ with GEOFFREY ROBERTS (eds.), *Ireland and the second world war: Politics, Society and Remembrance* (Dublin, 2000).

GORDON, LEONARD, *Brothers Against the Raj: A Biography of Indian Nationalists Sarat and Subhas Chandra Bose* (New York, 1990).

GRANT, DAVID, *Emerald Decision* (London, 1980).

GROSSE, PETER, *Gentleman Spy: The Life of Allen Dulles* (New York, 1994).

GRUNDLIGH, ALBERT, 'The King's Afrikaners? Enlistment and Ethnic Identity in the Union of South Africa's Defence Force During the second world war, 1939–1945', *Journal of African History*, 40: 3 (1990), 351–65.

GWYNN, CHARLES, *Imperial Policing* (London, 1934).

HAMILTON, HUGO, *The Speckled People* (London, 2003).

HAMMER, ELLEN, 'Insight on Vichy', *Political Science Quarterly*, 61: 2 (1946), 175–88.

HANLEY, BRIAN, *The IRA, 1926–1936* (Dublin, 2003).

HART, PETER, *The IRA and its Enemies* (Oxford, 1999).

____ *Mick: The Real Michael Collins* (London, 2005).

____ (ed.), *British Intelligence in Ireland, 1920–21: The Final Reports* (Cork, 2002).

HARTOG, RUDOLF, *The Sign of the Tiger: Subhas Chandra Bose and his Indian Legion in Germany, 1941–5* (New Delhi, 2001).

HAUNER, MILAN, *India in Axis Strategy: Germany, Japan, and Indian Nationalists in the second world war* (Stuttgart, 1981).

____ 'One Man Against the Empire: The Faqir of Ipi and the British in Central Asia on the Eve of and During the second world war', *Journal of Contemporary History*, 16 (1981), 183–212.

____ 'The Soviet Threat to Afghanistan and India, 1938–1940', *Modern Asian Studies*, 15: 2 (1981), 287–309.

HAUNER, MILAN, 'Afghanistan Between the Great Powers, 1938–1945', *International Journal of Middle Eastern Studies*, 14 (1982), 481–99.

HELMRICH, JONATHAN, 'The Negotiation of the Franco-Belgian Military Accord of 1920', *French Historical Studies*, 3: 3 (1964), 363–73.

HENNESSEY, THOMAS, *A History of Northern Ireland, 1920–1996* (Dublin, 1997).

HERZOG, CHAIM, *Living History: The Memoirs of a Great Israeli Freedom-Fighter, Soldier, Diplomat and Statesman* (1st edn., London, 1997; pbk edn., 1998).

HIGGINS, JACK, *The Eagle Has Landed* (London, 1975).

HINSLEY, F. H., and C. A. G. SIMKINS, *British Intelligence in the second world war*, vol. 4: *Security and Counter-Intelligence* (London, 1990).

HODSON, H. V., 'British Foreign Policy and the Dominions', *Foreign Affairs*, 17: 4 (July 1939), 753–63.

HOPKIRK, PETER, *On Secret Service East of Constantinople: The Plot to Bring Down the British Empire* (London, 1994; pbk. edn., 2006).

HORNE, JOHN, and ALAN KRAMER, *German Atrocities, 1914: A History of Denial* (New Haven, 2001).

HOWARD, MICHAEL, *British Intelligence in the second world war*, vol. v: *Strategic Deception* (London, 1990).

HUDSON, W. J., and H. J. W. STOKES (eds.), *Documents on Australian Foreign Policy 1937–49*, vol. iv: *July 1940–June 1941* (Canberra, 1980).

HULL, MARK, *Irish Secrets: German Espionage in Wartime Ireland, 1939–1945* (Dublin, 2003).

JACKSON, JULIAN, *The Fall of France: The Nazi Invasion of 1940* (Oxford, 2003).

JACKSON, PETER, *France and the Nazi Menace: Intelligence and Policy Making, 1933–1939* (Oxford, 2000).

JEFFERY, KEITH, *The GPO and the Easter Rising* (Dublin, 2006).

—— (ed.), *The Military Correspondence of Field Marshal Sir Henry Wilson, 1918–1922* (London, 1983).

—— and PETER HENNESSY, *States of Emergency: British Governments and Strikebreaking Since 1919* (London, 1983).

JENNINGS, ERIC, *Vichy in the Tropics: Pétain's National Revolution in Madagascar, Guadeloupe and Indochina, 1940–1944* (Stanford, 2001).

JENSEN, JOAN, *Passage from India: Asian Indian Immigrants to North America* (New Haven, 1988).

JONES, THOMAS, *A Diary with Letters, 1931–1950* (Oxford, 1954).

KAHN, DAVID, *Hitler's Spies* (1st edn., London, 1978; pbk. edn., 1982).

—— *The Reader of Gentlemen's Mail: Herbert O. Yardley and the Birth of American Code-breaking* (New Haven, 2004).

KANON, JOSEPH, *Alibi* (1st edn., London, 2005; pbk. edn., 2007).

KENNEDY, MICHAEL, *Ireland and the League of Nations: International Relations, Diplomacy and Politics* (Dublin, 1996).

—— ' "A Voyage of Exploration": Irish Diplomatic Perspectives on Egypt, Sudan and Palestine in the Inter-war years', in Miller, *Ireland and the Middle East*, 7–23.

KEOGH, DERMOT, *Ireland and the Vatican: The Politics and Diplomacy of Church–State Relations, 1922–1960* (Cork, 1995).

—— and MERVYN O'DRISCOLL (eds.), *Ireland in the second world war: Neutrality and Survival* (Cork, 2004).

KEOGH, NIALL, *Con Cremin, Ireland's Wartime Diplomat* (Cork, 2006).

KIMBALL, WARREN F., *Churchill and Roosevelt: The Complete Correspondence*, 3 vols. (Princeton, 1984).

KNIGHT, ALAN, 'Mexico, c.1930–1946', in Bethell, *Cambridge History of Latin America*, vii. 3–82.

LATHAM, R. D., *Naval Aviation in the first world war: Its Impact ond Influence* (London, 1996).

LE ROUX, LOUIS, *Patrick H. Pearse* (Dublin, n.d. [1932]).

LEVINE, PAUL, 'Swedish Neutrality During the second world war', in Wylie (ed.), *European Neutrals*, 304–30.

LEISTIKOW, GUNNAR, 'Denmark's Precarious Neutrality', *Foreign Affairs*, 17: 3 (Apr. 1939), 611–17.

LINGELBACH, W. E., 'Neutrality versus Alliances: Belgium and the Revolution in International Politics', *Proceedings of the American Philosophical Society*, 79: 4 (1936), 607–36.

LLOYD, LORNA, and ALAN JAMES, 'The External Representation of the Dominions, 1919–1948: Its Role in the Unravelling of the British Empire', *British Yearbook of International Law*, (1996), 500–21.

LYSAGHT, CHARLES, *Brendan Bracken* (London, 1980).

McGARRY, FEARGHAL, *Eoin O Duffy: A Self-Made Hero* (Oxford, 2005).

____ *Ireland and the Spanish Civil War* (Dublin, 2001).

McINTYRE, BEN, *Agent Zigzag: Lover, Traitor, Hero, Spy* (London, 2007).

MACKENZIE, W. J. M., *The Secret History of SOE: The Special Operations Executive, 1940–1945* (London, 2000).

McLOUGHLIN, BARRY, *Left to the Wolves: Irish Victims of Stalinist Terror* (Dublin, 2007).

McMAHON, DEIRDRE, *Republicans and Imperialists: Anglo-Irish Relations in the 1930s* (London, 1984).

McMAHON, PAUL, 'Covert Operations and official collaboration: British Intelligence's Dual Approach to Ireland During World War II', *Intelligence and National Security*, 18: 1 (spring, 2003), 41–64.

MAGAN, WILLIAM, *Middle Eastern Approaches: Memoirs of an Intelligence Officer* (Norwich, 2001).

MAHAN, A. T., *The Influence of Sea Power Upon History 1660–1783* (London, 1890).

MANNING, MAURICE, *The Blueshirts* (Dublin, 1974).

____ *James Dillon: A Biography* (Dublin, 1999).

MANSERGH, NICOLAS, *The Unresolved Question: The Anglo-Irish Settlement and its Undoing 1912–72* (London, 1992).

MASTERMAN, J. C., *On the Chariot Wheel: An Autobiography* (Oxford, 1975).

____ *The Double-Cross System in the War of 1939 to 1945* (New Haven, 1972).

MAUGHAM, W. SOMERSET, *Ashenden: Or the British Agent* (London, 1934).

MILLER, RORY (ed.), *Ireland and the Middle East: Trade, Society and Peace* (Dublin, 2007).

MONTAGU, EWAN, *The Man Who Never Was* (London, 1953).

MOORE, WALTER, *Schrödinger: Life and Thought* (Cambridge, 1989).

MUGGERIDGE, MALCOLM (ed.), *Ciano's Diaries, 1939–1943* (London, 1947).

MULLINS, GERRY, *Dublin Nazi No. 1: The Life of Adolf Mahr* (Dublin, 2007).

NICOSIA, FRANCIS R., ' "Drang nach Osten" Continued? Germany and Afghanistan During the Weimar Republic', *Journal of Contemporary History*, 32: 2 (1997), 235–57.

NÍ LOCHLAINN, AOIFE, 'Ailtirí na hAiséirighe: A Party of its Time?', in Keogh and O'Driscoll, *Ireland in World War Two*, 187–210.

NOEL, GERARD (ed.), *The Holy See and the War in Europe, 1939–1940* (English edn., London, 1968).

O'BRIEN, CONOR CRUISE, *Memoir: My Life and Themes* (Dublin, 1998).

O'CONNOR, EMMET, 'Communists, Russia, and the IRA, 1920–1923', *Historical Journal*, 46: 1 (2003), 115–31.

____ *Reds and the Green: Ireland, Russia and the Communist Internationals 1919–43* (Dublin, 2004).

O'DONOGHUE, DAVID, *Hitler's Irish Voices: The Story of German Radio's Wartime Irish Service* (Belfast, 1998).

O'DONOGHUE, FLORENCE, *No Other Law: The Story of Liam Lynch and the Irish Republican Army* (Dublin, 1954).

Ó DRISCEÓIL, DONAL, *Censorship in Ireland, 1939–1945: Neutrality, Politics and Society* (Cork, 1996).

O'DRISCOLL, MERVYN, *Ireland, Germany and the Nazis: Politics and Diplomacy, 1919–1939* (Dublin, 2004).

O'DUFFY, EOIN, *Crusade in Spain* (Dublin, 1938).

O'Halpin, Eunan, 'British Intelligence in Ireland, 1914–1921', in Andrew and Dilks, *The Missing Dimension*, 54–77.

——— *The Decline of the Union: British Government in Ireland, 1892–1920* (Dublin, 1987).

——— 'Financing British Intelligence: The Evidence up to 1945', in Robertson, *British and American Perspectives*, 187–217.

——— *Head of the Civil Service: A Study of Sir Warren Fisher* (London, 1989).

——— *Defending Ireland: The Irish State and its Enemies Since 1922* (Oxford, 1999).

——— 'Small States and Big Secrets: Understanding Sigint Cooperation Between Unequal Powers in the second world war', *Intelligence and National Security*, 17: 3 (2002), 1–16.

——— '"Weird Prophecies": British Intelligence and Anglo-Irish Relations, 1932–3', in Michael Kennedy and J. M. Skelly (eds.), *Irish Foreign Policy 1916–1966: From Independence Towards Interdependence* (Dublin, 2002).

——— 'Long Fellow, Long Story: MI5 and de Valera', *Irish Studies in International Affairs*, 14 (2003), 185–203.

——— 'The Liddell Diaries and British Intelligence History', *Intelligence and National Security*, 20: 4 (2005), 669–85.

——— 'Hitler's Irish Hideout', in Seaman, *Special Operations Executive*, 201–16.

——— 'The British Joint Intelligence Committee and Ireland, 1965–1972', IIIS Discussion Paper No. 211, Institute of International Integration Studies, Trinity College Dublin, www.tcd.ie/iiis.

——— (ed.), *MI5 and Ireland, 1939–1945: The Official History* (Dublin, 2003).

——— with ROBERT ARMSTRONG and JANE OHLMEYER (eds.), *Intelligence, Statecraft and International Power: Historical Studies XXV* (Dublin, 2006), 181–3.

Ó LONGAIGH, SEOSAMH, *Emergency Law in Independent Ireland, 1922–1948* (Dublin, 2005).

O'MALLEY, KATE, 'Indian Political Intelligence: The Monitoring of Real and Possible Danger?', in O'Halpin *et al.*, *Intelligence, Statecraft and International Power*, 175–85.

PEARTON, MAURICE, 'SOE in Romania', in Seaman, *Special Operations Executive*, 123–36.

PHILBY, KIM, *My Silent War* (London, 1968).

PIMLOTT, BEN (ed.), *The second world war Diaries of Hugh Dalton, 1939–1945* (London, 1986).

PIMLOTT, JOHN, 'The British Experience', in Ian Beckett (ed.), *The Roots of Counter-Insurgency: Armies and Guerilla Warfare, 1900–1945* (London, 1988), 17–39.

PORTER, IVOR, *Operation Anonymous: With SOE in Wartime Romania* (London, 1989).

PUIRSÉIL, NIAMH, *The Irish Labour Party, 1922–1973* (Dublin, 2007).

REEVES, CHRIS, '"Let Us Stand By Our Friends": British Policy Towards Ireland, 1949–59', *Irish Studies in International Affairs*, 11 (2000), 85–102.

REYNOLDS, DAVID, *Rich Relations: The American Occupation of Britain, 1942–1945* (London, 1995).

ROBERTSON, K. G. (ed.), *British and American Perspectives on Intelligence* (Basingstoke, 1987).

ROBERTS, GEOFFREY, 'Three Narratives of Neutrality: Historians and Ireland's War', in Girvin and Roberts, *Ireland and the second world war*, 165–79.

Rock, David, 'Argentina 1930–46', in Bethell, *Cambridge History of Latin America*, viii. 3–72.

Rosenberg, Joseph L., 'The 1941 Mission of Frank Aiken to the United States: An American Perspective', *Irish Historical Studies*, 22 (1980–1), 162–77.

Seaman, Mark, *Garbo: The Spy Who Saved D-Day* (London, 2000).

―――― ' "A New Instrument of War" ', in Seaman, *Special Operations Executive*, 7–21.

―――― (ed.), *Special Operations Executive: A New Kind of Warfare* (London, 2006).

Sexton, Brendan, *Ireland and the Crown, 1922–1936: The Governor-generalship of the Irish Free State* (Dublin, 1989).

Sloan, Geoffrey, *The Geopolitics of Anglo-Irish Relations in the Twentieth Century* (London, 1997).

Smith, Amanda (ed.), *Hostage to Fortune: The Letters of Joseph P. Kennedy* (New York, 2001).

Smith, Bradley F., *The Shadow Warriors: OSS and the Origins of the CIA* (London, 1983).

Smyllie, R. M., 'Unneutral Neutral Eire', *Foreign Affairs*, 24: 2 (Jan. 1946), 317–26.

Stephan, Enno, *Spies in Ireland* (London, 1963).

Stephens, Robert, *Nasser: A Political Biography* (London, 1971).

Strong, Kenneth, *Intelligence at the Top: The Recollections of an Intelligence Officer* (London, 1968).

Talwar, Bhagat Ram, *The Talwars of Pathan Land and Subhas Chandra's Great Escape* (New Delhi, 1976).

Taylor, Philip M., *British Propaganda in the Twentieth Century: Selling Democracy* (Edinburgh, 1999).

Thomas, Martin, 'France in British Signals Intelligence, 1939–1945', *French History*, 14: 2 (Mar. 2000), 41–56.

Thomas, R. T., *Britain and Vichy: The Dilemma of Anglo-French Relations 1940–42* (London, 1979).

Townshend, Charles, *The British Campaign in Ireland, 1919–1921: The Development of Political and Military Policies* (Cambridge, 1975).

Trench, Charles Chenevix, *The Frontier Scouts* (Oxford, 1985).

Van den Poel, Jean (ed.), *Selections from the Smuts Papers,* vol. vi: *December 1934–August 1945* (Cambridge, 1973).

Von Rintelen, Franz, *The Dark Invader: Wartime Reminiscences of a German Naval Intelligence Officer* (London, 1933).

Wark, Wesley, *The Ultimate Enemy: British Intelligence and Nazi Germany, 1933–1939* (London, 1985).

―――― 'Cryptographic Innocence: The Origins of Signals Intelligence in Canada in the second world war', *Journal of Contemporary History*, 22 (1987), 639–65.

Warren, Whitney, *Montenegro: The Crime of the Peace Conference* (London, 1922).

Wasserstein, Bernard, *Britain and the Jews of Europe, 1939–1945* (Oxford, 1979; Leicester, 1999).

Wheeler Bennett, John (ed.), *Action This Day: Working With Churchill* (London, 1968).

Whitehead, Laurence, 'Bolivia Since 1930', in Bethell, *Cambridge History of Latin America*, viii. 509–86.

Wilkinson, Peter, and Joan Bright Astley, *Gubbins and SOE* (London, 1993).

Wills, Clair, *That Neutral Island: A Cultural History of Ireland During the second world war* (London, 2007).

WYLIE, NEVILLE, ' "An Amateur Learns His Job"? Special Operations Executive in Portugal, 1940–42', *Journal of Contemporary History*, 36: 3 (2001), 441–57.

_____ *Britain, Switzerland and the second world war* (Oxford, 2003).

_____ (ed.), *European Neutrals and Non-Belligerents in the second world war* (Cambridge, 2002).

Index

Index